nickelodeon

THE LEGEND OF KORRA

RUINS OF THE EMPIRE

Written by
MICHAEL DANTE
DiMARTINO

Art by
MICHELLE WONG

Colors by
KILLIAN NG *with*
ADELE MATERA *(Part Three)*

Parts One and Two Lettering by
RACHEL DEERING

Part Three Lettering by
ARIANA MAHER

Covers by
MICHELLE WONG
with KILLIAN NG

DARK HORSE BOOKS

Publisher
MIKE RICHARDSON

Editor
RACHEL ROBERTS

Assistant Editor
JENNY BLENK

Collection Designer
SARAH TERRY

Digital Art Technician
ALLYSON HALLER

*Special thanks to Linda Lee, James Salerno, and Joan Hilty at Nickelodeon, to Dave Marshall
at Dark Horse, and to Bryan Konietzko, Michael Dante DiMartino, and Tim Hedrick.*

NEIL HANKERSON Executive Vice President TOM WEDDLE Chief Financial Officer RANDY STRADLEY
Vice President of Publishing NICK MCWHORTER Chief Business Development Officer DALE LAFOUNTAIN
Chief Information Officer MATT PARKINSON Vice President of Marketing VANESSA TODD-HOLMES Vice
President of Production and Scheduling MARK BERNARDI Vice President of Book Trade and Digital Sales KEN LIZZI
General Counsel DAVE MARSHALL Editor in Chief DAVEY ESTRADA Editorial Director CHRIS WARNER Senior
Books Editor CARY GRAZZINI Director of Specialty Projects LIA RIBACCHI Art Director MATT DRYER Director
of Digital Art and Prepress MICHAEL GOMBOS Senior Director of Licensed Publications KARI YADRO Director of
Custom Programs KARI TORSON Director of International Licensing SEAN BRICE Director of Trade Sales

1 3 5 7 9 10 8 6 4 2
Printed in China

ISBN 978-1-50670-893-5 Nick.com DarkHorse.com First edition: September 2020
Published by DARK HORSE BOOKS, a division of Dark Horse Comics LLC. 10956 SE Main Street, Milwaukie, OR 97222

To find a comics shop in your area, visit comicshoplocator.com

This book collects *The Legend of Korra—Ruins of the Empire* Parts 1 through 3.

Library of Congress Cataloging-in-Publication Data

Names: DiMartino, Michael Dante, writer. | Wong, Michelle (Comic book
 artist), artist. | Ng, Killian, colourist, artist. | Maher, Ariana,
 letterer. | Deering, Rachel, letterer.
Title: The legend of Korra : ruins of the empire library edition / written
 by Michael Dante DiMartino ; art by Michelle Wong ; colors by Killian Ng
 ; covers by Michelle Wong with
 Killian Ng.
Other titles: Ruins of the empire
Description: Library edition. | Milwaukie, OR : Dark Horse Books, 2020. |
 "The Legend of Korra created by Bryan Konietzko, Michael Dante
 DiMartino"
Identifiers: LCCN 2020021826 | ISBN 9781506708935 (hardcover)
Subjects: LCSH: Comic books, strips, etc.
Classification: LCC PN6728.L434 D545 2020 | DDC 741.5/973--dc23
LC record available at https://lccn.loc.gov/2020021826

Foreword

by MICHELLE WONG

This has undoubtedly been the greatest learning experience of my career. It feels like not too long ago I was still a bright-eyed aspiring comic book artist, reeling from the Book Four finale along with thousands of other fans around the world, and very convinced that working on something as awesome as *The Legend of Korra* was nothing more than a far-off dream.

Here I am now, able to say I crossed this one off the bucket list.

Ruins of the Empire picks up the narrative where Book Four left off in a way that had me pumping my fist in the air when my editors first told me about the premise. To me, *The Legend of Korra* is a series defined not only by its expansive plot and intricate world-building, but more importantly by the characters that drive its story. Like many others, I was captivated by Korra's fierce determination and Asami's dauntless grace, but I also have a soft spot for well-written villains, and Kuvira was my favorite of the bunch. It was a joy to delve into her backstory to see what makes her tick, and to add my own touches to her journey throughout this arc. I will probably always feel like bragging about how I officially drew kiddy Kuvira terrorizing people with her earthbending skills. I will always remember the joy of seeing fans get excited about another cute Korrasami moment. Above all else, I will always be proud that I got to be a part of this series, and I look forward to seeing where Korra's adventures take her next.

Thank you to Rachel Roberts, Jenny Blenk, and Joan Hilty for their amazing editorial work, as well as Dave Marshall for reaching out to me in the first place. I had been so nervous when submitting that very first style test back in 2018, but from start to finish the editing team has only been encouraging and dedicated to helping me improve my craft. Thank you to Anthony and all the lovely people at Dark Horse for making me feel welcome at NYCC; and to Killian, whose color work always blows me away. You are so spectacularly talented and working with you has been incredible. A great big thank-you to the fans who have been so endlessly supportive—your passion for this series is inspiring. Last but not least, thank you to Mike and Bryan for entrusting me with the task of drawing this story. It has been nothing short of an honor.

—Michelle Wong
April 2020

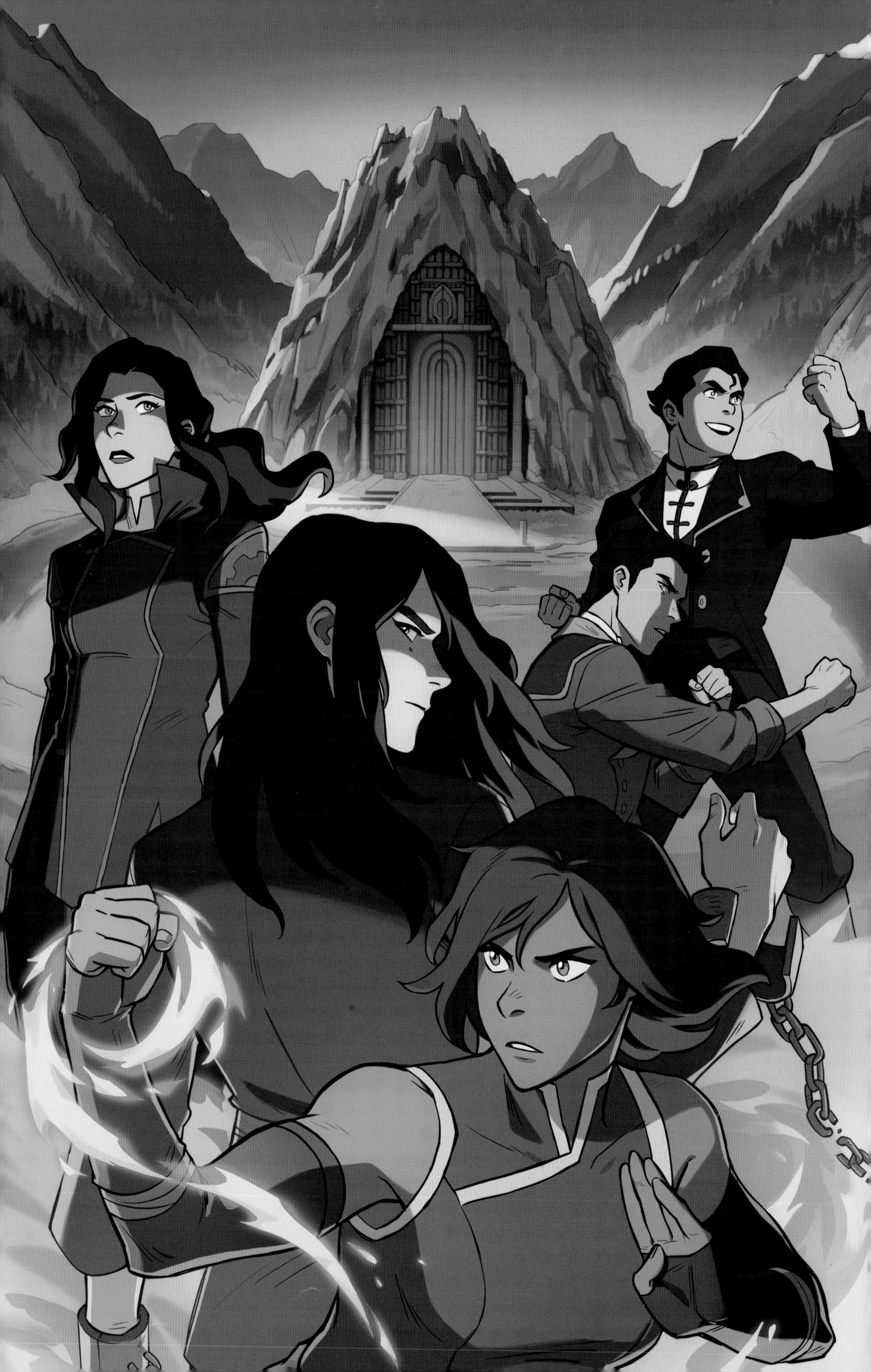

EARTH EMPIRE RE-EDUCATION CAMP, GAOLING.

THREE MONTHS AGO.

PLEASE TELL ME YOU MADE SOME PROGRESS SINCE THE LAST TIME WE SPOKE?

I'M GETTING BETTER RESPONSES FROM THE SUBJECTS, COMMANDER.

BUT THAT'S NOT WHY I'M HERE.

THEN ENLIGHTEN ME, DOCTOR SHENG--

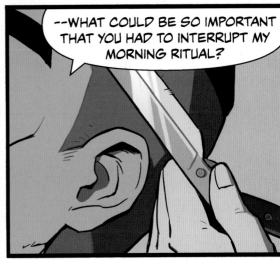

--WHAT COULD BE SO IMPORTANT THAT YOU HAD TO INTERRUPT MY MORNING RITUAL?

THE RADIO OPERATORS JUST HEARD FROM OUR FORCES IN REPUBLIC CITY.

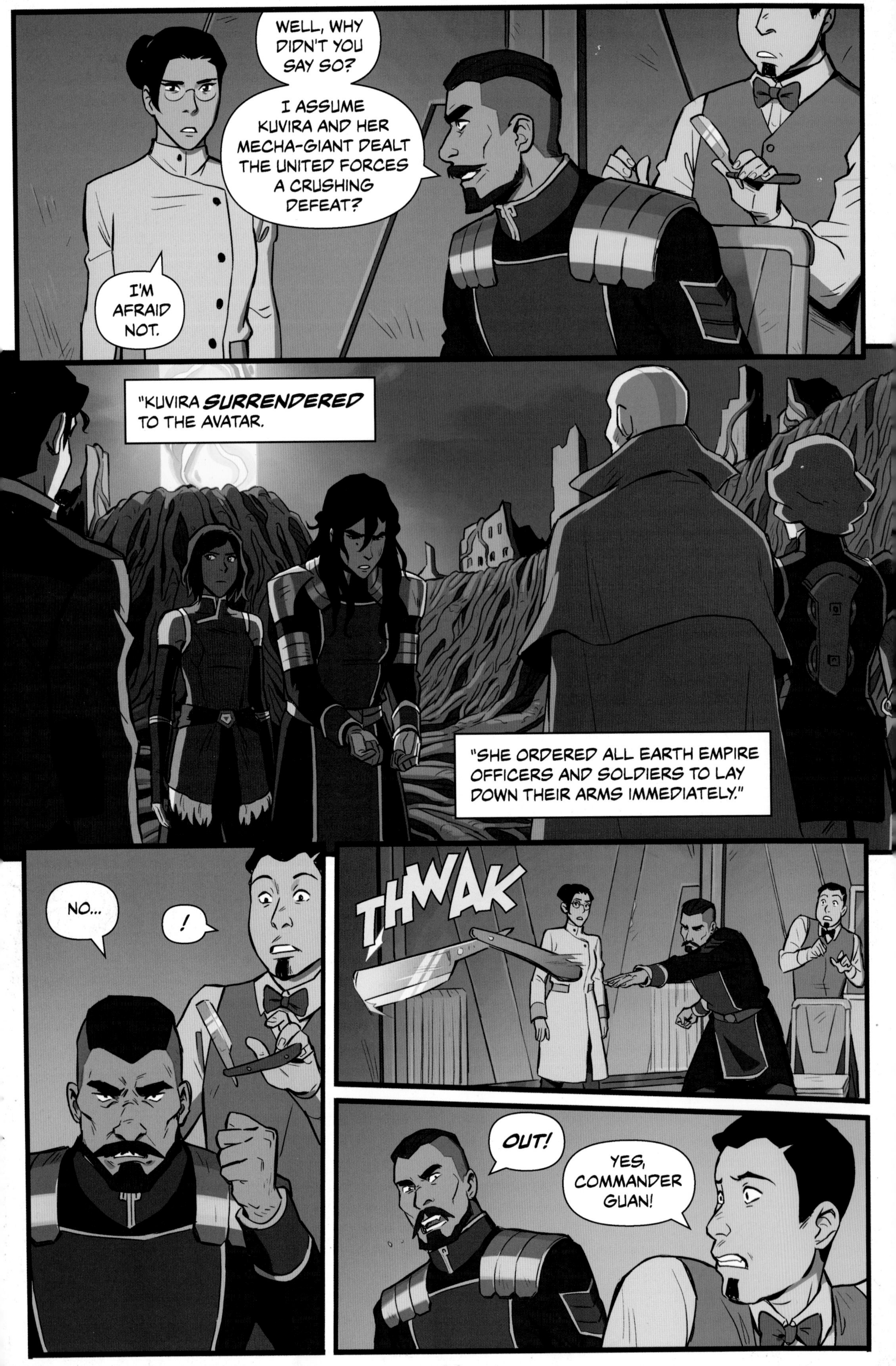
WELL, WHY DIDN'T YOU SAY SO?
I ASSUME KUVIRA AND HER MECHA-GIANT DEALT THE UNITED FORCES A CRUSHING DEFEAT?
I'M AFRAID NOT.
"KUVIRA **SURRENDERED** TO THE AVATAR.
"SHE ORDERED ALL EARTH EMPIRE OFFICERS AND SOLDIERS TO LAY DOWN THEIR ARMS IMMEDIATELY."
NO...
!
THWAK
OUT!
YES, COMMANDER GUAN!

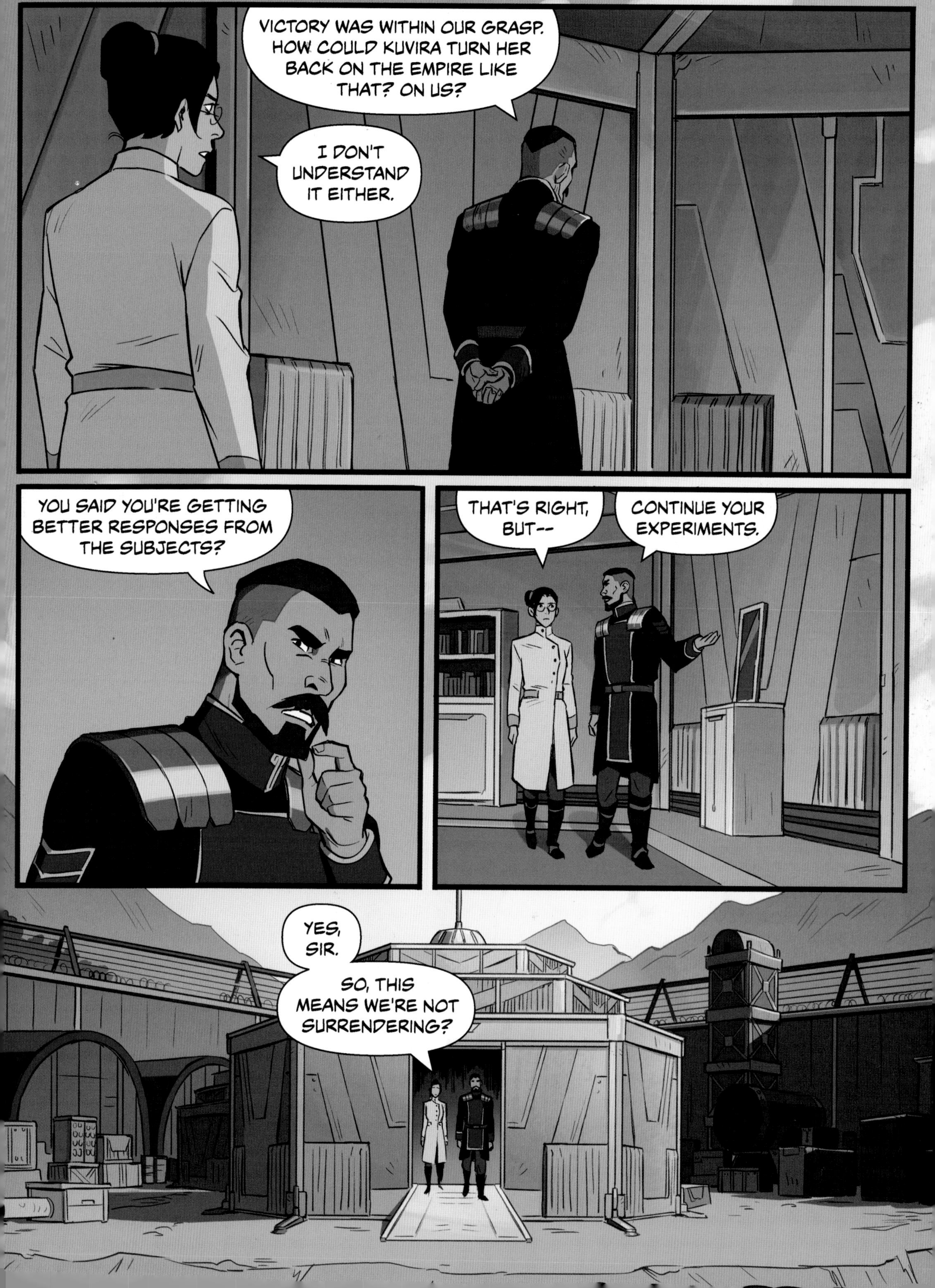
VICTORY WAS WITHIN OUR GRASP. HOW COULD KUVIRA TURN HER BACK ON THE EMPIRE LIKE THAT? ON US?
I DON'T UNDERSTAND IT EITHER.
YOU SAID YOU'RE GETTING BETTER RESPONSES FROM THE SUBJECTS?
THAT'S RIGHT, BUT--
CONTINUE YOUR EXPERIMENTS.
YES, SIR.
SO, THIS MEANS WE'RE NOT SURRENDERING?

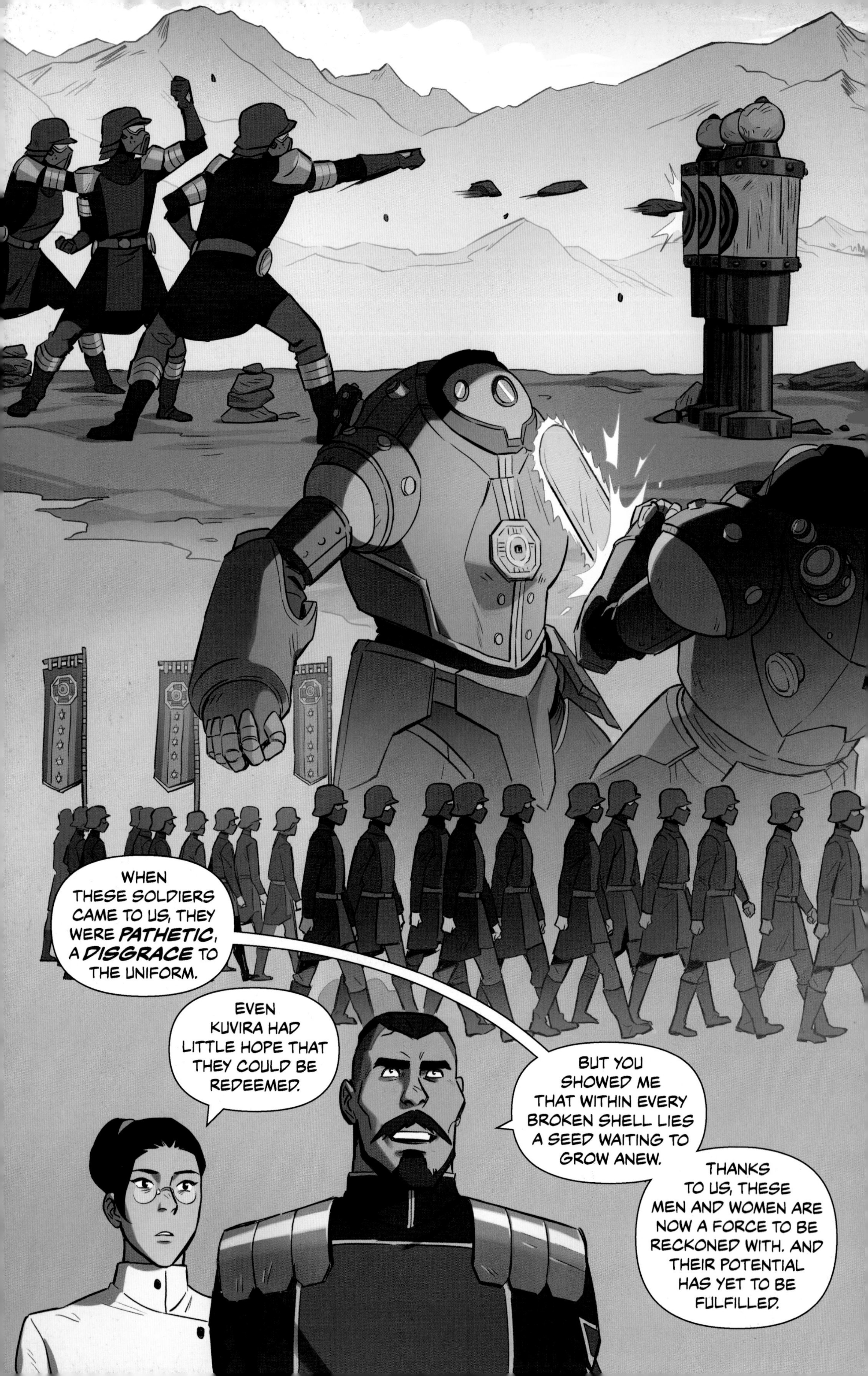
WHEN THESE SOLDIERS CAME TO US, THEY WERE *PATHETIC*, A *DISGRACE* TO THE UNIFORM.
EVEN KUVIRA HAD LITTLE HOPE THAT THEY COULD BE REDEEMED.
BUT YOU SHOWED ME THAT WITHIN EVERY BROKEN SHELL LIES A SEED WAITING TO GROW ANEW.
THANKS TO US, THESE MEN AND WOMEN ARE NOW A FORCE TO BE RECKONED WITH. AND THEIR POTENTIAL HAS YET TO BE FULFILLED.

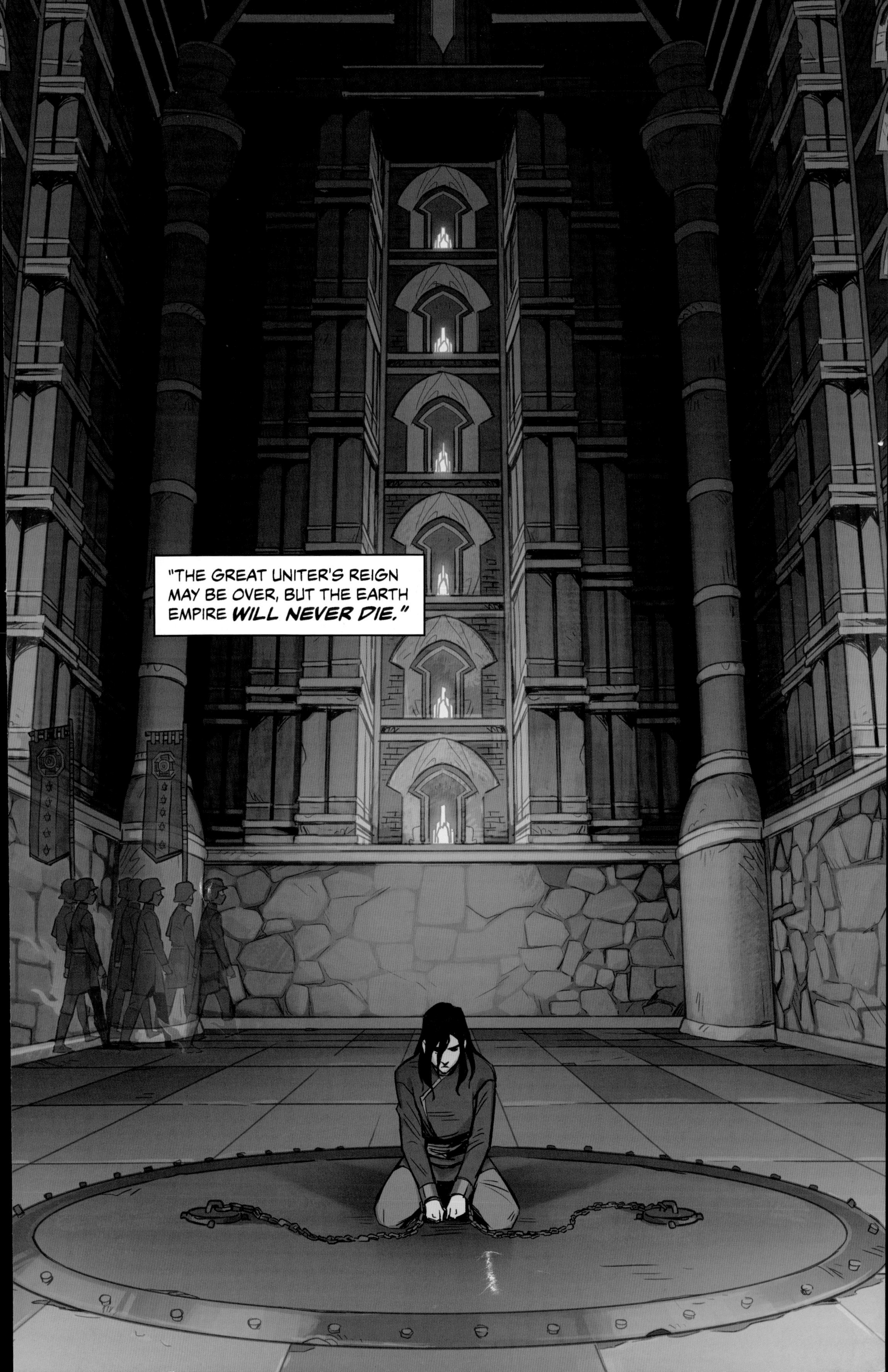
"THE GREAT UNITER'S REIGN MAY BE OVER, BUT THE EARTH EMPIRE ***WILL NEVER DIE.***"

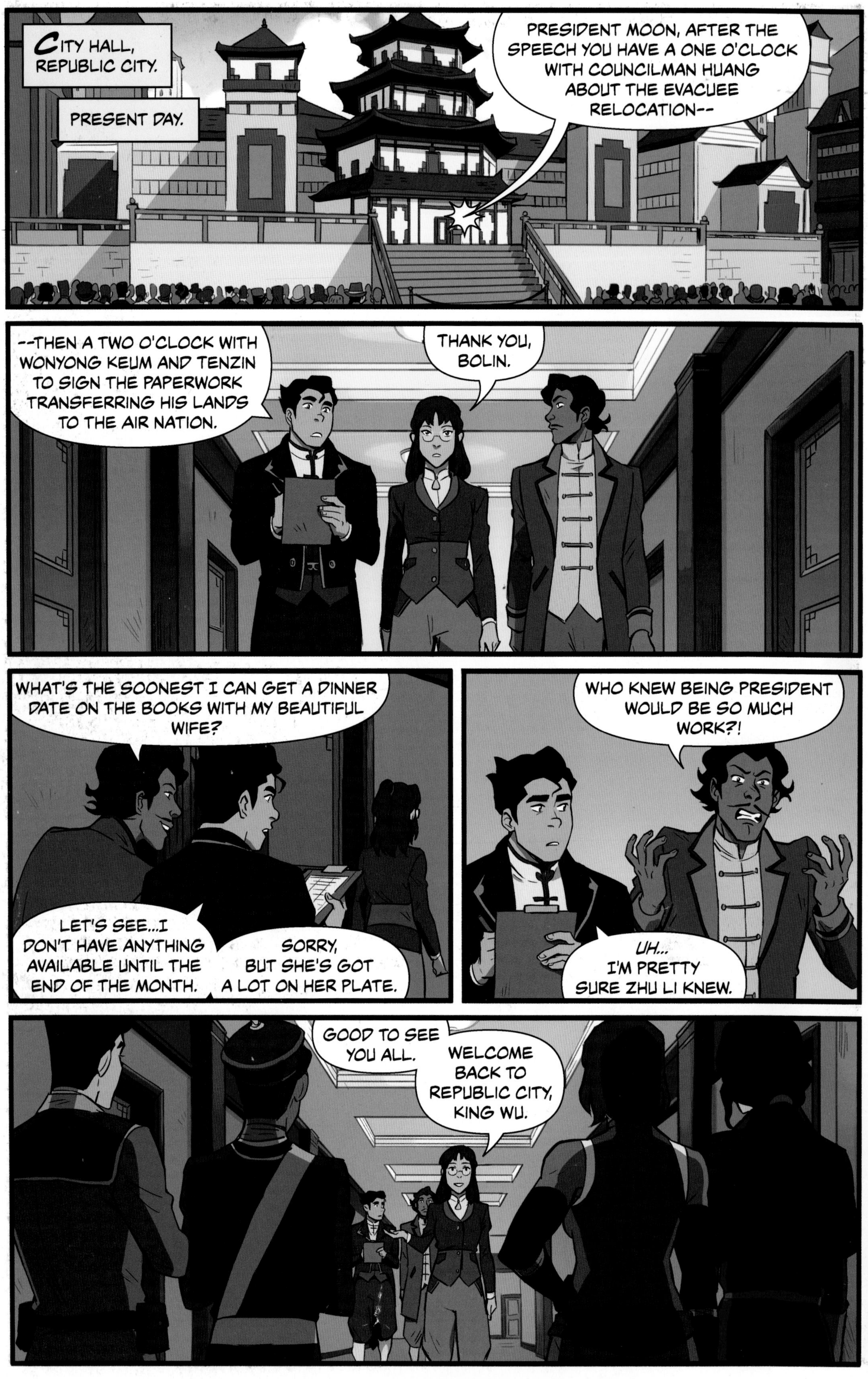
CITY HALL, REPUBLIC CITY.
PRESENT DAY.
PRESIDENT MOON, AFTER THE SPEECH YOU HAVE A ONE O'CLOCK WITH COUNCILMAN HUANG ABOUT THE EVACUEE RELOCATION--
--THEN A TWO O'CLOCK WITH WONYONG KEUM AND TENZIN TO SIGN THE PAPERWORK TRANSFERRING HIS LANDS TO THE AIR NATION.
THANK YOU, BOLIN.
WHAT'S THE SOONEST I CAN GET A DINNER DATE ON THE BOOKS WITH MY BEAUTIFUL WIFE?
LET'S SEE...I DON'T HAVE ANYTHING AVAILABLE UNTIL THE END OF THE MONTH.
SORRY, BUT SHE'S GOT A LOT ON HER PLATE.
WHO KNEW BEING PRESIDENT WOULD BE SO MUCH WORK?!
UH... I'M PRETTY SURE ZHU LI KNEW.
GOOD TO SEE YOU ALL.
WELCOME BACK TO REPUBLIC CITY, KING WU.

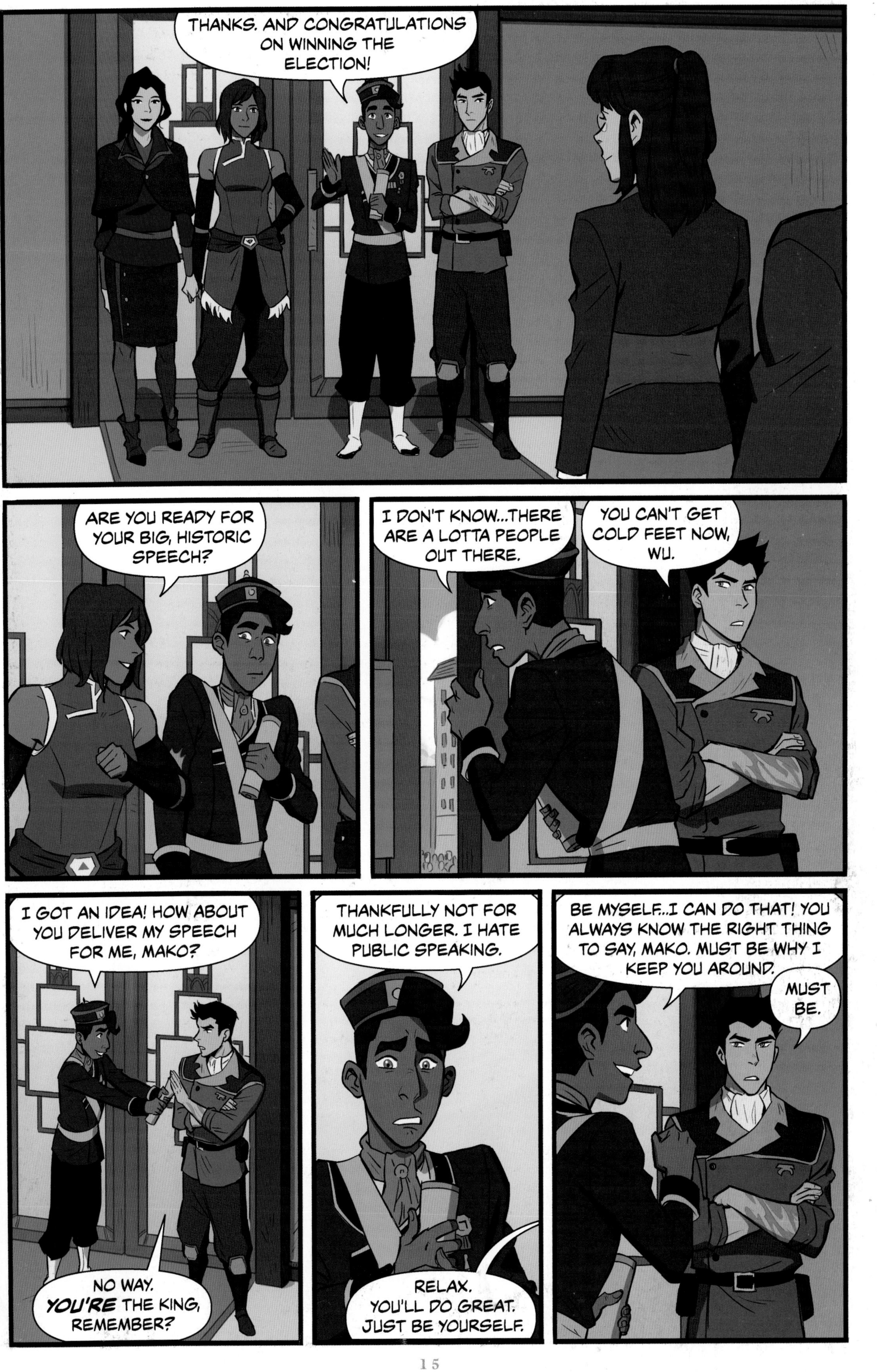
THANKS. AND CONGRATULATIONS ON WINNING THE ELECTION!
ARE YOU READY FOR YOUR BIG, HISTORIC SPEECH?
I DON'T KNOW...THERE ARE A LOTTA PEOPLE OUT THERE.
YOU CAN'T GET COLD FEET NOW, WU.
I GOT AN IDEA! HOW ABOUT YOU DELIVER MY SPEECH FOR ME, MAKO?
NO WAY. *YOU'RE* THE KING, REMEMBER?
THANKFULLY NOT FOR MUCH LONGER. I HATE PUBLIC SPEAKING.
RELAX. YOU'LL DO GREAT. JUST BE YOURSELF.
BE MYSELF...I CAN DO THAT! YOU ALWAYS KNOW THE RIGHT THING TO SAY, MAKO. MUST BE WHY I KEEP YOU AROUND.
MUST BE.

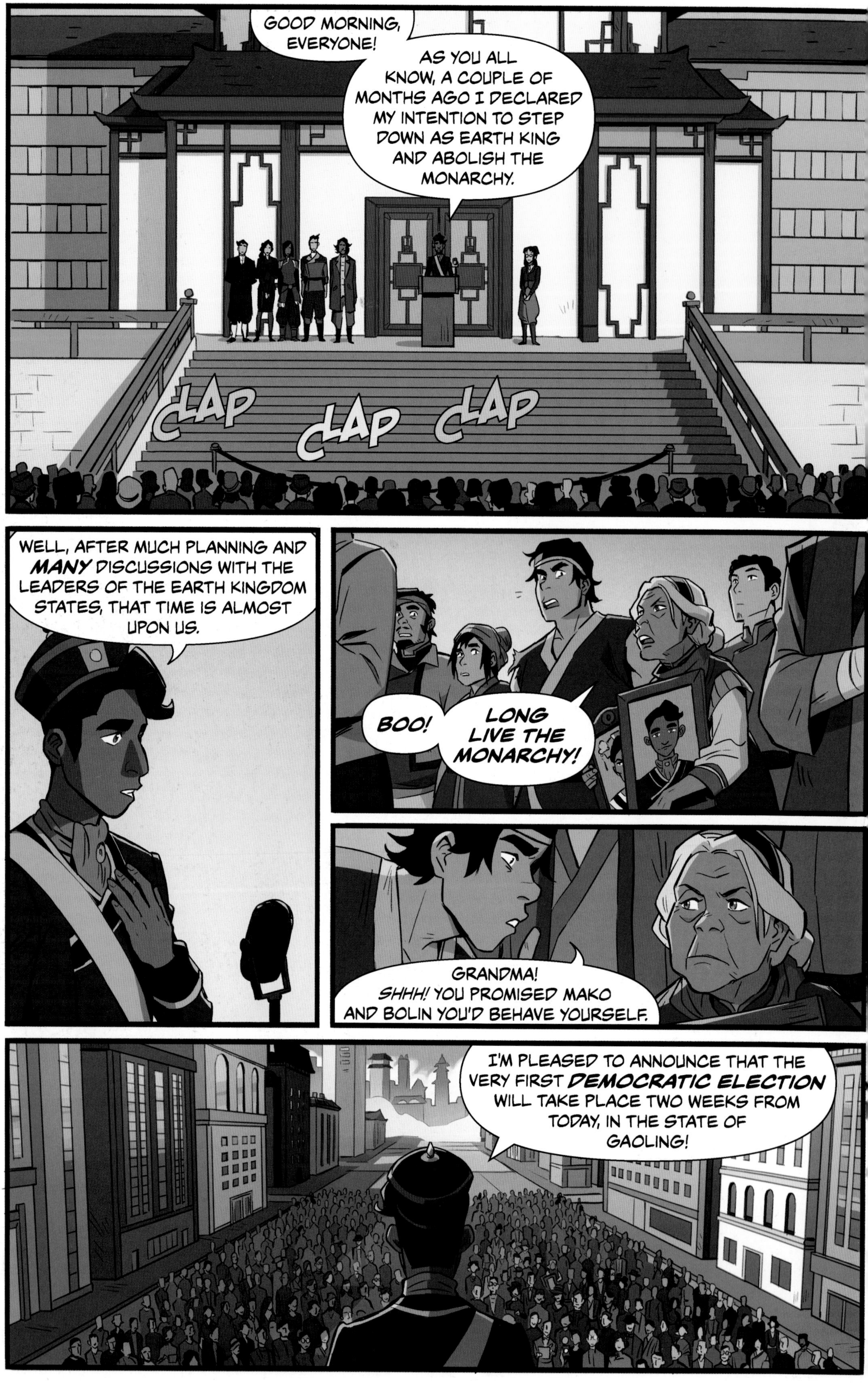
GOOD MORNING, EVERYONE!
AS YOU ALL KNOW, A COUPLE OF MONTHS AGO I DECLARED MY INTENTION TO STEP DOWN AS EARTH KING AND ABOLISH THE MONARCHY.
CLAP CLAP CLAP
WELL, AFTER MUCH PLANNING AND MANY DISCUSSIONS WITH THE LEADERS OF THE EARTH KINGDOM STATES, THAT TIME IS ALMOST UPON US.
BOO!
LONG LIVE THE MONARCHY!
GRANDMA! SHHH! YOU PROMISED MAKO AND BOLIN YOU'D BEHAVE YOURSELF.
I'M PLEASED TO ANNOUNCE THAT THE VERY FIRST DEMOCRATIC ELECTION WILL TAKE PLACE TWO WEEKS FROM TODAY, IN THE STATE OF GAOLING!

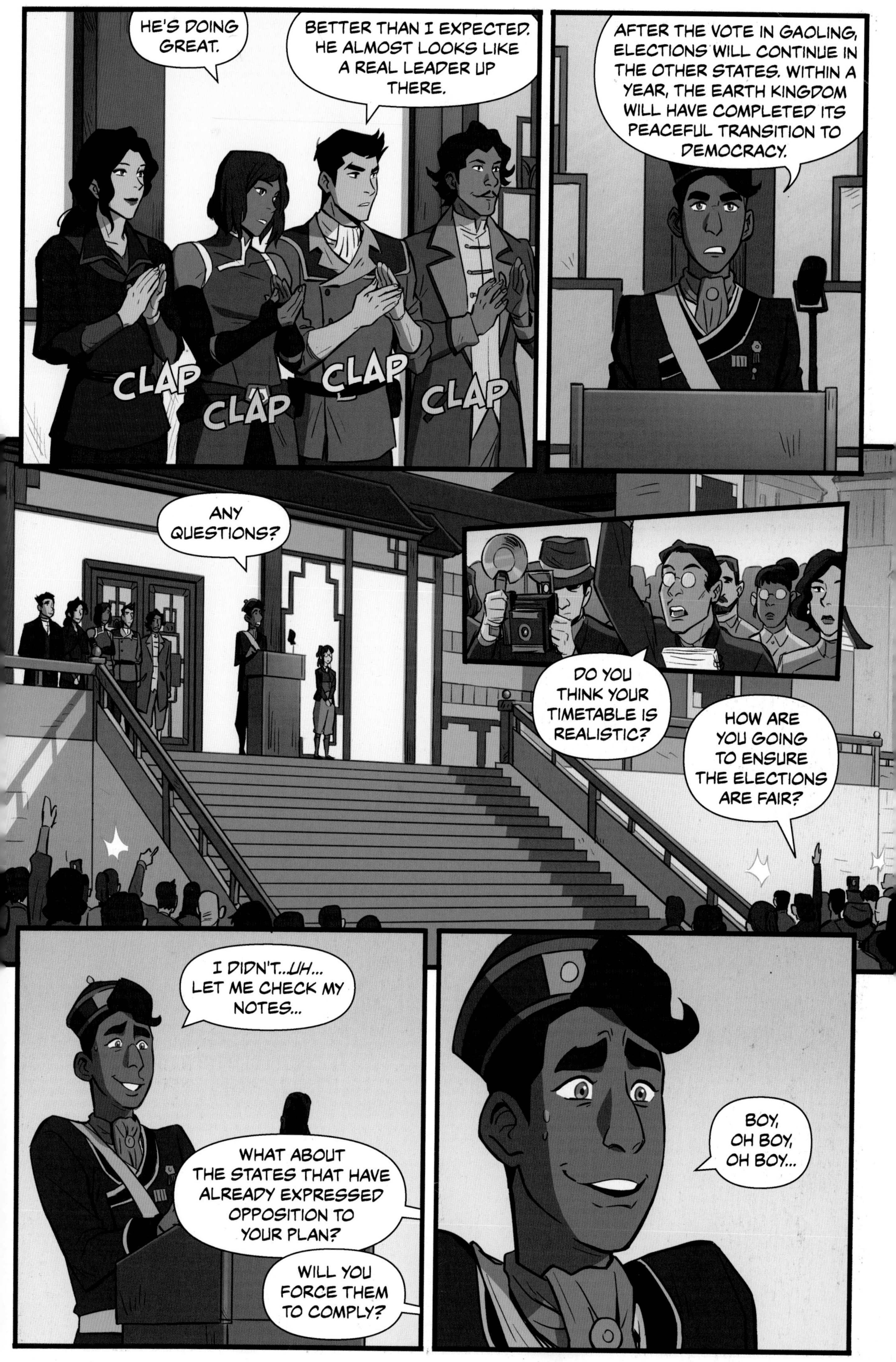
HE'S DOING GREAT.
BETTER THAN I EXPECTED. HE ALMOST LOOKS LIKE A REAL LEADER UP THERE.
CLAP
CLAP
CLAP
CLAP
AFTER THE VOTE IN GAOLING, ELECTIONS WILL CONTINUE IN THE OTHER STATES. WITHIN A YEAR, THE EARTH KINGDOM WILL HAVE COMPLETED ITS PEACEFUL TRANSITION TO DEMOCRACY.
ANY QUESTIONS?
DO YOU THINK YOUR TIMETABLE IS REALISTIC?
HOW ARE YOU GOING TO ENSURE THE ELECTIONS ARE FAIR?
I DIDN'T...*UH*... LET ME CHECK MY NOTES...
WHAT ABOUT THE STATES THAT HAVE ALREADY EXPRESSED OPPOSITION TO YOUR PLAN?
WILL YOU FORCE THEM TO COMPLY?
BOY, OH BOY, OH BOY...

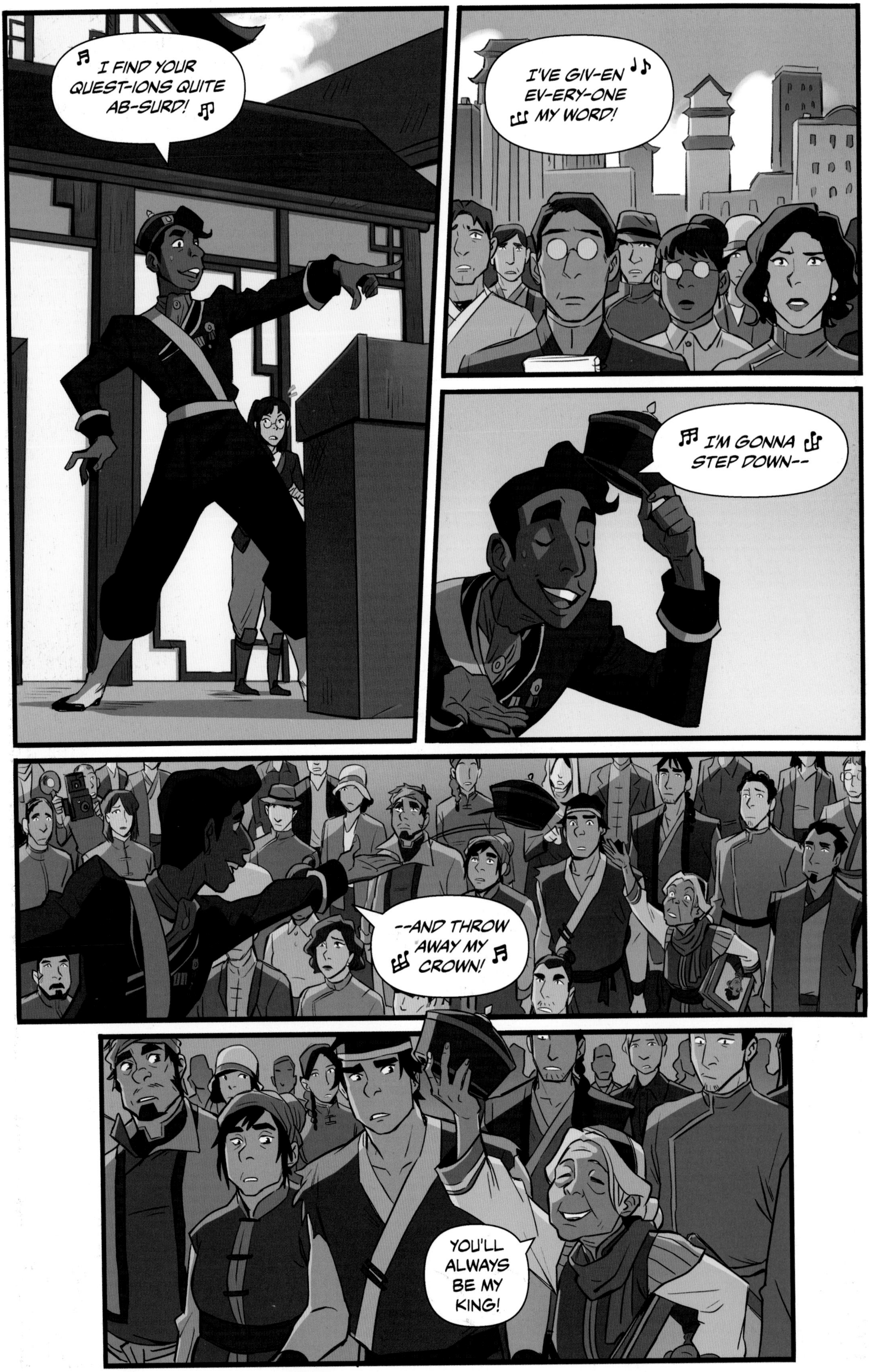
I FIND YOUR QUEST-IONS QUITE AB-SURD!
I'VE GIV-EN EV-ERY-ONE MY WORD!
I'M GONNA STEP DOWN--
--AND THROW AWAY MY CROWN!
YOU'LL ALWAYS BE MY KING!

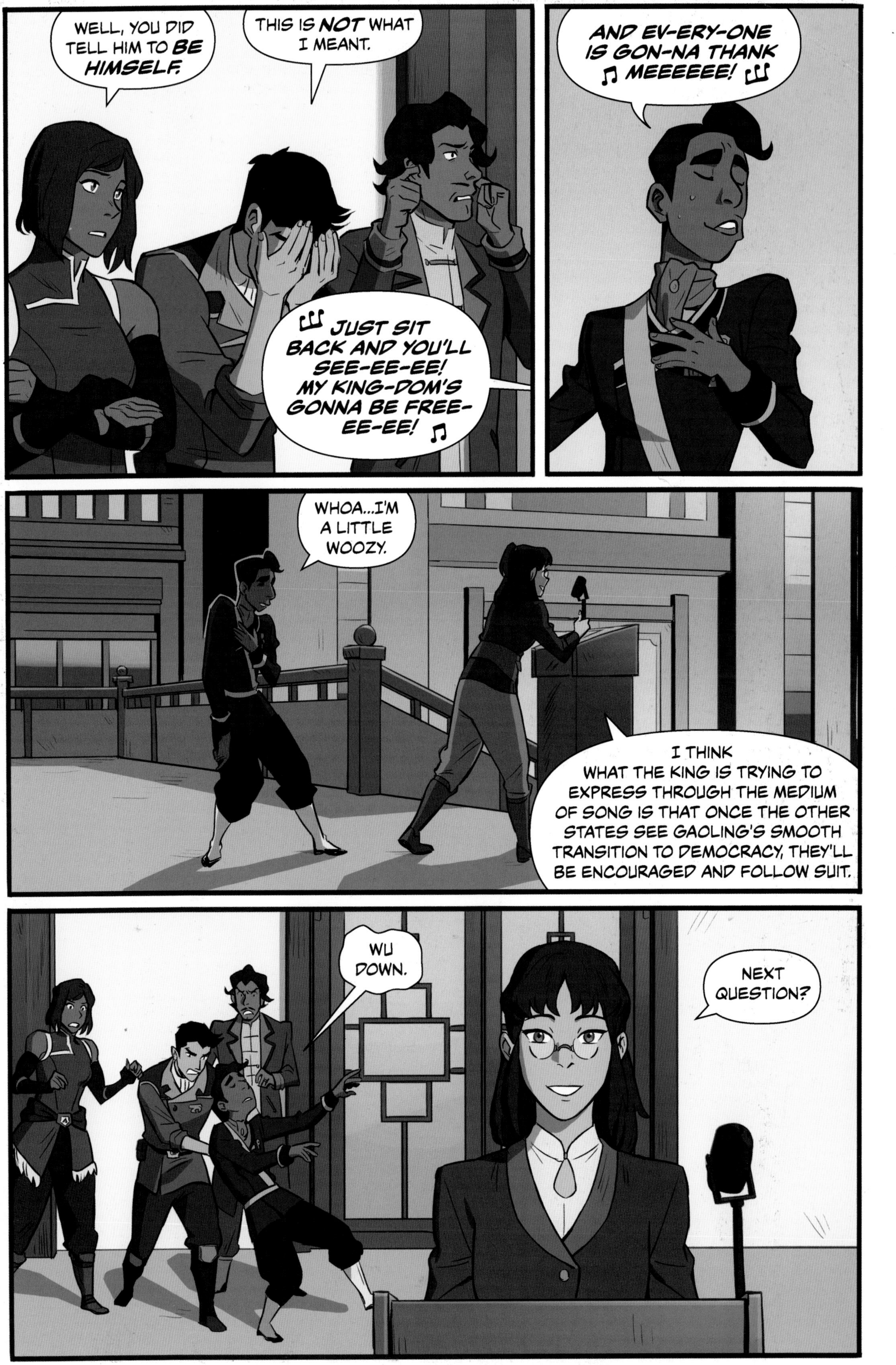

WELL, YOU DID TELL HIM TO BE HIMSELF.
THIS IS NOT WHAT I MEANT.
JUST SIT BACK AND YOU'LL SEE-EE-EE! MY KING-DOM'S GONNA BE FREE-EE-EE!
AND EV-ERY-ONE IS GON-NA THANK MEEEEEE!
WHOA...I'M A LITTLE WOOZY.
I THINK WHAT THE KING IS TRYING TO EXPRESS THROUGH THE MEDIUM OF SONG IS THAT ONCE THE OTHER STATES SEE GAOLING'S SMOOTH TRANSITION TO DEMOCRACY, THEY'LL BE ENCOURAGED AND FOLLOW SUIT.
WU DOWN.
NEXT QUESTION?

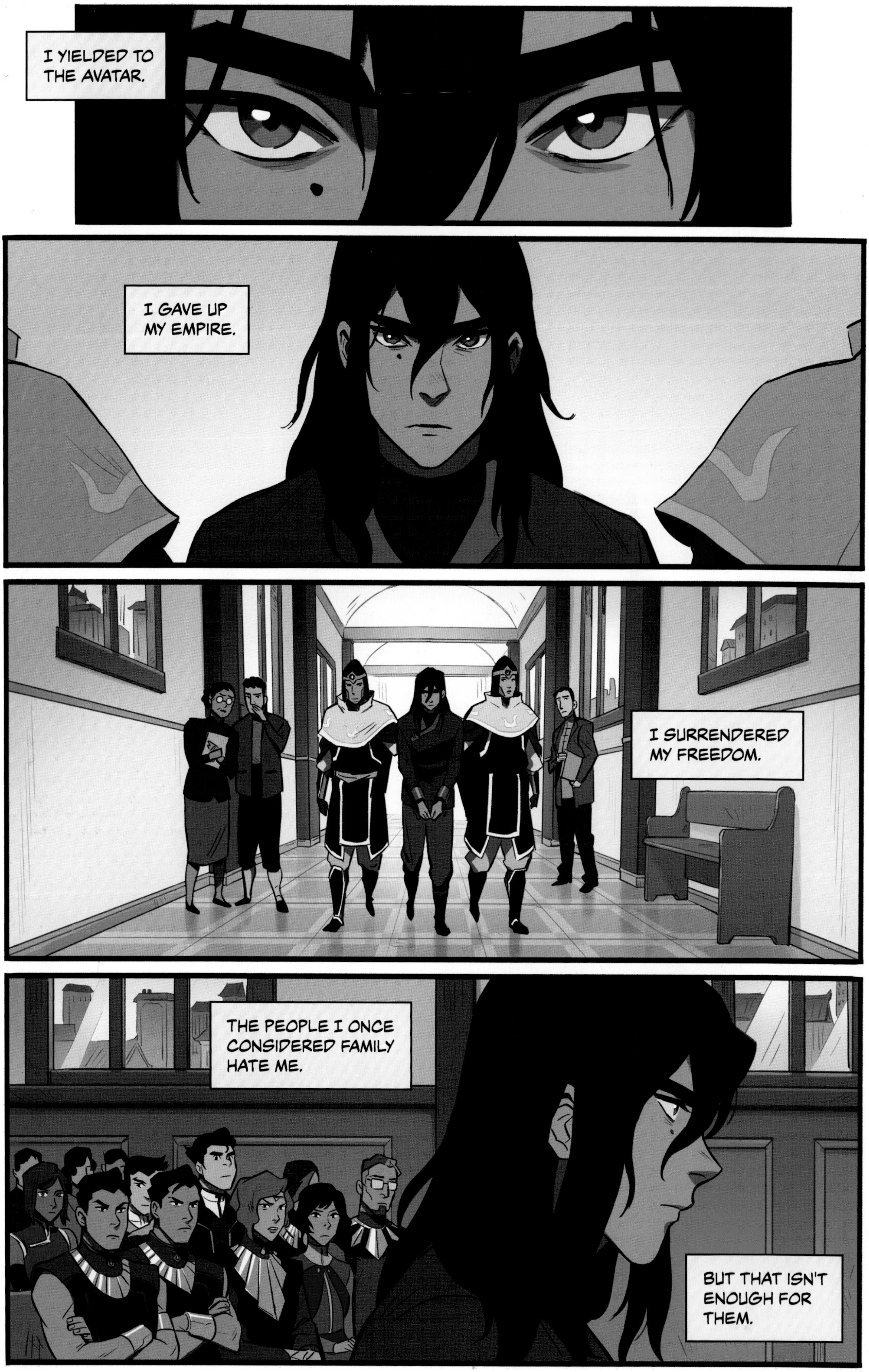
I YIELDED TO THE AVATAR.
I GAVE UP MY EMPIRE.
I SURRENDERED MY FREEDOM.
THE PEOPLE I ONCE CONSIDERED FAMILY HATE ME.
BUT THAT ISN'T ENOUGH FOR THEM.

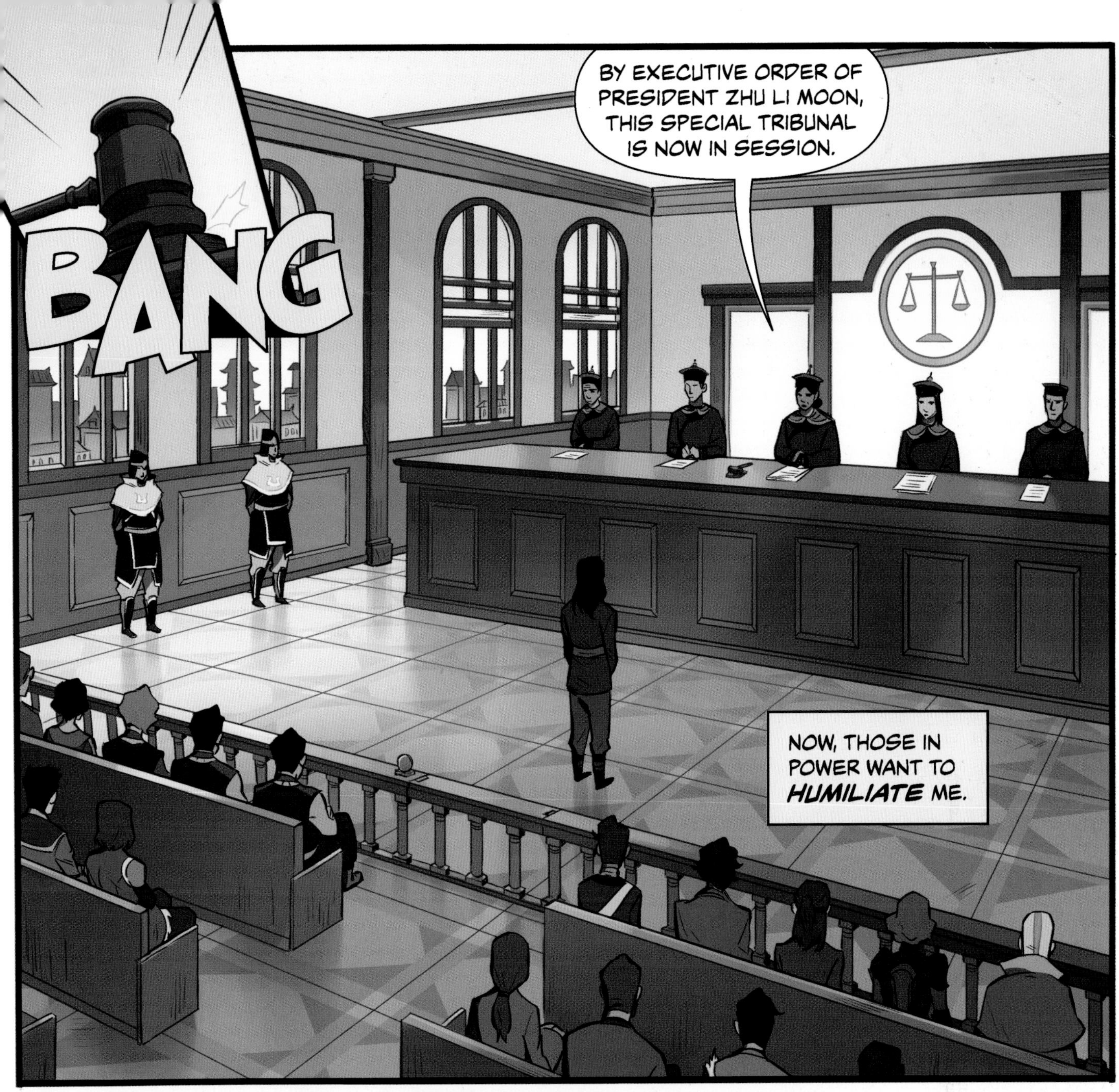
BANG
BY EXECUTIVE ORDER OF PRESIDENT ZHU LI MOON, THIS SPECIAL TRIBUNAL IS NOW IN SESSION.
NOW, THOSE IN POWER WANT TO HUMILIATE ME.

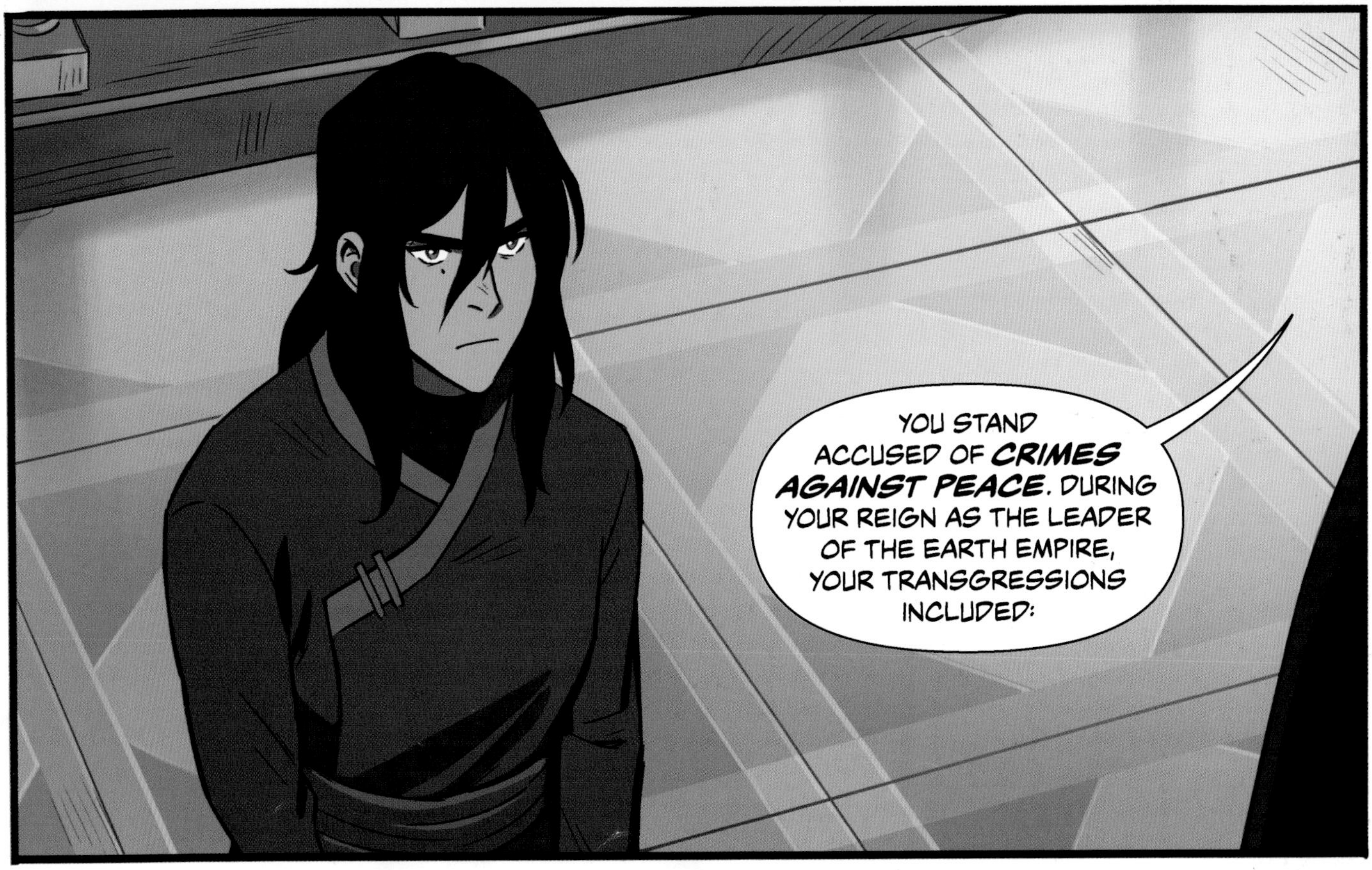
YOU STAND ACCUSED OF CRIMES AGAINST PEACE. DURING YOUR REIGN AS THE LEADER OF THE EARTH EMPIRE, YOUR TRANSGRESSIONS INCLUDED:

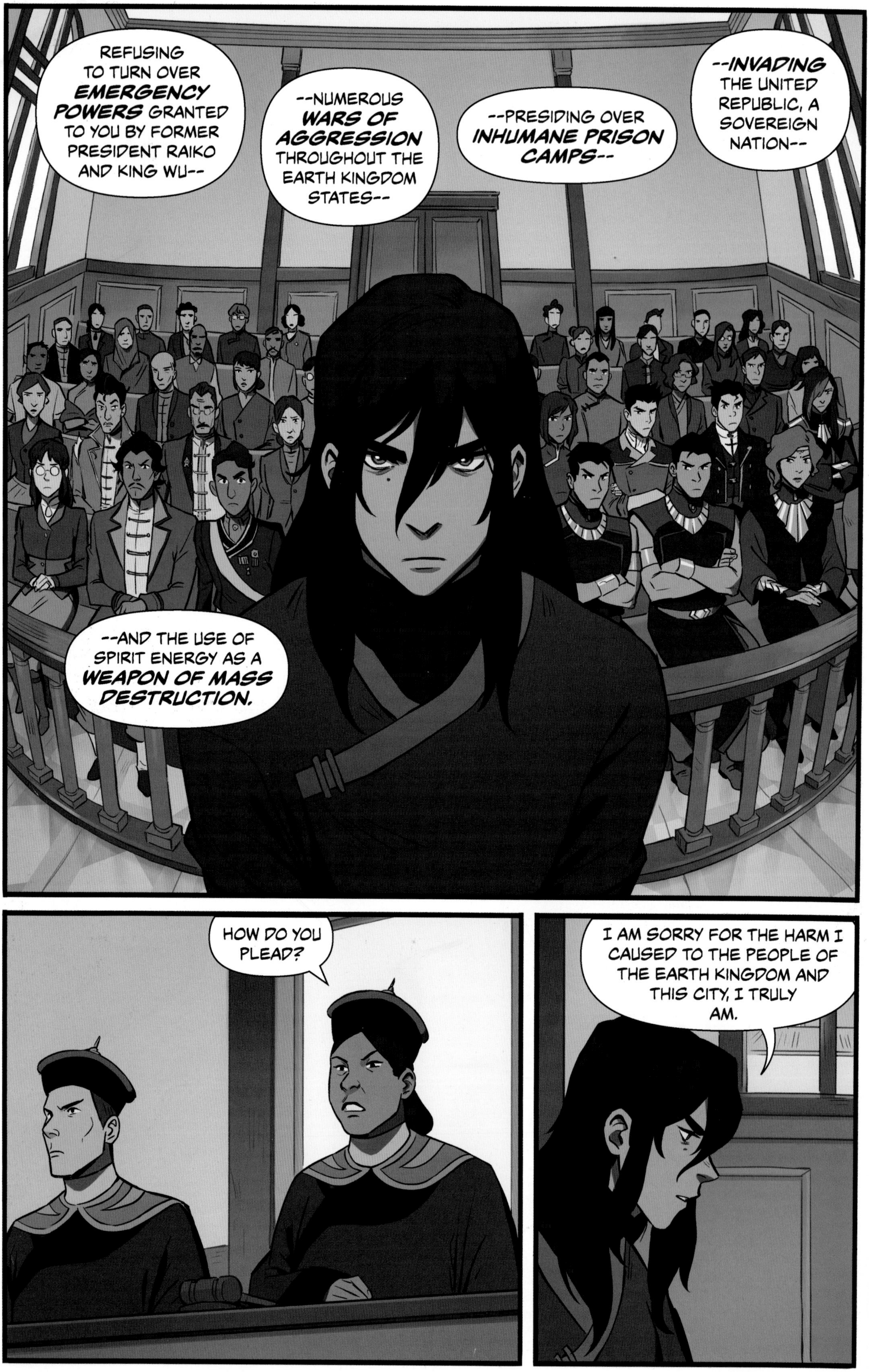
REFUSING TO TURN OVER **EMERGENCY POWERS** GRANTED TO YOU BY FORMER PRESIDENT RAIKO AND KING WU--
--NUMEROUS **WARS OF AGGRESSION** THROUGHOUT THE EARTH KINGDOM STATES--
--PRESIDING OVER **INHUMANE PRISON CAMPS**--
--**INVADING** THE UNITED REPUBLIC, A SOVEREIGN NATION--
--AND THE USE OF SPIRIT ENERGY AS A **WEAPON OF MASS DESTRUCTION.**
HOW DO YOU PLEAD?
I AM SORRY FOR THE HARM I CAUSED TO THE PEOPLE OF THE EARTH KINGDOM AND THIS CITY, I TRULY AM.

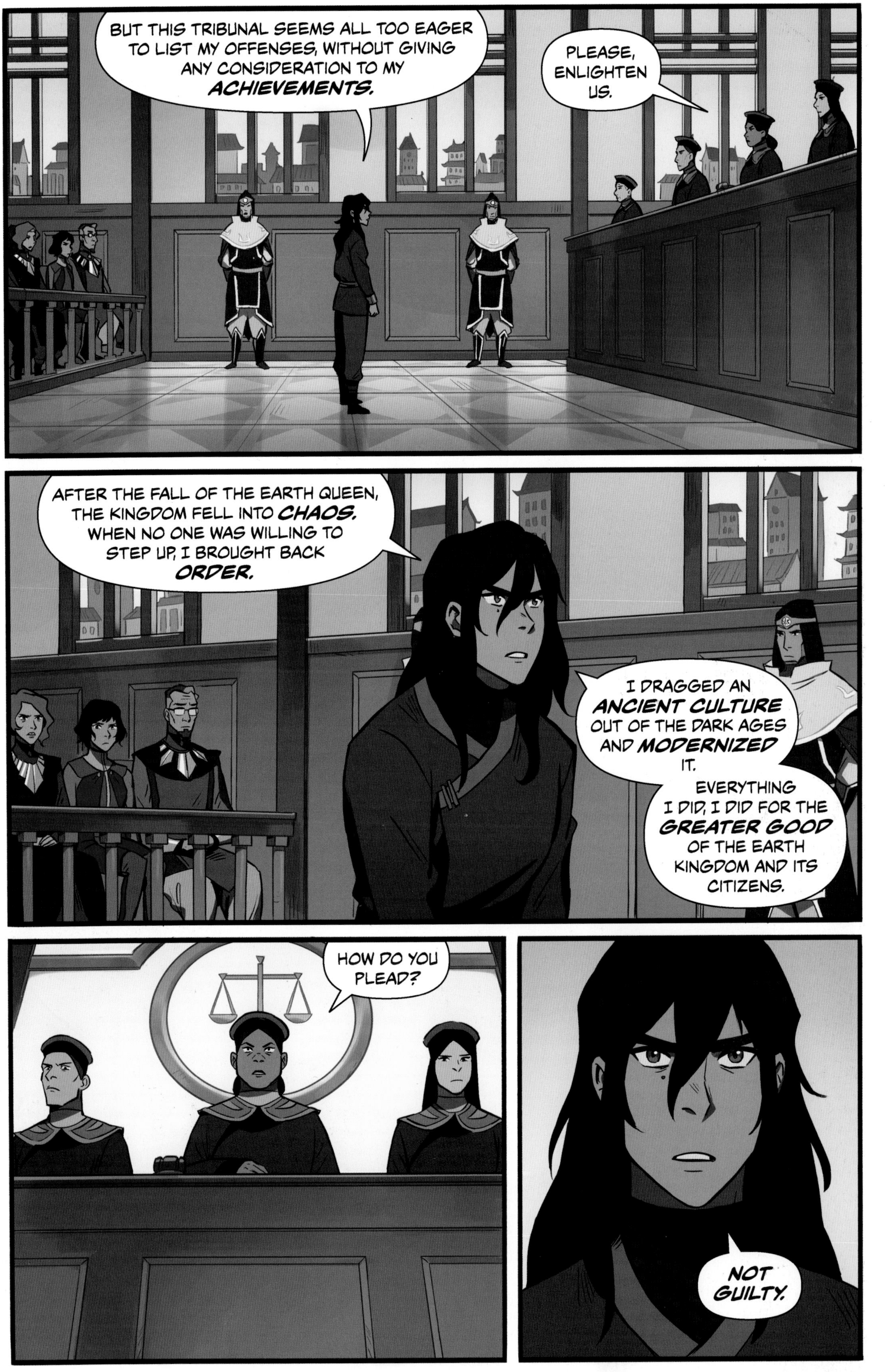
BUT THIS TRIBUNAL SEEMS ALL TOO EAGER TO LIST MY OFFENSES, WITHOUT GIVING ANY CONSIDERATION TO MY ACHIEVEMENTS.
PLEASE, ENLIGHTEN US.
AFTER THE FALL OF THE EARTH QUEEN, THE KINGDOM FELL INTO CHAOS. WHEN NO ONE WAS WILLING TO STEP UP, I BROUGHT BACK ORDER.
I DRAGGED AN ANCIENT CULTURE OUT OF THE DARK AGES AND MODERNIZED IT.
EVERYTHING I DID, I DID FOR THE GREATER GOOD OF THE EARTH KINGDOM AND ITS CITIZENS.
HOW DO YOU PLEAD?
NOT GUILTY.

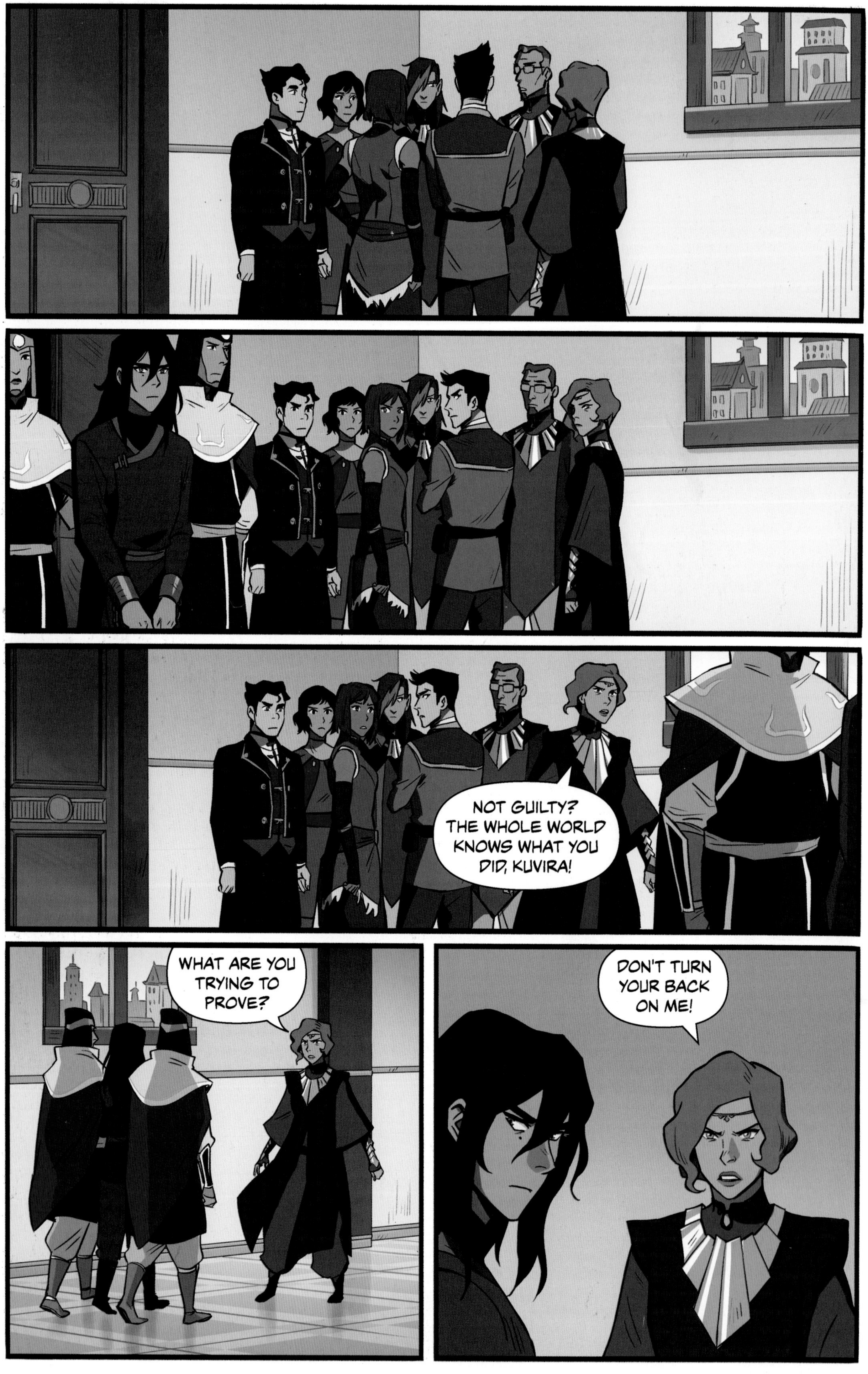
NOT GUILTY? THE WHOLE WORLD KNOWS WHAT YOU DID, KUVIRA!
WHAT ARE YOU TRYING TO PROVE?
DON'T TURN YOUR BACK ON ME!

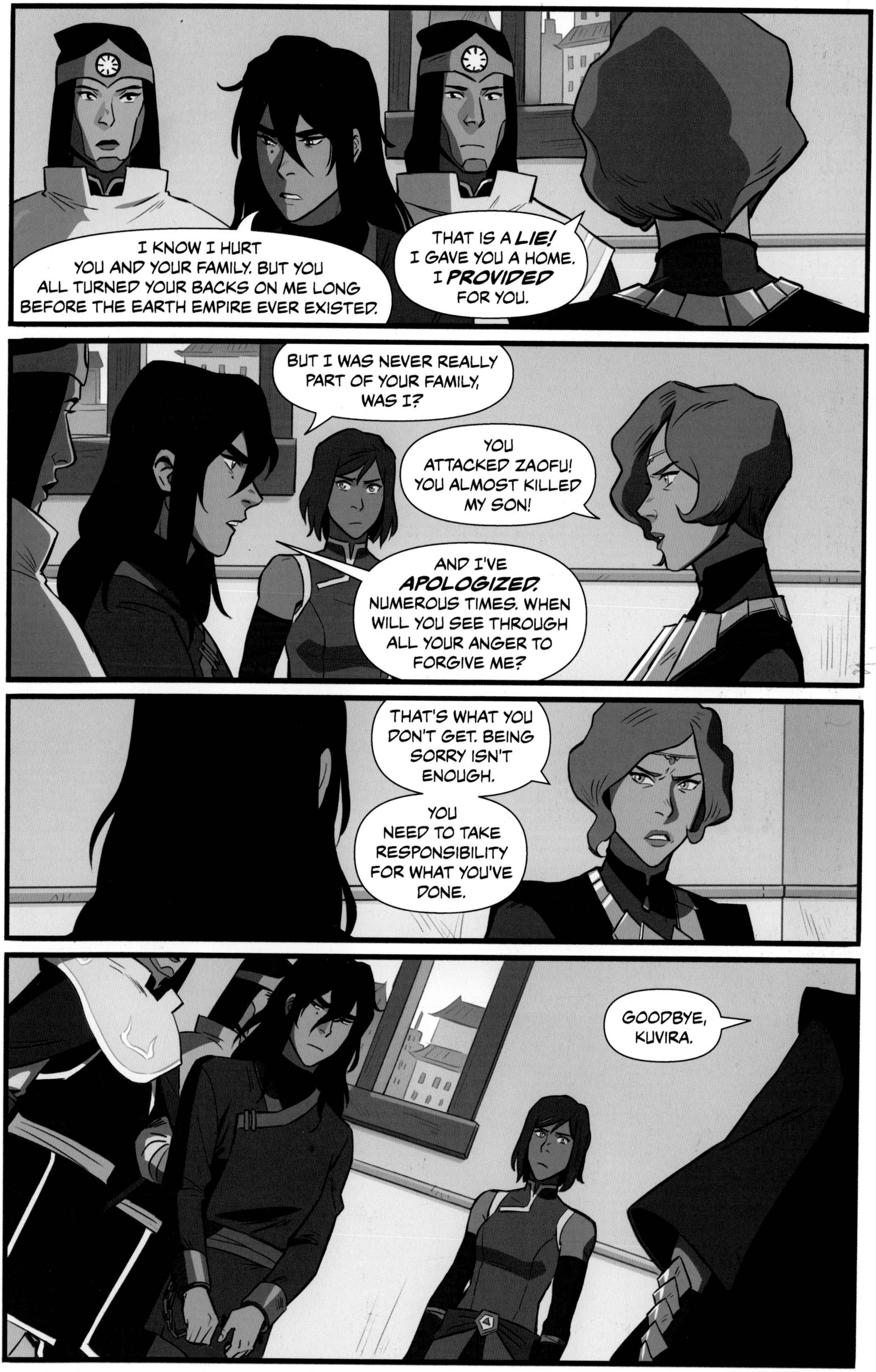
I KNOW I HURT YOU AND YOUR FAMILY. BUT YOU ALL TURNED YOUR BACKS ON ME LONG BEFORE THE EARTH EMPIRE EVER EXISTED.
THAT IS A ***LIE!*** I GAVE YOU A HOME. I ***PROVIDED*** FOR YOU.
BUT I WAS NEVER REALLY PART OF YOUR FAMILY, WAS I?
YOU ATTACKED ZAOFU! YOU ALMOST KILLED MY SON!
AND I'VE ***APOLOGIZED.*** NUMEROUS TIMES. WHEN WILL YOU SEE THROUGH ALL YOUR ANGER TO FORGIVE ME?
THAT'S WHAT YOU DON'T GET. BEING SORRY ISN'T ENOUGH.
YOU NEED TO TAKE RESPONSIBILITY FOR WHAT YOU'VE DONE.
GOODBYE, KUVIRA.

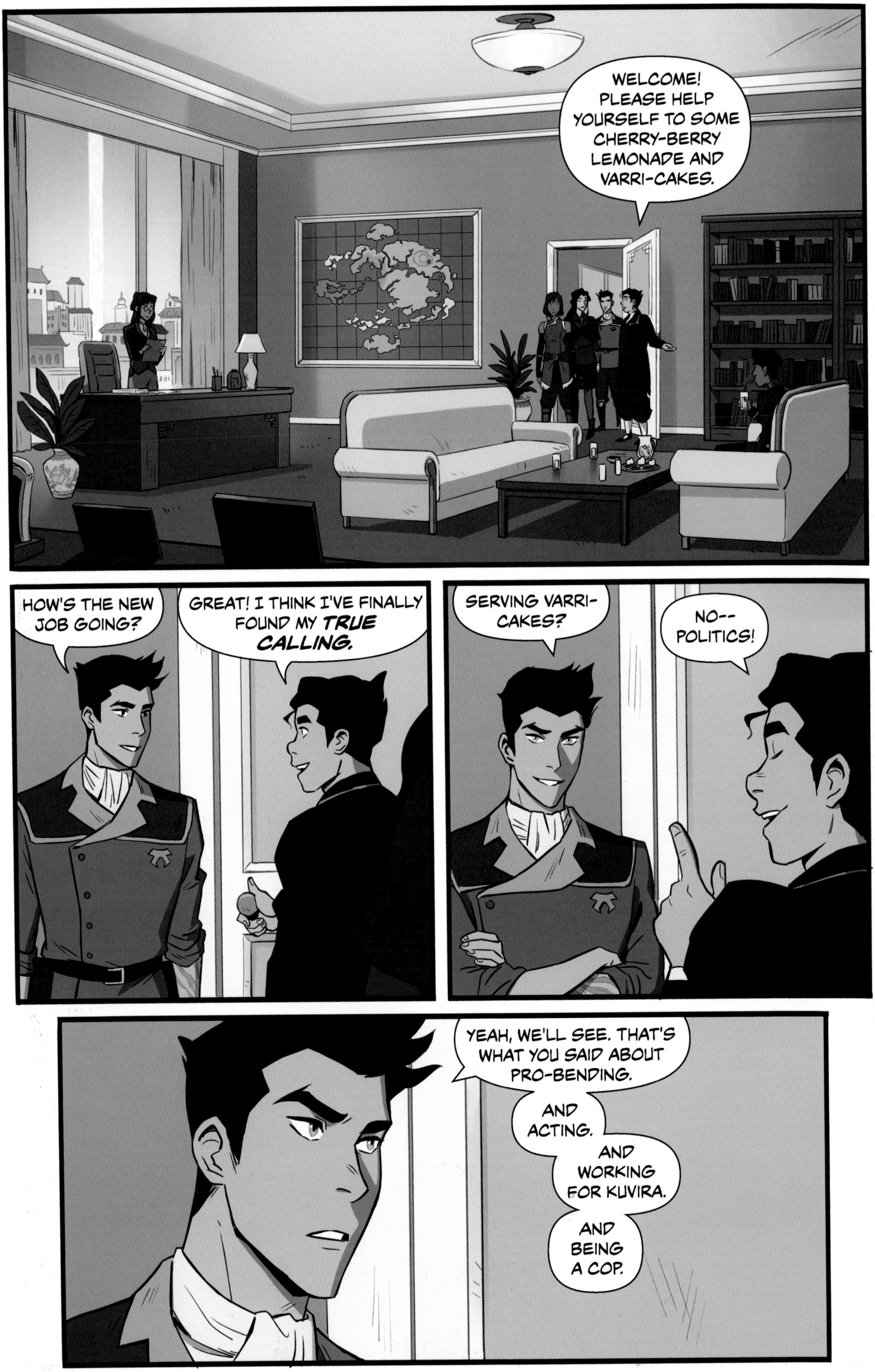
WELCOME! PLEASE HELP YOURSELF TO SOME CHERRY-BERRY LEMONADE AND VARRI-CAKES.
HOW'S THE NEW JOB GOING?
GREAT! I THINK I'VE FINALLY FOUND MY *TRUE CALLING.*
SERVING VARRI-CAKES?
NO-- POLITICS!
YEAH, WE'LL SEE. THAT'S WHAT YOU SAID ABOUT PRO-BENDING.
AND ACTING.
AND WORKING FOR KUVIRA.
AND BEING A COP.

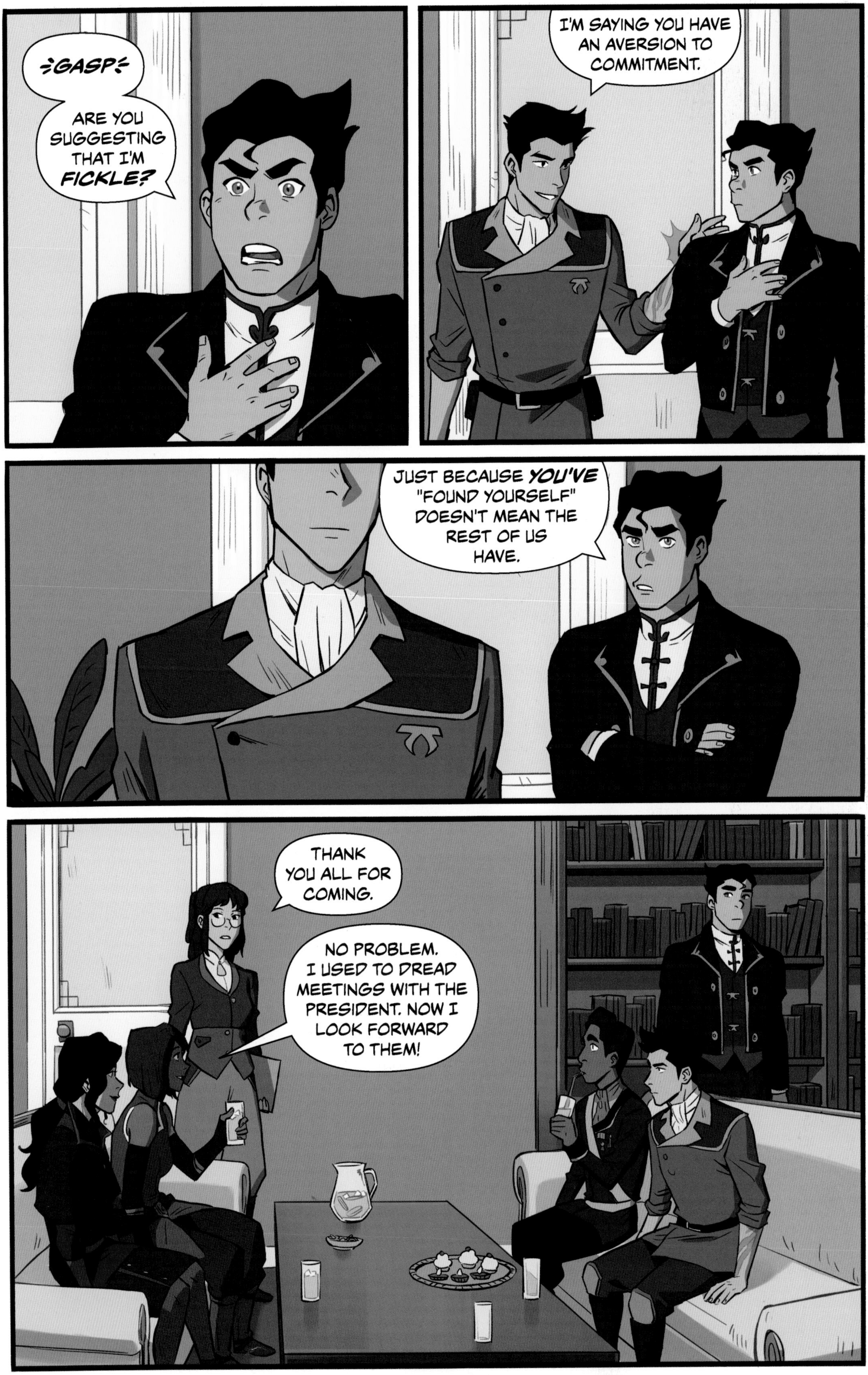

GASP
ARE YOU SUGGESTING THAT I'M FICKLE?
I'M SAYING YOU HAVE AN AVERSION TO COMMITMENT.
JUST BECAUSE YOU'VE "FOUND YOURSELF" DOESN'T MEAN THE REST OF US HAVE.
THANK YOU ALL FOR COMING.
NO PROBLEM. I USED TO DREAD MEETINGS WITH THE PRESIDENT. NOW I LOOK FORWARD TO THEM!

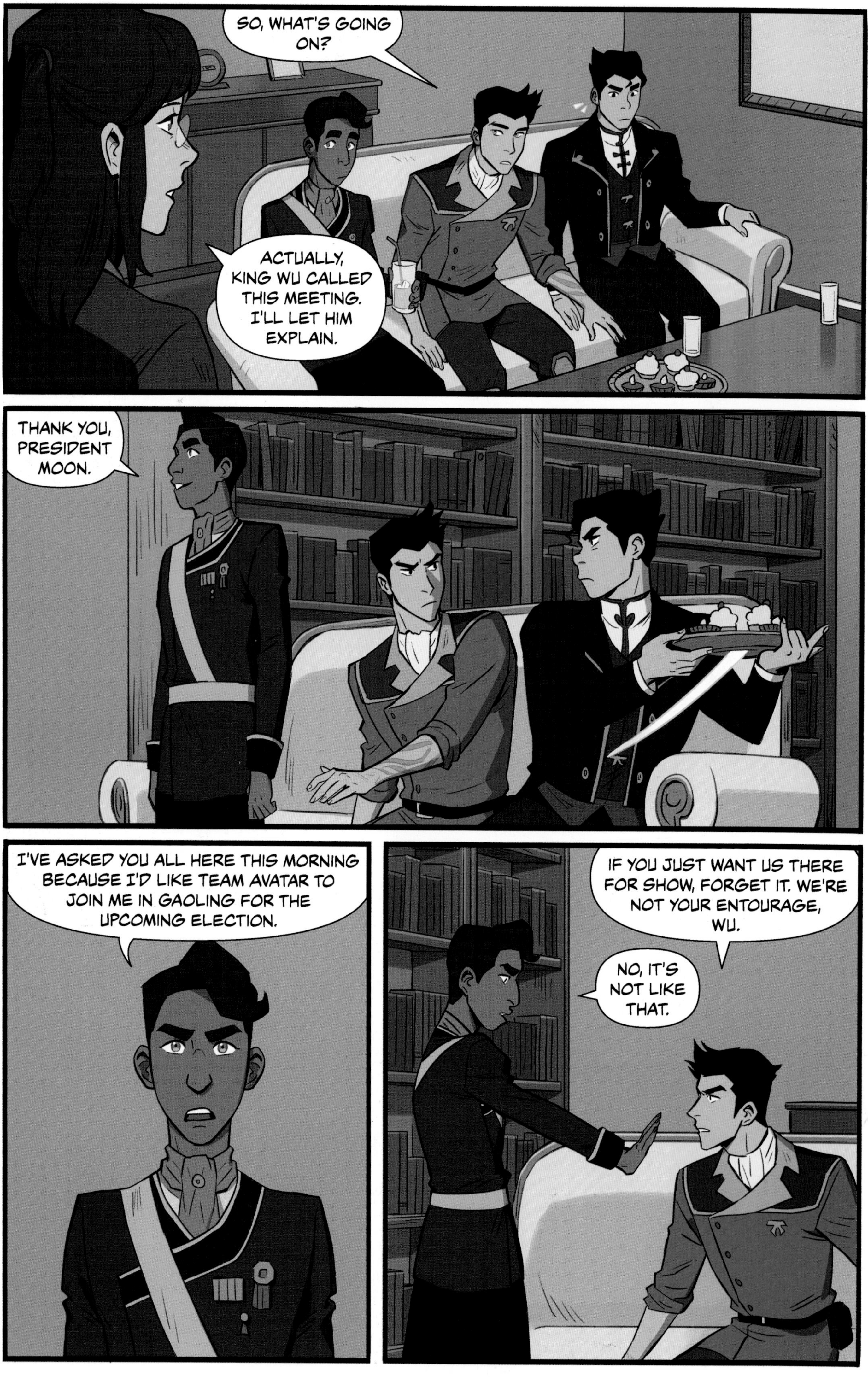

SO, WHAT'S GOING ON?
ACTUALLY, KING WU CALLED THIS MEETING. I'LL LET HIM EXPLAIN.
THANK YOU, PRESIDENT MOON.
I'VE ASKED YOU ALL HERE THIS MORNING BECAUSE I'D LIKE TEAM AVATAR TO JOIN ME IN GAOLING FOR THE UPCOMING ELECTION.
IF YOU JUST WANT US THERE FOR SHOW, FORGET IT. WE'RE NOT YOUR ENTOURAGE, WU.
NO, IT'S NOT LIKE THAT.

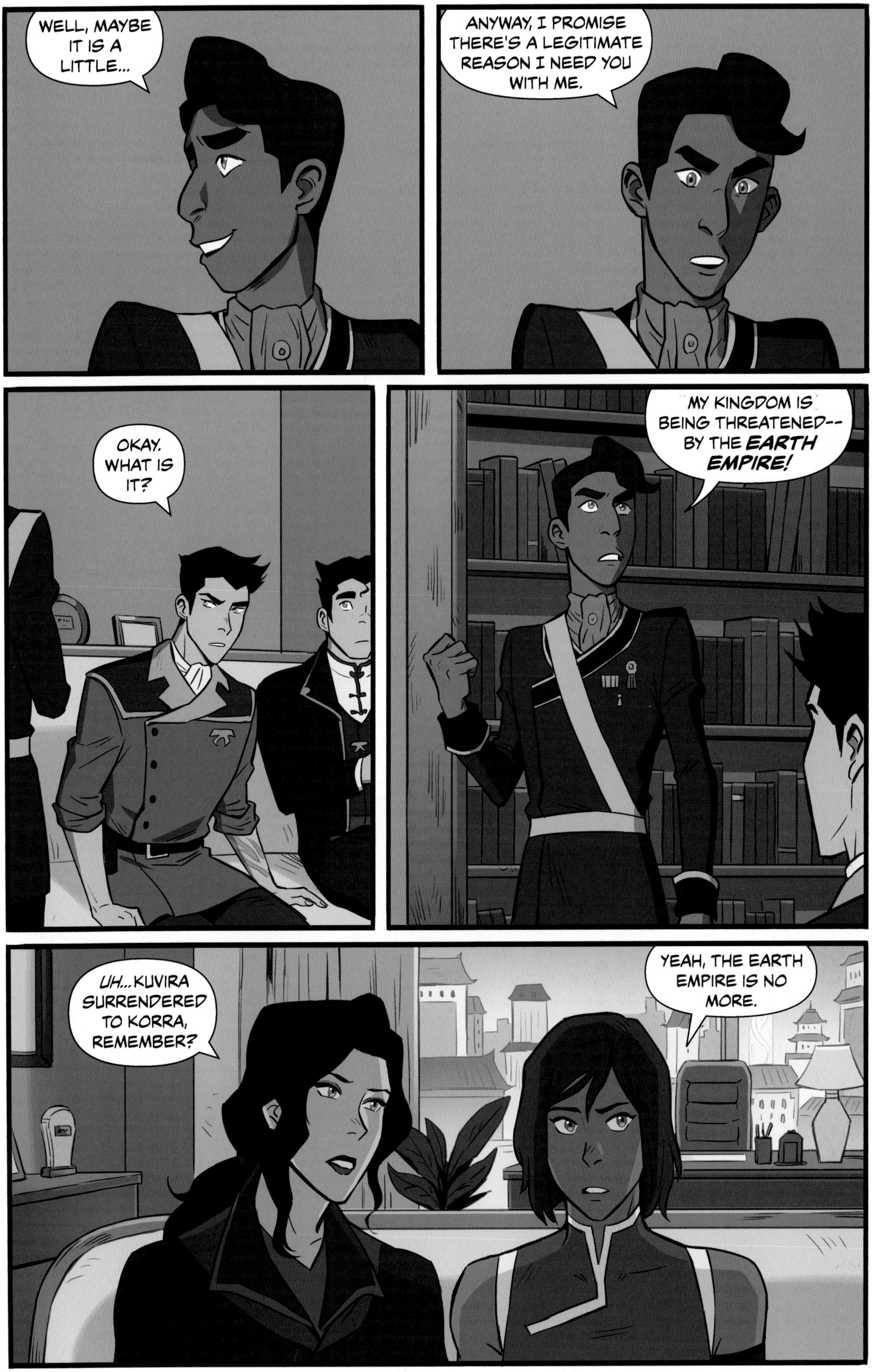
WELL, MAYBE IT IS A LITTLE...
ANYWAY, I PROMISE THERE'S A LEGITIMATE REASON I NEED YOU WITH ME.
OKAY. WHAT IS IT?
MY KINGDOM IS BEING THREATENED-- BY THE EARTH EMPIRE!
UH... KUVIRA SURRENDERED TO KORRA, REMEMBER?
YEAH, THE EARTH EMPIRE IS NO MORE.

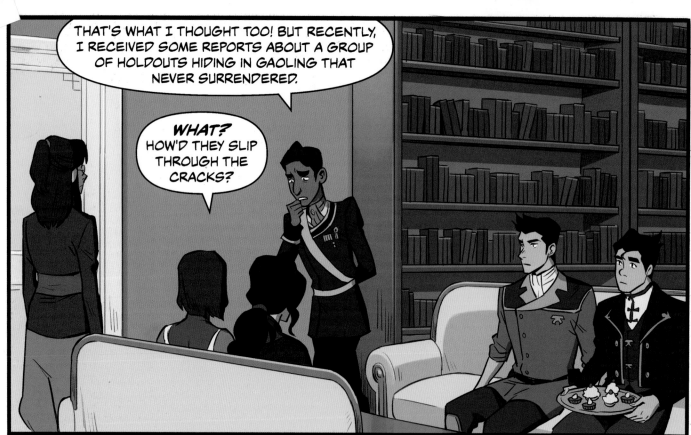

THAT'S WHAT I THOUGHT TOO! BUT RECENTLY, I RECEIVED SOME REPORTS ABOUT A GROUP OF HOLDOUTS HIDING IN GAOLING THAT NEVER SURRENDERED.

WHAT? HOW'D THEY SLIP THROUGH THE CRACKS?

KUVIRA GUTTED THE EARTH KINGDOM ARMY WHEN SHE TOOK POWER. WE'VE BEEN DOING OUR BEST TO ROUND UP EARTH EMPIRE STRAGGLERS, BUT THE ARMY IS STILL UNDERSTAFFED.

THE LEADER OF THE HOLDOUTS IS ONE OF KUVIRA'S FORMER COMMANDERS--

--A MAN BY THE NAME OF GUAN.

AND YOU'RE WORRIED GUAN AND HIS TROOPS MIGHT DISRUPT THE ELECTION?

YES! I COULDN'T GET A WINK OF SLEEP LAST NIGHT!

IF COMMANDER GUAN DOES TRY TO STOP PEOPLE FROM VOTING, IT MIGHT GIVE THE OTHER STATES AN EXCUSE TO CALL OFF THEIR ELECTIONS.

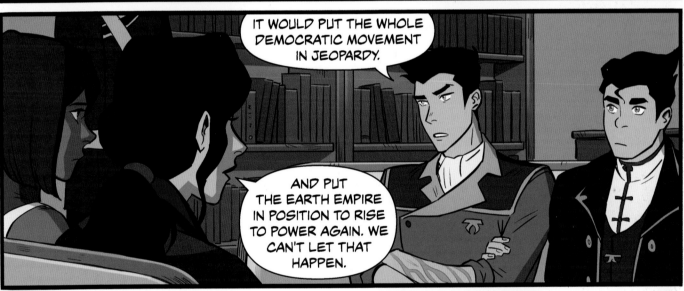

IT WOULD PUT THE WHOLE DEMOCRATIC MOVEMENT IN JEOPARDY.

AND PUT THE EARTH EMPIRE IN POSITION TO RISE TO POWER AGAIN. WE CAN'T LET THAT HAPPEN.

I THINK IT WOULD BE A GOOD IDEA FOR THE AVATAR TO STAND WITH KING WU, AS A SYMBOL OF BALANCE AND PEACE.

AGREED.

IF GUAN TRIES ANYTHING, WE'LL KEEP YOU SAFE.

YES YES YES!

31

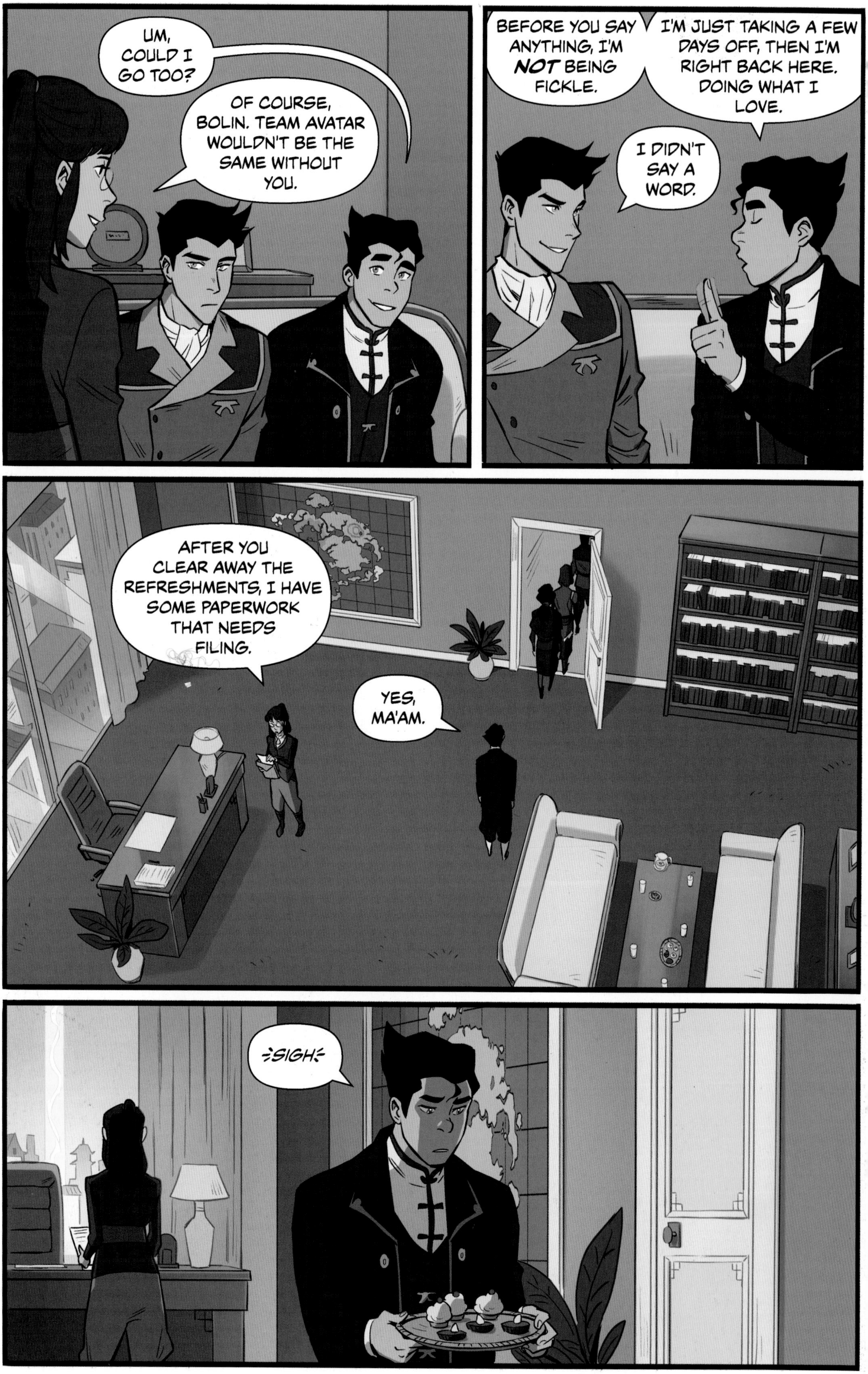
UM, COULD I GO TOO?
OF COURSE, BOLIN. TEAM AVATAR WOULDN'T BE THE SAME WITHOUT YOU.
BEFORE YOU SAY ANYTHING, I'M **NOT** BEING FICKLE.
I'M JUST TAKING A FEW DAYS OFF, THEN I'M RIGHT BACK HERE. DOING WHAT I LOVE.
I DIDN'T SAY A WORD.
AFTER YOU CLEAR AWAY THE REFRESHMENTS, I HAVE SOME PAPERWORK THAT NEEDS FILING.
YES, MA'AM.
SIGH

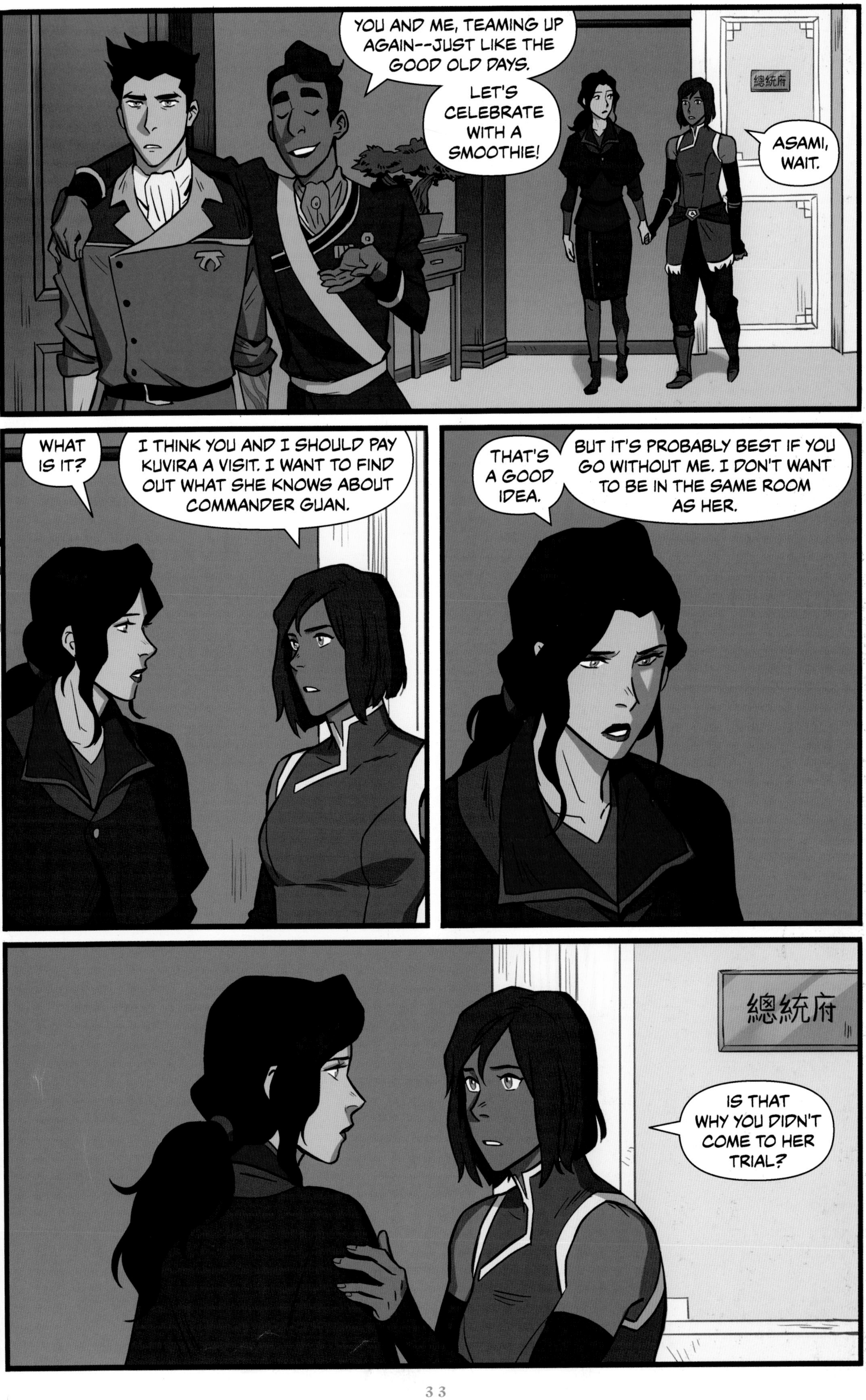
YOU AND ME, TEAMING UP AGAIN--JUST LIKE THE GOOD OLD DAYS.
LET'S CELEBRATE WITH A SMOOTHIE!
ASAMI, WAIT.
總統府
WHAT IS IT?
I THINK YOU AND I SHOULD PAY KUVIRA A VISIT. I WANT TO FIND OUT WHAT SHE KNOWS ABOUT COMMANDER GUAN.
THAT'S A GOOD IDEA.
BUT IT'S PROBABLY BEST IF YOU GO WITHOUT ME. I DON'T WANT TO BE IN THE SAME ROOM AS HER.
總統府
IS THAT WHY YOU DIDN'T COME TO HER TRIAL?

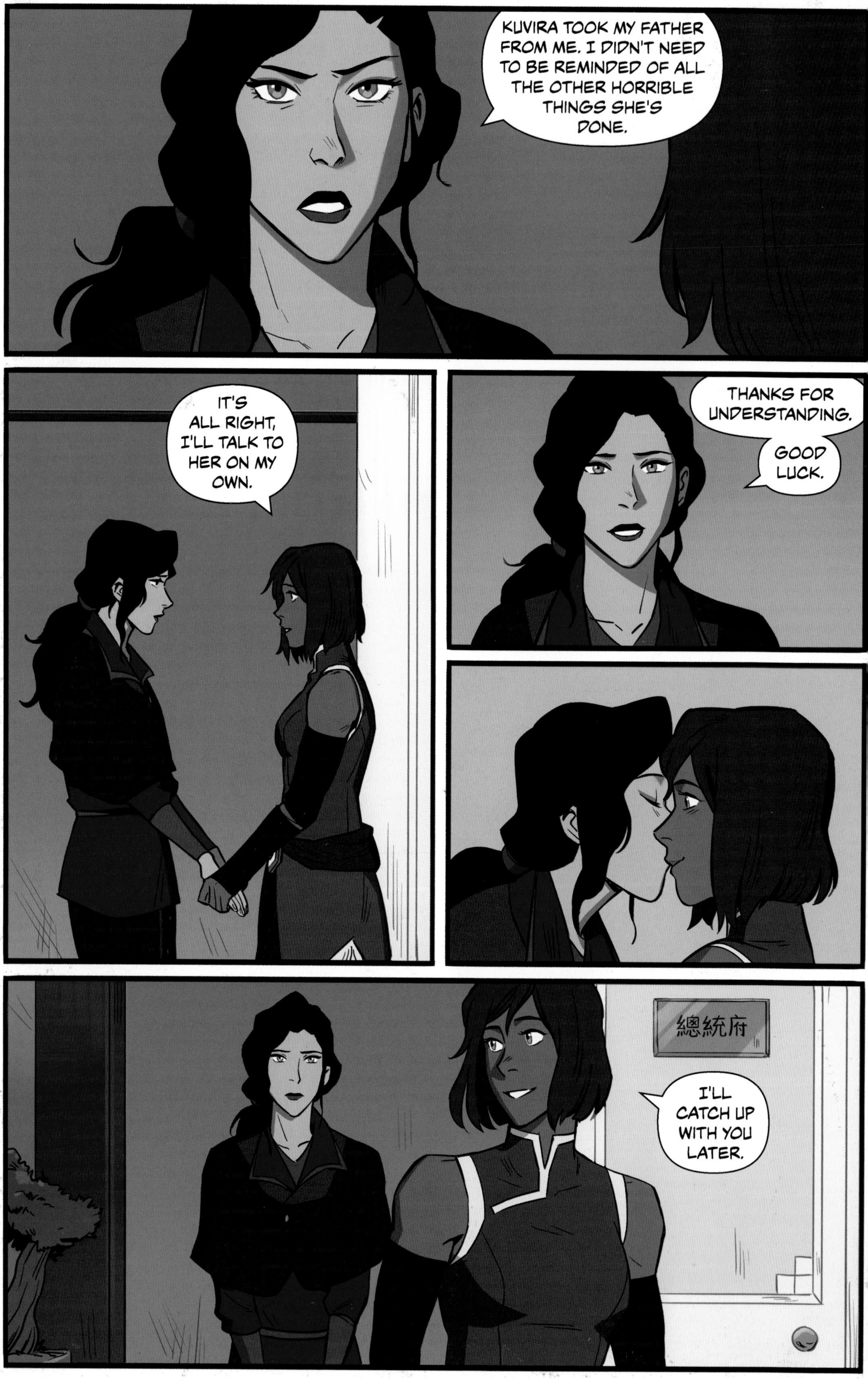
KUVIRA TOOK MY FATHER FROM ME. I DIDN'T NEED TO BE REMINDED OF ALL THE OTHER HORRIBLE THINGS SHE'S DONE.
IT'S ALL RIGHT, I'LL TALK TO HER ON MY OWN.
THANKS FOR UNDERSTANDING.
GOOD LUCK.
總統府
I'LL CATCH UP WITH YOU LATER.

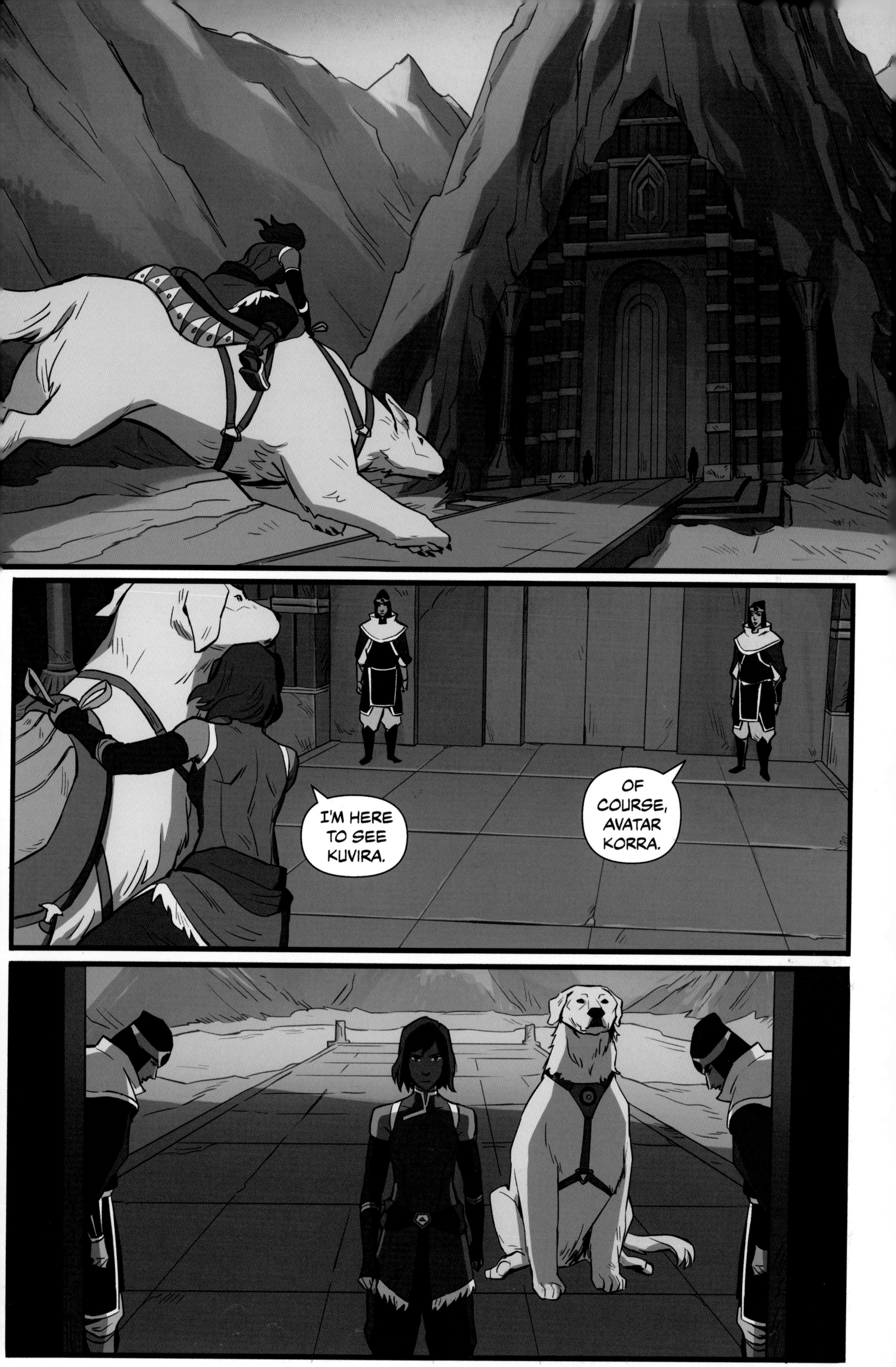
I'M HERE TO SEE KUVIRA.
OF COURSE, AVATAR KORRA.

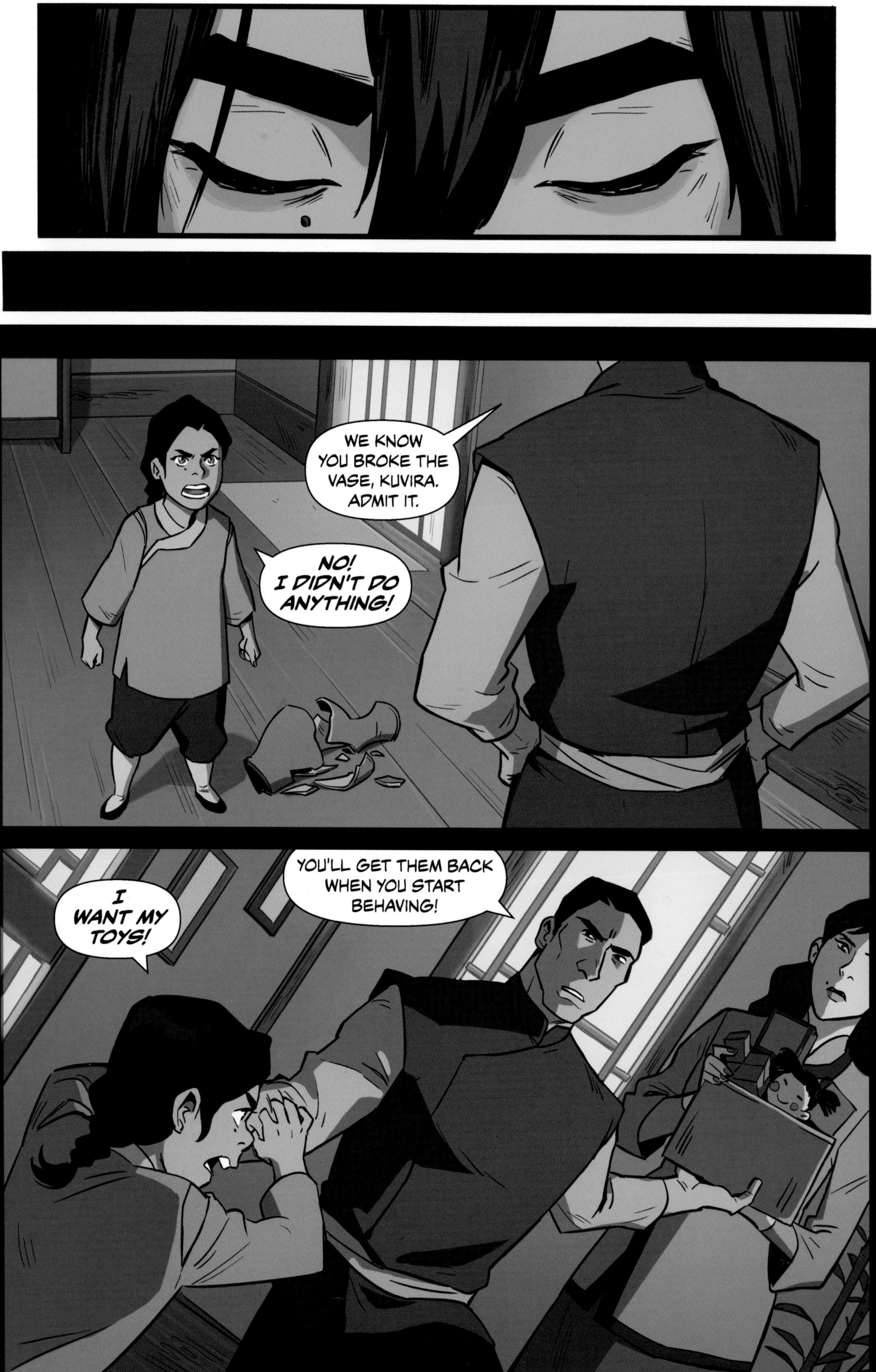
WE KNOW YOU BROKE THE VASE, KUVIRA. ADMIT IT.
NO! I DIDN'T DO ANYTHING!
I WANT MY TOYS!
YOU'LL GET THEM BACK WHEN YOU START BEHAVING!

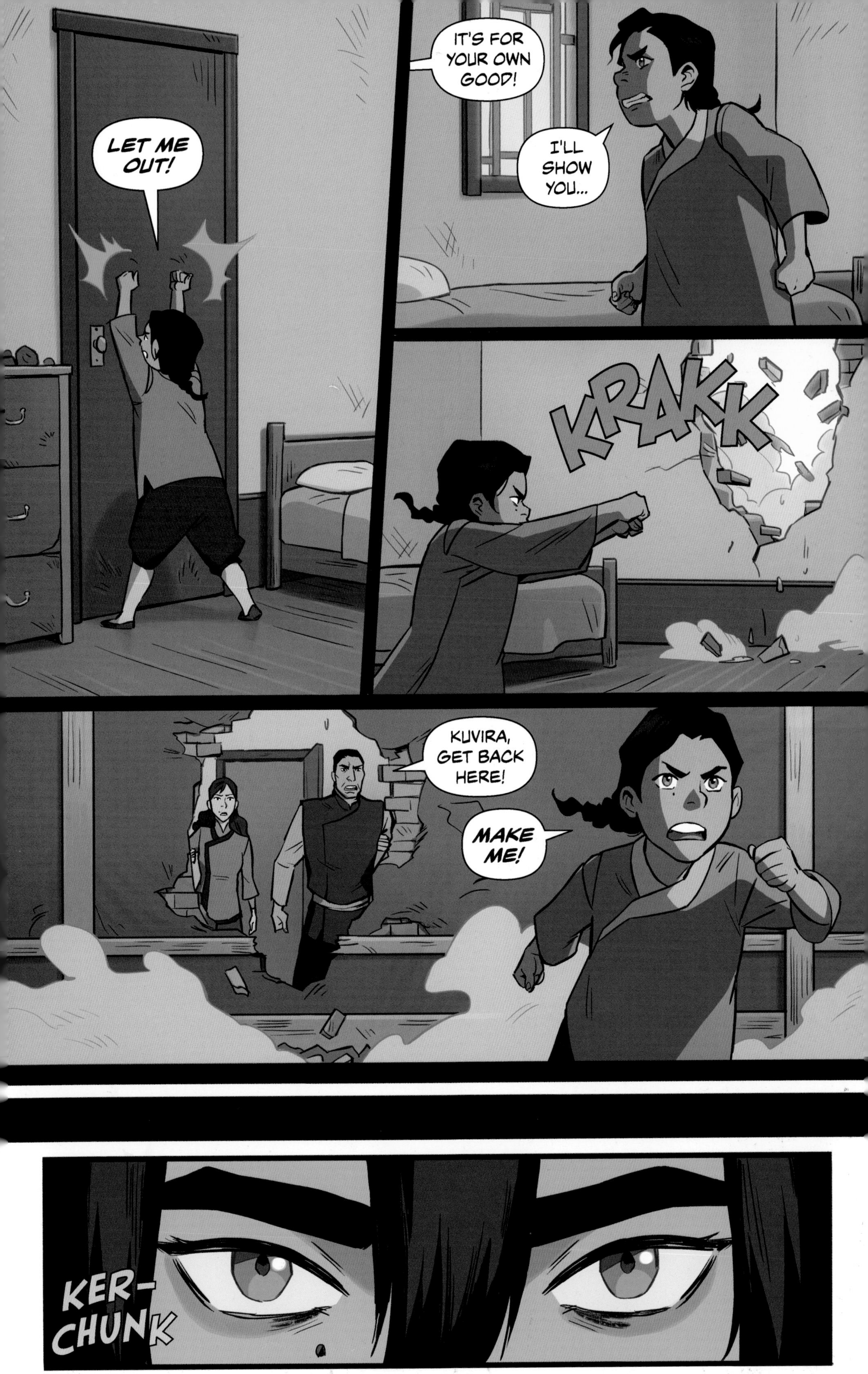

LET ME OUT!
IT'S FOR YOUR OWN GOOD!
I'LL SHOW YOU...
KRAKK
KUVIRA, GET BACK HERE!
MAKE ME!
KER-CHUNK

HELLO, KUVIRA.

I HAD A FEELING YOU WERE GOING TO BE MY FIRST VISITOR.

I NEED YOUR HELP.

WITH WHAT?

TELL ME ABOUT COMMANDER GUAN.

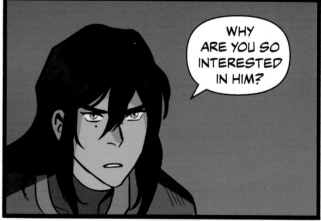

WHY ARE YOU SO INTERESTED IN HIM?

WERE YOU AWARE HE AND HIS TROOPS NEVER SURRENDERED?

WHAT?

NO, I WASN'T.

GUAN IS A CUNNING STRATEGIST WITH A KEEN MIND. I PUT HIM IN CHARGE OF MY SOUTHERN FORCES BECAUSE I KNEW HE COULD KEEP THAT REGION IN LINE.

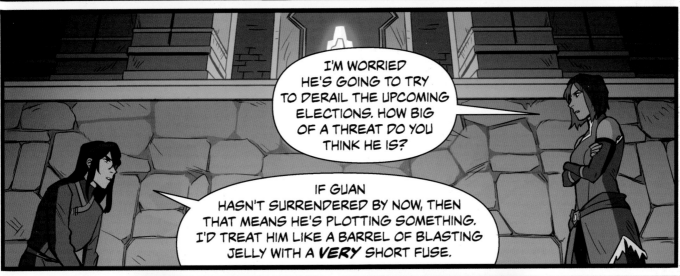

I'M WORRIED HE'S GOING TO TRY TO DERAIL THE UPCOMING ELECTIONS. HOW BIG OF A THREAT DO YOU THINK HE IS?

IF GUAN HASN'T SURRENDERED BY NOW, THEN THAT MEANS HE'S PLOTTING SOMETHING. I'D TREAT HIM LIKE A BARREL OF BLASTING JELLY WITH A *VERY* SHORT FUSE.

IF YOU WERE IN MY POSITION, HOW WOULD YOU DEAL WITH HIM?

I'D TAKE SOMEONE WITH ME WHO GUAN RESPECTS. SOMEONE WHO CAN REASON WITH HIM AND BRING HIM INTO LINE.

YOU WANT ME TO BRING *YOU?*

GUAN'S NOT GOING TO ROLL OVER JUST BECAUSE THE AVATAR ASKS HIM TO--

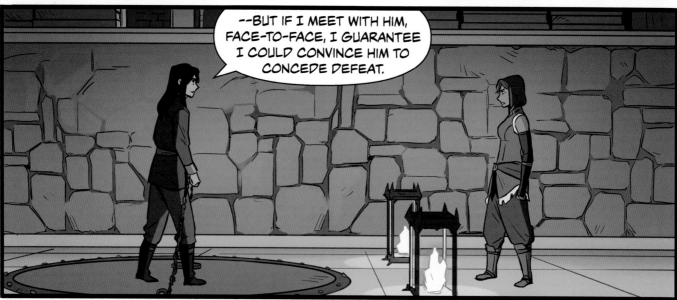

--BUT IF I MEET WITH HIM, FACE-TO-FACE, I GUARANTEE I COULD CONVINCE HIM TO CONCEDE DEFEAT.

THEN YOU AND KING WU CAN CARRY ON WITH YOUR LITTLE ELECTION.

THINK IT OVER. I'LL BE HERE WHEN YOU NEED ME.

AND YOU WILL.

THANKS FOR THE INFO. BUT I CAN HANDLE GUAN WITHOUT YOU.

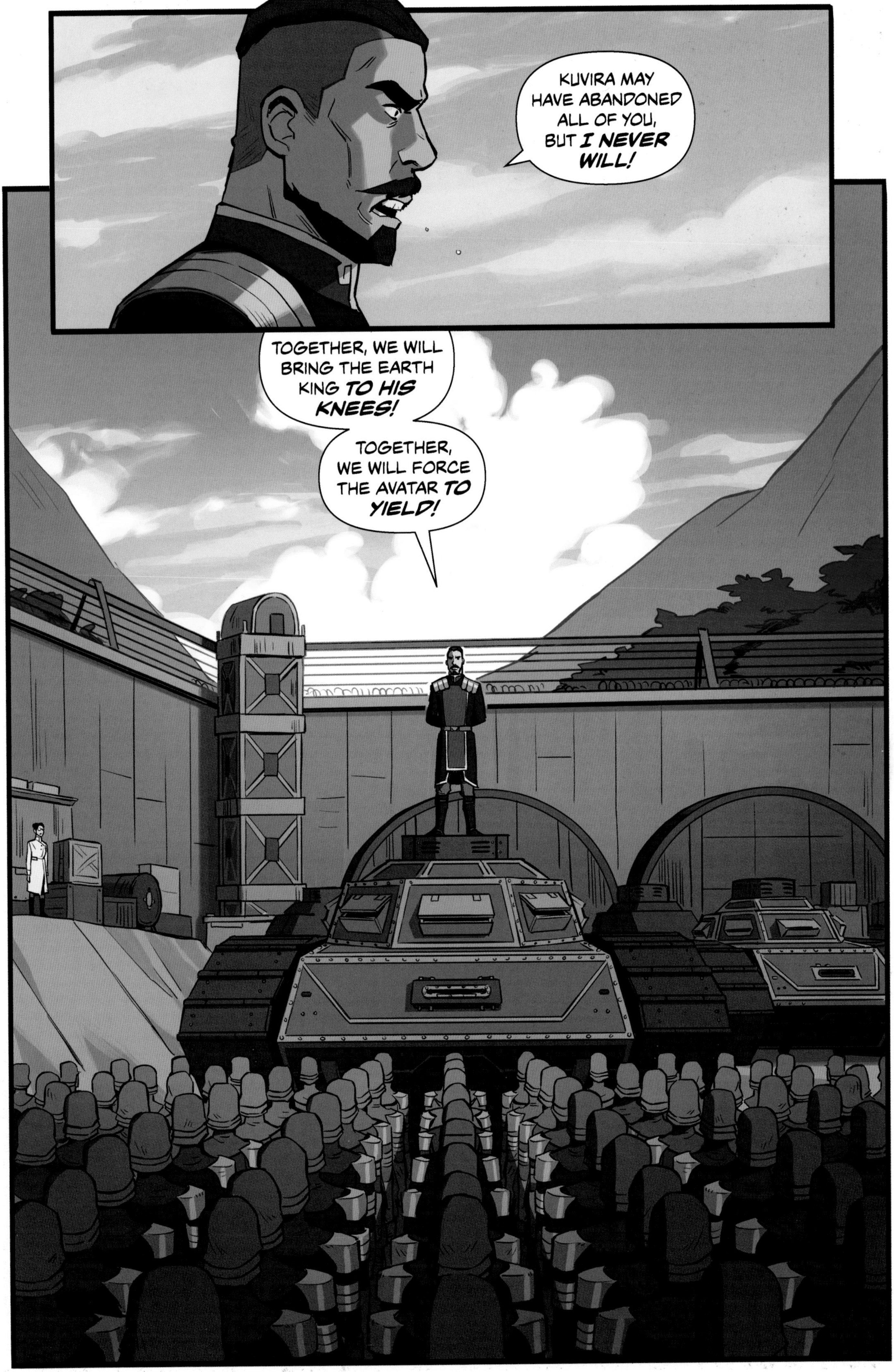
KUVIRA MAY HAVE ABANDONED ALL OF YOU, BUT I NEVER WILL!
TOGETHER, WE WILL BRING THE EARTH KING TO HIS KNEES!
TOGETHER, WE WILL FORCE THE AVATAR TO YIELD!

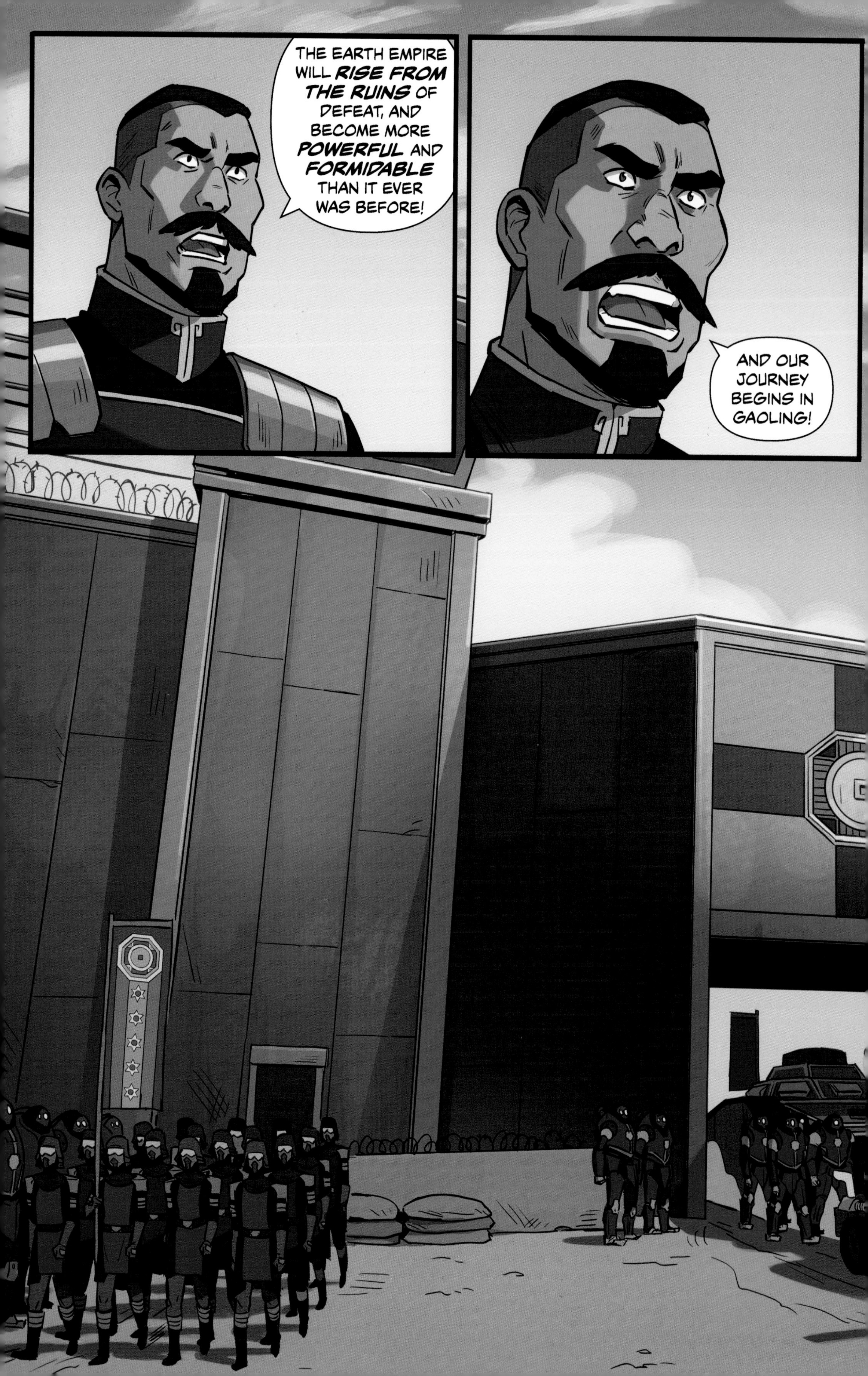
THE EARTH EMPIRE WILL RISE FROM THE RUINS OF DEFEAT, AND BECOME MORE POWERFUL AND FORMIDABLE THAN IT EVER WAS BEFORE!
AND OUR JOURNEY BEGINS IN GAOLING!

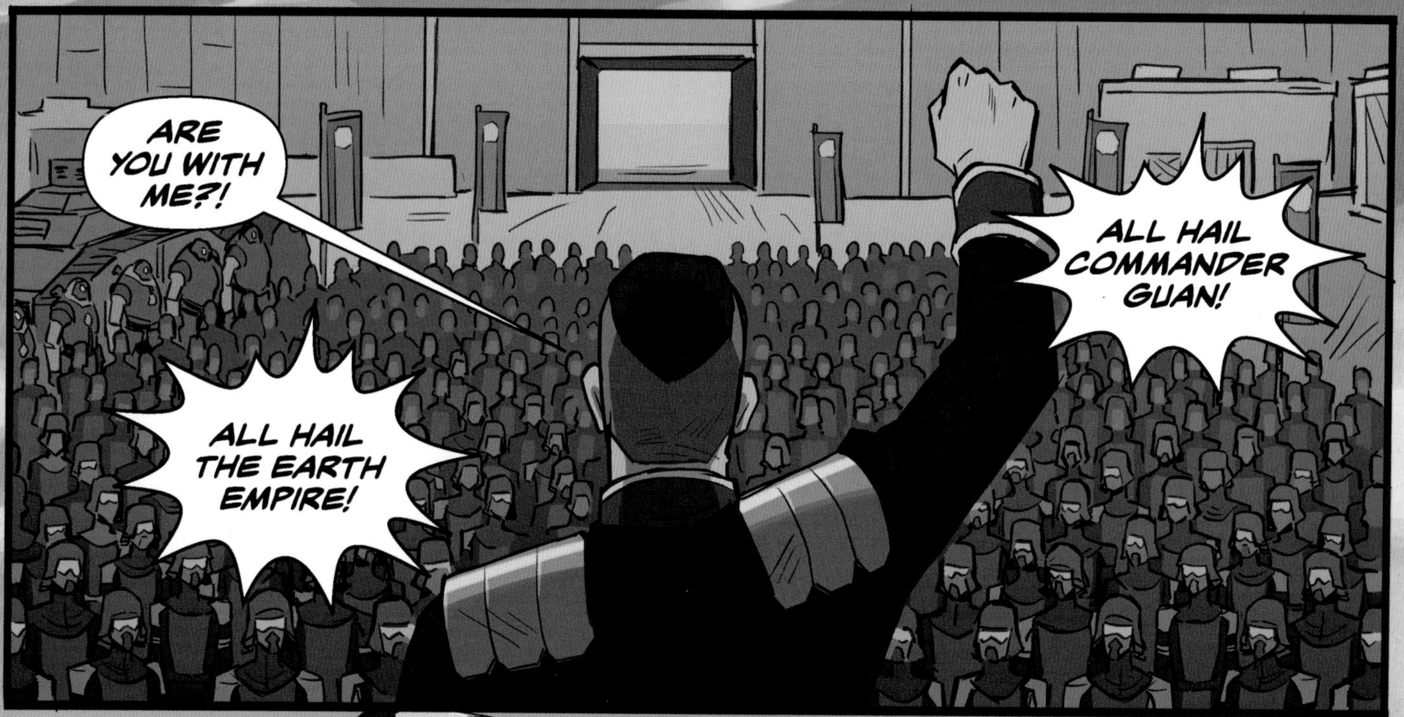
ARE YOU WITH ME?!
ALL HAIL COMMANDER GUAN!
ALL HAIL THE EARTH EMPIRE!

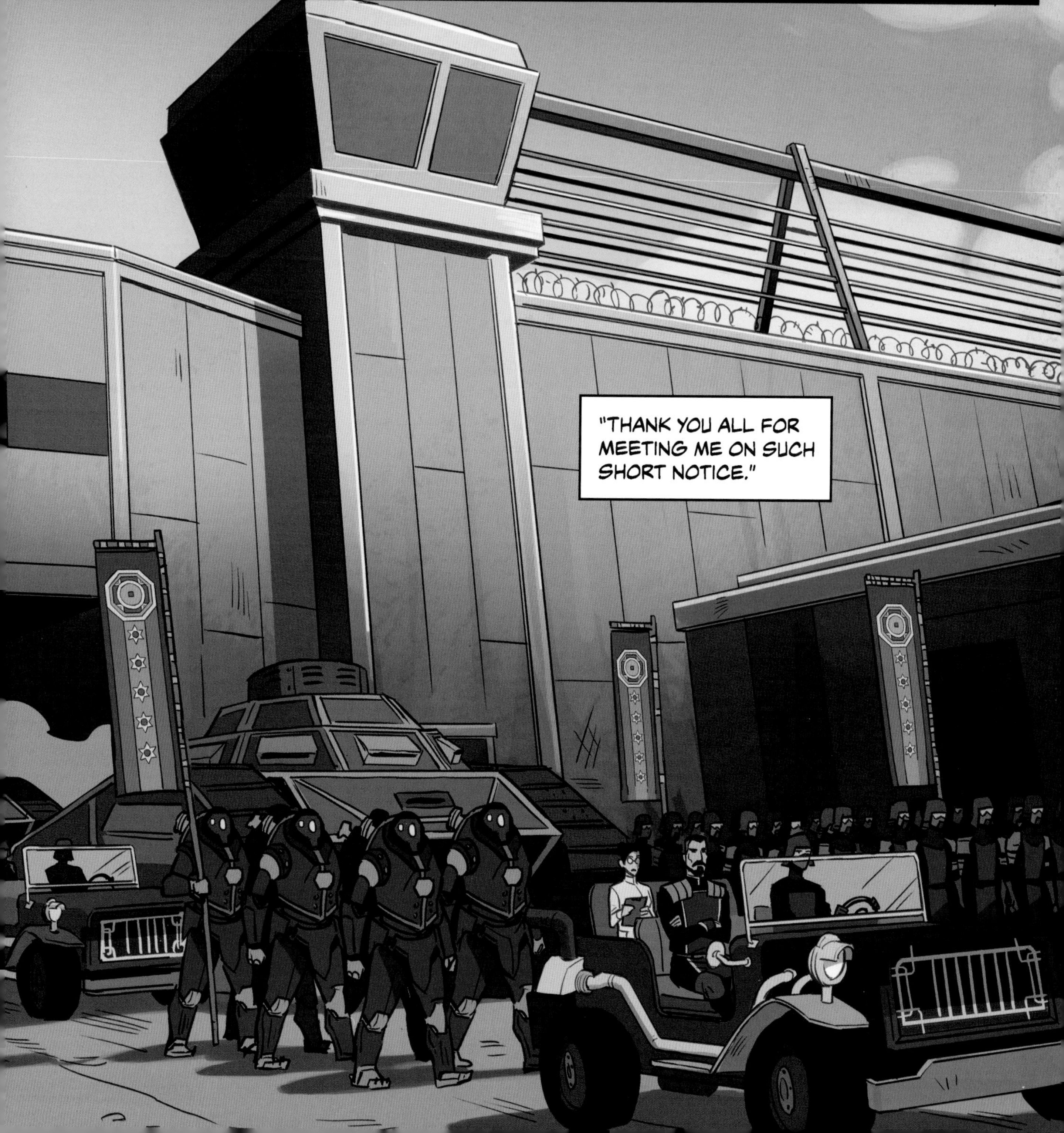
"THANK YOU ALL FOR MEETING ME ON SUCH SHORT NOTICE."

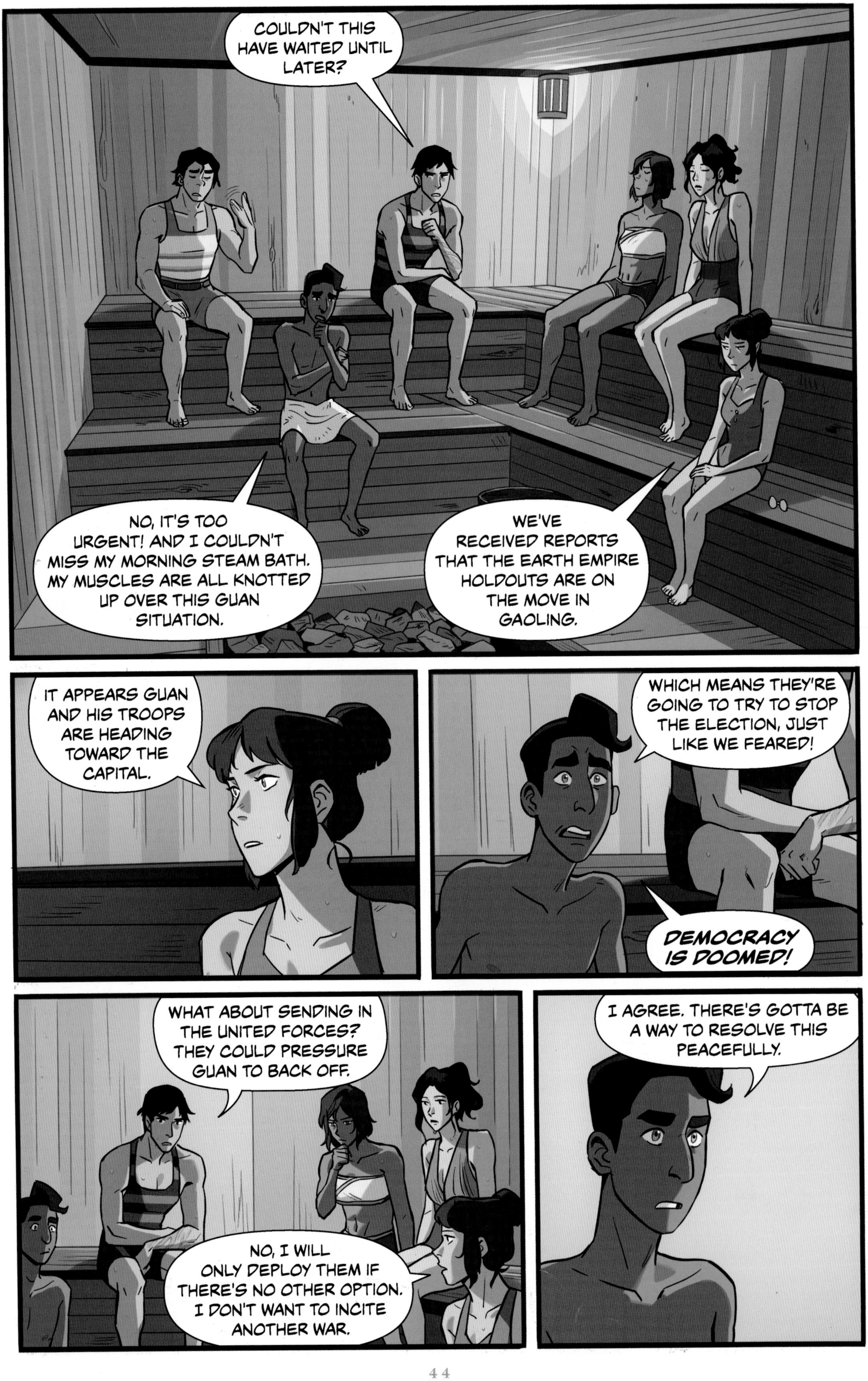
COULDN'T THIS HAVE WAITED UNTIL LATER?
NO, IT'S TOO URGENT! AND I COULDN'T MISS MY MORNING STEAM BATH. MY MUSCLES ARE ALL KNOTTED UP OVER THIS GUAN SITUATION.
WE'VE RECEIVED REPORTS THAT THE EARTH EMPIRE HOLDOUTS ARE ON THE MOVE IN GAOLING.
IT APPEARS GUAN AND HIS TROOPS ARE HEADING TOWARD THE CAPITAL.
WHICH MEANS THEY'RE GOING TO TRY TO STOP THE ELECTION, JUST LIKE WE FEARED!
DEMOCRACY IS DOOMED!
WHAT ABOUT SENDING IN THE UNITED FORCES? THEY COULD PRESSURE GUAN TO BACK OFF.
NO, I WILL ONLY DEPLOY THEM IF THERE'S NO OTHER OPTION. I DON'T WANT TO INCITE ANOTHER WAR.
I AGREE. THERE'S GOTTA BE A WAY TO RESOLVE THIS PEACEFULLY.

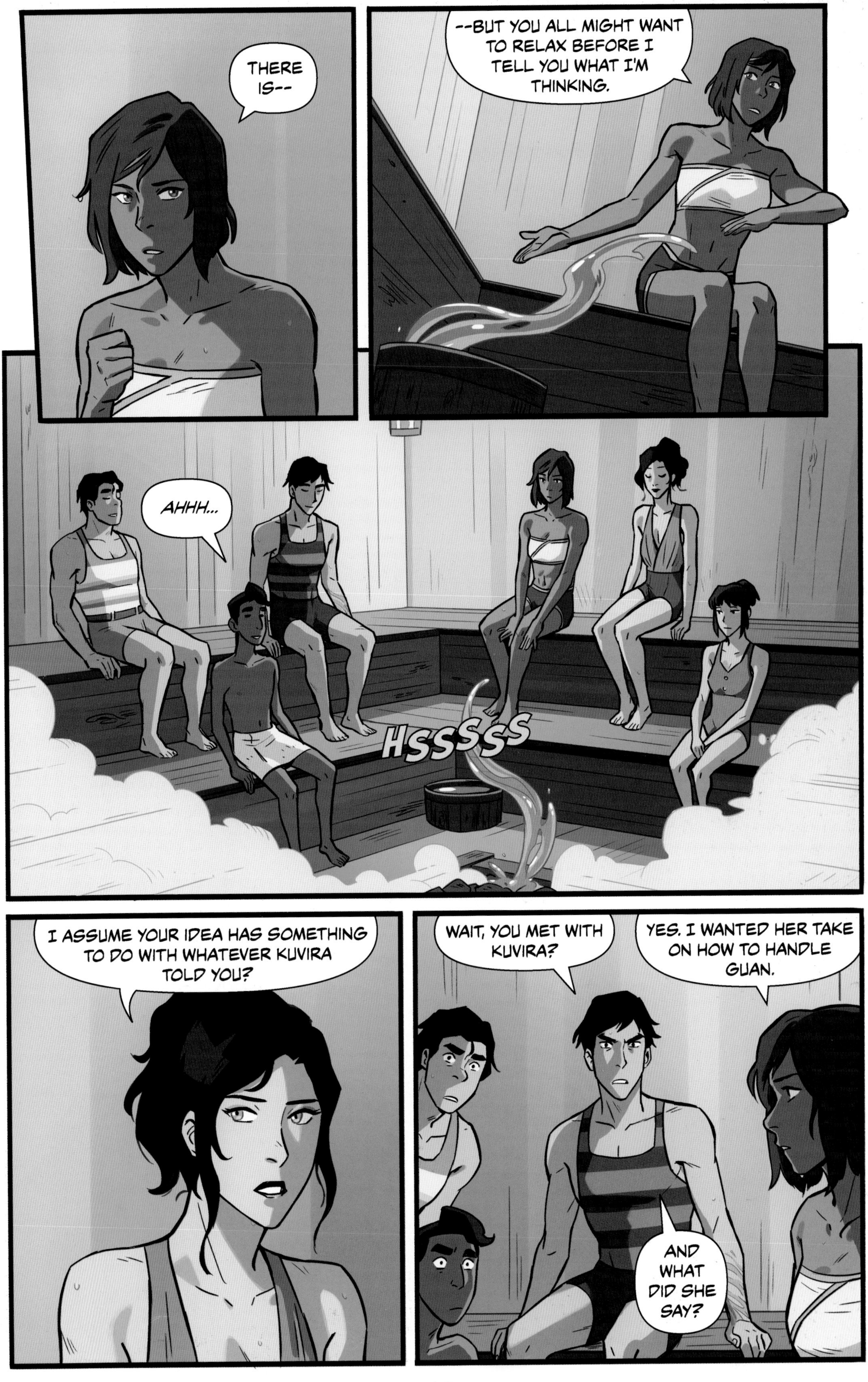
THERE IS--
--BUT YOU ALL MIGHT WANT TO RELAX BEFORE I TELL YOU WHAT I'M THINKING.
AHHH...
HSSSSS
I ASSUME YOUR IDEA HAS SOMETHING TO DO WITH WHATEVER KUVIRA TOLD YOU?
WAIT, YOU MET WITH KUVIRA?
YES. I WANTED HER TAKE ON HOW TO HANDLE GUAN.
AND WHAT DID SHE SAY?

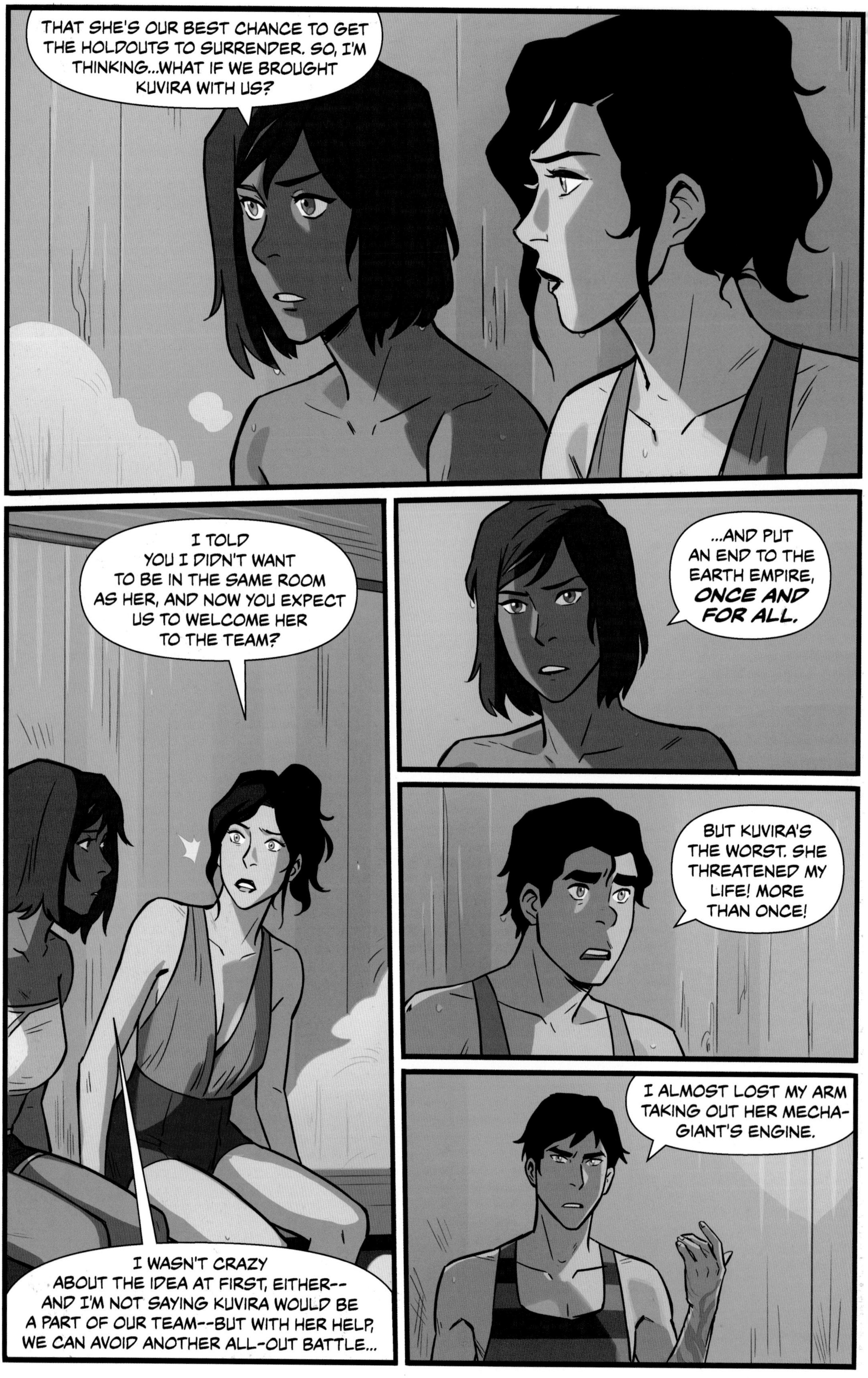
THAT SHE'S OUR BEST CHANCE TO GET THE HOLDOUTS TO SURRENDER. SO, I'M THINKING...WHAT IF WE BROUGHT KUVIRA WITH US?
...AND PUT AN END TO THE EARTH EMPIRE, ONCE AND FOR ALL.
I TOLD YOU I DIDN'T WANT TO BE IN THE SAME ROOM AS HER, AND NOW YOU EXPECT US TO WELCOME HER TO THE TEAM?
BUT KUVIRA'S THE WORST. SHE THREATENED MY LIFE! MORE THAN ONCE!
I ALMOST LOST MY ARM TAKING OUT HER MECHA-GIANT'S ENGINE.
I WASN'T CRAZY ABOUT THE IDEA AT FIRST, EITHER-- AND I'M NOT SAYING KUVIRA WOULD BE A PART OF OUR TEAM--BUT WITH HER HELP, WE CAN AVOID ANOTHER ALL-OUT BATTLE...

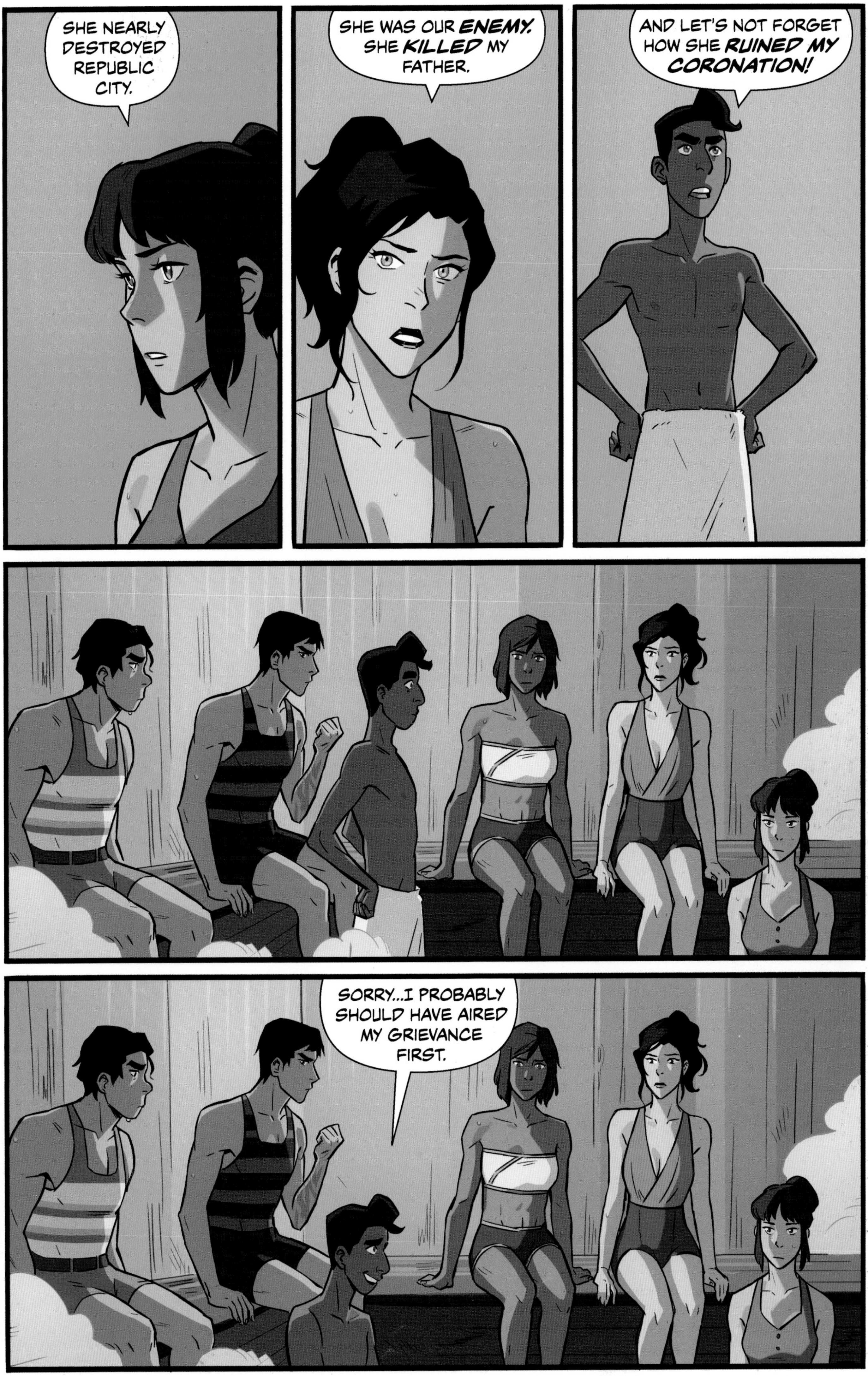
SHE NEARLY DESTROYED REPUBLIC CITY.
SHE WAS OUR ENEMY. SHE KILLED MY FATHER.
AND LET'S NOT FORGET HOW SHE RUINED MY CORONATION!
SORRY...I PROBABLY SHOULD HAVE AIRED MY GRIEVANCE FIRST.

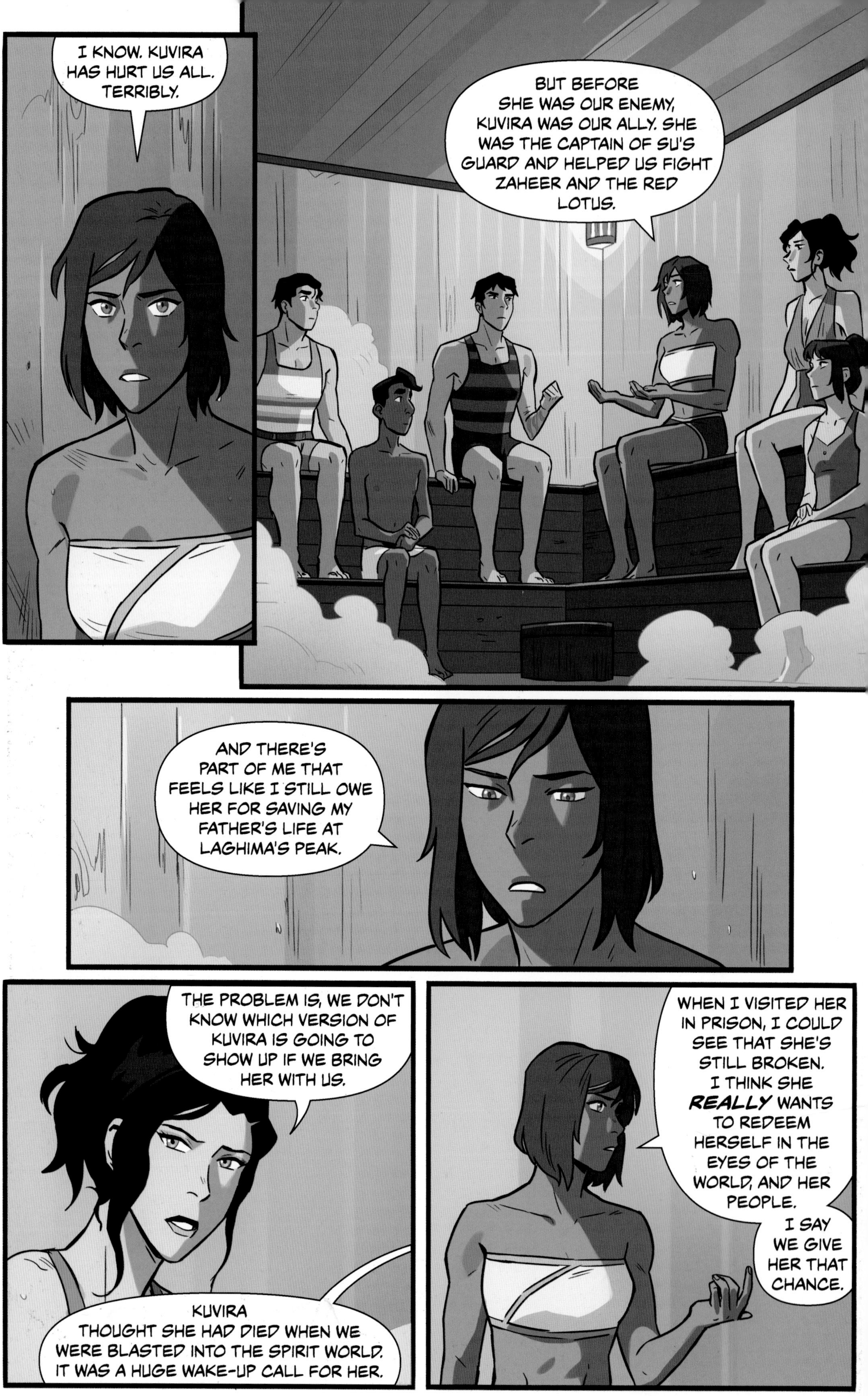
I KNOW. KUVIRA HAS HURT US ALL. TERRIBLY.
BUT BEFORE SHE WAS OUR ENEMY, KUVIRA WAS OUR ALLY. SHE WAS THE CAPTAIN OF SU'S GUARD AND HELPED US FIGHT ZAHEER AND THE RED LOTUS.
AND THERE'S PART OF ME THAT FEELS LIKE I STILL OWE HER FOR SAVING MY FATHER'S LIFE AT LAGHIMA'S PEAK.
THE PROBLEM IS, WE DON'T KNOW WHICH VERSION OF KUVIRA IS GOING TO SHOW UP IF WE BRING HER WITH US.
KUVIRA THOUGHT SHE HAD DIED WHEN WE WERE BLASTED INTO THE SPIRIT WORLD. IT WAS A HUGE WAKE-UP CALL FOR HER.
WHEN I VISITED HER IN PRISON, I COULD SEE THAT SHE'S STILL BROKEN. I THINK SHE ***REALLY*** WANTS TO REDEEM HERSELF IN THE EYES OF THE WORLD, AND HER PEOPLE.
I SAY WE GIVE HER THAT CHANCE.

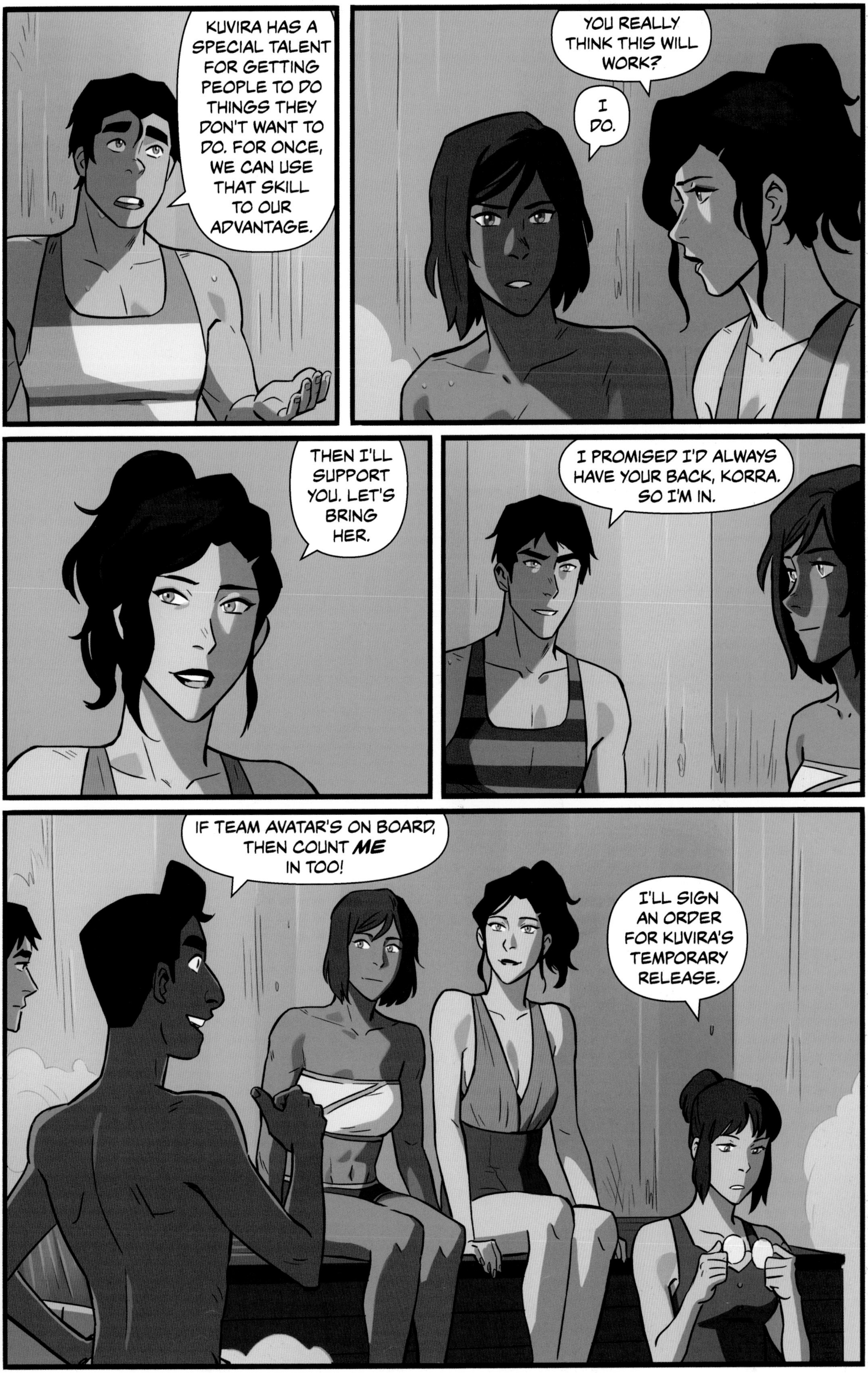
KUVIRA HAS A SPECIAL TALENT FOR GETTING PEOPLE TO DO THINGS THEY DON'T WANT TO DO. FOR ONCE, WE CAN USE THAT SKILL TO OUR ADVANTAGE.
YOU REALLY THINK THIS WILL WORK?
I DO.
THEN I'LL SUPPORT YOU. LET'S BRING HER.
I PROMISED I'D ALWAYS HAVE YOUR BACK, KORRA. SO I'M IN.
IF TEAM AVATAR'S ON BOARD, THEN COUNT ***ME*** IN TOO!
I'LL SIGN AN ORDER FOR KUVIRA'S TEMPORARY RELEASE.

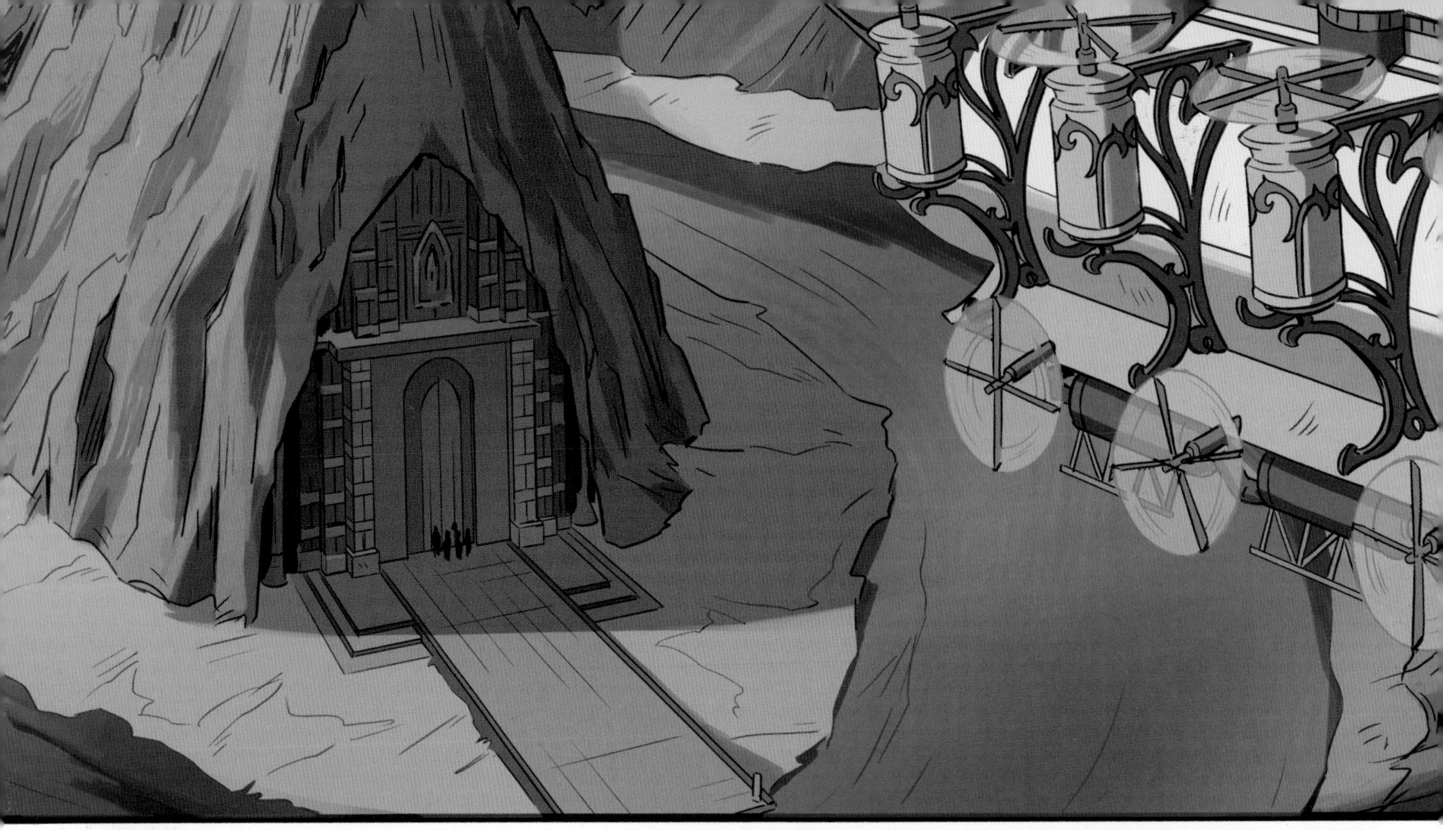

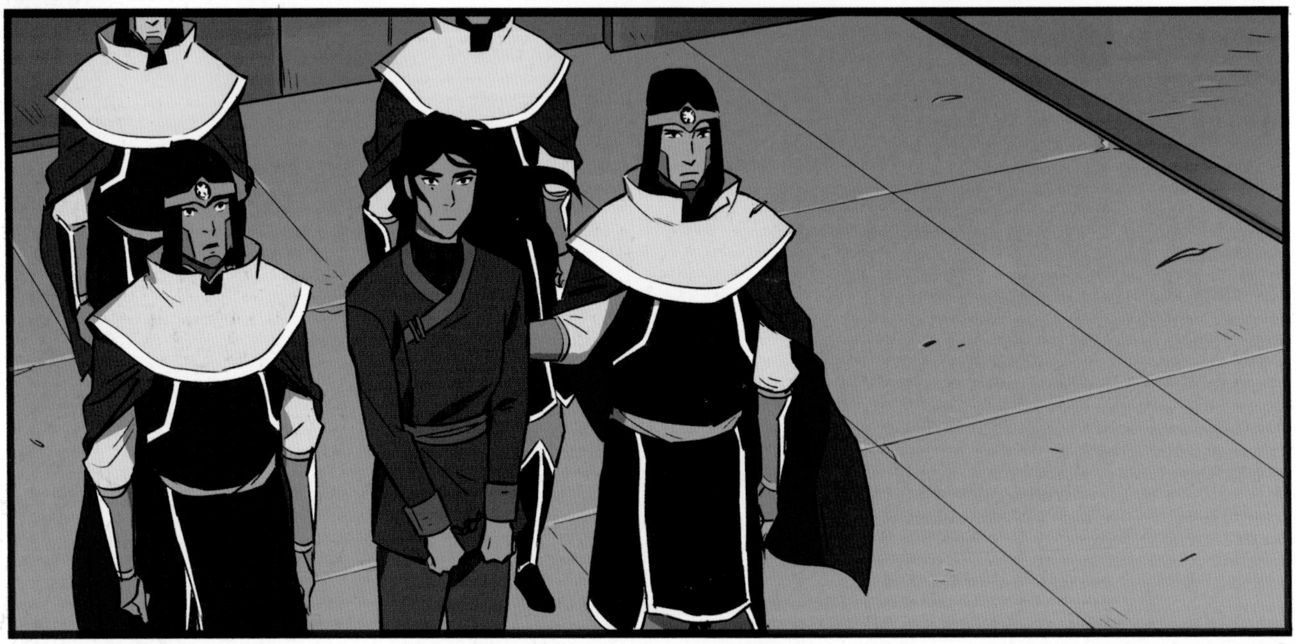

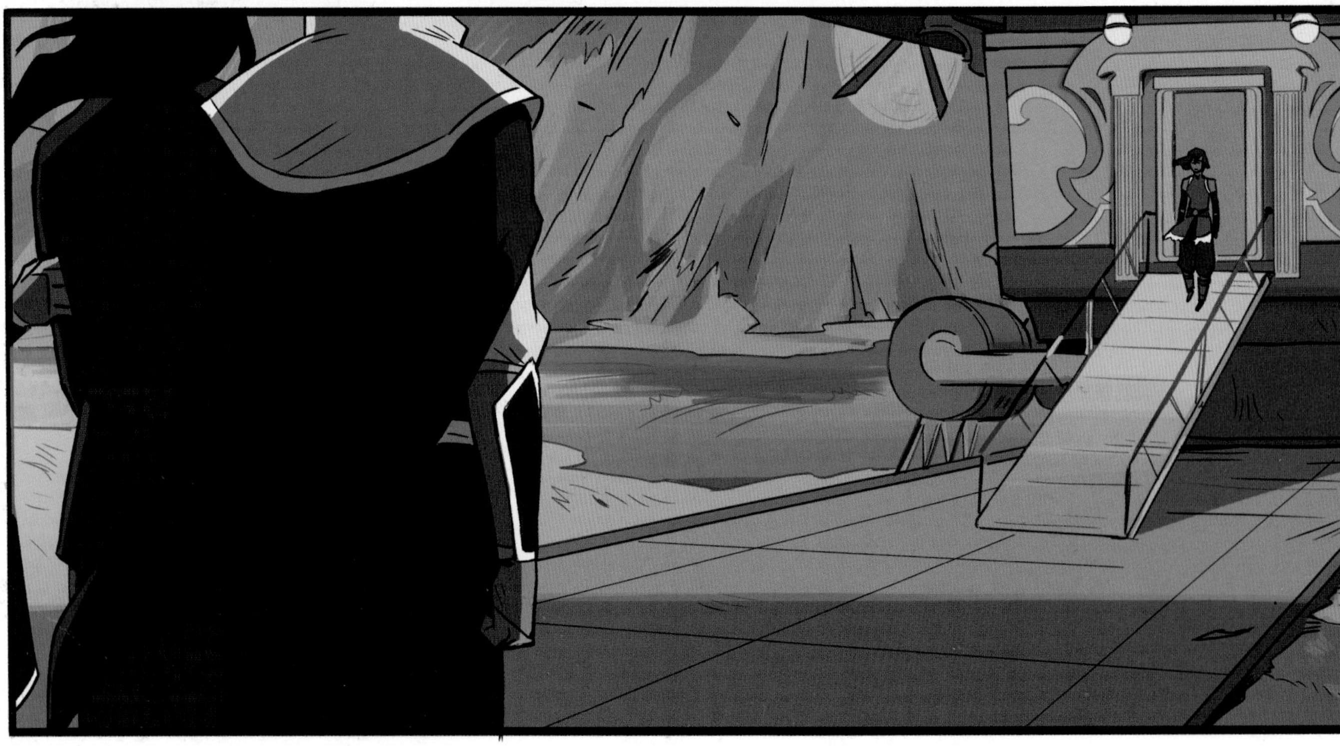

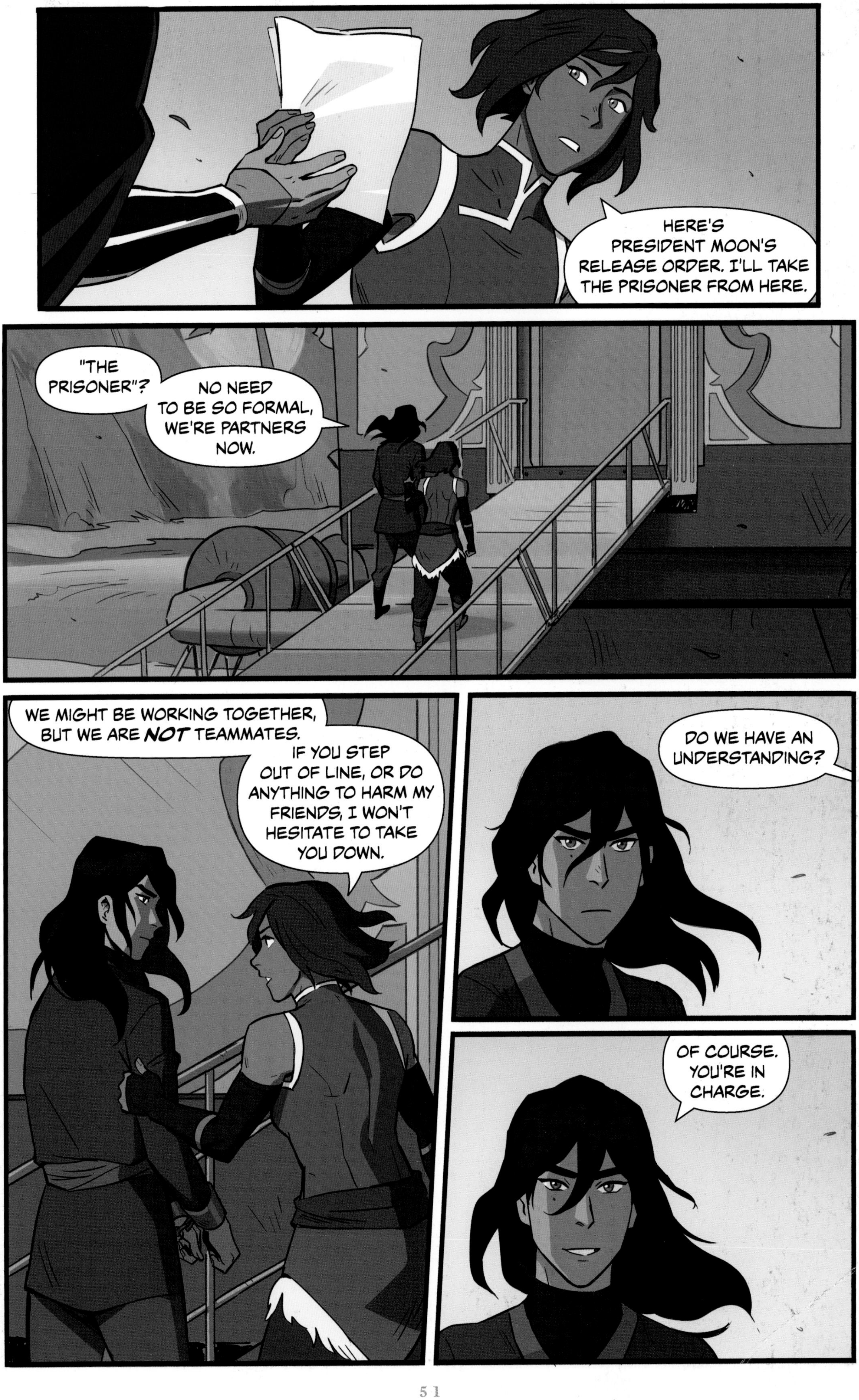
HERE'S PRESIDENT MOON'S RELEASE ORDER. I'LL TAKE THE PRISONER FROM HERE.
"THE PRISONER"?
NO NEED TO BE SO FORMAL, WE'RE PARTNERS NOW.
WE MIGHT BE WORKING TOGETHER, BUT WE ARE *NOT* TEAMMATES.
IF YOU STEP OUT OF LINE, OR DO ANYTHING TO HARM MY FRIENDS, I WON'T HESITATE TO TAKE YOU DOWN.
DO WE HAVE AN UNDERSTANDING?
OF COURSE. YOU'RE IN CHARGE.

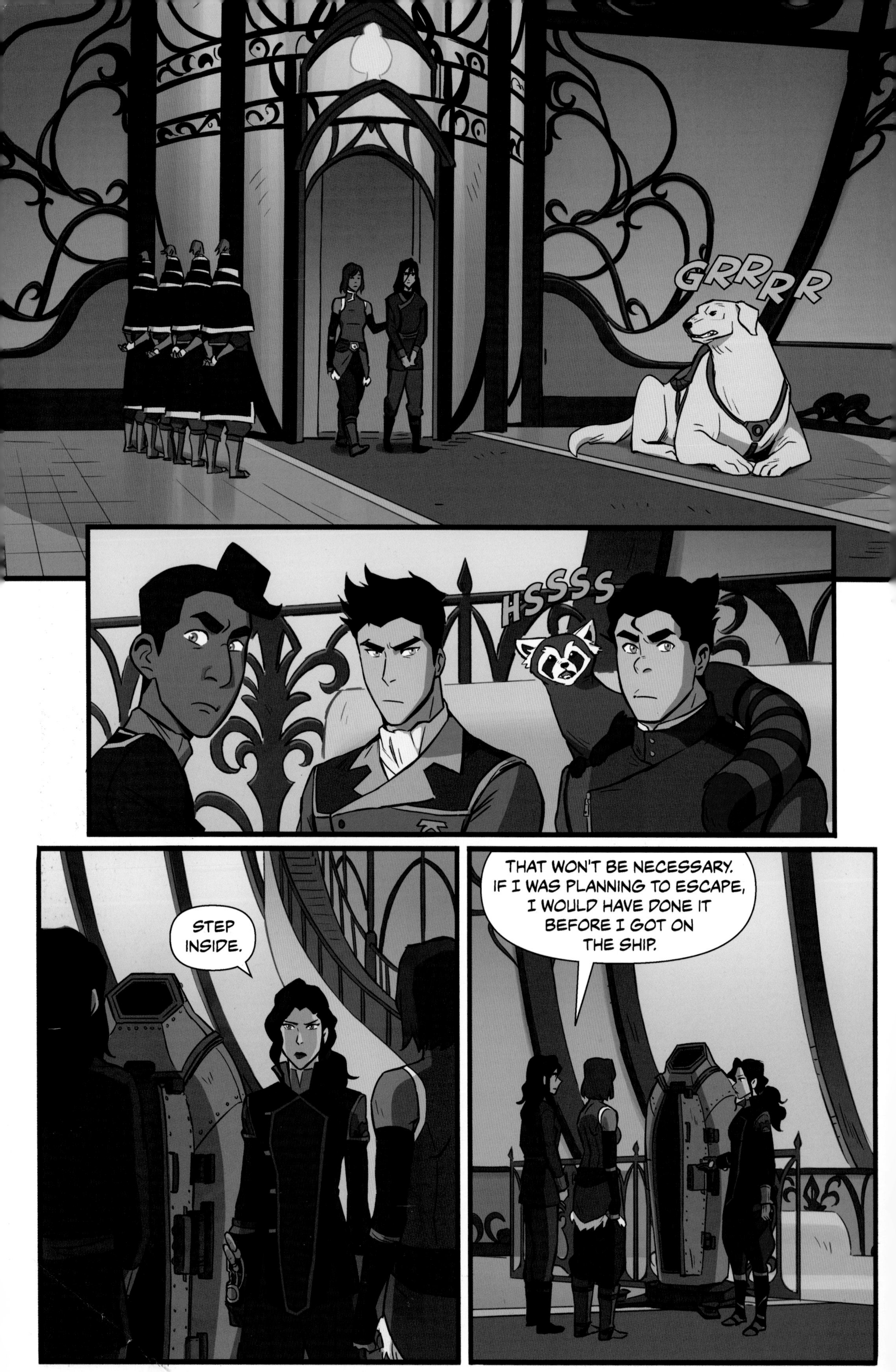
GRRRR
HSSSS
STEP INSIDE.
THAT WON'T BE NECESSARY. IF I WAS PLANNING TO ESCAPE, I WOULD HAVE DONE IT BEFORE I GOT ON THE SHIP.

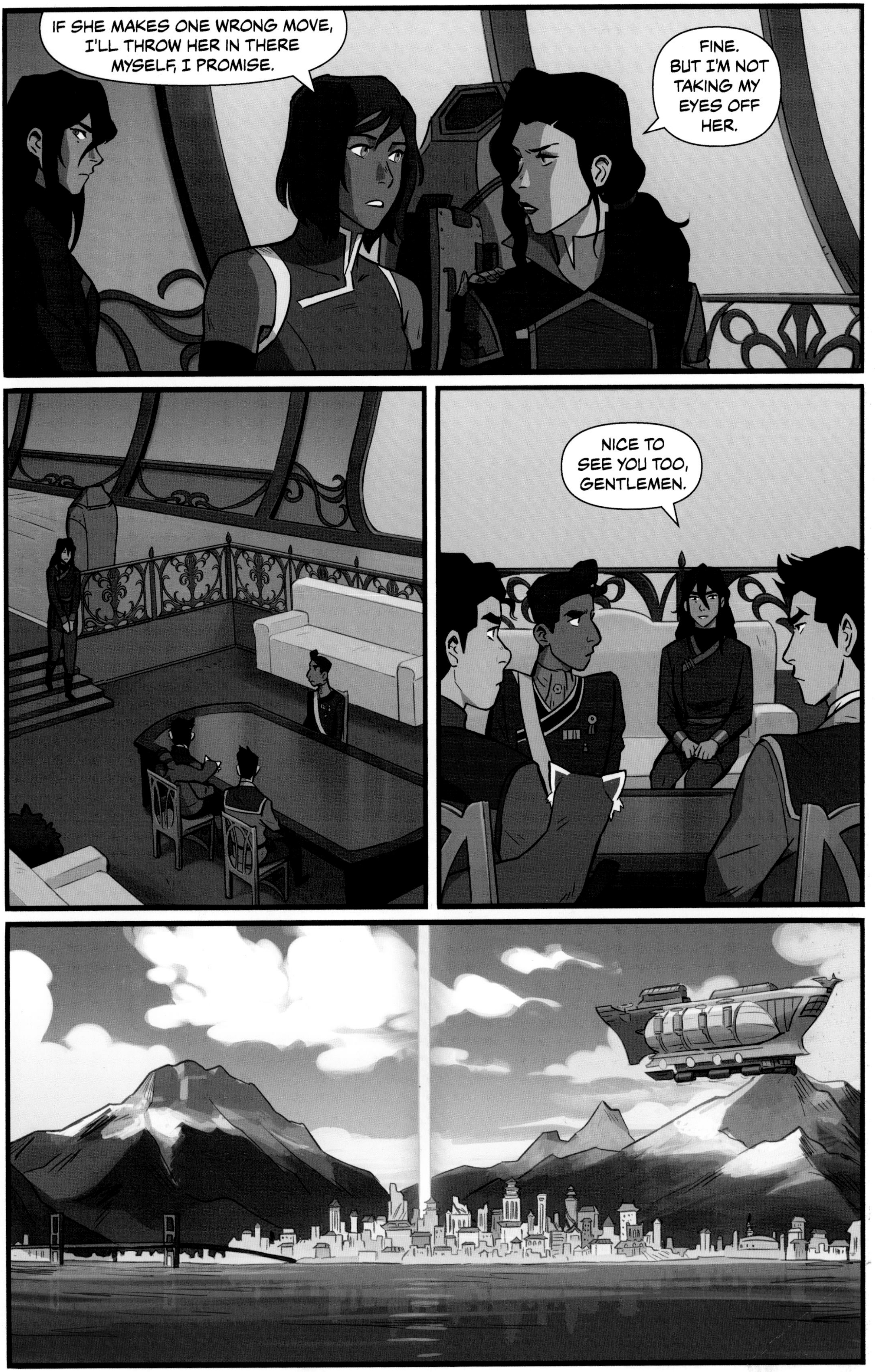
IF SHE MAKES ONE WRONG MOVE, I'LL THROW HER IN THERE MYSELF, I PROMISE.
FINE. BUT I'M NOT TAKING MY EYES OFF HER.
NICE TO SEE YOU TOO, GENTLEMEN.

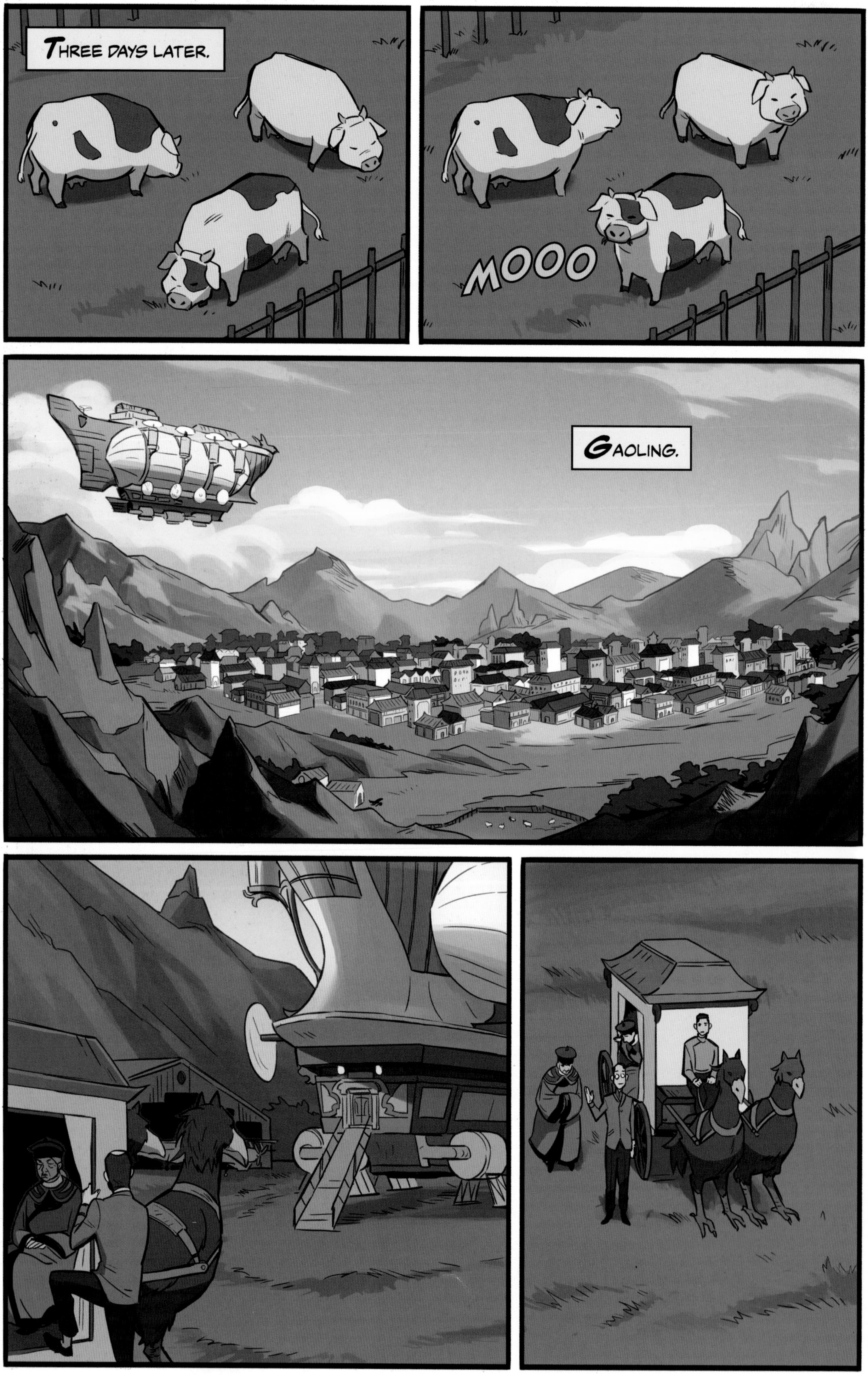
THREE DAYS LATER.
MOOO
GAOLING.

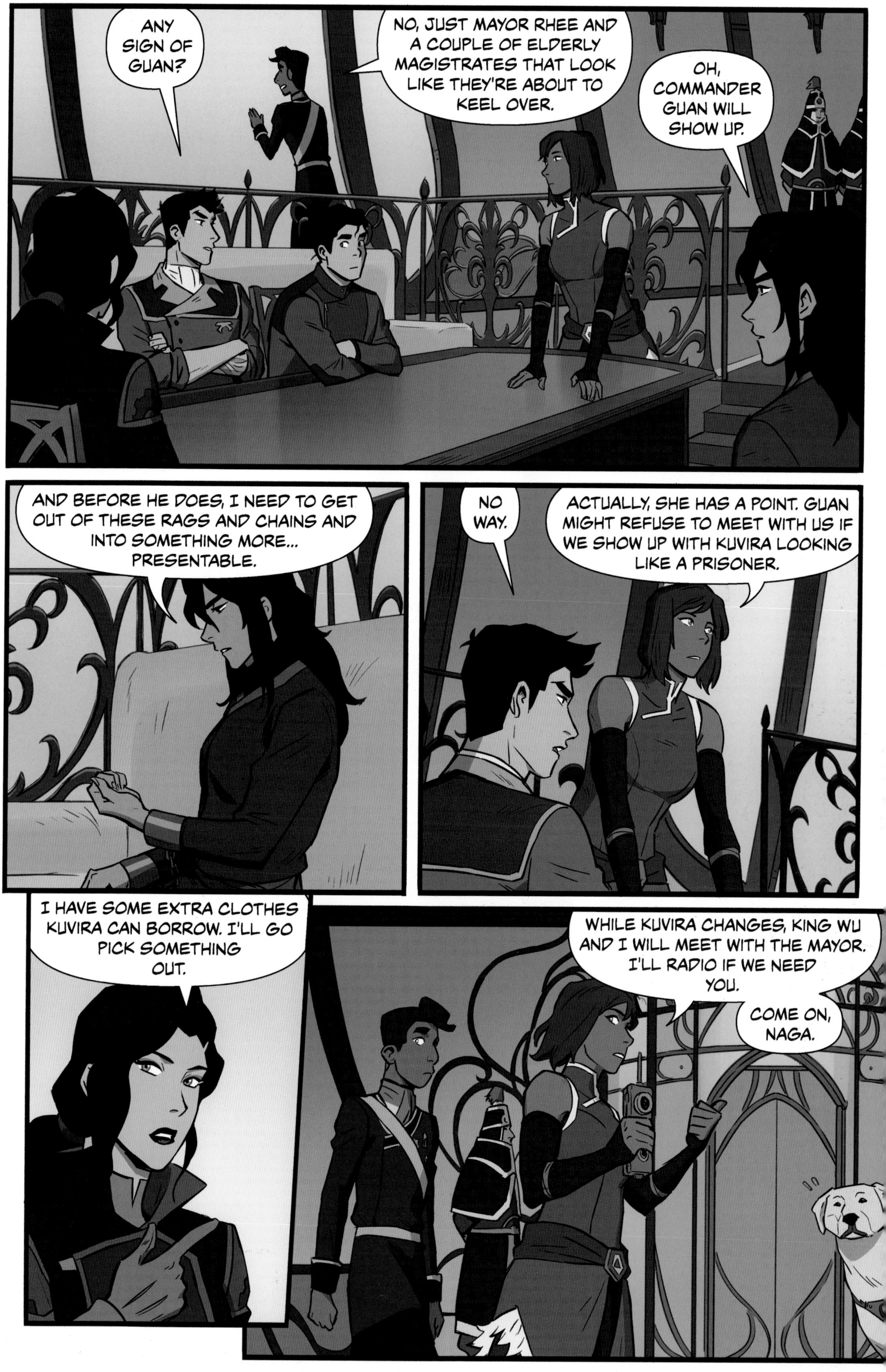
ANY SIGN OF GUAN?
NO, JUST MAYOR RHEE AND A COUPLE OF ELDERLY MAGISTRATES THAT LOOK LIKE THEY'RE ABOUT TO KEEL OVER.
OH, COMMANDER GUAN WILL SHOW UP.
AND BEFORE HE DOES, I NEED TO GET OUT OF THESE RAGS AND CHAINS AND INTO SOMETHING MORE... PRESENTABLE.
NO WAY.
ACTUALLY, SHE HAS A POINT. GUAN MIGHT REFUSE TO MEET WITH US IF WE SHOW UP WITH KUVIRA LOOKING LIKE A PRISONER.
I HAVE SOME EXTRA CLOTHES KUVIRA CAN BORROW. I'LL GO PICK SOMETHING OUT.
WHILE KUVIRA CHANGES, KING WU AND I WILL MEET WITH THE MAYOR. I'LL RADIO IF WE NEED YOU.
COME ON, NAGA.

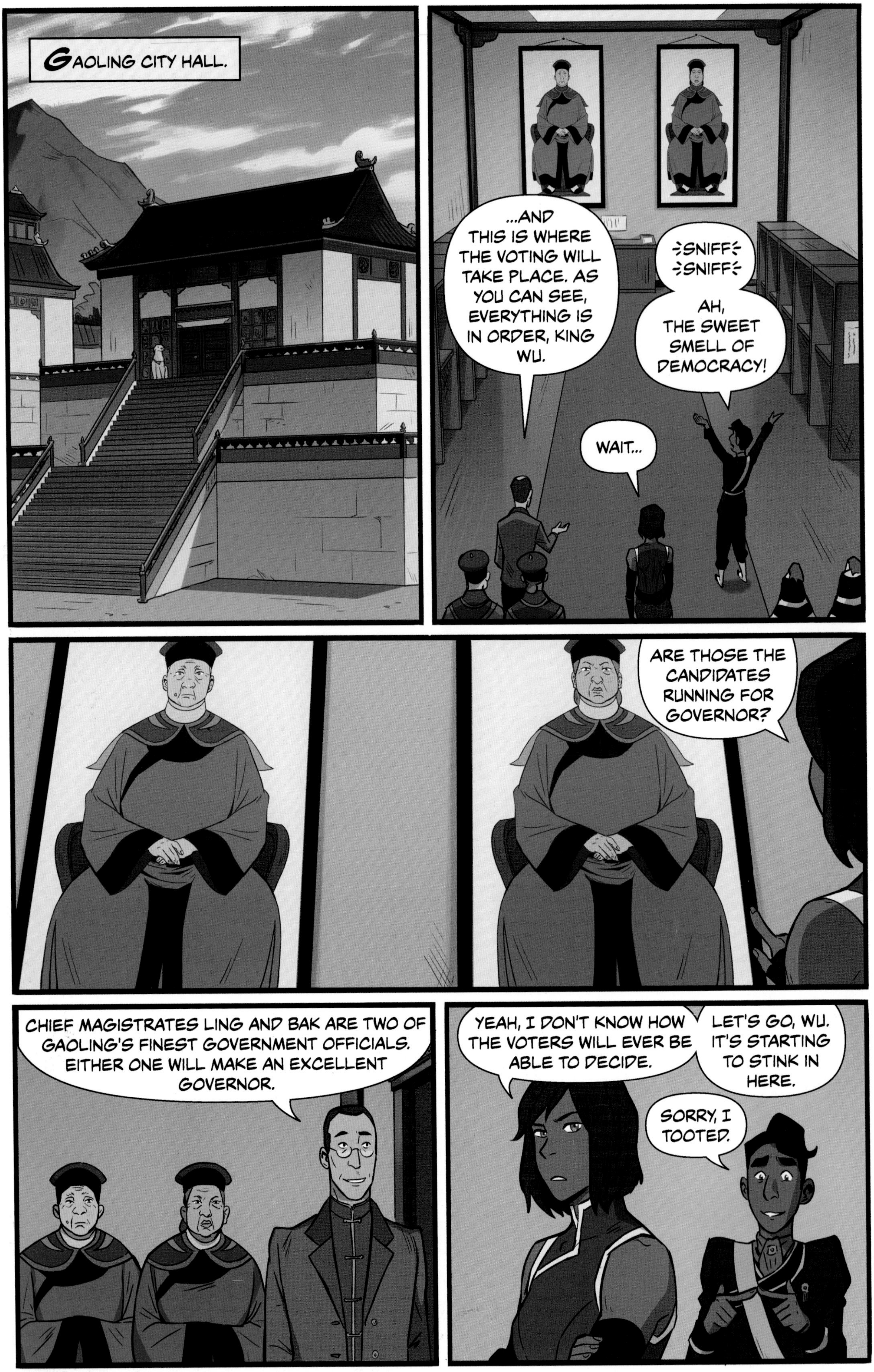
GAOLING CITY HALL.
...AND THIS IS WHERE THE VOTING WILL TAKE PLACE. AS YOU CAN SEE, EVERYTHING IS IN ORDER, KING WU.
SNIFF SNIFF
AH, THE SWEET SMELL OF DEMOCRACY!
WAIT...
ARE THOSE THE CANDIDATES RUNNING FOR GOVERNOR?
CHIEF MAGISTRATES LING AND BAK ARE TWO OF GAOLING'S FINEST GOVERNMENT OFFICIALS. EITHER ONE WILL MAKE AN EXCELLENT GOVERNOR.
YEAH, I DON'T KNOW HOW THE VOTERS WILL EVER BE ABLE TO DECIDE.
LET'S GO, WU. IT'S STARTING TO STINK IN HERE.
SORRY, I TOOTED.

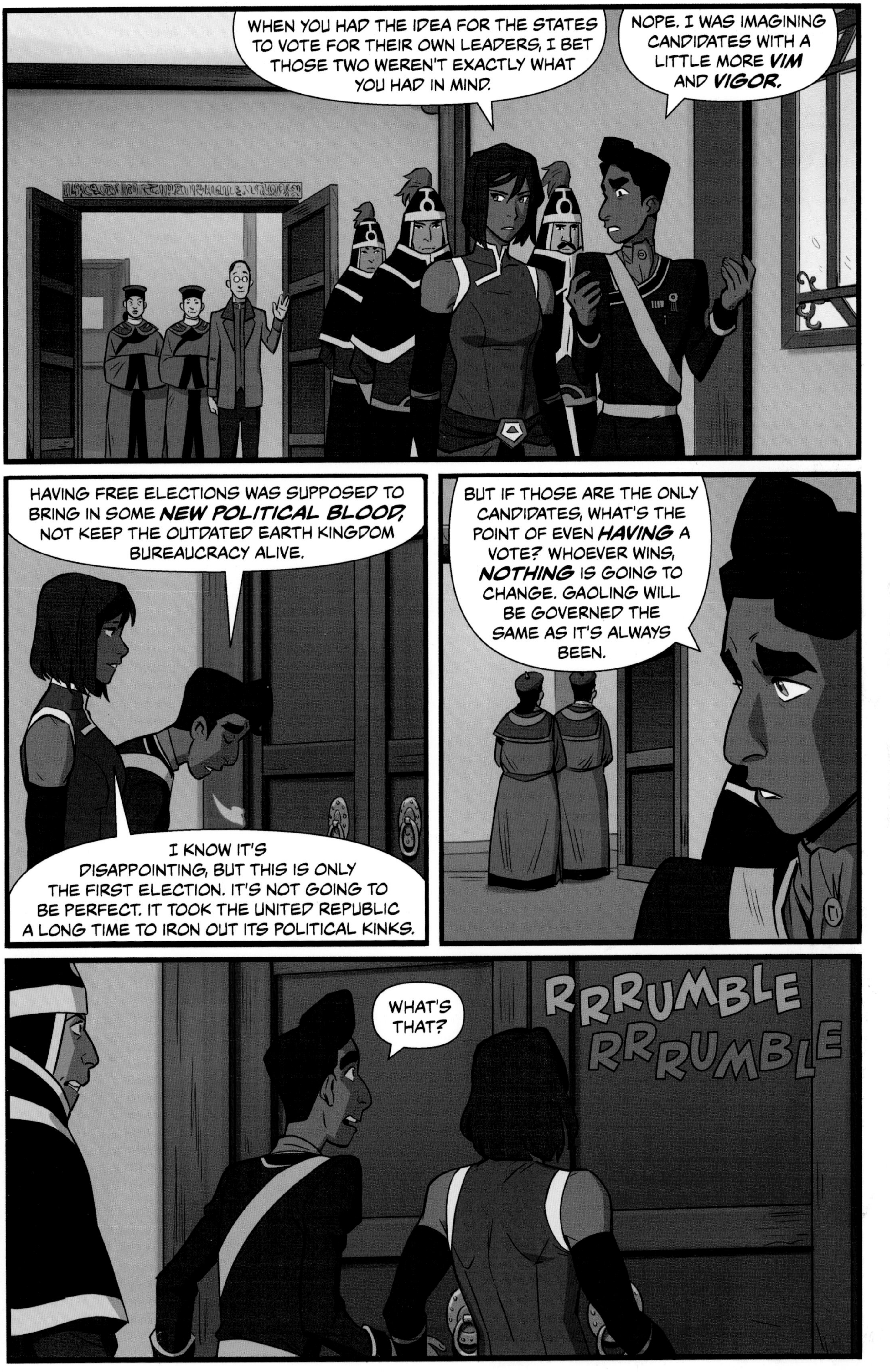
WHEN YOU HAD THE IDEA FOR THE STATES TO VOTE FOR THEIR OWN LEADERS, I BET THOSE TWO WEREN'T EXACTLY WHAT YOU HAD IN MIND.
NOPE. I WAS IMAGINING CANDIDATES WITH A LITTLE MORE *VIM* AND *VIGOR.*
HAVING FREE ELECTIONS WAS SUPPOSED TO BRING IN SOME *NEW POLITICAL BLOOD,* NOT KEEP THE OUTDATED EARTH KINGDOM BUREAUCRACY ALIVE.
I KNOW IT'S DISAPPOINTING, BUT THIS IS ONLY THE FIRST ELECTION. IT'S NOT GOING TO BE PERFECT. IT TOOK THE UNITED REPUBLIC A LONG TIME TO IRON OUT ITS POLITICAL KINKS.
BUT IF THOSE ARE THE ONLY CANDIDATES, WHAT'S THE POINT OF EVEN *HAVING* A VOTE? WHOEVER WINS, *NOTHING* IS GOING TO CHANGE. GAOLING WILL BE GOVERNED THE SAME AS IT'S ALWAYS BEEN.
WHAT'S THAT?
RRRUMBLE
RRRUMBLE

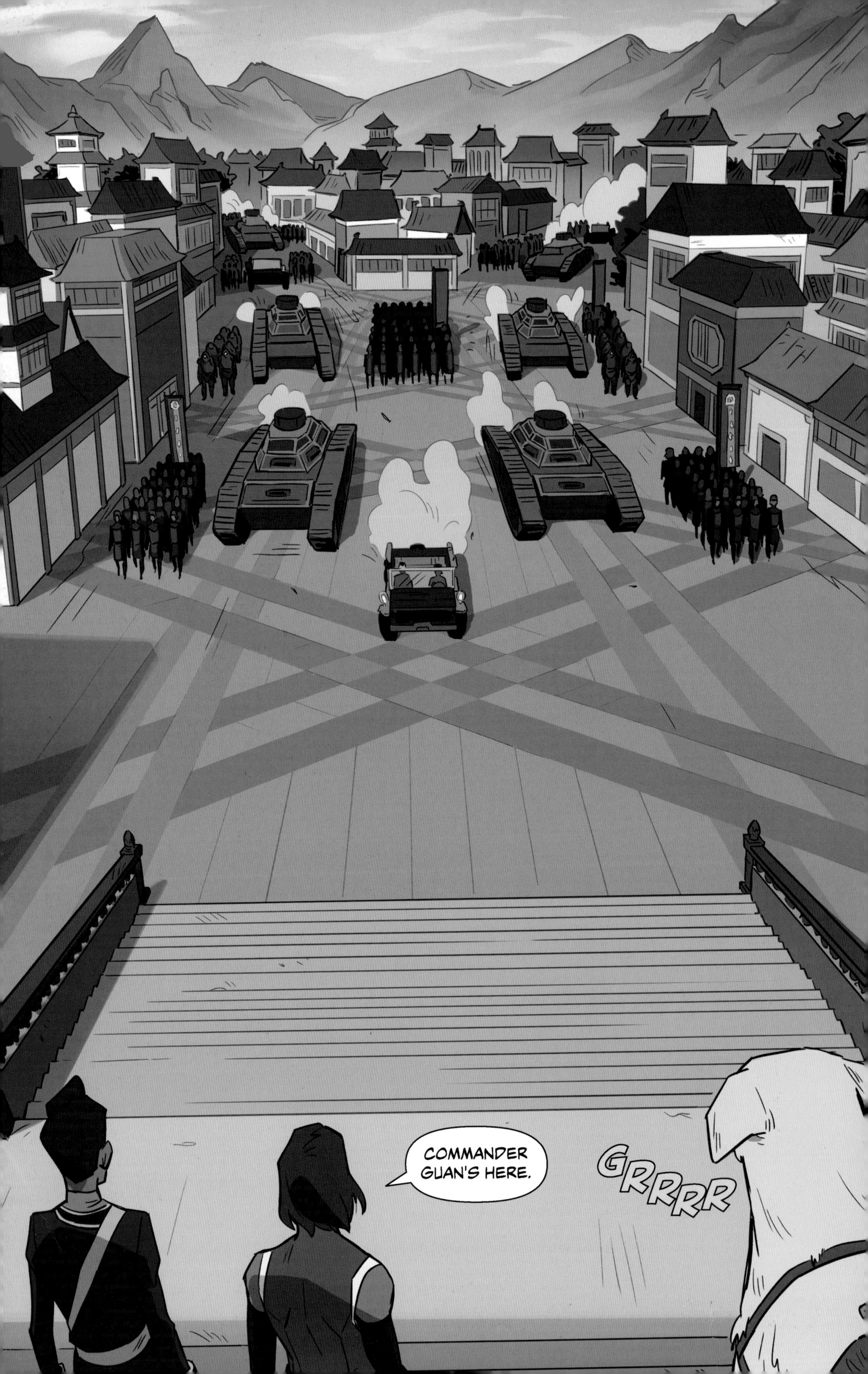
COMMANDER GUAN'S HERE.
GRRRR

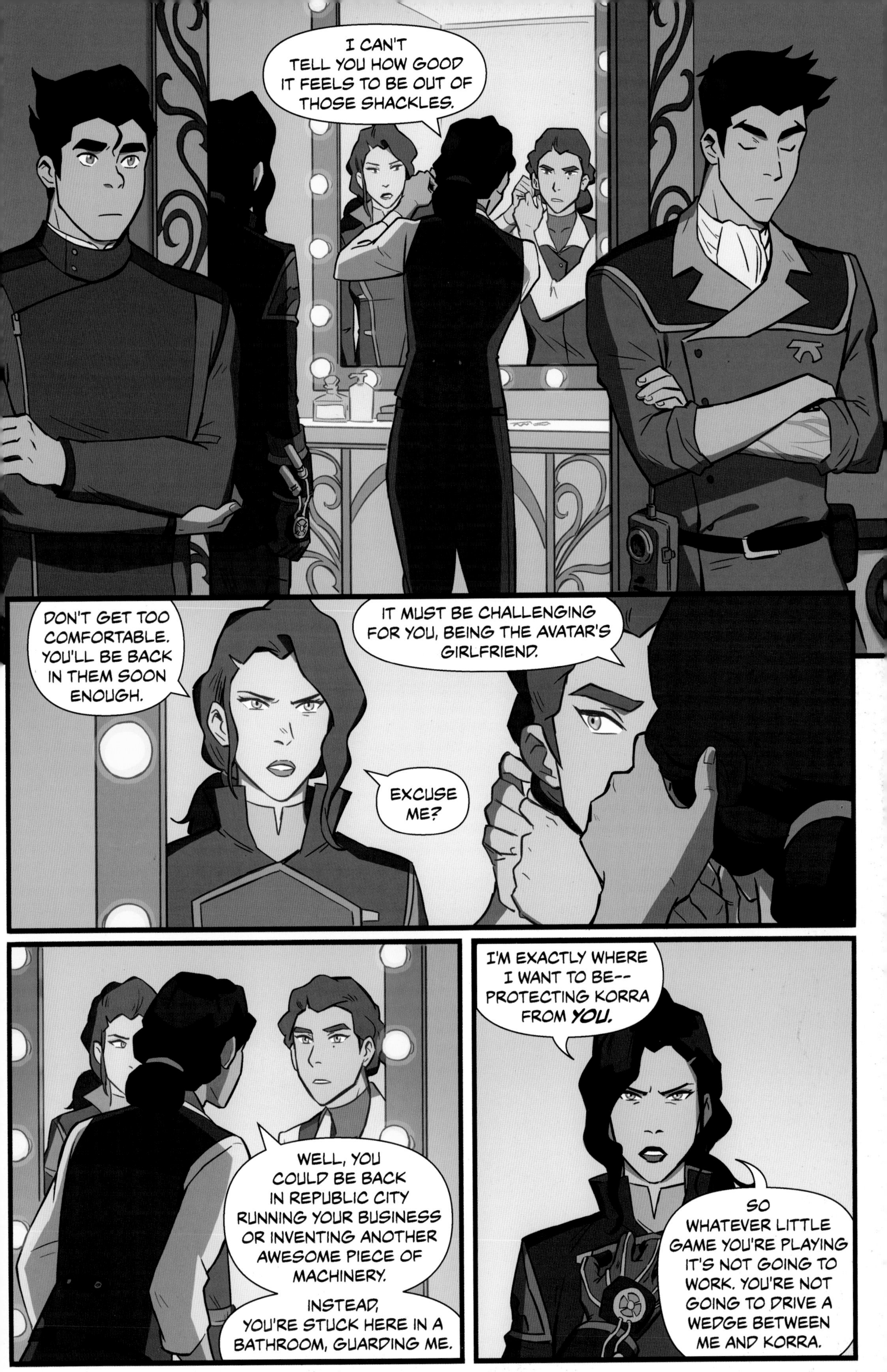
I CAN'T TELL YOU HOW GOOD IT FEELS TO BE OUT OF THOSE SHACKLES.
DON'T GET TOO COMFORTABLE. YOU'LL BE BACK IN THEM SOON ENOUGH.
IT MUST BE CHALLENGING FOR YOU, BEING THE AVATAR'S GIRLFRIEND.
EXCUSE ME?
WELL, YOU COULD BE BACK IN REPUBLIC CITY RUNNING YOUR BUSINESS OR INVENTING ANOTHER AWESOME PIECE OF MACHINERY.
INSTEAD, YOU'RE STUCK HERE IN A BATHROOM, GUARDING ME.
I'M EXACTLY WHERE I WANT TO BE-- PROTECTING KORRA FROM *YOU.*
SO WHATEVER LITTLE GAME YOU'RE PLAYING IT'S NOT GOING TO WORK. YOU'RE NOT GOING TO DRIVE A WEDGE BETWEEN ME AND KORRA.

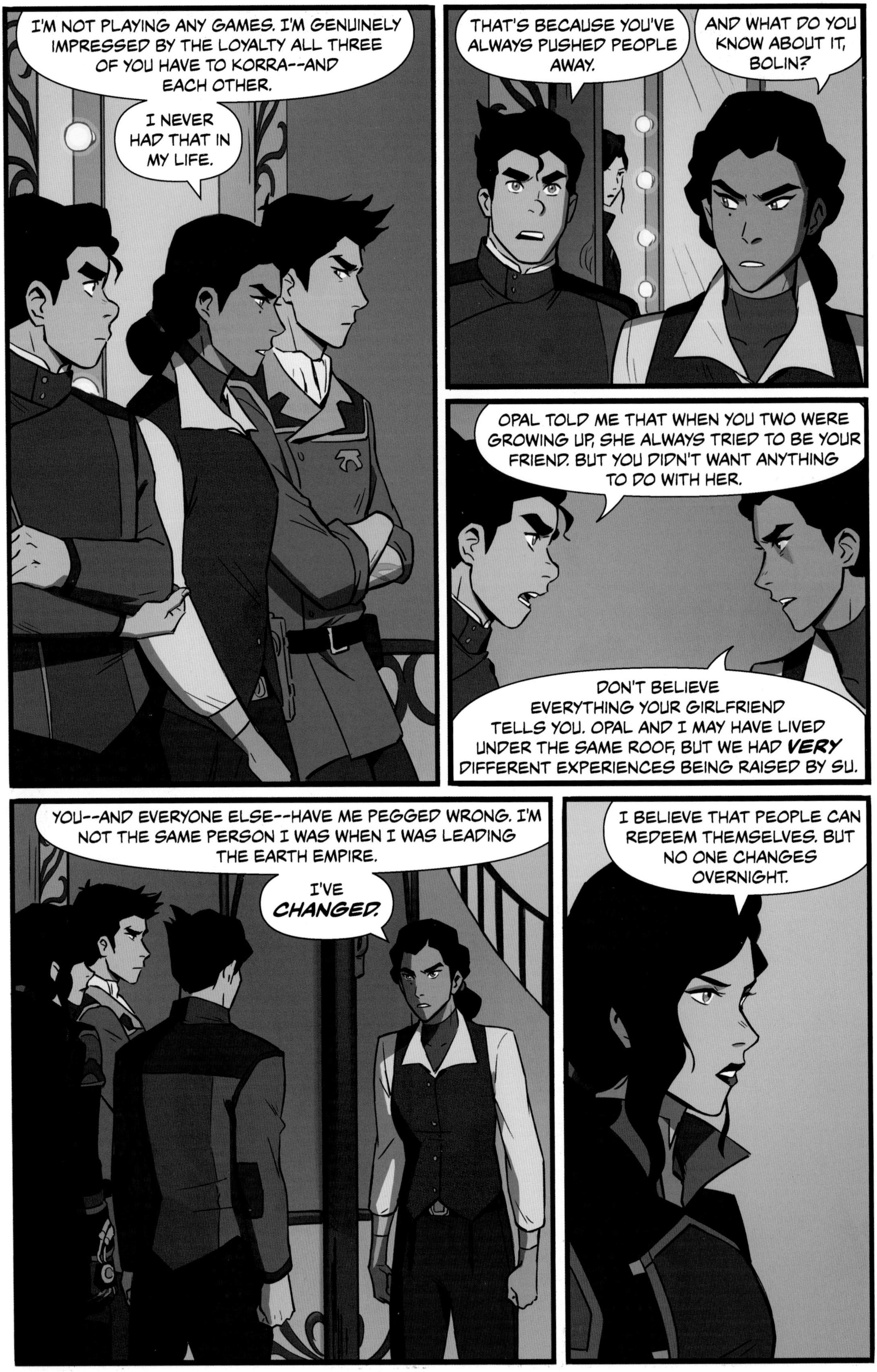
I'M NOT PLAYING ANY GAMES. I'M GENUINELY IMPRESSED BY THE LOYALTY ALL THREE OF YOU HAVE TO KORRA--AND EACH OTHER.
I NEVER HAD THAT IN MY LIFE.
THAT'S BECAUSE YOU'VE ALWAYS PUSHED PEOPLE AWAY.
AND WHAT DO YOU KNOW ABOUT IT, BOLIN?
OPAL TOLD ME THAT WHEN YOU TWO WERE GROWING UP, SHE ALWAYS TRIED TO BE YOUR FRIEND. BUT YOU DIDN'T WANT ANYTHING TO DO WITH HER.
DON'T BELIEVE EVERYTHING YOUR GIRLFRIEND TELLS YOU. OPAL AND I MAY HAVE LIVED UNDER THE SAME ROOF, BUT WE HAD VERY DIFFERENT EXPERIENCES BEING RAISED BY SU.
YOU--AND EVERYONE ELSE--HAVE ME PEGGED WRONG. I'M NOT THE SAME PERSON I WAS WHEN I WAS LEADING THE EARTH EMPIRE.
I'VE CHANGED.
I BELIEVE THAT PEOPLE CAN REDEEM THEMSELVES. BUT NO ONE CHANGES OVERNIGHT.

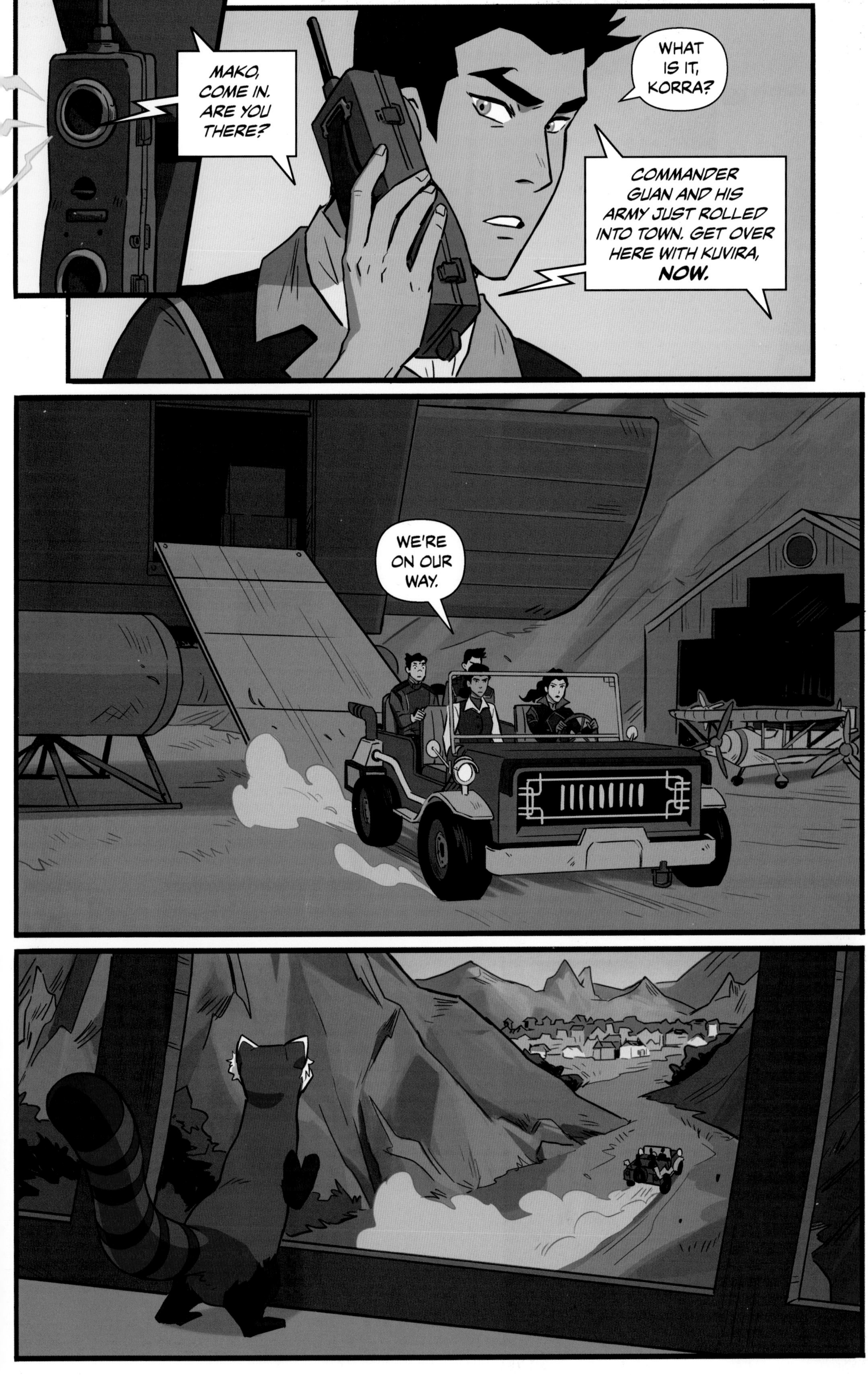
MAKO, COME IN. ARE YOU THERE?
WHAT IS IT, KORRA?
COMMANDER GUAN AND HIS ARMY JUST ROLLED INTO TOWN. GET OVER HERE WITH KUVIRA, NOW.
WE'RE ON OUR WAY.

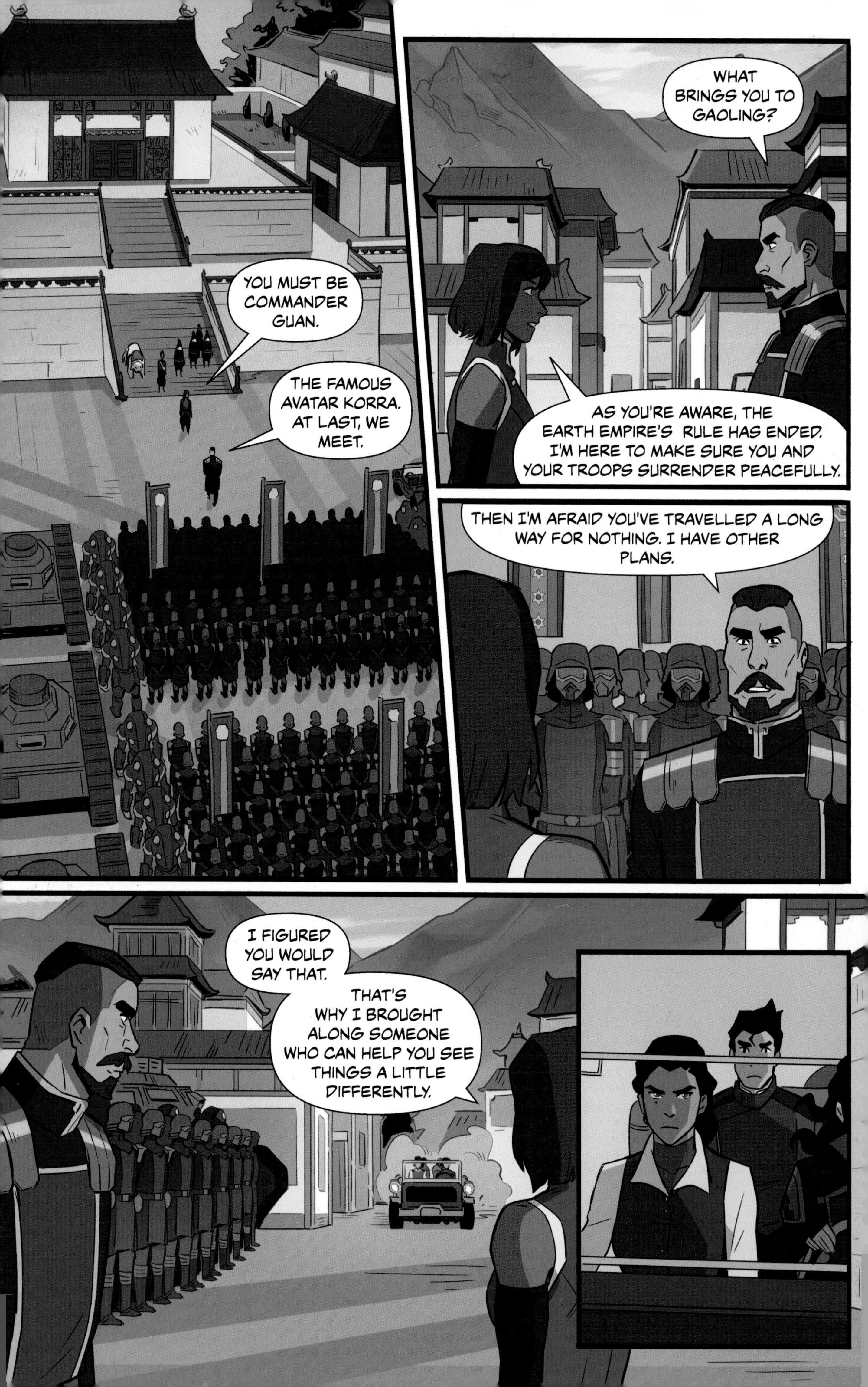

YOU MUST BE COMMANDER GUAN.
THE FAMOUS AVATAR KORRA. AT LAST, WE MEET.
WHAT BRINGS YOU TO GAOLING?
AS YOU'RE AWARE, THE EARTH EMPIRE'S RULE HAS ENDED. I'M HERE TO MAKE SURE YOU AND YOUR TROOPS SURRENDER PEACEFULLY.
THEN I'M AFRAID YOU'VE TRAVELLED A LONG WAY FOR NOTHING. I HAVE OTHER PLANS.
I FIGURED YOU WOULD SAY THAT.
THAT'S WHY I BROUGHT ALONG SOMEONE WHO CAN HELP YOU SEE THINGS A LITTLE DIFFERENTLY.

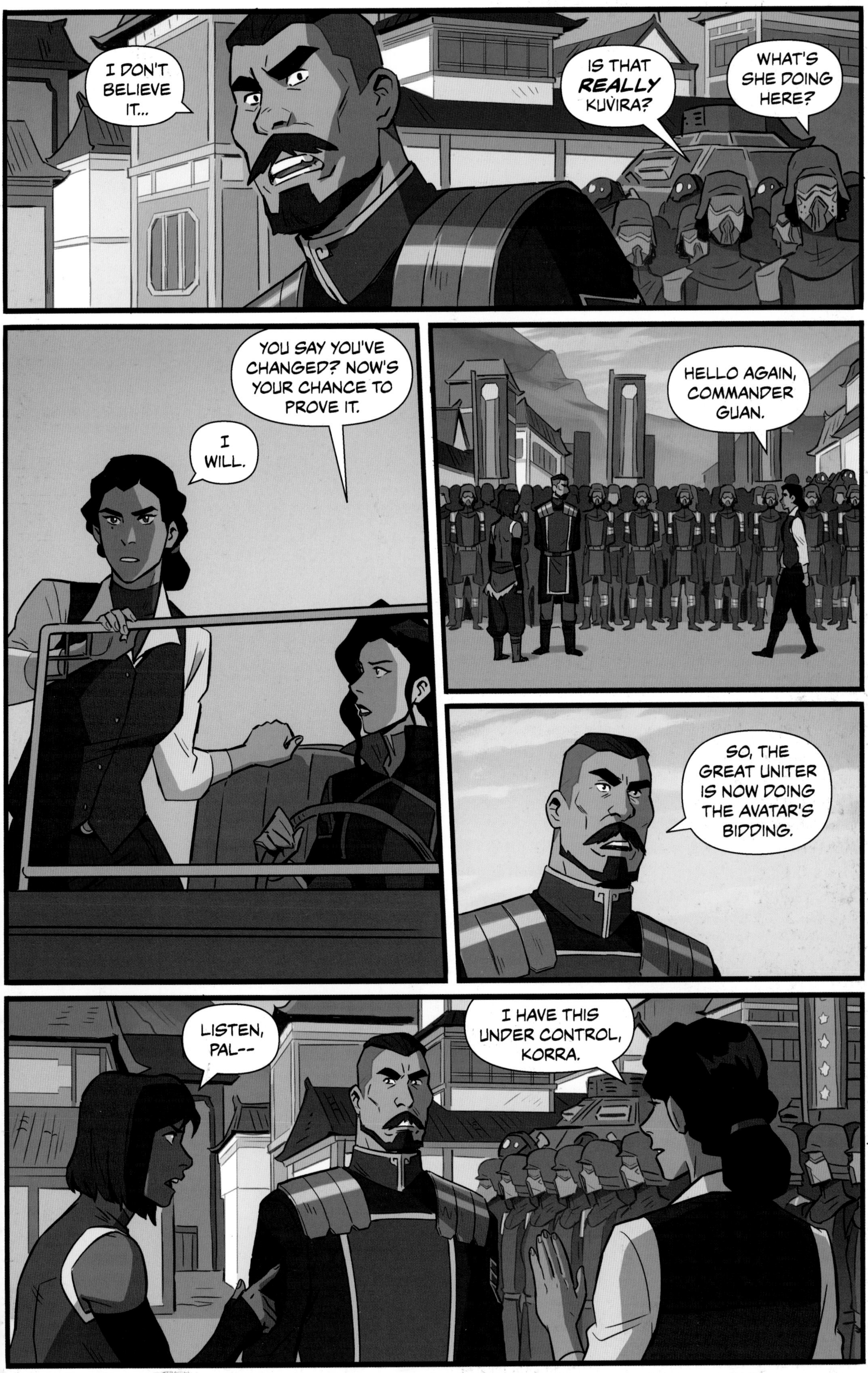
I DON'T BELIEVE IT...
IS THAT REALLY KUVIRA?
WHAT'S SHE DOING HERE?
YOU SAY YOU'VE CHANGED? NOW'S YOUR CHANCE TO PROVE IT.
I WILL.
HELLO AGAIN, COMMANDER GUAN.
SO, THE GREAT UNITER IS NOW DOING THE AVATAR'S BIDDING.
LISTEN, PAL--
I HAVE THIS UNDER CONTROL, KORRA.

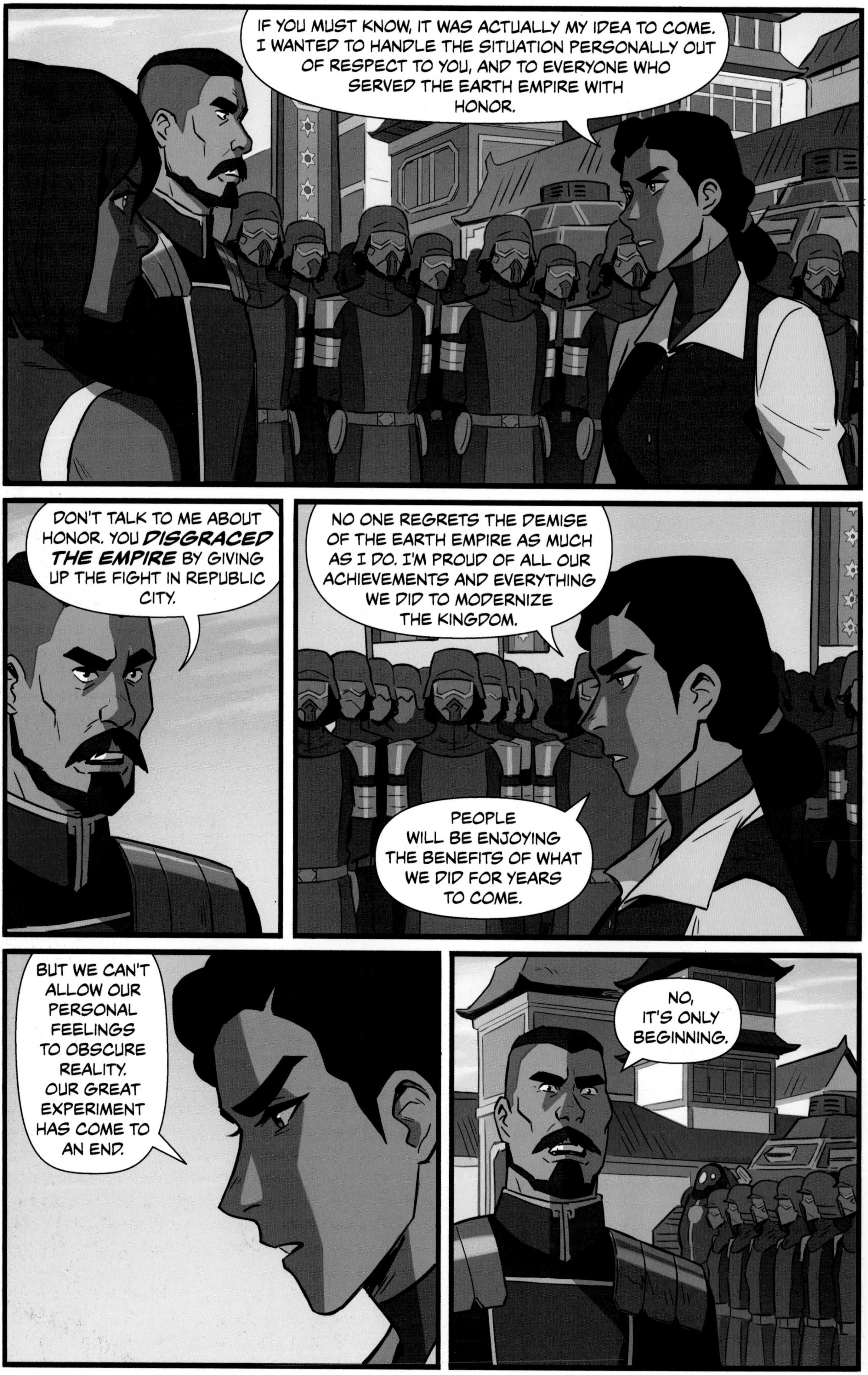
IF YOU MUST KNOW, IT WAS ACTUALLY MY IDEA TO COME. I WANTED TO HANDLE THE SITUATION PERSONALLY OUT OF RESPECT TO YOU, AND TO EVERYONE WHO SERVED THE EARTH EMPIRE WITH HONOR.
DON'T TALK TO ME ABOUT HONOR. YOU ***DISGRACED THE EMPIRE*** BY GIVING UP THE FIGHT IN REPUBLIC CITY.
NO ONE REGRETS THE DEMISE OF THE EARTH EMPIRE AS MUCH AS I DO. I'M PROUD OF ALL OUR ACHIEVEMENTS AND EVERYTHING WE DID TO MODERNIZE THE KINGDOM.
PEOPLE WILL BE ENJOYING THE BENEFITS OF WHAT WE DID FOR YEARS TO COME.
BUT WE CAN'T ALLOW OUR PERSONAL FEELINGS TO OBSCURE REALITY. OUR GREAT EXPERIMENT HAS COME TO AN END.
NO, IT'S ONLY BEGINNING.

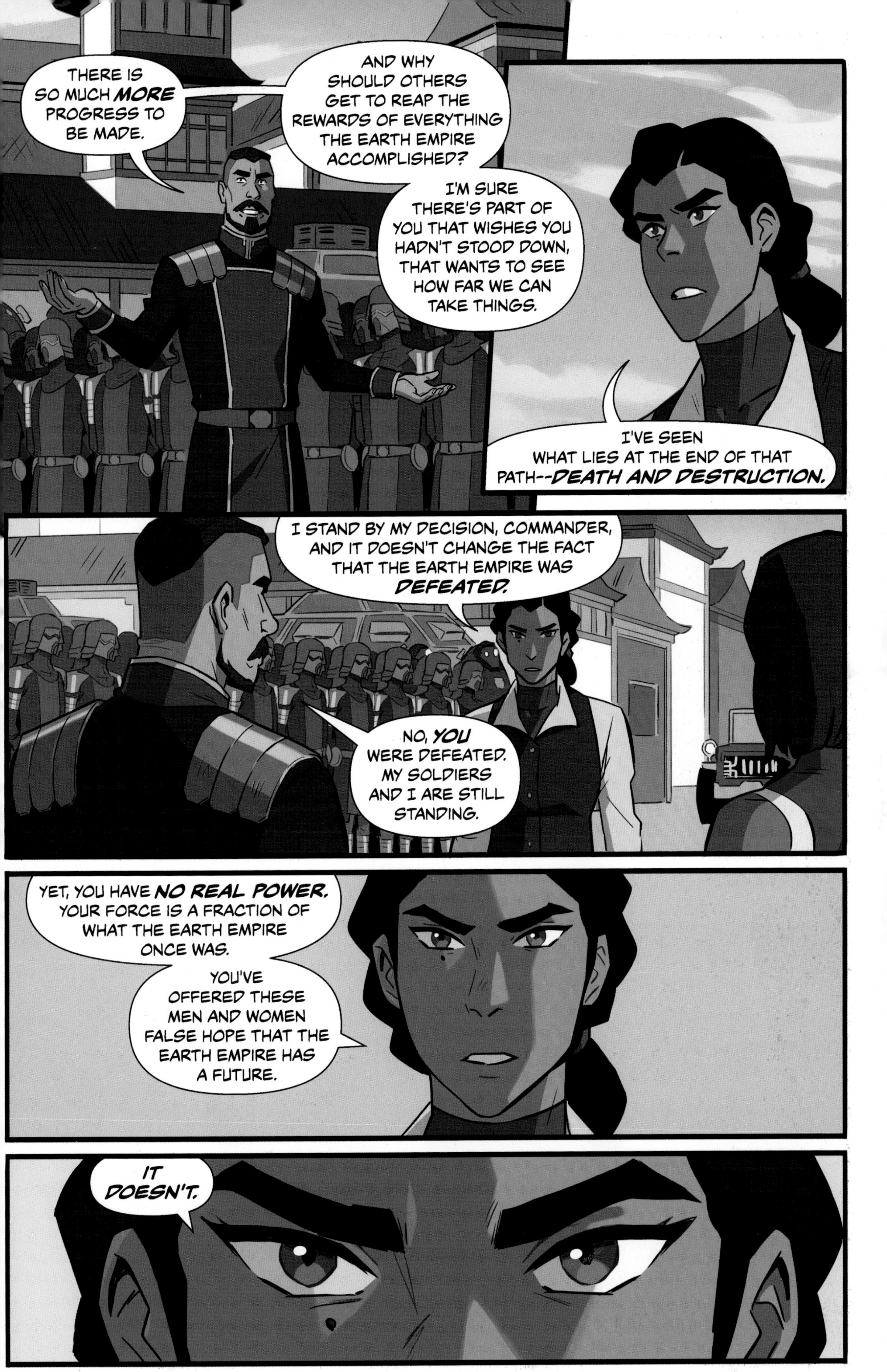
THERE IS SO MUCH MORE PROGRESS TO BE MADE.
AND WHY SHOULD OTHERS GET TO REAP THE REWARDS OF EVERYTHING THE EARTH EMPIRE ACCOMPLISHED?
I'M SURE THERE'S PART OF YOU THAT WISHES YOU HADN'T STOOD DOWN, THAT WANTS TO SEE HOW FAR WE CAN TAKE THINGS.
I'VE SEEN WHAT LIES AT THE END OF THAT PATH--DEATH AND DESTRUCTION.
I STAND BY MY DECISION, COMMANDER, AND IT DOESN'T CHANGE THE FACT THAT THE EARTH EMPIRE WAS DEFEATED.
NO, YOU WERE DEFEATED. MY SOLDIERS AND I ARE STILL STANDING.
YET, YOU HAVE NO REAL POWER. YOUR FORCE IS A FRACTION OF WHAT THE EARTH EMPIRE ONCE WAS.
YOU'VE OFFERED THESE MEN AND WOMEN FALSE HOPE THAT THE EARTH EMPIRE HAS A FUTURE.
IT DOESN'T.

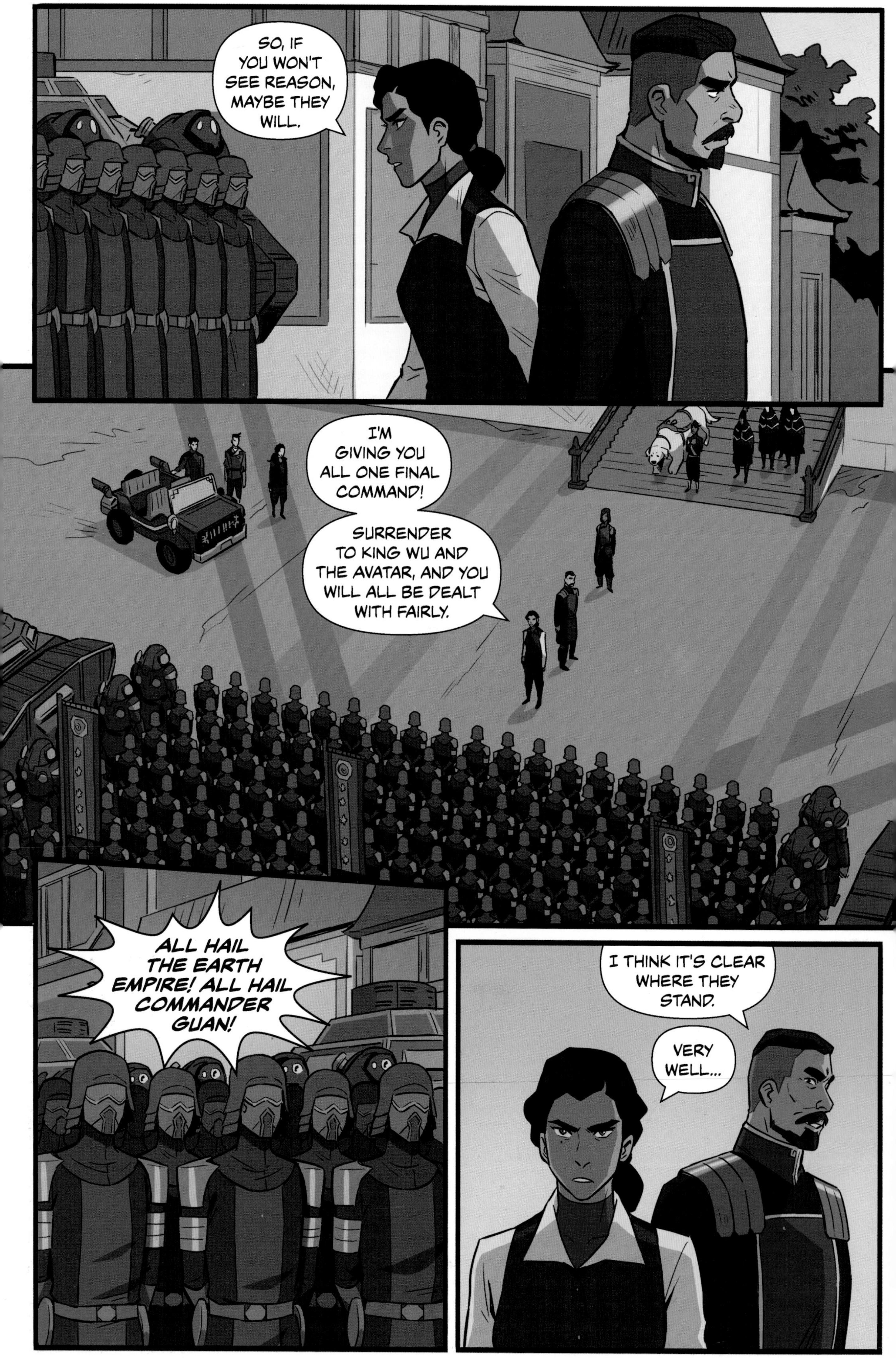
SO, IF YOU WON'T SEE REASON, MAYBE THEY WILL.
I'M GIVING YOU ALL ONE FINAL COMMAND!
SURRENDER TO KING WU AND THE AVATAR, AND YOU WILL ALL BE DEALT WITH FAIRLY.
ALL HAIL THE EARTH EMPIRE! ALL HAIL COMMANDER GUAN!
I THINK IT'S CLEAR WHERE THEY STAND.
VERY WELL...

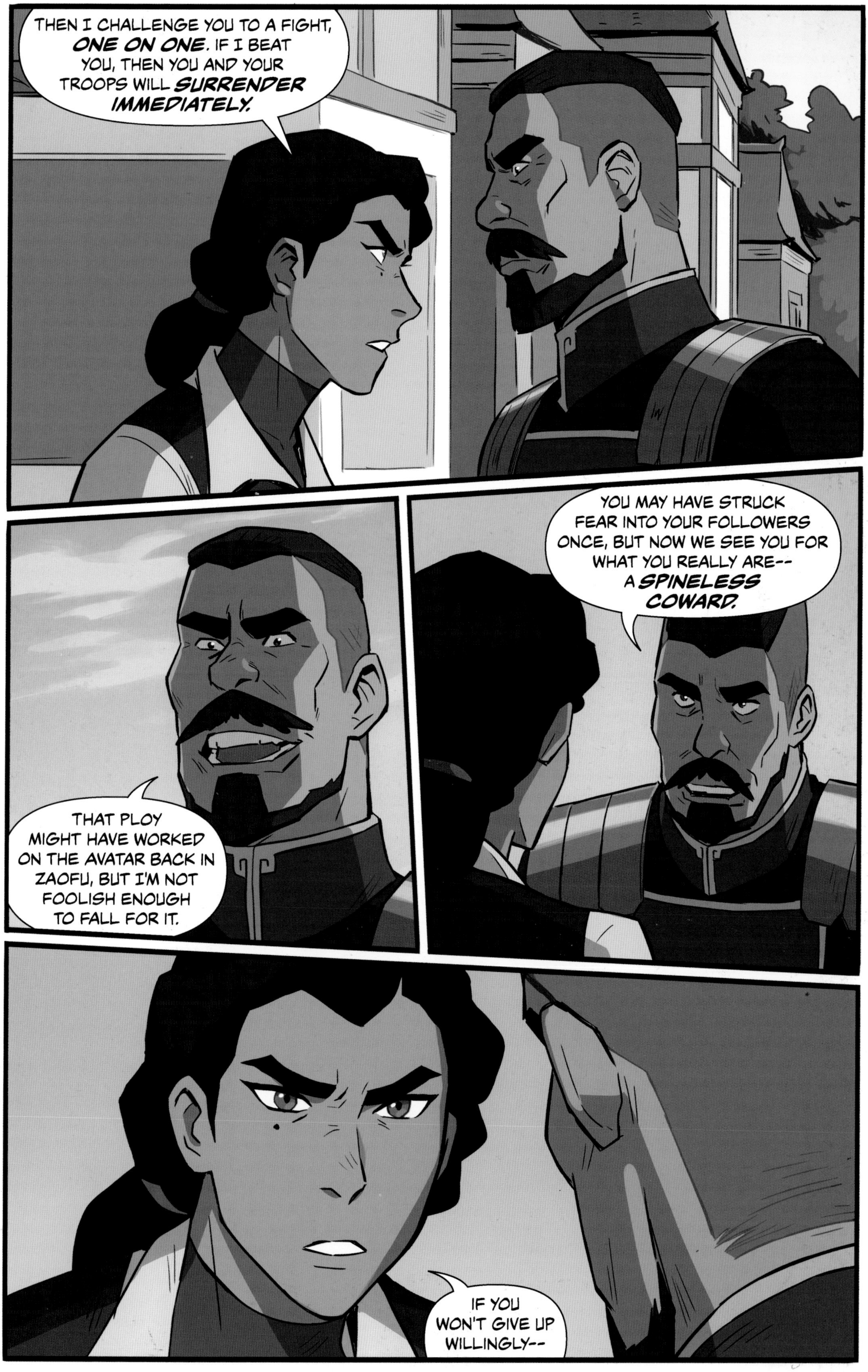
THEN I CHALLENGE YOU TO A FIGHT, ONE ON ONE. IF I BEAT YOU, THEN YOU AND YOUR TROOPS WILL SURRENDER IMMEDIATELY.
THAT PLOY MIGHT HAVE WORKED ON THE AVATAR BACK IN ZAOFU, BUT I'M NOT FOOLISH ENOUGH TO FALL FOR IT.
YOU MAY HAVE STRUCK FEAR INTO YOUR FOLLOWERS ONCE, BUT NOW WE SEE YOU FOR WHAT YOU REALLY ARE-- A SPINELESS COWARD.
IF YOU WON'T GIVE UP WILLINGLY--

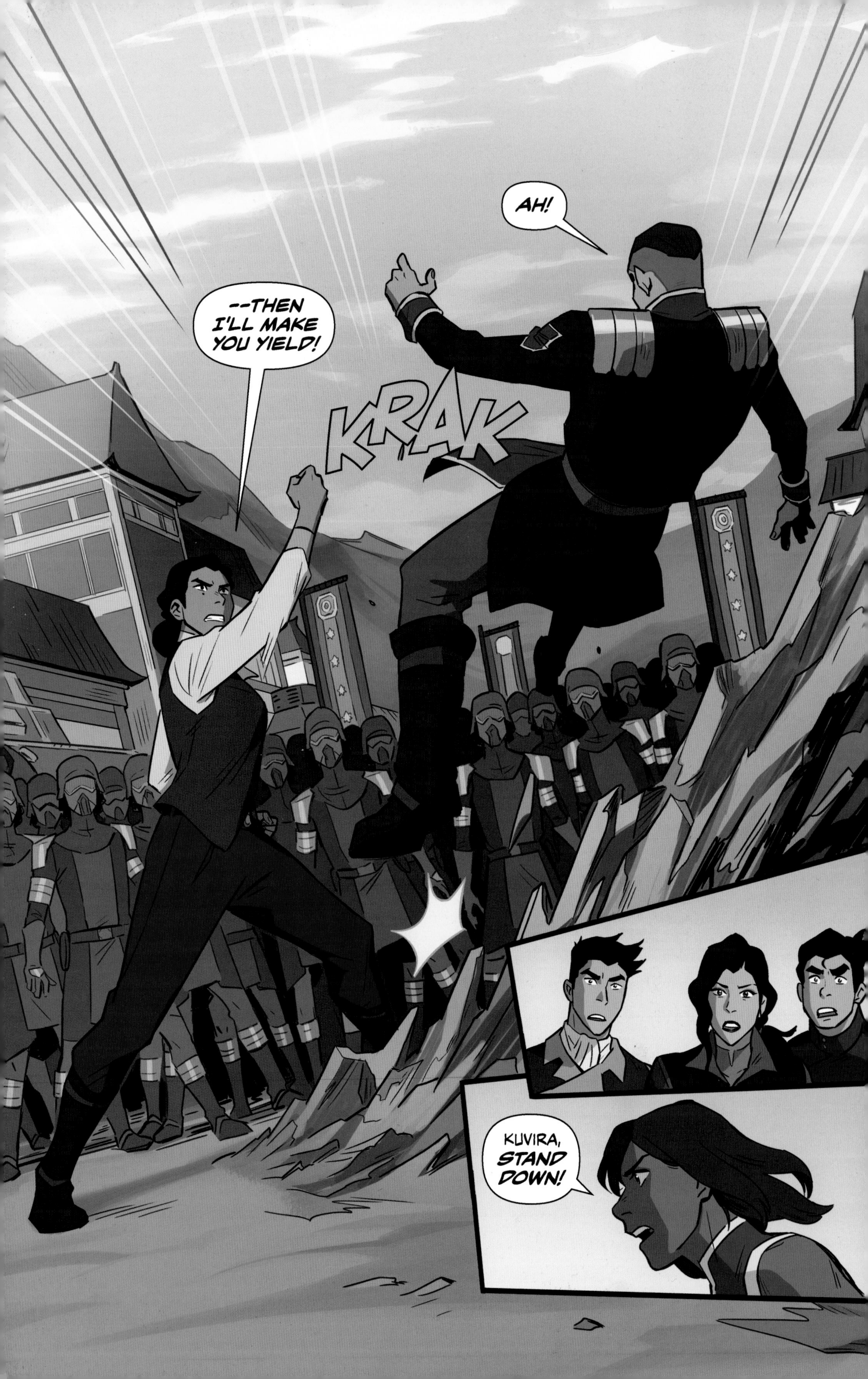
--THEN I'LL MAKE YOU YIELD!
AH!
KRAK
KUVIRA, STAND DOWN!

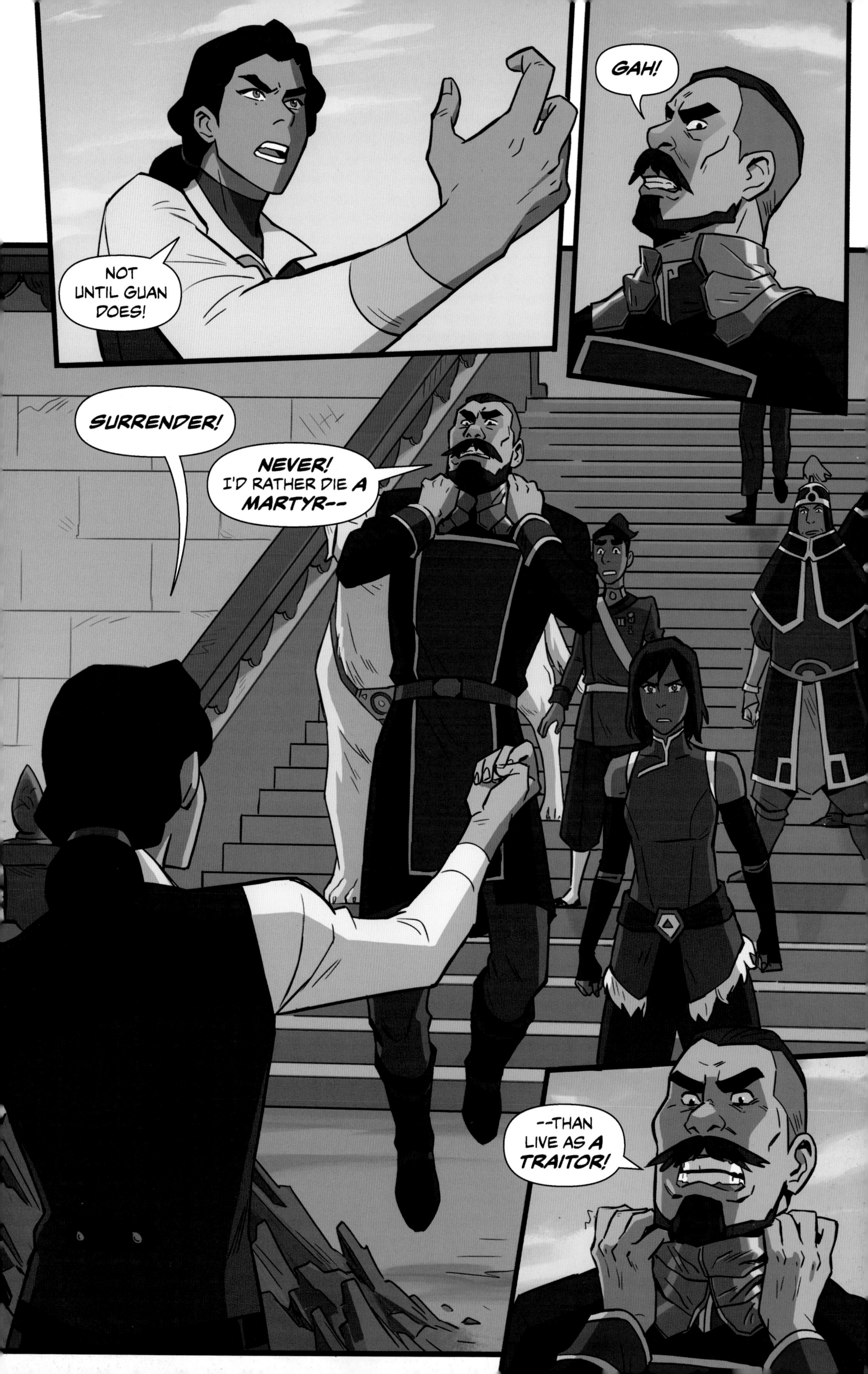
NOT UNTIL GUAN DOES!
GAH!
SURRENDER!
NEVER! I'D RATHER DIE A MARTYR--
--THAN LIVE AS A TRAITOR!

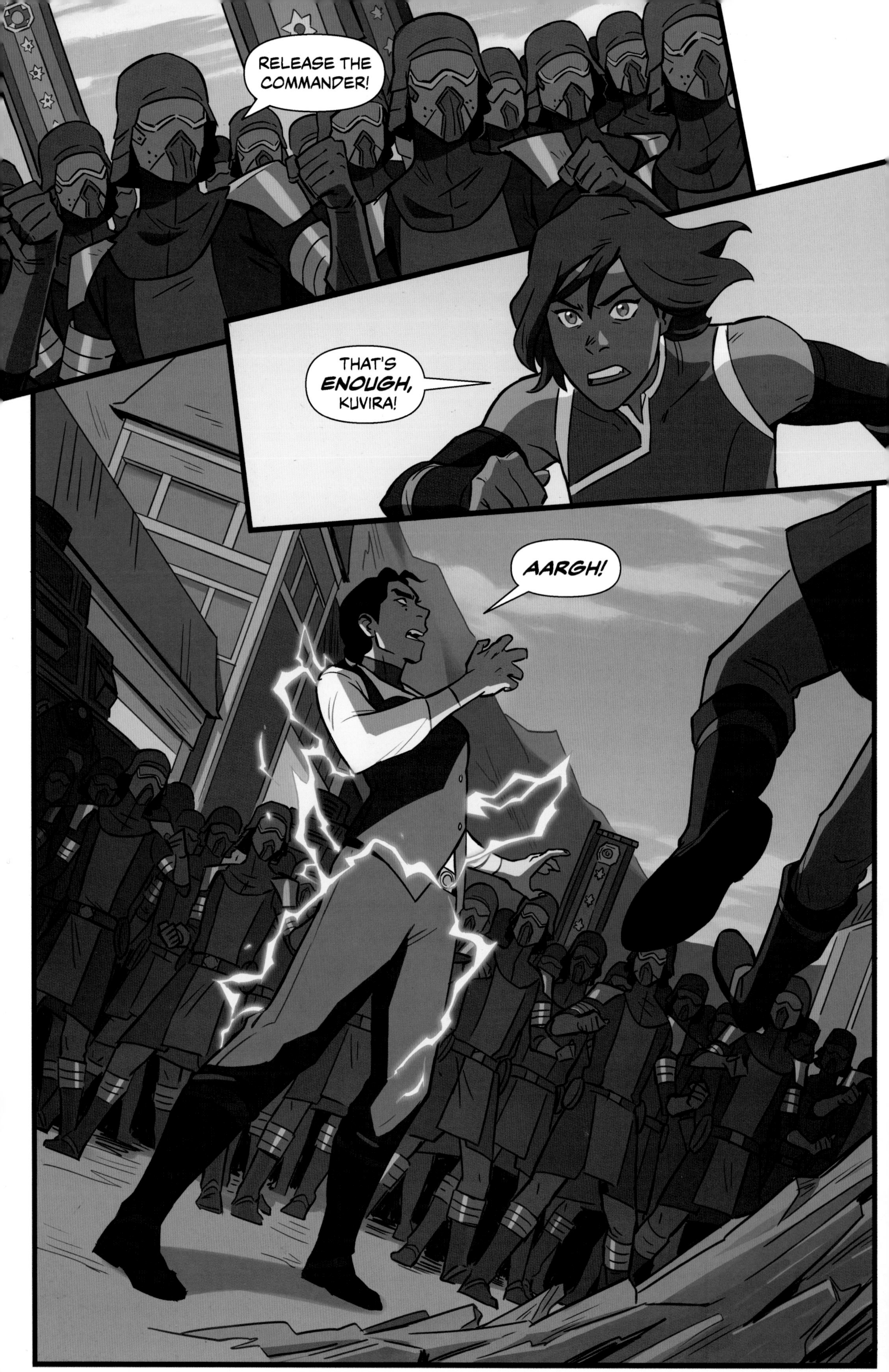
RELEASE THE COMMANDER!
THAT'S ENOUGH, KUVIRA!
AARGH!

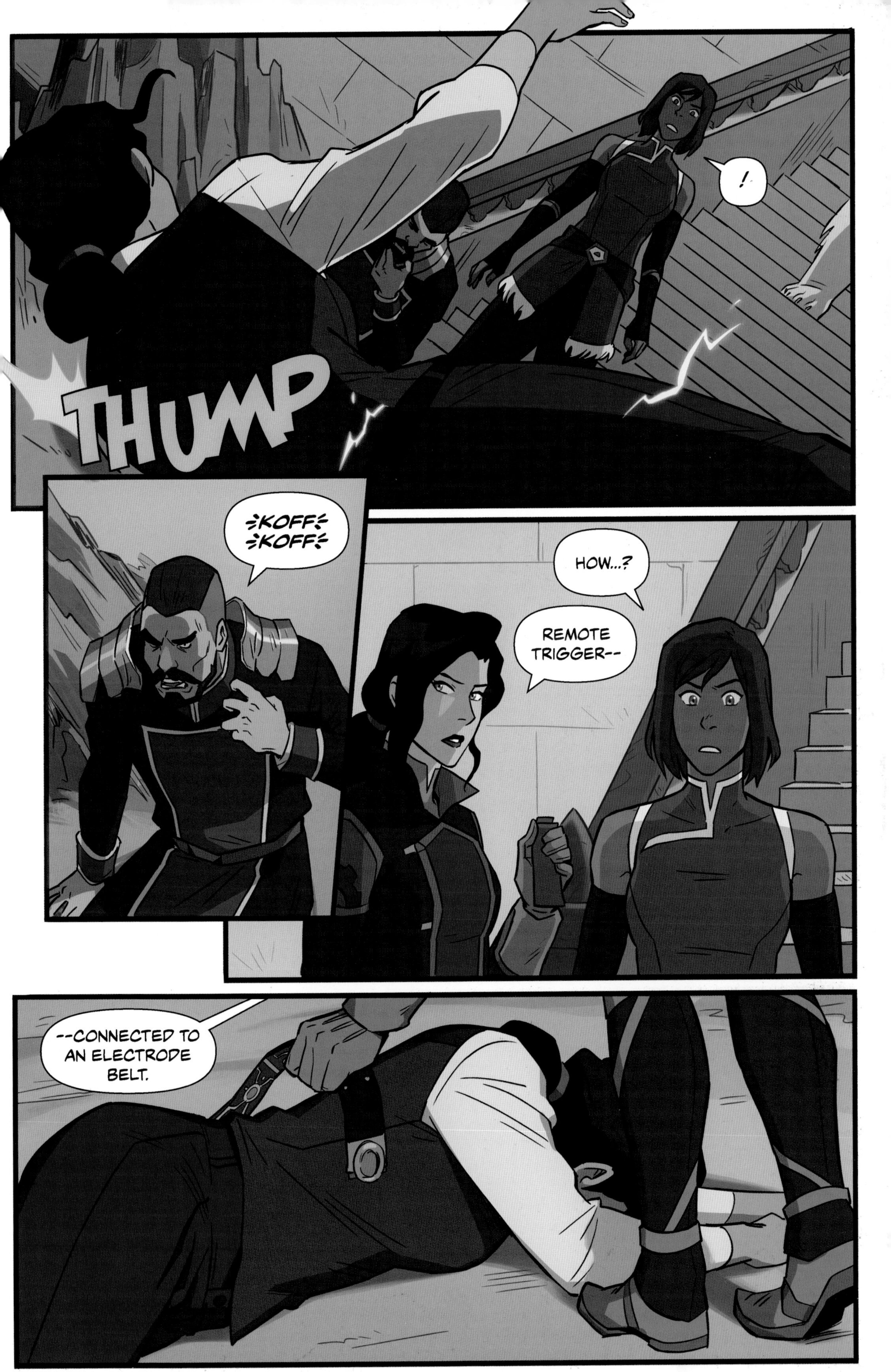
!
THUMP
KOFF
KOFF
HOW...?
REMOTE TRIGGER--
--CONNECTED TO AN ELECTRODE BELT.

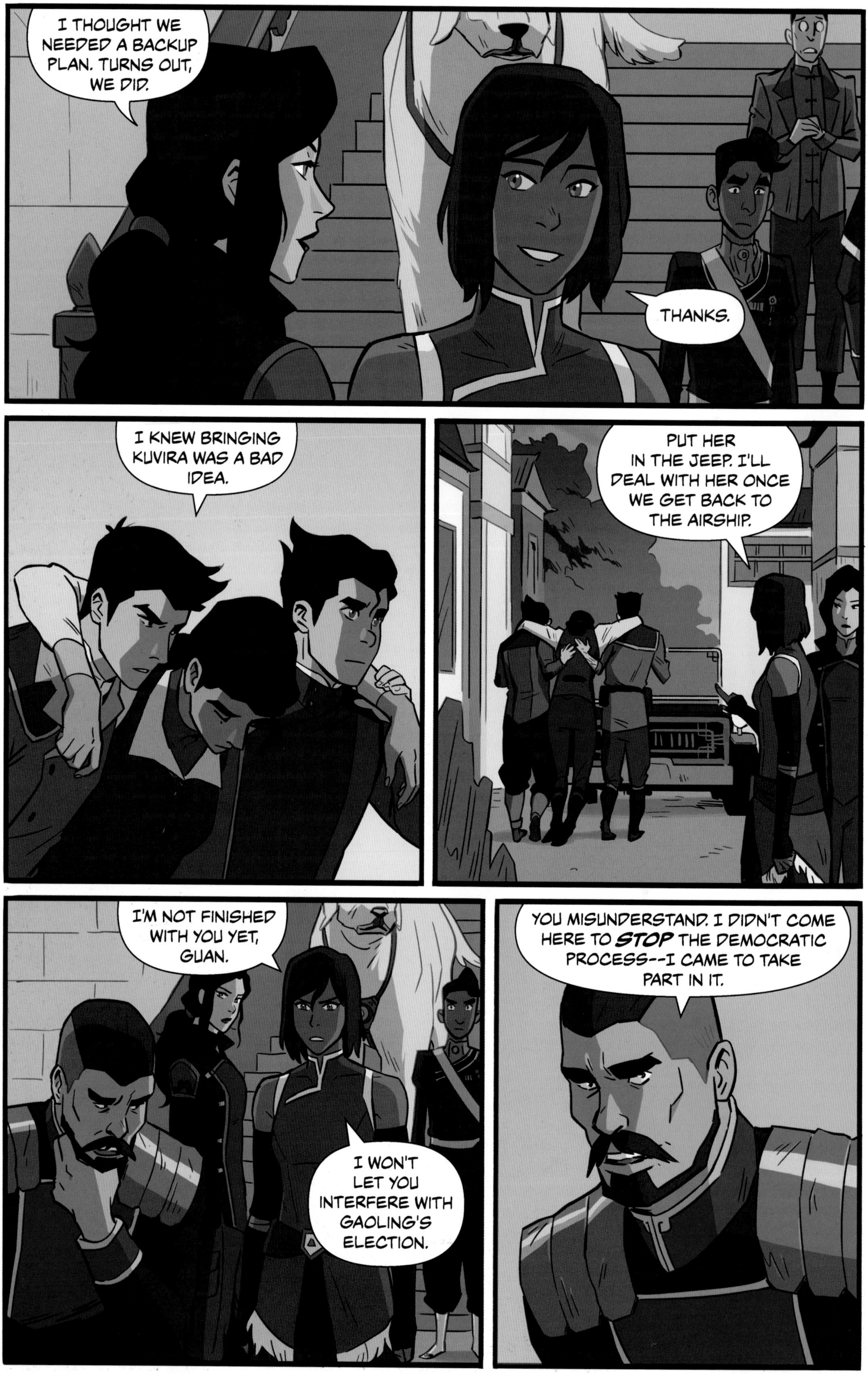
I THOUGHT WE NEEDED A BACKUP PLAN. TURNS OUT, WE DID.
THANKS.
I KNEW BRINGING KUVIRA WAS A BAD IDEA.
PUT HER IN THE JEEP. I'LL DEAL WITH HER ONCE WE GET BACK TO THE AIRSHIP.
I'M NOT FINISHED WITH YOU YET, GUAN.
I WON'T LET YOU INTERFERE WITH GAOLING'S ELECTION.
YOU MISUNDERSTAND. I DIDN'T COME HERE TO STOP THE DEMOCRATIC PROCESS--I CAME TO TAKE PART IN IT.

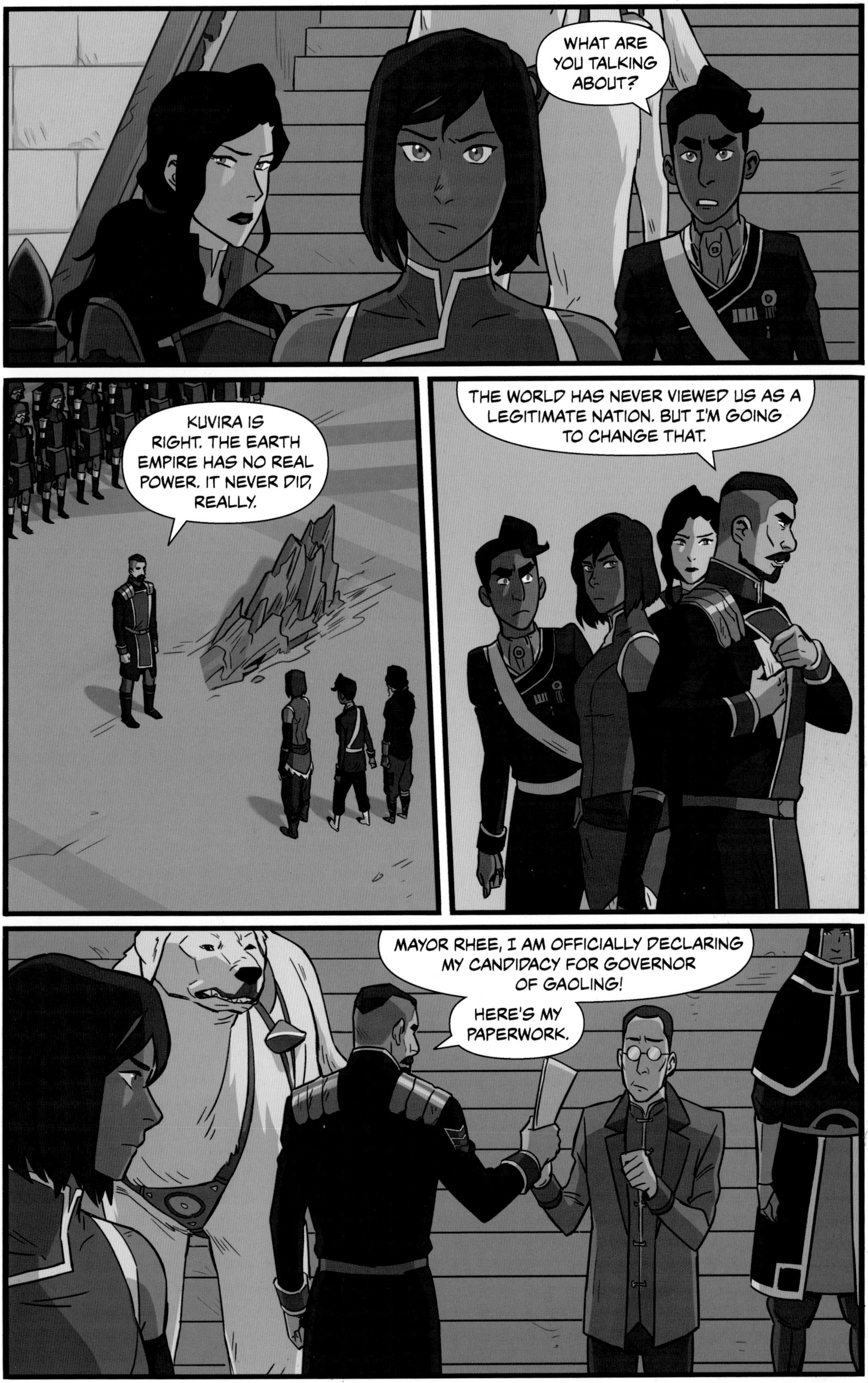
WHAT ARE YOU TALKING ABOUT?
KUVIRA IS RIGHT. THE EARTH EMPIRE HAS NO REAL POWER. IT NEVER DID, REALLY.
THE WORLD HAS NEVER VIEWED US AS A LEGITIMATE NATION. BUT I'M GOING TO CHANGE THAT.
MAYOR RHEE, I AM OFFICIALLY DECLARING MY CANDIDACY FOR GOVERNOR OF GAOLING!
HERE'S MY PAPERWORK.

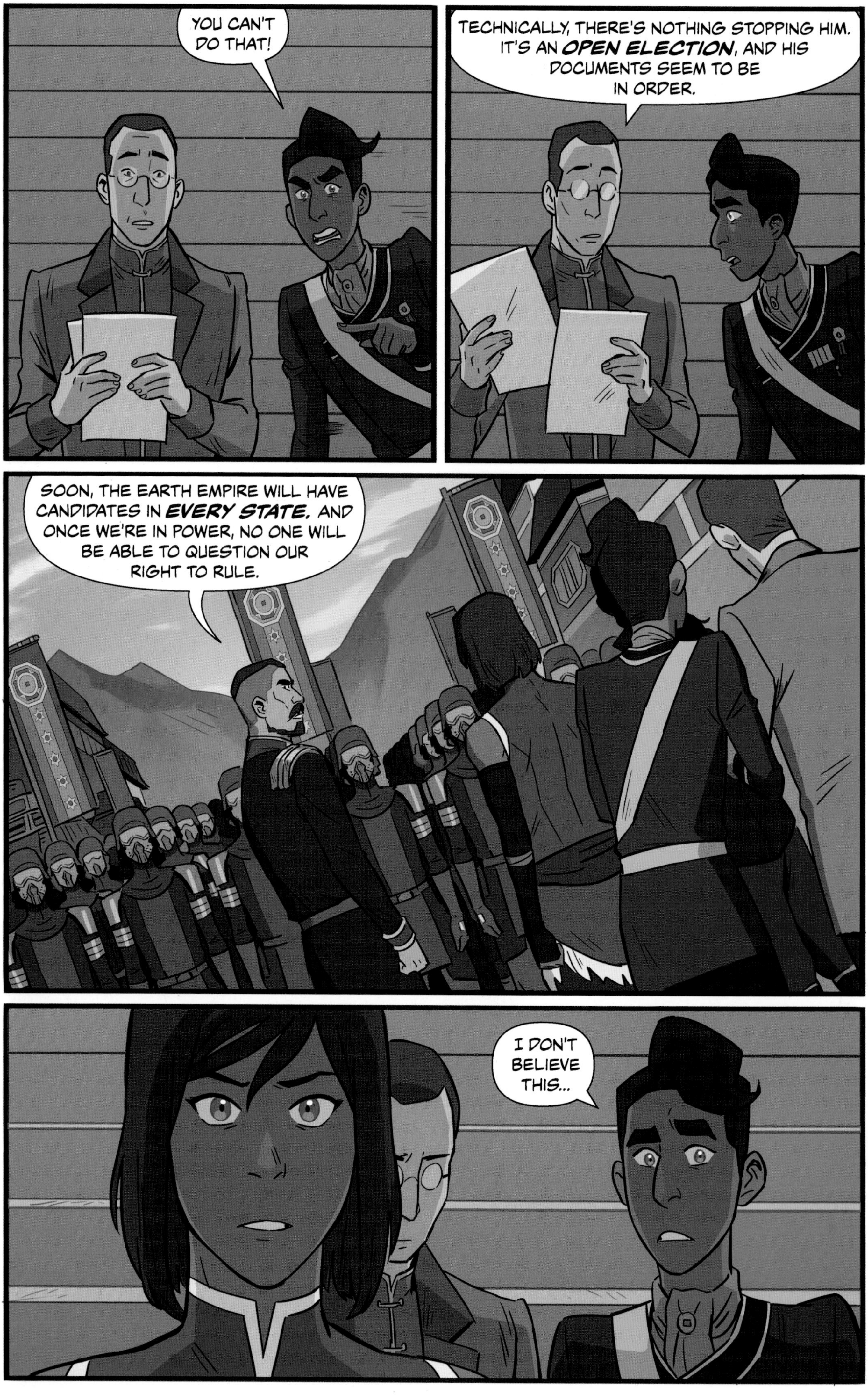
YOU CAN'T DO THAT!
TECHNICALLY, THERE'S NOTHING STOPPING HIM. IT'S AN *OPEN ELECTION*, AND HIS DOCUMENTS SEEM TO BE IN ORDER.
SOON, THE EARTH EMPIRE WILL HAVE CANDIDATES IN *EVERY STATE*, AND ONCE WE'RE IN POWER, NO ONE WILL BE ABLE TO QUESTION OUR RIGHT TO RULE.
I DON'T BELIEVE THIS...

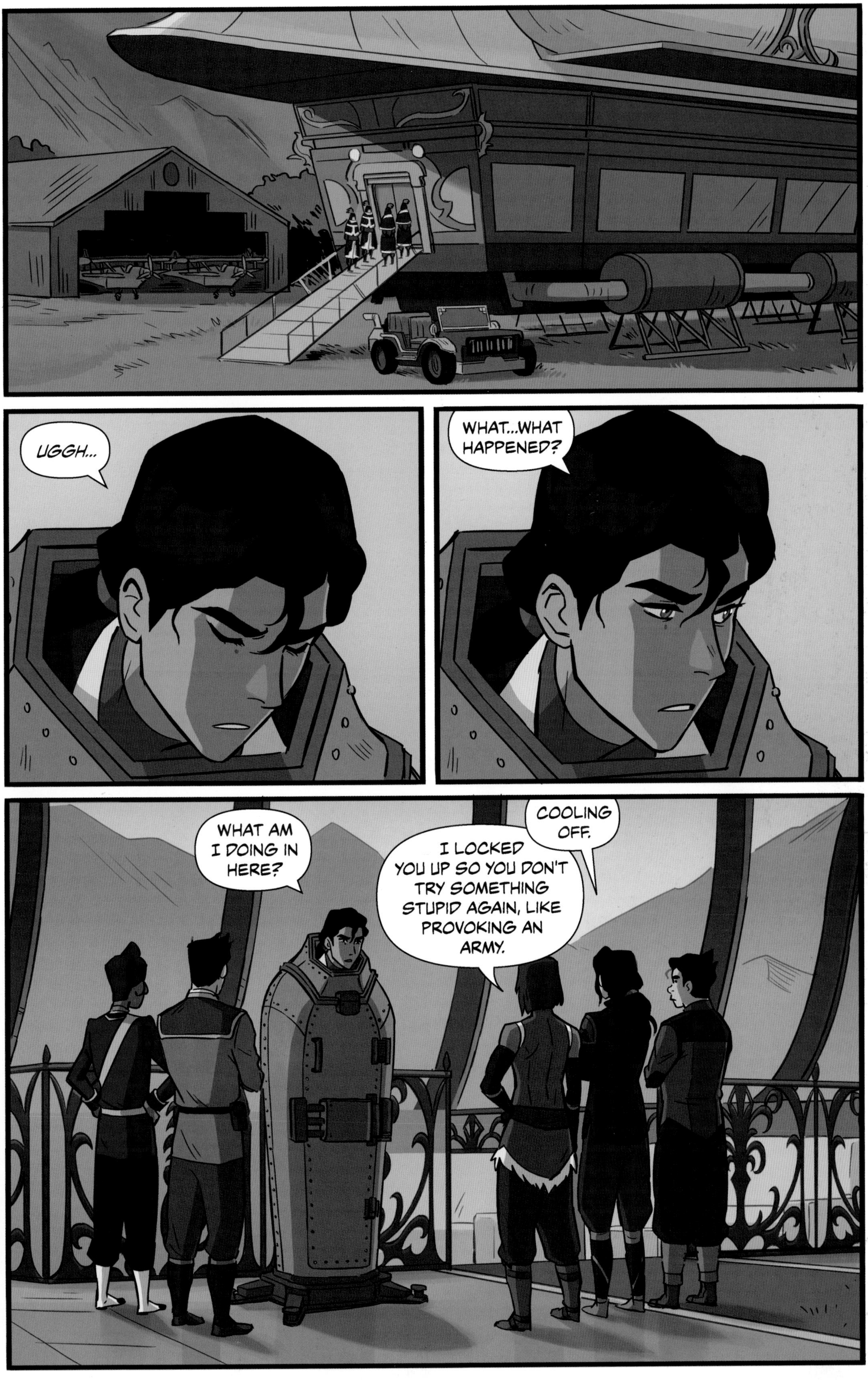
UGGH...
WHAT...WHAT HAPPENED?
WHAT AM I DOING IN HERE?
I LOCKED YOU UP SO YOU DON'T TRY SOMETHING STUPID AGAIN, LIKE PROVOKING AN ARMY.
COOLING OFF.

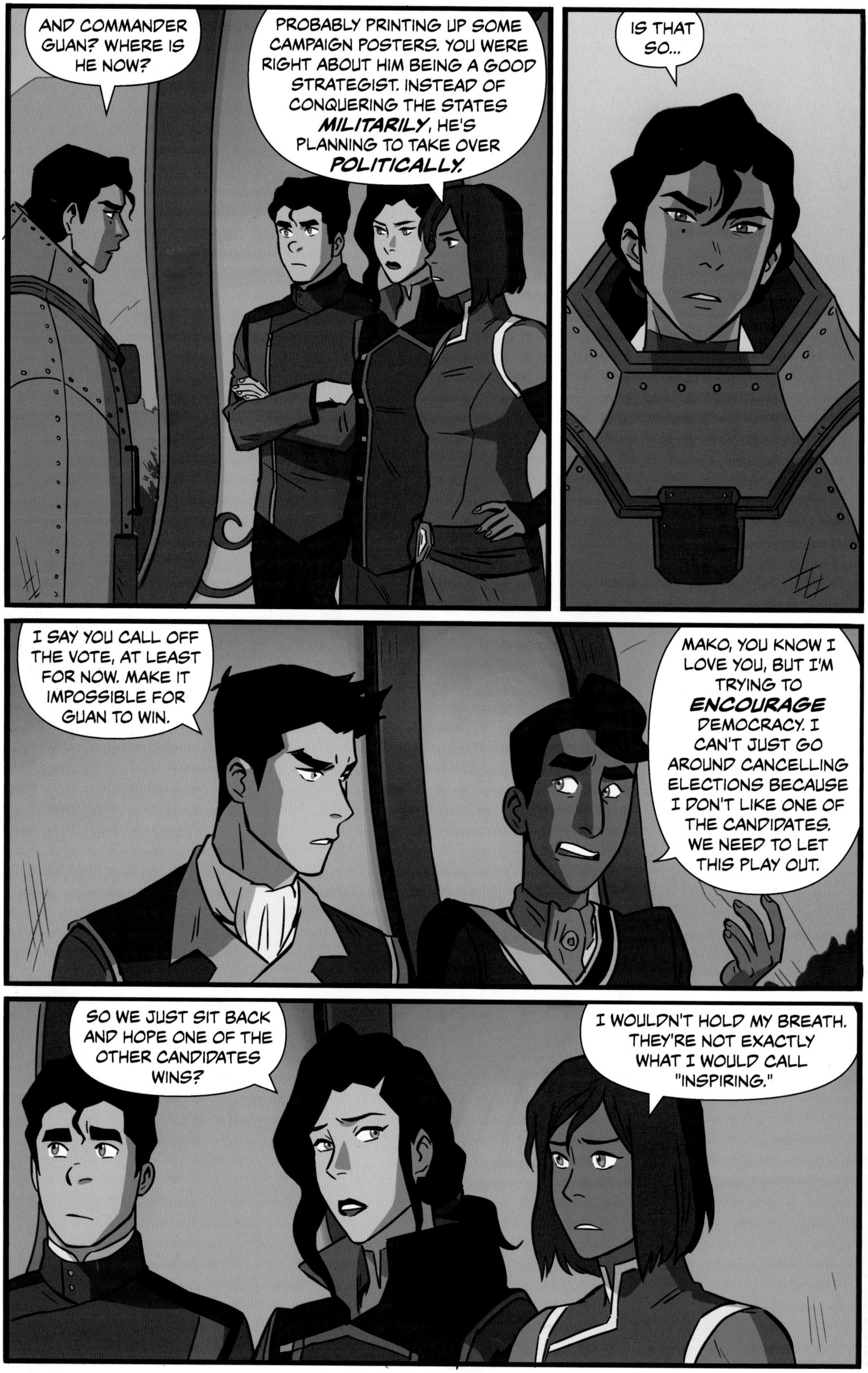

AND COMMANDER GUAN? WHERE IS HE NOW?
PROBABLY PRINTING UP SOME CAMPAIGN POSTERS. YOU WERE RIGHT ABOUT HIM BEING A GOOD STRATEGIST. INSTEAD OF CONQUERING THE STATES MILITARILY, HE'S PLANNING TO TAKE OVER POLITICALLY.
IS THAT SO...
I SAY YOU CALL OFF THE VOTE, AT LEAST FOR NOW. MAKE IT IMPOSSIBLE FOR GUAN TO WIN.
MAKO, YOU KNOW I LOVE YOU, BUT I'M TRYING TO ENCOURAGE DEMOCRACY. I CAN'T JUST GO AROUND CANCELLING ELECTIONS BECAUSE I DON'T LIKE ONE OF THE CANDIDATES. WE NEED TO LET THIS PLAY OUT.
SO WE JUST SIT BACK AND HOPE ONE OF THE OTHER CANDIDATES WINS?
I WOULDN'T HOLD MY BREATH. THEY'RE NOT EXACTLY WHAT I WOULD CALL "INSPIRING."

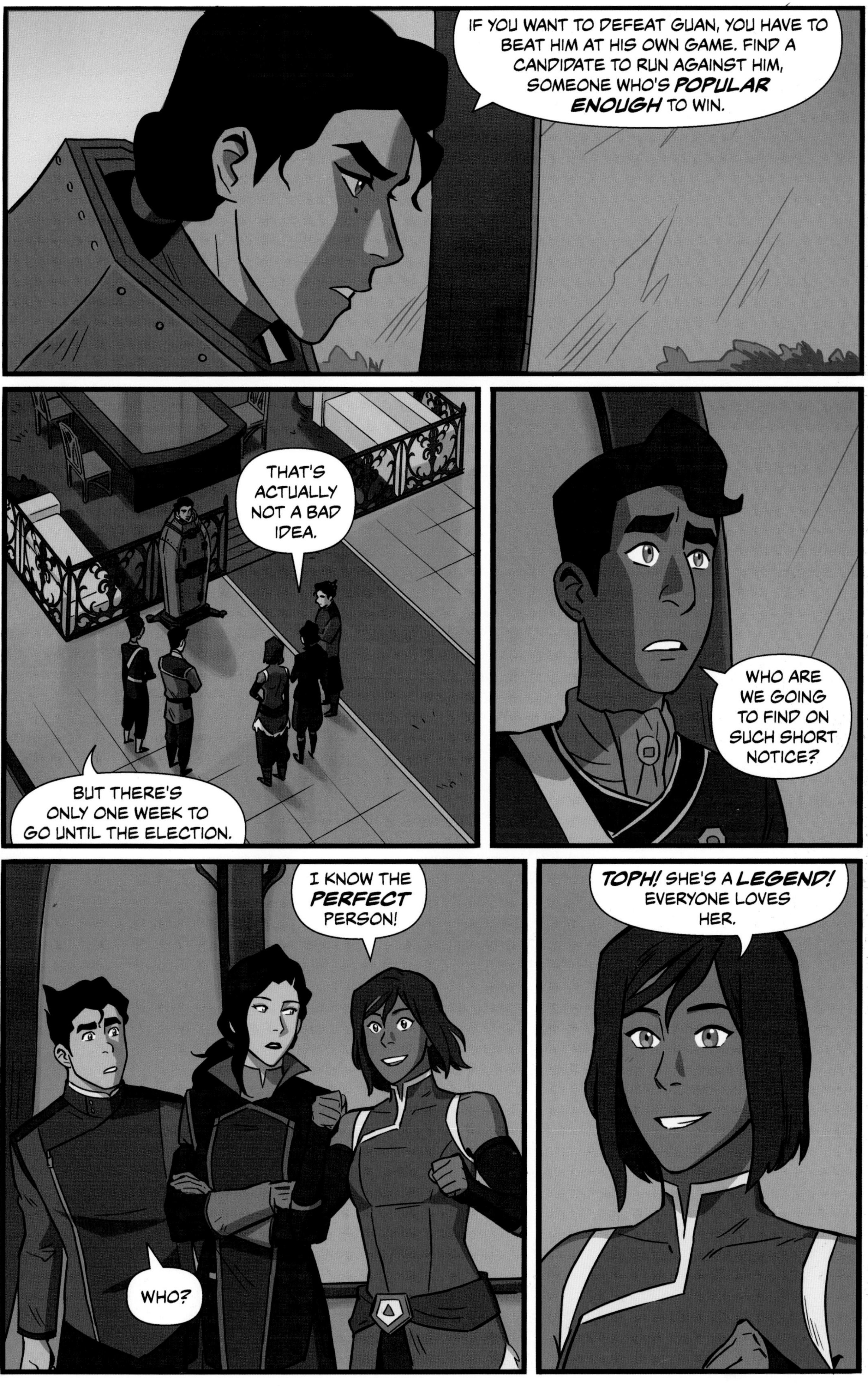
IF YOU WANT TO DEFEAT GUAN, YOU HAVE TO BEAT HIM AT HIS OWN GAME. FIND A CANDIDATE TO RUN AGAINST HIM, SOMEONE WHO'S POPULAR ENOUGH TO WIN.
THAT'S ACTUALLY NOT A BAD IDEA.
BUT THERE'S ONLY ONE WEEK TO GO UNTIL THE ELECTION.
WHO ARE WE GOING TO FIND ON SUCH SHORT NOTICE?
I KNOW THE PERFECT PERSON!
WHO?
TOPH! SHE'S A LEGEND! EVERYONE LOVES HER.

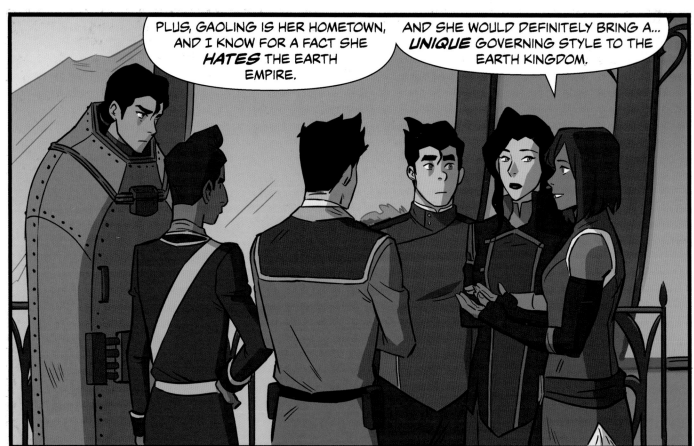

PLUS, GAOLING IS HER HOMETOWN, AND I KNOW FOR A FACT SHE *HATES* THE EARTH EMPIRE.

AND SHE WOULD DEFINITELY BRING A... *UNIQUE* GOVERNING STYLE TO THE EARTH KINGDOM.

SOUNDS GOOD TO ME!

THERE'S ONE ITSY BITSY PROBLEM. LAST TIME I SAW TOPH, SHE DIDN'T SEEM TOO KEEN ON GETTING INVOLVED WITH WORLD AFFAIRS.

THEN WE'LL JUST HAVE TO CONVINCE HER.

YOU SHOULD HAVE SEEN KUVIRA, DOCTOR SHENG.

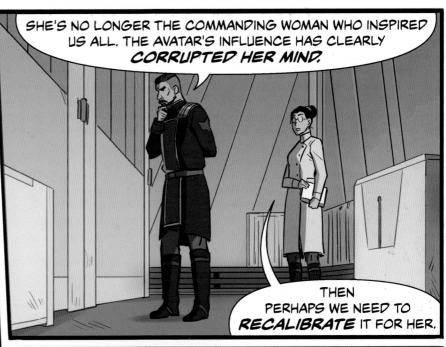

SHE'S NO LONGER THE COMMANDING WOMAN WHO INSPIRED US ALL. THE AVATAR'S INFLUENCE HAS CLEARLY *CORRUPTED HER MIND.*

THEN PERHAPS WE NEED TO *RECALIBRATE* IT FOR HER.

PERHAPS...

BUT AT THE MOMENT, WE HAVE AN ELECTION TO PREPARE FOR.

YOU MENTIONED THE FIRST CAMPAIGN RECRUITS HAVE ARRIVED?

RIGHT THROUGH HERE, SIR.

YOU'LL BE PLEASED TO HEAR THAT THEY'RE RESPONDING QUITE WELL TO OUR MESSAGING.

EXCELLENT.

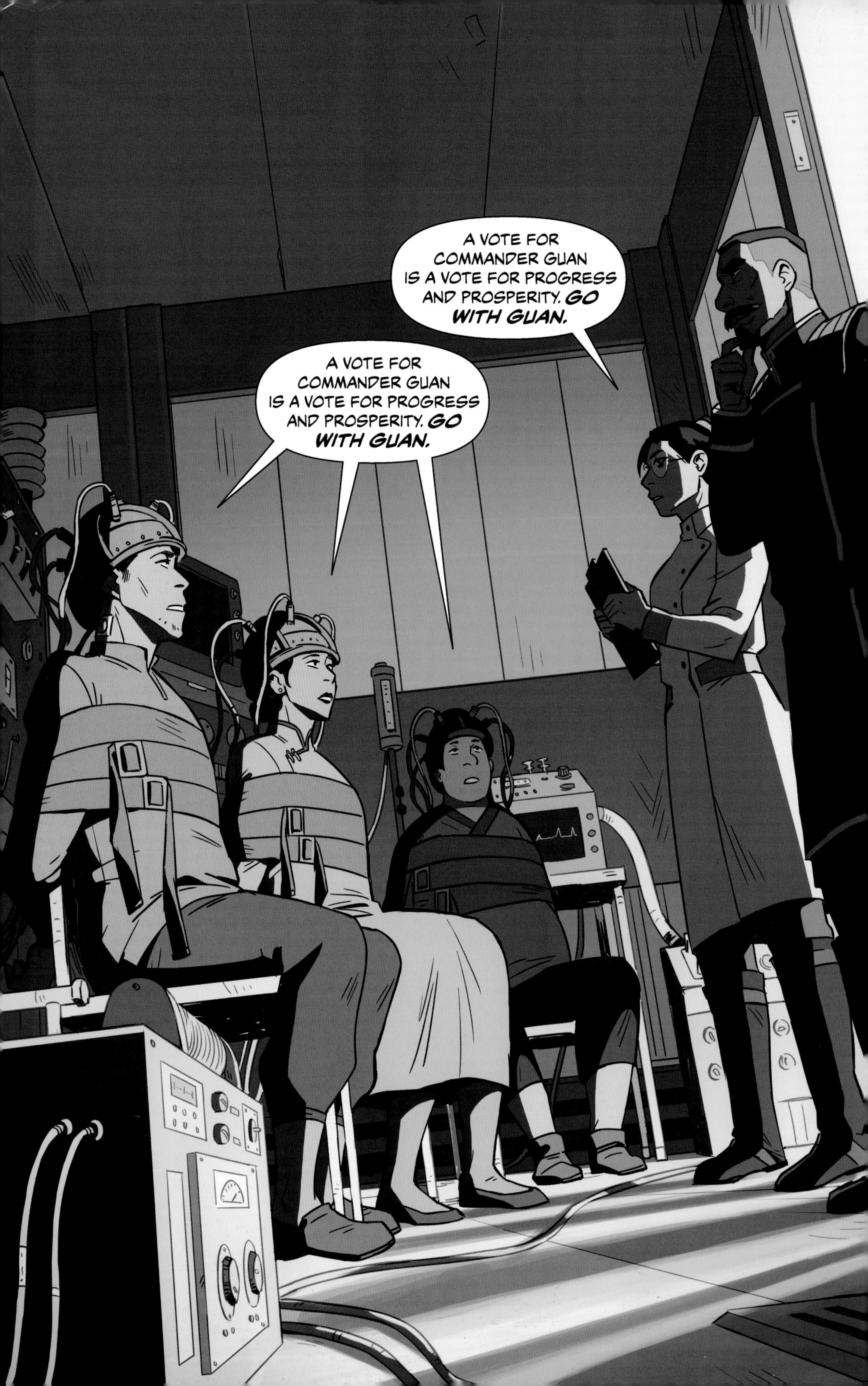
A VOTE FOR COMMANDER GUAN IS A VOTE FOR PROGRESS AND PROSPERITY. GO WITH GUAN.
A VOTE FOR COMMANDER GUAN IS A VOTE FOR PROGRESS AND PROSPERITY. GO WITH GUAN.

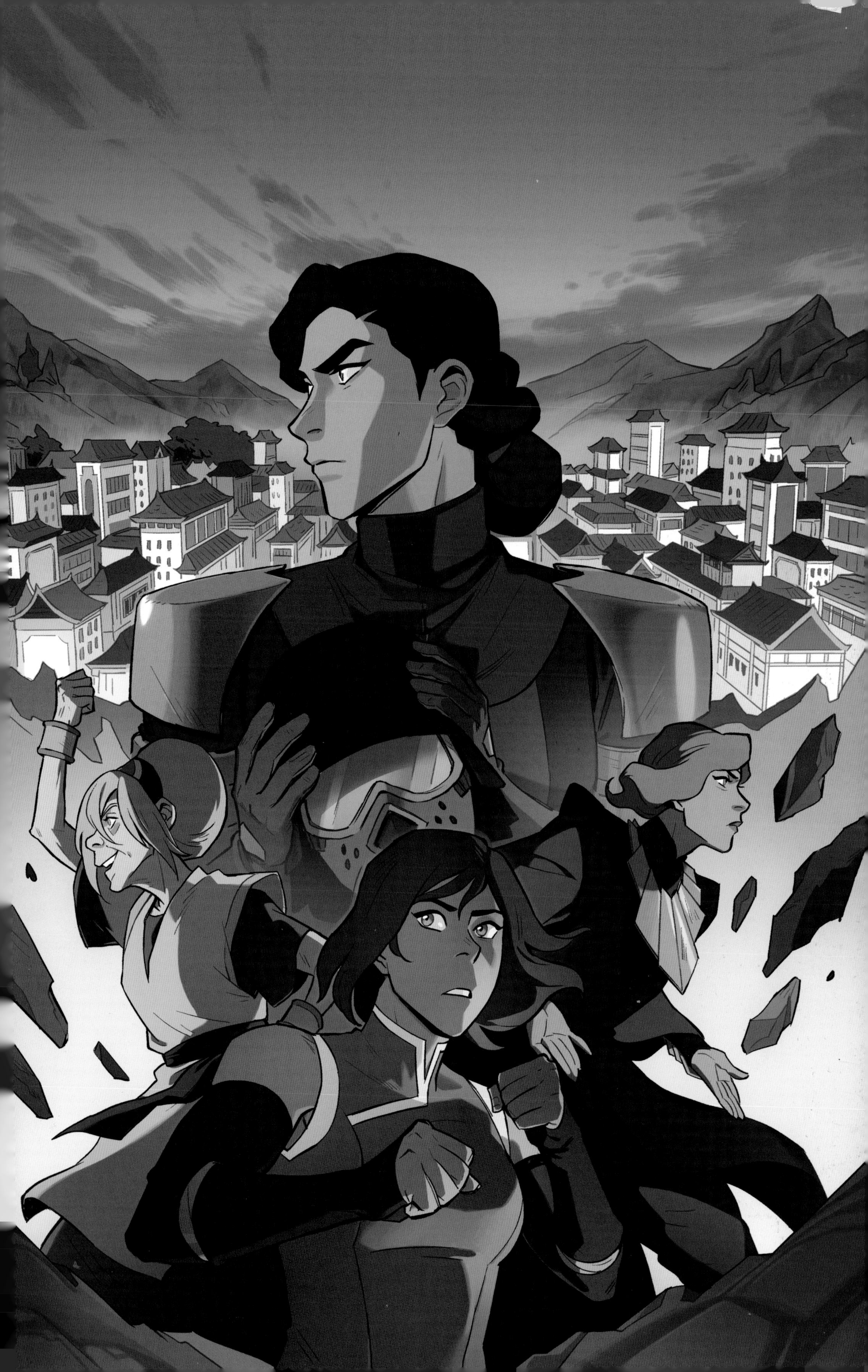

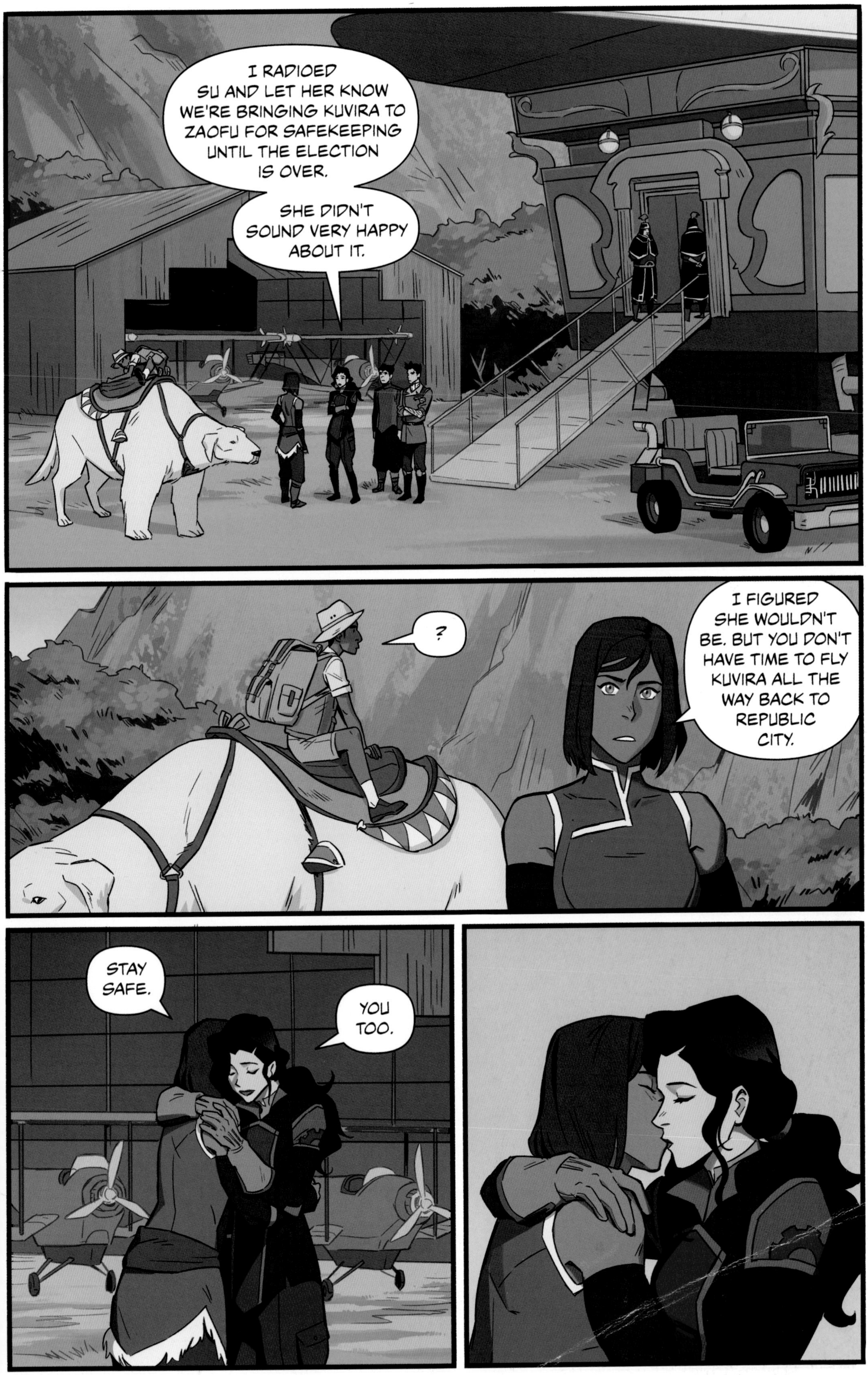
I RADIOED SU AND LET HER KNOW WE'RE BRINGING KUVIRA TO ZAOFU FOR SAFEKEEPING UNTIL THE ELECTION IS OVER.
SHE DIDN'T SOUND VERY HAPPY ABOUT IT.
?
I FIGURED SHE WOULDN'T BE. BUT YOU DON'T HAVE TIME TO FLY KUVIRA ALL THE WAY BACK TO REPUBLIC CITY.
STAY SAFE.
YOU TOO.

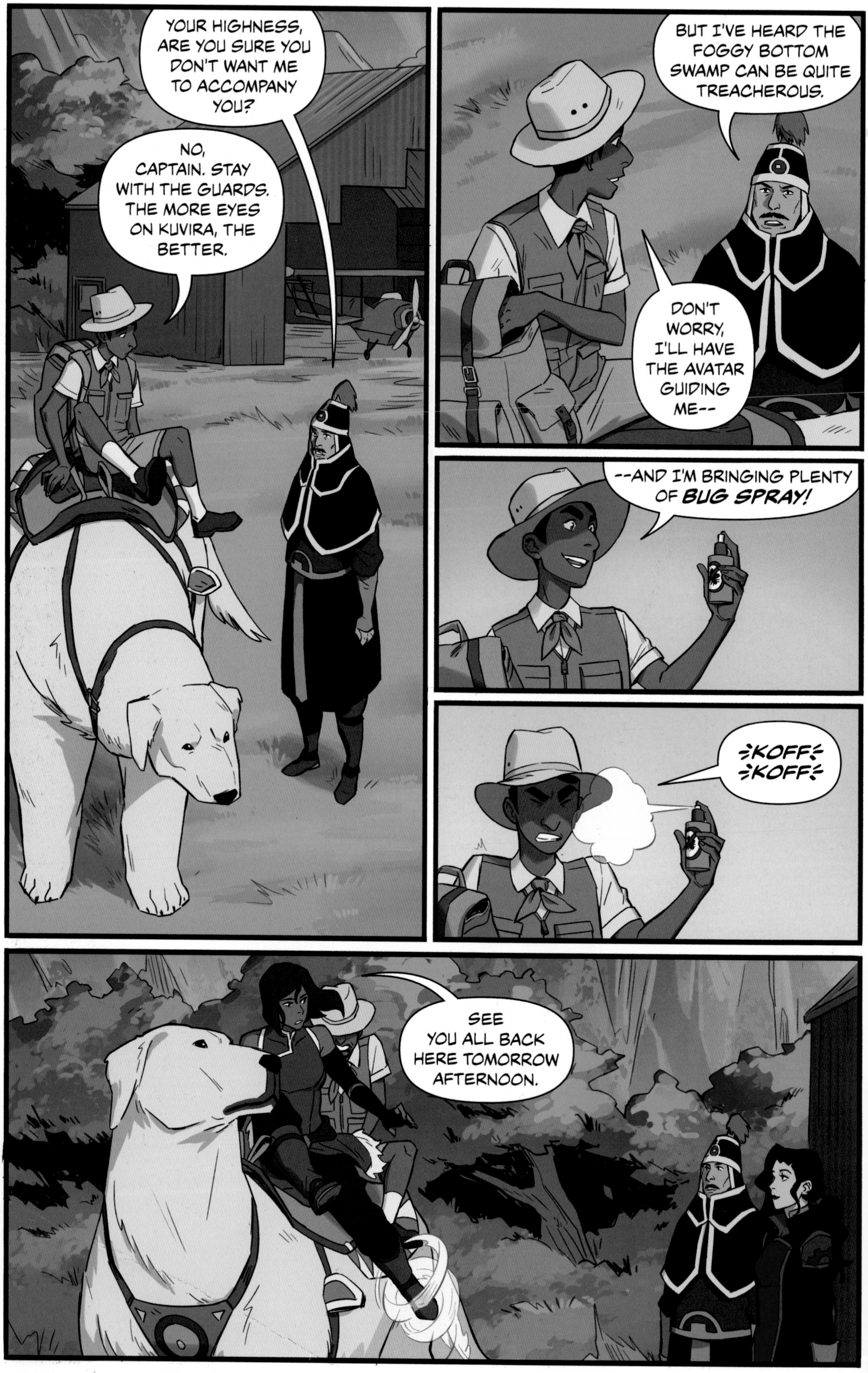
YOUR HIGHNESS, ARE YOU SURE YOU DON'T WANT ME TO ACCOMPANY YOU?
NO, CAPTAIN. STAY WITH THE GUARDS. THE MORE EYES ON KUVIRA, THE BETTER.
BUT I'VE HEARD THE FOGGY BOTTOM SWAMP CAN BE QUITE TREACHEROUS.
DON'T WORRY, I'LL HAVE THE AVATAR GUIDING ME--
--AND I'M BRINGING PLENTY OF BUG SPRAY!
KOFF KOFF
SEE YOU ALL BACK HERE TOMORROW AFTERNOON.

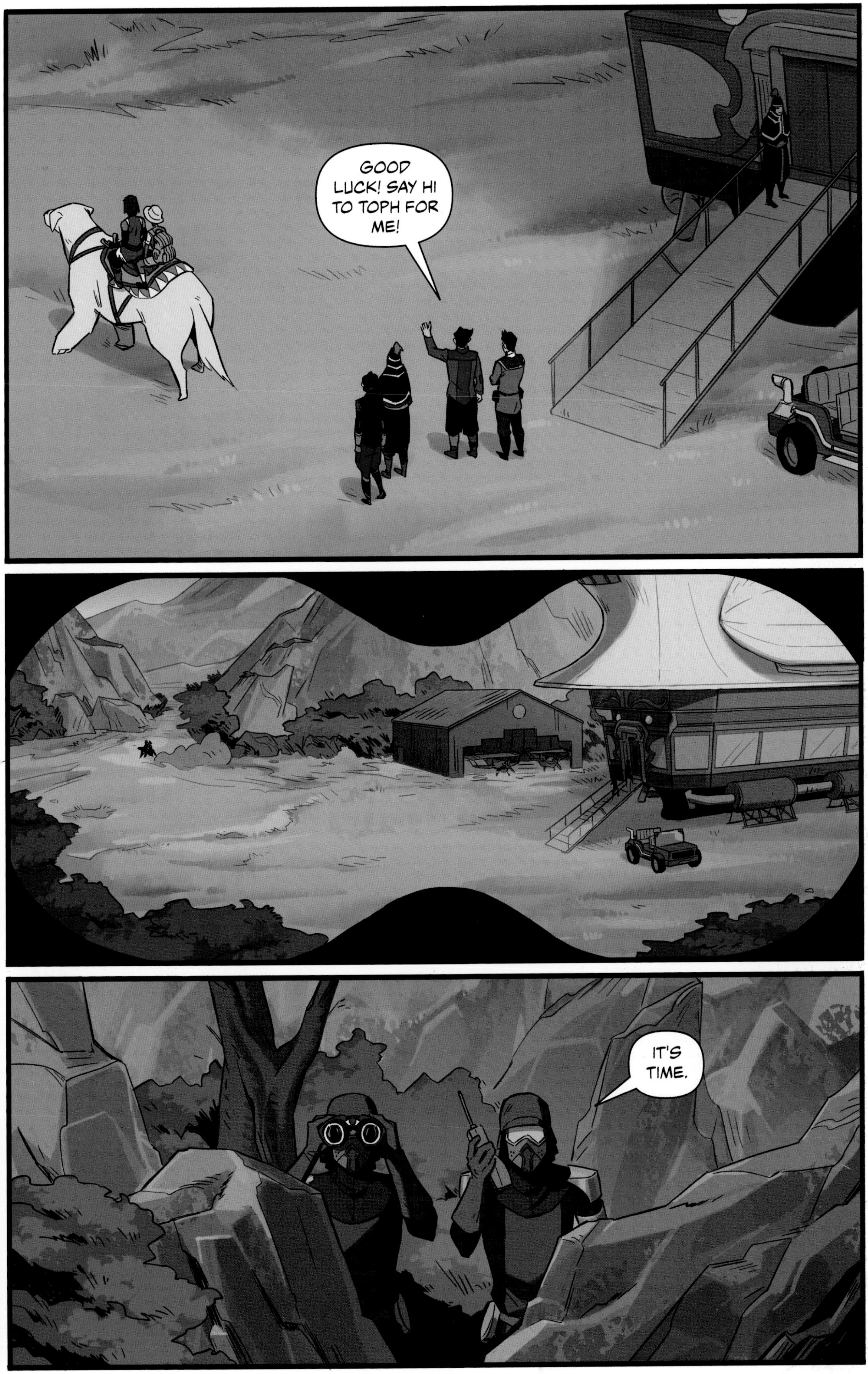
GOOD LUCK! SAY HI TO TOPH FOR ME!
IT'S TIME.

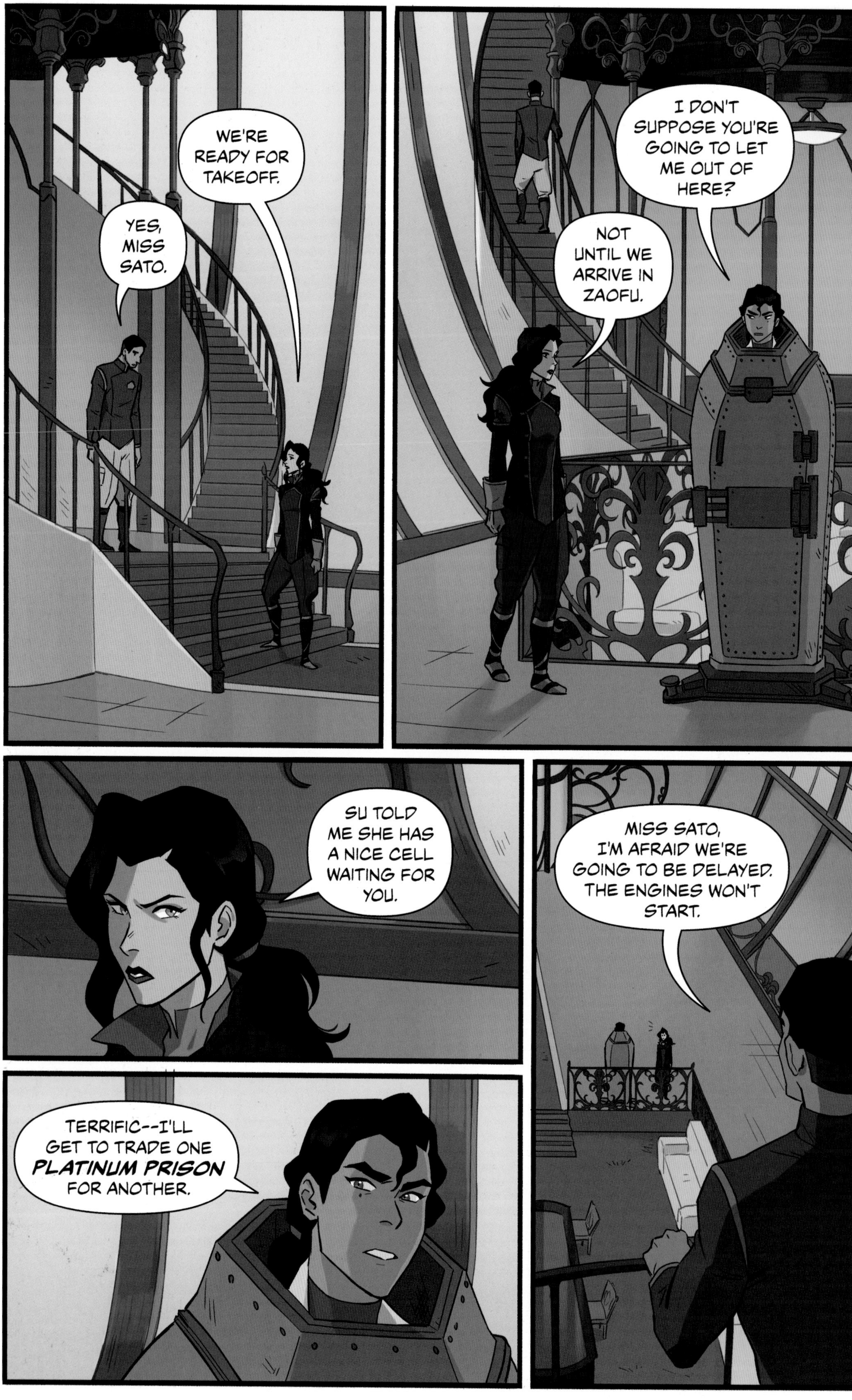
WE'RE READY FOR TAKEOFF.
YES, MISS SATO.
I DON'T SUPPOSE YOU'RE GOING TO LET ME OUT OF HERE?
NOT UNTIL WE ARRIVE IN ZAOFU.
SU TOLD ME SHE HAS A NICE CELL WAITING FOR YOU.
TERRIFIC--I'LL GET TO TRADE ONE ***PLATINUM PRISON*** FOR ANOTHER.
MISS SATO, I'M AFRAID WE'RE GOING TO BE DELAYED. THE ENGINES WON'T START.

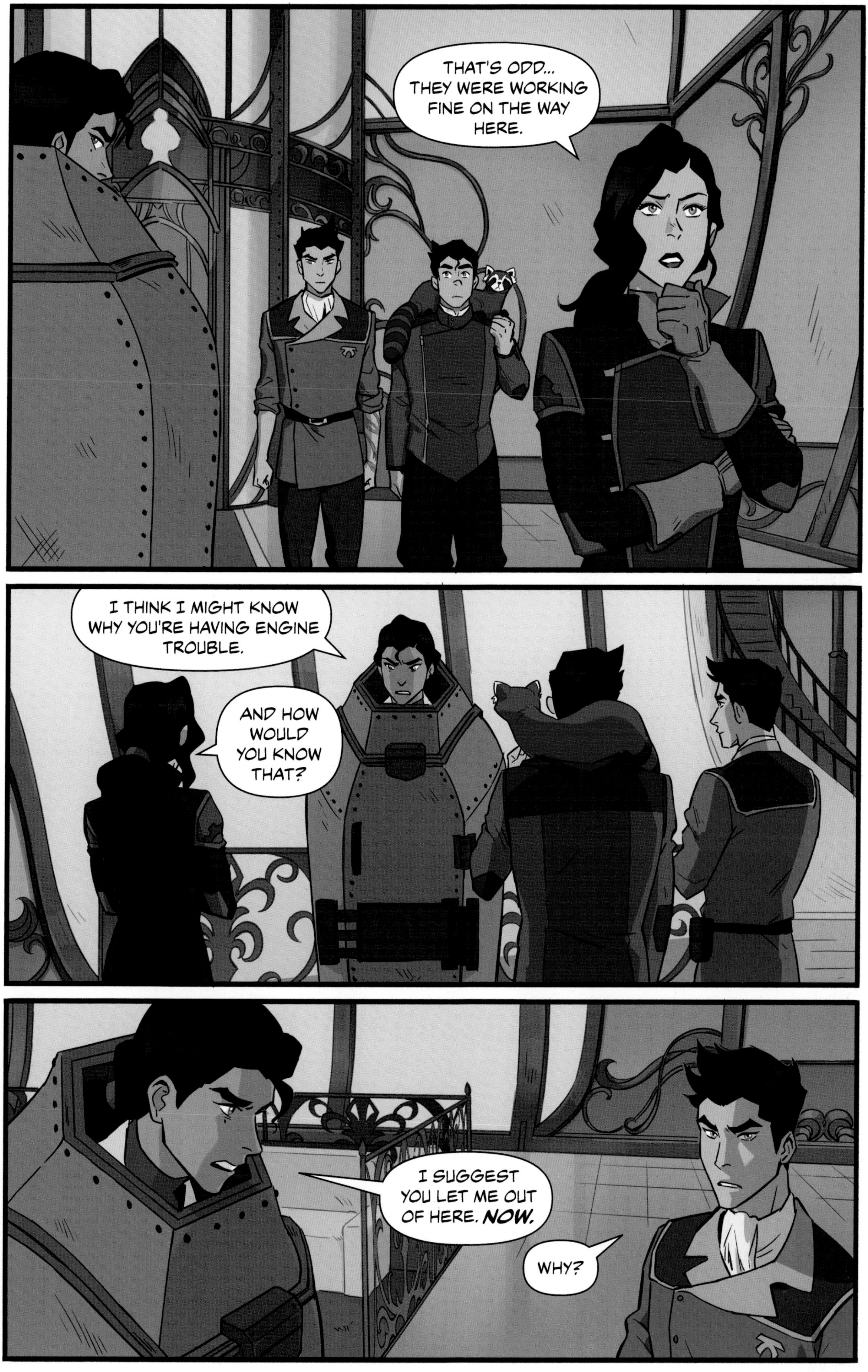
THAT'S ODD... THEY WERE WORKING FINE ON THE WAY HERE.
I THINK I MIGHT KNOW WHY YOU'RE HAVING ENGINE TROUBLE.
AND HOW WOULD YOU KNOW THAT?
I SUGGEST YOU LET ME OUT OF HERE. **NOW.**
WHY?

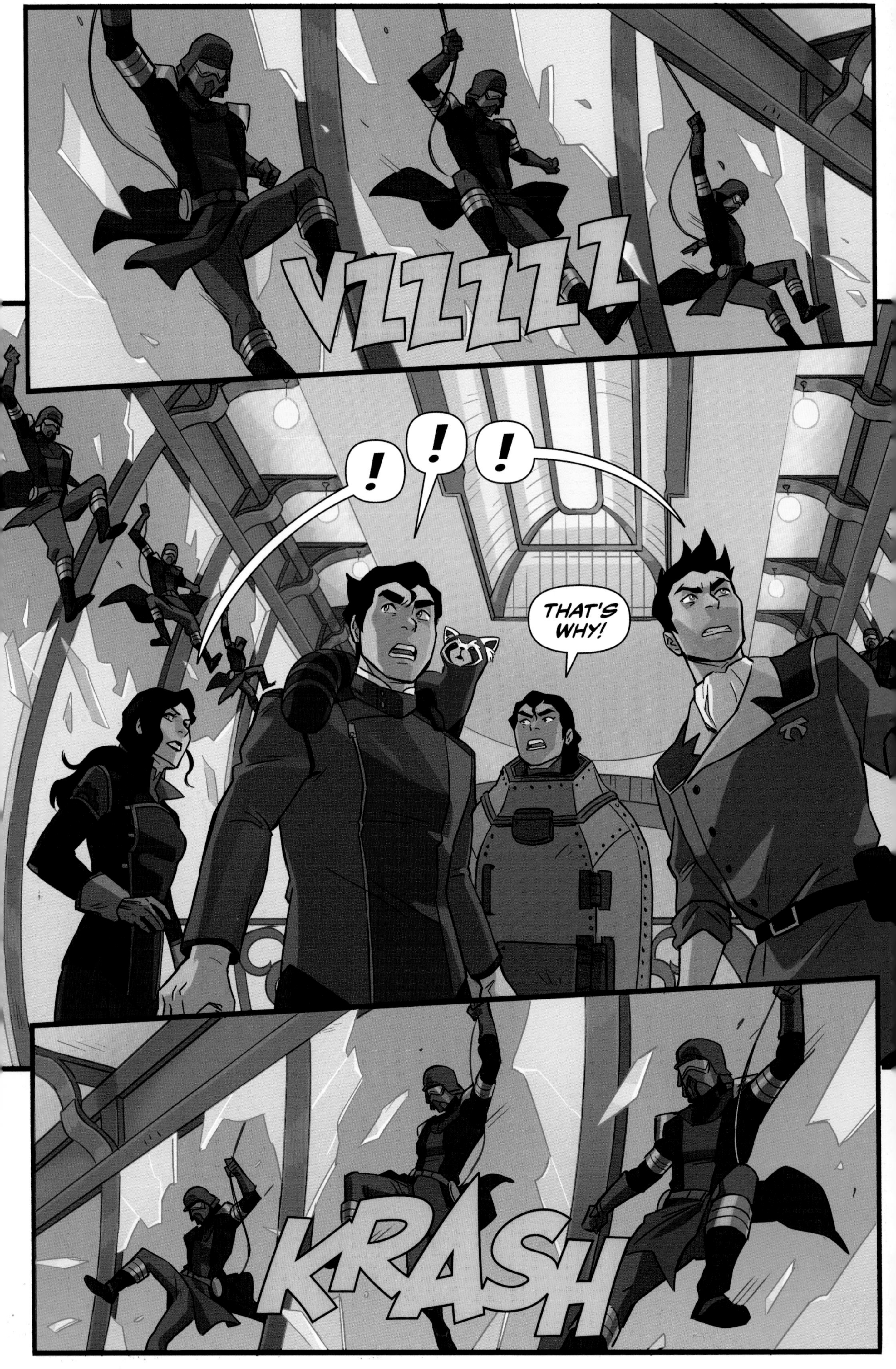
VZZZZZ
!
!
!
THAT'S WHY!
KRASH

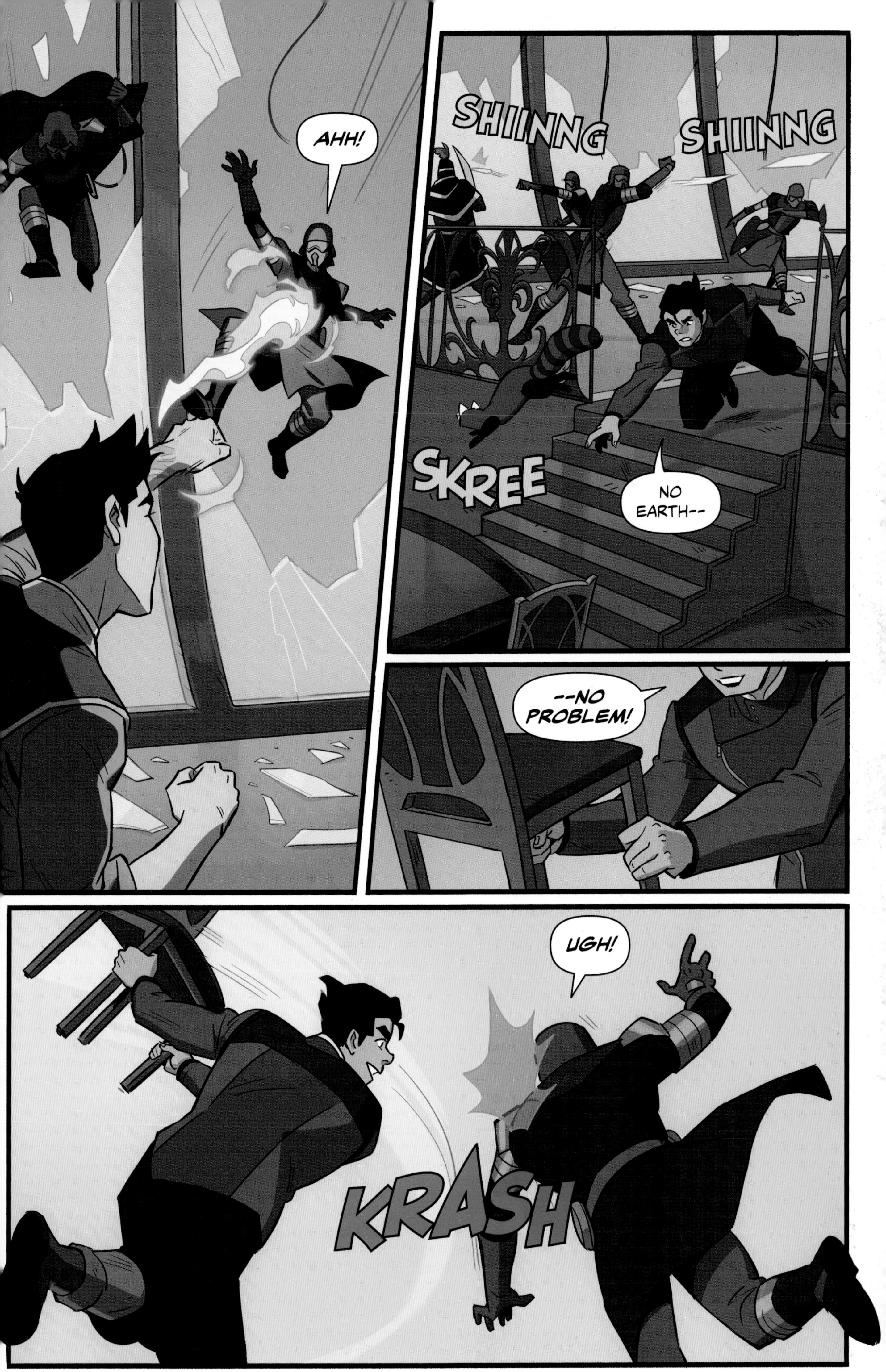
AHH!
SHIINNG
SHIINNG
SKREE
NO EARTH--
--NO PROBLEM!
UGH!
KRASH

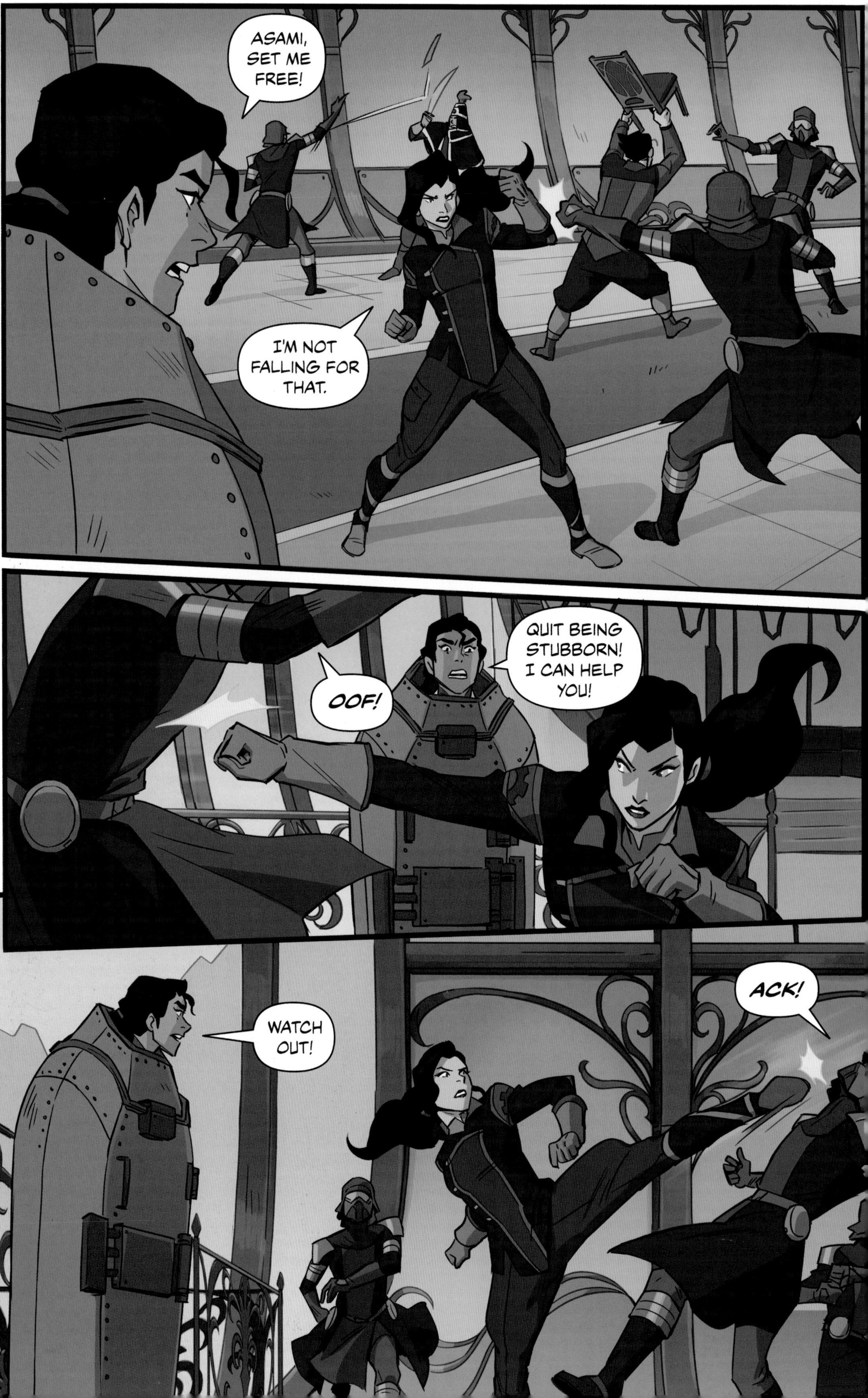
ASAMI, SET ME FREE!
I'M NOT FALLING FOR THAT.
OOF!
QUIT BEING STUBBORN! I CAN HELP YOU!
WATCH OUT!
ACK!

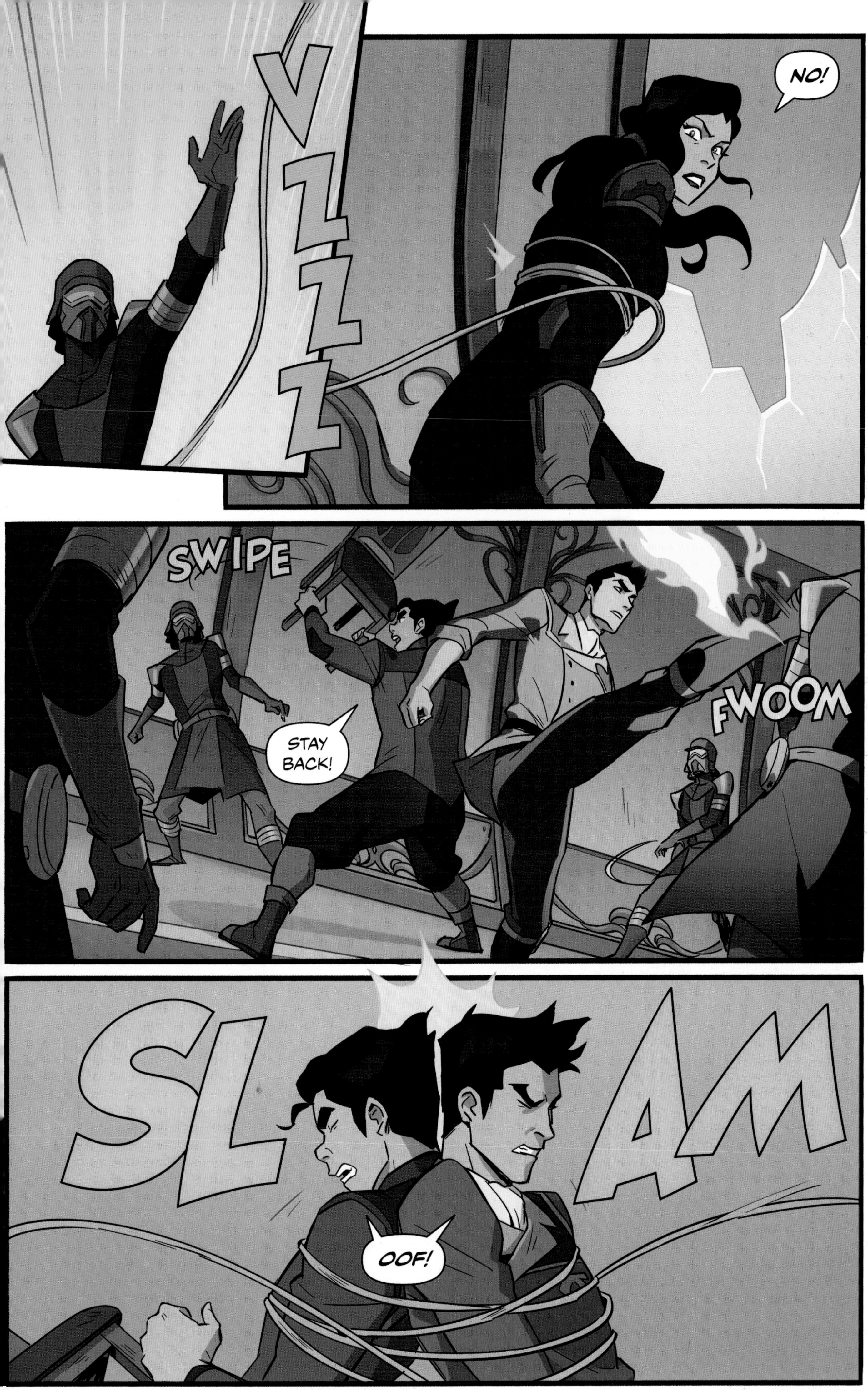
VZZZZ
NO!
SWIPE
STAY BACK!
FWOOM
SLAM
OOF!

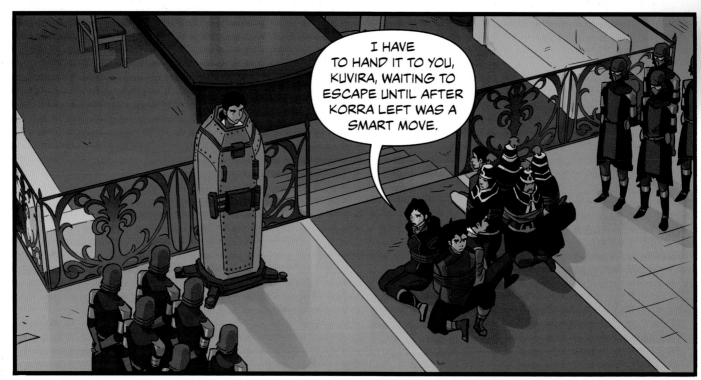

I HAVE TO HAND IT TO YOU, KUVIRA, WAITING TO ESCAPE UNTIL AFTER KORRA LEFT WAS A SMART MOVE.

YOU FOOLS, THIS WASN'T MY DOING--

DING

IT WAS HIS.

HELLO AGAIN, KUVIRA.

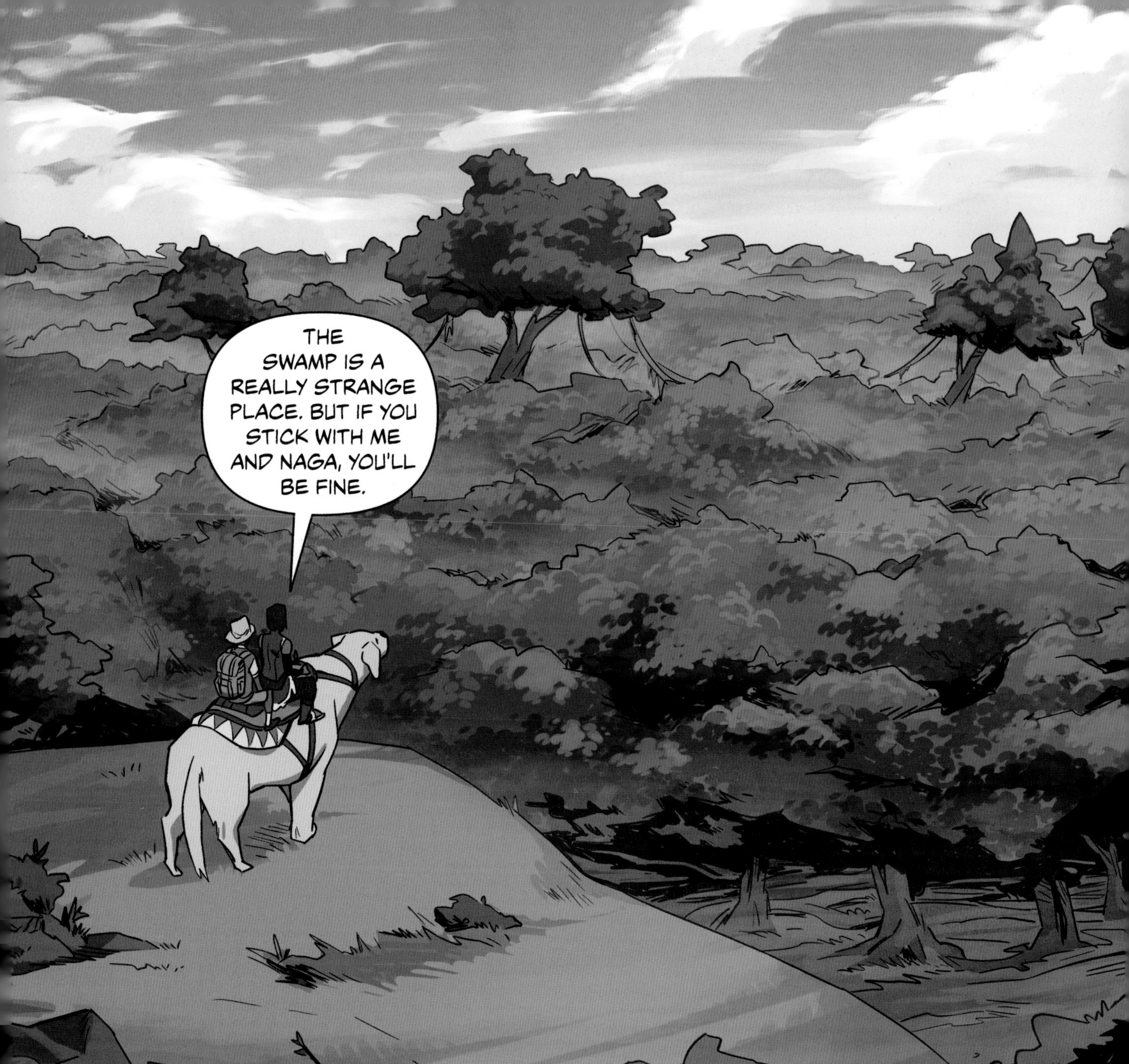
THE SWAMP IS A REALLY STRANGE PLACE. BUT IF YOU STICK WITH ME AND NAGA, YOU'LL BE FINE.

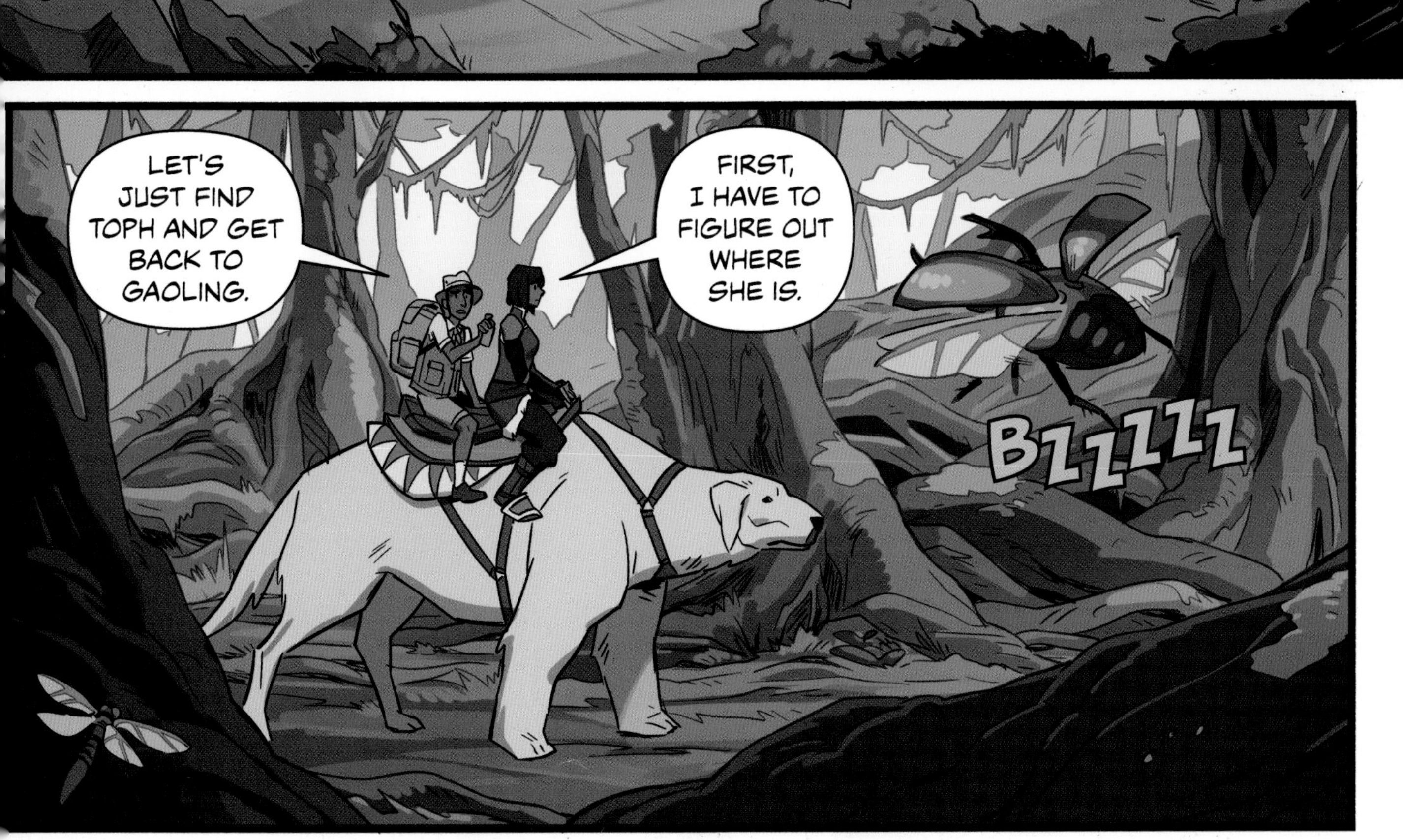
LET'S JUST FIND TOPH AND GET BACK TO GAOLING.
FIRST, I HAVE TO FIGURE OUT WHERE SHE IS.
BZZZZZ

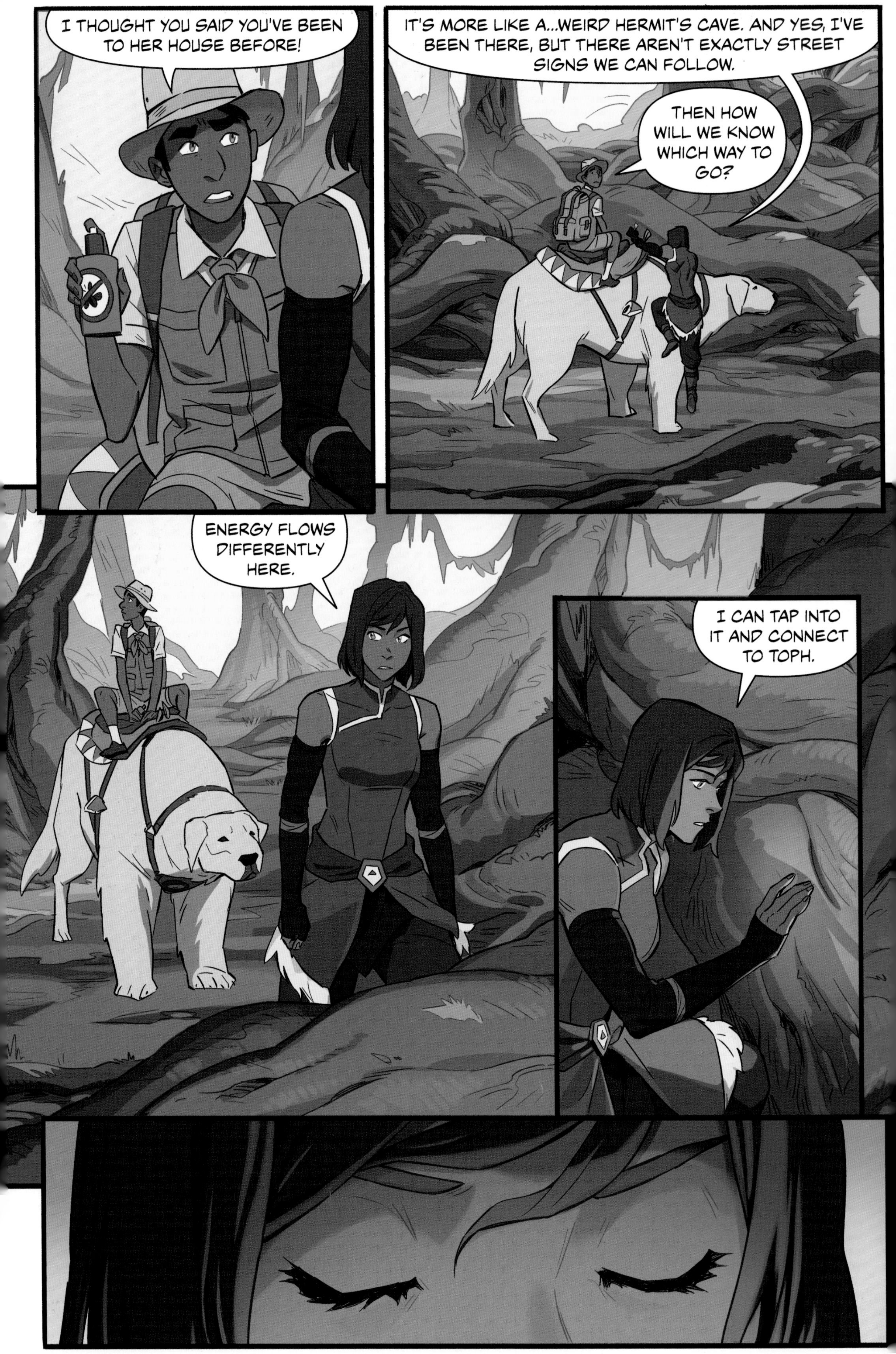
I THOUGHT YOU SAID YOU'VE BEEN TO HER HOUSE BEFORE!
IT'S MORE LIKE A...WEIRD HERMIT'S CAVE. AND YES, I'VE BEEN THERE, BUT THERE AREN'T EXACTLY STREET SIGNS WE CAN FOLLOW.
THEN HOW WILL WE KNOW WHICH WAY TO GO?
ENERGY FLOWS DIFFERENTLY HERE.
I CAN TAP INTO IT AND CONNECT TO TOPH.

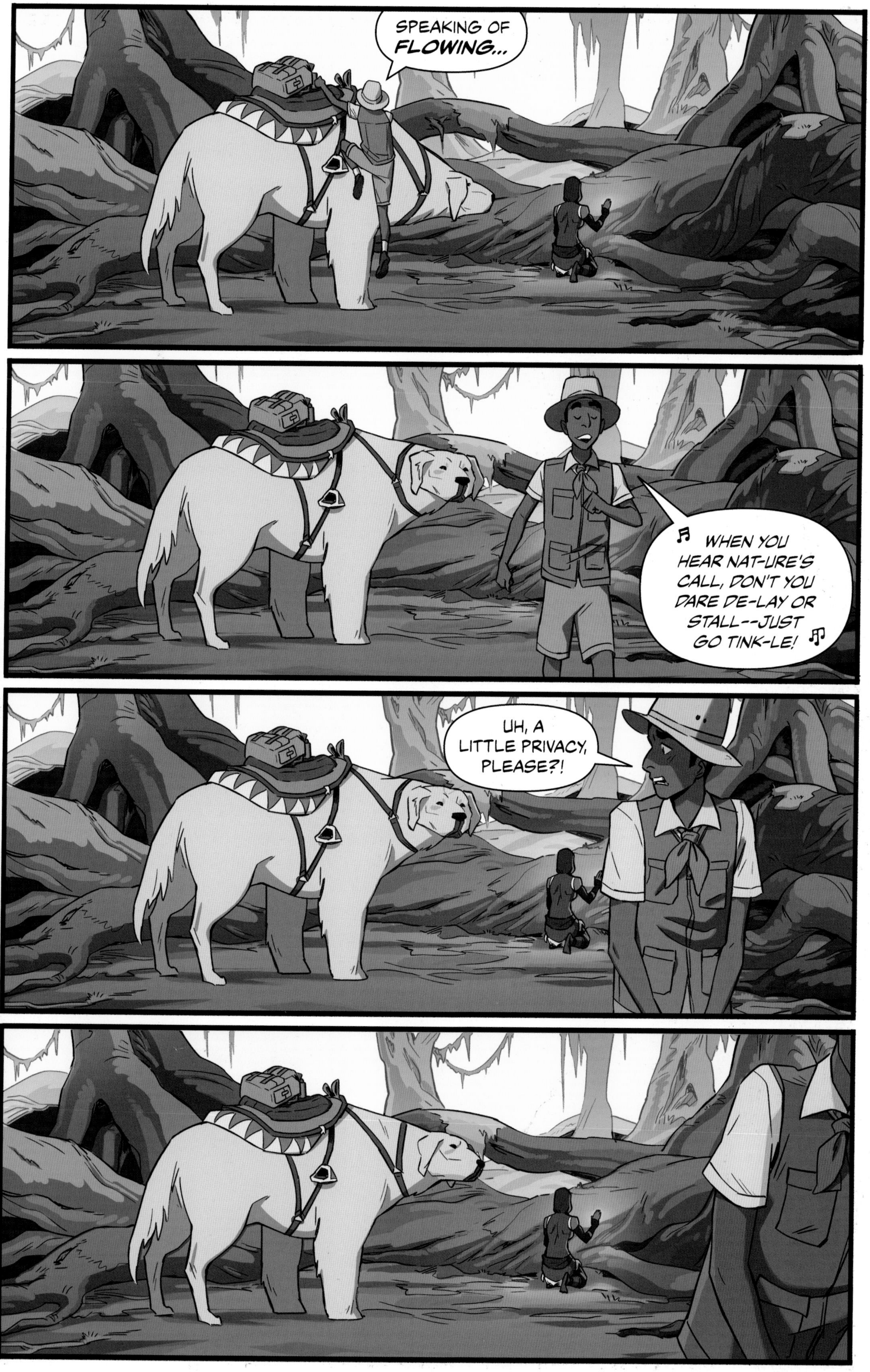
SPEAKING OF FLOWING...
♬ WHEN YOU HEAR NAT-URE'S CALL, DON'T YOU DARE DE-LAY OR STALL--JUST GO TINK-LE! ♫
UH, A LITTLE PRIVACY, PLEASE?!

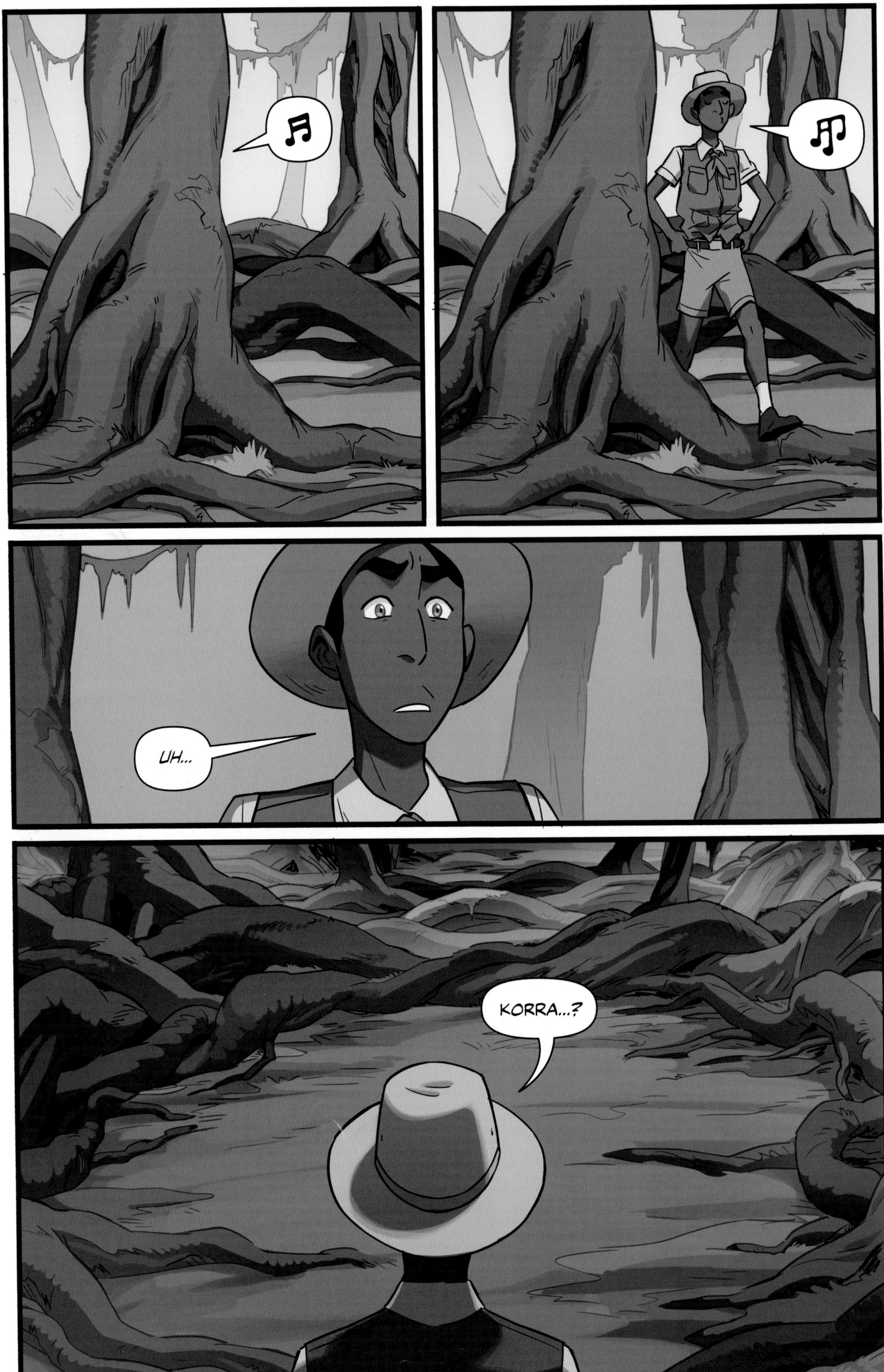
♬
♫
UH...
KORRA...?

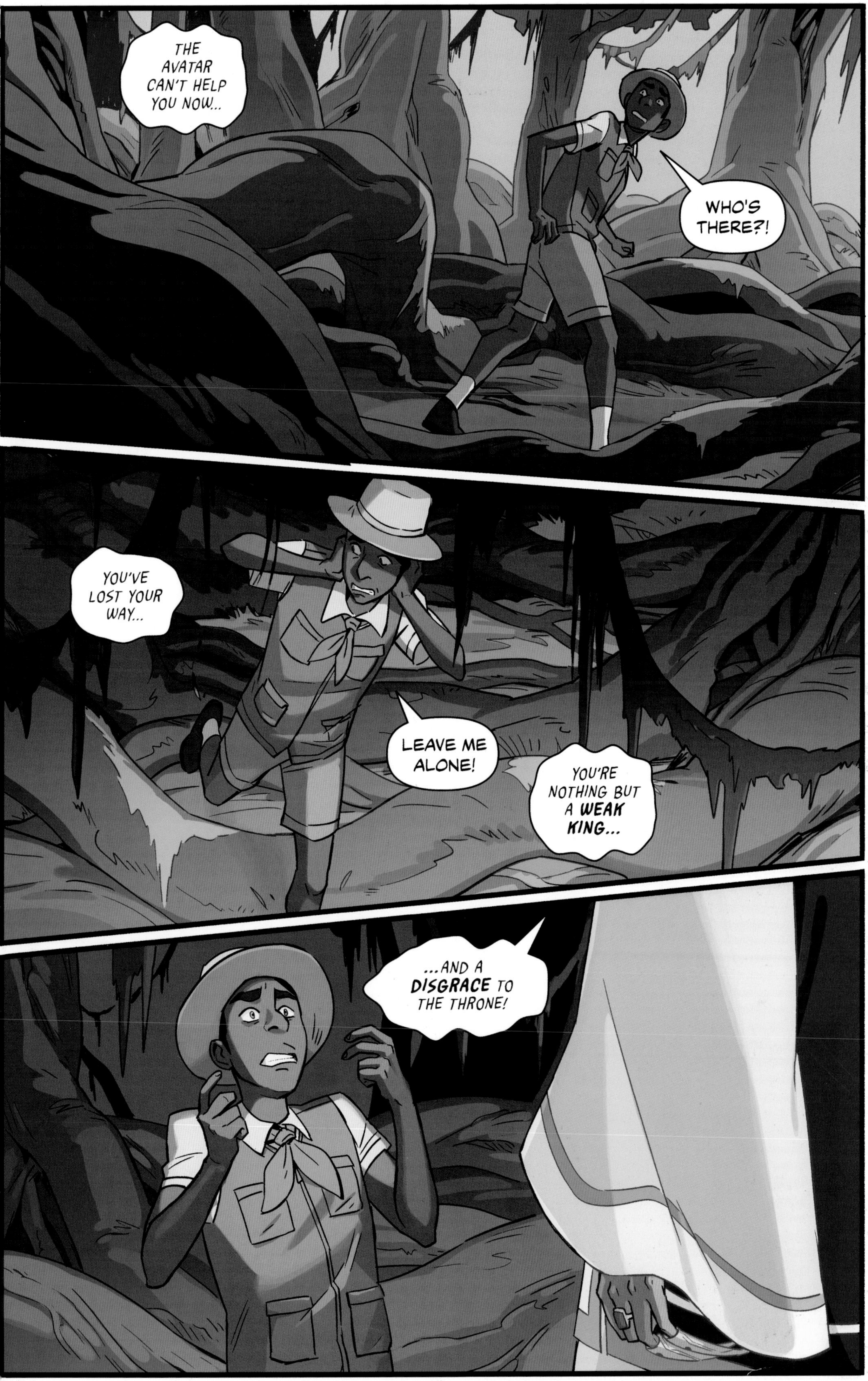
THE AVATAR CAN'T HELP YOU NOW...
WHO'S THERE?!
YOU'VE LOST YOUR WAY...
LEAVE ME ALONE!
YOU'RE NOTHING BUT A WEAK KING...
...AND A DISGRACE TO THE THRONE!

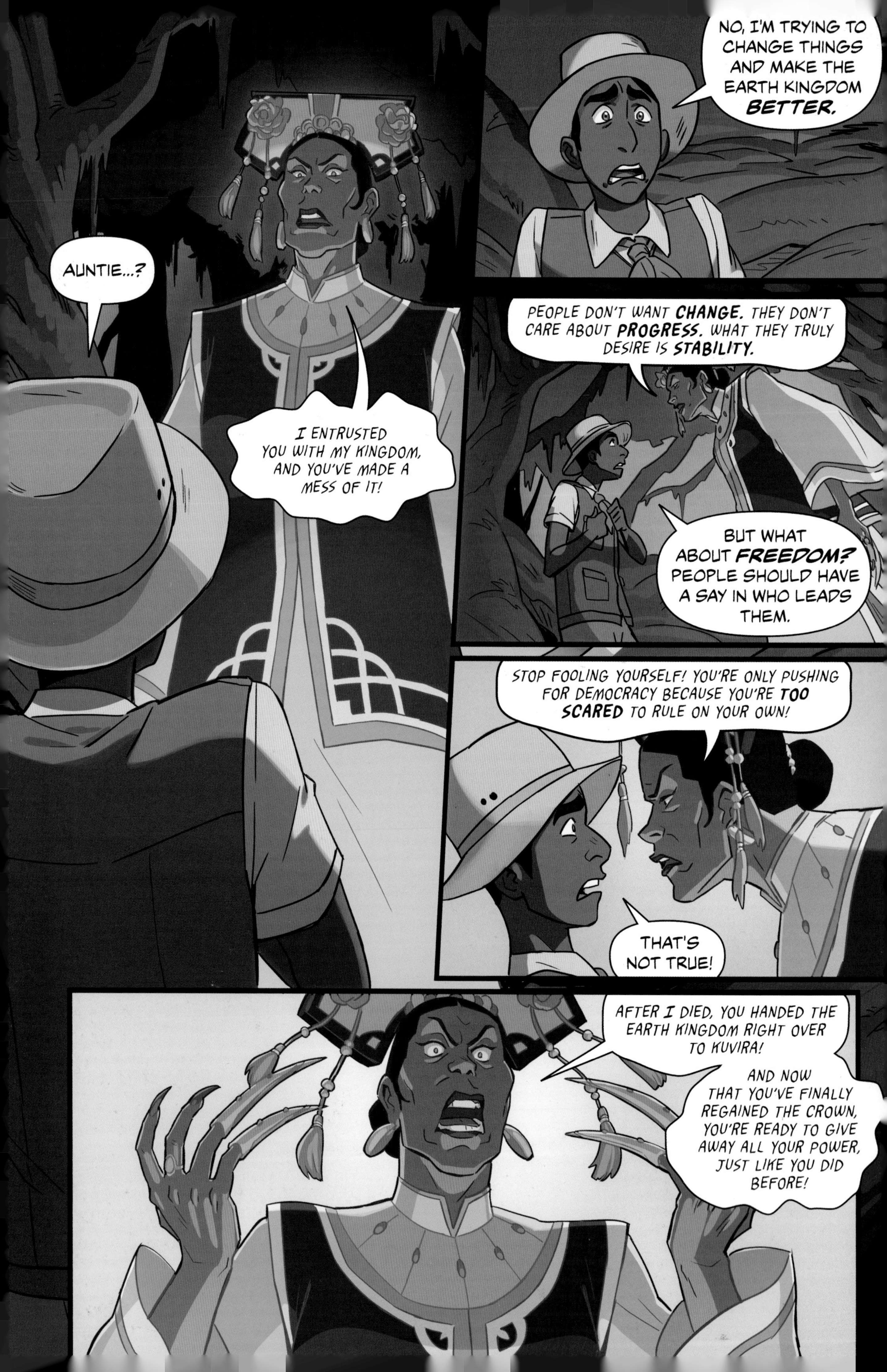
AUNTIE...?
I ENTRUSTED YOU WITH MY KINGDOM, AND YOU'VE MADE A MESS OF IT!
NO, I'M TRYING TO CHANGE THINGS AND MAKE THE EARTH KINGDOM BETTER.
PEOPLE DON'T WANT CHANGE. THEY DON'T CARE ABOUT PROGRESS. WHAT THEY TRULY DESIRE IS STABILITY.
BUT WHAT ABOUT FREEDOM? PEOPLE SHOULD HAVE A SAY IN WHO LEADS THEM.
STOP FOOLING YOURSELF! YOU'RE ONLY PUSHING FOR DEMOCRACY BECAUSE YOU'RE TOO SCARED TO RULE ON YOUR OWN!
THAT'S NOT TRUE!
AFTER I DIED, YOU HANDED THE EARTH KINGDOM RIGHT OVER TO KUVIRA!
AND NOW THAT YOU'VE FINALLY REGAINED THE CROWN, YOU'RE READY TO GIVE AWAY ALL YOUR POWER, JUST LIKE YOU DID BEFORE!

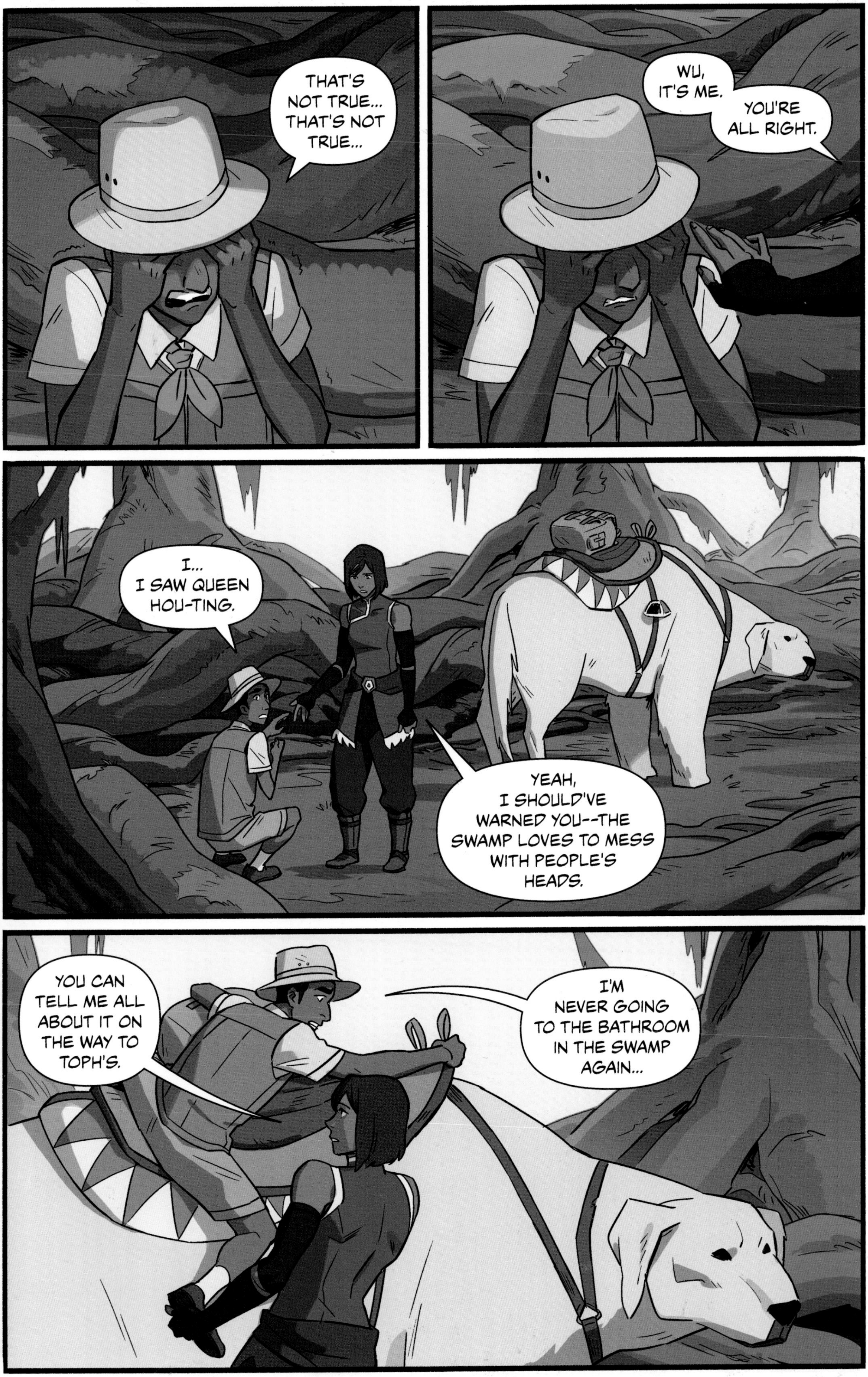
THAT'S NOT TRUE... THAT'S NOT TRUE...
WU, IT'S ME.
YOU'RE ALL RIGHT.
I... I SAW QUEEN HOU-TING.
YEAH, I SHOULD'VE WARNED YOU--THE SWAMP LOVES TO MESS WITH PEOPLE'S HEADS.
YOU CAN TELL ME ALL ABOUT IT ON THE WAY TO TOPH'S.
I'M NEVER GOING TO THE BATHROOM IN THE SWAMP AGAIN...

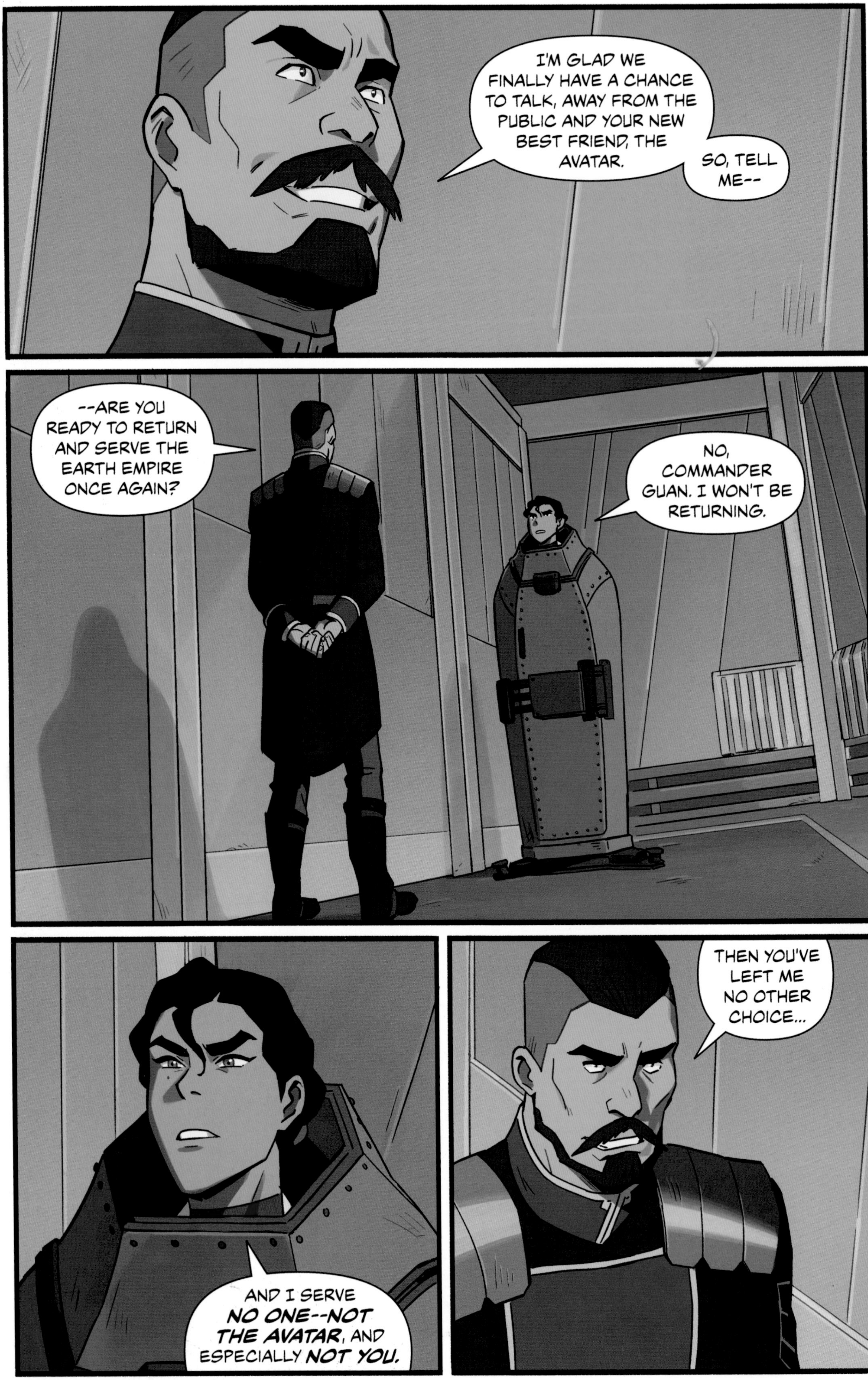
I'M GLAD WE FINALLY HAVE A CHANCE TO TALK, AWAY FROM THE PUBLIC AND YOUR NEW BEST FRIEND, THE AVATAR.
SO, TELL ME--
--ARE YOU READY TO RETURN AND SERVE THE EARTH EMPIRE ONCE AGAIN?
NO, COMMANDER GUAN. I WON'T BE RETURNING.
AND I SERVE **NO ONE--NOT THE AVATAR**, AND ESPECIALLY **NOT YOU.**
THEN YOU'VE LEFT ME NO OTHER CHOICE...

KER-CHUNK

MMMPH!

RELEASE THEM AT ONCE!

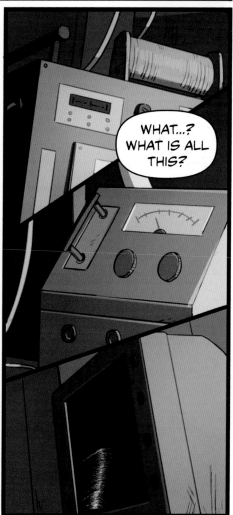

WHAT...? WHAT IS ALL THIS?

YOU REMEMBER DR. SHENG, DON'T YOU? SHE WORKED VERY CLOSELY WITH YOUR FORMER FIANCÉ.

HELLO, KUVIRA.

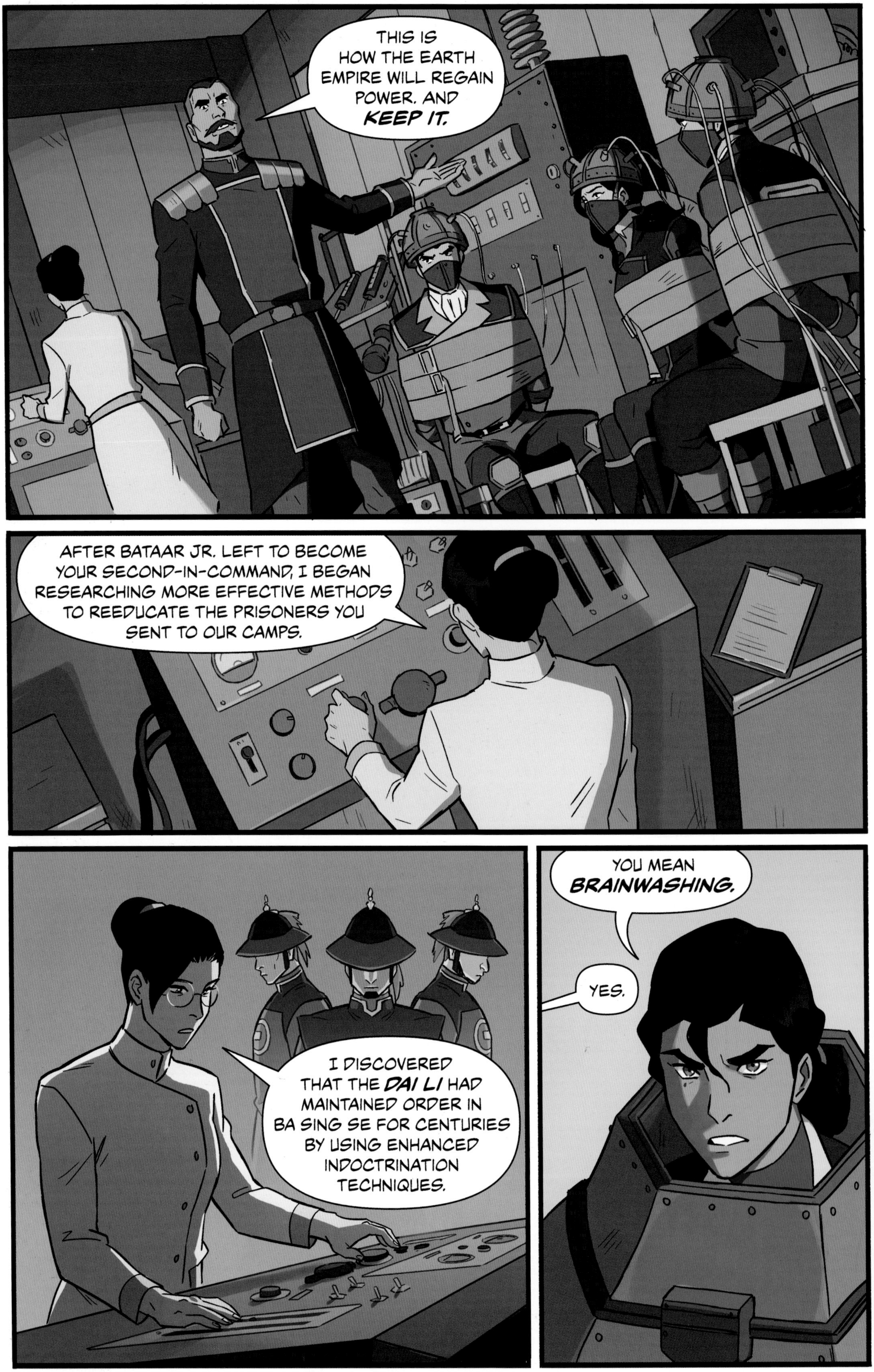
THIS IS HOW THE EARTH EMPIRE WILL REGAIN POWER. AND **KEEP IT.**
AFTER BATAAR JR. LEFT TO BECOME YOUR SECOND-IN-COMMAND, I BEGAN RESEARCHING MORE EFFECTIVE METHODS TO REEDUCATE THE PRISONERS YOU SENT TO OUR CAMPS.
I DISCOVERED THAT THE ***DAI LI*** HAD MAINTAINED ORDER IN BA SING SE FOR CENTURIES BY USING ENHANCED INDOCTRINATION TECHNIQUES.
YOU MEAN **BRAINWASHING.**
YES.

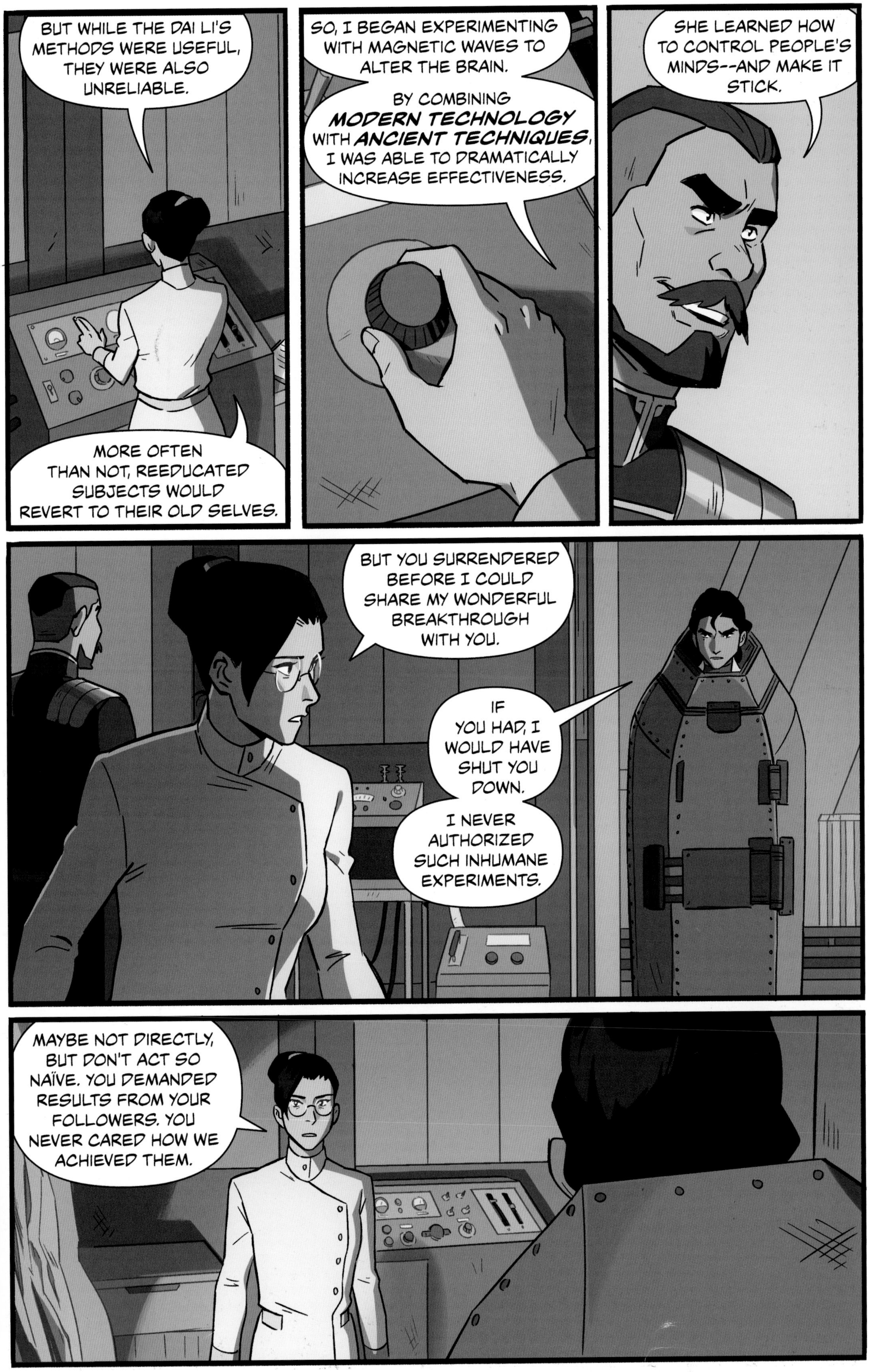

BUT WHILE THE DAI LI'S METHODS WERE USEFUL, THEY WERE ALSO UNRELIABLE.
MORE OFTEN THAN NOT, REEDUCATED SUBJECTS WOULD REVERT TO THEIR OLD SELVES.
SO, I BEGAN EXPERIMENTING WITH MAGNETIC WAVES TO ALTER THE BRAIN.
BY COMBINING MODERN TECHNOLOGY WITH ANCIENT TECHNIQUES, I WAS ABLE TO DRAMATICALLY INCREASE EFFECTIVENESS.
SHE LEARNED HOW TO CONTROL PEOPLE'S MINDS--AND MAKE IT STICK.
BUT YOU SURRENDERED BEFORE I COULD SHARE MY WONDERFUL BREAKTHROUGH WITH YOU.
IF YOU HAD, I WOULD HAVE SHUT YOU DOWN.
I NEVER AUTHORIZED SUCH INHUMANE EXPERIMENTS.
MAYBE NOT DIRECTLY, BUT DON'T ACT SO NAÏVE. YOU DEMANDED RESULTS FROM YOUR FOLLOWERS. YOU NEVER CARED HOW WE ACHIEVED THEM.

NO... THAT'S NOT TRUE.

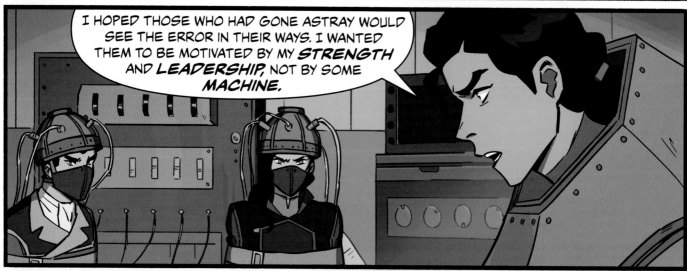

I HOPED THOSE WHO HAD GONE ASTRAY WOULD SEE THE ERROR IN THEIR WAYS. I WANTED THEM TO BE MOTIVATED BY MY *STRENGTH* AND *LEADERSHIP*, NOT BY SOME *MACHINE*.

YOU MIGHT CHANGE YOUR OPINION ONCE YOU SEE WHAT DR. SHENG AND I HAVE ACCOMPLISHED IN YOUR ABSENCE. I THINK YOU'LL BE QUITE IMPRESSED.

PLEASE, DON'T!

MMMPH!

ASAMI, YOU HAVE TO KNOW, I DIDN'T MEAN FOR ANY OF THIS TO HAPPEN.

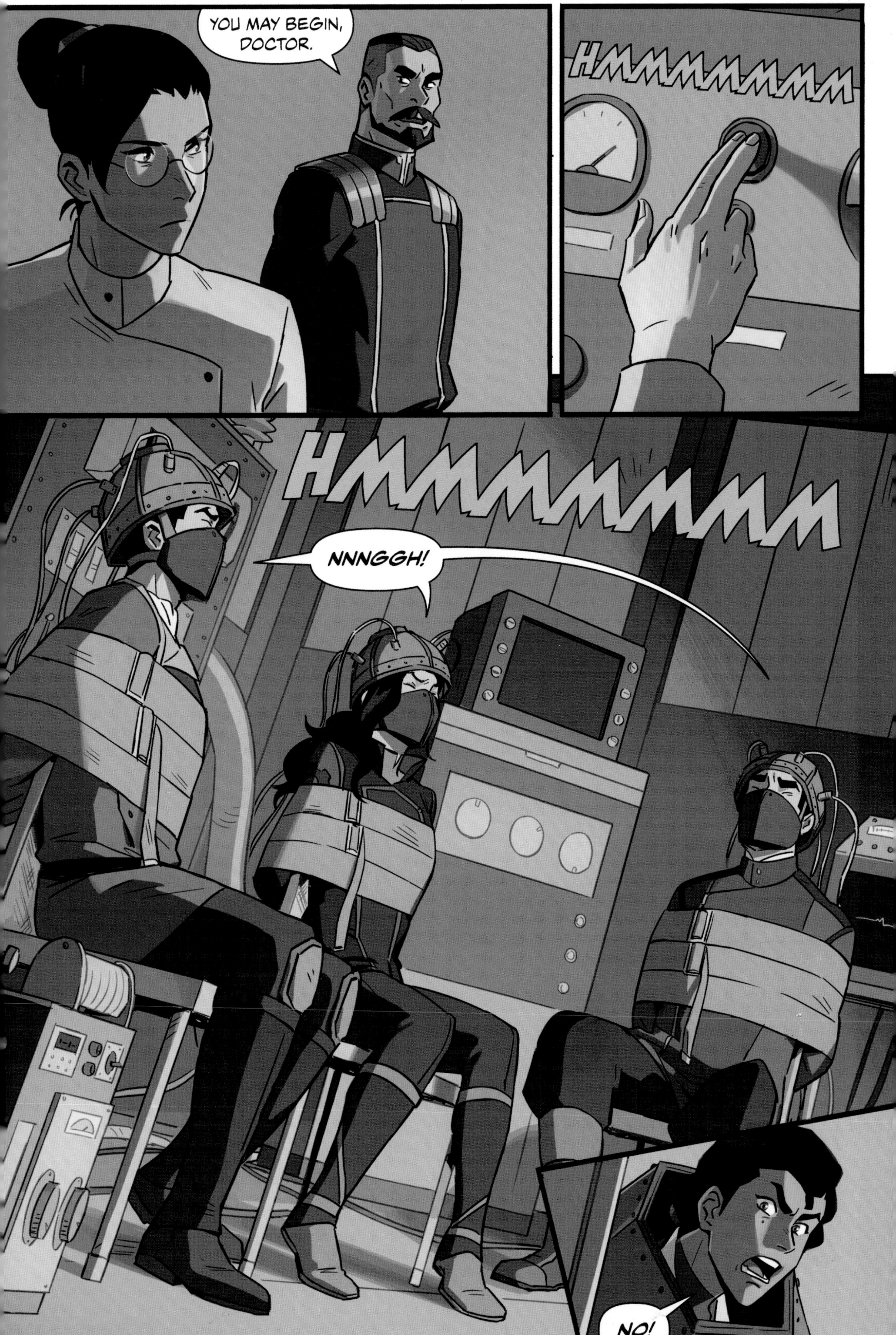
YOU MAY BEGIN, DOCTOR.
HMMMMMMMMM
HMMMMMMMMM
NNNGGH!
NO!

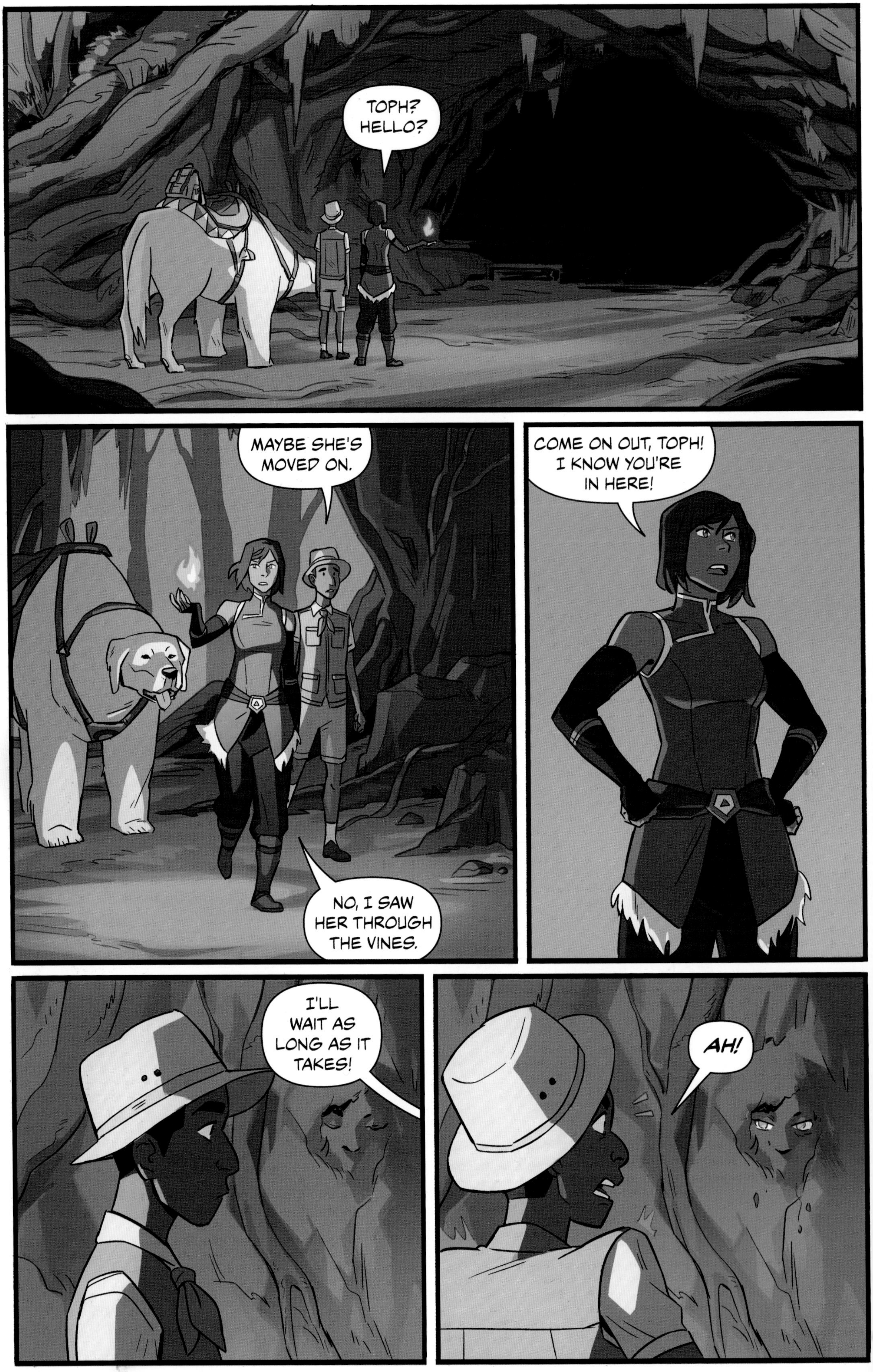
TOPH? HELLO?
MAYBE SHE'S MOVED ON.
NO, I SAW HER THROUGH THE VINES.
COME ON OUT, TOPH! I KNOW YOU'RE IN HERE!
I'LL WAIT AS LONG AS IT TAKES!
AH!

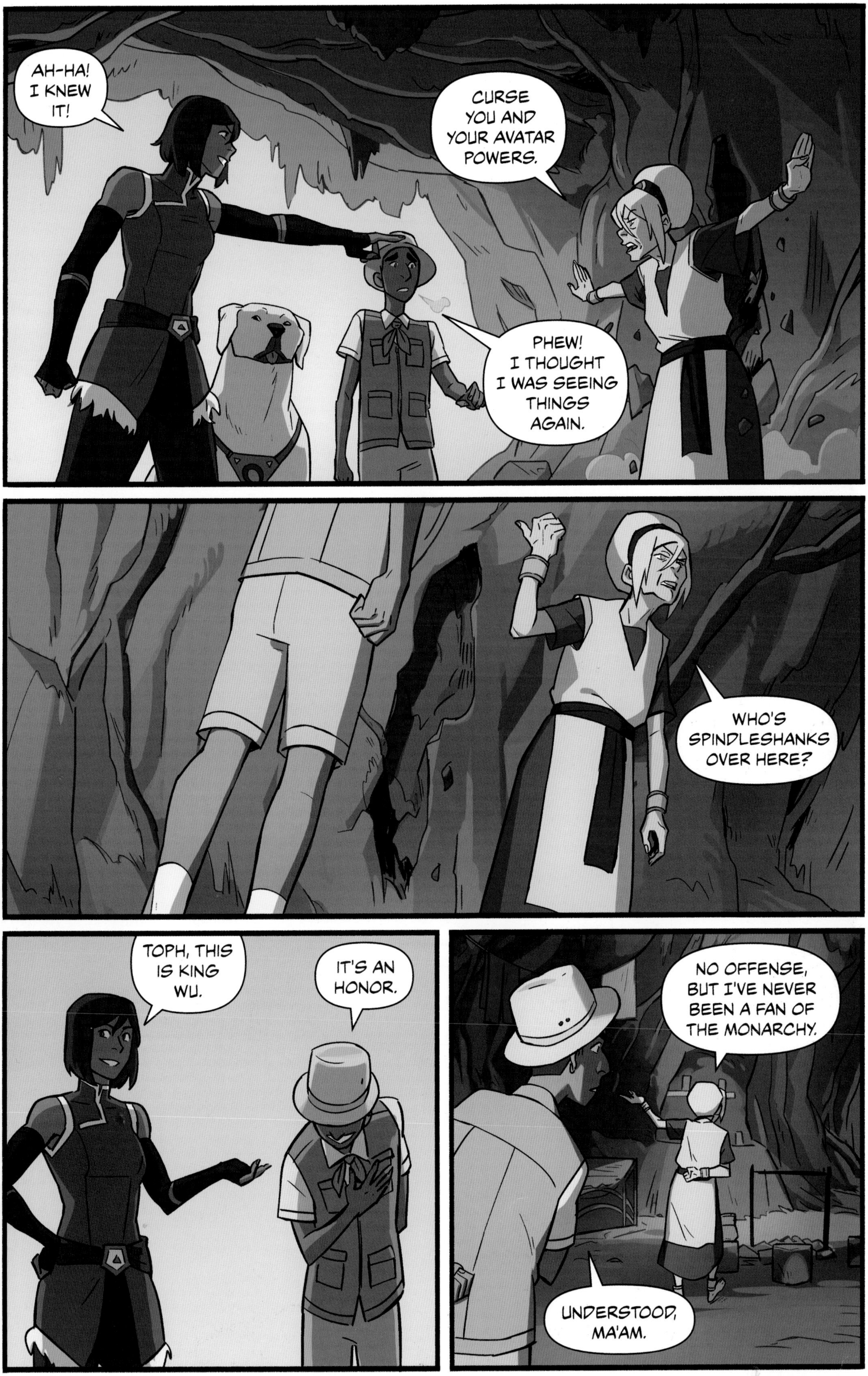
AH-HA! I KNEW IT!
CURSE YOU AND YOUR AVATAR POWERS.
PHEW! I THOUGHT I WAS SEEING THINGS AGAIN.
WHO'S SPINDLESHANKS OVER HERE?
TOPH, THIS IS KING WU.
IT'S AN HONOR.
NO OFFENSE, BUT I'VE NEVER BEEN A FAN OF THE MONARCHY.
UNDERSTOOD, MA'AM.

WHAT DO YOU WANT, KORRA?

CAN'T AN OLD FRIEND POP BY TO SAY "HELLO"?

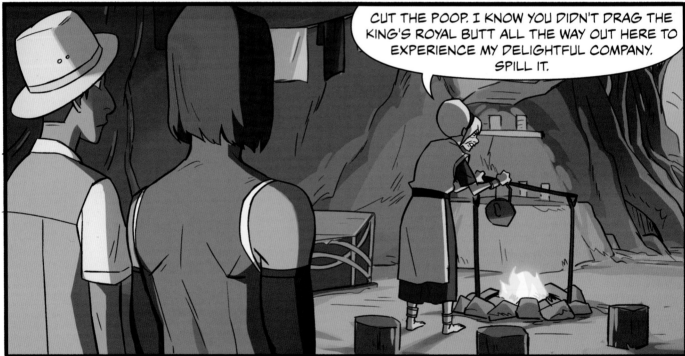

CUT THE POOP. I KNOW YOU DIDN'T DRAG THE KING'S ROYAL BUTT ALL THE WAY OUT HERE TO EXPERIENCE MY DELIGHTFUL COMPANY. SPILL IT.

FINE. I ASSUME YOU HEARD THAT KUVIRA AND HER ARMY SURRENDERED IN REPUBLIC CITY?

YUP. GOOD RIDDANCE.

WELL, IT TURNS OUT NOT *EVERYONE* SURRENDERED...

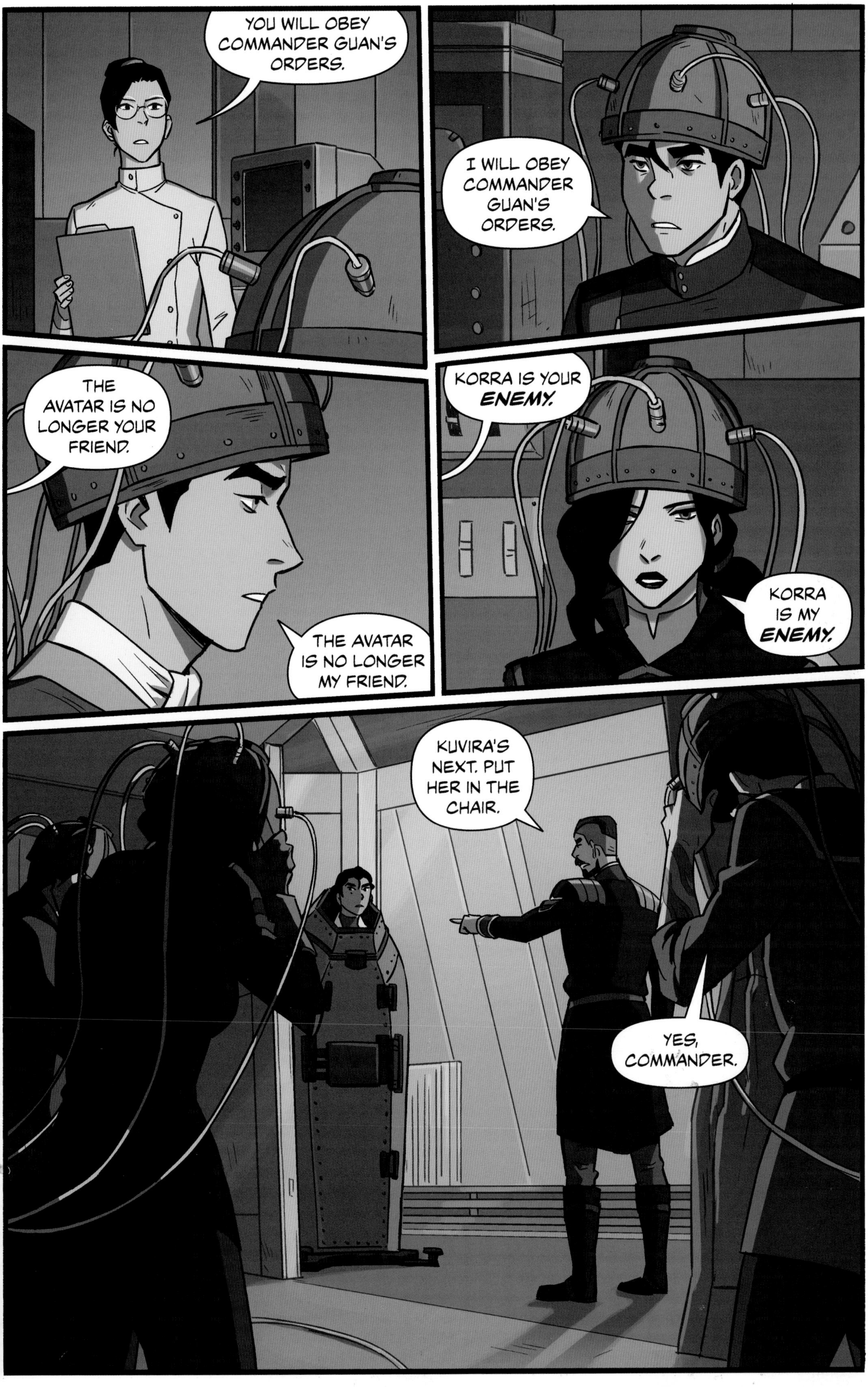
YOU WILL OBEY COMMANDER GUAN'S ORDERS.
I WILL OBEY COMMANDER GUAN'S ORDERS.
THE AVATAR IS NO LONGER YOUR FRIEND.
THE AVATAR IS NO LONGER MY FRIEND.
KORRA IS YOUR ENEMY.
KORRA IS MY ENEMY.
KUVIRA'S NEXT. PUT HER IN THE CHAIR.
YES, COMMANDER.

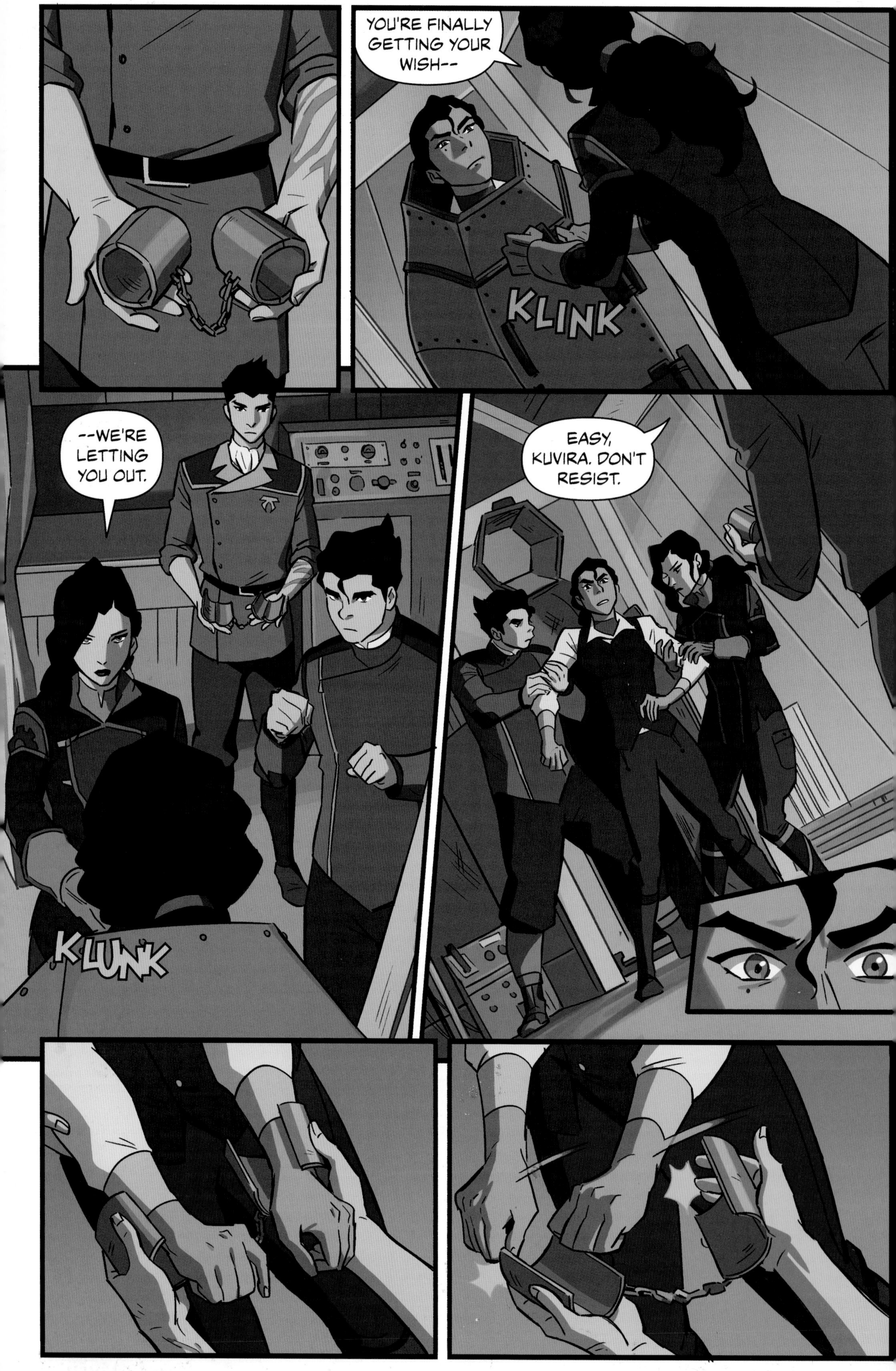
YOU'RE FINALLY GETTING YOUR WISH--
KLINK
--WE'RE LETTING YOU OUT.
KLUNK
EASY, KUVIRA. DON'T RESIST.

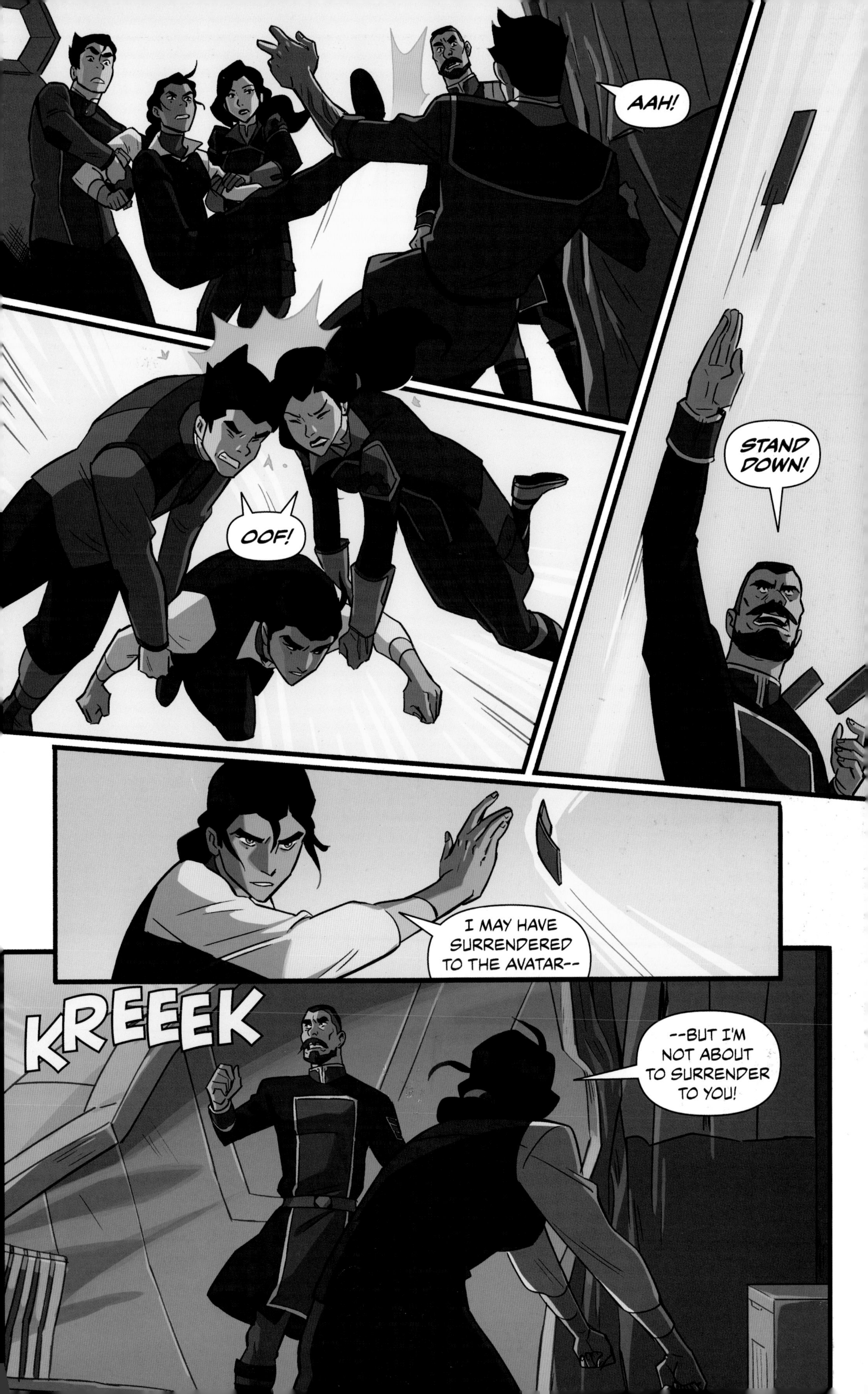
AAH!
OOF!
STAND DOWN!
I MAY HAVE SURRENDERED TO THE AVATAR--
KREEEK
--BUT I'M NOT ABOUT TO SURRENDER TO YOU!

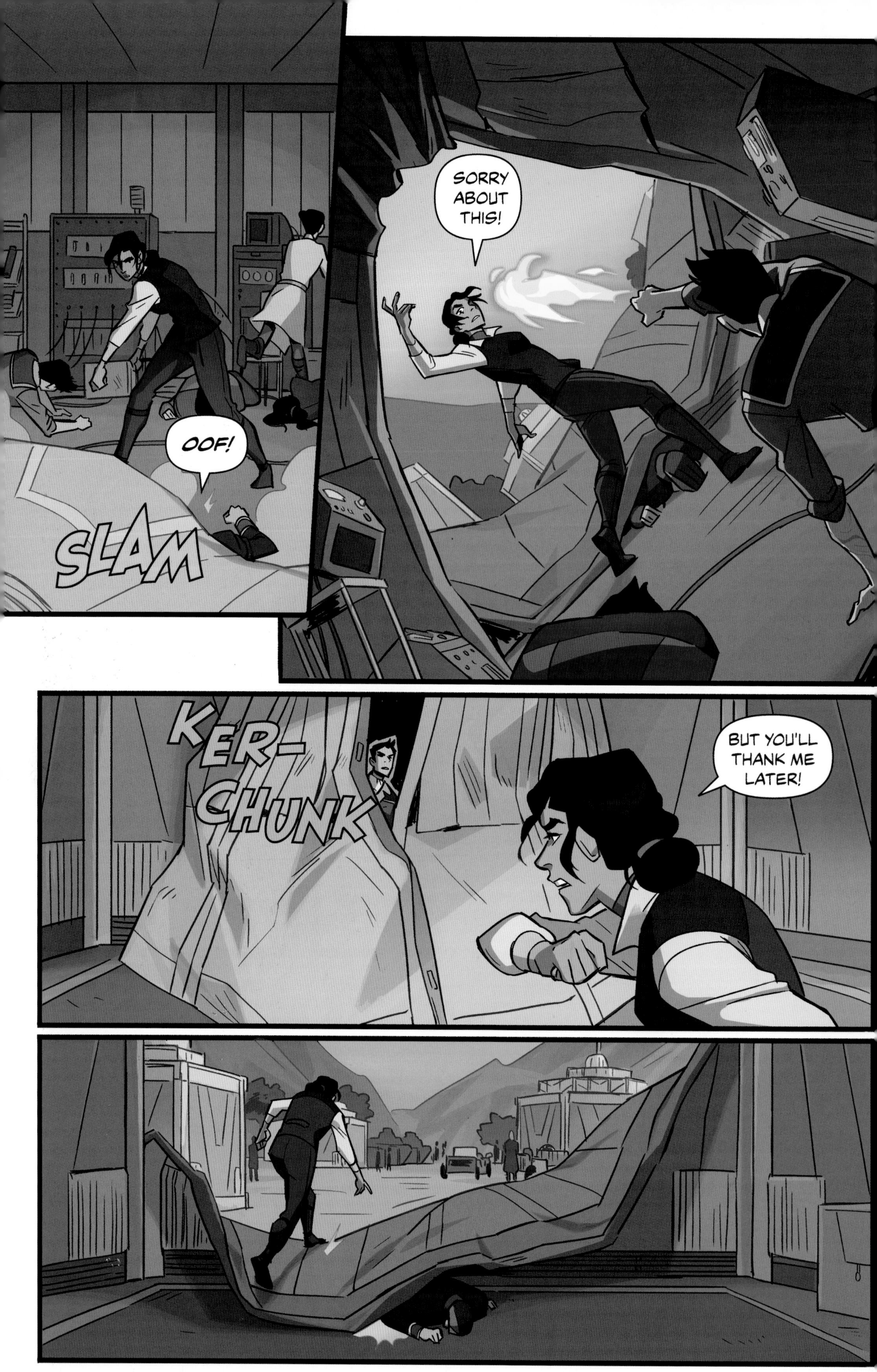
OOF!
SLAM
SORRY ABOUT THIS!
KER-CHUNK
BUT YOU'LL THANK ME LATER!

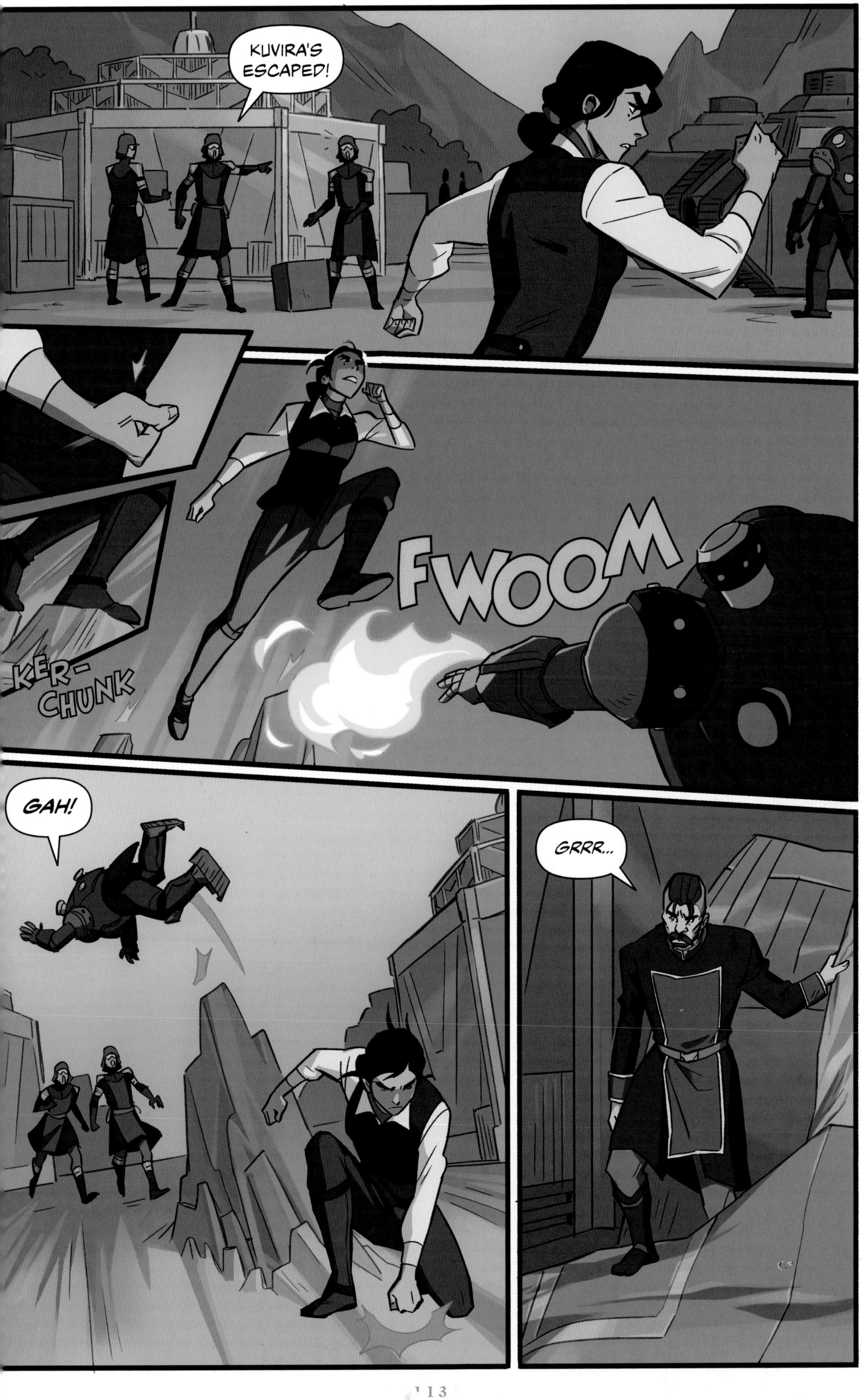
KUVIRA'S ESCAPED!
FWOOM
KER-CHUNK
GAH!
GRRR...

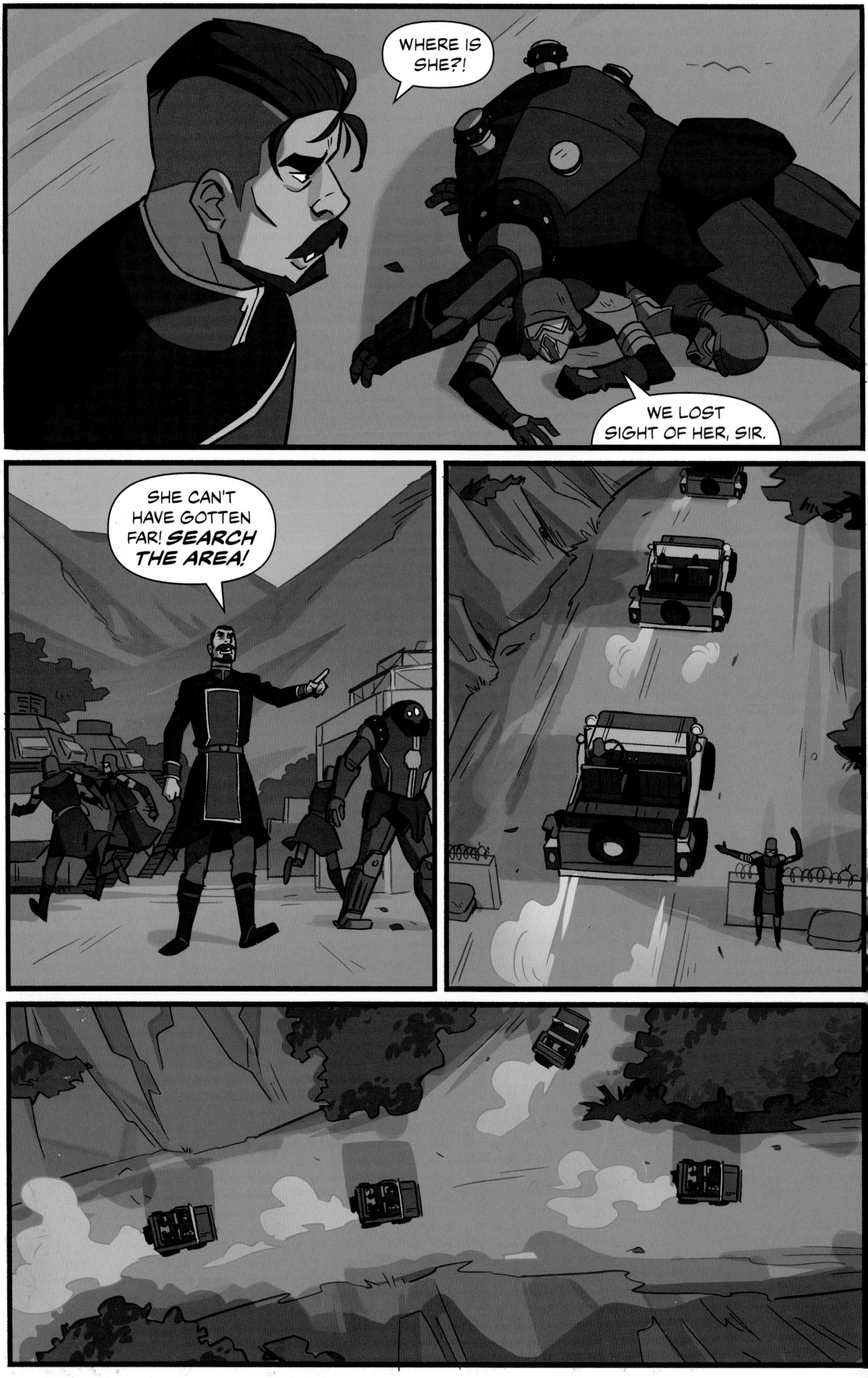
WHERE IS SHE?!
WE LOST SIGHT OF HER, SIR.
SHE CAN'T HAVE GOTTEN FAR! SEARCH THE AREA!

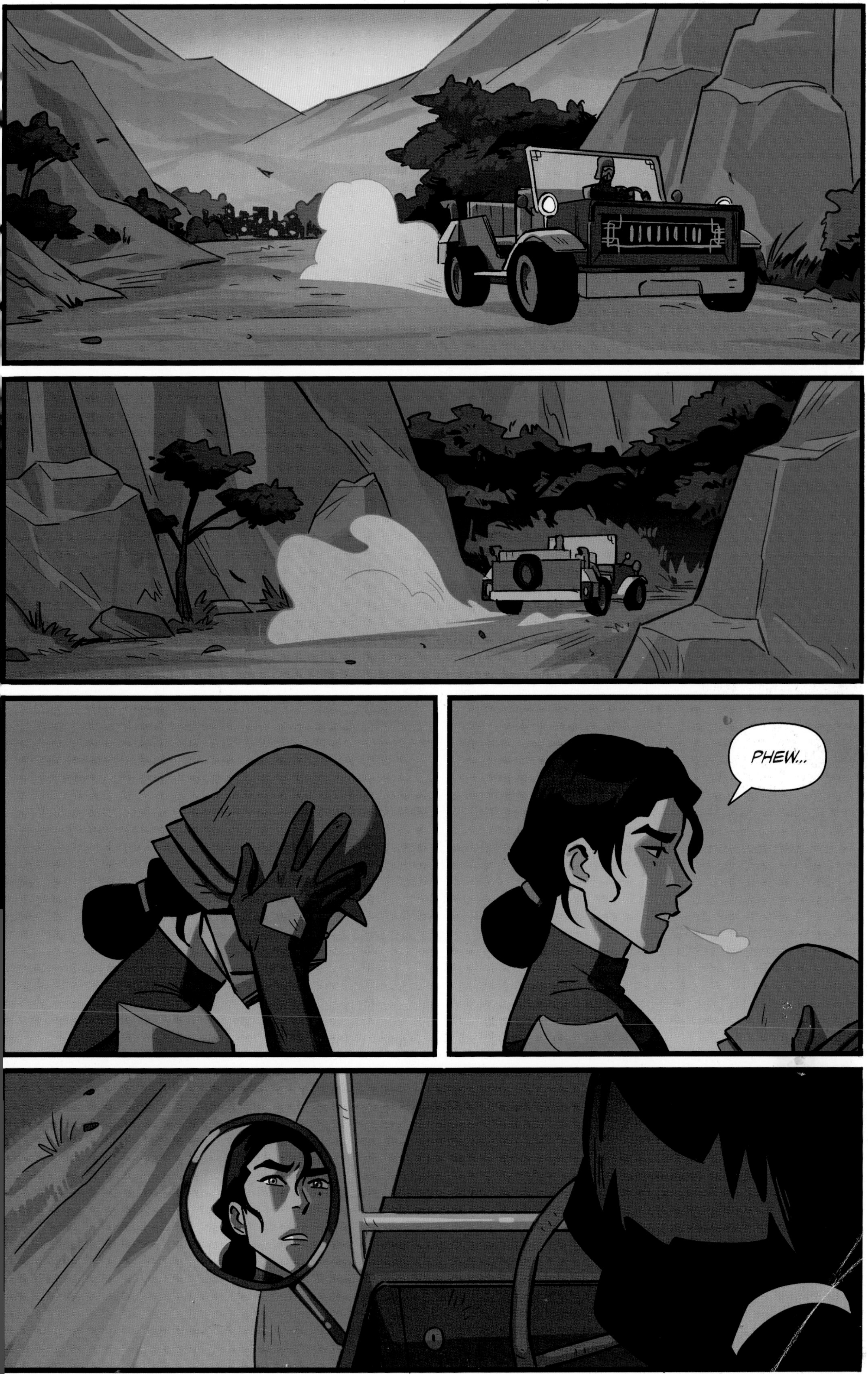
PHEW...

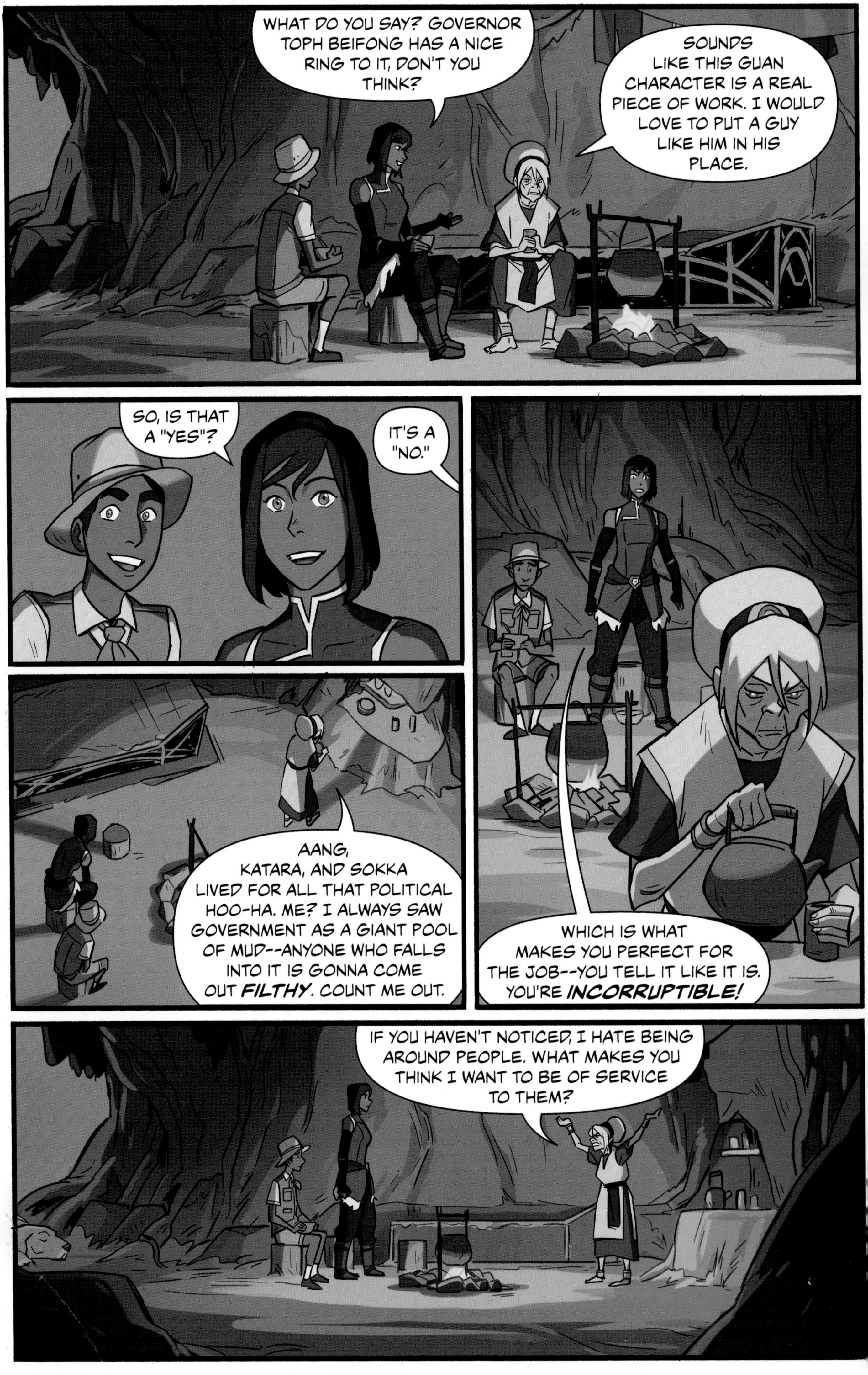
WHAT DO YOU SAY? GOVERNOR TOPH BEIFONG HAS A NICE RING TO IT, DON'T YOU THINK?
SOUNDS LIKE THIS GUAN CHARACTER IS A REAL PIECE OF WORK. I WOULD LOVE TO PUT A GUY LIKE HIM IN HIS PLACE.
SO, IS THAT A "YES"?
IT'S A "NO."
AANG, KATARA, AND SOKKA LIVED FOR ALL THAT POLITICAL HOO-HA. ME? I ALWAYS SAW GOVERNMENT AS A GIANT POOL OF MUD--ANYONE WHO FALLS INTO IT IS GONNA COME OUT FILTHY. COUNT ME OUT.
WHICH IS WHAT MAKES YOU PERFECT FOR THE JOB--YOU TELL IT LIKE IT IS. YOU'RE INCORRUPTIBLE!
IF YOU HAVEN'T NOTICED, I HATE BEING AROUND PEOPLE. WHAT MAKES YOU THINK I WANT TO BE OF SERVICE TO THEM?

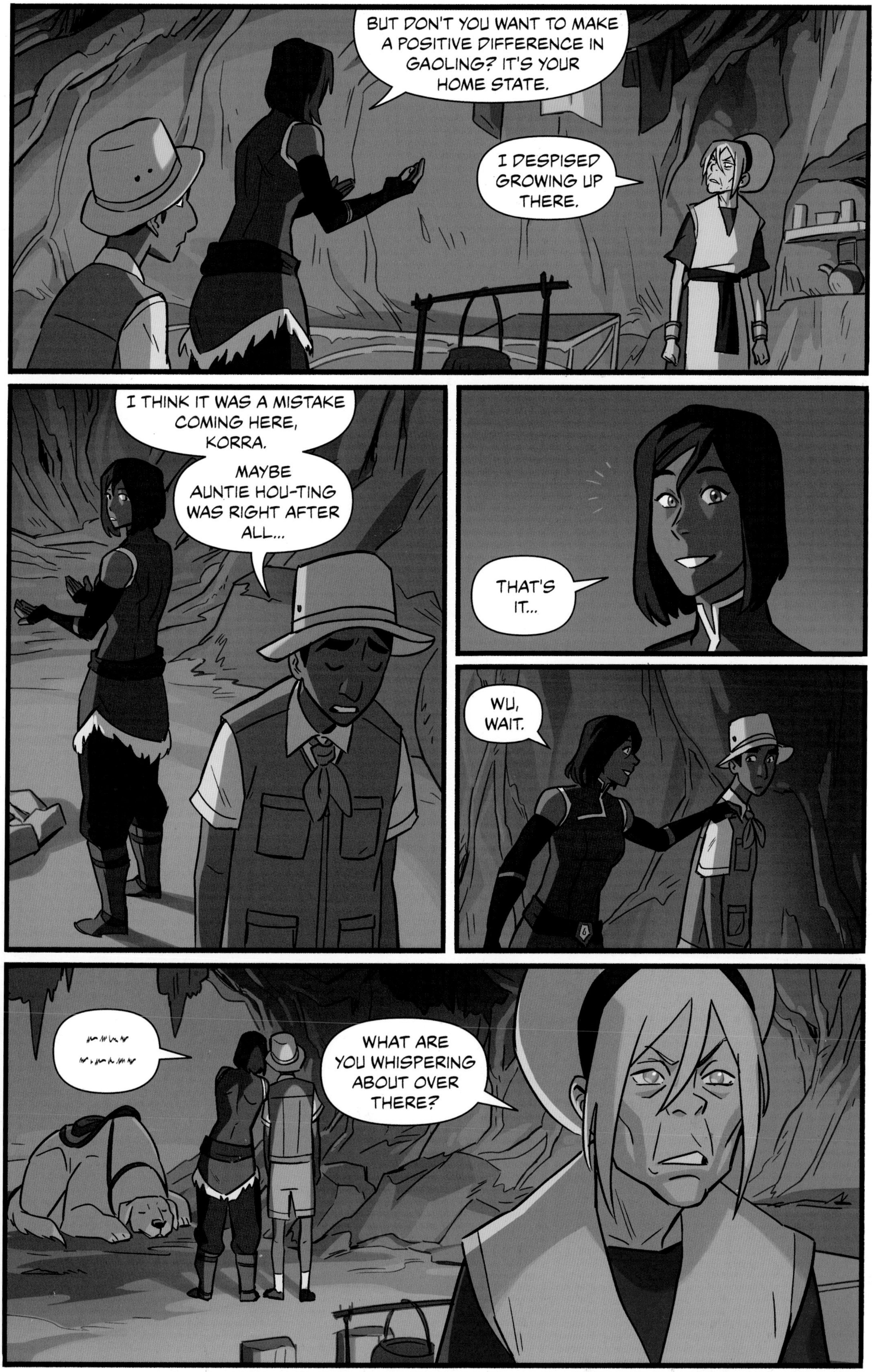
BUT DON'T YOU WANT TO MAKE A POSITIVE DIFFERENCE IN GAOLING? IT'S YOUR HOME STATE.
I DESPISED GROWING UP THERE.
I THINK IT WAS A MISTAKE COMING HERE, KORRA.
MAYBE AUNTIE HOU-TING WAS RIGHT AFTER ALL...
THAT'S IT...
WU, WAIT.
WHAT ARE YOU WHISPERING ABOUT OVER THERE?

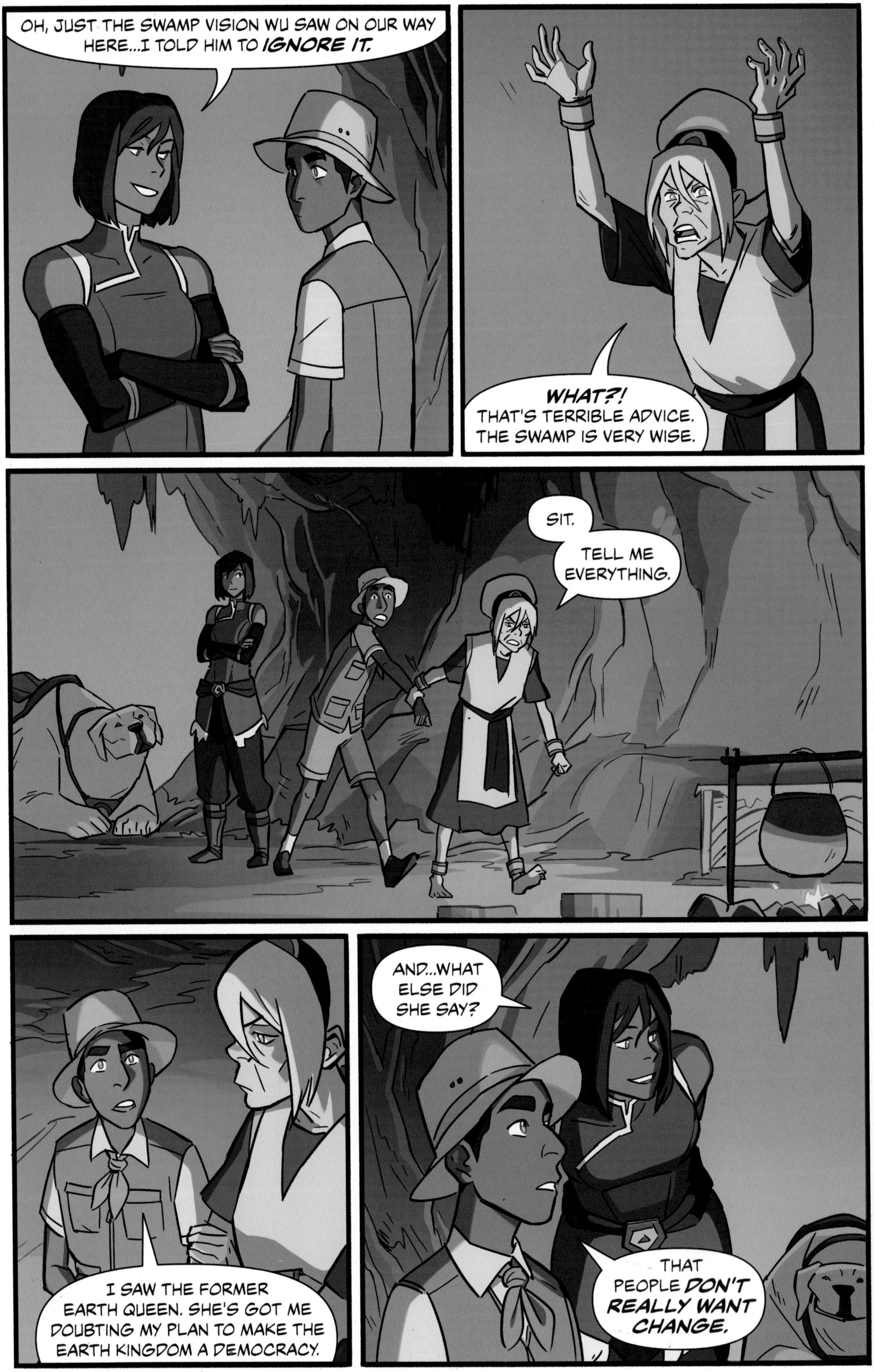
OH, JUST THE SWAMP VISION WU SAW ON OUR WAY HERE...I TOLD HIM TO IGNORE IT.
WHAT?! THAT'S TERRIBLE ADVICE. THE SWAMP IS VERY WISE.
SIT.
TELL ME EVERYTHING.
I SAW THE FORMER EARTH QUEEN. SHE'S GOT ME DOUBTING MY PLAN TO MAKE THE EARTH KINGDOM A DEMOCRACY.
AND...WHAT ELSE DID SHE SAY?
THAT PEOPLE DON'T REALLY WANT CHANGE.

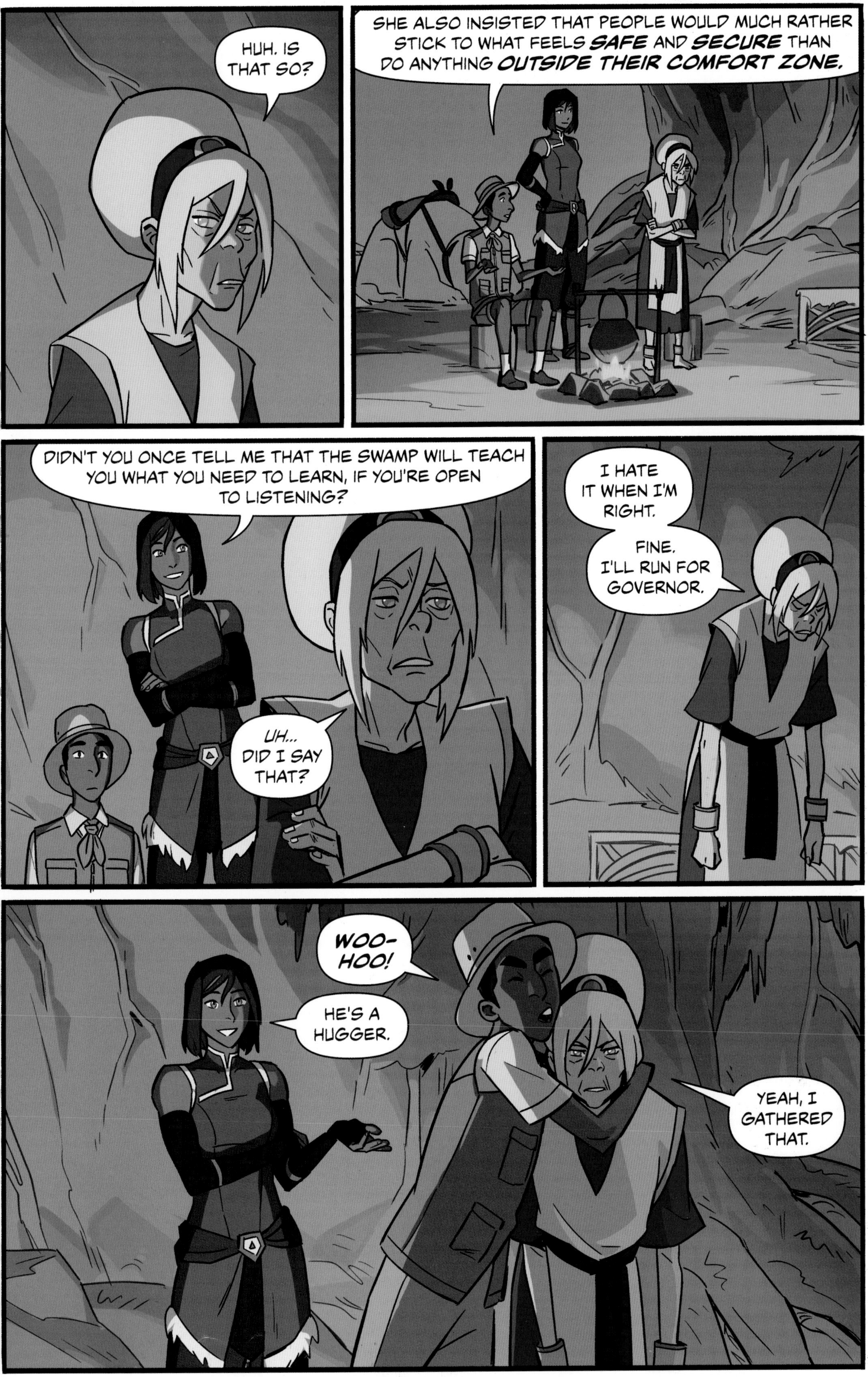
HUH. IS THAT SO?
SHE ALSO INSISTED THAT PEOPLE WOULD MUCH RATHER STICK TO WHAT FEELS SAFE AND SECURE THAN DO ANYTHING OUTSIDE THEIR COMFORT ZONE.
DIDN'T YOU ONCE TELL ME THAT THE SWAMP WILL TEACH YOU WHAT YOU NEED TO LEARN, IF YOU'RE OPEN TO LISTENING?
UH... DID I SAY THAT?
I HATE IT WHEN I'M RIGHT.
FINE. I'LL RUN FOR GOVERNOR.
WOO-HOO!
HE'S A HUGGER.
YEAH, I GATHERED THAT.

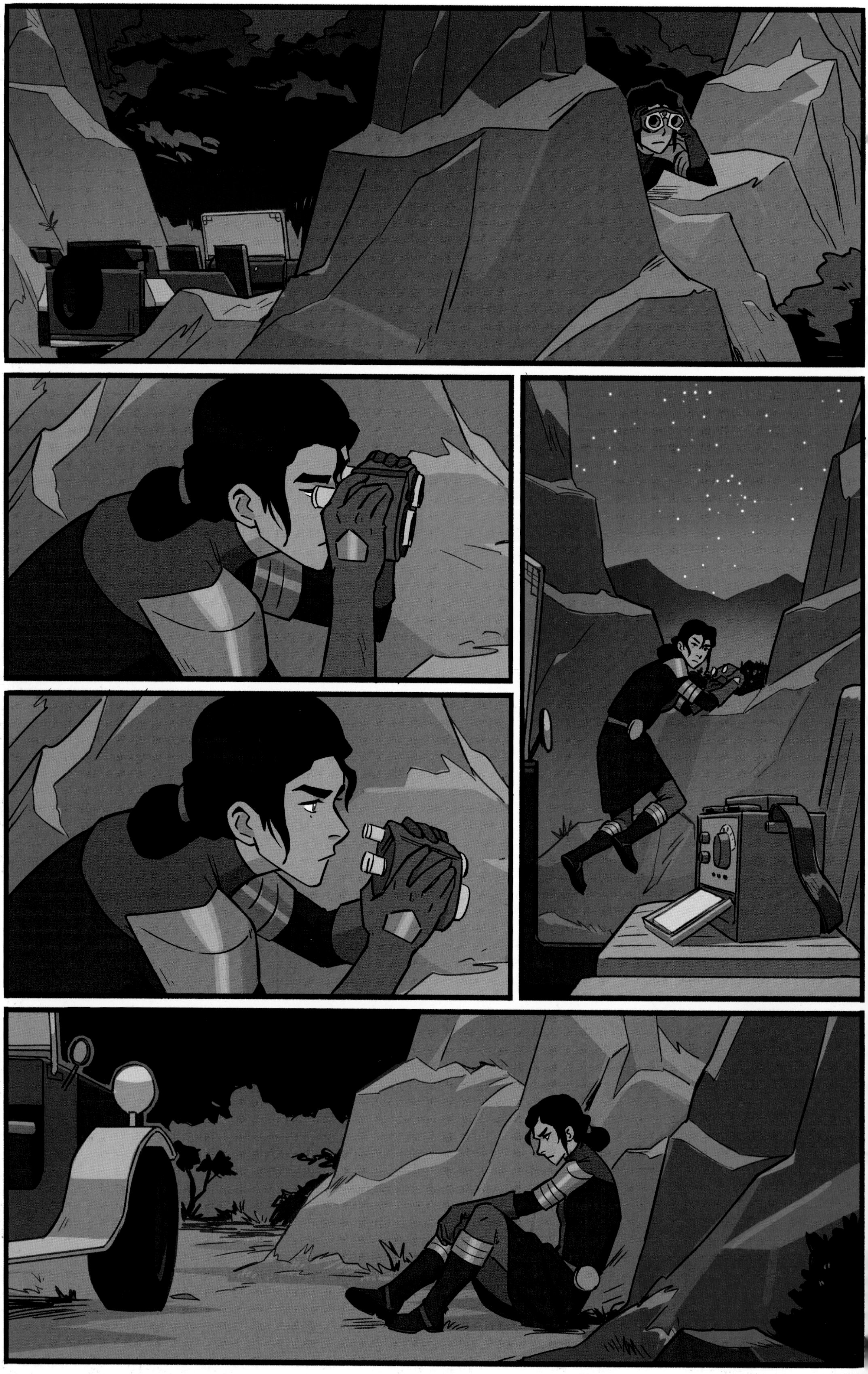

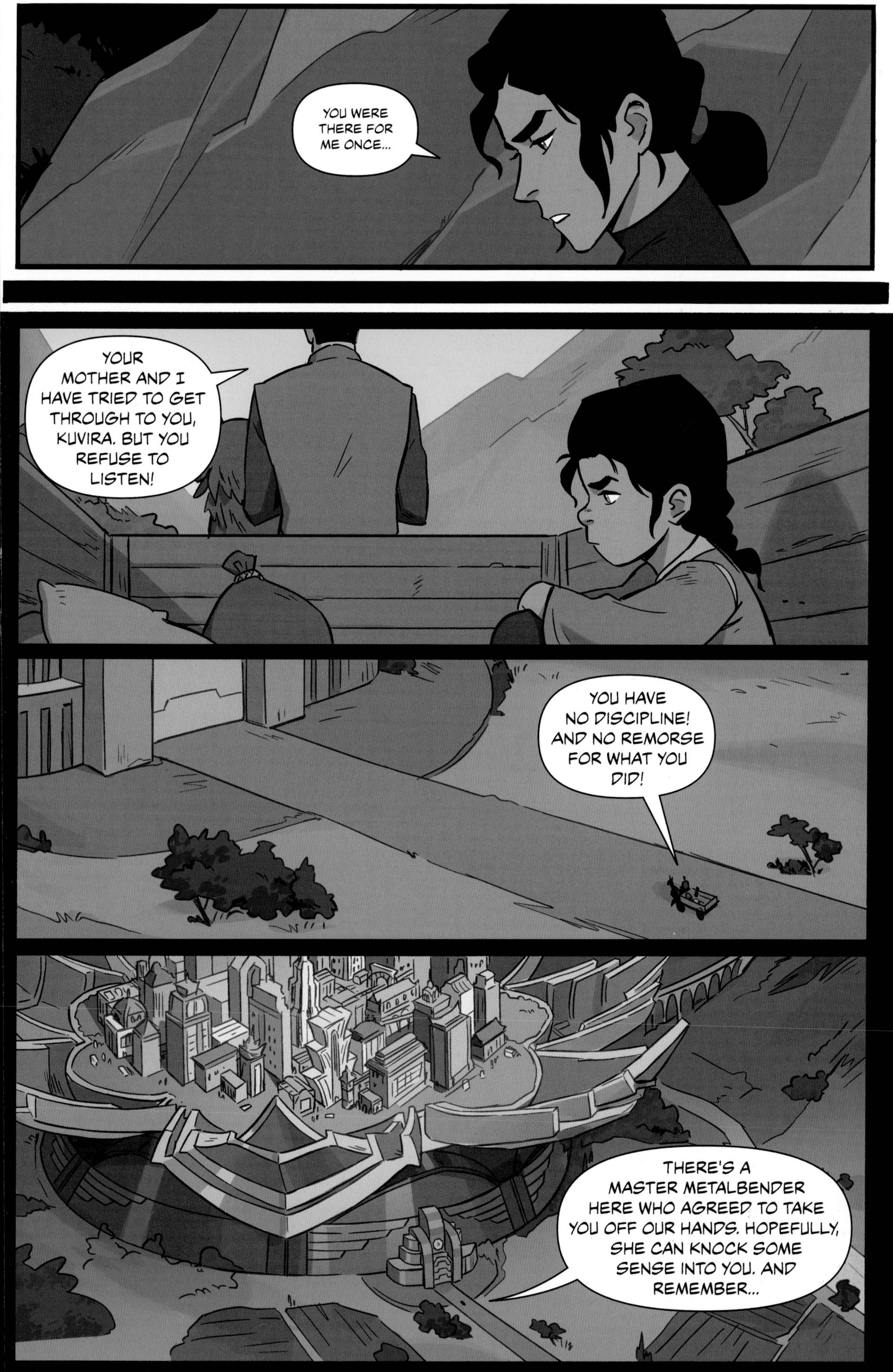
YOU WERE THERE FOR ME ONCE...
YOUR MOTHER AND I HAVE TRIED TO GET THROUGH TO YOU, KUVIRA. BUT YOU REFUSE TO LISTEN!
YOU HAVE NO DISCIPLINE! AND NO REMORSE FOR WHAT YOU DID!
THERE'S A MASTER METALBENDER HERE WHO AGREED TO TAKE YOU OFF OUR HANDS. HOPEFULLY, SHE CAN KNOCK SOME SENSE INTO YOU. AND REMEMBER...

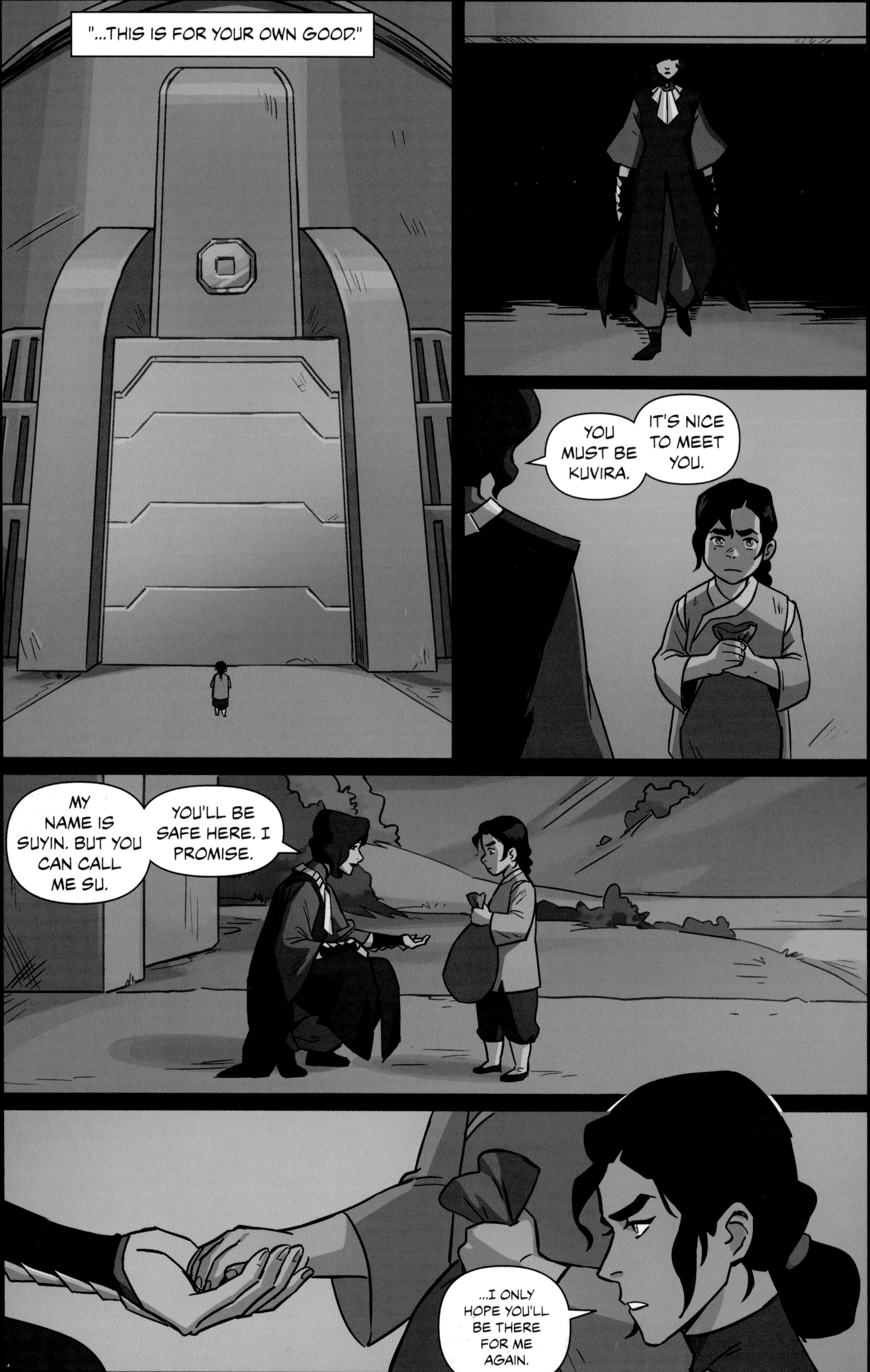
"...THIS IS FOR YOUR OWN GOOD."
YOU MUST BE KUVIRA.
IT'S NICE TO MEET YOU.
MY NAME IS SUYIN. BUT YOU CAN CALL ME SU.
YOU'LL BE SAFE HERE. I PROMISE.
...I ONLY HOPE YOU'LL BE THERE FOR ME AGAIN.

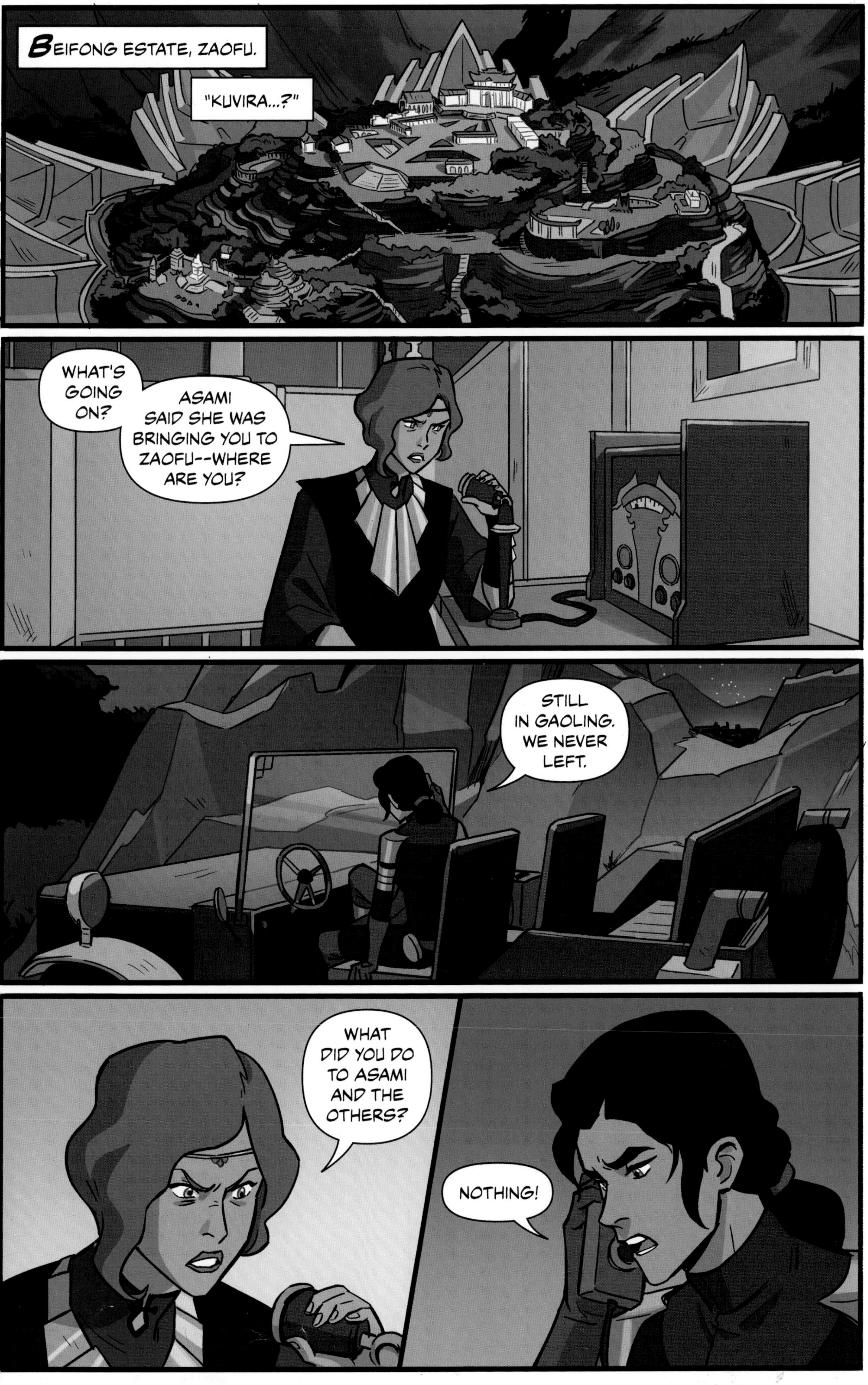
BEIFONG ESTATE, ZAOFU.
"KUVIRA...?"
WHAT'S GOING ON?
ASAMI SAID SHE WAS BRINGING YOU TO ZAOFU--WHERE ARE YOU?
STILL IN GAOLING. WE NEVER LEFT.
WHAT DID YOU DO TO ASAMI AND THE OTHERS?
NOTHING!

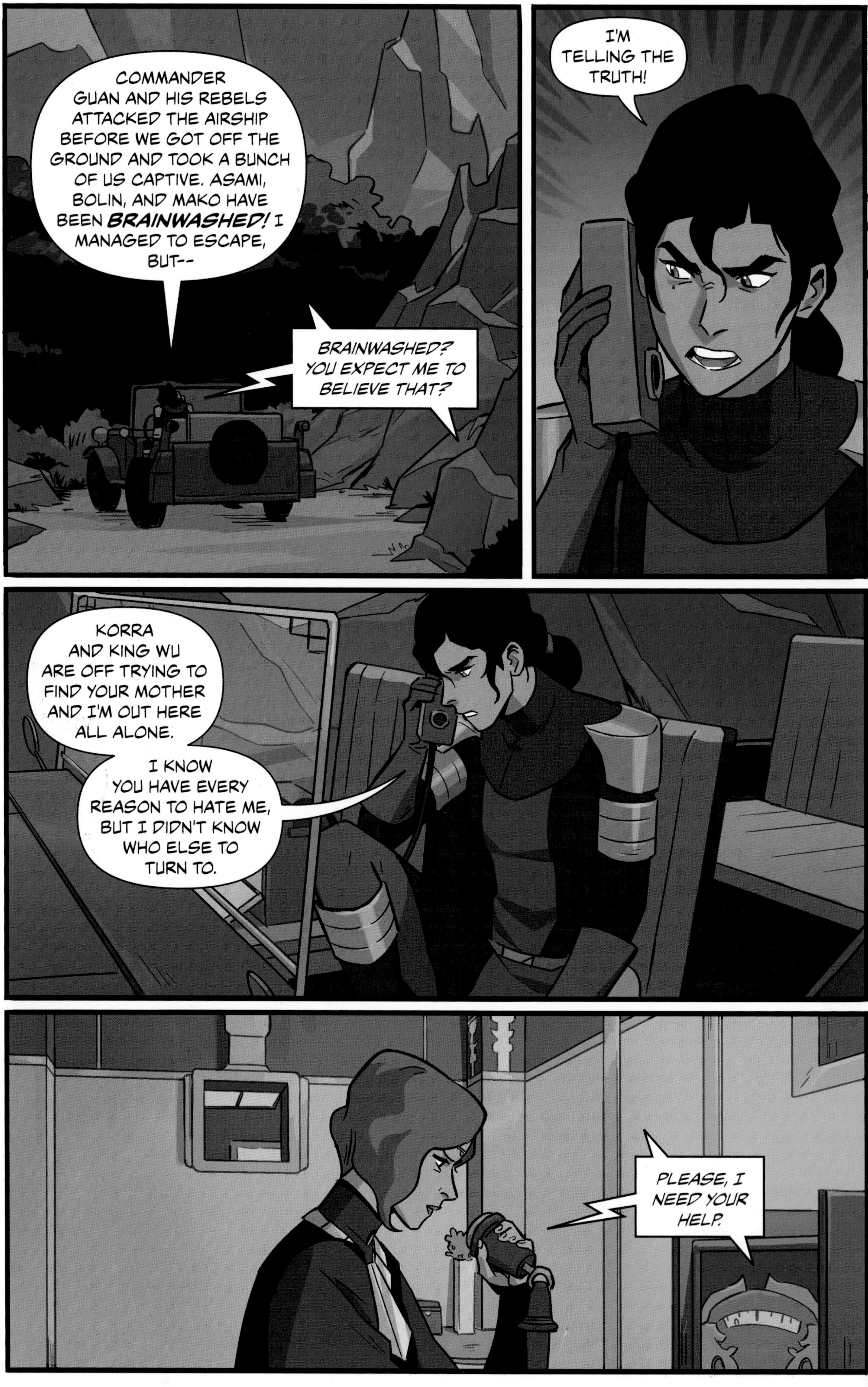
COMMANDER GUAN AND HIS REBELS ATTACKED THE AIRSHIP BEFORE WE GOT OFF THE GROUND AND TOOK A BUNCH OF US CAPTIVE. ASAMI, BOLIN, AND MAKO HAVE BEEN BRAINWASHED! I MANAGED TO ESCAPE, BUT--
BRAINWASHED? YOU EXPECT ME TO BELIEVE THAT?
I'M TELLING THE TRUTH!
KORRA AND KING WU ARE OFF TRYING TO FIND YOUR MOTHER AND I'M OUT HERE ALL ALONE.
I KNOW YOU HAVE EVERY REASON TO HATE ME, BUT I DIDN'T KNOW WHO ELSE TO TURN TO.
PLEASE, I NEED YOUR HELP.

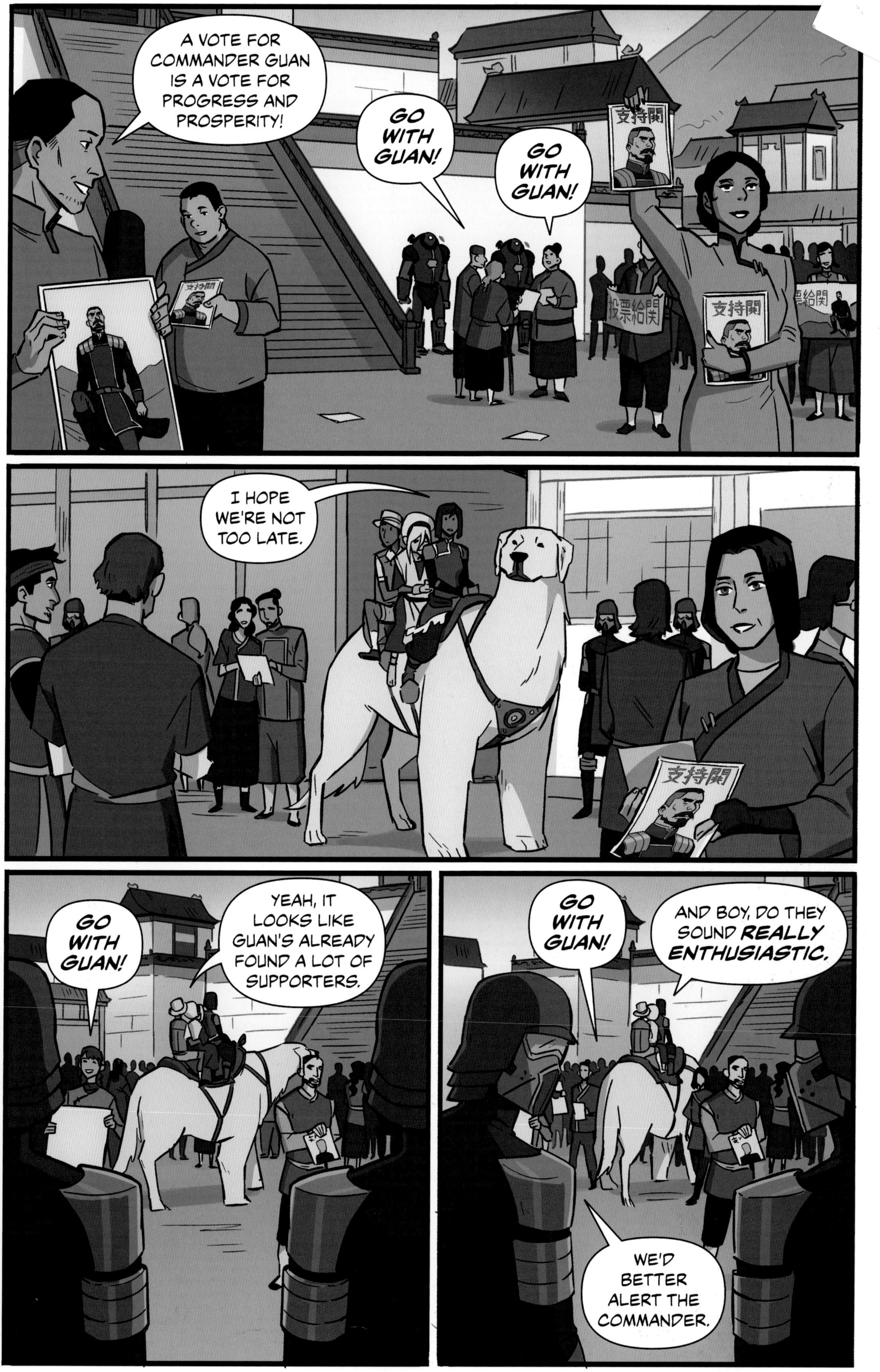
A VOTE FOR COMMANDER GUAN IS A VOTE FOR PROGRESS AND PROSPERITY!
GO WITH GUAN!
GO WITH GUAN!
支持関
投票給関
I HOPE WE'RE NOT TOO LATE.
支持関
GO WITH GUAN!
YEAH, IT LOOKS LIKE GUAN'S ALREADY FOUND A LOT OF SUPPORTERS.
GO WITH GUAN!
AND BOY, DO THEY SOUND **REALLY ENTHUSIASTIC.**
WE'D BETTER ALERT THE COMMANDER.

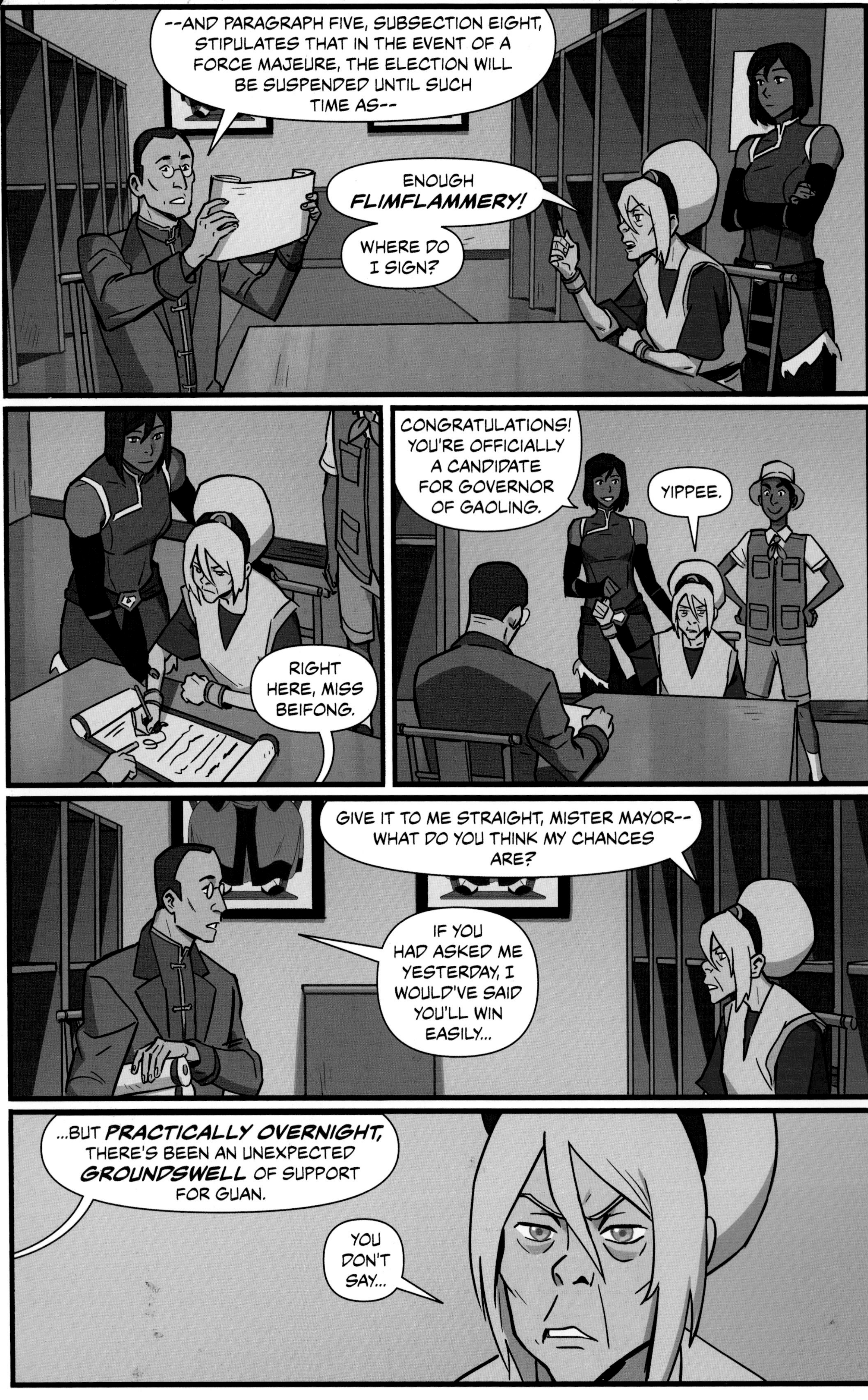
--AND PARAGRAPH FIVE, SUBSECTION EIGHT, STIPULATES THAT IN THE EVENT OF A FORCE MAJEURE, THE ELECTION WILL BE SUSPENDED UNTIL SUCH TIME AS--
ENOUGH FLIMFLAMMERY!
WHERE DO I SIGN?
RIGHT HERE, MISS BEIFONG.
CONGRATULATIONS! YOU'RE OFFICIALLY A CANDIDATE FOR GOVERNOR OF GAOLING.
YIPPEE.
GIVE IT TO ME STRAIGHT, MISTER MAYOR-- WHAT DO YOU THINK MY CHANCES ARE?
IF YOU HAD ASKED ME YESTERDAY, I WOULD'VE SAID YOU'LL WIN EASILY...
...BUT PRACTICALLY OVERNIGHT, THERE'S BEEN AN UNEXPECTED GROUNDSWELL OF SUPPORT FOR GUAN.
YOU DON'T SAY...

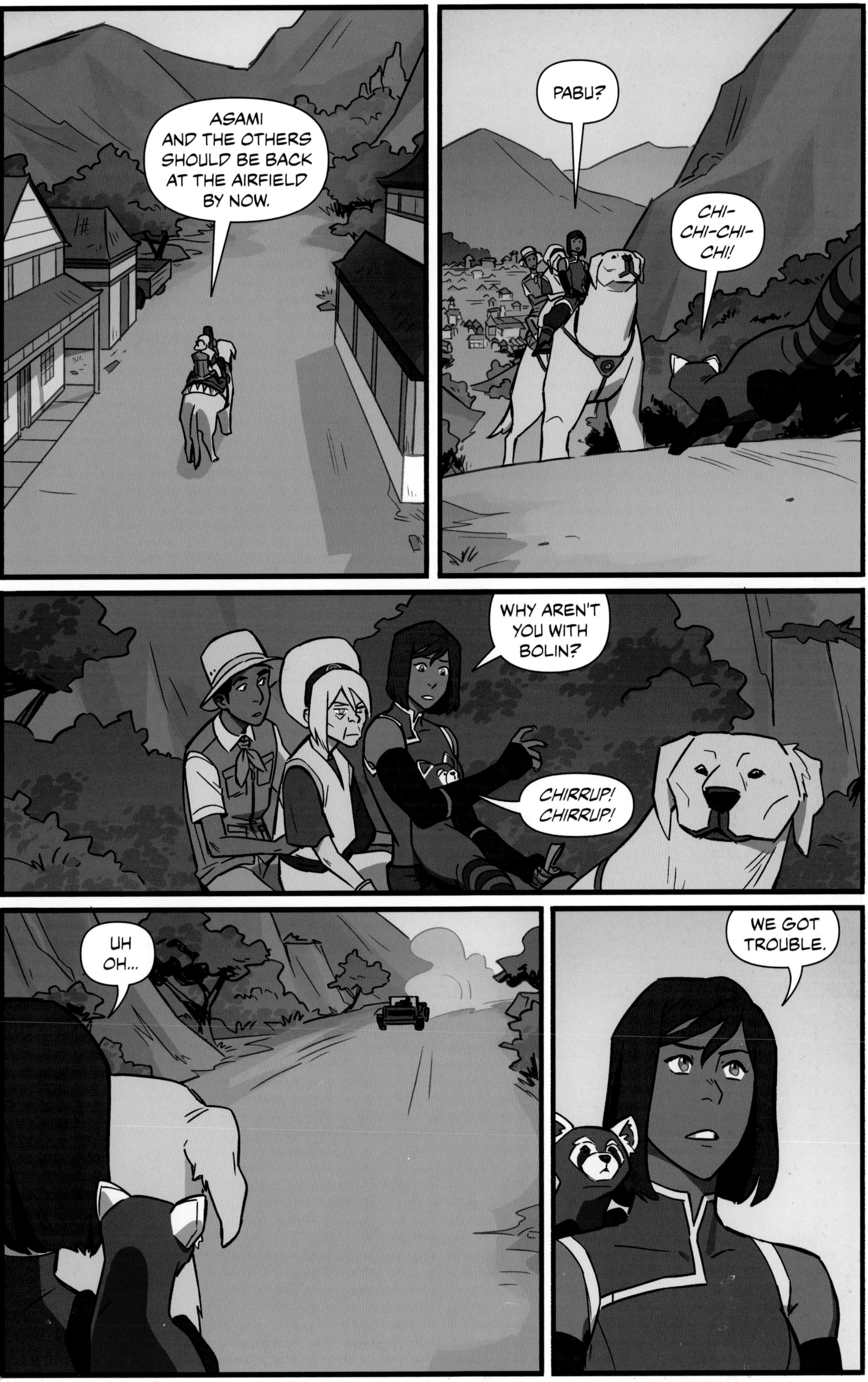
ASAMI AND THE OTHERS SHOULD BE BACK AT THE AIRFIELD BY NOW.
PABU?
CHI-CHI-CHI-CHI!
WHY AREN'T YOU WITH BOLIN?
CHIRRUP! CHIRRUP!
UH OH...
WE GOT TROUBLE.

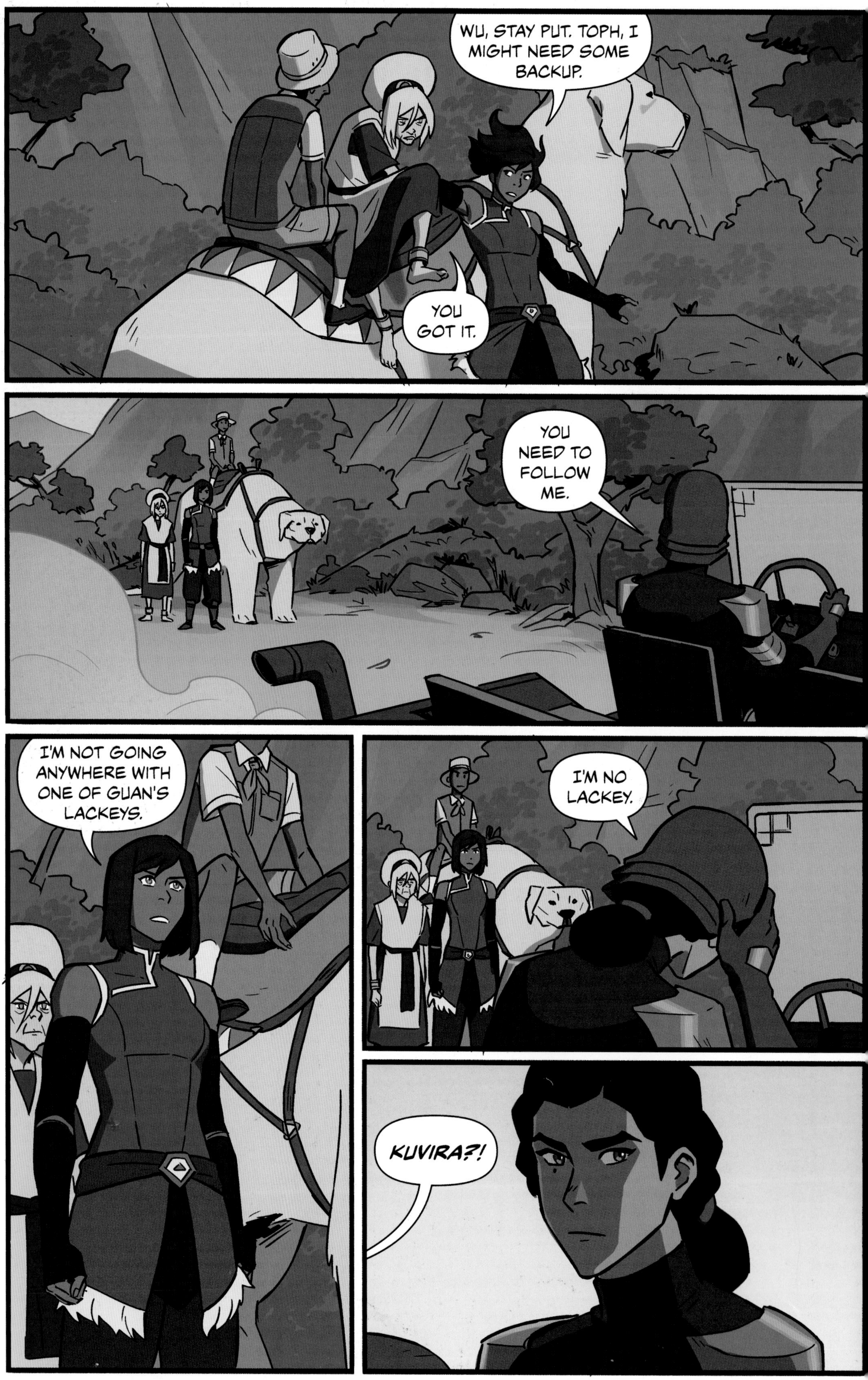
WU, STAY PUT. TOPH, I MIGHT NEED SOME BACKUP.
YOU GOT IT.
YOU NEED TO FOLLOW ME.
I'M NOT GOING ANYWHERE WITH ONE OF GUAN'S LACKEYS.
I'M NO LACKEY.
KUVIRA?!

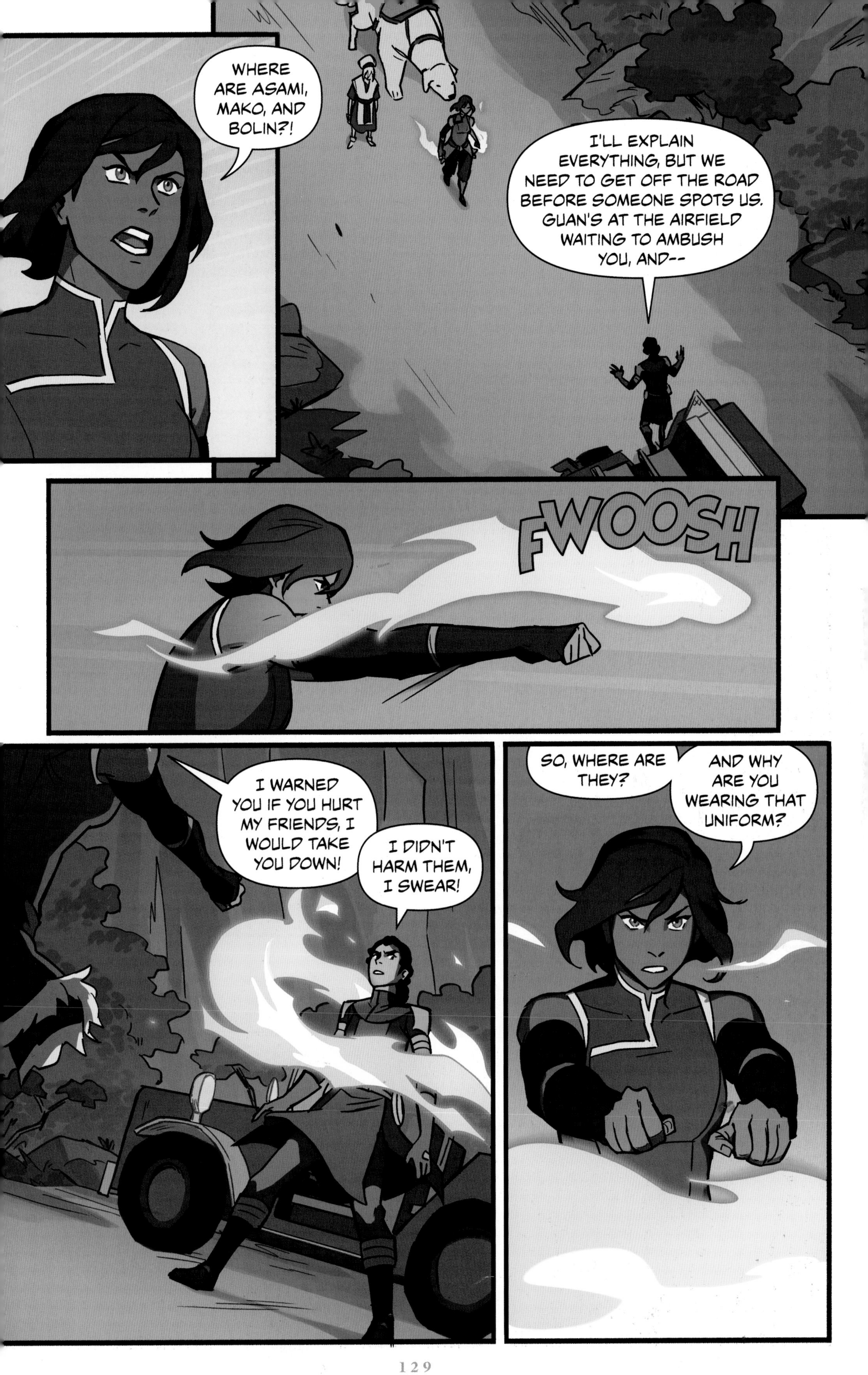
WHERE ARE ASAMI, MAKO, AND BOLIN?!
I'LL EXPLAIN EVERYTHING, BUT WE NEED TO GET OFF THE ROAD BEFORE SOMEONE SPOTS US. GUAN'S AT THE AIRFIELD WAITING TO AMBUSH YOU, AND--
FWOOSH
I WARNED YOU IF YOU HURT MY FRIENDS, I WOULD TAKE YOU DOWN!
I DIDN'T HARM THEM, I SWEAR!
SO, WHERE ARE THEY?
AND WHY ARE YOU WEARING THAT UNIFORM?

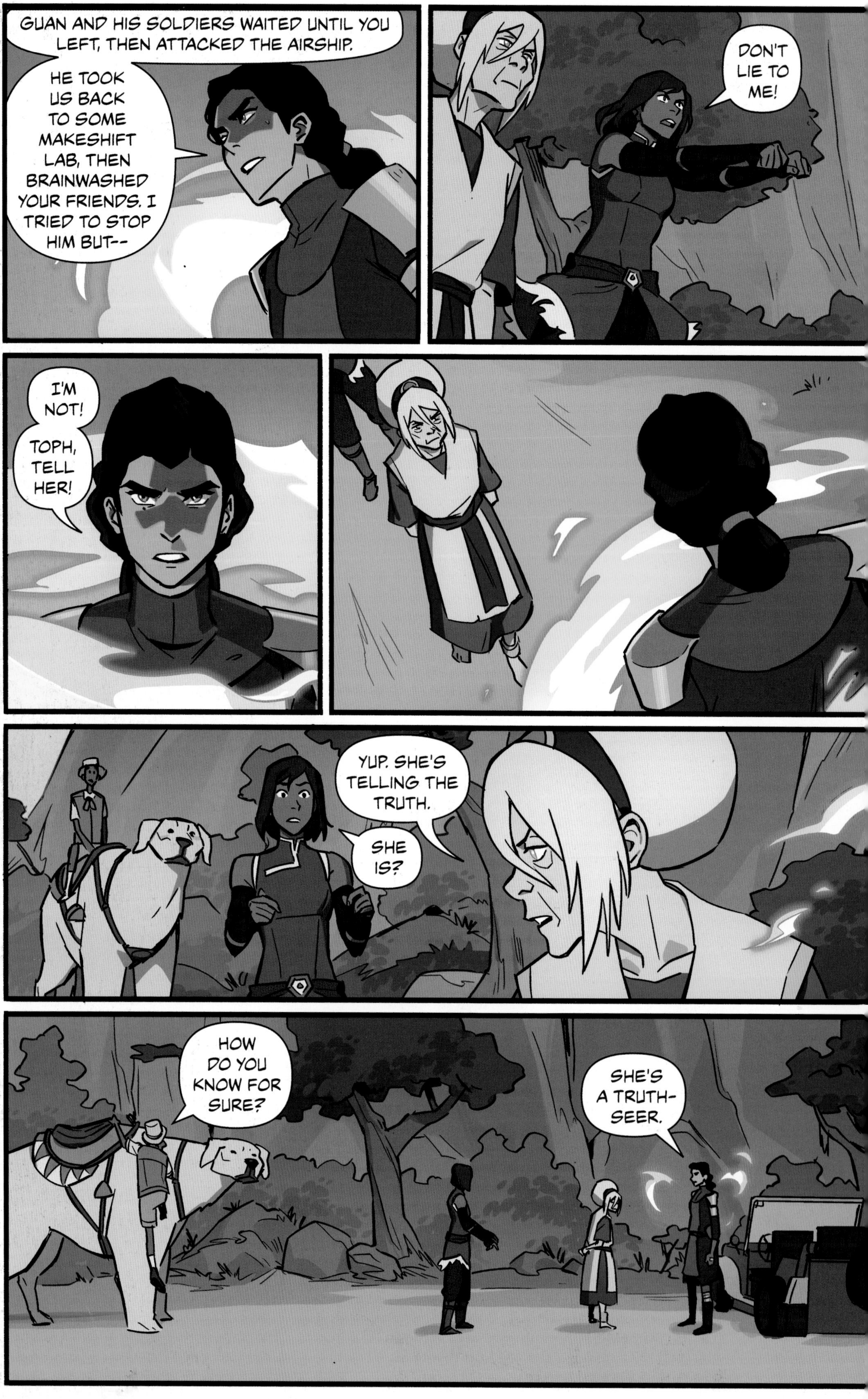
GUAN AND HIS SOLDIERS WAITED UNTIL YOU LEFT, THEN ATTACKED THE AIRSHIP.
HE TOOK US BACK TO SOME MAKESHIFT LAB, THEN BRAINWASHED YOUR FRIENDS. I TRIED TO STOP HIM BUT--
DON'T LIE TO ME!
I'M NOT!
TOPH, TELL HER!
YUP. SHE'S TELLING THE TRUTH.
SHE IS?
HOW DO YOU KNOW FOR SURE?
SHE'S A TRUTH-SEER.

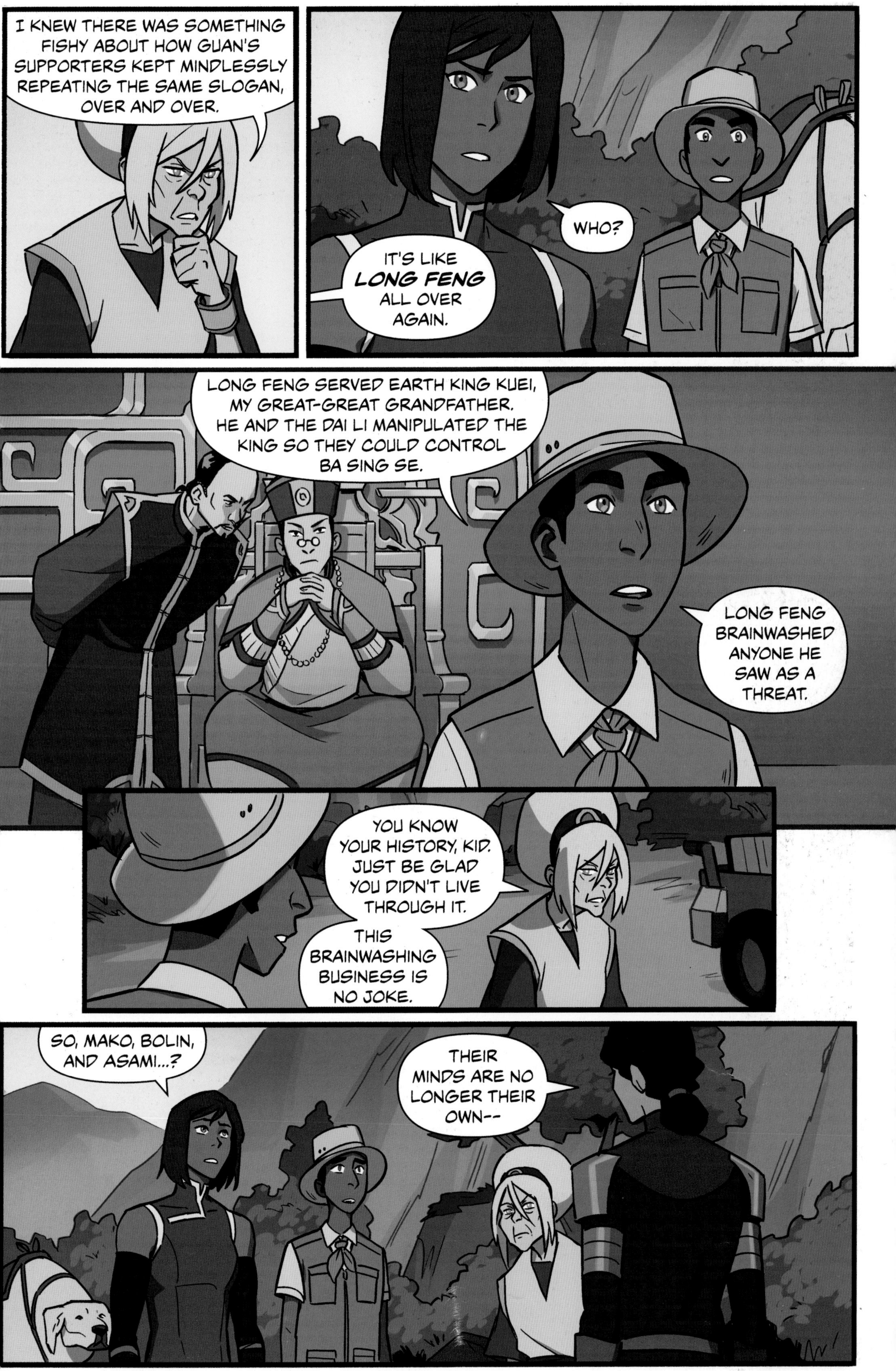
I KNEW THERE WAS SOMETHING FISHY ABOUT HOW GUAN'S SUPPORTERS KEPT MINDLESSLY REPEATING THE SAME SLOGAN, OVER AND OVER.
IT'S LIKE LONG FENG ALL OVER AGAIN.
WHO?
LONG FENG SERVED EARTH KING KUEI, MY GREAT-GREAT GRANDFATHER. HE AND THE DAI LI MANIPULATED THE KING SO THEY COULD CONTROL BA SING SE.
LONG FENG BRAINWASHED ANYONE HE SAW AS A THREAT.
YOU KNOW YOUR HISTORY, KID. JUST BE GLAD YOU DIDN'T LIVE THROUGH IT.
THIS BRAINWASHING BUSINESS IS NO JOKE.
SO, MAKO, BOLIN, AND ASAMI...?
THEIR MINDS ARE NO LONGER THEIR OWN--

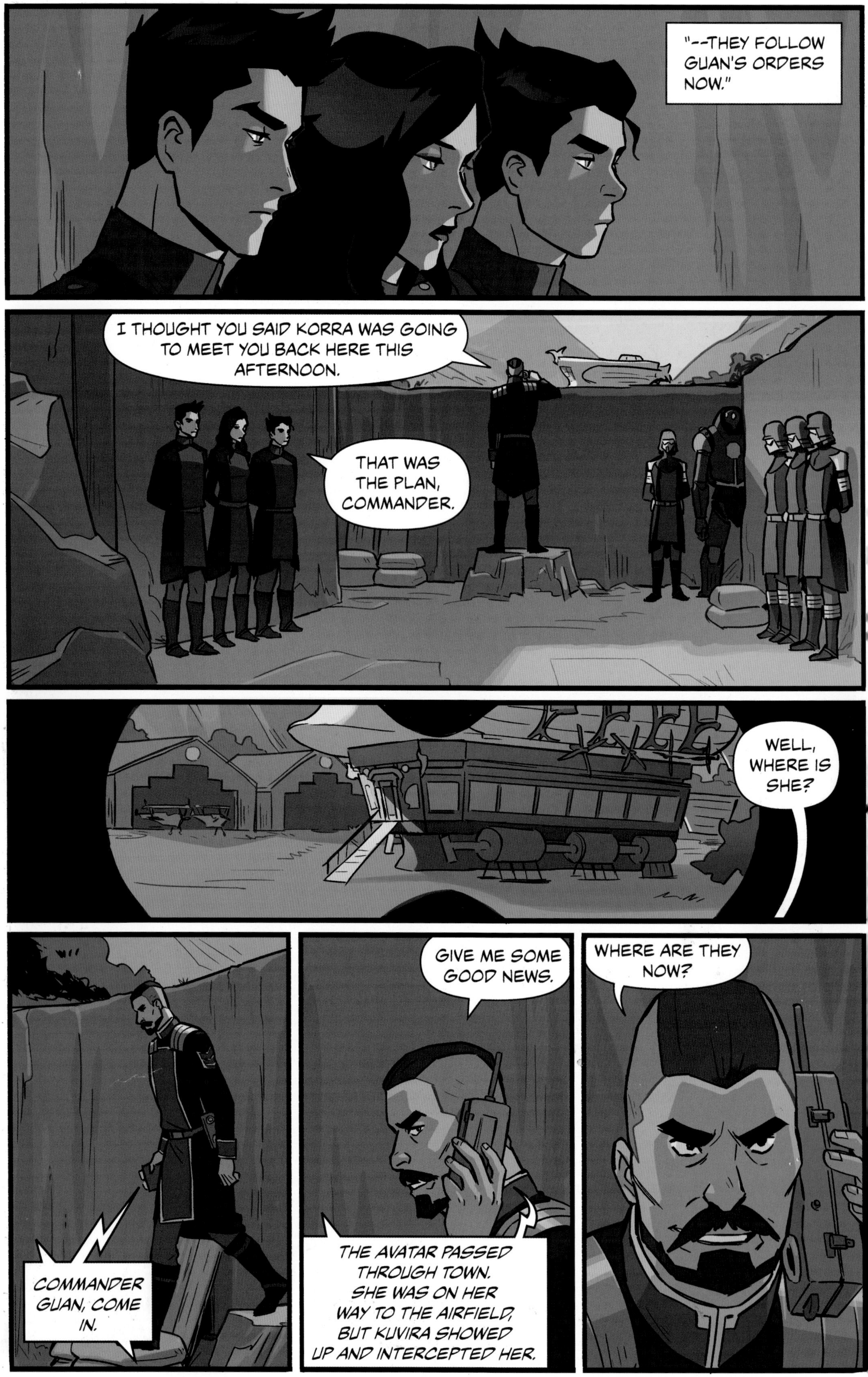
"--THEY FOLLOW GUAN'S ORDERS NOW."
I THOUGHT YOU SAID KORRA WAS GOING TO MEET YOU BACK HERE THIS AFTERNOON.
THAT WAS THE PLAN, COMMANDER.
WELL, WHERE IS SHE?
COMMANDER GUAN, COME IN.
GIVE ME SOME GOOD NEWS.
THE AVATAR PASSED THROUGH TOWN. SHE WAS ON HER WAY TO THE AIRFIELD, BUT KUVIRA SHOWED UP AND INTERCEPTED HER.
WHERE ARE THEY NOW?

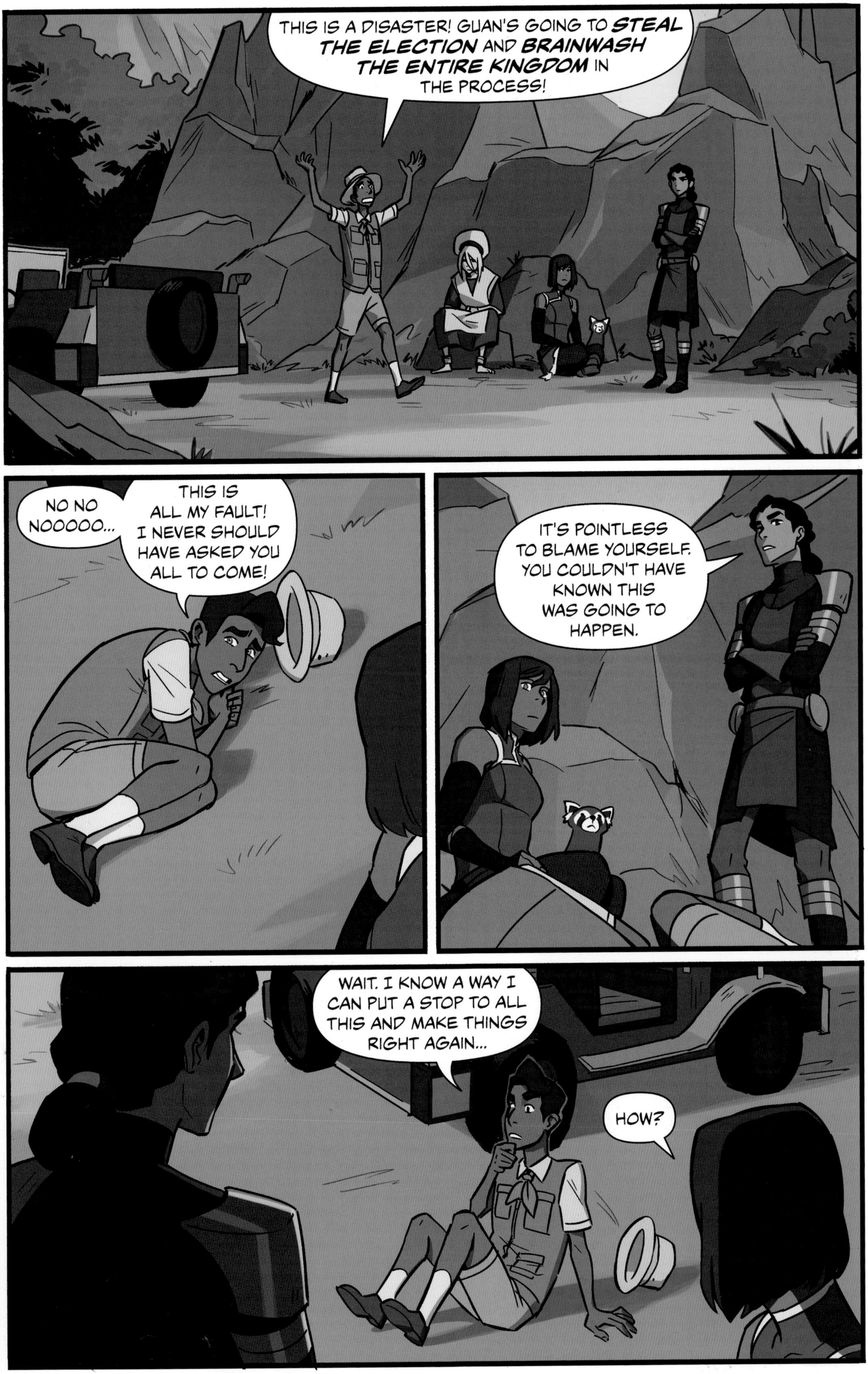
THIS IS A DISASTER! GUAN'S GOING TO **STEAL THE ELECTION** AND **BRAINWASH THE ENTIRE KINGDOM** IN THE PROCESS!
NO NO NOOOOO...
THIS IS ALL MY FAULT! I NEVER SHOULD HAVE ASKED YOU ALL TO COME!
IT'S POINTLESS TO BLAME YOURSELF. YOU COULDN'T HAVE KNOWN THIS WAS GOING TO HAPPEN.
WAIT. I KNOW A WAY I CAN PUT A STOP TO ALL THIS AND MAKE THINGS RIGHT AGAIN...
HOW?

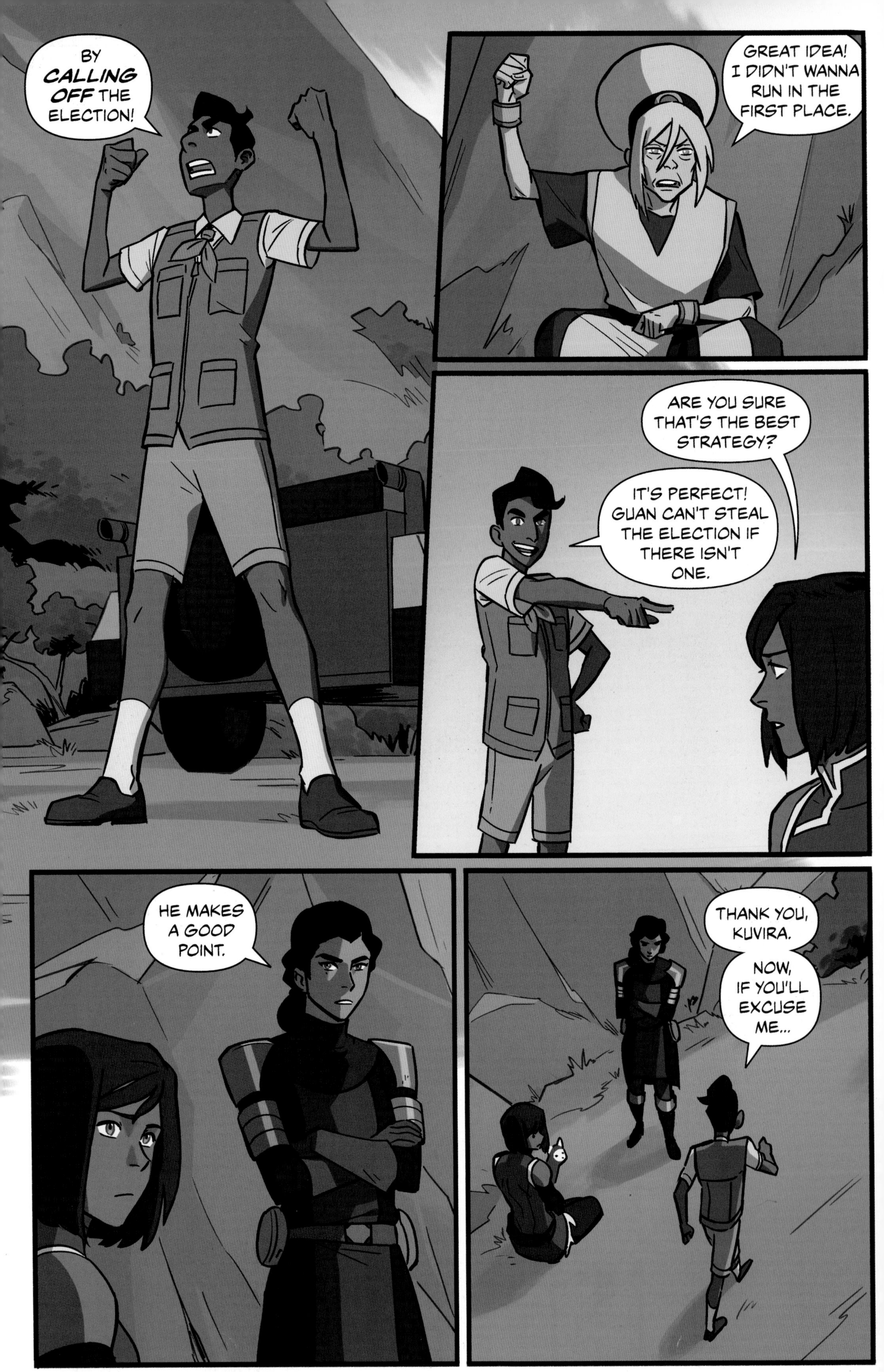
BY CALLING OFF THE ELECTION!
GREAT IDEA! I DIDN'T WANNA RUN IN THE FIRST PLACE.
ARE YOU SURE THAT'S THE BEST STRATEGY?
IT'S PERFECT! GUAN CAN'T STEAL THE ELECTION IF THERE ISN'T ONE.
HE MAKES A GOOD POINT.
THANK YOU, KUVIRA.
NOW, IF YOU'LL EXCUSE ME...

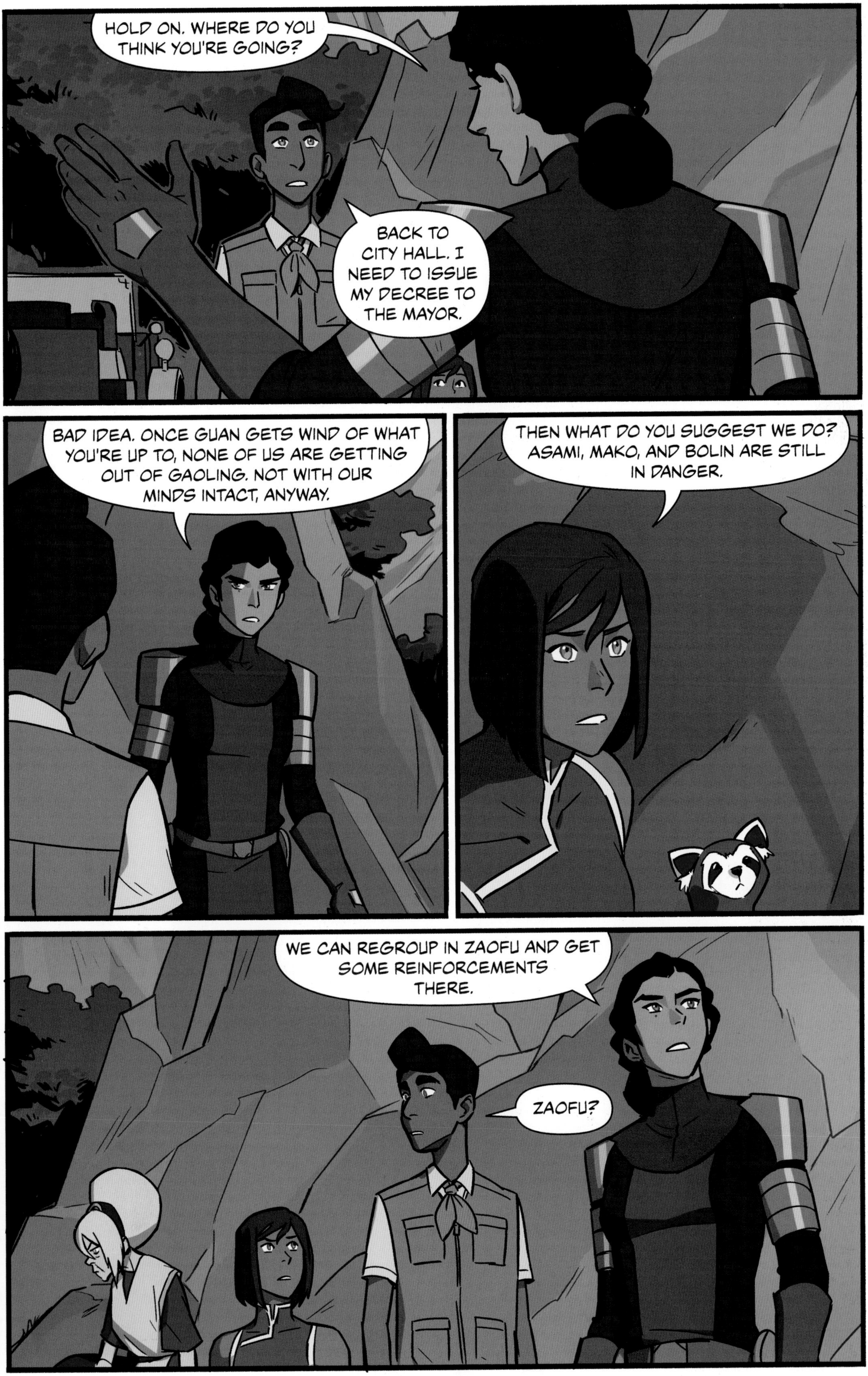
HOLD ON. WHERE DO YOU THINK YOU'RE GOING?
BACK TO CITY HALL. I NEED TO ISSUE MY DECREE TO THE MAYOR.
BAD IDEA. ONCE GUAN GETS WIND OF WHAT YOU'RE UP TO, NONE OF US ARE GETTING OUT OF GAOLING. NOT WITH OUR MINDS INTACT, ANYWAY.
THEN WHAT DO YOU SUGGEST WE DO? ASAMI, MAKO, AND BOLIN ARE STILL IN DANGER.
WE CAN REGROUP IN ZAOFU AND GET SOME REINFORCEMENTS THERE.
ZAOFU?

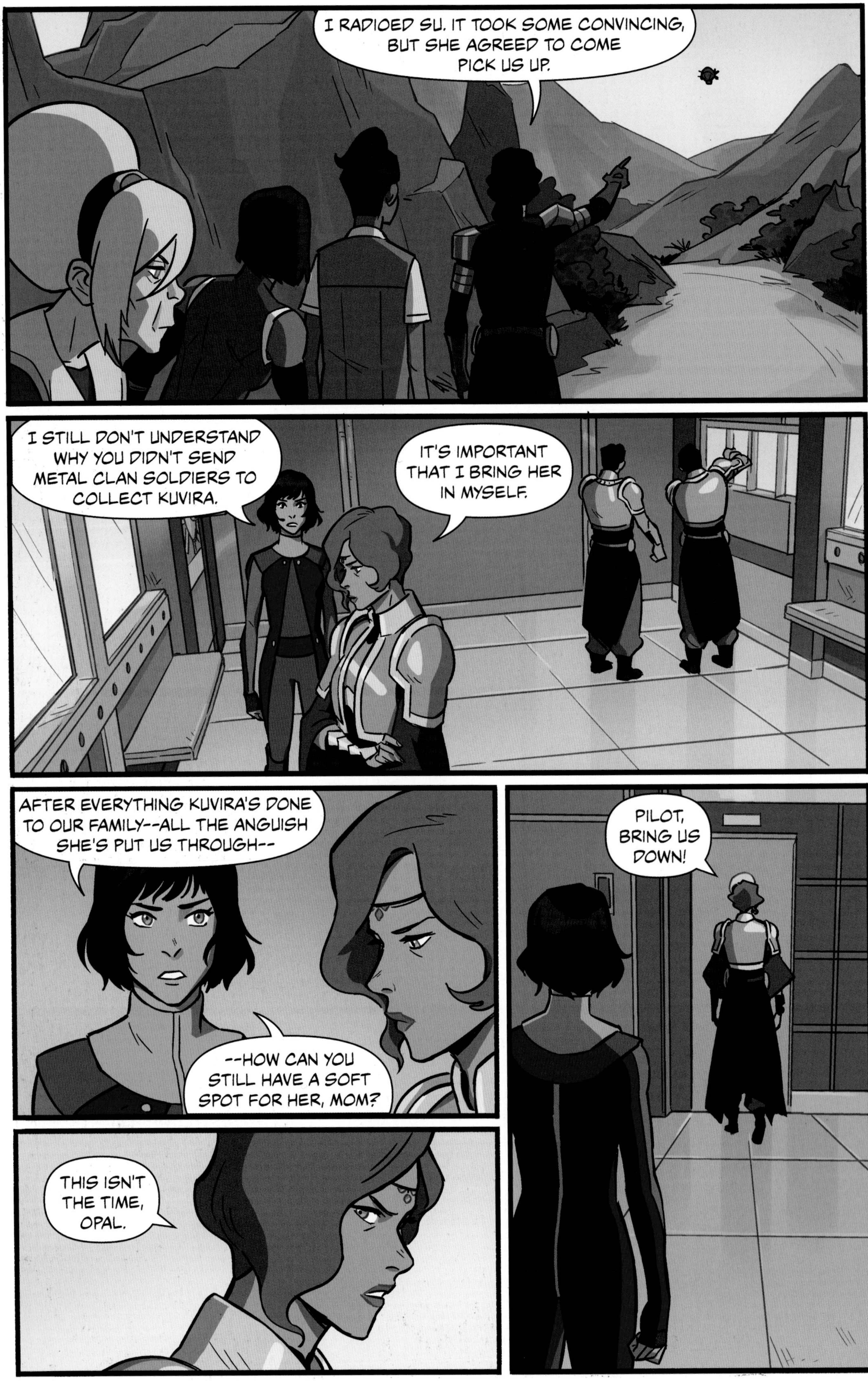
I RADIOED SU. IT TOOK SOME CONVINCING, BUT SHE AGREED TO COME PICK US UP.
I STILL DON'T UNDERSTAND WHY YOU DIDN'T SEND METAL CLAN SOLDIERS TO COLLECT KUVIRA.
IT'S IMPORTANT THAT I BRING HER IN MYSELF.
AFTER EVERYTHING KUVIRA'S DONE TO OUR FAMILY--ALL THE ANGUISH SHE'S PUT US THROUGH--
--HOW CAN YOU STILL HAVE A SOFT SPOT FOR HER, MOM?
THIS ISN'T THE TIME, OPAL.
PILOT, BRING US DOWN!

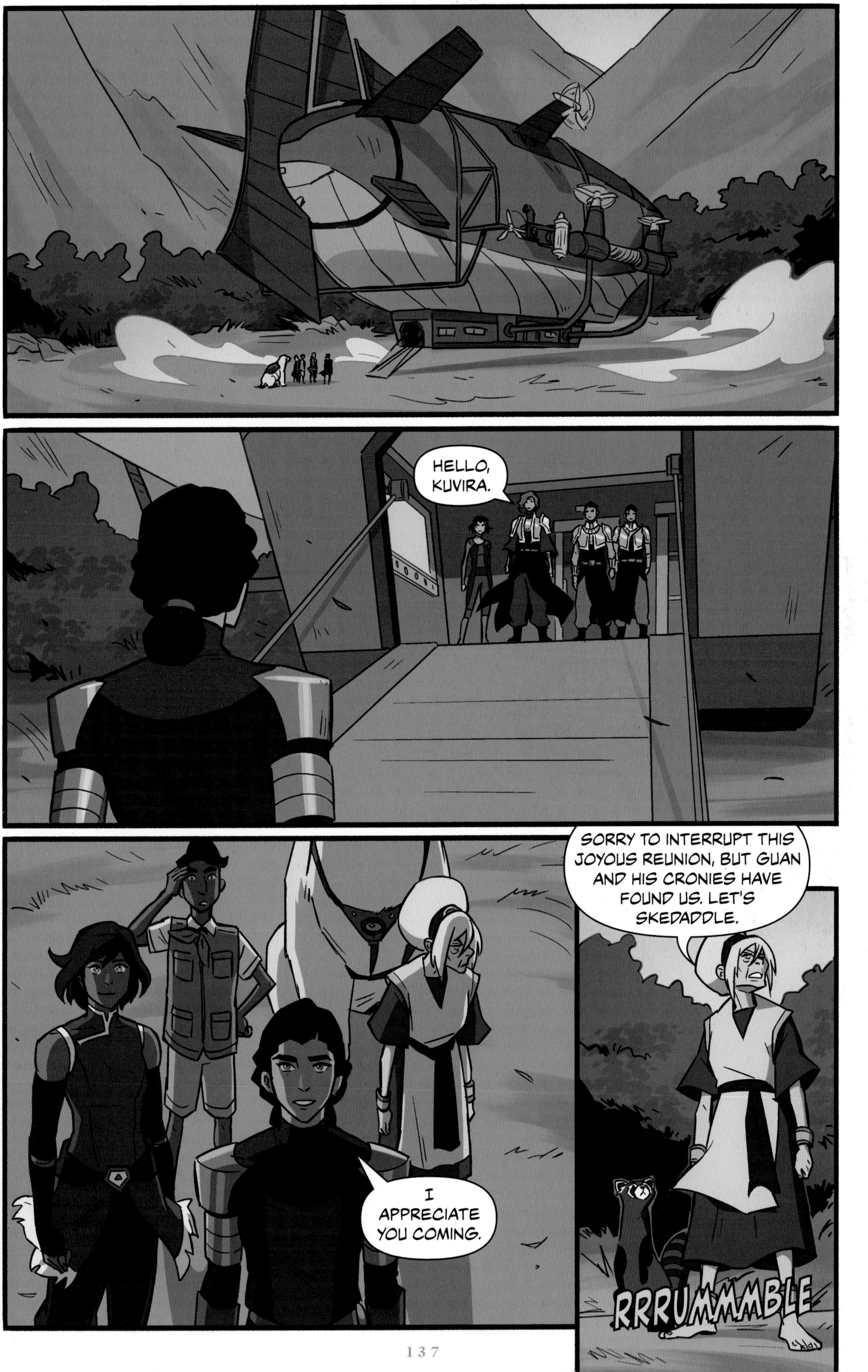
HELLO, KUVIRA.
I APPRECIATE YOU COMING.
SORRY TO INTERRUPT THIS JOYOUS REUNION, BUT GUAN AND HIS CRONIES HAVE FOUND US. LET'S SKEDADDLE.
RRRUMMMBLE

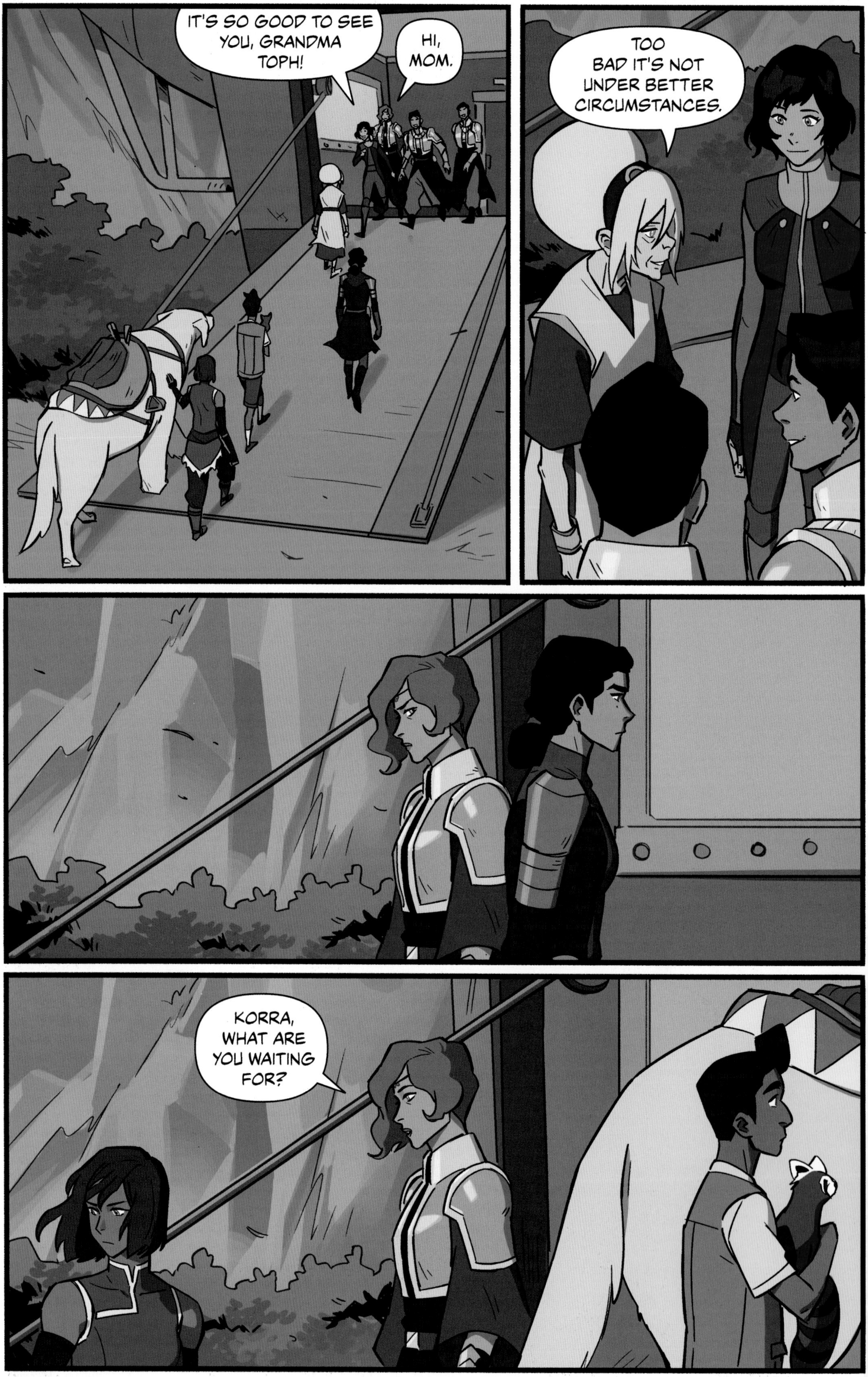
IT'S SO GOOD TO SEE YOU, GRANDMA TOPH!
HI, MOM.
TOO BAD IT'S NOT UNDER BETTER CIRCUMSTANCES.
KORRA, WHAT ARE YOU WAITING FOR?

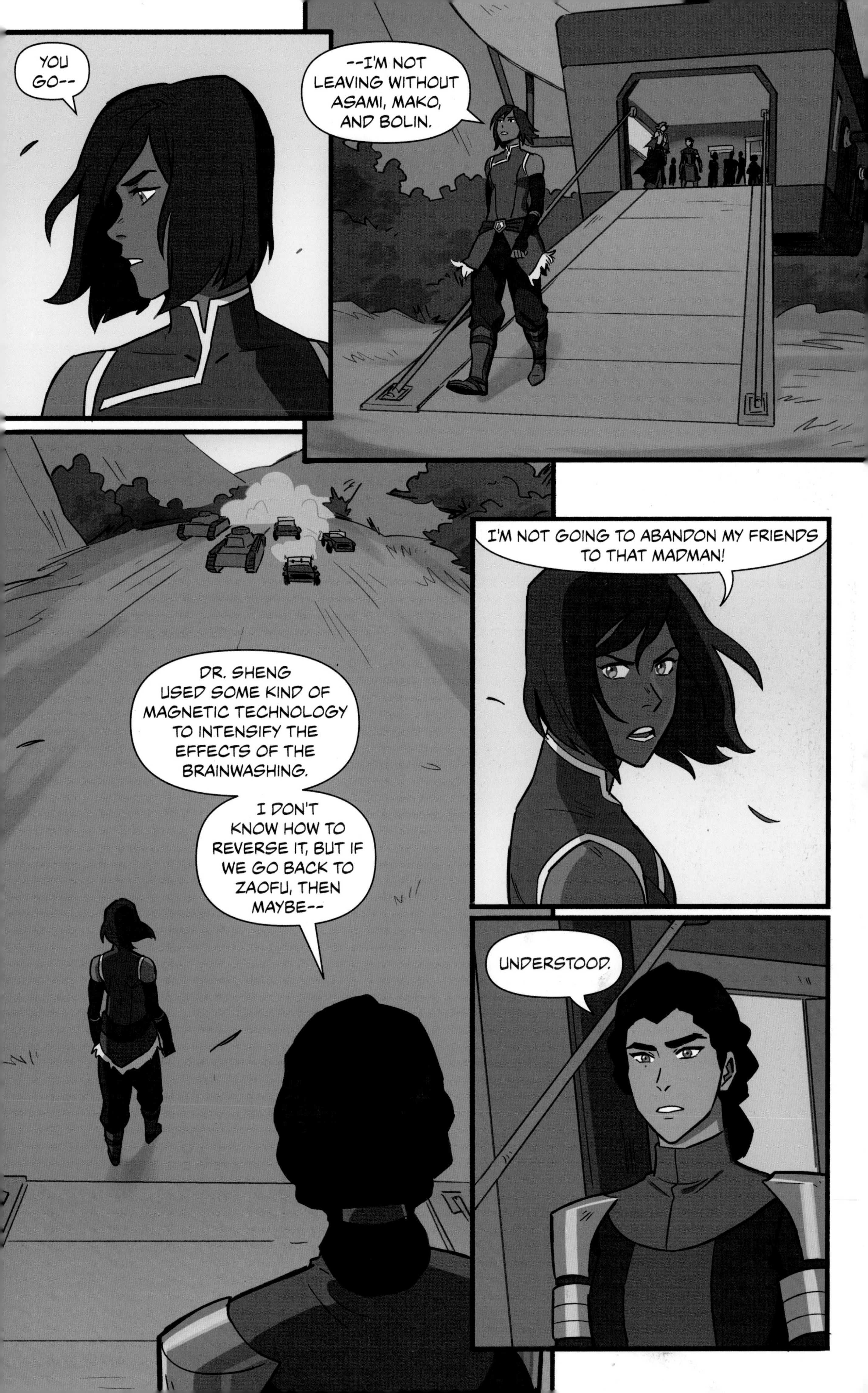
YOU GO--
--I'M NOT LEAVING WITHOUT ASAMI, MAKO, AND BOLIN.
I'M NOT GOING TO ABANDON MY FRIENDS TO THAT MADMAN!
DR. SHENG USED SOME KIND OF MAGNETIC TECHNOLOGY TO INTENSIFY THE EFFECTS OF THE BRAINWASHING.
I DON'T KNOW HOW TO REVERSE IT, BUT IF WE GO BACK TO ZAOFU, THEN MAYBE--
UNDERSTOOD.

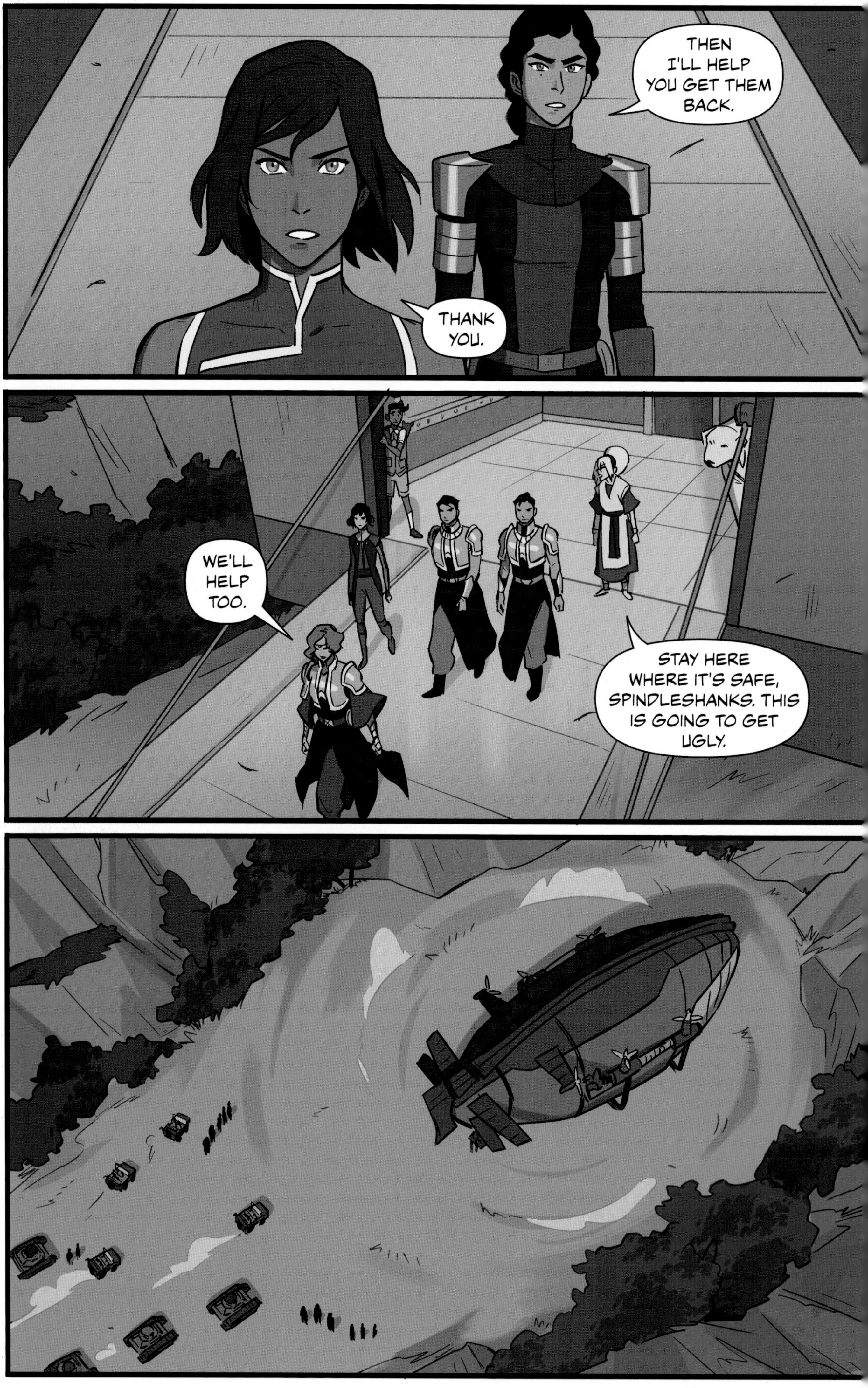
THEN I'LL HELP YOU GET THEM BACK.
THANK YOU.
WE'LL HELP TOO.
STAY HERE WHERE IT'S SAFE, SPINDLESHANKS. THIS IS GOING TO GET UGLY.

THE AVATAR IS YOUR ENEMY.
BRING HER TO ME.
YES, COMMANDER GUAN.

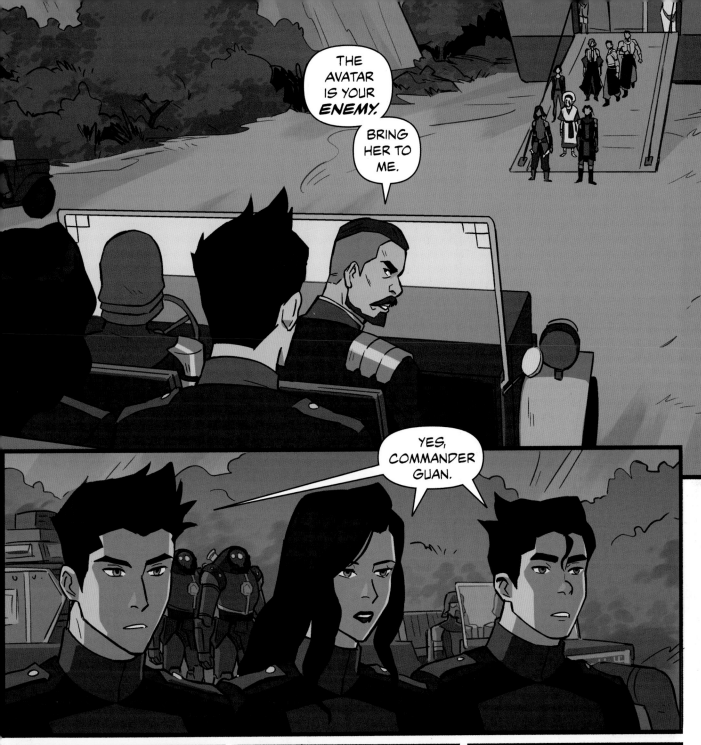

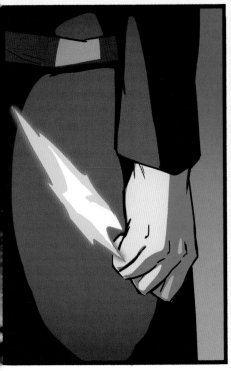

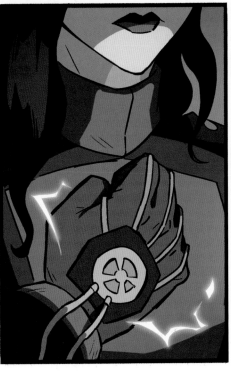

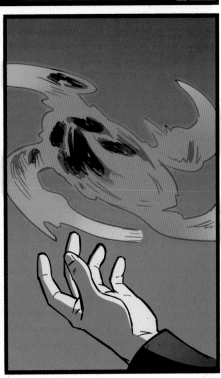

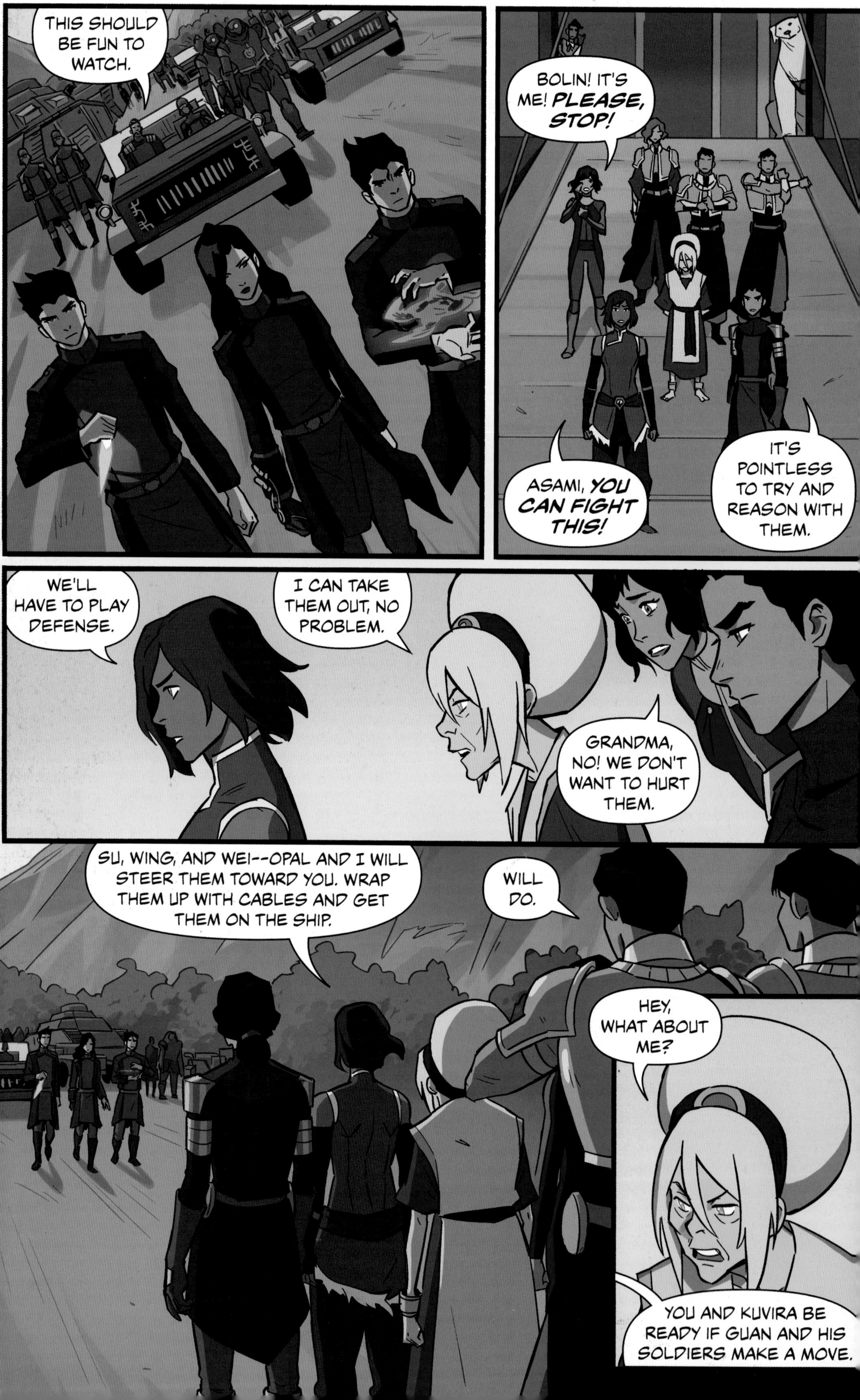

THIS SHOULD BE FUN TO WATCH.
BOLIN! IT'S ME! PLEASE, STOP!
ASAMI, YOU CAN FIGHT THIS!
IT'S POINTLESS TO TRY AND REASON WITH THEM.
WE'LL HAVE TO PLAY DEFENSE.
I CAN TAKE THEM OUT, NO PROBLEM.
GRANDMA, NO! WE DON'T WANT TO HURT THEM.
SU, WING, AND WEI--OPAL AND I WILL STEER THEM TOWARD YOU. WRAP THEM UP WITH CABLES AND GET THEM ON THE SHIP.
WILL DO.
HEY, WHAT ABOUT ME?
YOU AND KUVIRA BE READY IF GUAN AND HIS SOLDIERS MAKE A MOVE.

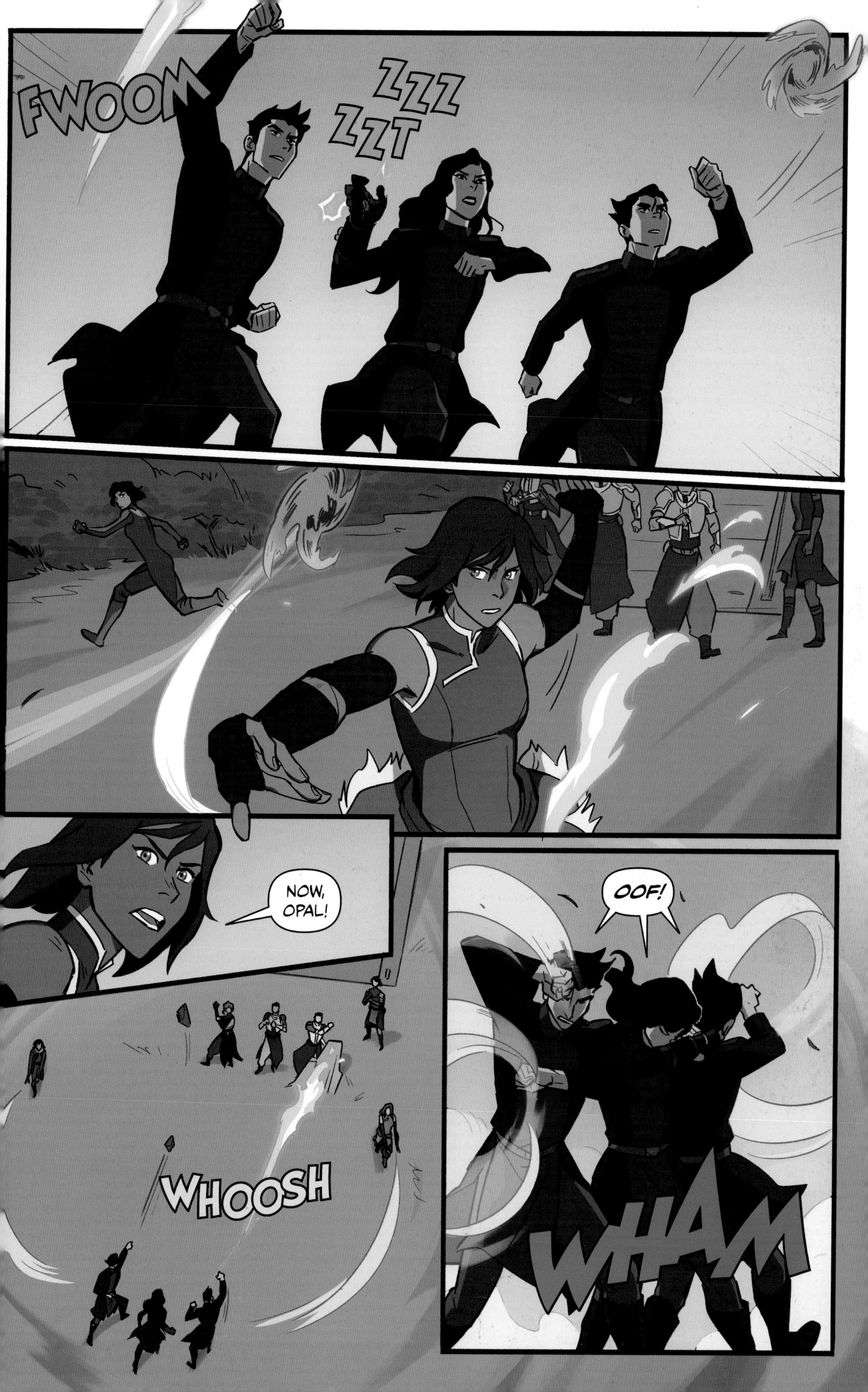
FWOOM
ZZZ
ZZT
NOW, OPAL!
WHOOSH
OOF!
WHAM

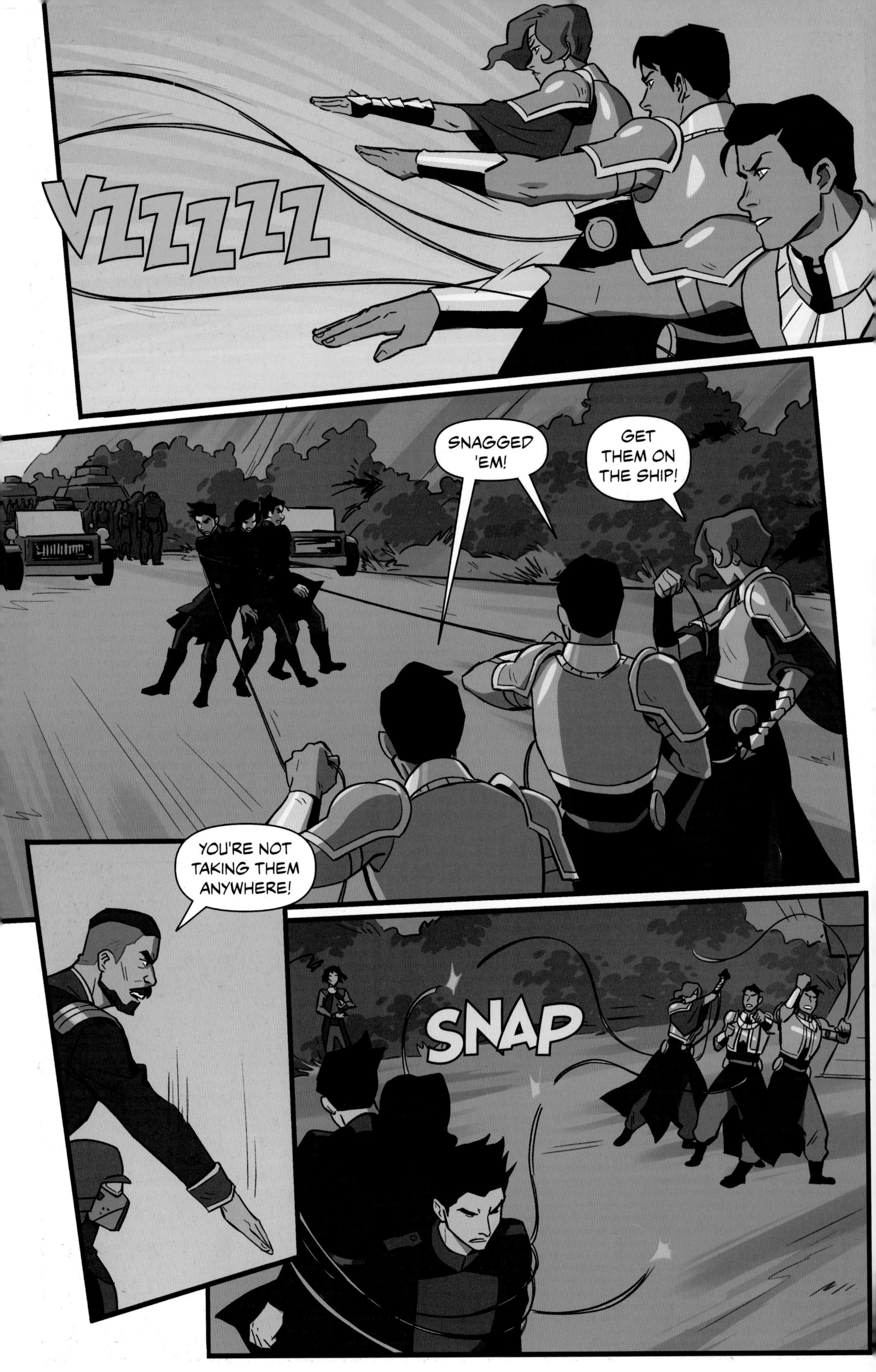
VZZZZZZ
SNAGGED 'EM!
GET THEM ON THE SHIP!
YOU'RE NOT TAKING THEM ANYWHERE!
SNAP

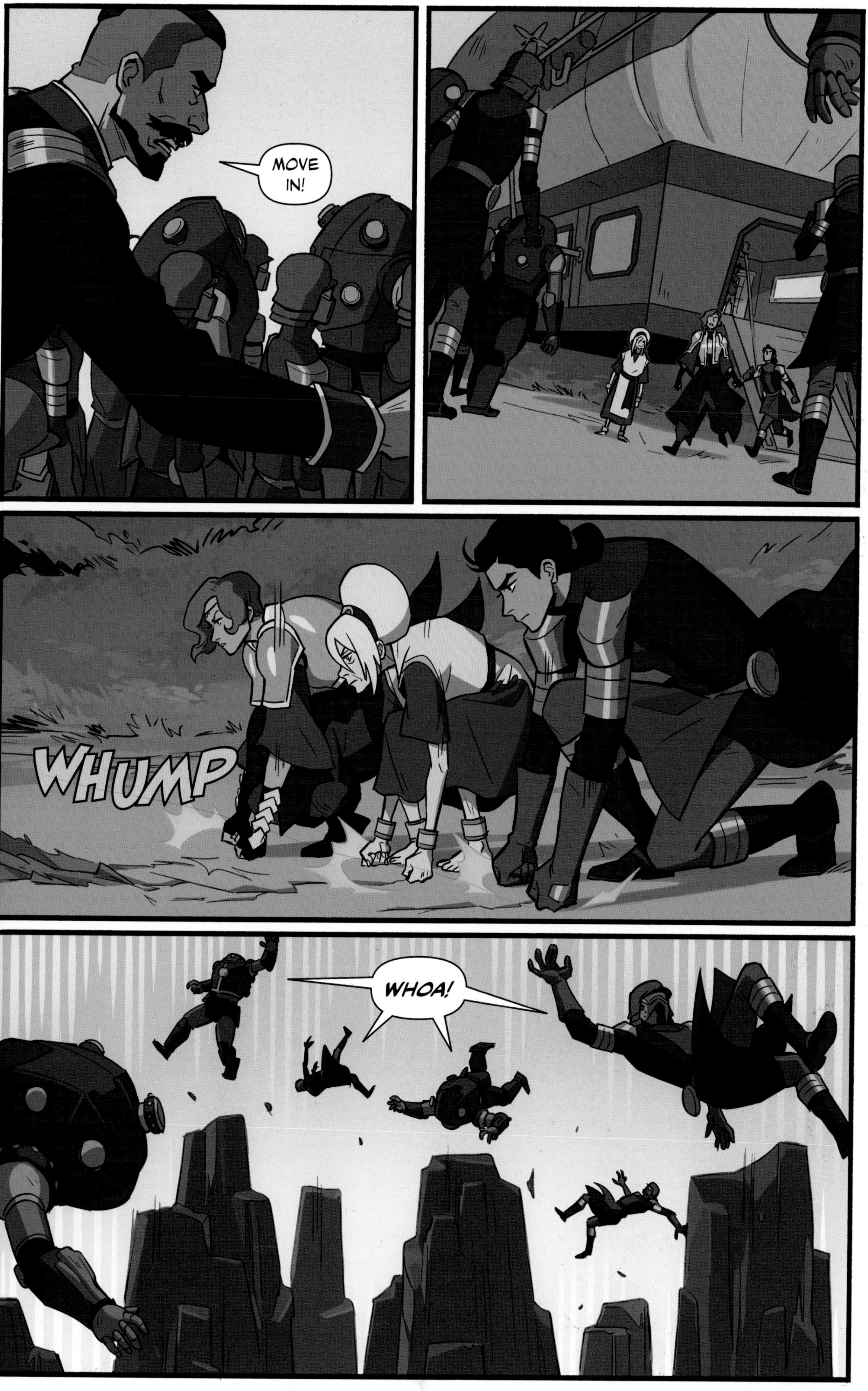
MOVE IN!
WHUMP
WHOA!

BOLIN! STOP!

WHOOSH

UGH!

OPAL!

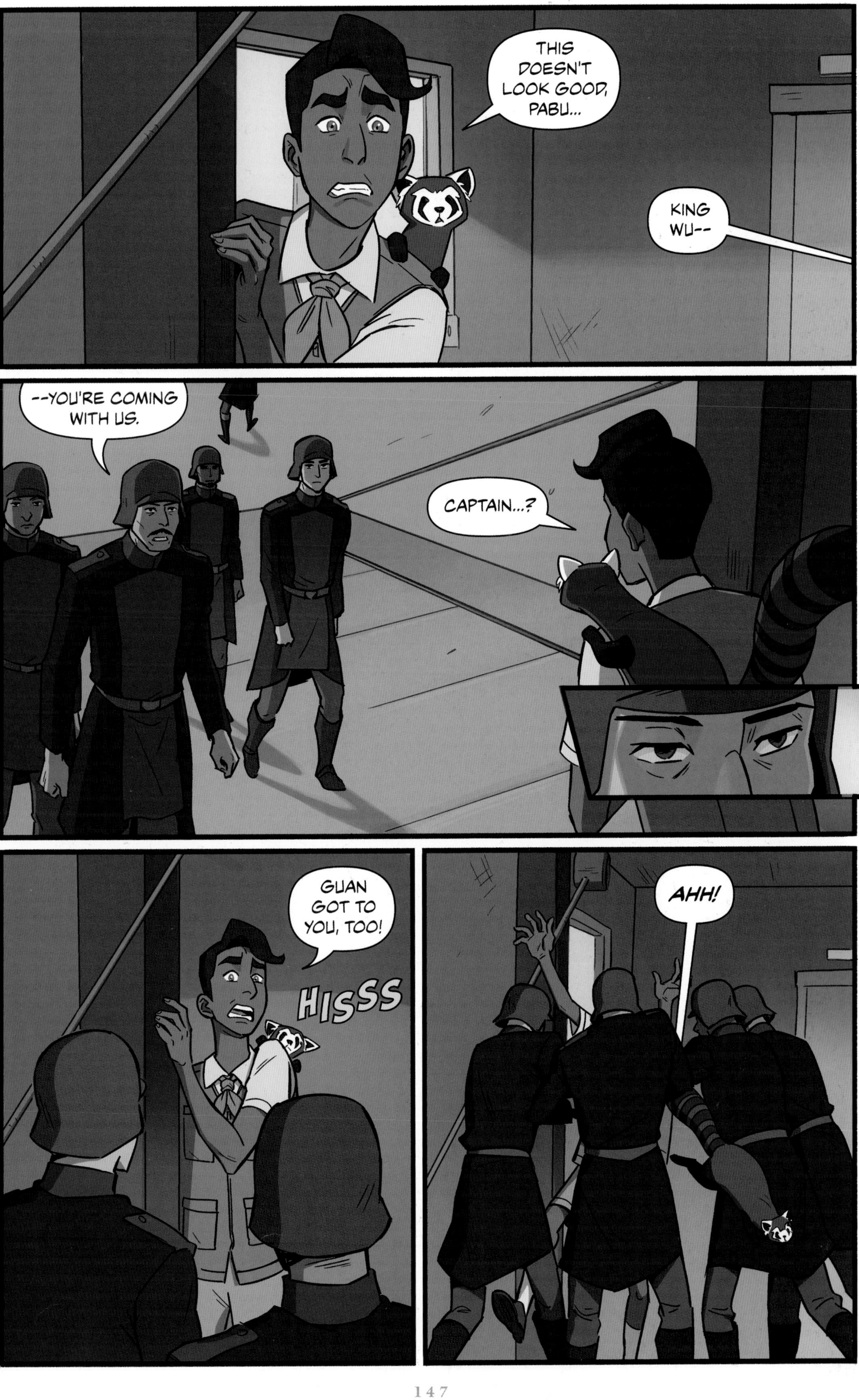
THIS DOESN'T LOOK GOOD, PABU...
KING WU--
--YOU'RE COMING WITH US.
CAPTAIN...?
GUAN GOT TO YOU, TOO!
HISSS
AHH!

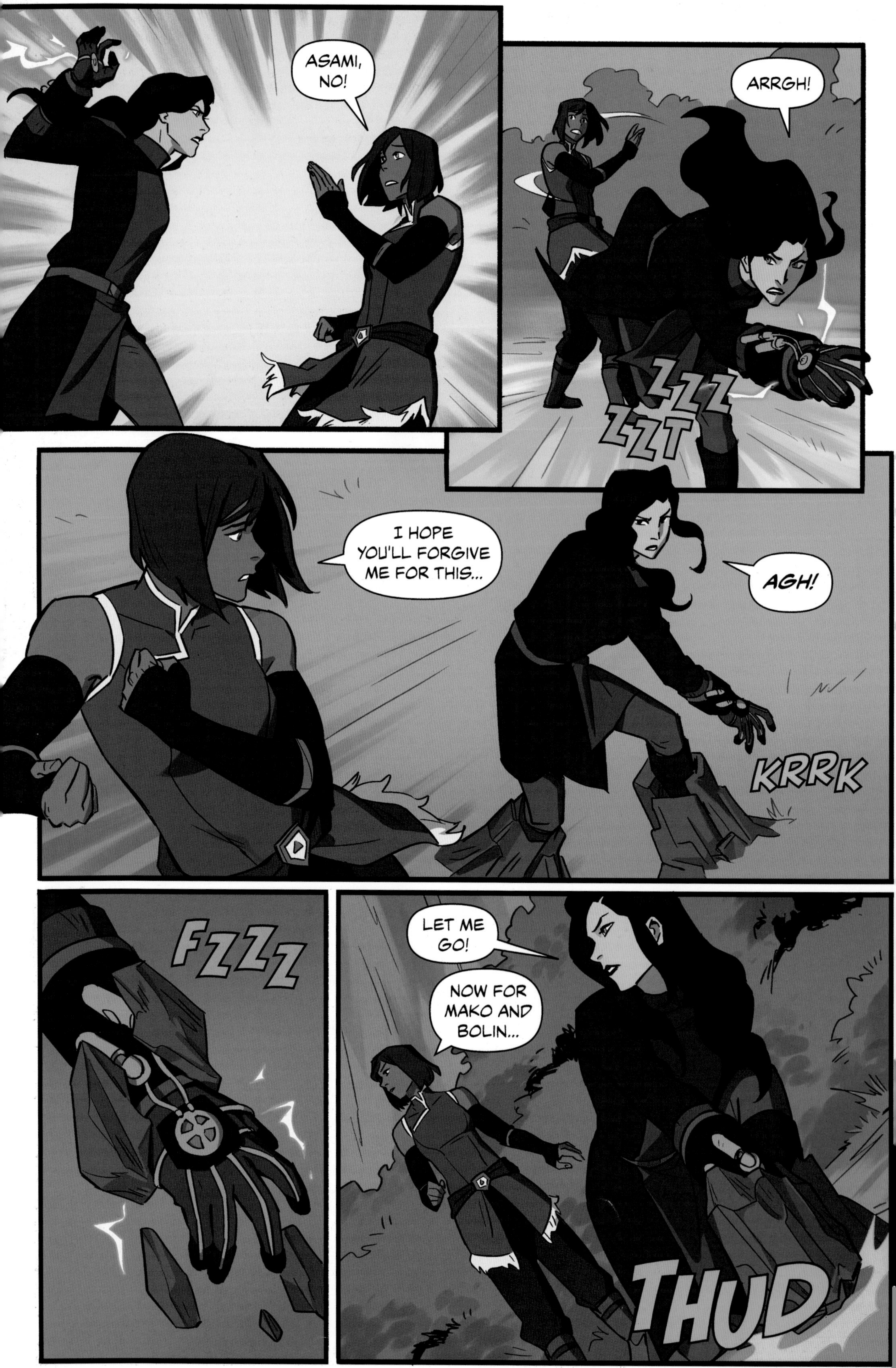
ASAMI, NO!
ARRGH!
ZZZ ZZT
I HOPE YOU'LL FORGIVE ME FOR THIS...
AGH!
KRRK
FZZZ
LET ME GO!
NOW FOR MAKO AND BOLIN...
THUD

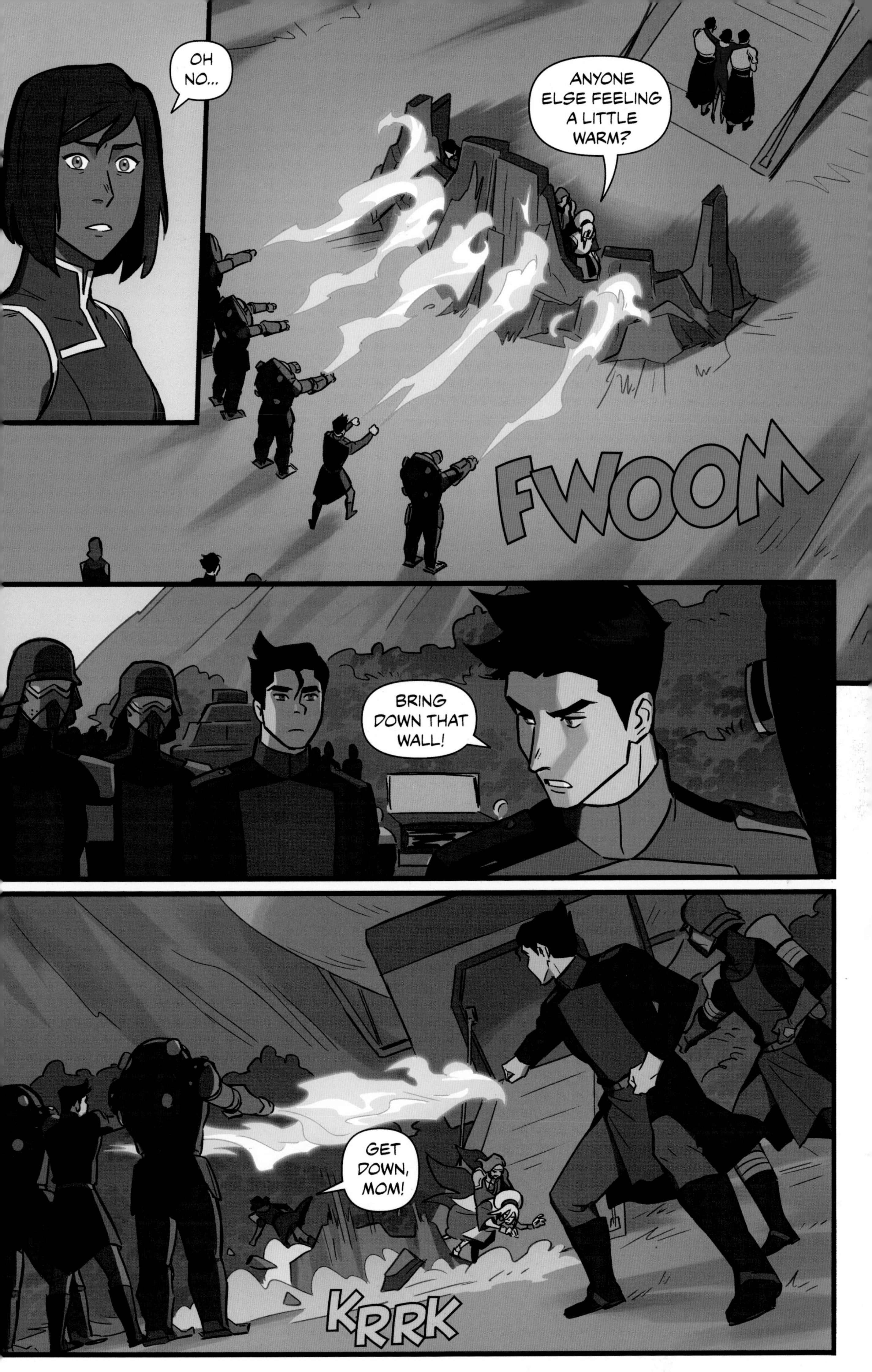
OH NO...
ANYONE ELSE FEELING A LITTLE WARM?
FWOOM
BRING DOWN THAT WALL!
GET DOWN, MOM!
KRRK

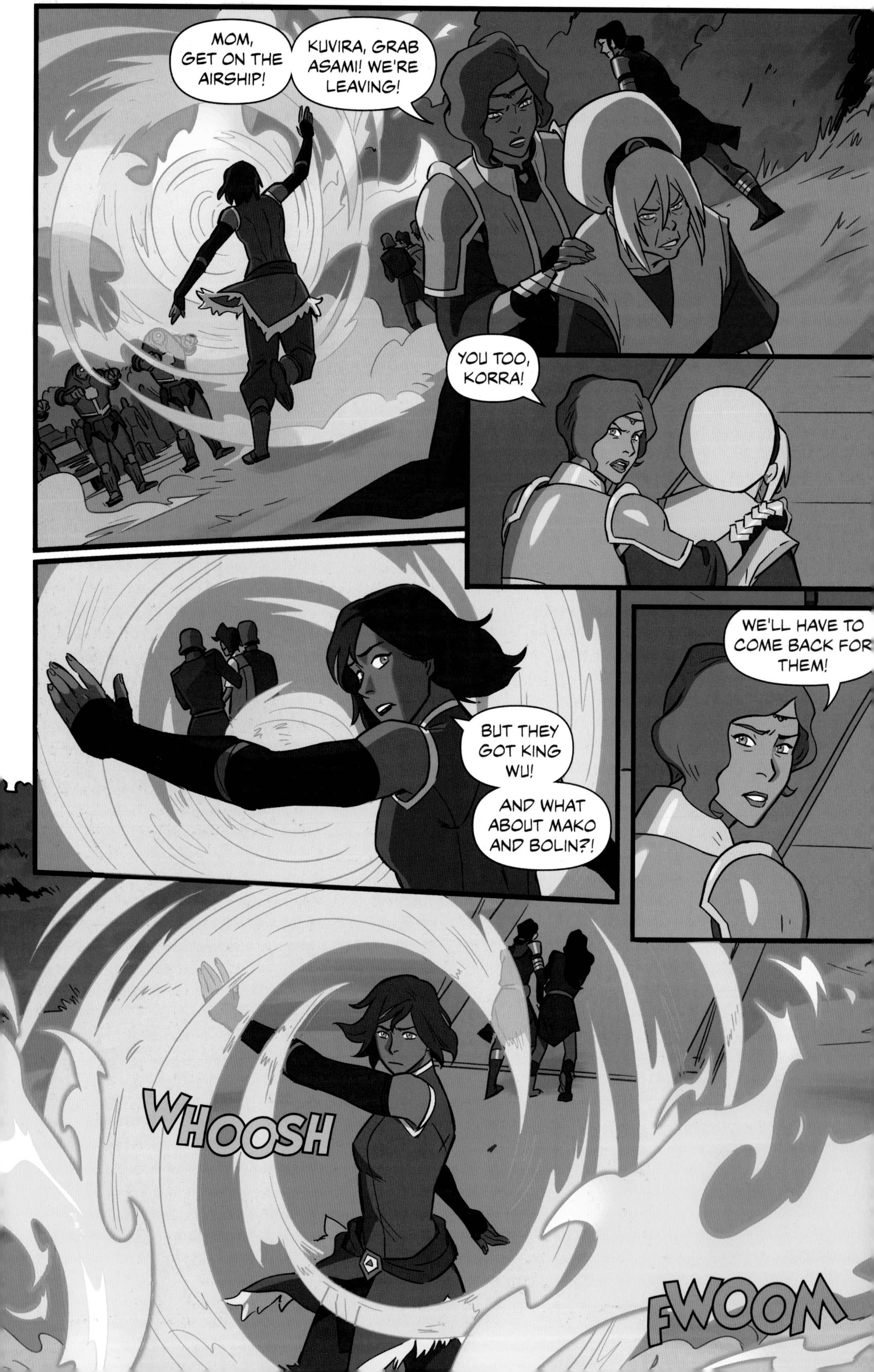
MOM, GET ON THE AIRSHIP!
KUVIRA, GRAB ASAMI! WE'RE LEAVING!
YOU TOO, KORRA!
BUT THEY GOT KING WU!
AND WHAT ABOUT MAKO AND BOLIN?!
WE'LL HAVE TO COME BACK FOR THEM!
WHOOSH
FWOOM

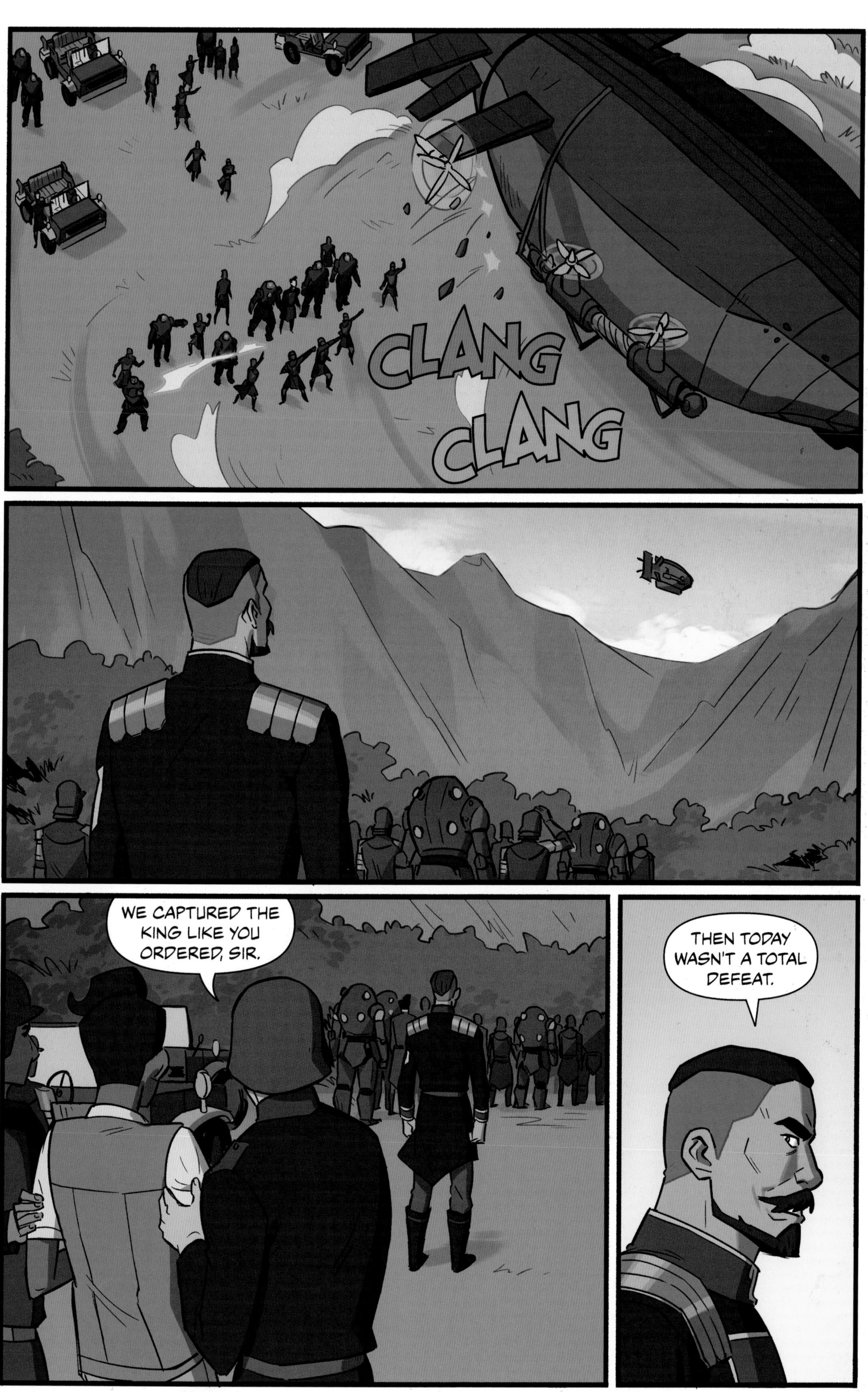
CLANG
CLANG
WE CAPTURED THE KING LIKE YOU ORDERED, SIR.
THEN TODAY WASN'T A TOTAL DEFEAT.

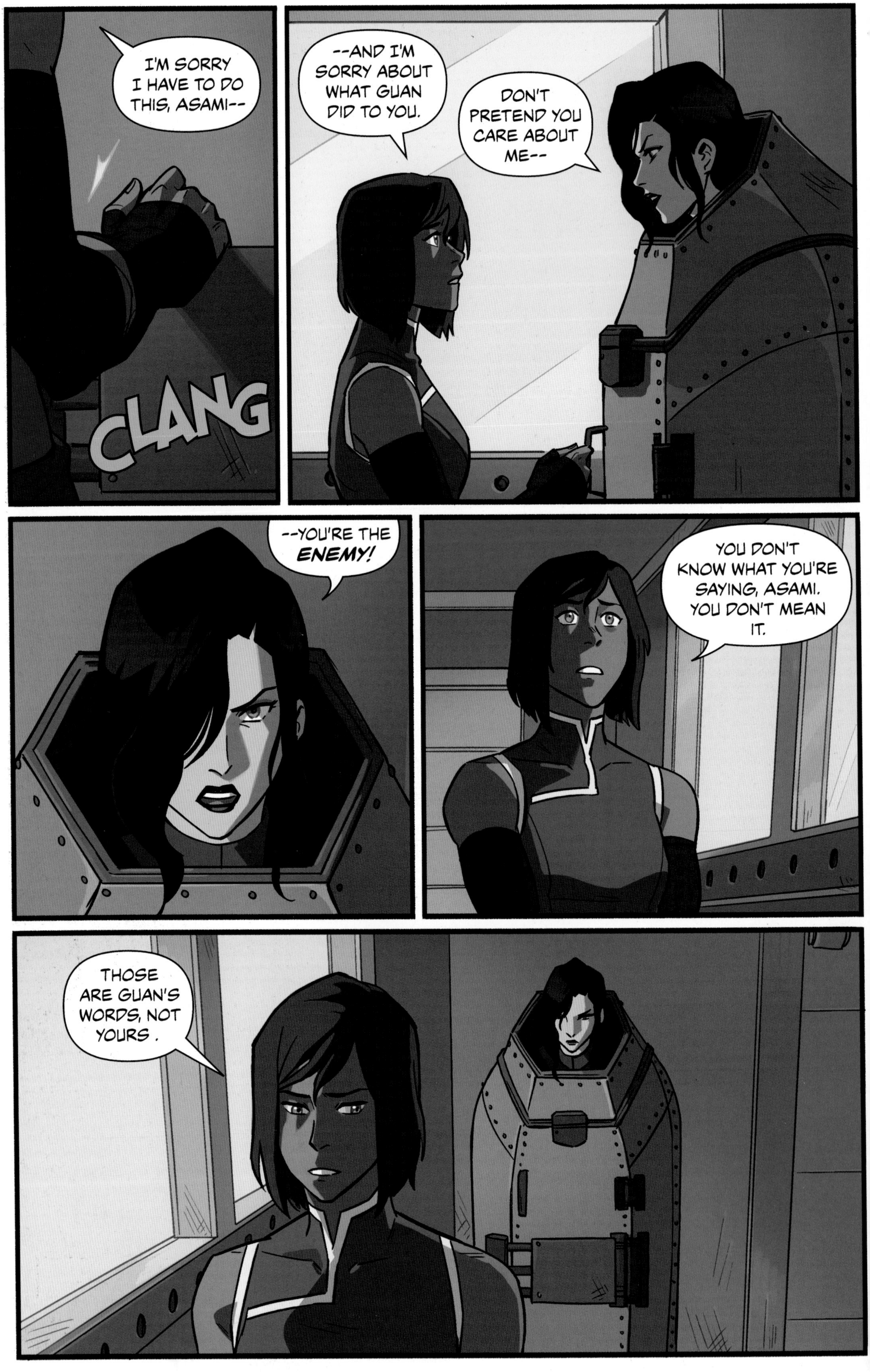
I'M SORRY I HAVE TO DO THIS, ASAMI--
CLANG
--AND I'M SORRY ABOUT WHAT GUAN DID TO YOU.
DON'T PRETEND YOU CARE ABOUT ME--
--YOU'RE THE *ENEMY!*
YOU DON'T KNOW WHAT YOU'RE SAYING, ASAMI. YOU DON'T MEAN IT.
THOSE ARE GUAN'S WORDS, NOT YOURS .

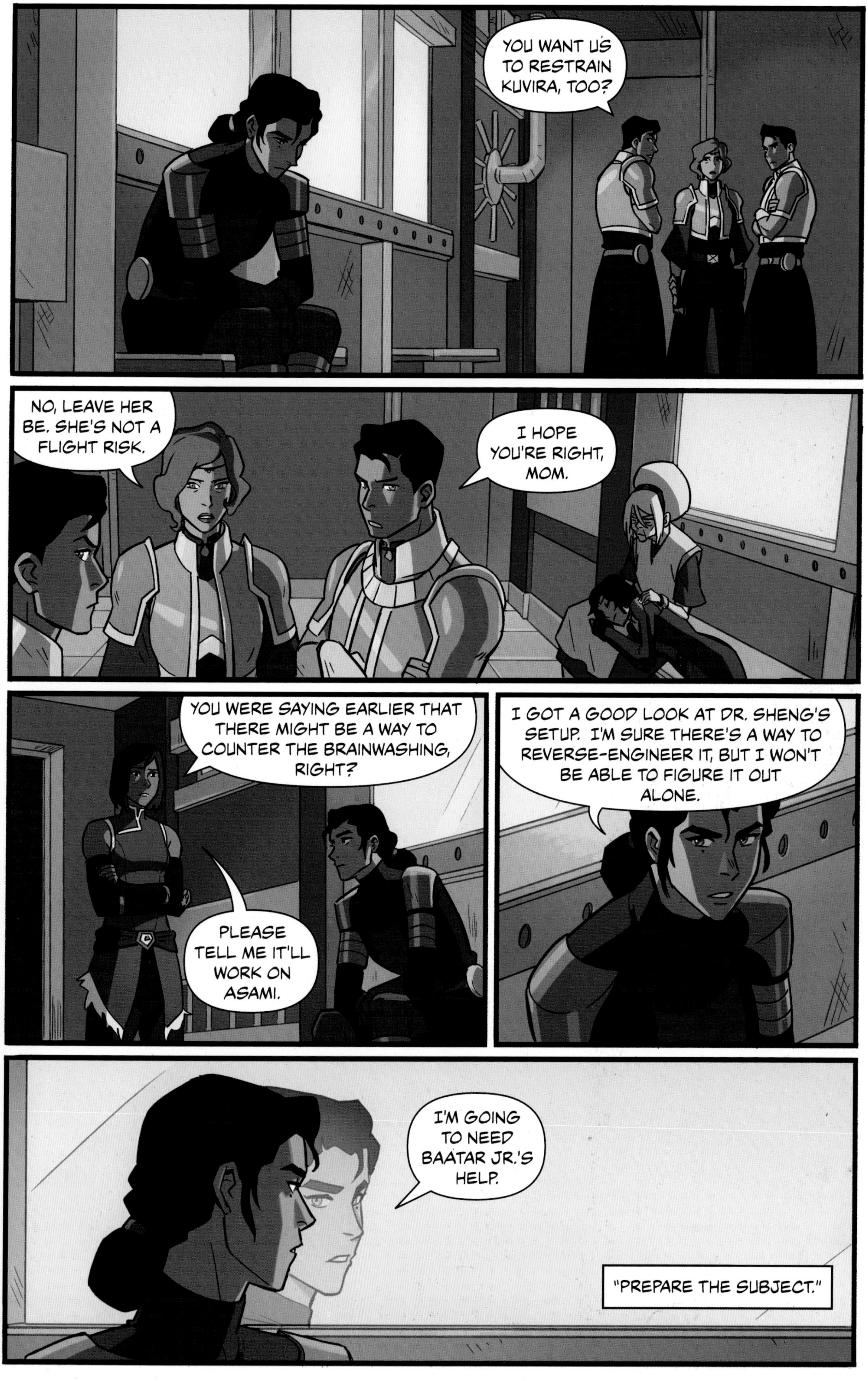
YOU WANT US TO RESTRAIN KUVIRA, TOO?
NO, LEAVE HER BE. SHE'S NOT A FLIGHT RISK.
I HOPE YOU'RE RIGHT, MOM.
YOU WERE SAYING EARLIER THAT THERE MIGHT BE A WAY TO COUNTER THE BRAINWASHING, RIGHT?
PLEASE TELL ME IT'LL WORK ON ASAMI.
I GOT A GOOD LOOK AT DR. SHENG'S SETUP. I'M SURE THERE'S A WAY TO REVERSE-ENGINEER IT, BUT I WON'T BE ABLE TO FIGURE IT OUT ALONE.
I'M GOING TO NEED BAATAR JR.'S HELP.
"PREPARE THE SUBJECT."

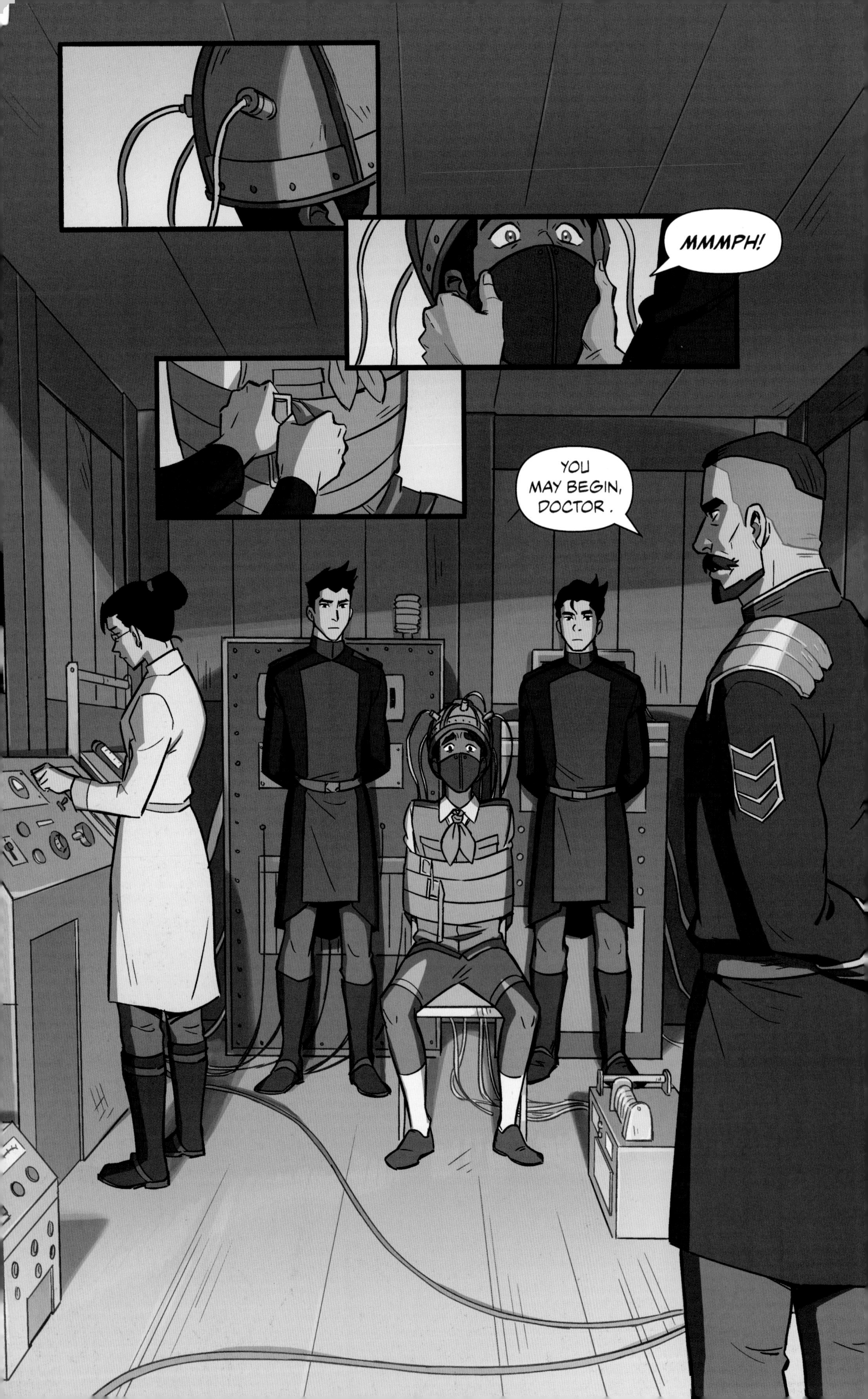
MMMPH!
YOU MAY BEGIN, DOCTOR.

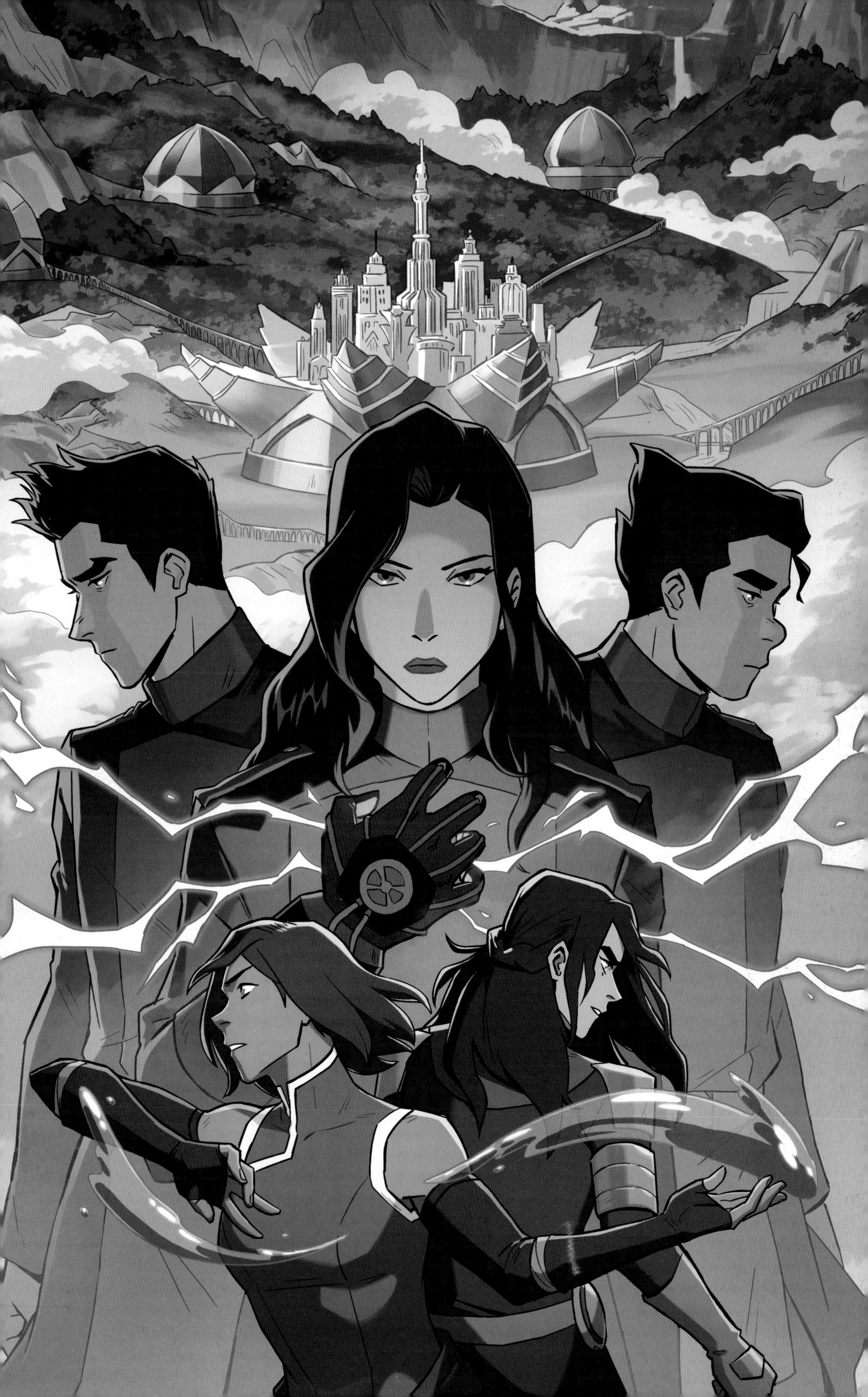

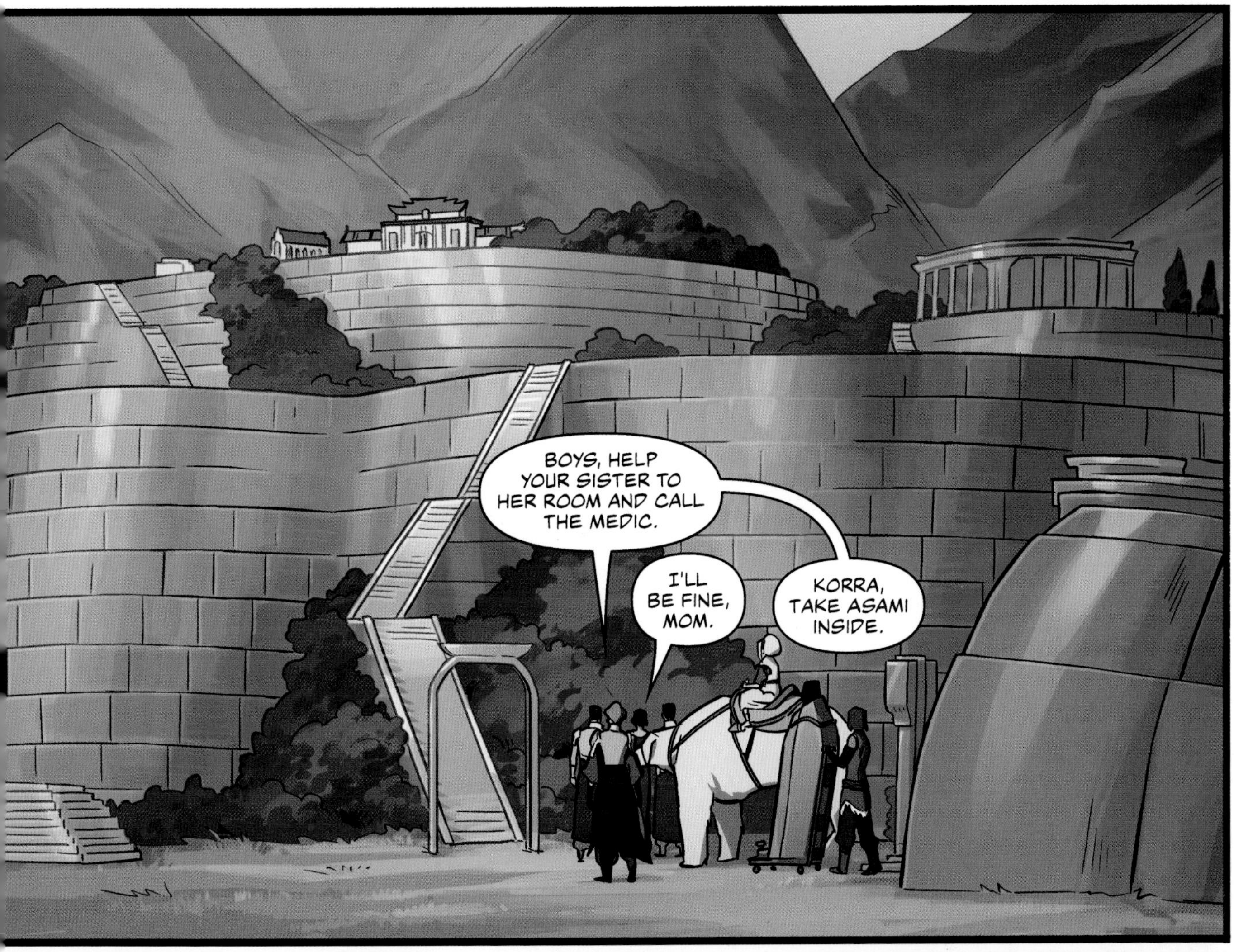
BOYS, HELP YOUR SISTER TO HER ROOM AND CALL THE MEDIC.
I'LL BE FINE, MOM.
KORRA, TAKE ASAMI INSIDE.

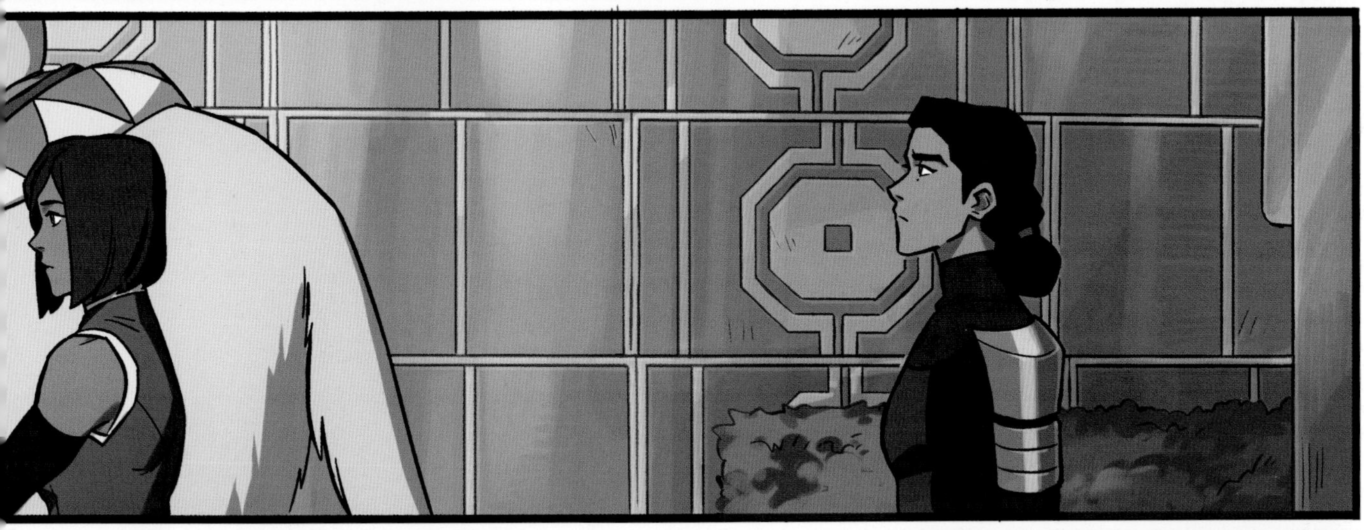

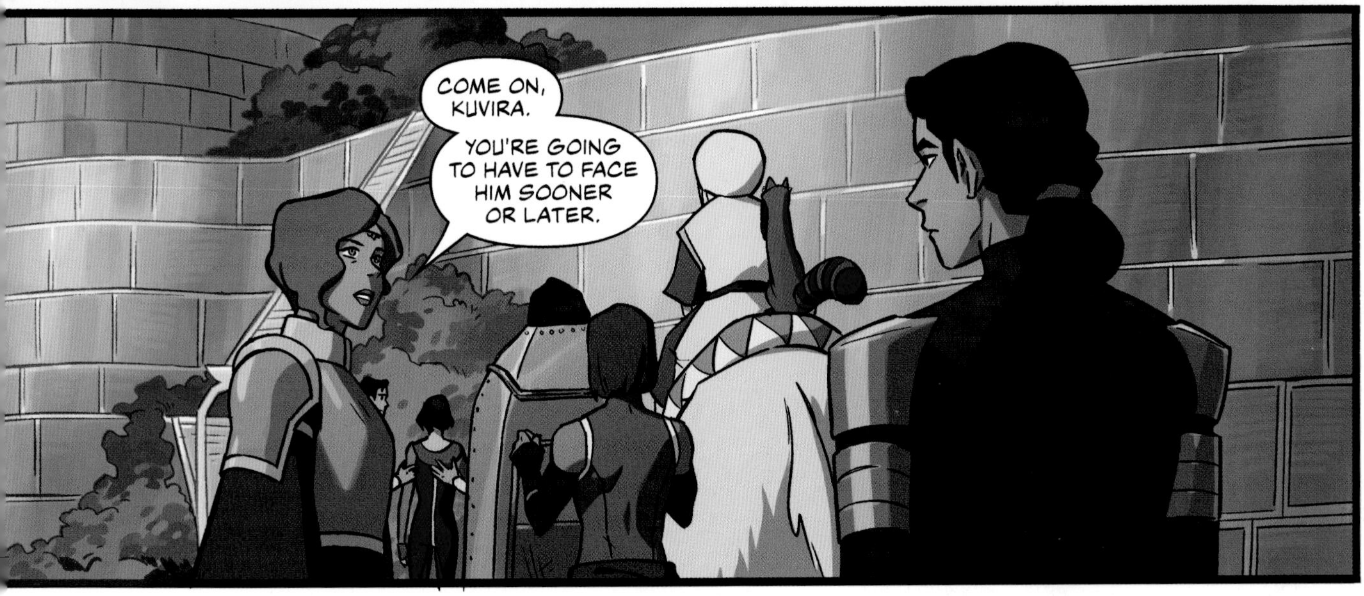
COME ON, KUVIRA.
YOU'RE GOING TO HAVE TO FACE HIM SOONER OR LATER.

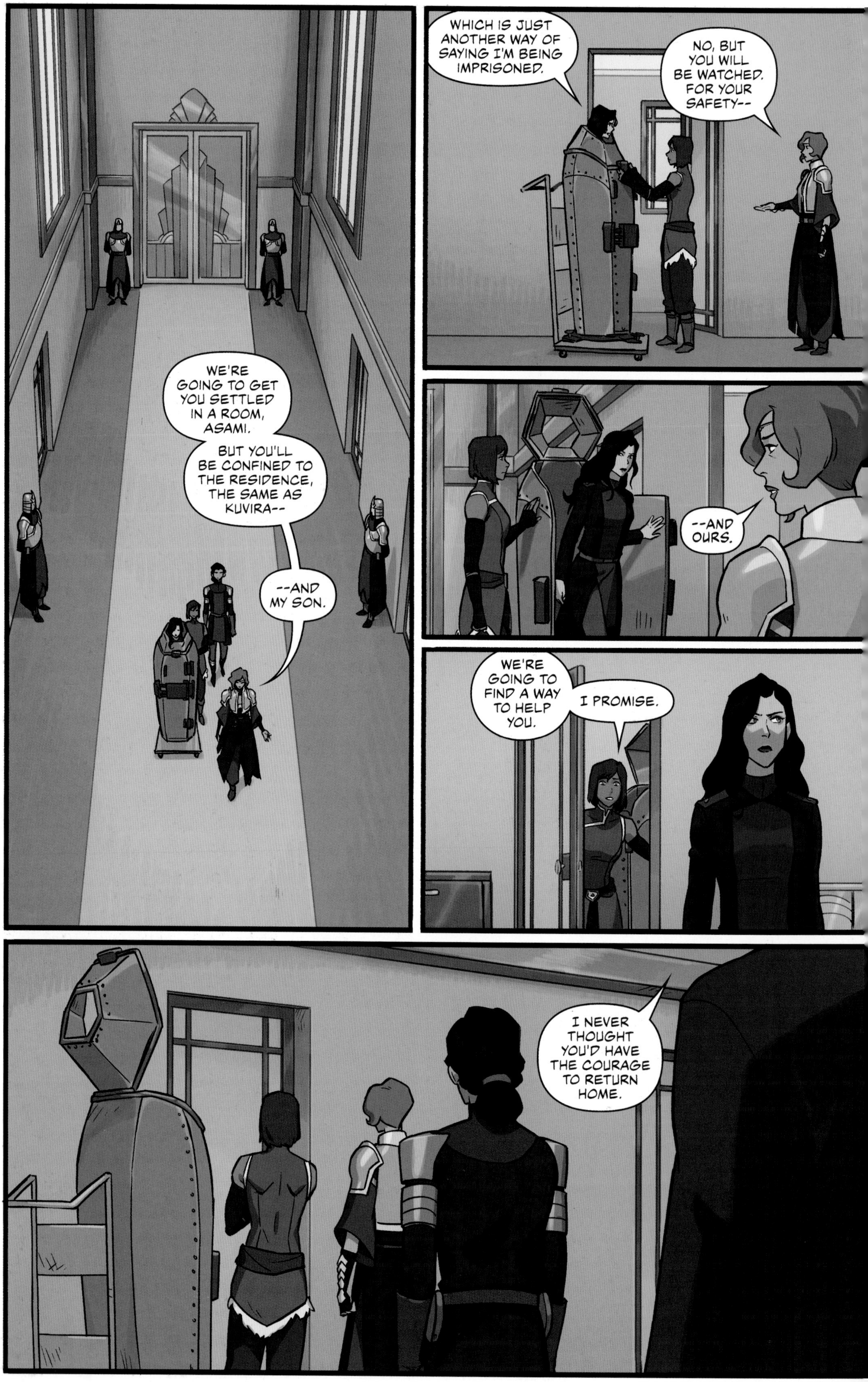
WE'RE GOING TO GET YOU SETTLED IN A ROOM, ASAMI.
BUT YOU'LL BE CONFINED TO THE RESIDENCE, THE SAME AS KUVIRA--
--AND MY SON.
WHICH IS JUST ANOTHER WAY OF SAYING I'M BEING IMPRISONED.
NO, BUT YOU WILL BE WATCHED. FOR YOUR SAFETY--
--AND OURS.
WE'RE GOING TO FIND A WAY TO HELP YOU.
I PROMISE.
I NEVER THOUGHT YOU'D HAVE THE COURAGE TO RETURN HOME.

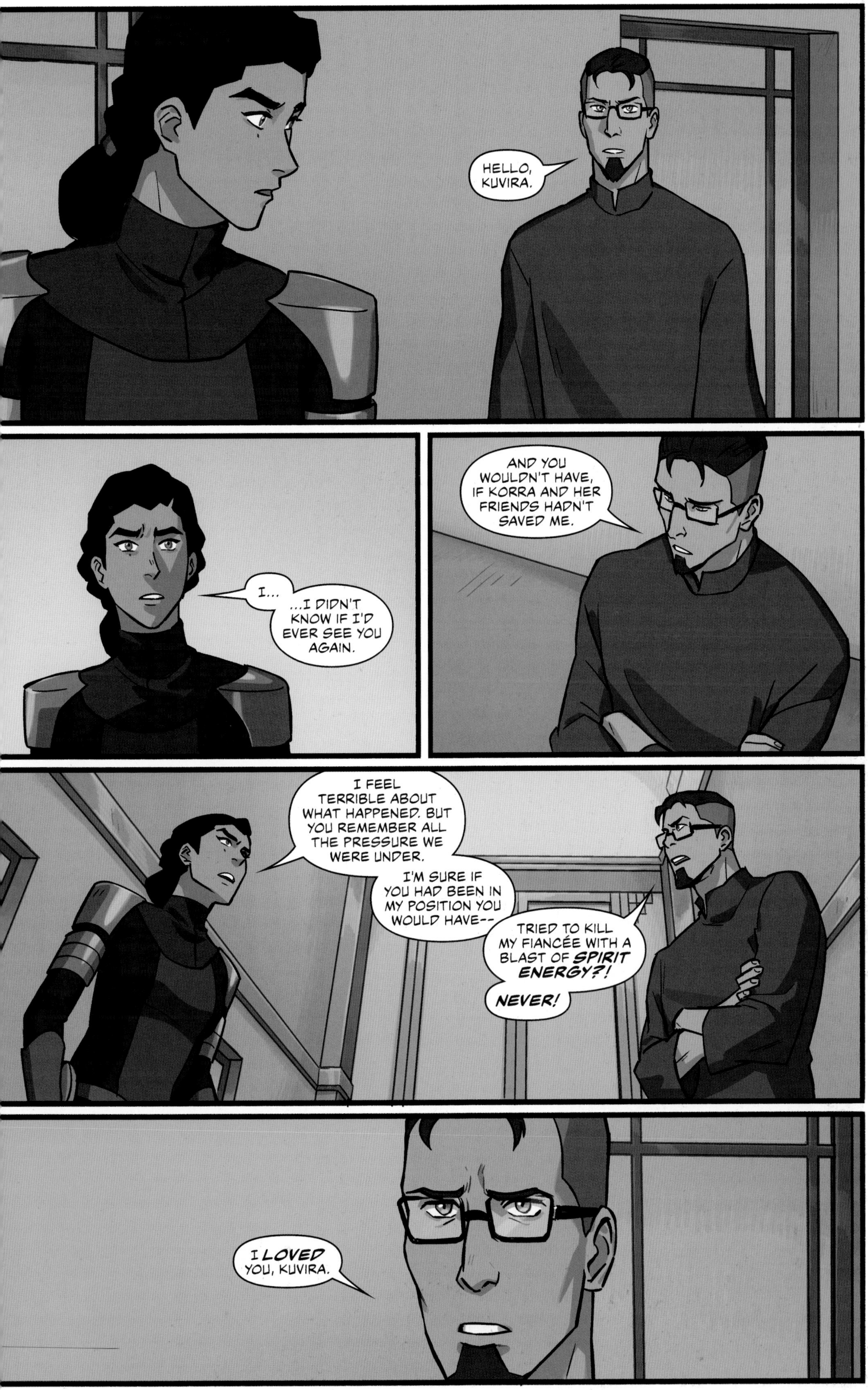
HELLO, KUVIRA.
I... ...I DIDN'T KNOW IF I'D EVER SEE YOU AGAIN.
AND YOU WOULDN'T HAVE, IF KORRA AND HER FRIENDS HADN'T SAVED ME.
I FEEL TERRIBLE ABOUT WHAT HAPPENED. BUT YOU REMEMBER ALL THE PRESSURE WE WERE UNDER.
I'M SURE IF YOU HAD BEEN IN MY POSITION YOU WOULD HAVE--
TRIED TO KILL MY FIANCÉE WITH A BLAST OF SPIRIT ENERGY?!
NEVER!
I LOVED YOU, KUVIRA.

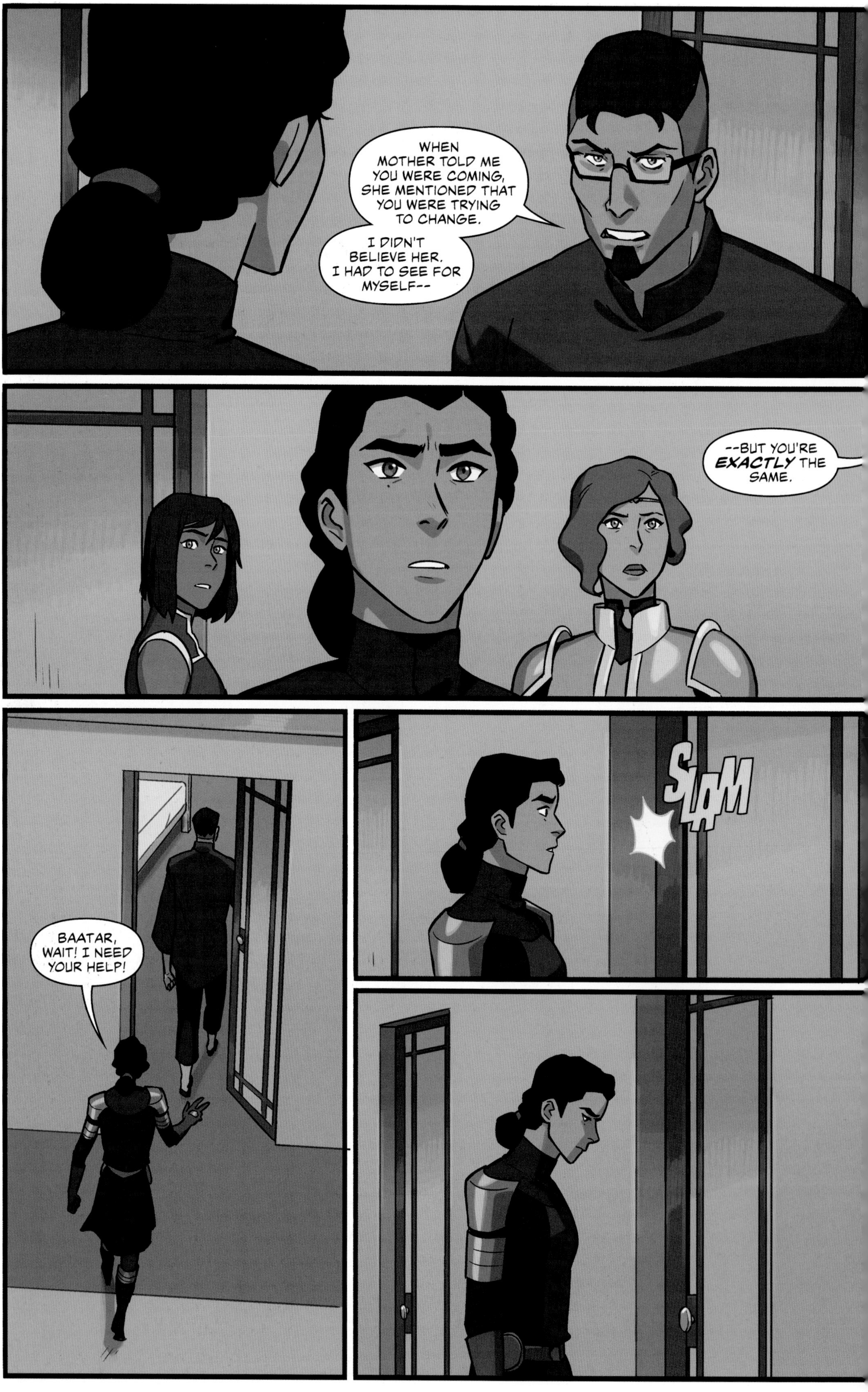
WHEN MOTHER TOLD ME YOU WERE COMING, SHE MENTIONED THAT YOU WERE TRYING TO CHANGE.
I DIDN'T BELIEVE HER. I HAD TO SEE FOR MYSELF--
--BUT YOU'RE *EXACTLY* THE SAME.
BAATAR, WAIT! I NEED YOUR HELP!
SLAM

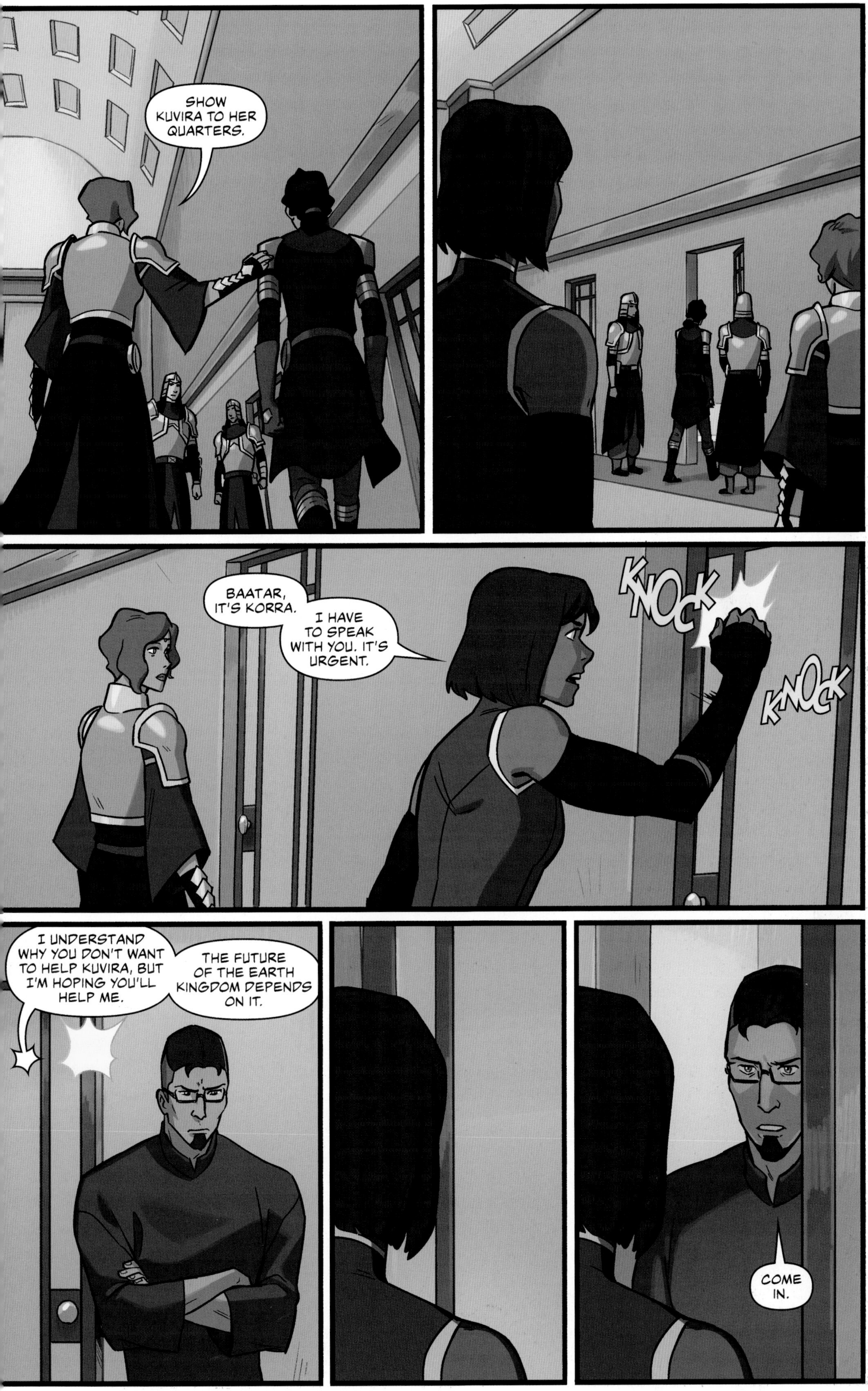
SHOW KUVIRA TO HER QUARTERS.
BAATAR, IT'S KORRA.
I HAVE TO SPEAK WITH YOU. IT'S URGENT.
KNOCK
KNOCK
I UNDERSTAND WHY YOU DON'T WANT TO HELP KUVIRA, BUT I'M HOPING YOU'LL HELP ME.
THE FUTURE OF THE EARTH KINGDOM DEPENDS ON IT.
COME IN.

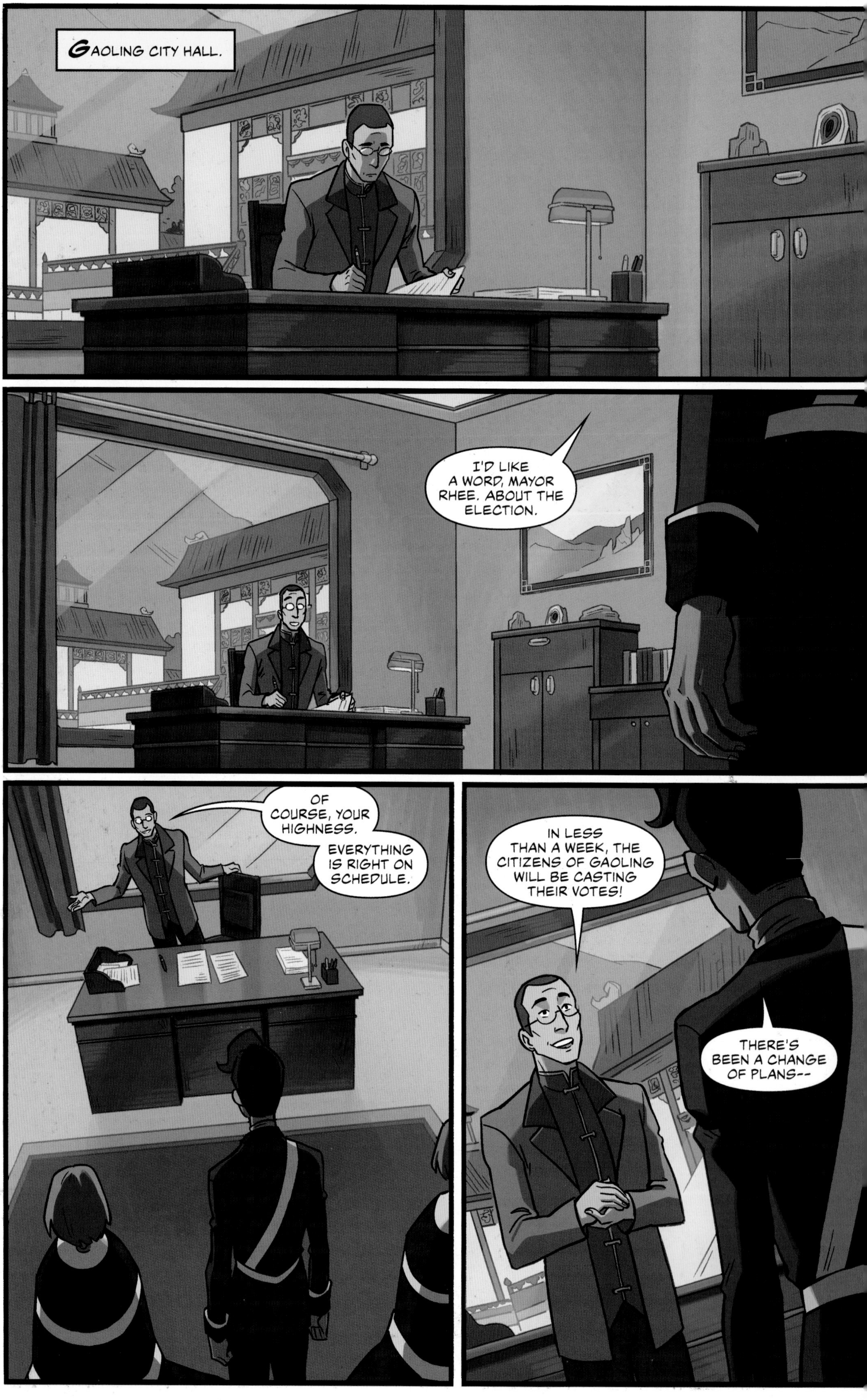
GAOLING CITY HALL.
I'D LIKE A WORD, MAYOR RHEE. ABOUT THE ELECTION.
OF COURSE, YOUR HIGHNESS.
EVERYTHING IS RIGHT ON SCHEDULE.
IN LESS THAN A WEEK, THE CITIZENS OF GAOLING WILL BE CASTING THEIR VOTES!
THERE'S BEEN A CHANGE OF PLANS--

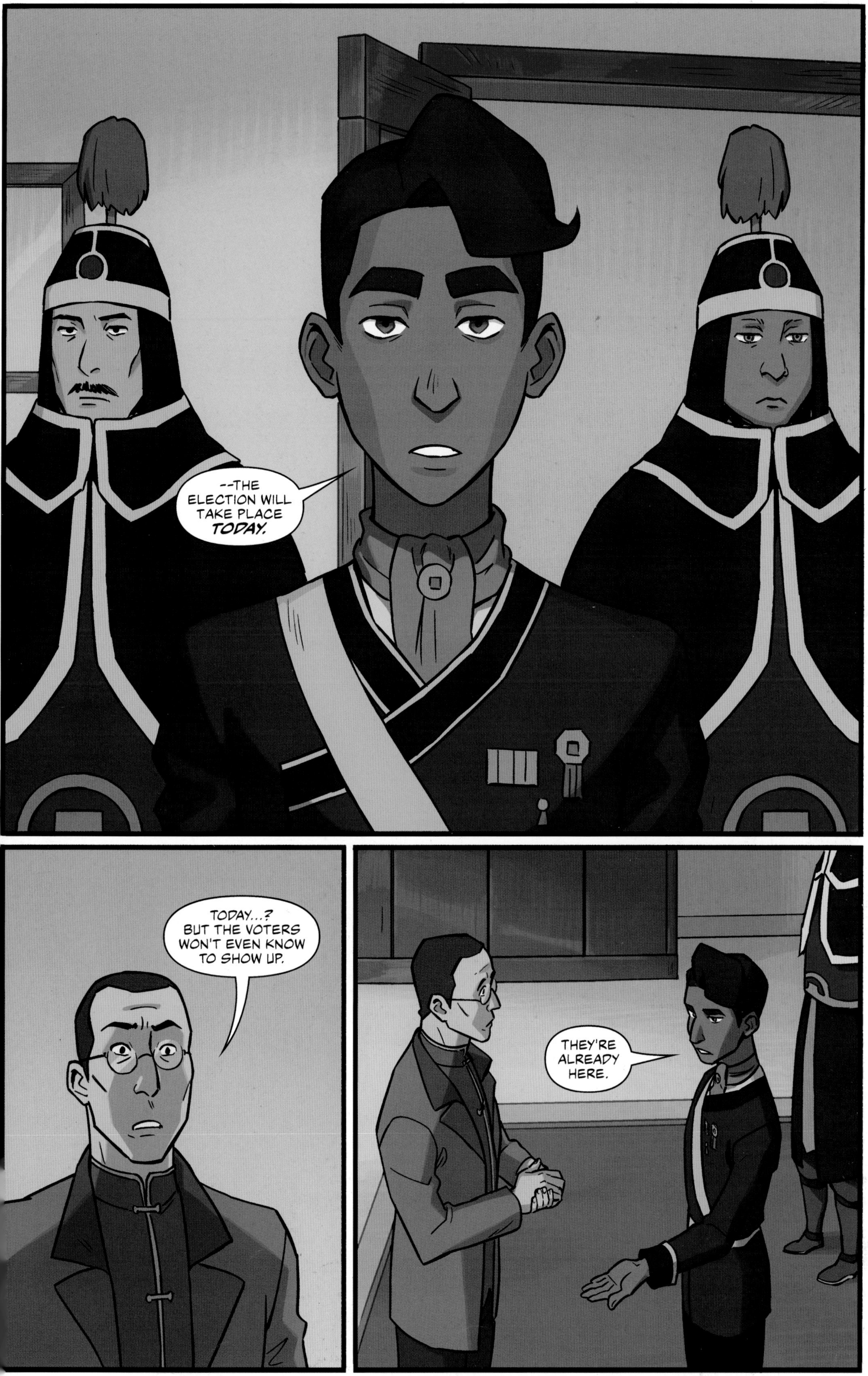
--THE ELECTION WILL TAKE PLACE *TODAY.*
TODAY...? BUT THE VOTERS WON'T EVEN KNOW TO SHOW UP.
THEY'RE ALREADY HERE.

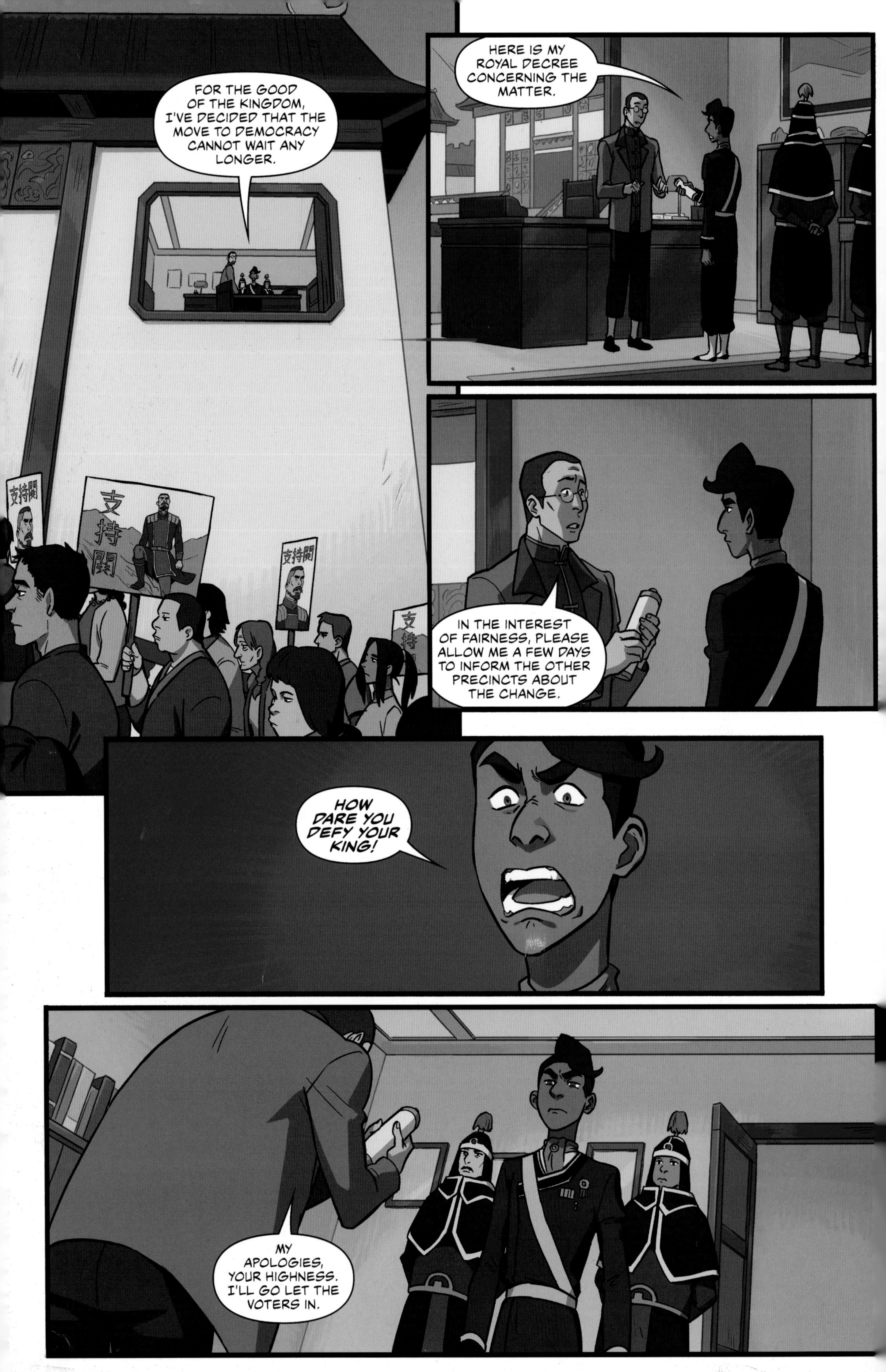
FOR THE GOOD OF THE KINGDOM, I'VE DECIDED THAT THE MOVE TO DEMOCRACY CANNOT WAIT ANY LONGER.
HERE IS MY ROYAL DECREE CONCERNING THE MATTER.
IN THE INTEREST OF FAIRNESS, PLEASE ALLOW ME A FEW DAYS TO INFORM THE OTHER PRECINCTS ABOUT THE CHANGE.
HOW DARE YOU DEFY YOUR KING!
MY APOLOGIES, YOUR HIGHNESS. I'LL GO LET THE VOTERS IN.

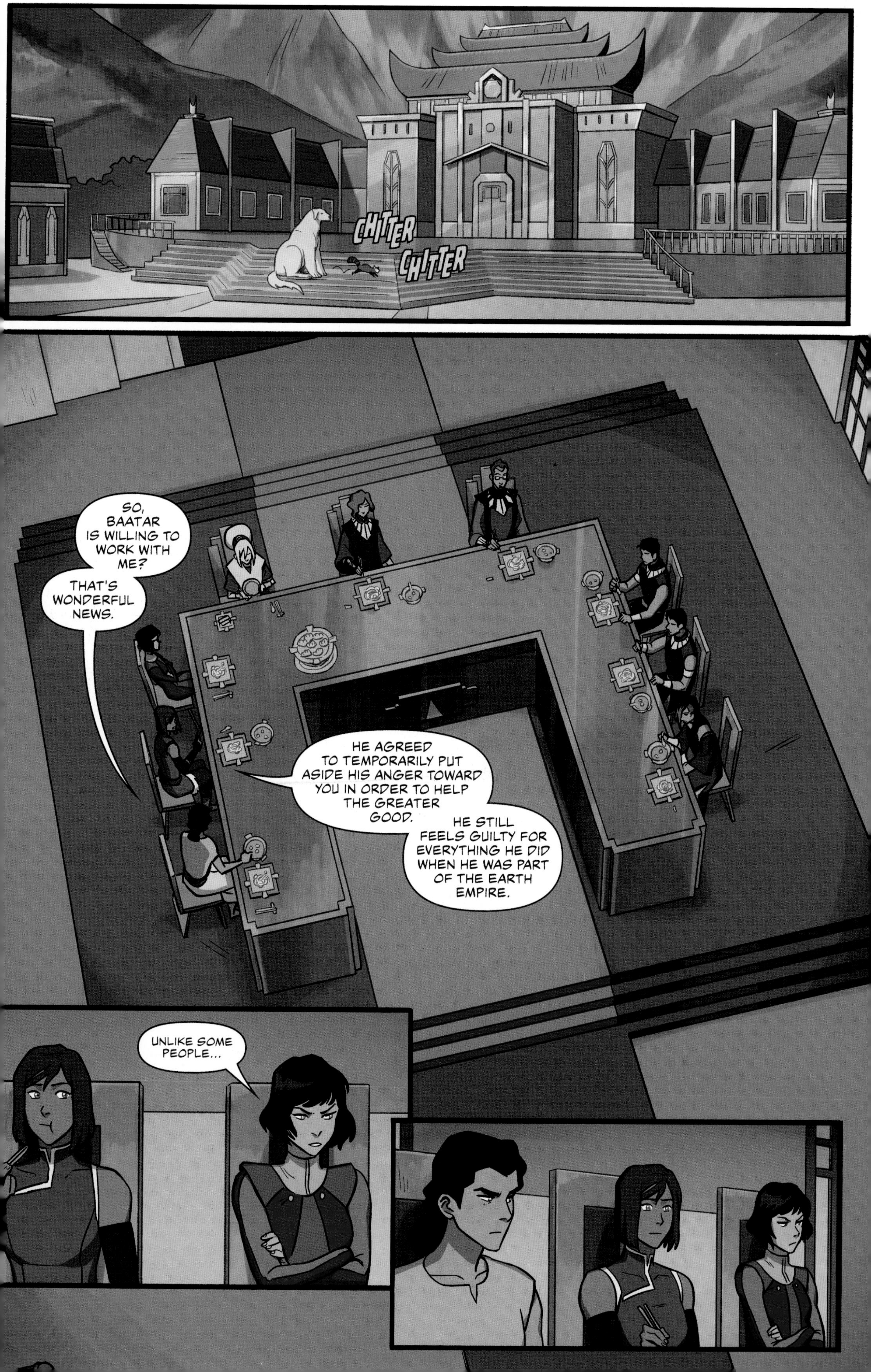
CHITTER
CHITTER
SO, BAATAR IS WILLING TO WORK WITH ME?
THAT'S WONDERFUL NEWS.
HE AGREED TO TEMPORARILY PUT ASIDE HIS ANGER TOWARD YOU IN ORDER TO HELP THE GREATER GOOD.
HE STILL FEELS GUILTY FOR EVERYTHING HE DID WHEN HE WAS PART OF THE EARTH EMPIRE.
UNLIKE SOME PEOPLE...

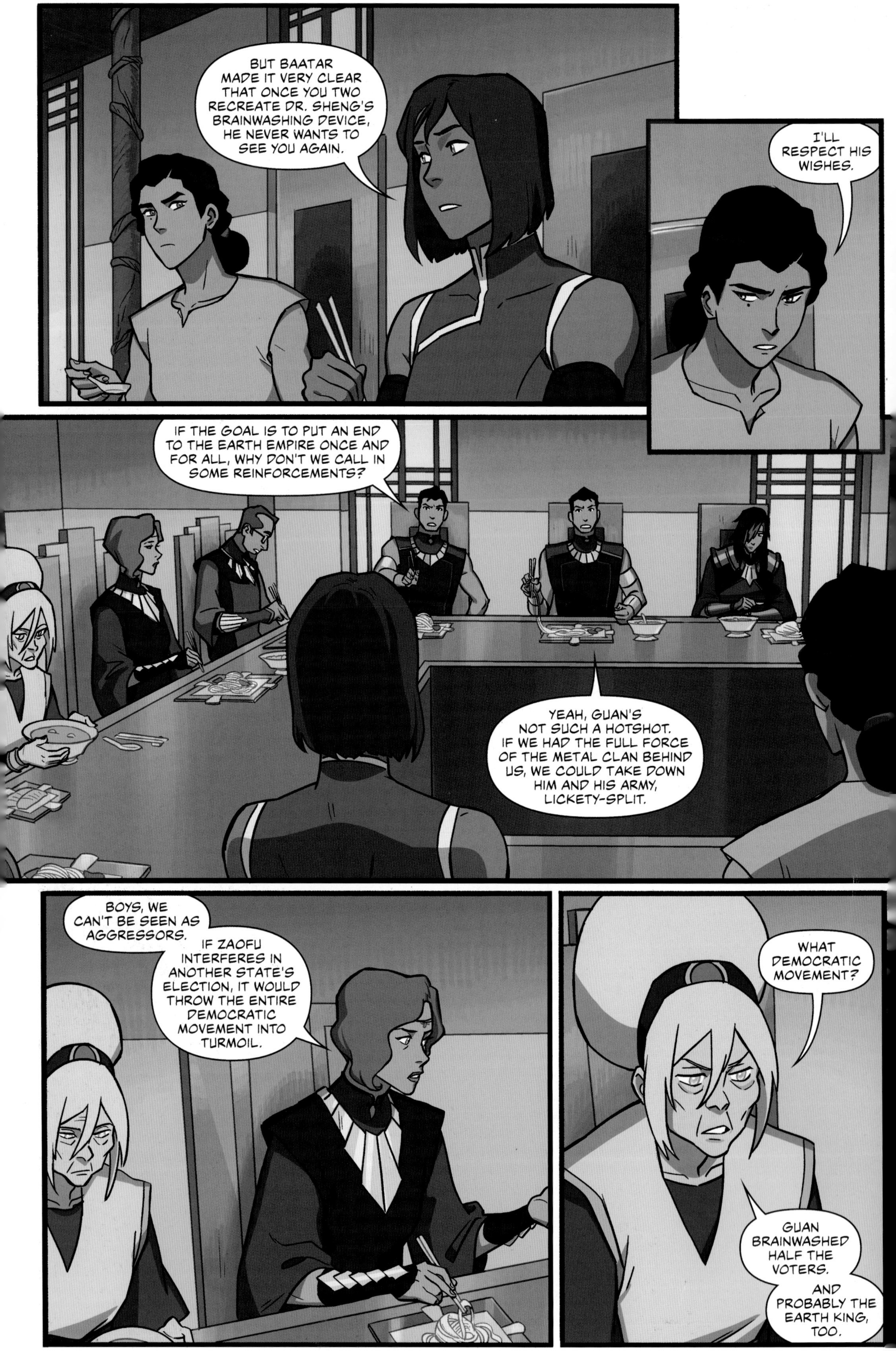
BUT BAATAR MADE IT VERY CLEAR THAT ONCE YOU TWO RECREATE DR. SHENG'S BRAINWASHING DEVICE, HE NEVER WANTS TO SEE YOU AGAIN.
I'LL RESPECT HIS WISHES.
IF THE GOAL IS TO PUT AN END TO THE EARTH EMPIRE ONCE AND FOR ALL, WHY DON'T WE CALL IN SOME REINFORCEMENTS?
YEAH, GUAN'S NOT SUCH A HOTSHOT. IF WE HAD THE FULL FORCE OF THE METAL CLAN BEHIND US, WE COULD TAKE DOWN HIM AND HIS ARMY, LICKETY-SPLIT.
BOYS, WE CAN'T BE SEEN AS AGGRESSORS.
IF ZAOFU INTERFERES IN ANOTHER STATE'S ELECTION, IT WOULD THROW THE ENTIRE DEMOCRATIC MOVEMENT INTO TURMOIL.
WHAT DEMOCRATIC MOVEMENT?
GUAN BRAINWASHED HALF THE VOTERS.
AND PROBABLY THE EARTH KING, TOO.

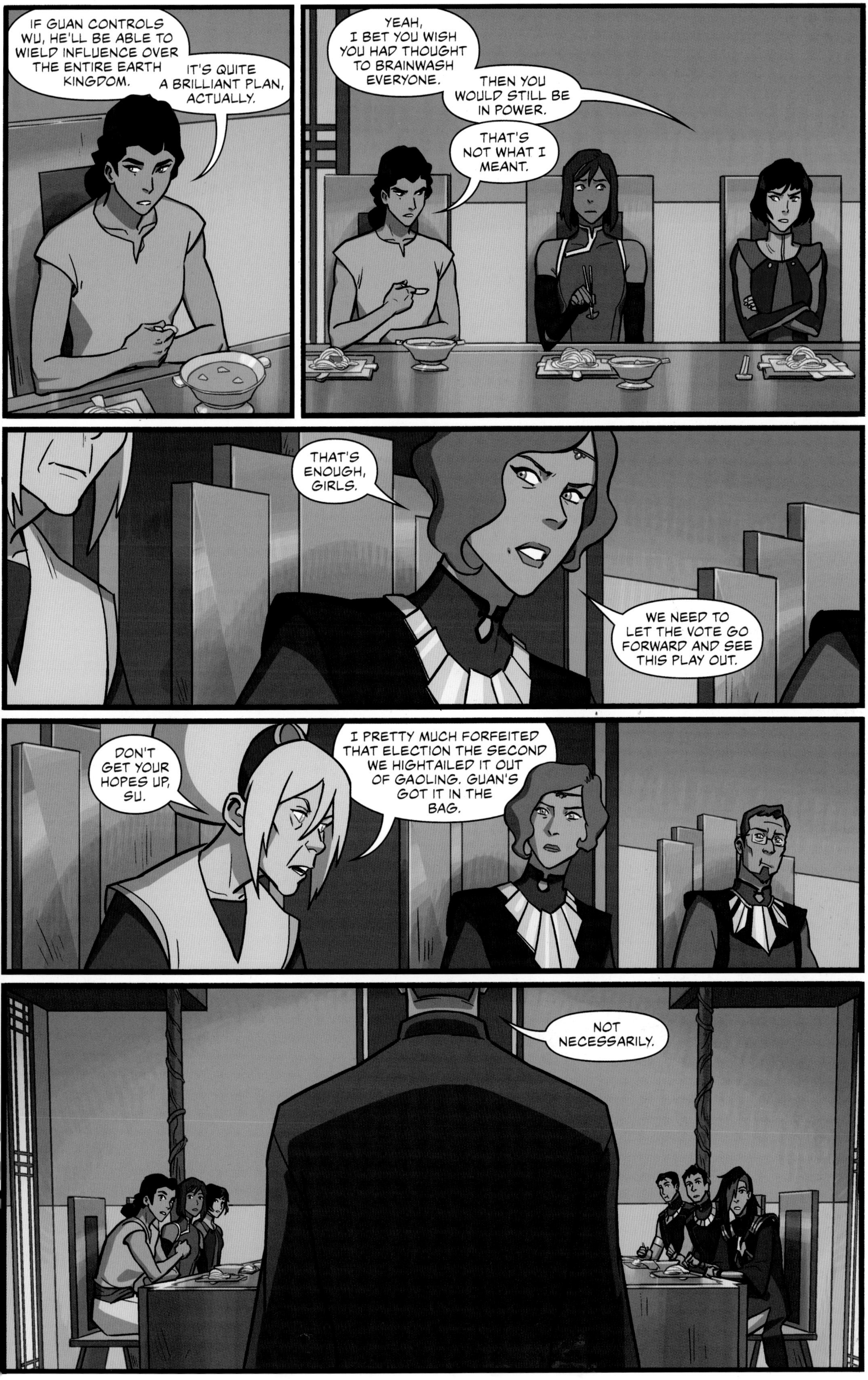
IF GUAN CONTROLS WU, HE'LL BE ABLE TO WIELD INFLUENCE OVER THE ENTIRE EARTH KINGDOM.
IT'S QUITE A BRILLIANT PLAN, ACTUALLY.
YEAH, I BET YOU WISH YOU HAD THOUGHT TO BRAINWASH EVERYONE.
THEN YOU WOULD STILL BE IN POWER.
THAT'S NOT WHAT I MEANT.
THAT'S ENOUGH, GIRLS.
WE NEED TO LET THE VOTE GO FORWARD AND SEE THIS PLAY OUT.
DON'T GET YOUR HOPES UP, SU.
I PRETTY MUCH FORFEITED THAT ELECTION THE SECOND WE HIGHTAILED IT OUT OF GAOLING. GUAN'S GOT IT IN THE BAG.
NOT NECESSARILY.

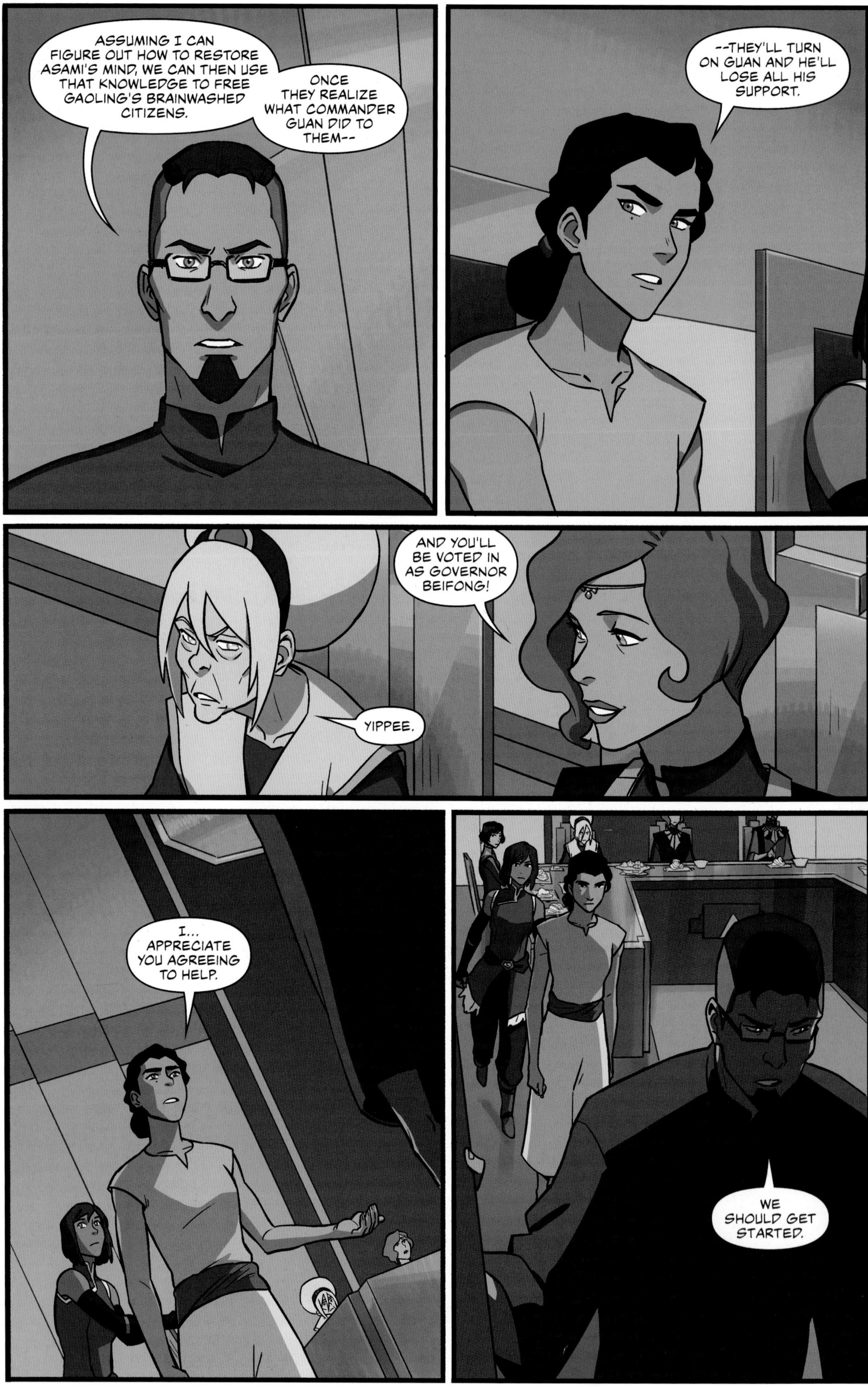
ASSUMING I CAN FIGURE OUT HOW TO RESTORE ASAMI'S MIND, WE CAN THEN USE THAT KNOWLEDGE TO FREE GAOLING'S BRAINWASHED CITIZENS.
ONCE THEY REALIZE WHAT COMMANDER GUAN DID TO THEM--
--THEY'LL TURN ON GUAN AND HE'LL LOSE ALL HIS SUPPORT.
AND YOU'LL BE VOTED IN AS GOVERNOR BEIFONG!
YIPPEE.
I... APPRECIATE YOU AGREEING TO HELP.
WE SHOULD GET STARTED.

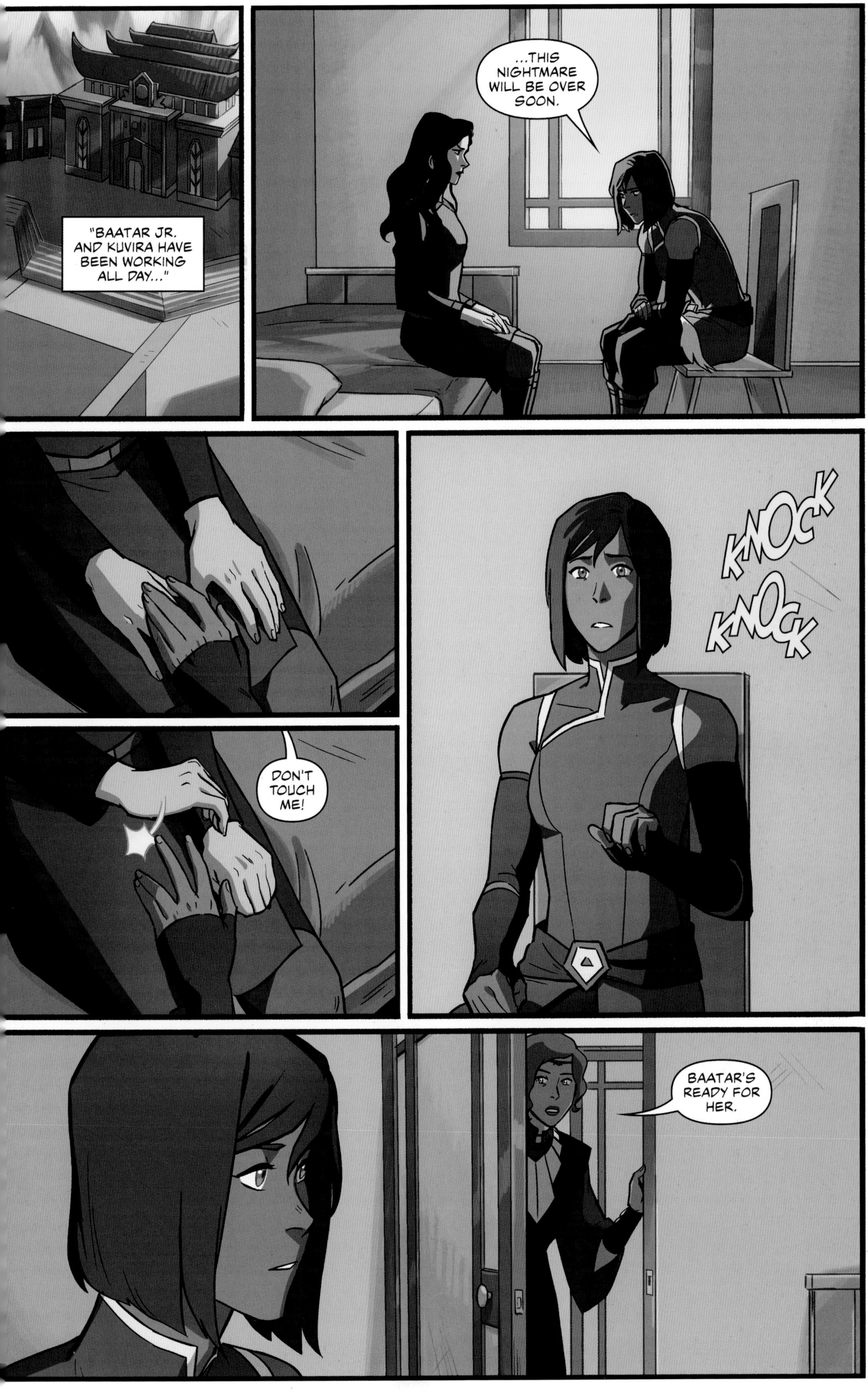
"BAATAR JR. AND KUVIRA HAVE BEEN WORKING ALL DAY..."
...THIS NIGHTMARE WILL BE OVER SOON.
DON'T TOUCH ME!
KNOCK KNOCK
BAATAR'S READY FOR HER.

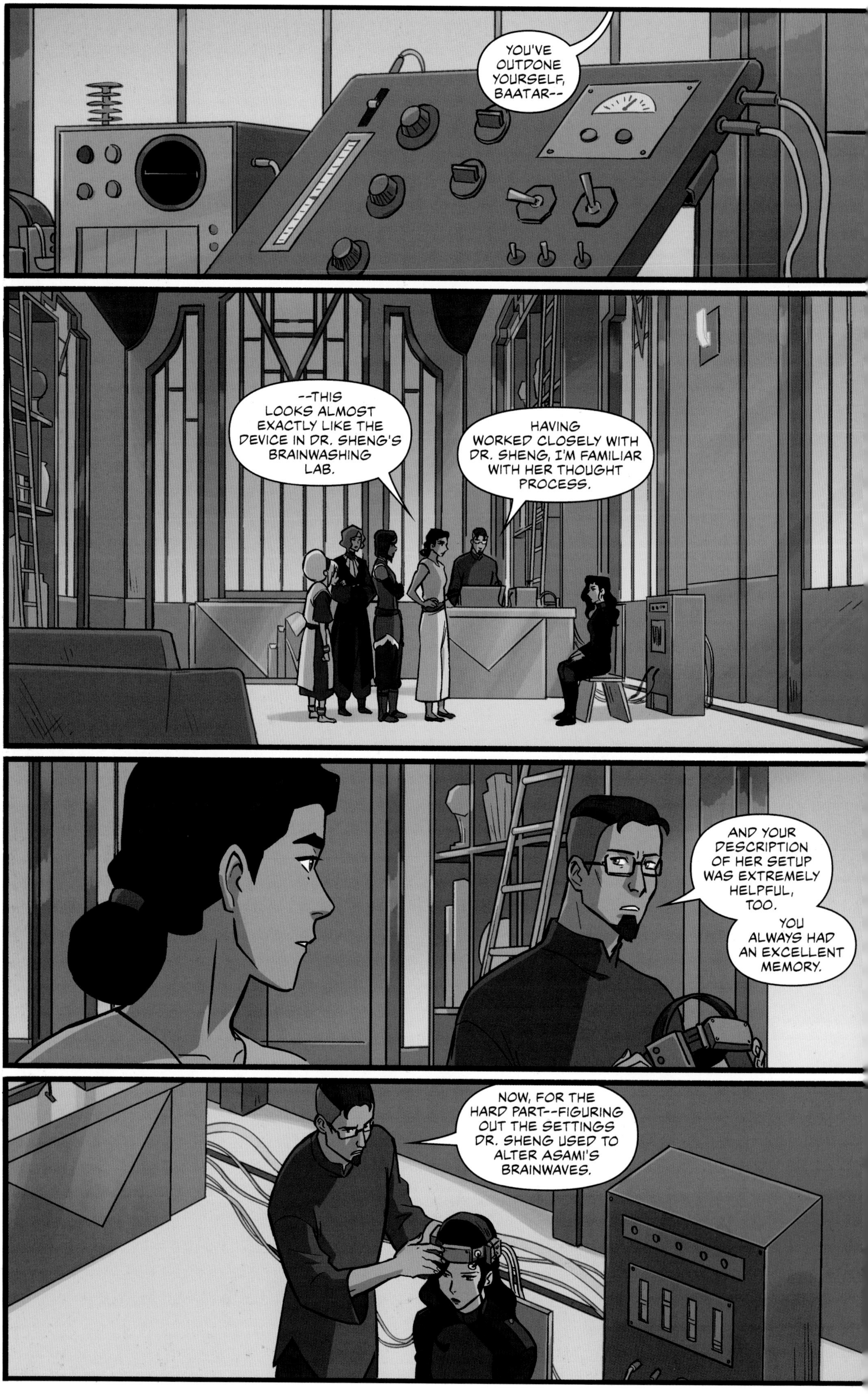
YOU'VE OUTDONE YOURSELF, BAATAR--
--THIS LOOKS ALMOST EXACTLY LIKE THE DEVICE IN DR. SHENG'S BRAINWASHING LAB.
HAVING WORKED CLOSELY WITH DR. SHENG, I'M FAMILIAR WITH HER THOUGHT PROCESS.
AND YOUR DESCRIPTION OF HER SETUP WAS EXTREMELY HELPFUL, TOO.
YOU ALWAYS HAD AN EXCELLENT MEMORY.
NOW, FOR THE HARD PART--FIGURING OUT THE SETTINGS DR. SHENG USED TO ALTER ASAMI'S BRAINWAVES.

I'LL BEGIN WITH LOW-INTENSITY ELECTROMAGNETIC PULSES.

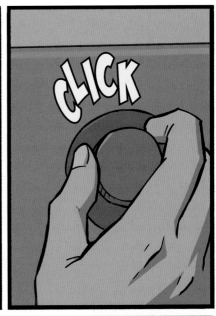

CLICK

YOU WILL NO LONGER OBEY COMMANDER GUAN'S ORDERS.

THE AVATAR IS NO LONGER YOUR ENEMY.

YOUR MIND IS YOURS AGAIN.

I AM ONLY LOYAL TO COMMANDER GUAN.

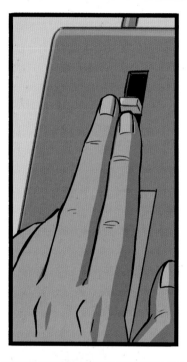

YOU WILL NO LONGER OBEY COMMANDER GUAN'S ORDERS.

THE AVATAR IS NO LONGER YOUR ENEMY.

YOUR MIND IS YOURS AGAIN.

I AM ONLY LOYAL TO COMMANDER GUAN.

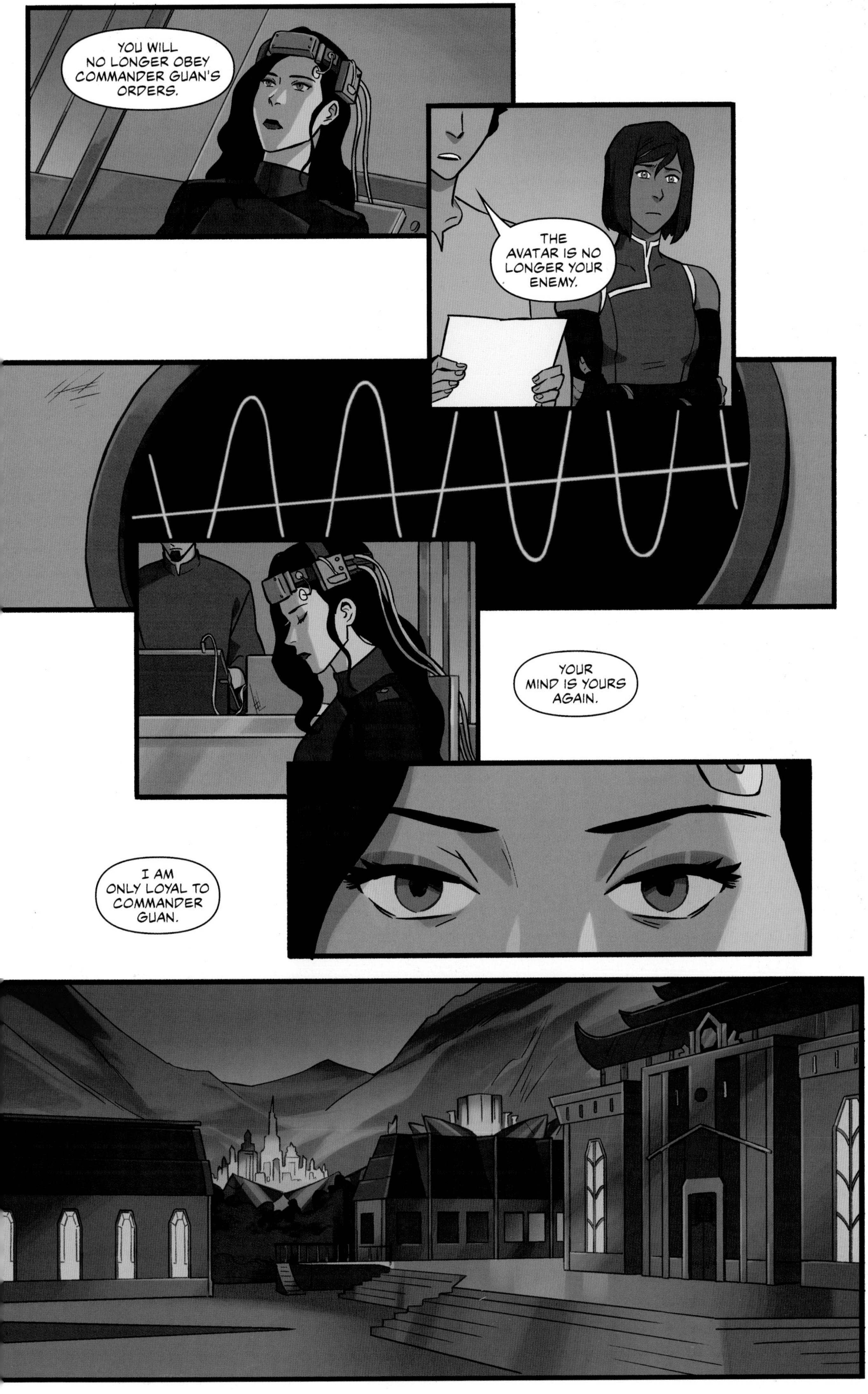
YOU WILL NO LONGER OBEY COMMANDER GUAN'S ORDERS.
THE AVATAR IS NO LONGER YOUR ENEMY.
YOUR MIND IS YOURS AGAIN.
I AM ONLY LOYAL TO COMMANDER GUAN.

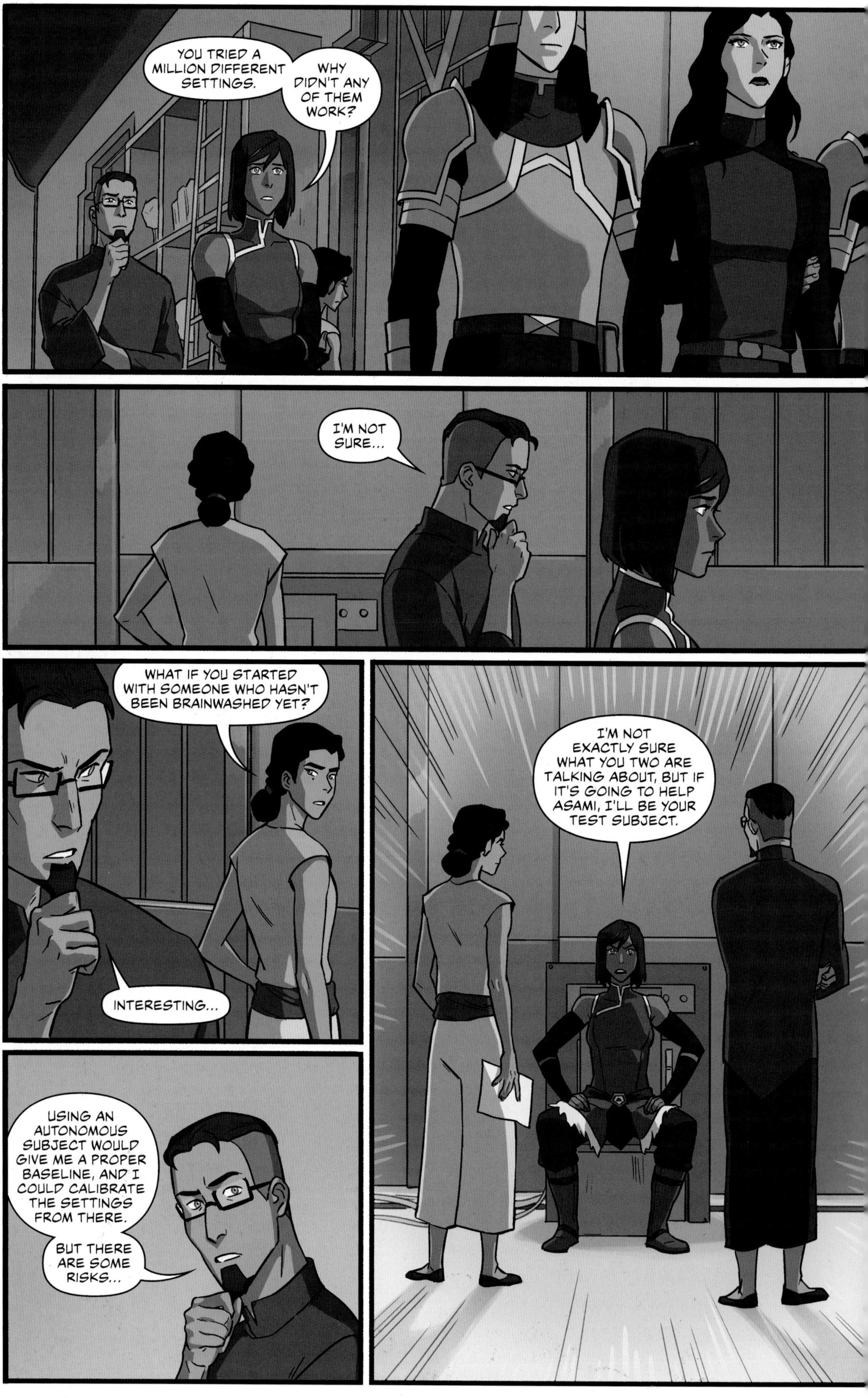
YOU TRIED A MILLION DIFFERENT SETTINGS.
WHY DIDN'T ANY OF THEM WORK?
I'M NOT SURE...
WHAT IF YOU STARTED WITH SOMEONE WHO HASN'T BEEN BRAINWASHED YET?
INTERESTING...
I'M NOT EXACTLY SURE WHAT YOU TWO ARE TALKING ABOUT, BUT IF IT'S GOING TO HELP ASAMI, I'LL BE YOUR TEST SUBJECT.
USING AN AUTONOMOUS SUBJECT WOULD GIVE ME A PROPER BASELINE, AND I COULD CALIBRATE THE SETTINGS FROM THERE.
BUT THERE ARE SOME RISKS...

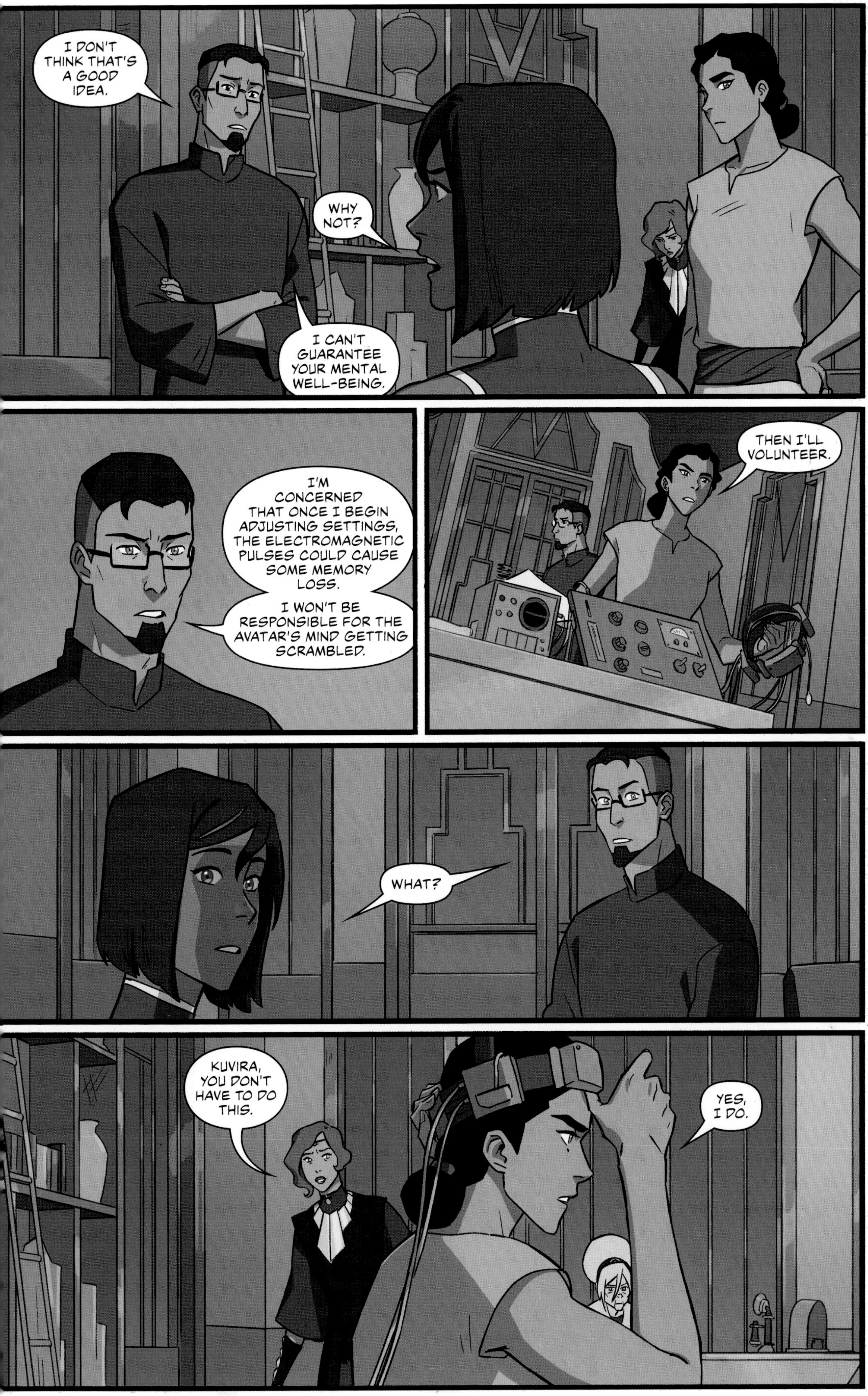
I DON'T THINK THAT'S A GOOD IDEA.
WHY NOT?
I CAN'T GUARANTEE YOUR MENTAL WELL-BEING.
I'M CONCERNED THAT ONCE I BEGIN ADJUSTING SETTINGS, THE ELECTROMAGNETIC PULSES COULD CAUSE SOME MEMORY LOSS.
I WON'T BE RESPONSIBLE FOR THE AVATAR'S MIND GETTING SCRAMBLED.
THEN I'LL VOLUNTEER.
WHAT?
KUVIRA, YOU DON'T HAVE TO DO THIS.
YES, I DO.

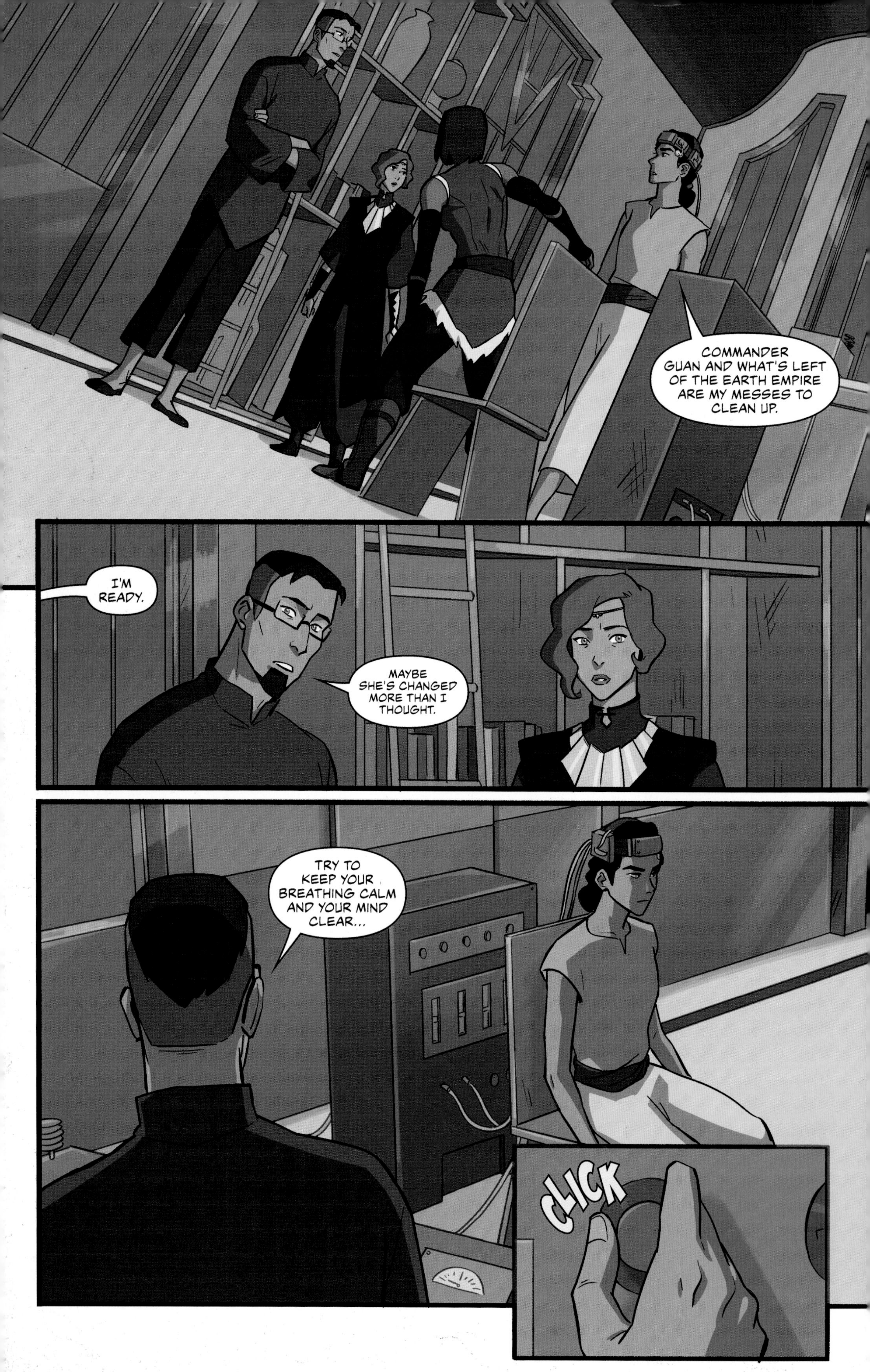
COMMANDER GUAN AND WHAT'S LEFT OF THE EARTH EMPIRE ARE MY MESSES TO CLEAN UP.
I'M READY.
MAYBE SHE'S CHANGED MORE THAN I THOUGHT.
TRY TO KEEP YOUR BREATHING CALM AND YOUR MIND CLEAR...
CLICK

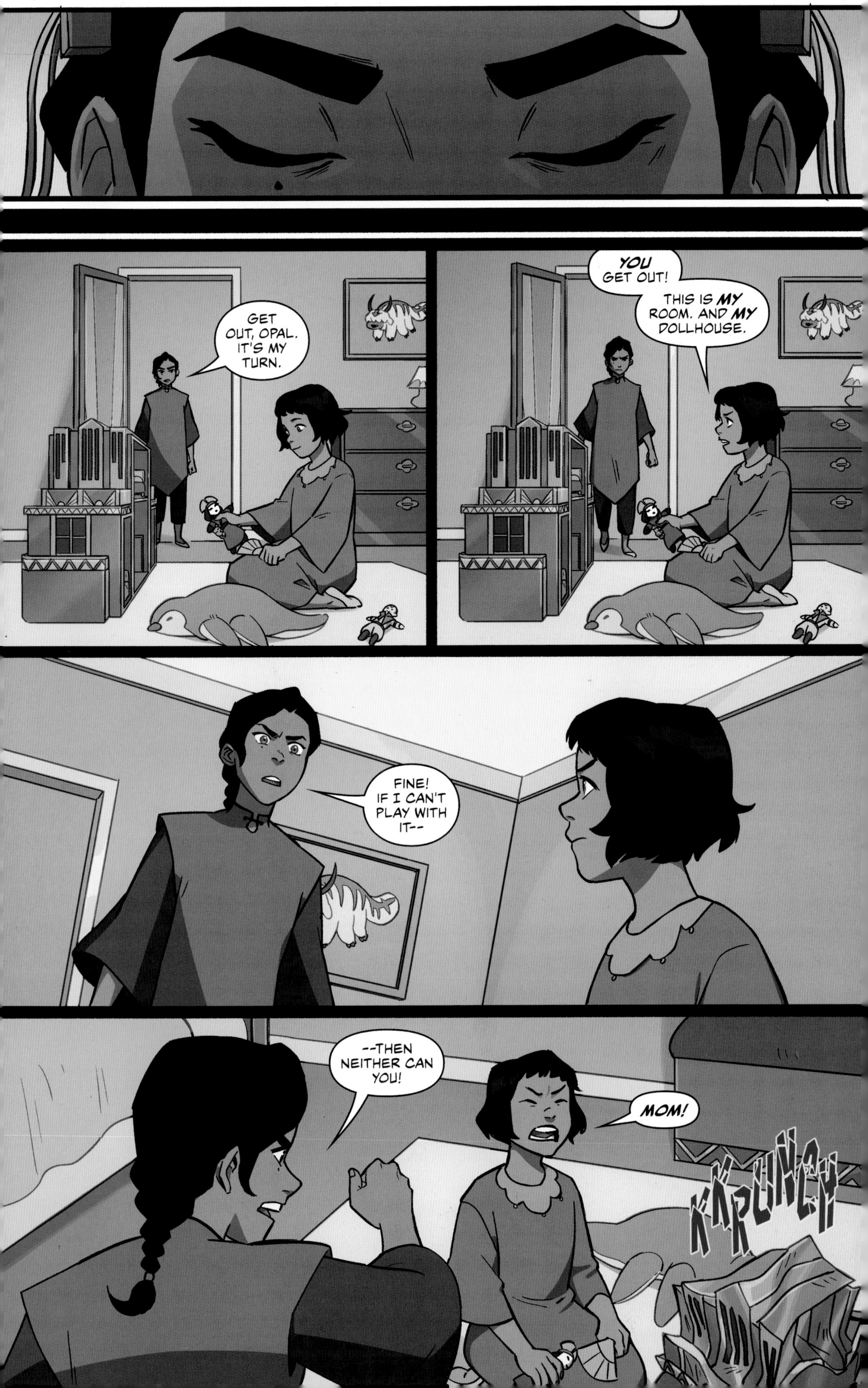
GET OUT, OPAL. IT'S MY TURN.
YOU GET OUT!
THIS IS MY ROOM. AND MY DOLLHOUSE.
FINE! IF I CAN'T PLAY WITH IT--
--THEN NEITHER CAN YOU!
MOM!
KKRUNCH

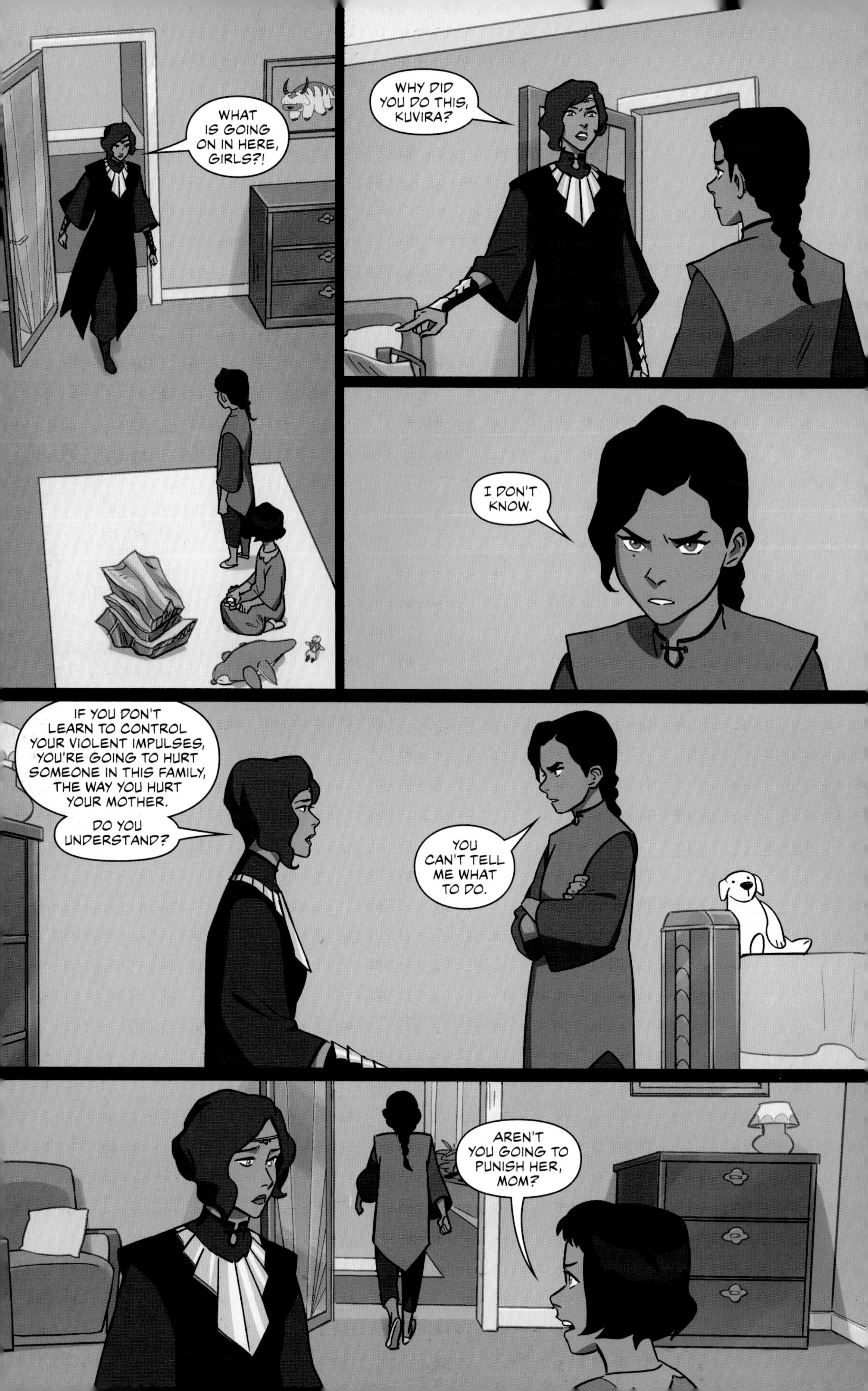
WHAT IS GOING ON IN HERE, GIRLS?!
WHY DID YOU DO THIS, KUVIRA?
I DON'T KNOW.
IF YOU DON'T LEARN TO CONTROL YOUR VIOLENT IMPULSES, YOU'RE GOING TO HURT SOMEONE IN THIS FAMILY, THE WAY YOU HURT YOUR MOTHER.
DO YOU UNDERSTAND?
YOU CAN'T TELL ME WHAT TO DO.
AREN'T YOU GOING TO PUNISH HER, MOM?

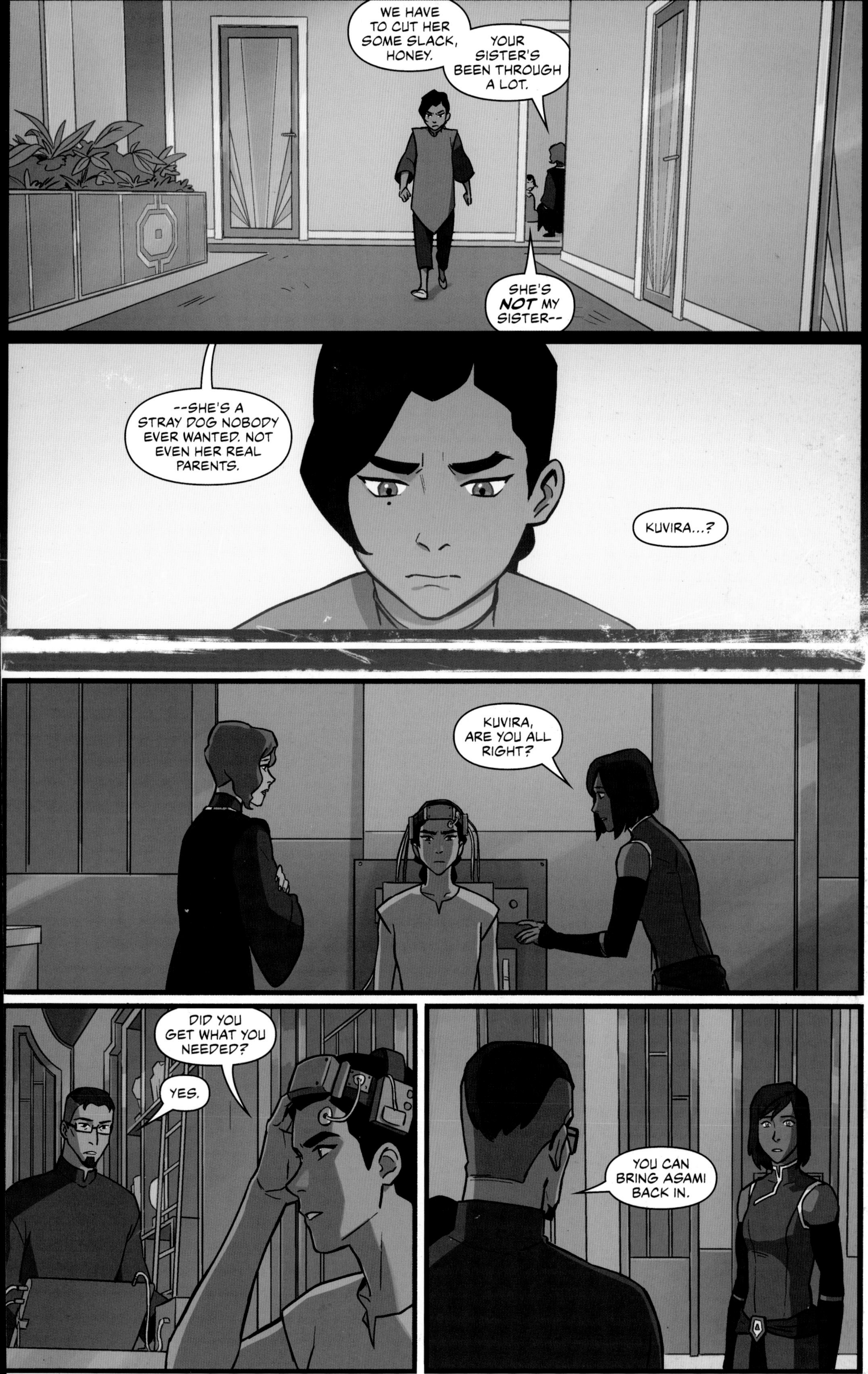
WE HAVE TO CUT HER SOME SLACK, HONEY.
YOUR SISTER'S BEEN THROUGH A LOT.
SHE'S ***NOT*** MY SISTER--
--SHE'S A STRAY DOG NOBODY EVER WANTED. NOT EVEN HER REAL PARENTS.
KUVIRA...?
KUVIRA, ARE YOU ALL RIGHT?
DID YOU GET WHAT YOU NEEDED?
YES.
YOU CAN BRING ASAMI BACK IN.

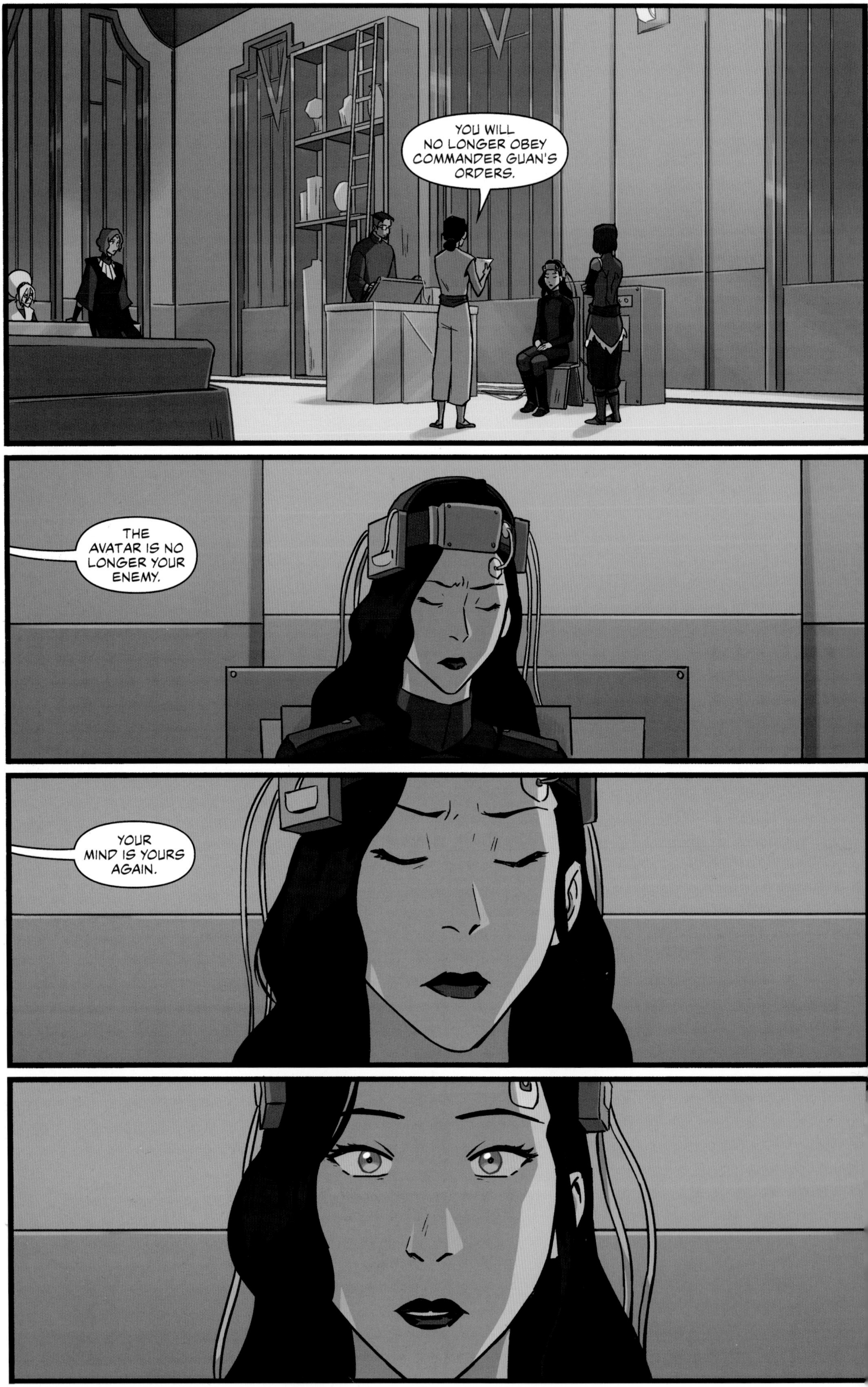
YOU WILL NO LONGER OBEY COMMANDER GUAN'S ORDERS.
THE AVATAR IS NO LONGER YOUR ENEMY.
YOUR MIND IS YOURS AGAIN.

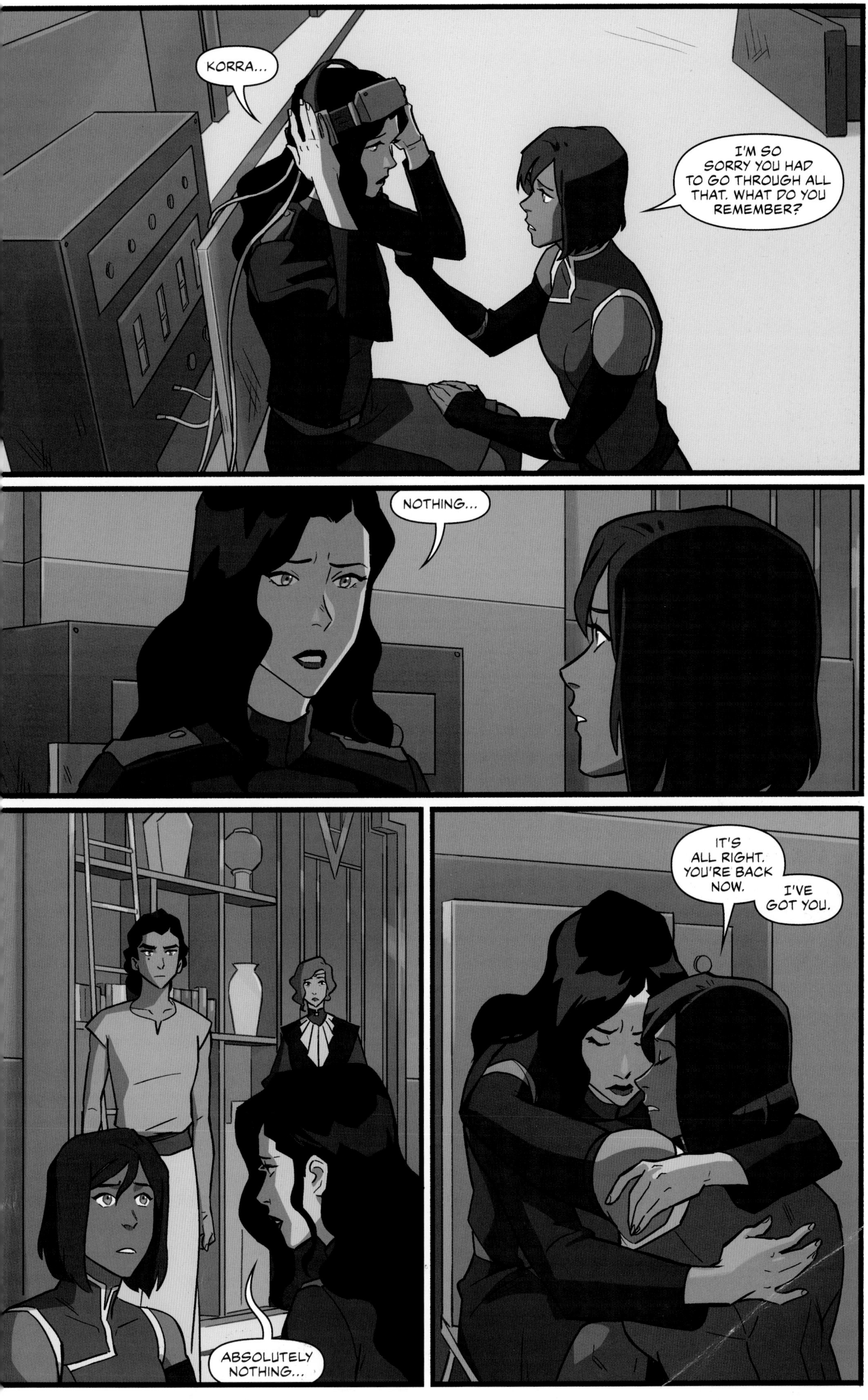
KORRA...
I'M SO SORRY YOU HAD TO GO THROUGH ALL THAT. WHAT DO YOU REMEMBER?
NOTHING...
ABSOLUTELY NOTHING...
IT'S ALL RIGHT. YOU'RE BACK NOW.
I'VE GOT YOU.

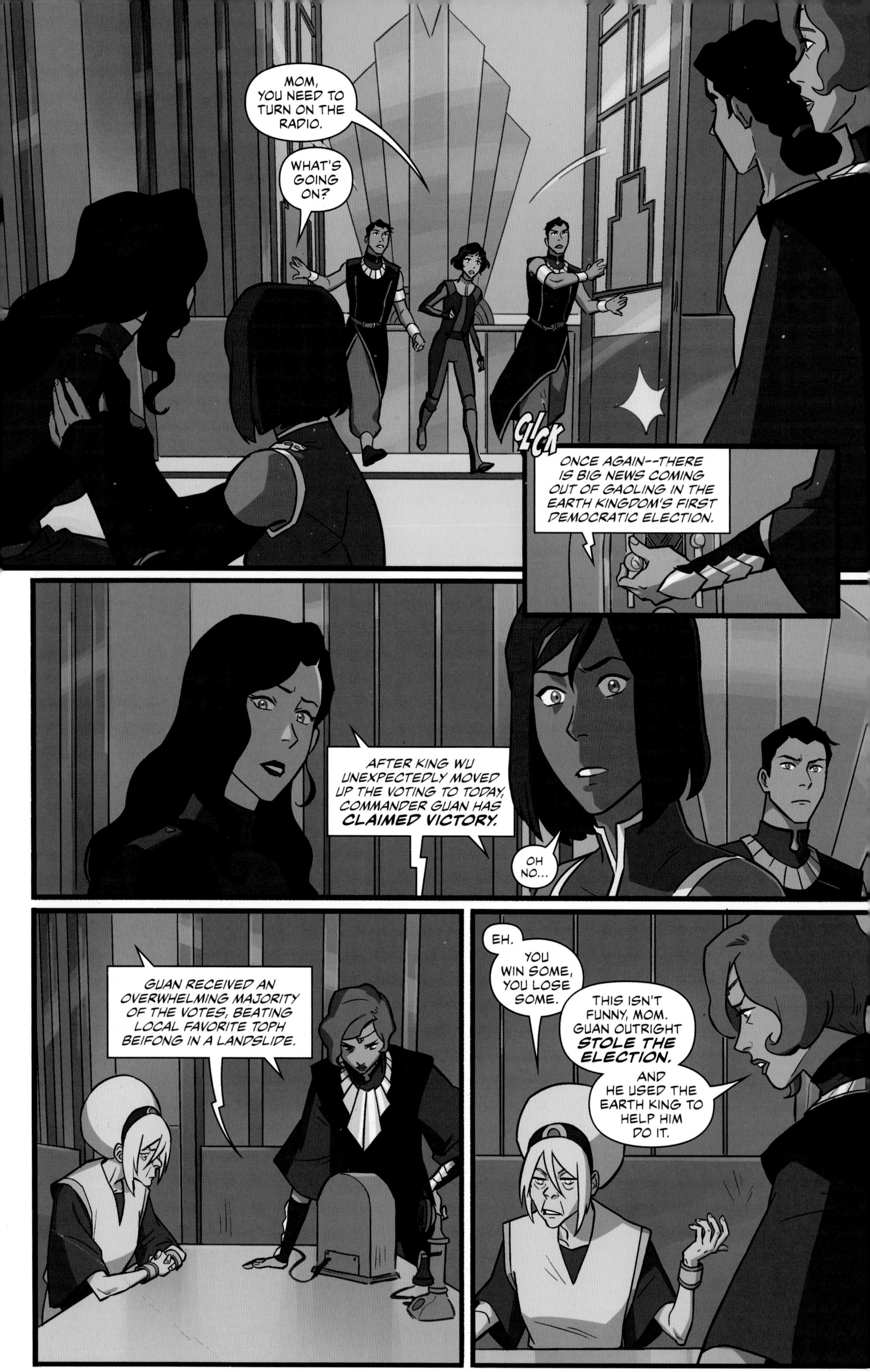
MOM, YOU NEED TO TURN ON THE RADIO.
WHAT'S GOING ON?
CLICK
ONCE AGAIN--THERE IS BIG NEWS COMING OUT OF GAOLING IN THE EARTH KINGDOM'S FIRST DEMOCRATIC ELECTION.
AFTER KING WU UNEXPECTEDLY MOVED UP THE VOTING TO TODAY, COMMANDER GUAN HAS **CLAIMED VICTORY.**
OH NO...
GUAN RECEIVED AN OVERWHELMING MAJORITY OF THE VOTES, BEATING LOCAL FAVORITE TOPH BEIFONG IN A LANDSLIDE.
EH.
YOU WIN SOME, YOU LOSE SOME.
THIS ISN'T FUNNY, MOM. GUAN OUTRIGHT **STOLE THE ELECTION.**
AND HE USED THE EARTH KING TO HELP HIM DO IT.

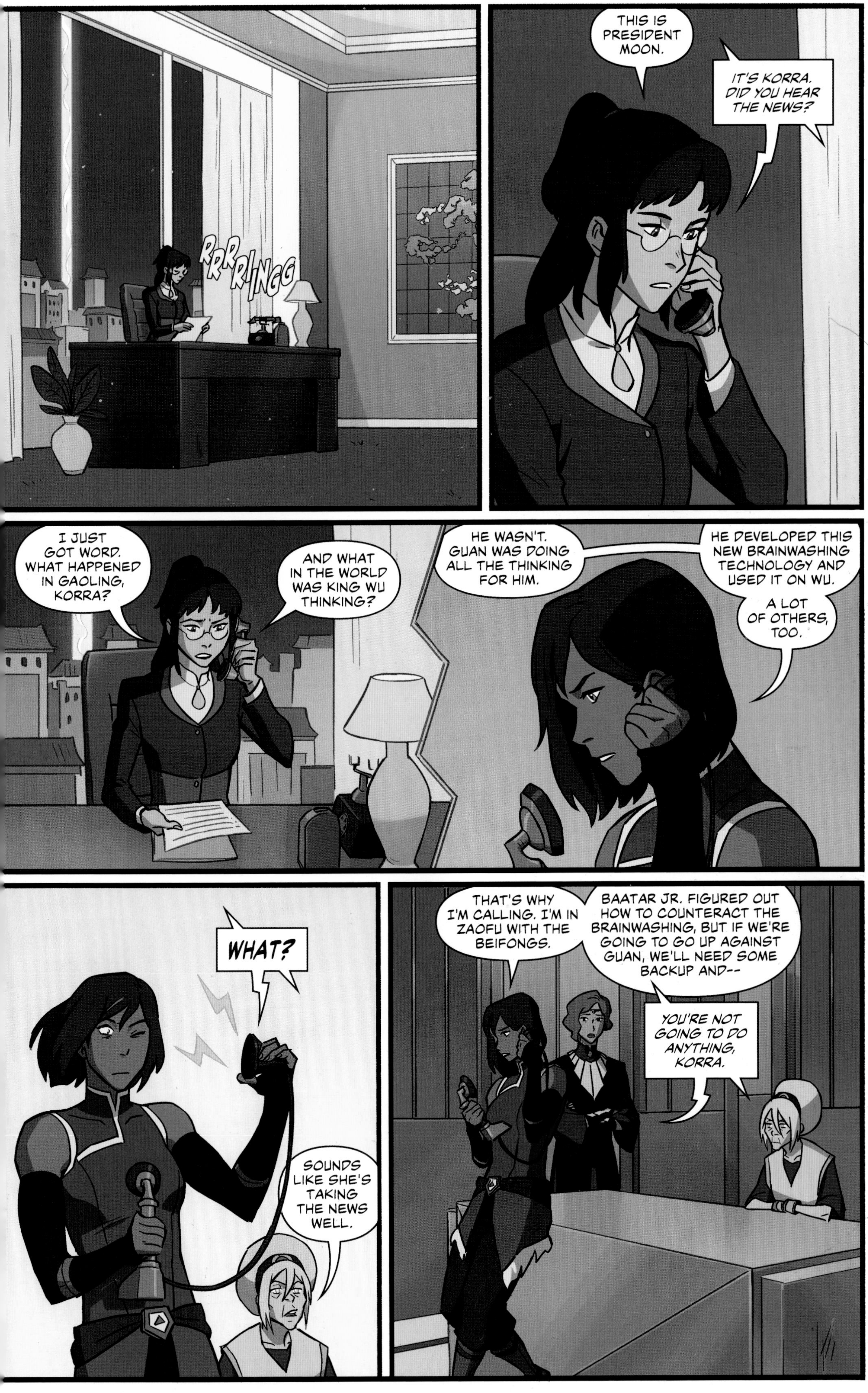
RRRRINGG
THIS IS PRESIDENT MOON.
IT'S KORRA. DID YOU HEAR THE NEWS?
I JUST GOT WORD. WHAT HAPPENED IN GAOLING, KORRA?
AND WHAT IN THE WORLD WAS KING WU THINKING?
HE WASN'T. GUAN WAS DOING ALL THE THINKING FOR HIM.
HE DEVELOPED THIS NEW BRAINWASHING TECHNOLOGY AND USED IT ON WU.
A LOT OF OTHERS, TOO.
WHAT?
SOUNDS LIKE SHE'S TAKING THE NEWS WELL.
THAT'S WHY I'M CALLING. I'M IN ZAOFU WITH THE BEIFONGS.
BAATAR JR. FIGURED OUT HOW TO COUNTERACT THE BRAINWASHING, BUT IF WE'RE GOING TO GO UP AGAINST GUAN, WE'LL NEED SOME BACKUP AND--
YOU'RE NOT GOING TO DO ANYTHING, KORRA.

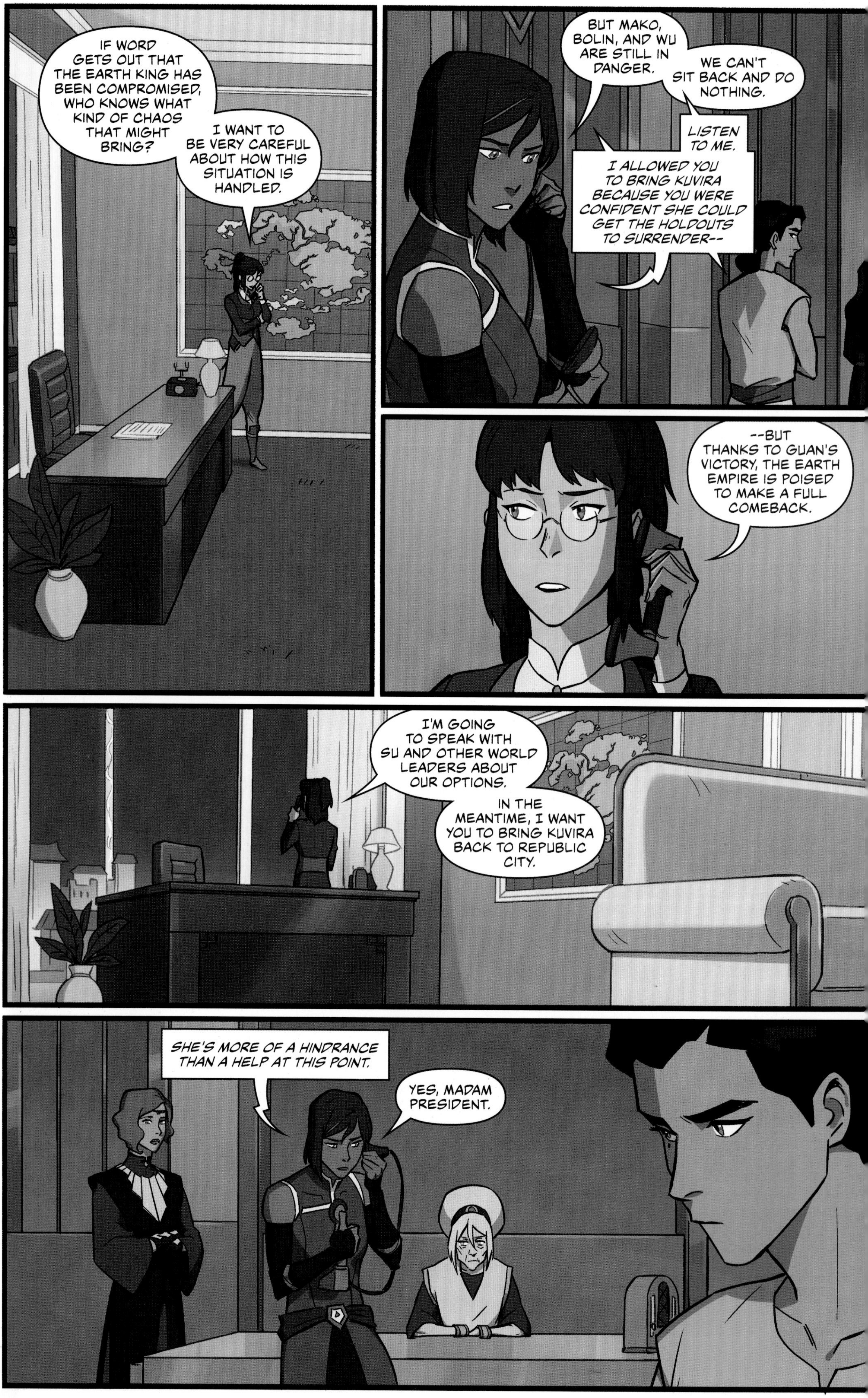
IF WORD GETS OUT THAT THE EARTH KING HAS BEEN COMPROMISED, WHO KNOWS WHAT KIND OF CHAOS THAT MIGHT BRING?
I WANT TO BE VERY CAREFUL ABOUT HOW THIS SITUATION IS HANDLED.
BUT MAKO, BOLIN, AND WU ARE STILL IN DANGER.
WE CAN'T SIT BACK AND DO NOTHING.
LISTEN TO ME.
I ALLOWED YOU TO BRING KUVIRA BECAUSE YOU WERE CONFIDENT SHE COULD GET THE HOLDOUTS TO SURRENDER--
--BUT THANKS TO GUAN'S VICTORY, THE EARTH EMPIRE IS POISED TO MAKE A FULL COMEBACK.
I'M GOING TO SPEAK WITH SU AND OTHER WORLD LEADERS ABOUT OUR OPTIONS.
IN THE MEANTIME, I WANT YOU TO BRING KUVIRA BACK TO REPUBLIC CITY.
SHE'S MORE OF A HINDRANCE THAN A HELP AT THIS POINT.
YES, MADAM PRESIDENT.

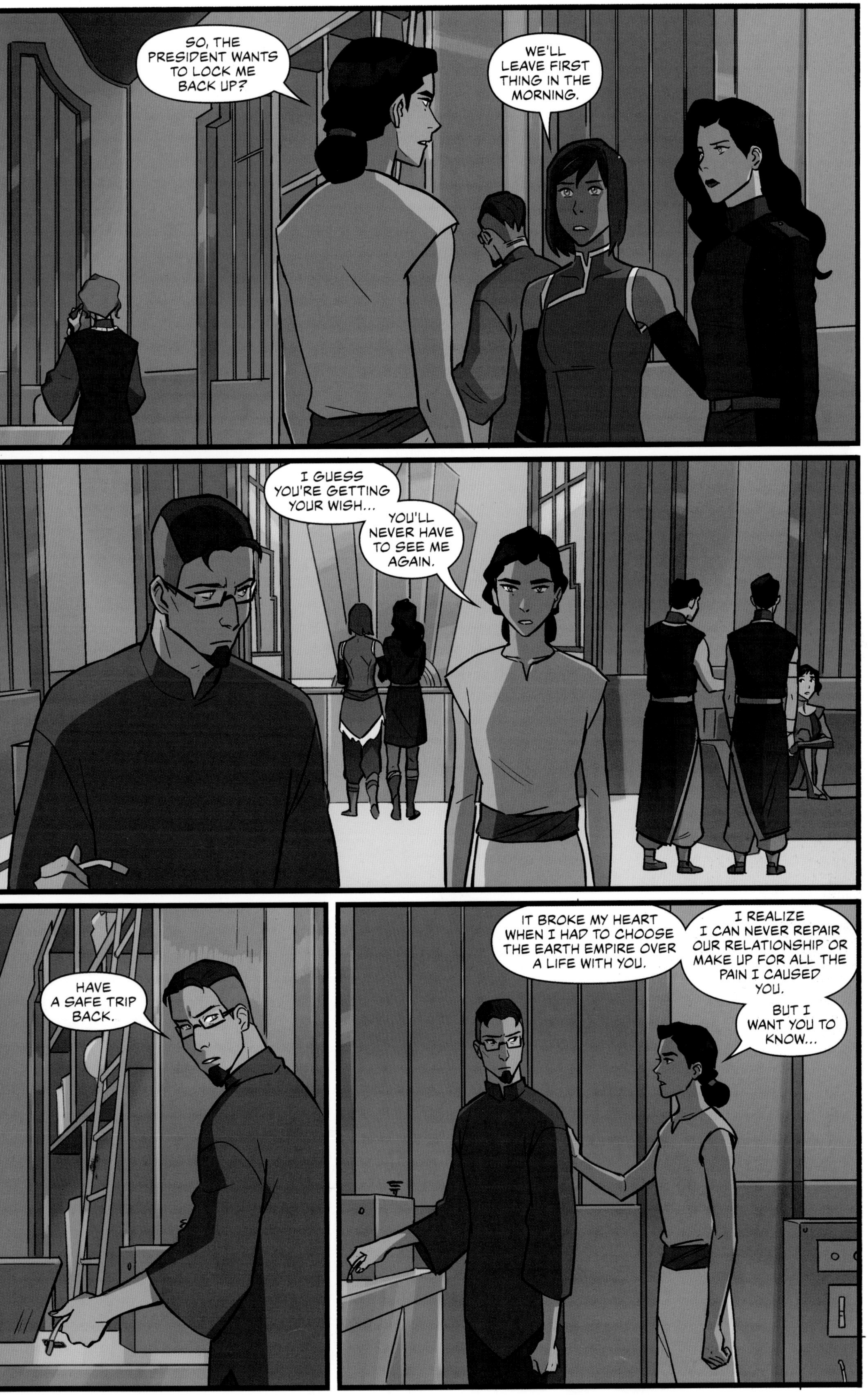
SO, THE PRESIDENT WANTS TO LOCK ME BACK UP?
WE'LL LEAVE FIRST THING IN THE MORNING.
I GUESS YOU'RE GETTING YOUR WISH...
YOU'LL NEVER HAVE TO SEE ME AGAIN.
HAVE A SAFE TRIP BACK.
IT BROKE MY HEART WHEN I HAD TO CHOOSE THE EARTH EMPIRE OVER A LIFE WITH YOU.
I REALIZE I CAN NEVER REPAIR OUR RELATIONSHIP OR MAKE UP FOR ALL THE PAIN I CAUSED YOU.
BUT I WANT YOU TO KNOW...

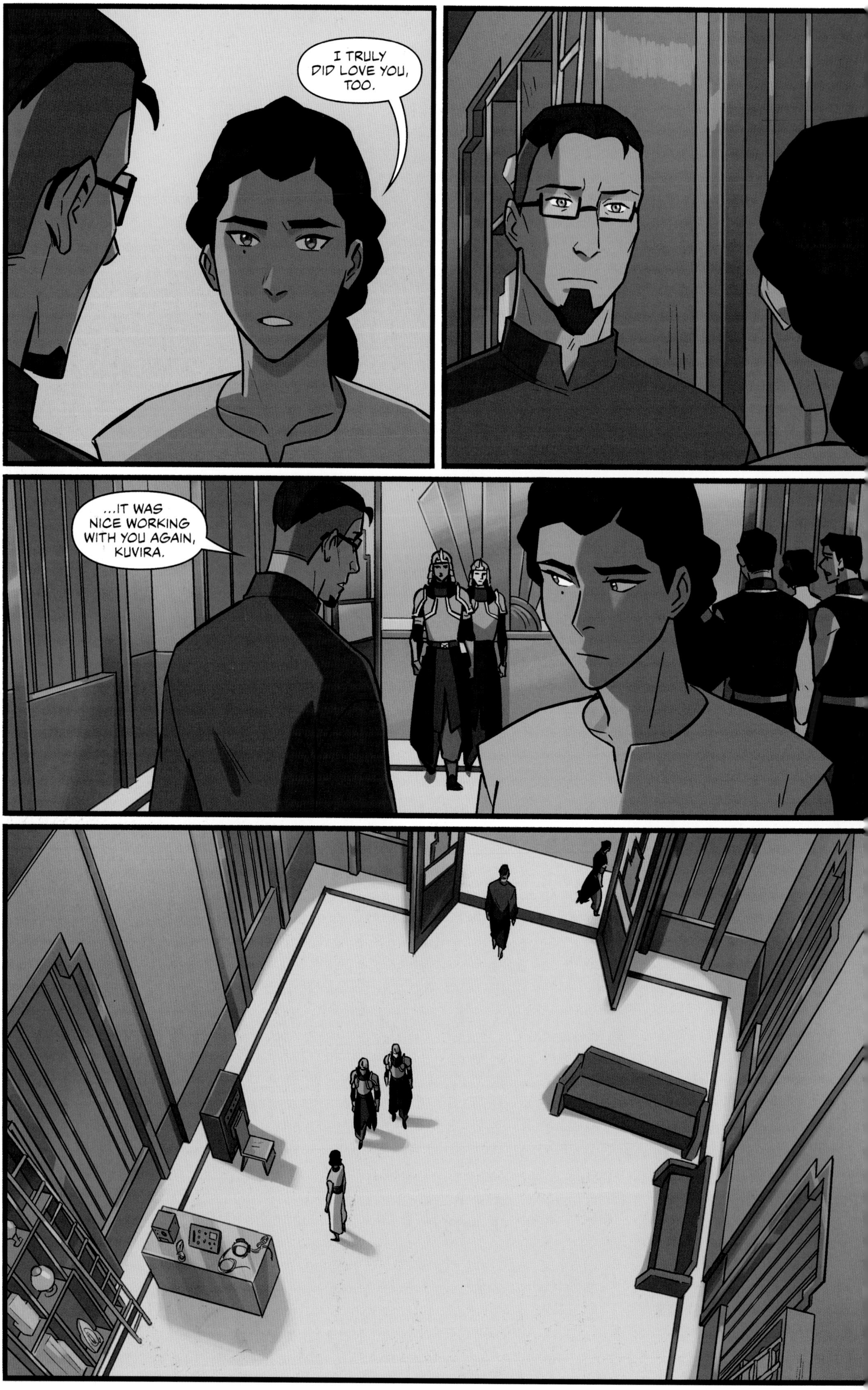
I TRULY DID LOVE YOU, TOO.
...IT WAS NICE WORKING WITH YOU AGAIN, KUVIRA.

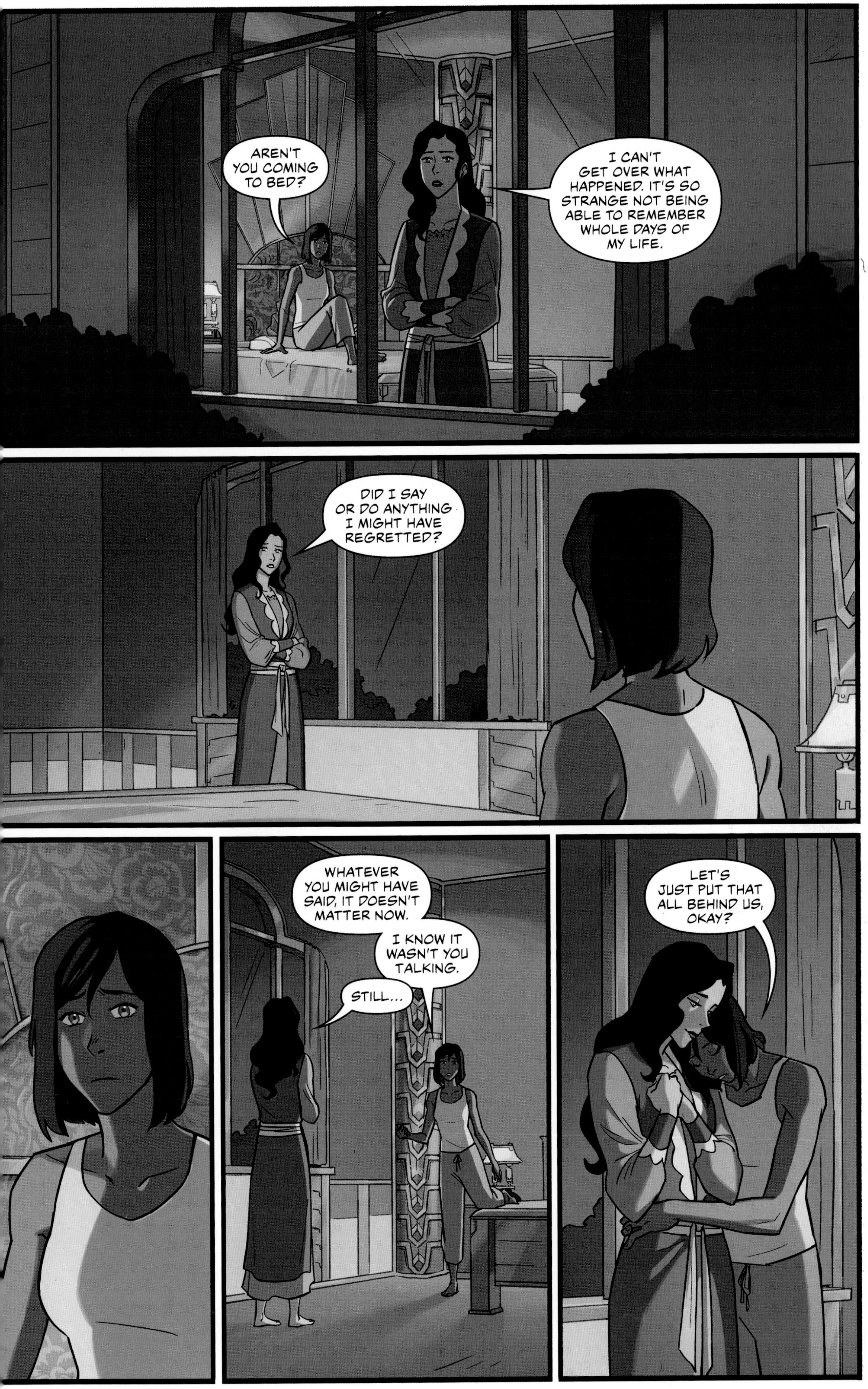
AREN'T YOU COMING TO BED?
I CAN'T GET OVER WHAT HAPPENED. IT'S SO STRANGE NOT BEING ABLE TO REMEMBER WHOLE DAYS OF MY LIFE.
DID I SAY OR DO ANYTHING I MIGHT HAVE REGRETTED?
WHATEVER YOU MIGHT HAVE SAID, IT DOESN'T MATTER NOW.
I KNOW IT WASN'T YOU TALKING.
STILL...
LET'S JUST PUT THAT ALL BEHIND US, OKAY?

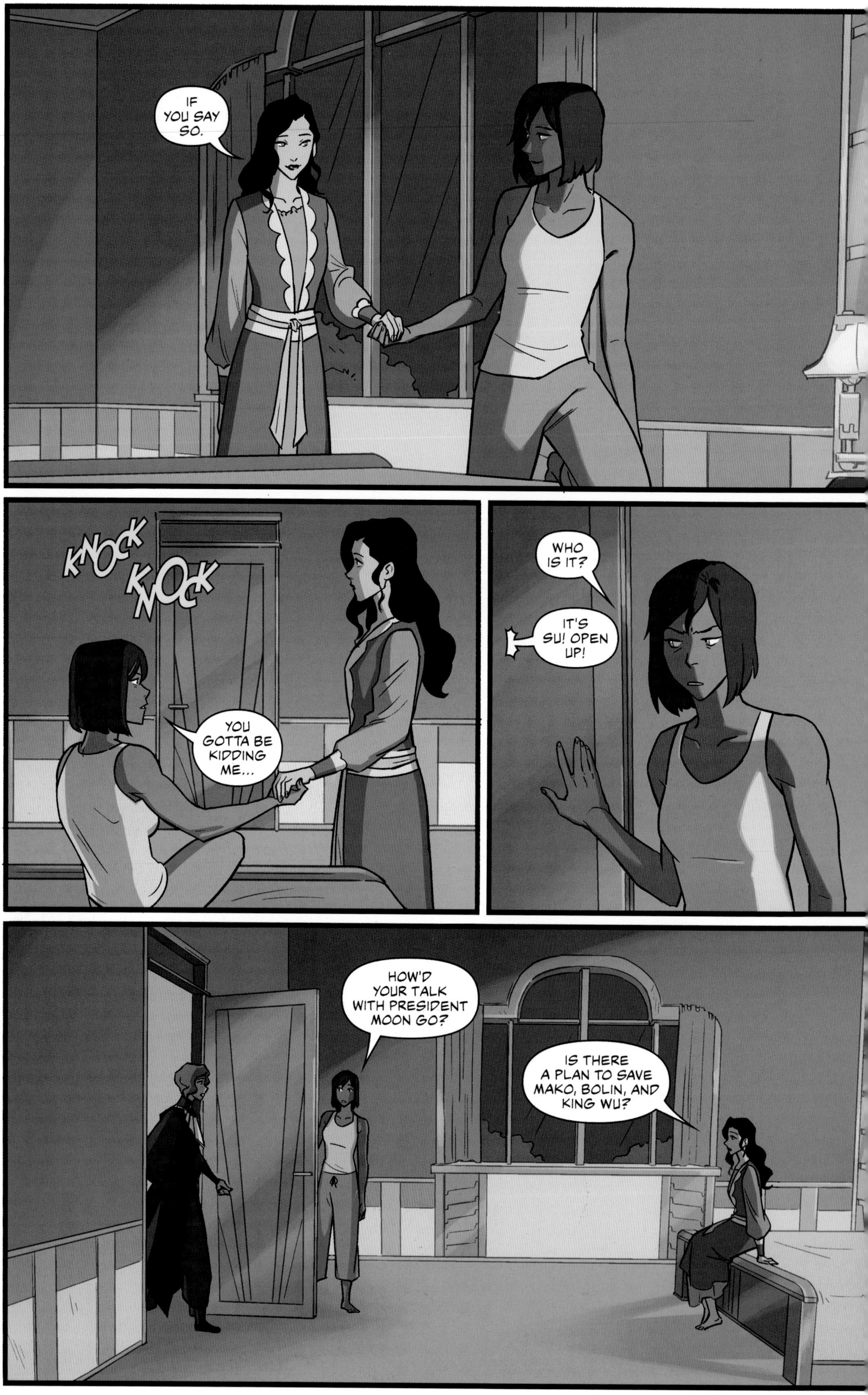
IF YOU SAY SO.
KNOCK KNOCK
YOU GOTTA BE KIDDING ME...
WHO IS IT?
IT'S SU! OPEN UP!
HOW'D YOUR TALK WITH PRESIDENT MOON GO?
IS THERE A PLAN TO SAVE MAKO, BOLIN, AND KING WU?

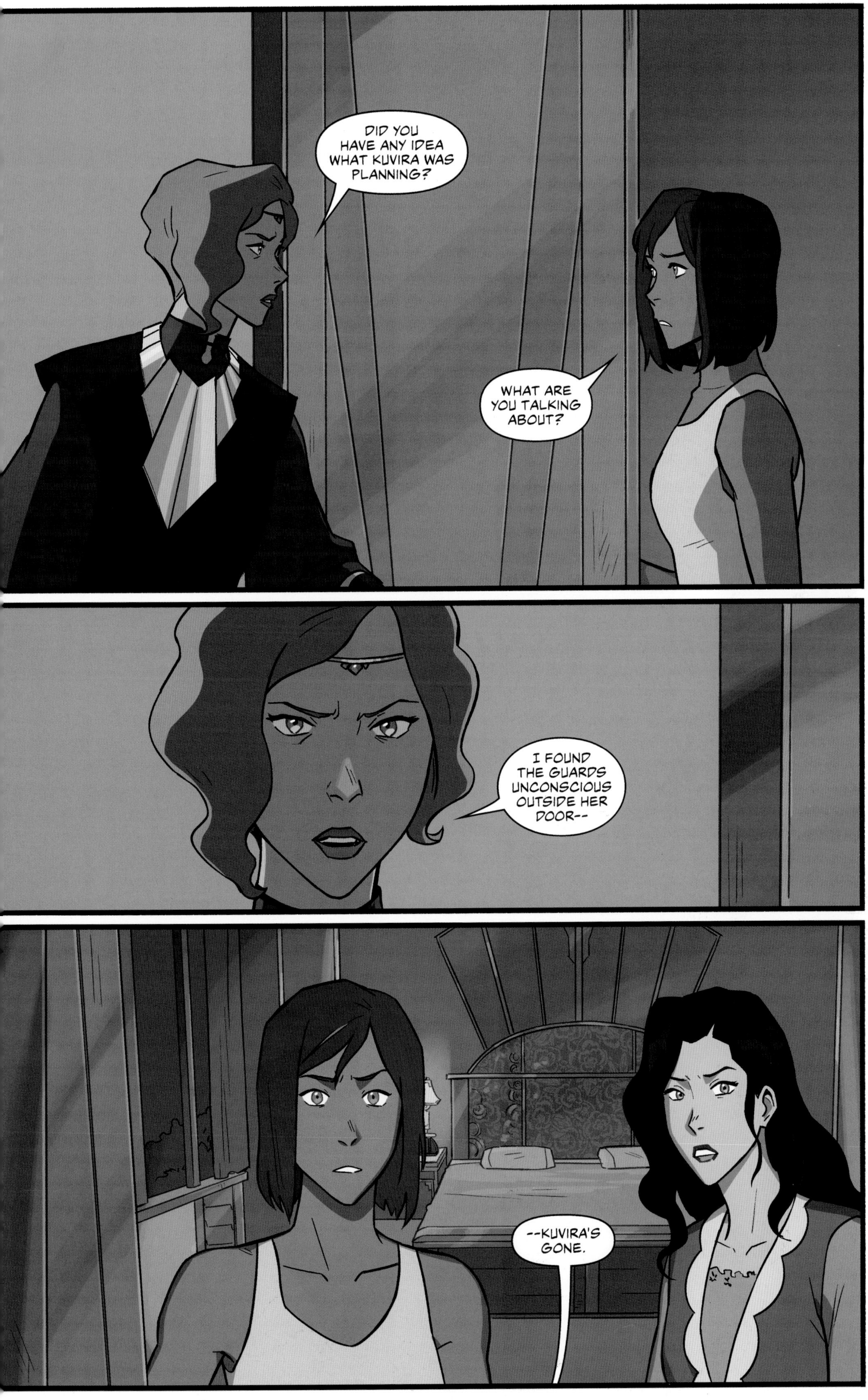
DID YOU HAVE ANY IDEA WHAT KUVIRA WAS PLANNING?
WHAT ARE YOU TALKING ABOUT?
I FOUND THE GUARDS UNCONSCIOUS OUTSIDE HER DOOR--
--KUVIRA'S GONE.

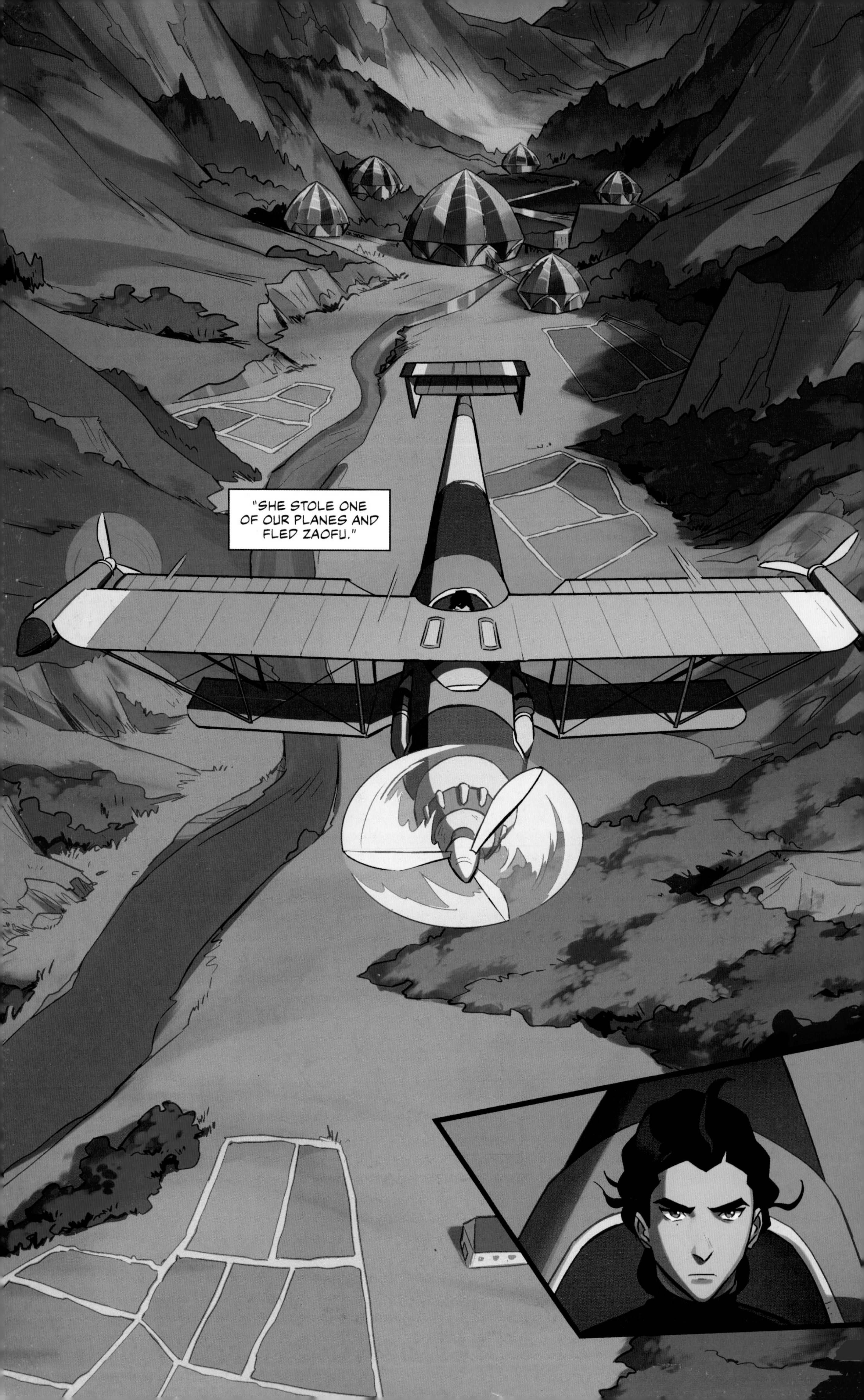
"SHE STOLE ONE OF OUR PLANES AND FLED ZAOFU."

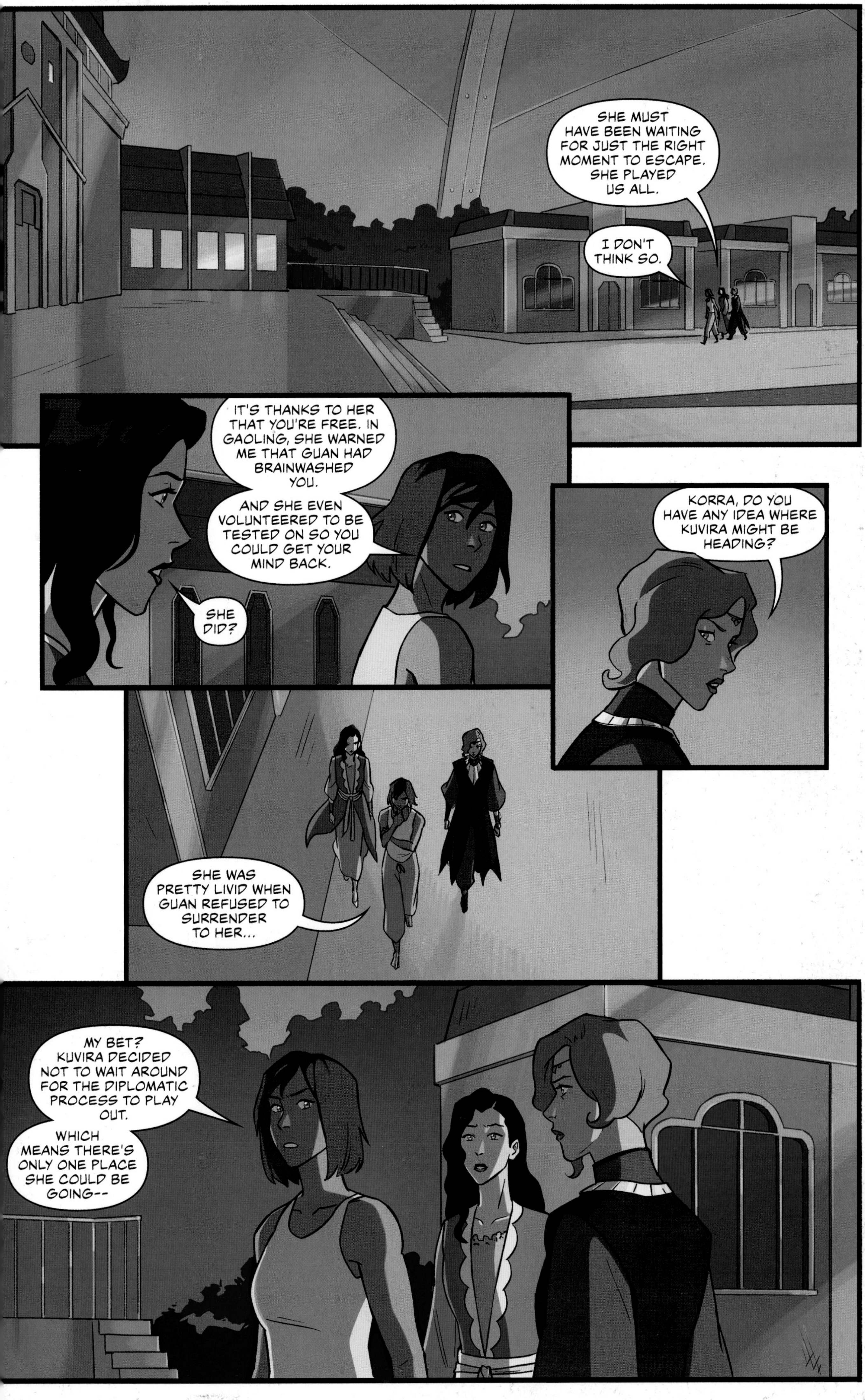
SHE MUST HAVE BEEN WAITING FOR JUST THE RIGHT MOMENT TO ESCAPE. SHE PLAYED US ALL.
I DON'T THINK SO.
IT'S THANKS TO HER THAT YOU'RE FREE. IN GAOLING, SHE WARNED ME THAT GUAN HAD BRAINWASHED YOU.
AND SHE EVEN VOLUNTEERED TO BE TESTED ON SO YOU COULD GET YOUR MIND BACK.
SHE DID?
KORRA, DO YOU HAVE ANY IDEA WHERE KUVIRA MIGHT BE HEADING?
SHE WAS PRETTY LIVID WHEN GUAN REFUSED TO SURRENDER TO HER...
MY BET? KUVIRA DECIDED NOT TO WAIT AROUND FOR THE DIPLOMATIC PROCESS TO PLAY OUT.
WHICH MEANS THERE'S ONLY ONE PLACE SHE COULD BE GOING--

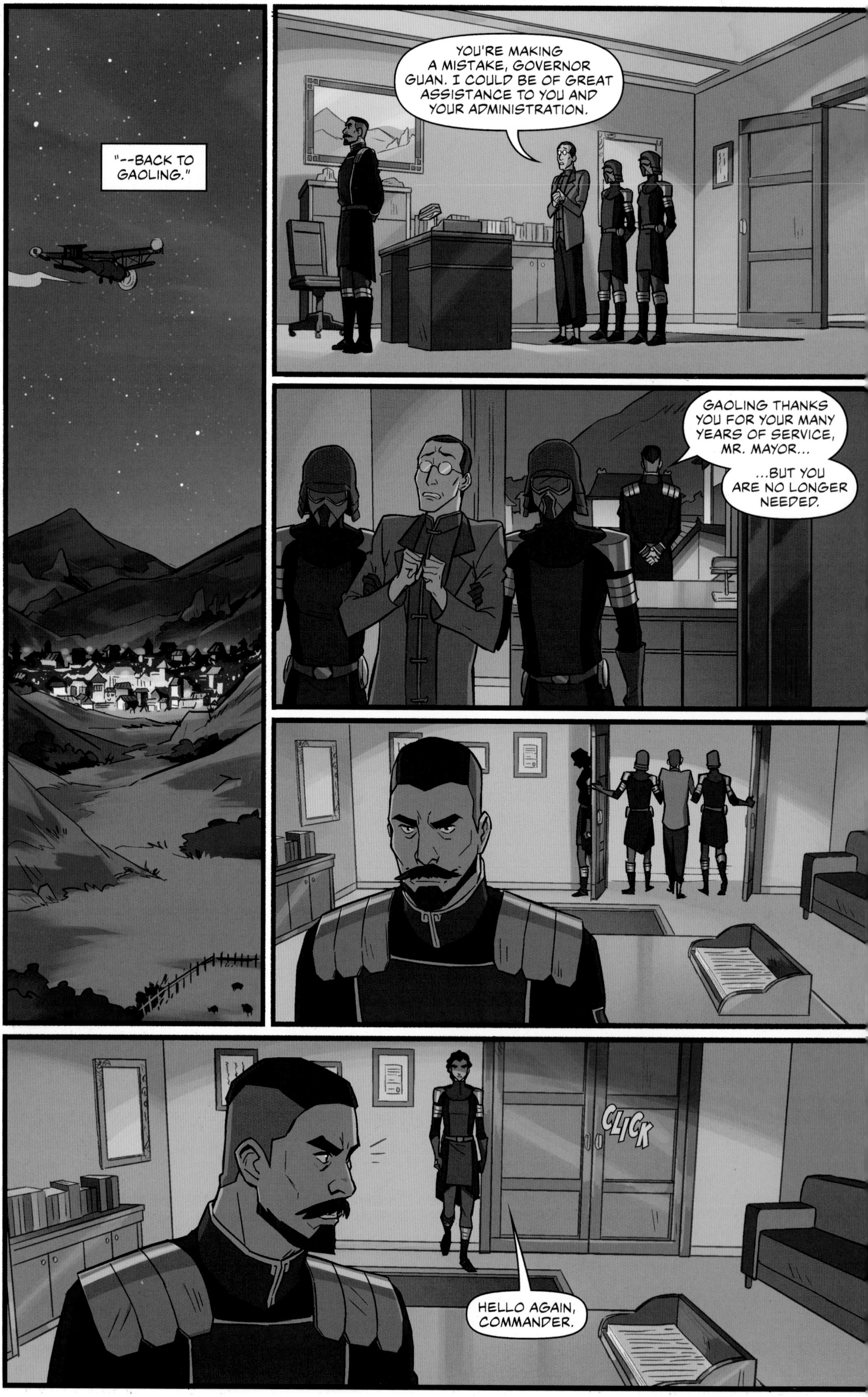
"--BACK TO GAOLING."
YOU'RE MAKING A MISTAKE, GOVERNOR GUAN. I COULD BE OF GREAT ASSISTANCE TO YOU AND YOUR ADMINISTRATION.
GAOLING THANKS YOU FOR YOUR MANY YEARS OF SERVICE, MR. MAYOR...
...BUT YOU ARE NO LONGER NEEDED.
CLICK
HELLO AGAIN, COMMANDER.

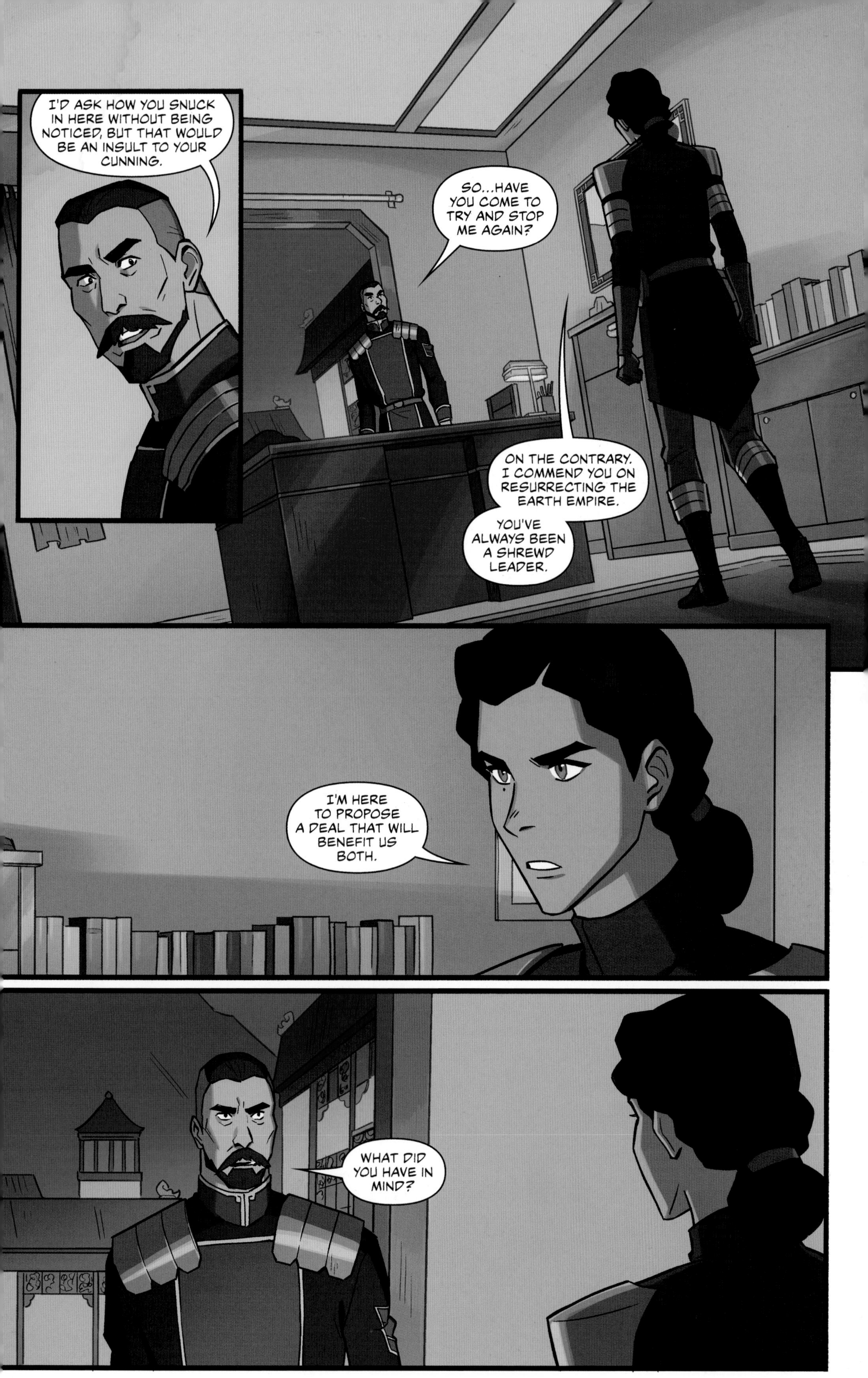
I'D ASK HOW YOU SNUCK IN HERE WITHOUT BEING NOTICED, BUT THAT WOULD BE AN INSULT TO YOUR CUNNING.
SO...HAVE YOU COME TO TRY AND STOP ME AGAIN?
ON THE CONTRARY. I COMMEND YOU ON RESURRECTING THE EARTH EMPIRE.
YOU'VE ALWAYS BEEN A SHREWD LEADER.
I'M HERE TO PROPOSE A DEAL THAT WILL BENEFIT US BOTH.
WHAT DID YOU HAVE IN MIND?

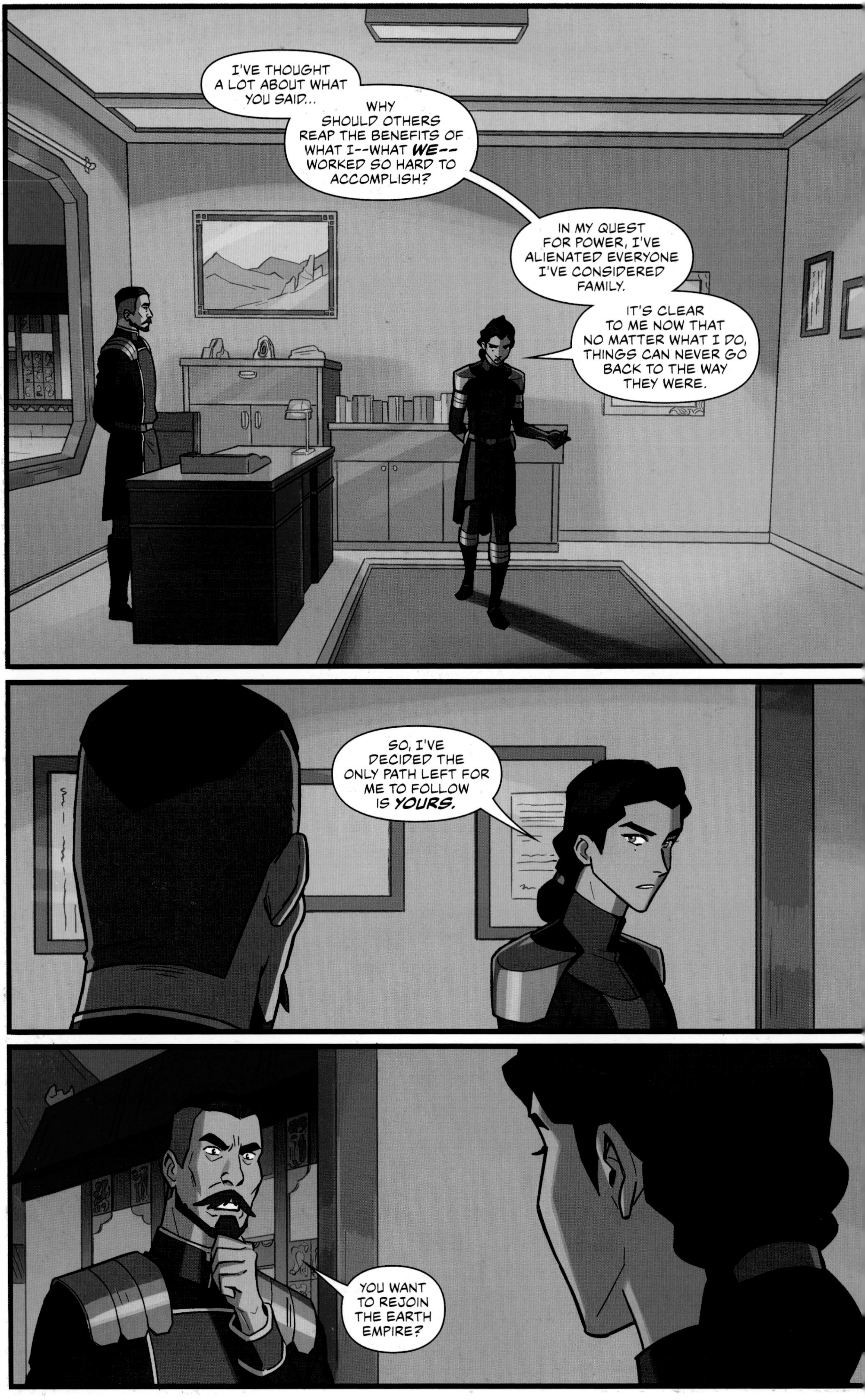
I'VE THOUGHT A LOT ABOUT WHAT YOU SAID...
WHY SHOULD OTHERS REAP THE BENEFITS OF WHAT I--WHAT WE-- WORKED SO HARD TO ACCOMPLISH?
IN MY QUEST FOR POWER, I'VE ALIENATED EVERYONE I'VE CONSIDERED FAMILY.
IT'S CLEAR TO ME NOW THAT NO MATTER WHAT I DO, THINGS CAN NEVER GO BACK TO THE WAY THEY WERE.
SO, I'VE DECIDED THE ONLY PATH LEFT FOR ME TO FOLLOW IS YOURS.
YOU WANT TO REJOIN THE EARTH EMPIRE?

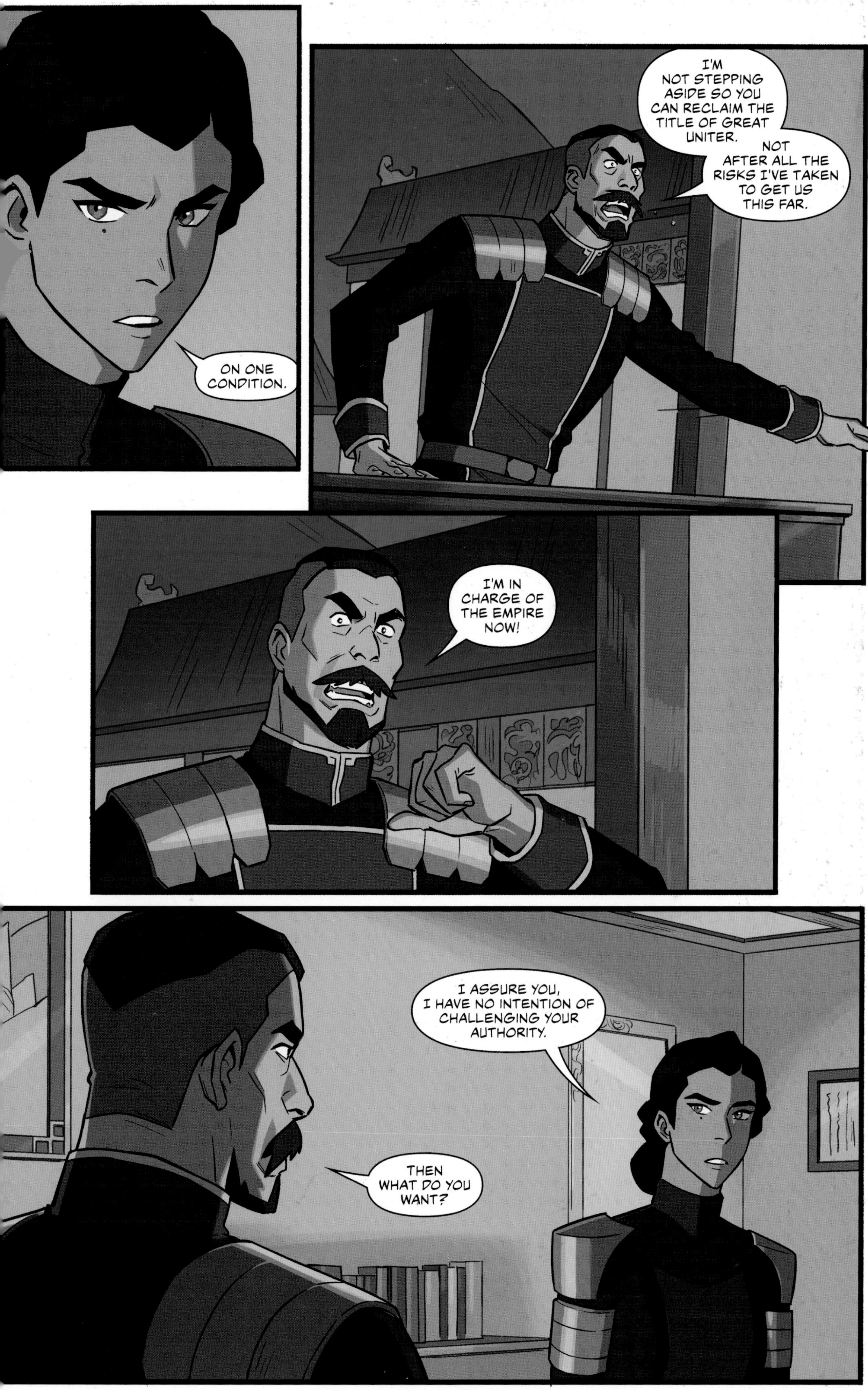
ON ONE CONDITION.
I'M NOT STEPPING ASIDE SO YOU CAN RECLAIM THE TITLE OF GREAT UNITER.
NOT AFTER ALL THE RISKS I'VE TAKEN TO GET US THIS FAR.
I'M IN CHARGE OF THE EMPIRE NOW!
I ASSURE YOU, I HAVE NO INTENTION OF CHALLENGING YOUR AUTHORITY.
THEN WHAT DO YOU WANT?

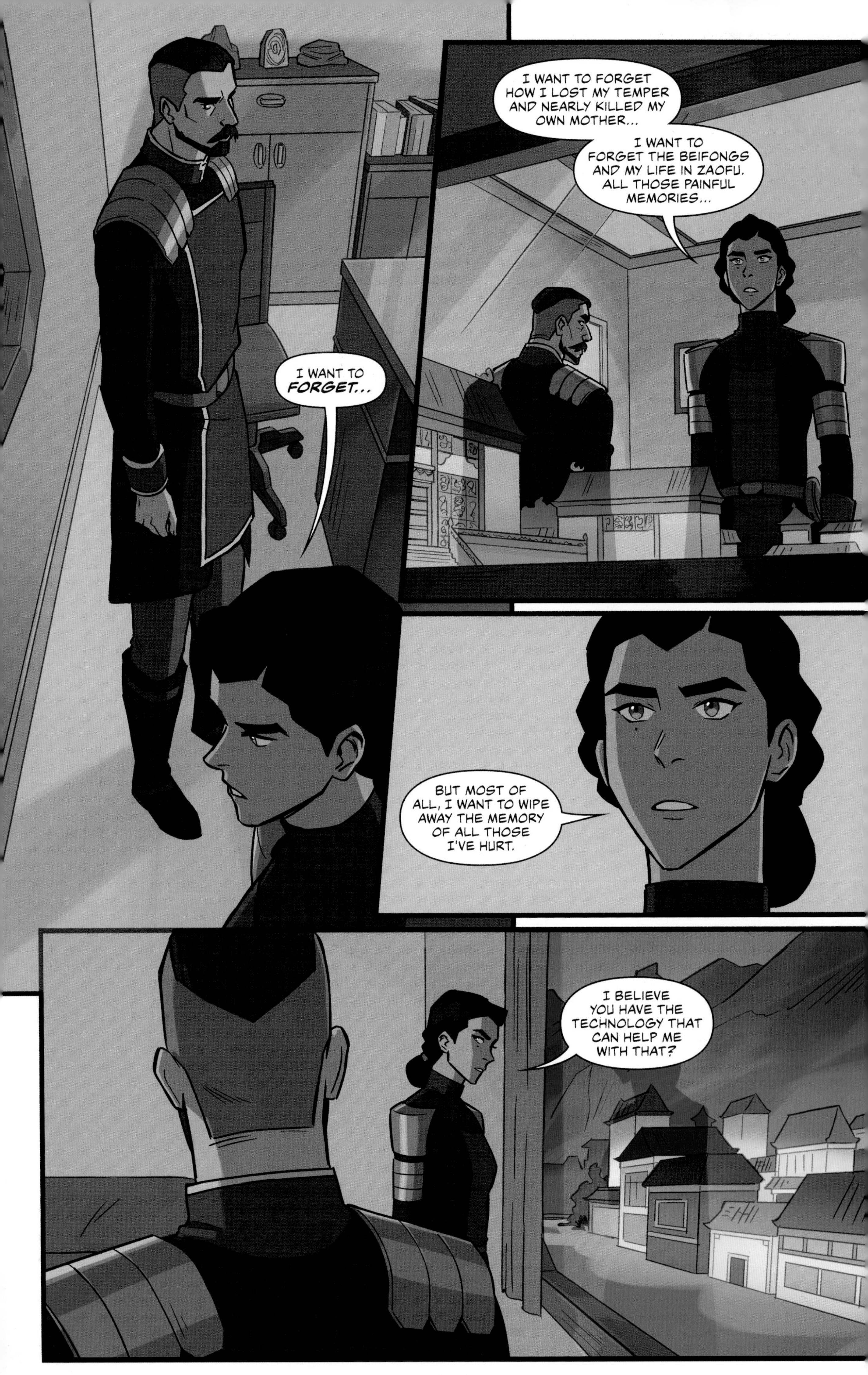
I WANT TO FORGET...
I WANT TO FORGET HOW I LOST MY TEMPER AND NEARLY KILLED MY OWN MOTHER...
I WANT TO FORGET THE BEIFONGS AND MY LIFE IN ZAOFU. ALL THOSE PAINFUL MEMORIES...
BUT MOST OF ALL, I WANT TO WIPE AWAY THE MEMORY OF ALL THOSE I'VE HURT.
I BELIEVE YOU HAVE THE TECHNOLOGY THAT CAN HELP ME WITH THAT?

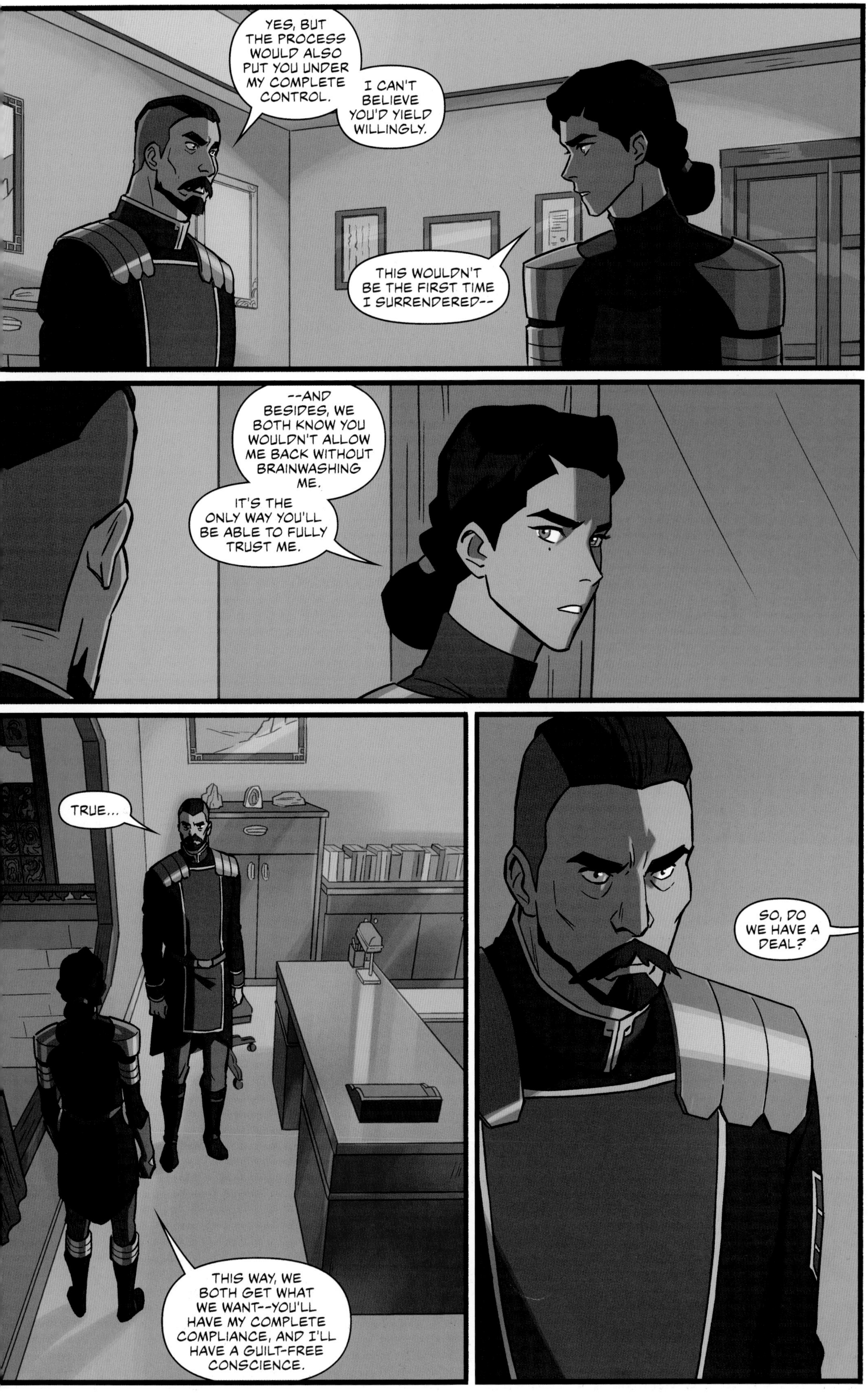
YES, BUT THE PROCESS WOULD ALSO PUT YOU UNDER MY COMPLETE CONTROL.
I CAN'T BELIEVE YOU'D YIELD WILLINGLY.
THIS WOULDN'T BE THE FIRST TIME I SURRENDERED--
--AND BESIDES, WE BOTH KNOW YOU WOULDN'T ALLOW ME BACK WITHOUT BRAINWASHING ME.
IT'S THE ONLY WAY YOU'LL BE ABLE TO FULLY TRUST ME.
TRUE...
THIS WAY, WE BOTH GET WHAT WE WANT--YOU'LL HAVE MY COMPLETE COMPLIANCE, AND I'LL HAVE A GUILT-FREE CONSCIENCE.
SO, DO WE HAVE A DEAL?

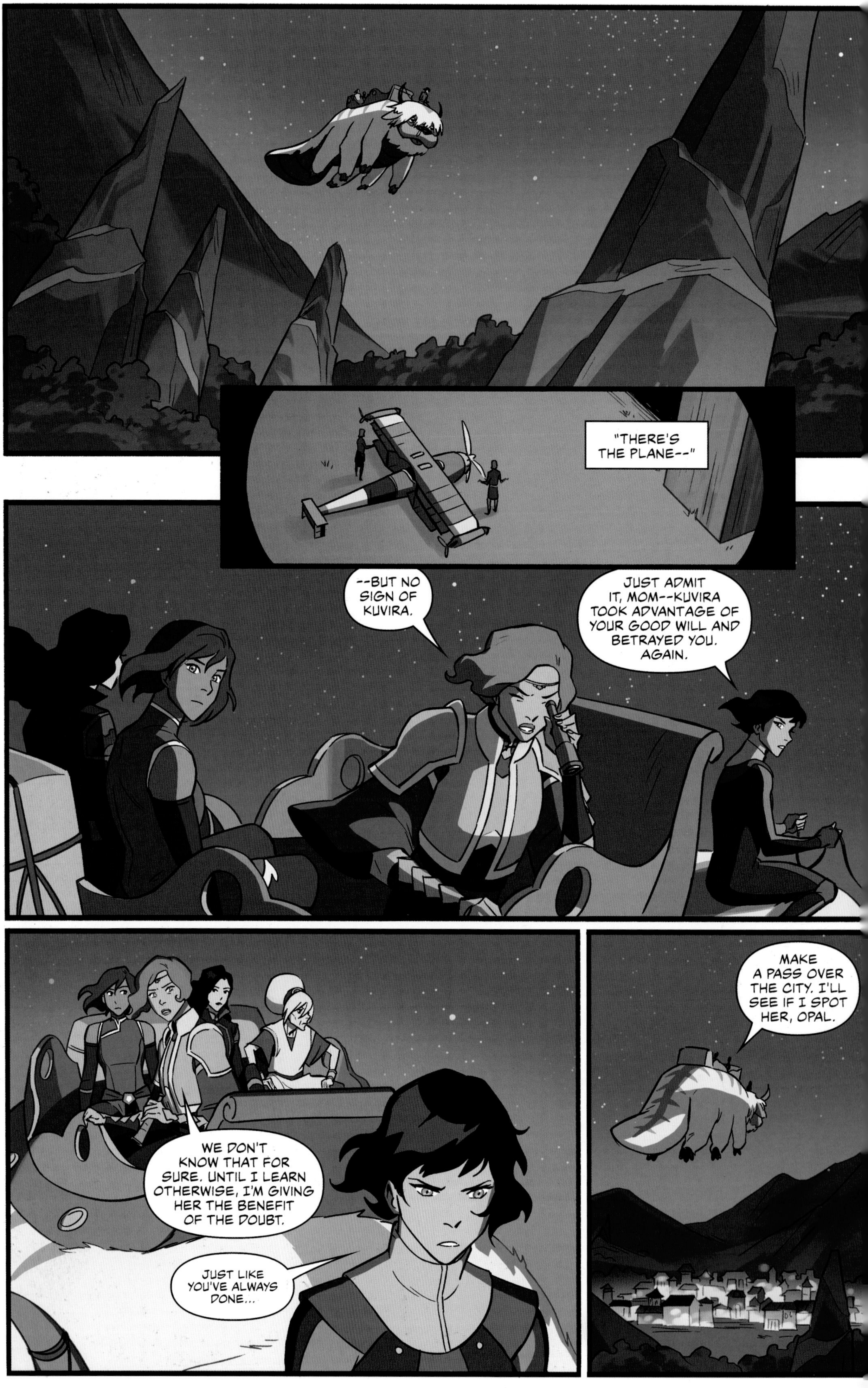
"THERE'S THE PLANE--"
--BUT NO SIGN OF KUVIRA.
JUST ADMIT IT, MOM--KUVIRA TOOK ADVANTAGE OF YOUR GOOD WILL AND BETRAYED YOU. AGAIN.
WE DON'T KNOW THAT FOR SURE. UNTIL I LEARN OTHERWISE, I'M GIVING HER THE BENEFIT OF THE DOUBT.
JUST LIKE YOU'VE ALWAYS DONE...
MAKE A PASS OVER THE CITY. I'LL SEE IF I SPOT HER, OPAL.

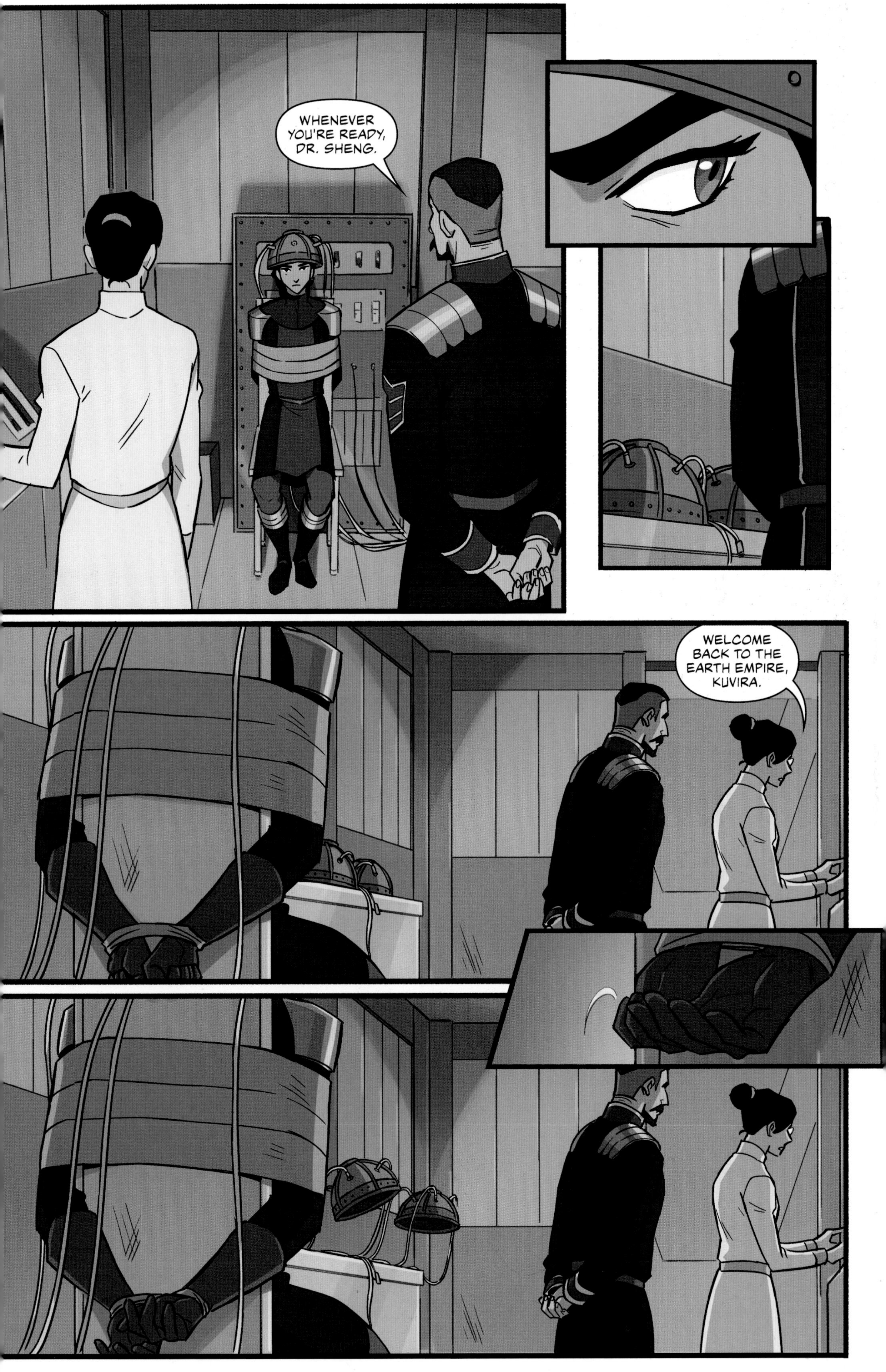
WHENEVER YOU'RE READY, DR. SHENG.
WELCOME BACK TO THE EARTH EMPIRE, KUVIRA.

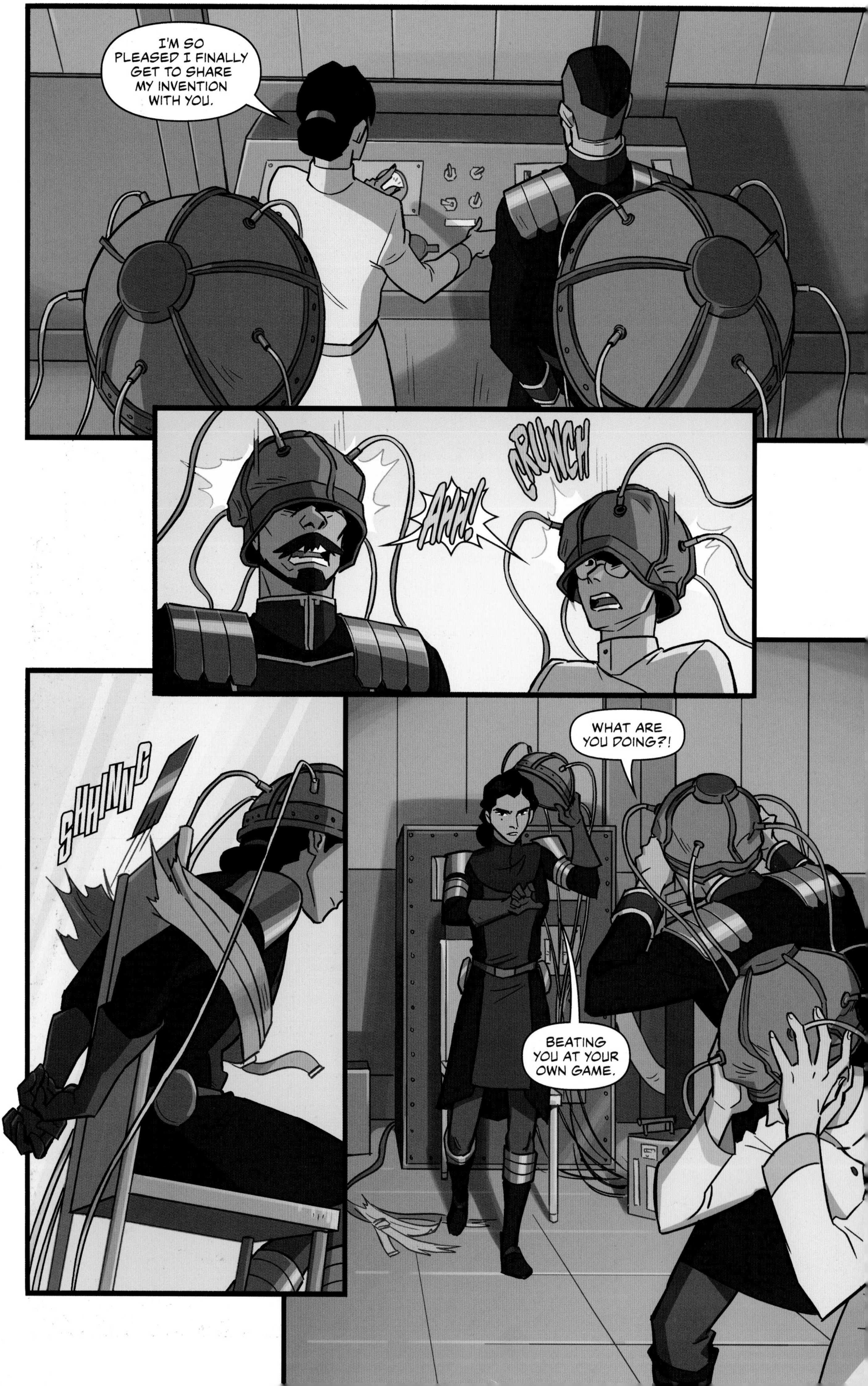
I'M SO PLEASED I FINALLY GET TO SHARE MY INVENTION WITH YOU.
CRUNCH
AHH!
SHHINNG
WHAT ARE YOU DOING?!
BEATING YOU AT YOUR OWN GAME.

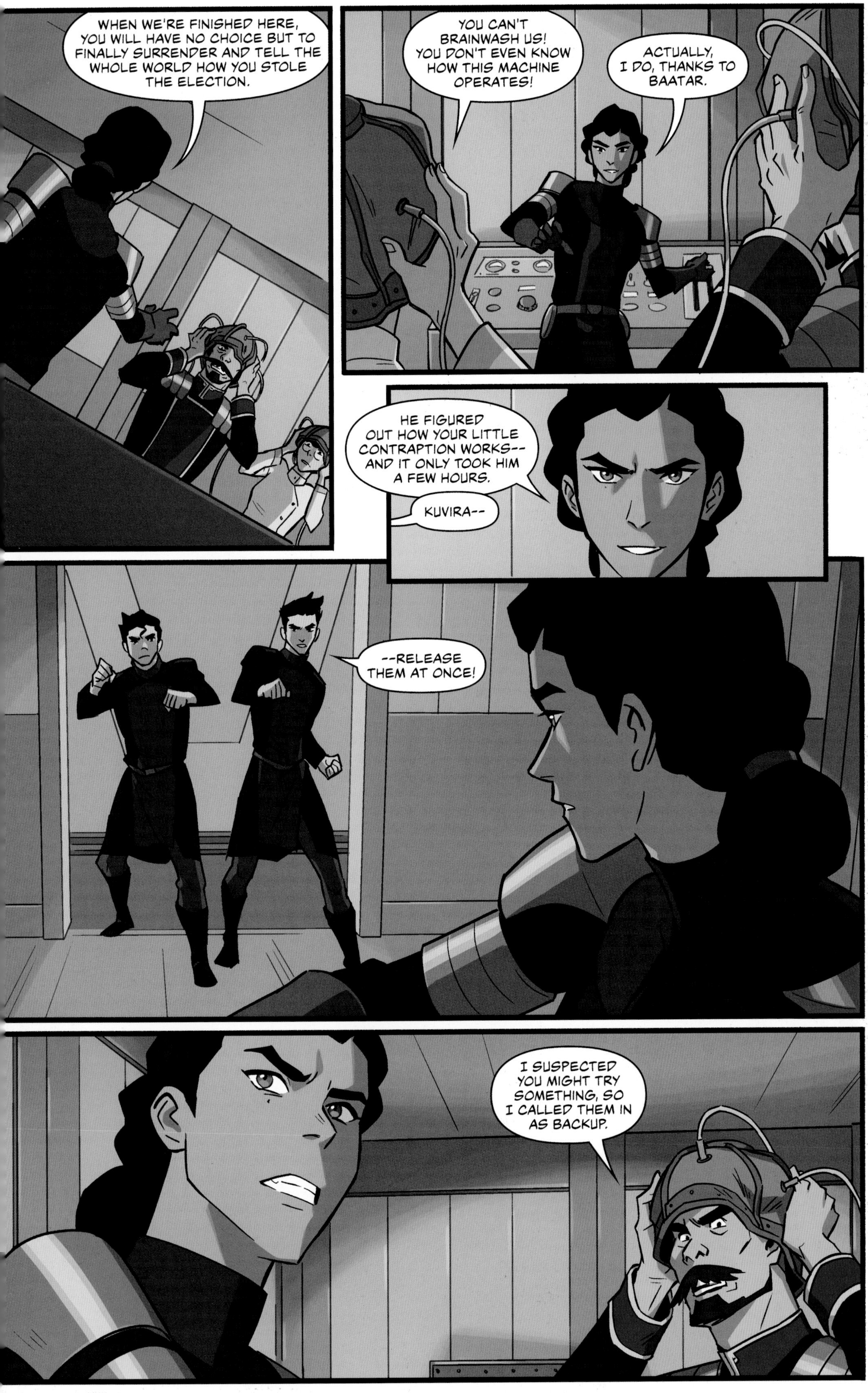
WHEN WE'RE FINISHED HERE, YOU WILL HAVE NO CHOICE BUT TO FINALLY SURRENDER AND TELL THE WHOLE WORLD HOW YOU STOLE THE ELECTION.
YOU CAN'T BRAINWASH US! YOU DON'T EVEN KNOW HOW THIS MACHINE OPERATES!
ACTUALLY, I DO, THANKS TO BAATAR.
HE FIGURED OUT HOW YOUR LITTLE CONTRAPTION WORKS-- AND IT ONLY TOOK HIM A FEW HOURS.
KUVIRA--
--RELEASE THEM AT ONCE!
I SUSPECTED YOU MIGHT TRY SOMETHING, SO I CALLED THEM IN AS BACKUP.

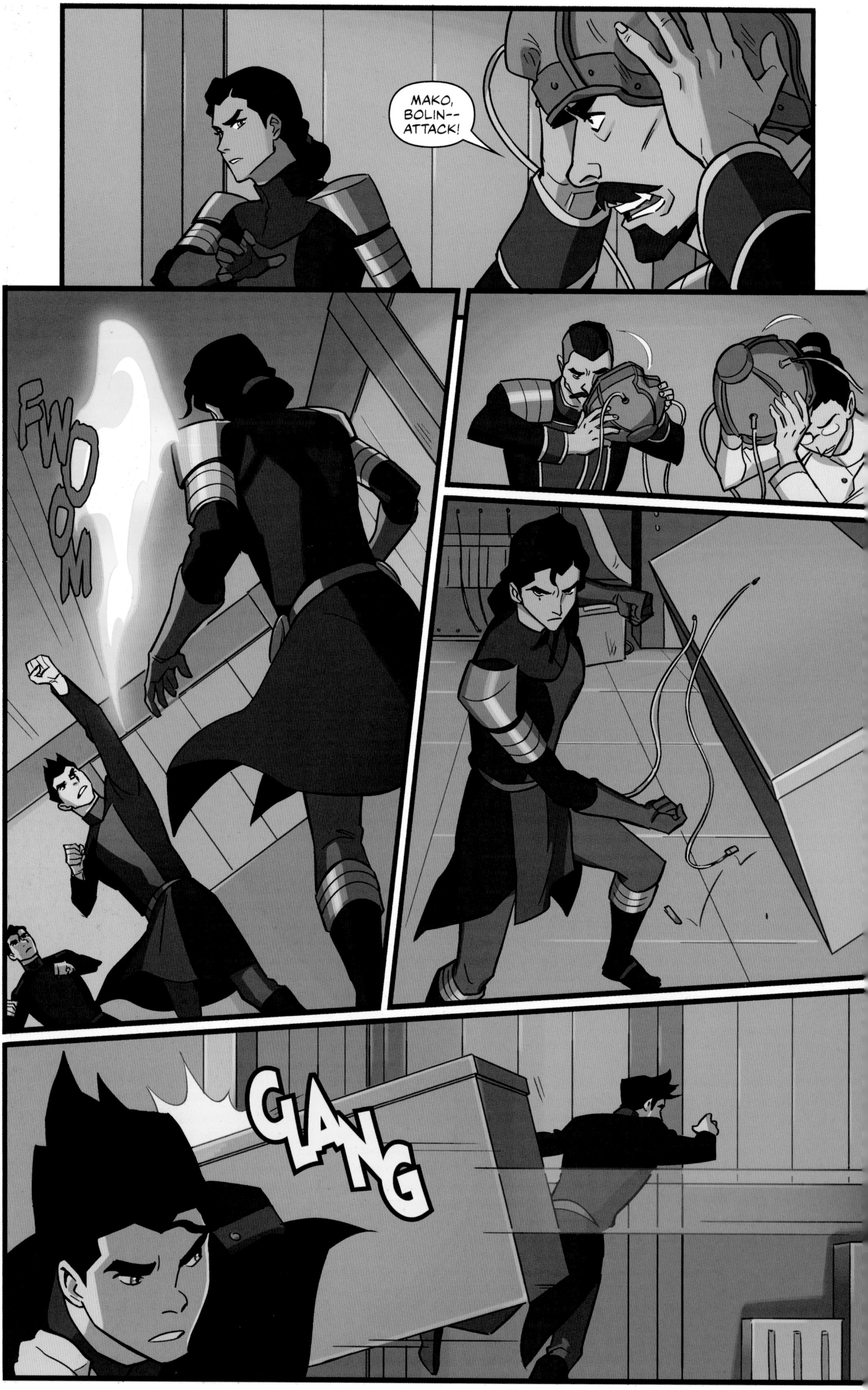
MAKO, BOLIN-- ATTACK!
FWOOM
CLANG

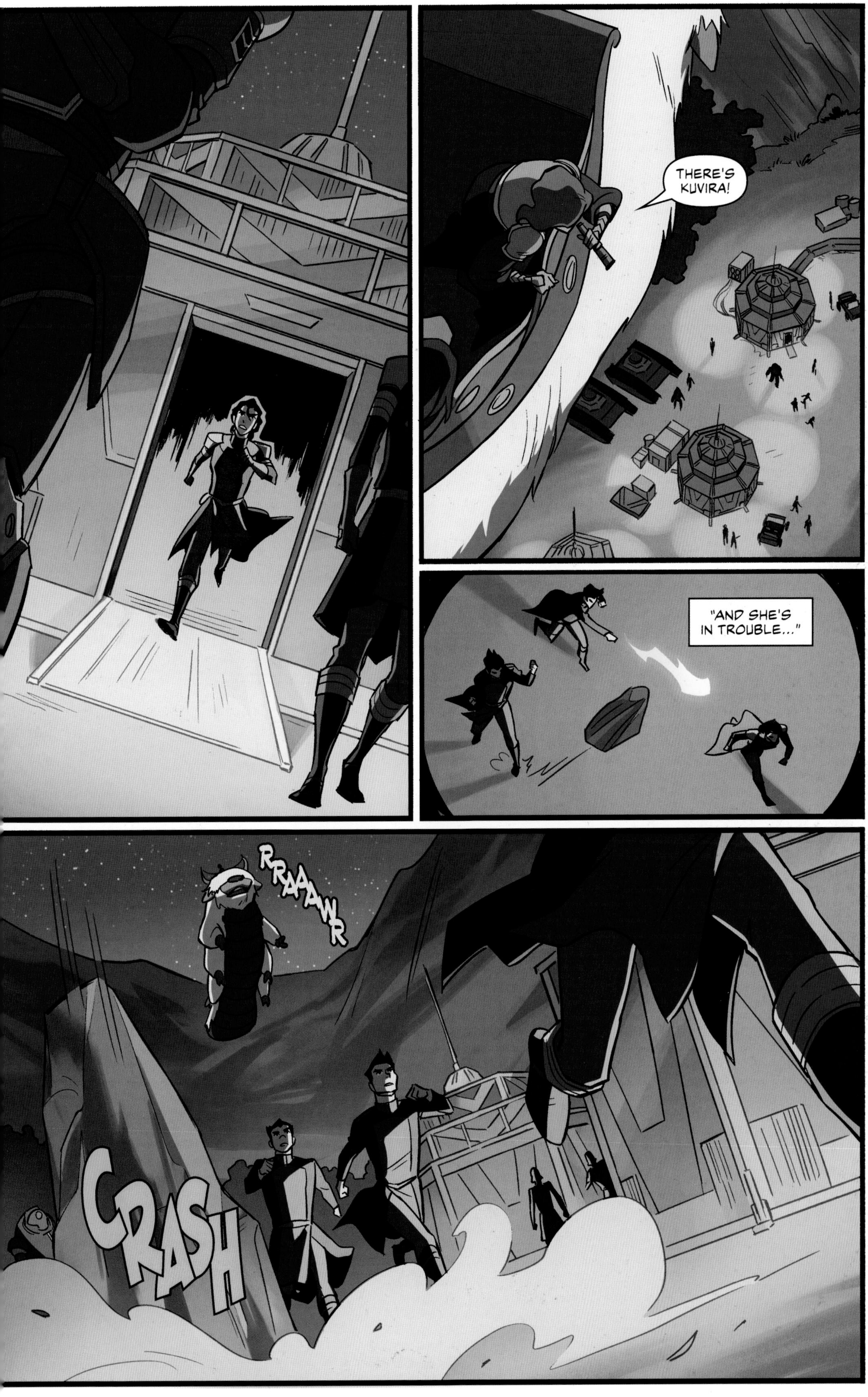
THERE'S KUVIRA!
"AND SHE'S IN TROUBLE..."
RRAAAAWR
CRASH

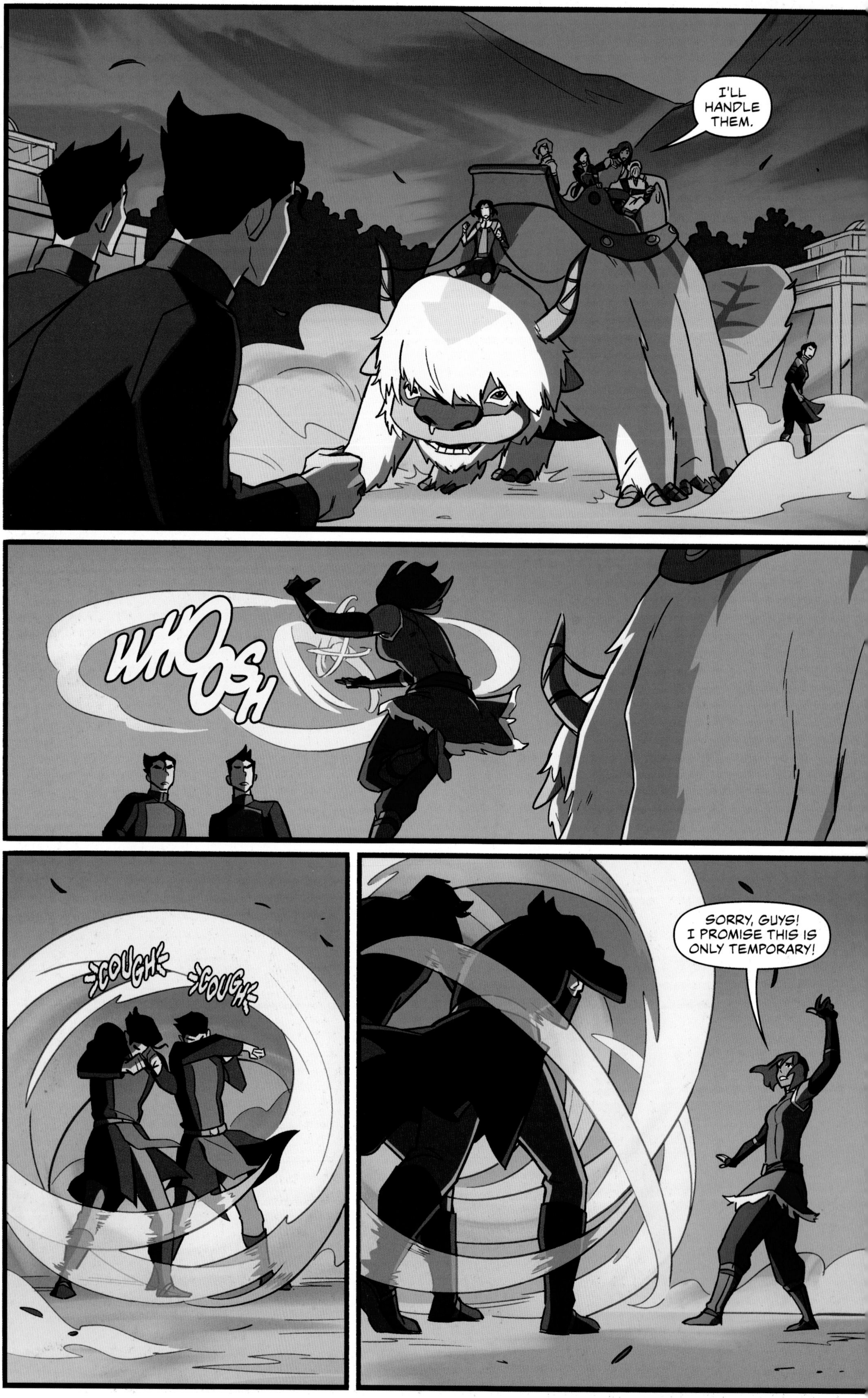
I'LL HANDLE THEM.
WHOOSH
COUGH
COUGH
SORRY, GUYS! I PROMISE THIS IS ONLY TEMPORARY!

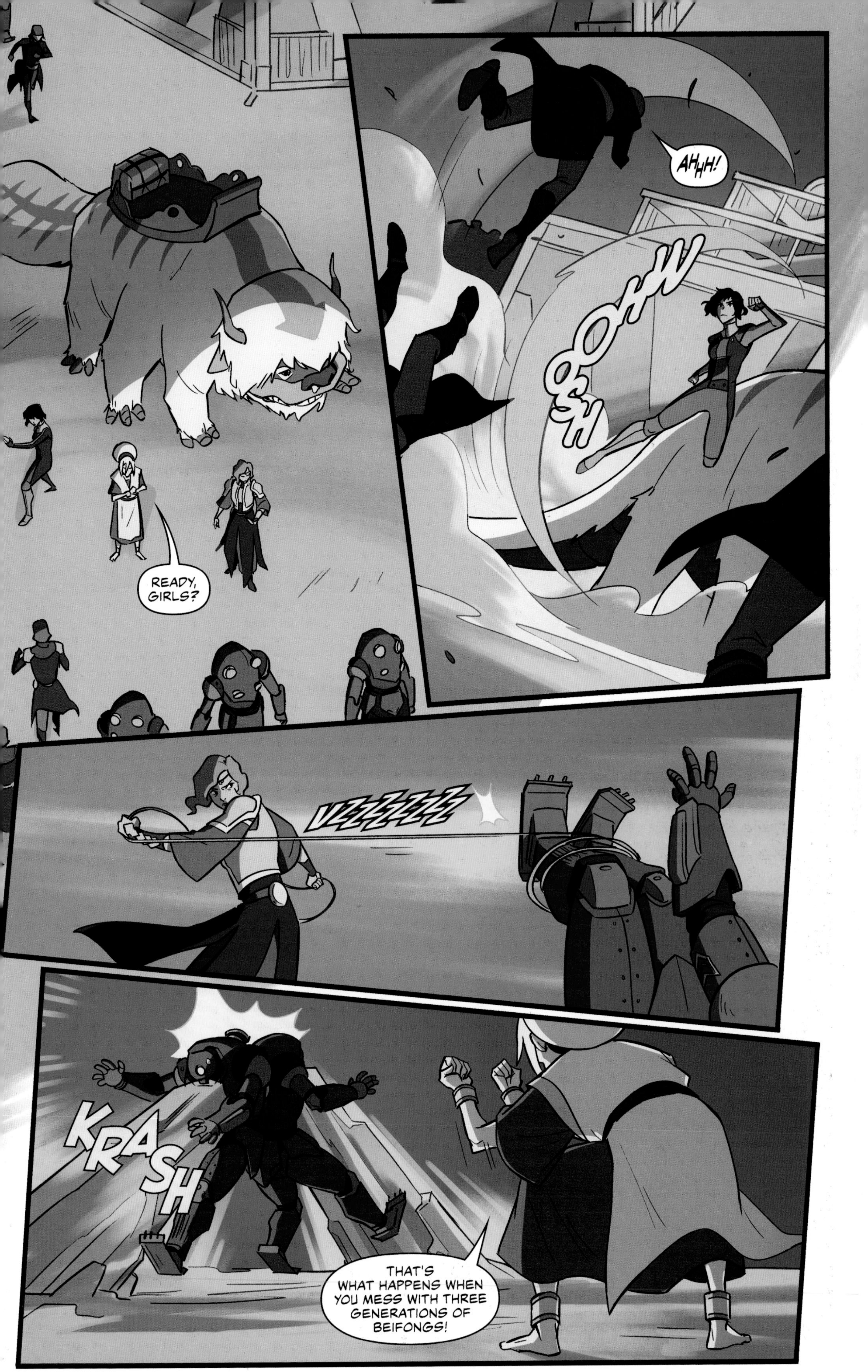
READY, GIRLS?
AHHH!
WHOOSH
VZZZZZZ
KRASH
THAT'S WHAT HAPPENS WHEN YOU MESS WITH THREE GENERATIONS OF BEIFONGS!

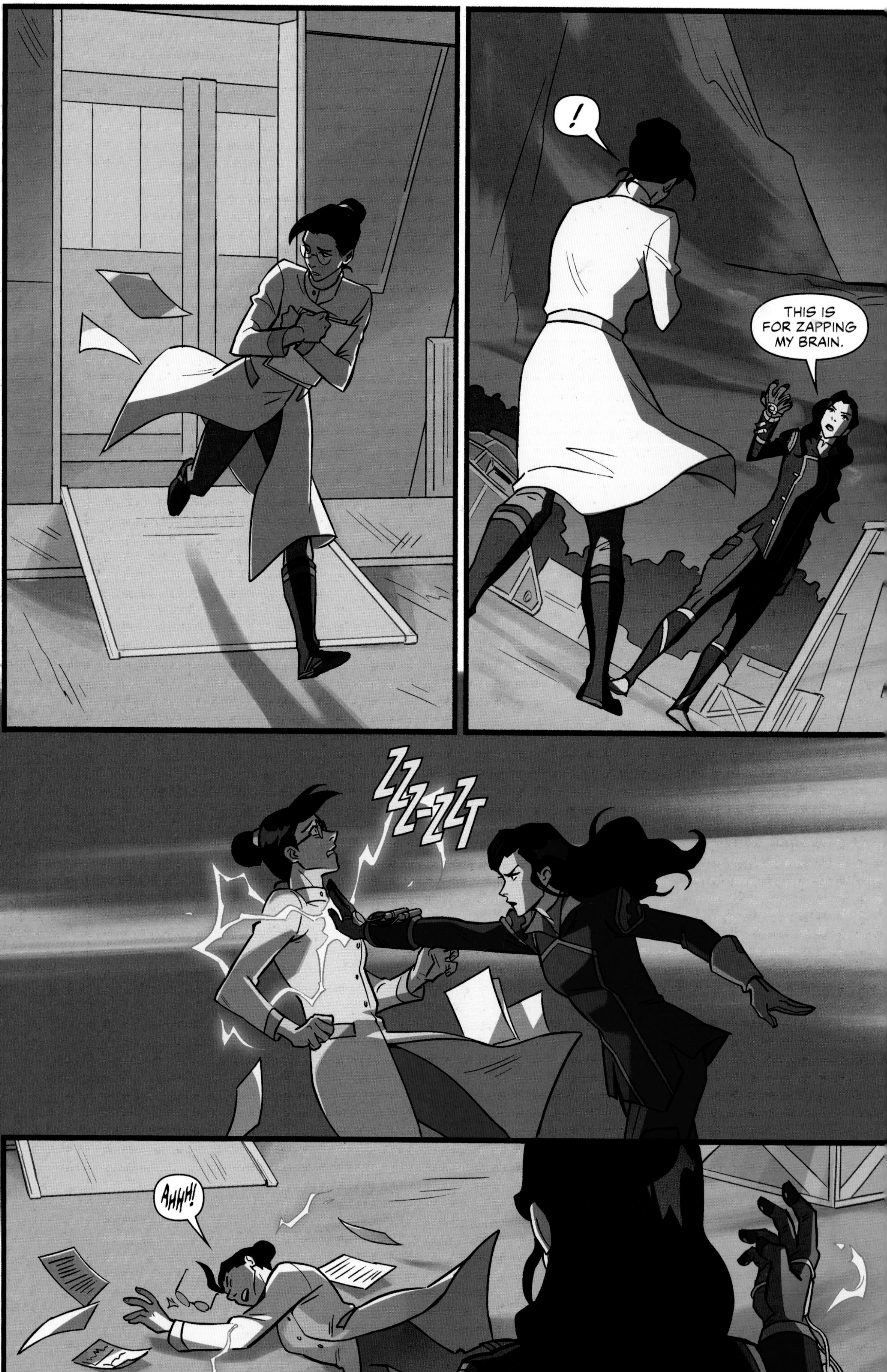
!
THIS IS FOR ZAPPING MY BRAIN.
ZZZ-ZZT
AHHH!

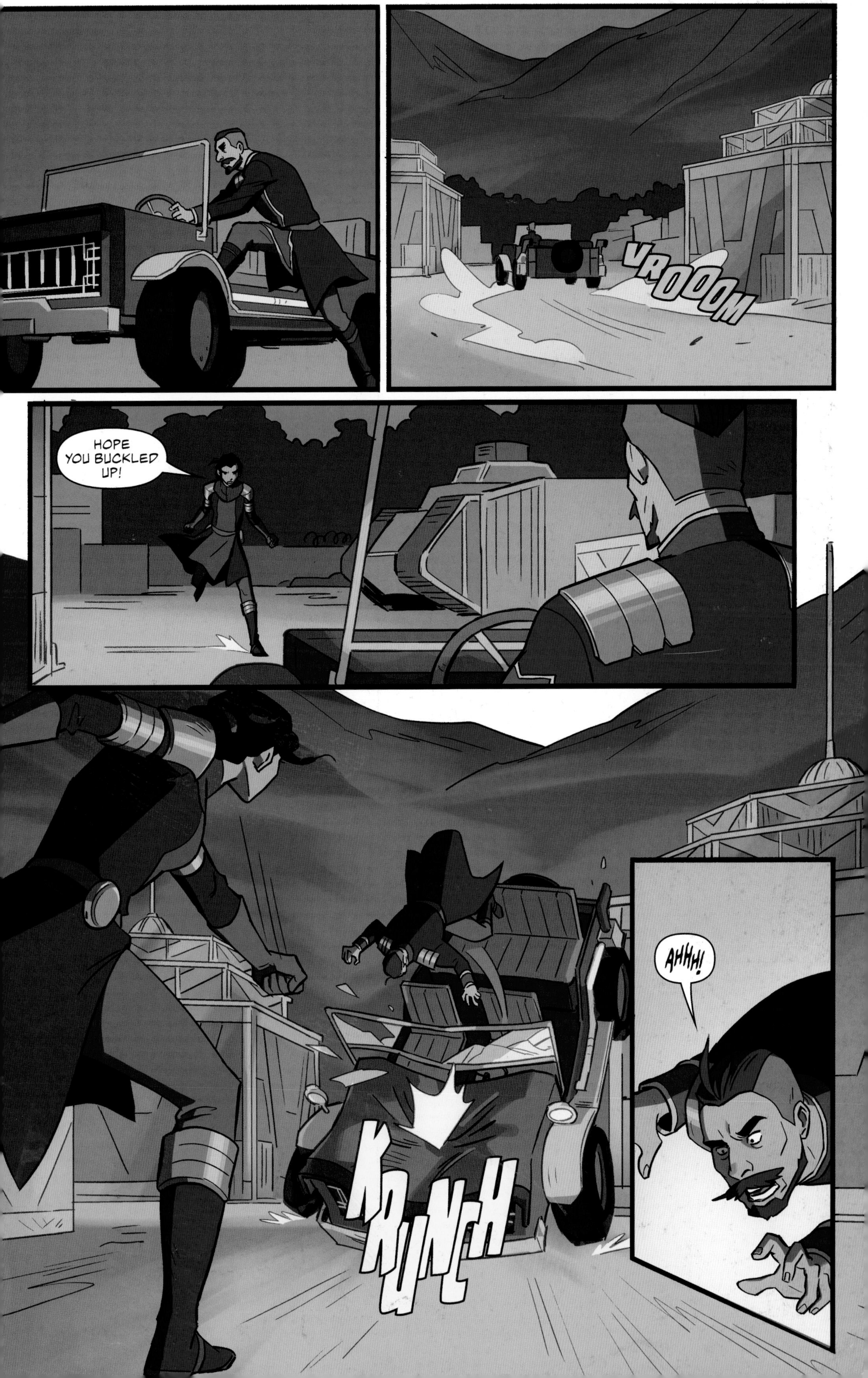
VROOOM
HOPE YOU BUCKLED UP!
AHHH!
KRUNCH

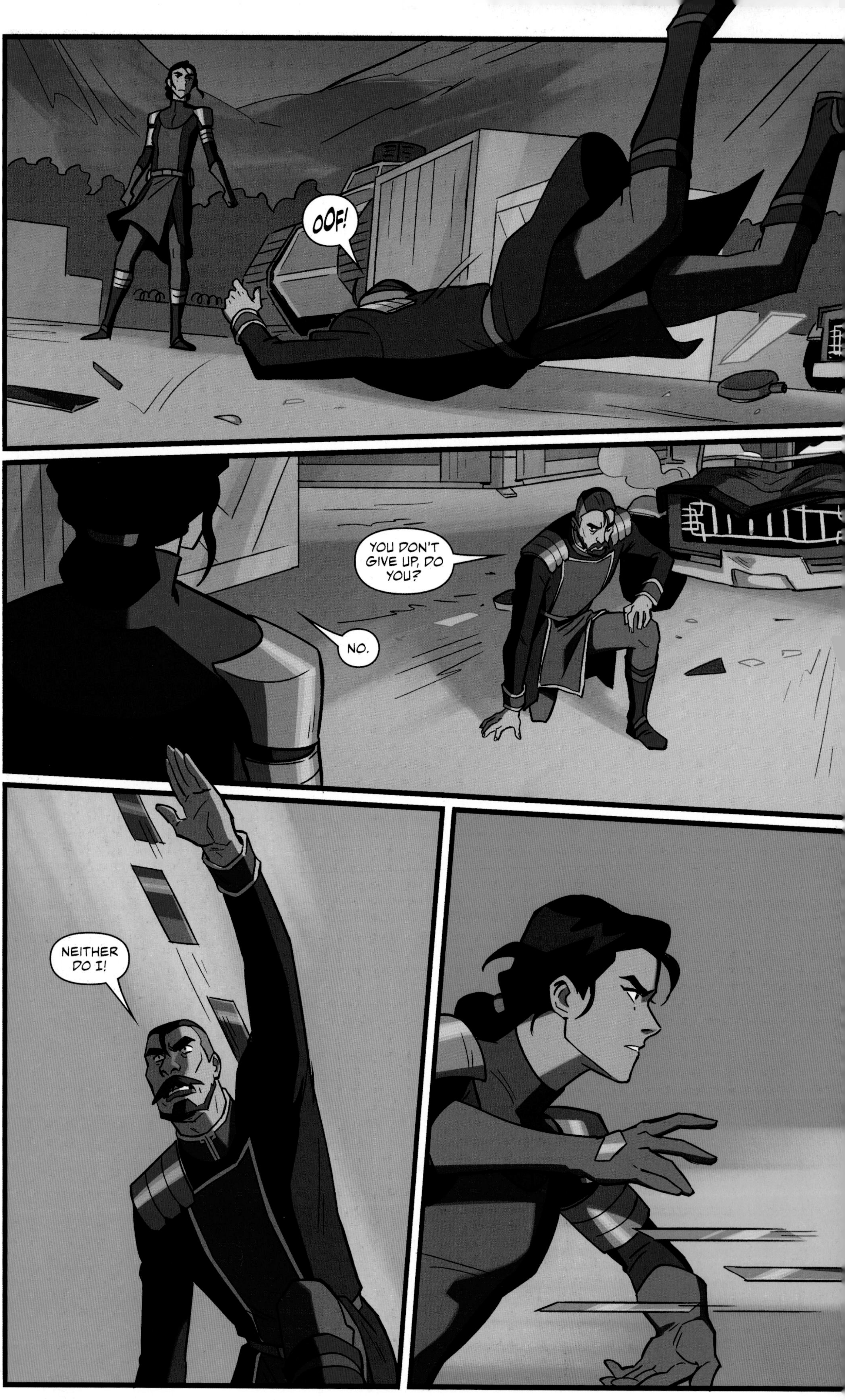
OOF!
YOU DON'T GIVE UP, DO YOU?
NO.
NEITHER DO I!

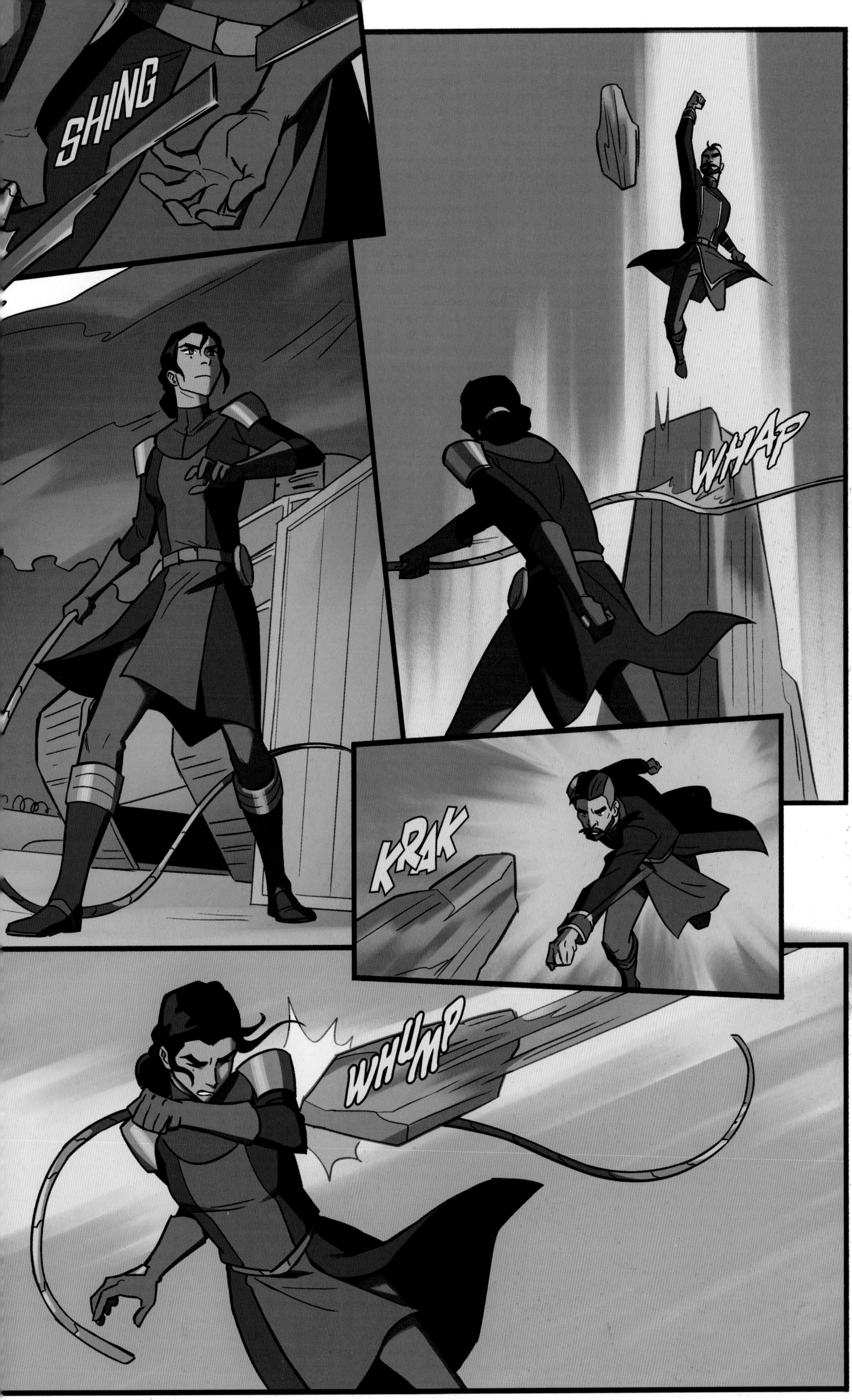
SHING
WHAP
KRAK
WHUMP

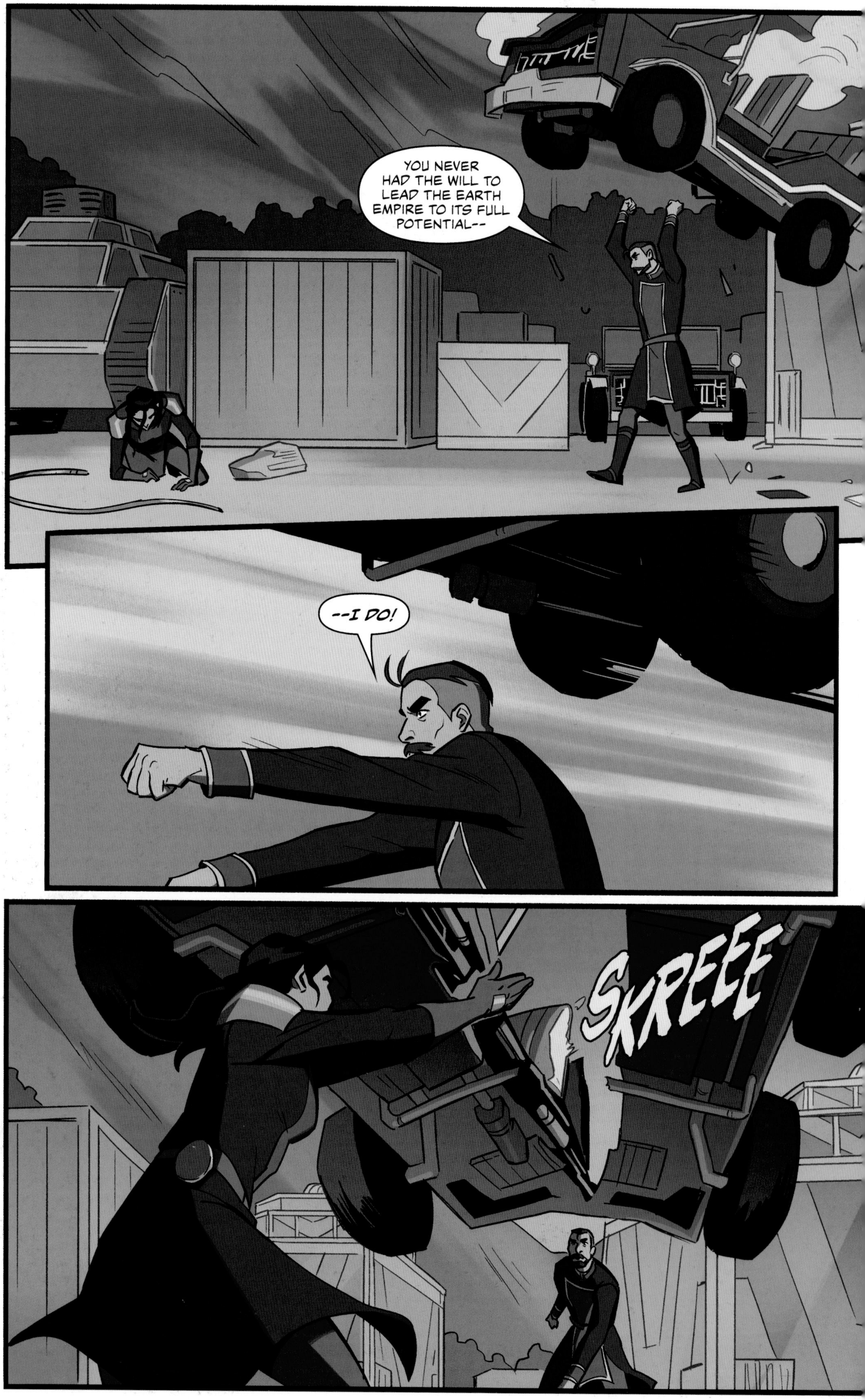
YOU NEVER HAD THE WILL TO LEAD THE EARTH EMPIRE TO ITS FULL POTENTIAL--
--I DO!
SKREEE

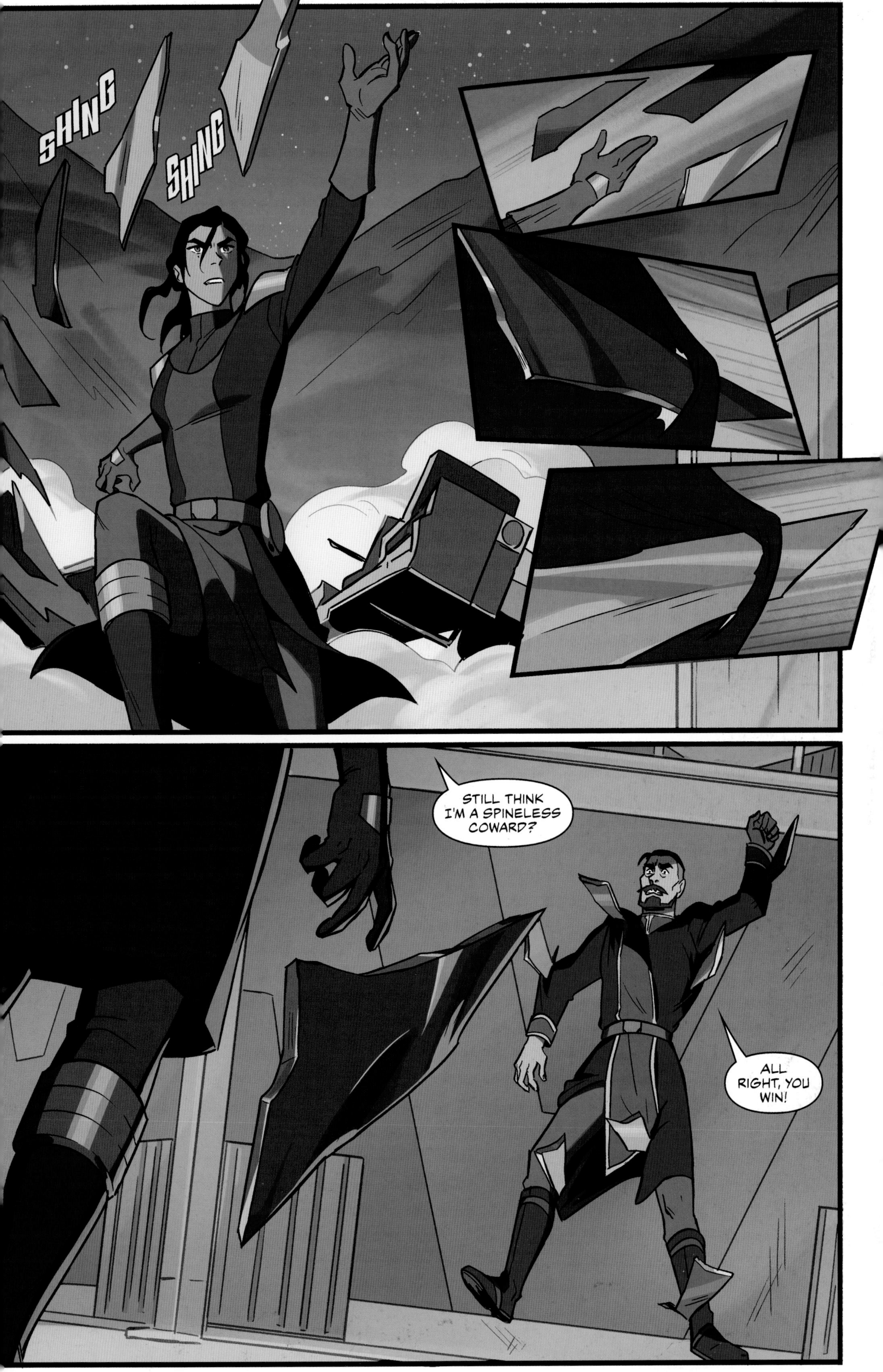
SHING
SHING
STILL THINK I'M A SPINELESS COWARD?
ALL RIGHT, YOU WIN!

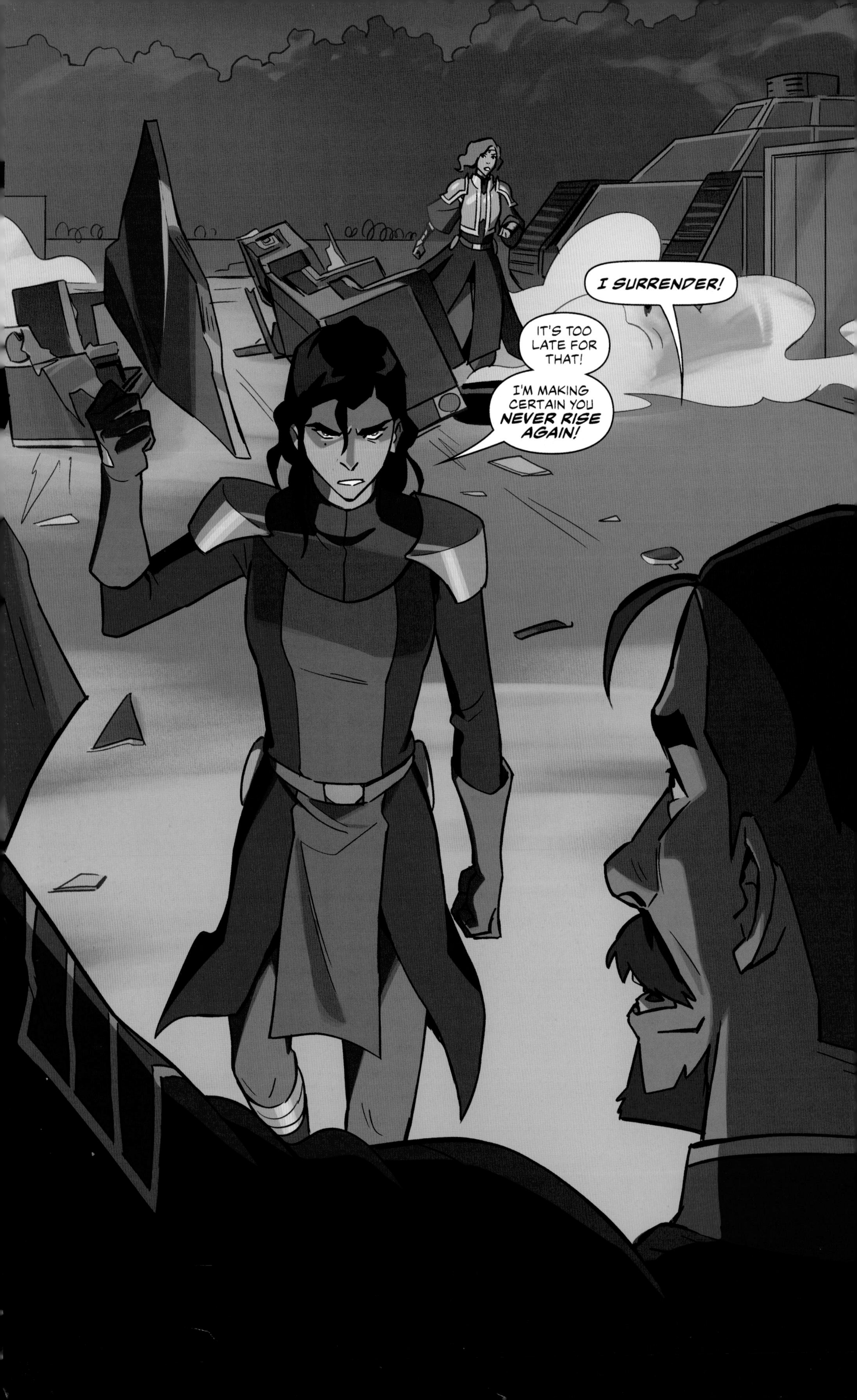
I SURRENDER!
IT'S TOO LATE FOR THAT!
I'M MAKING CERTAIN YOU NEVER RISE AGAIN!

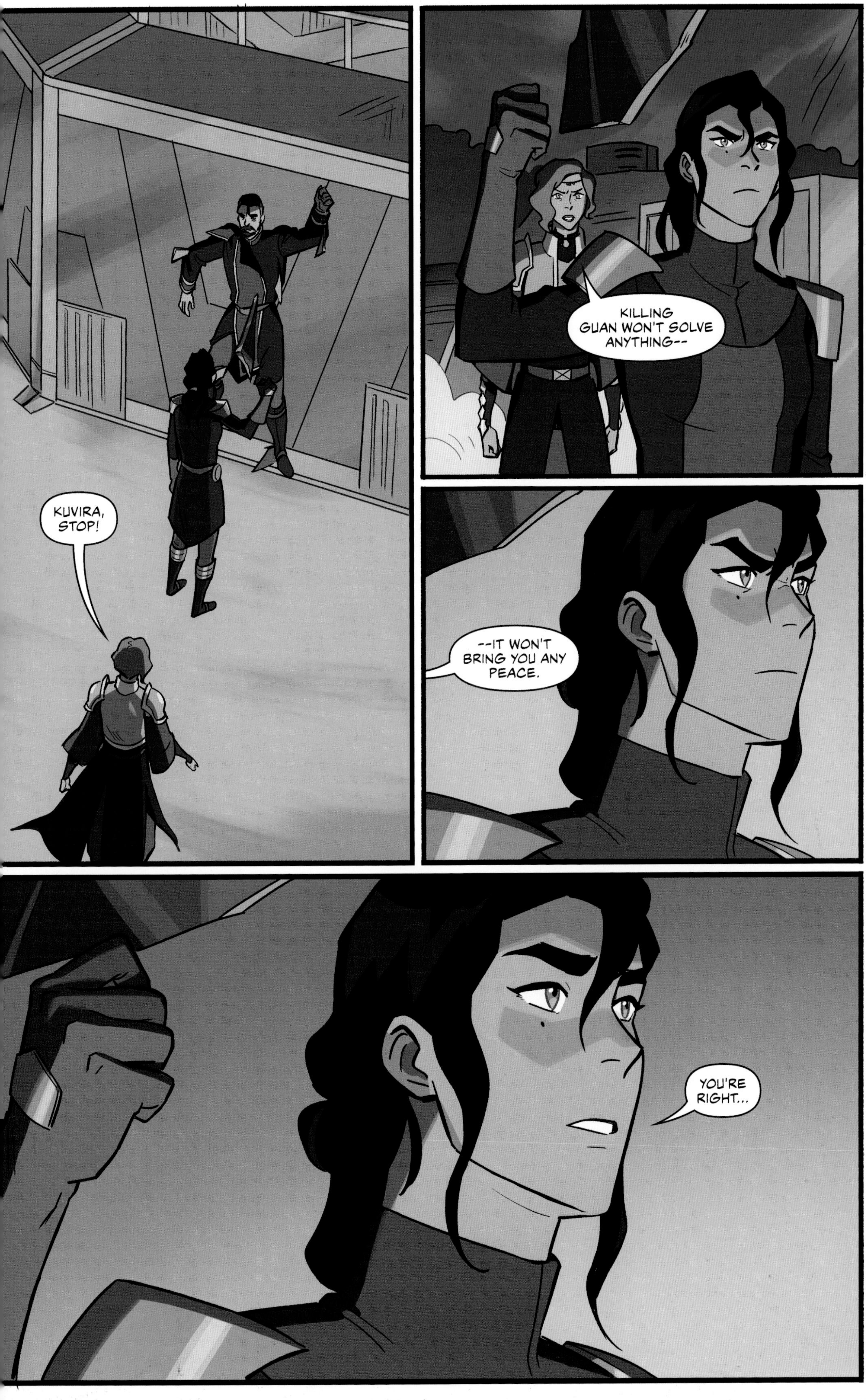
KILLING GUAN WON'T SOLVE ANYTHING--
KUVIRA, STOP!
--IT WON'T BRING YOU ANY PEACE.
YOU'RE RIGHT...

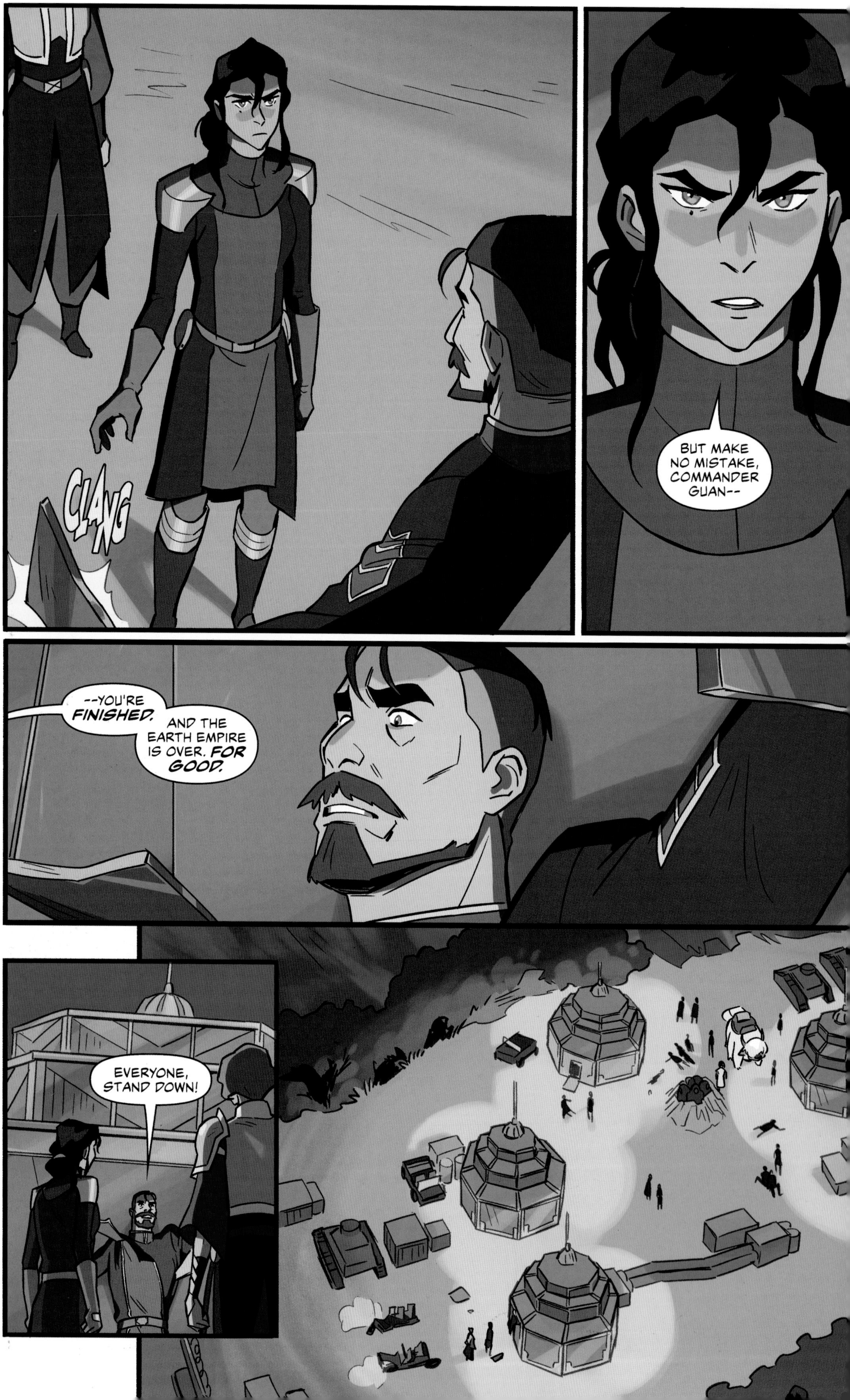
CLANG
BUT MAKE NO MISTAKE, COMMANDER GUAN--
--YOU'RE FINISHED.
AND THE EARTH EMPIRE IS OVER. FOR GOOD.
EVERYONE, STAND DOWN!

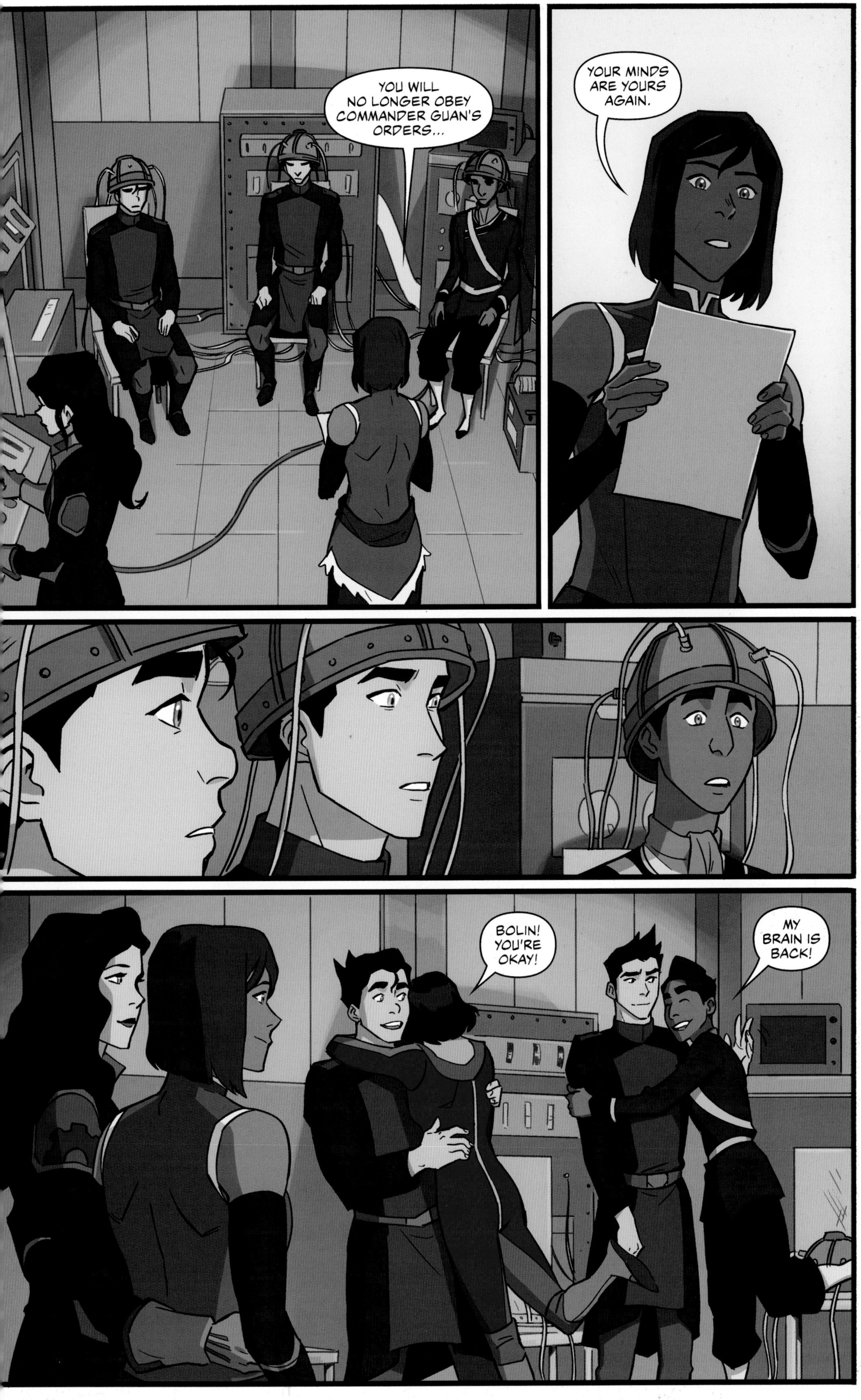
YOU WILL NO LONGER OBEY COMMANDER GUAN'S ORDERS...
YOUR MINDS ARE YOURS AGAIN.
BOLIN! YOU'RE OKAY!
MY BRAIN IS BACK!

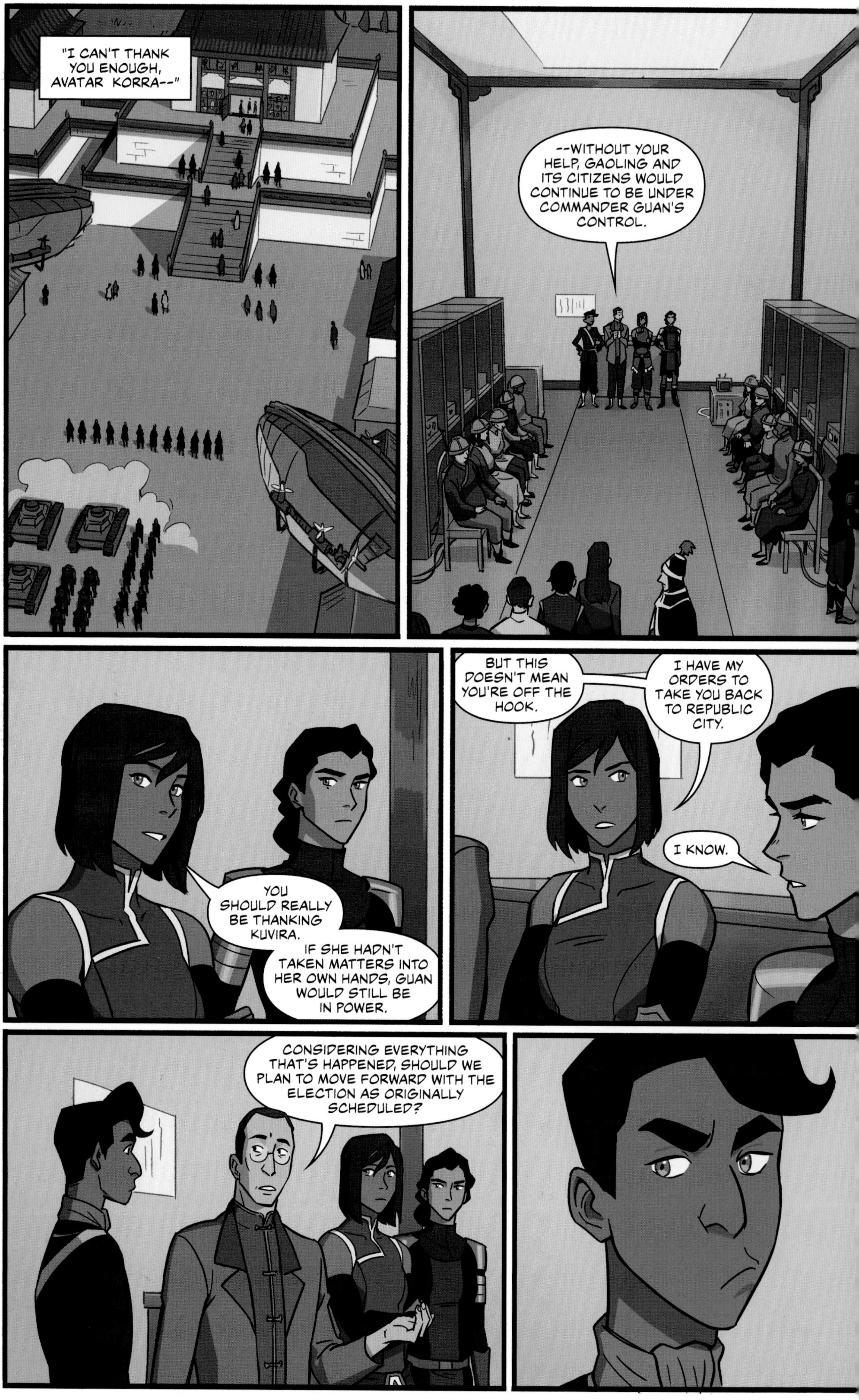
"I CAN'T THANK YOU ENOUGH, AVATAR KORRA--"
--WITHOUT YOUR HELP, GAOLING AND ITS CITIZENS WOULD CONTINUE TO BE UNDER COMMANDER GUAN'S CONTROL.
YOU SHOULD REALLY BE THANKING KUVIRA.
IF SHE HADN'T TAKEN MATTERS INTO HER OWN HANDS, GUAN WOULD STILL BE IN POWER.
BUT THIS DOESN'T MEAN YOU'RE OFF THE HOOK.
I HAVE MY ORDERS TO TAKE YOU BACK TO REPUBLIC CITY.
I KNOW.
CONSIDERING EVERYTHING THAT'S HAPPENED, SHOULD WE PLAN TO MOVE FORWARD WITH THE ELECTION AS ORIGINALLY SCHEDULED?

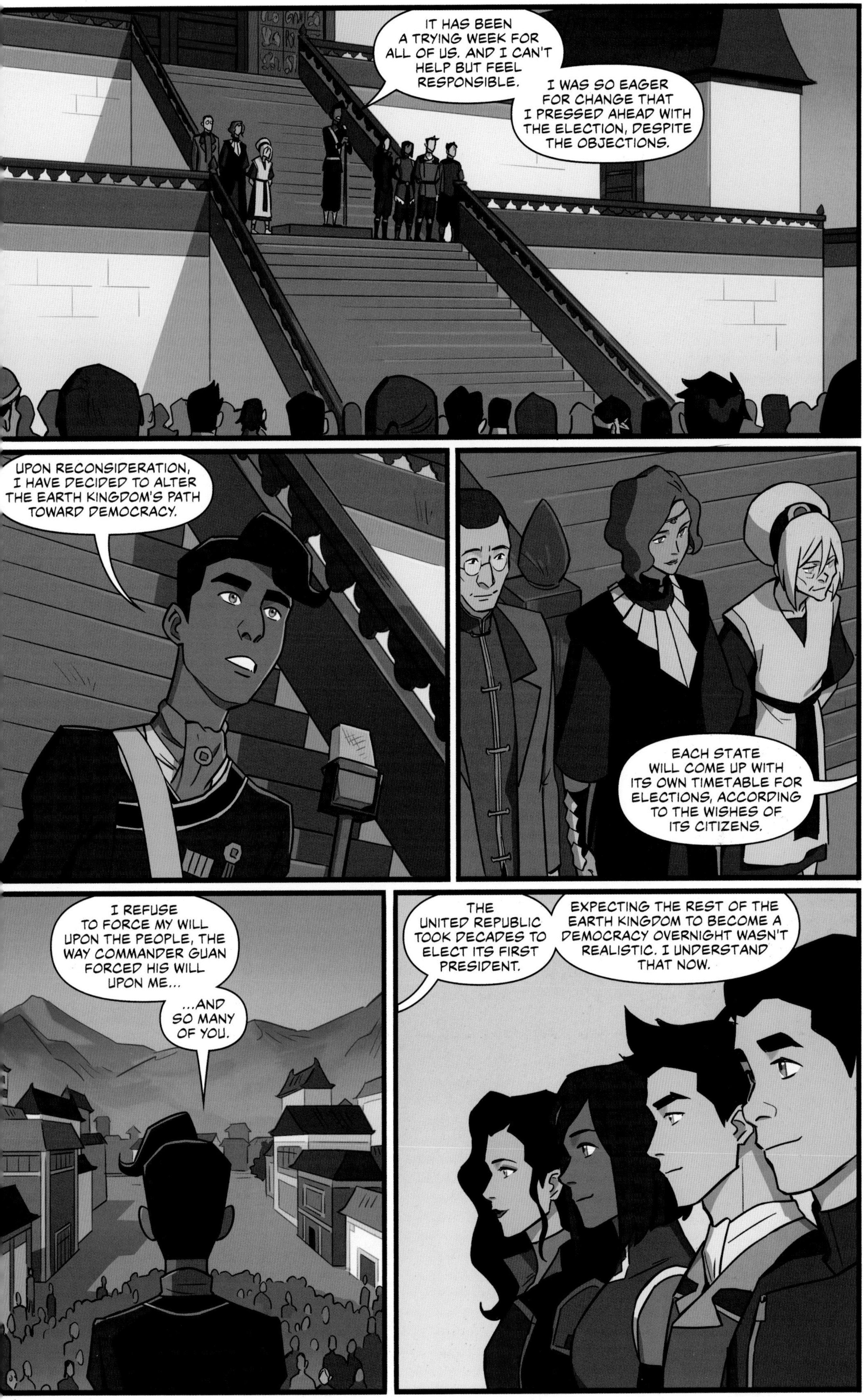
IT HAS BEEN A TRYING WEEK FOR ALL OF US. AND I CAN'T HELP BUT FEEL RESPONSIBLE.
I WAS SO EAGER FOR CHANGE THAT I PRESSED AHEAD WITH THE ELECTION, DESPITE THE OBJECTIONS.
UPON RECONSIDERATION, I HAVE DECIDED TO ALTER THE EARTH KINGDOM'S PATH TOWARD DEMOCRACY.
EACH STATE WILL COME UP WITH ITS OWN TIMETABLE FOR ELECTIONS, ACCORDING TO THE WISHES OF ITS CITIZENS.
I REFUSE TO FORCE MY WILL UPON THE PEOPLE, THE WAY COMMANDER GUAN FORCED HIS WILL UPON ME...
...AND SO MANY OF YOU.
THE UNITED REPUBLIC TOOK DECADES TO ELECT ITS FIRST PRESIDENT.
EXPECTING THE REST OF THE EARTH KINGDOM TO BECOME A DEMOCRACY OVERNIGHT WASN'T REALISTIC. I UNDERSTAND THAT NOW.

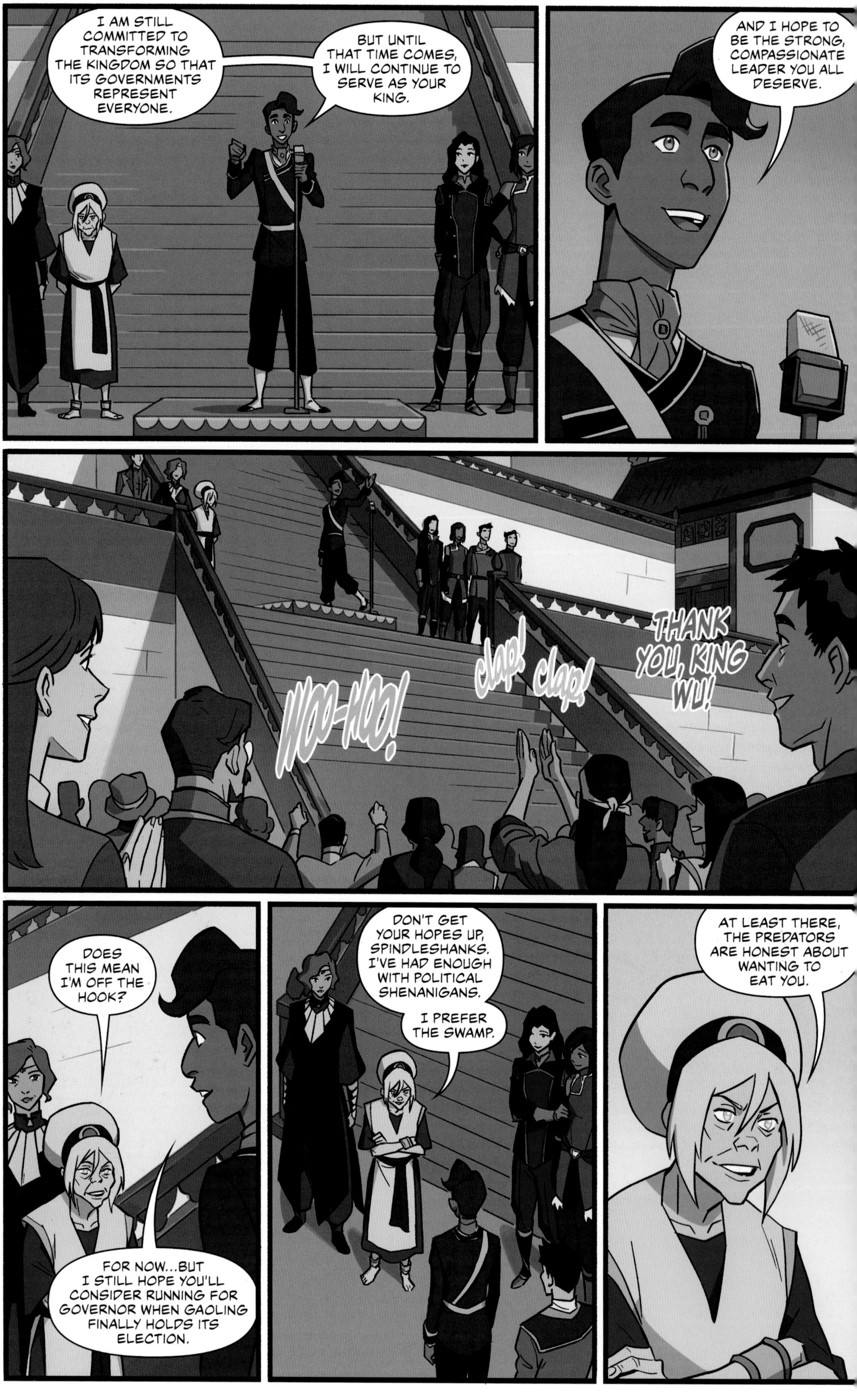
I AM STILL COMMITTED TO TRANSFORMING THE KINGDOM SO THAT ITS GOVERNMENTS REPRESENT EVERYONE.
BUT UNTIL THAT TIME COMES, I WILL CONTINUE TO SERVE AS YOUR KING.
AND I HOPE TO BE THE STRONG, COMPASSIONATE LEADER YOU ALL DESERVE.
WOO-HOO!
CLAP! CLAP!
THANK YOU, KING WU!
DOES THIS MEAN I'M OFF THE HOOK?
FOR NOW...BUT I STILL HOPE YOU'LL CONSIDER RUNNING FOR GOVERNOR WHEN GAOLING FINALLY HOLDS ITS ELECTION.
DON'T GET YOUR HOPES UP, SPINDLESHANKS. I'VE HAD ENOUGH WITH POLITICAL SHENANIGANS.
I PREFER THE SWAMP.
AT LEAST THERE, THE PREDATORS ARE HONEST ABOUT WANTING TO EAT YOU.

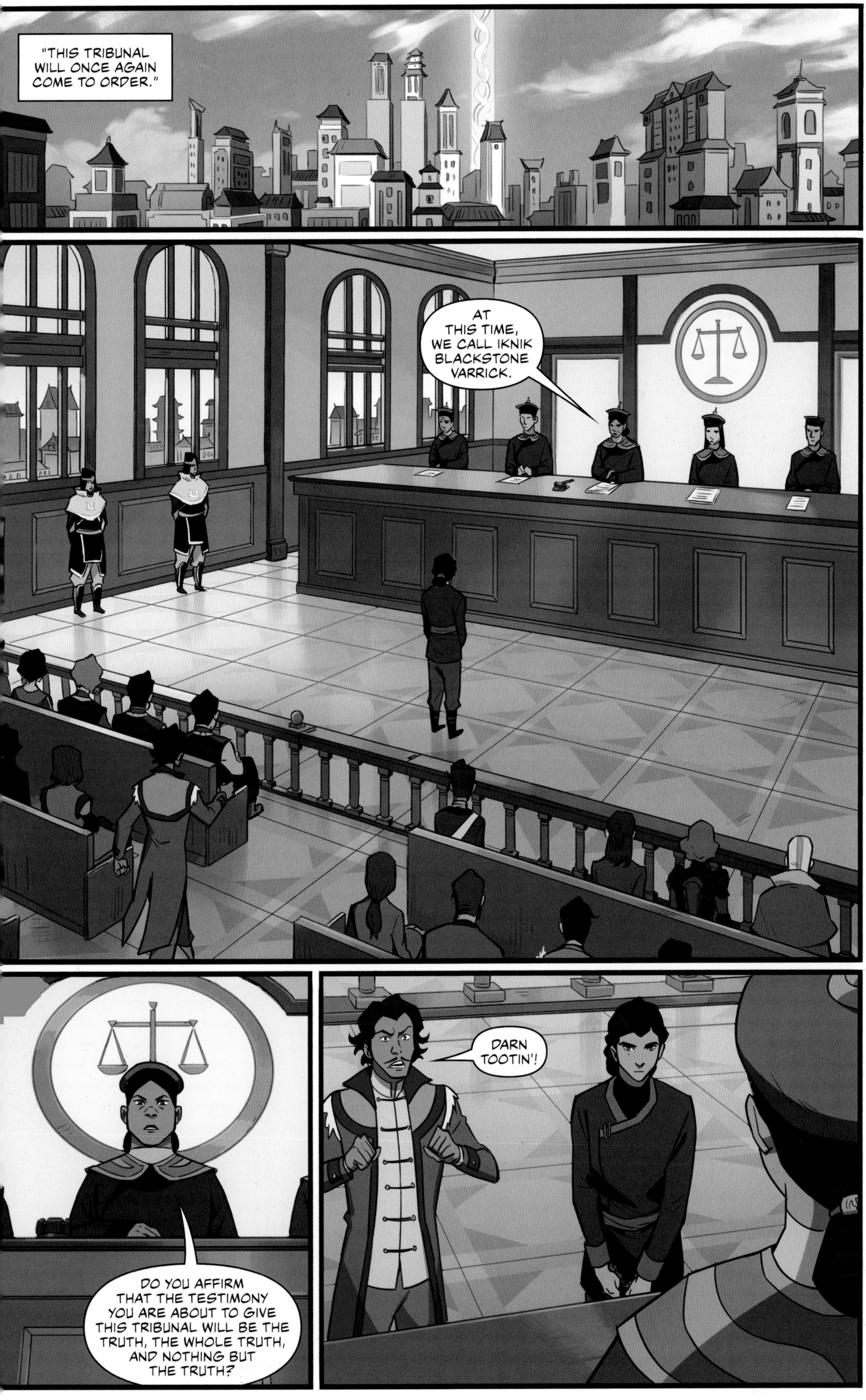
"THIS TRIBUNAL WILL ONCE AGAIN COME TO ORDER."
AT THIS TIME, WE CALL IKNIK BLACKSTONE VARRICK.
DO YOU AFFIRM THAT THE TESTIMONY YOU ARE ABOUT TO GIVE THIS TRIBUNAL WILL BE THE TRUTH, THE WHOLE TRUTH, AND NOTHING BUT THE TRUTH?
DARN TOOTIN'!

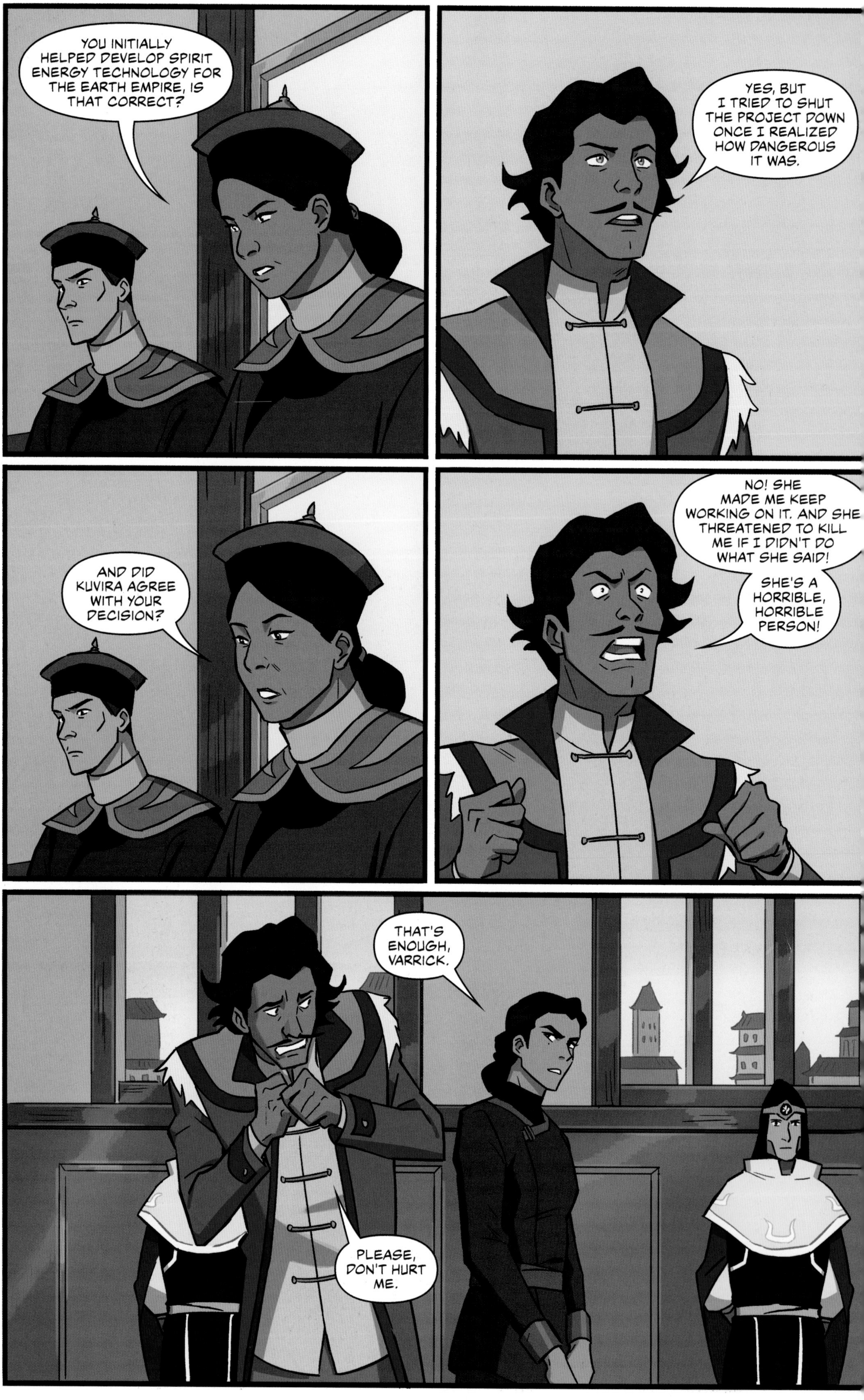
YOU INITIALLY HELPED DEVELOP SPIRIT ENERGY TECHNOLOGY FOR THE EARTH EMPIRE, IS THAT CORRECT?
YES, BUT I TRIED TO SHUT THE PROJECT DOWN ONCE I REALIZED HOW DANGEROUS IT WAS.
AND DID KUVIRA AGREE WITH YOUR DECISION?
NO! SHE MADE ME KEEP WORKING ON IT. AND SHE THREATENED TO KILL ME IF I DIDN'T DO WHAT SHE SAID!
SHE'S A HORRIBLE, HORRIBLE PERSON!
THAT'S ENOUGH, VARRICK.
PLEASE, DON'T HURT ME.

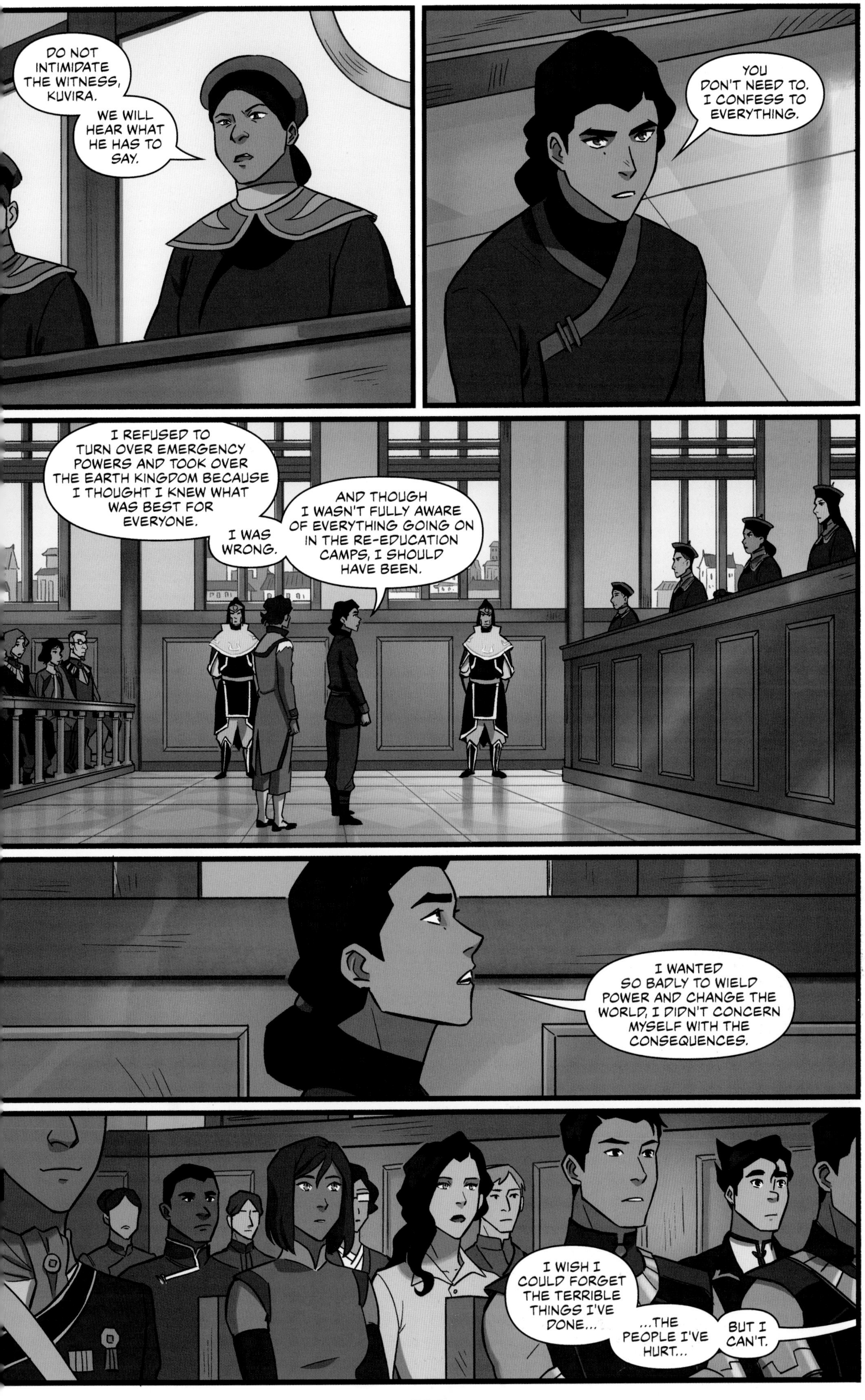
DO NOT INTIMIDATE THE WITNESS, KUVIRA.
WE WILL HEAR WHAT HE HAS TO SAY.
YOU DON'T NEED TO. I CONFESS TO EVERYTHING.
I REFUSED TO TURN OVER EMERGENCY POWERS AND TOOK OVER THE EARTH KINGDOM BECAUSE I THOUGHT I KNEW WHAT WAS BEST FOR EVERYONE.
I WAS WRONG.
AND THOUGH I WASN'T FULLY AWARE OF EVERYTHING GOING ON IN THE RE-EDUCATION CAMPS, I SHOULD HAVE BEEN.
I WANTED SO BADLY TO WIELD POWER AND CHANGE THE WORLD, I DIDN'T CONCERN MYSELF WITH THE CONSEQUENCES.
I WISH I COULD FORGET THE TERRIBLE THINGS I'VE DONE...
...THE PEOPLE I'VE HURT...
BUT I CAN'T.

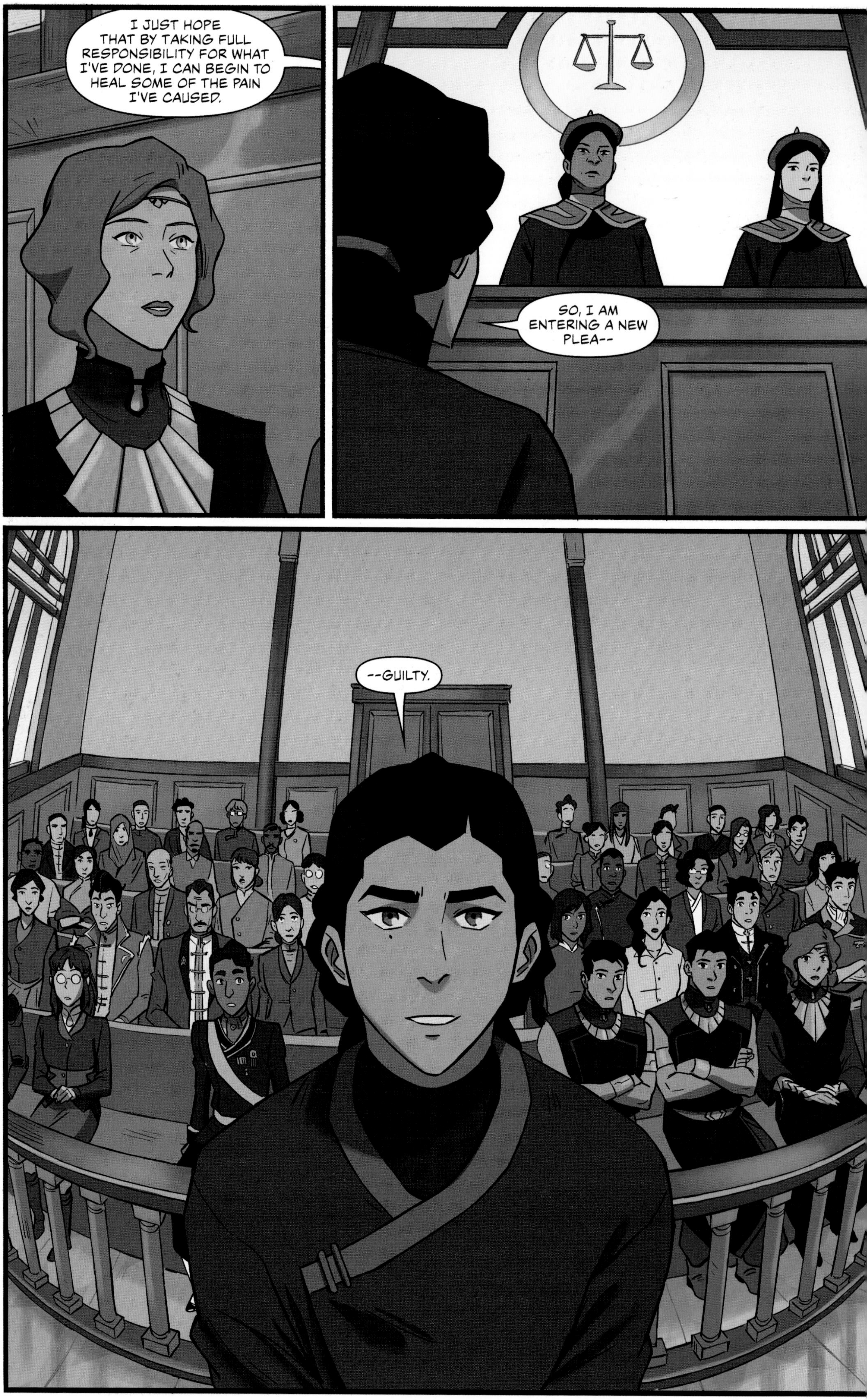
I JUST HOPE THAT BY TAKING FULL RESPONSIBILITY FOR WHAT I'VE DONE, I CAN BEGIN TO HEAL SOME OF THE PAIN I'VE CAUSED.
SO, I AM ENTERING A NEW PLEA--
--GUILTY.

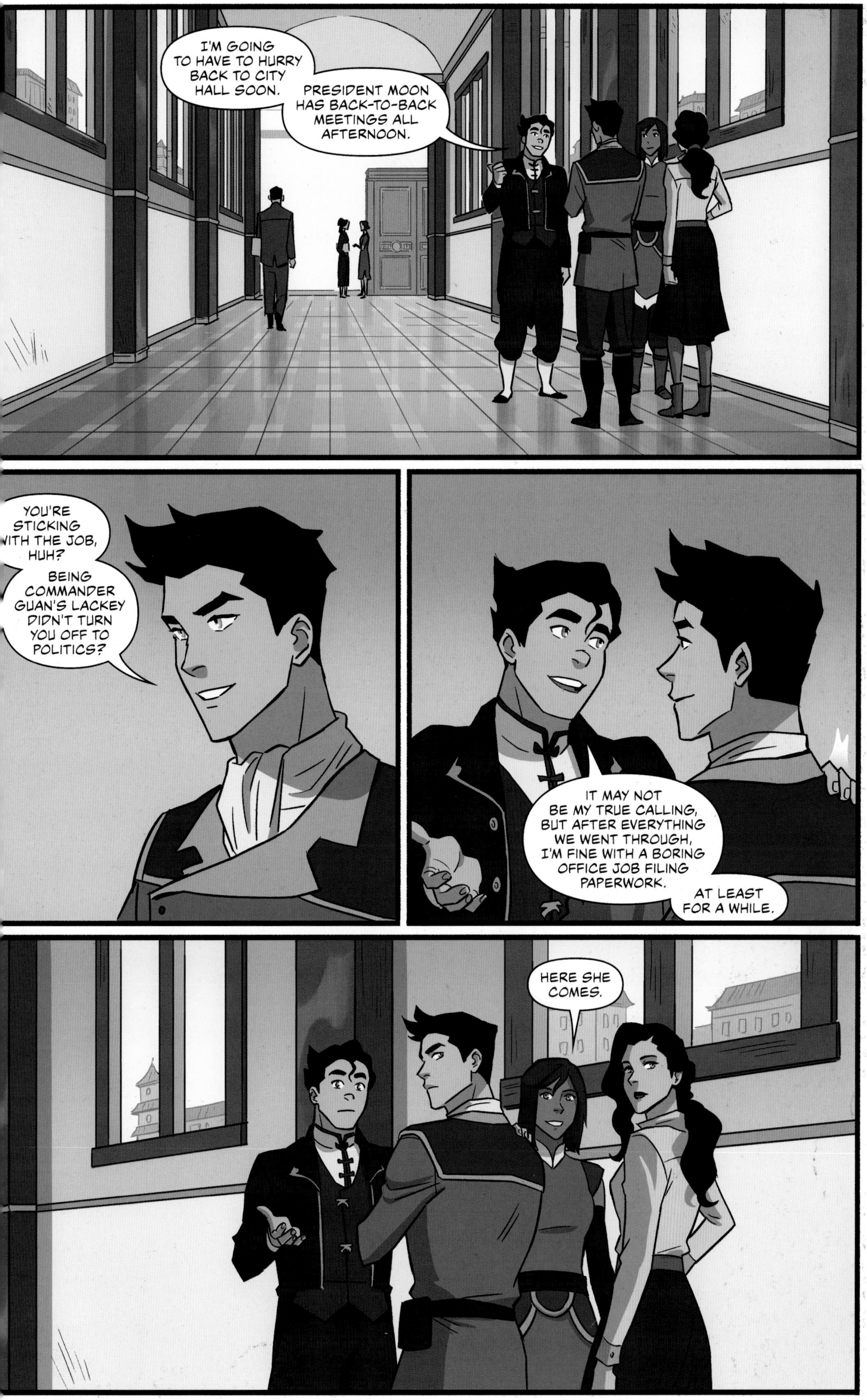
I'M GOING TO HAVE TO HURRY BACK TO CITY HALL SOON.
PRESIDENT MOON HAS BACK-TO-BACK MEETINGS ALL AFTERNOON.
YOU'RE STICKING WITH THE JOB, HUH?
BEING COMMANDER GUAN'S LACKEY DIDN'T TURN YOU OFF TO POLITICS?
IT MAY NOT BE MY TRUE CALLING, BUT AFTER EVERYTHING WE WENT THROUGH, I'M FINE WITH A BORING OFFICE JOB FILING PAPERWORK.
AT LEAST FOR A WHILE.
HERE SHE COMES.

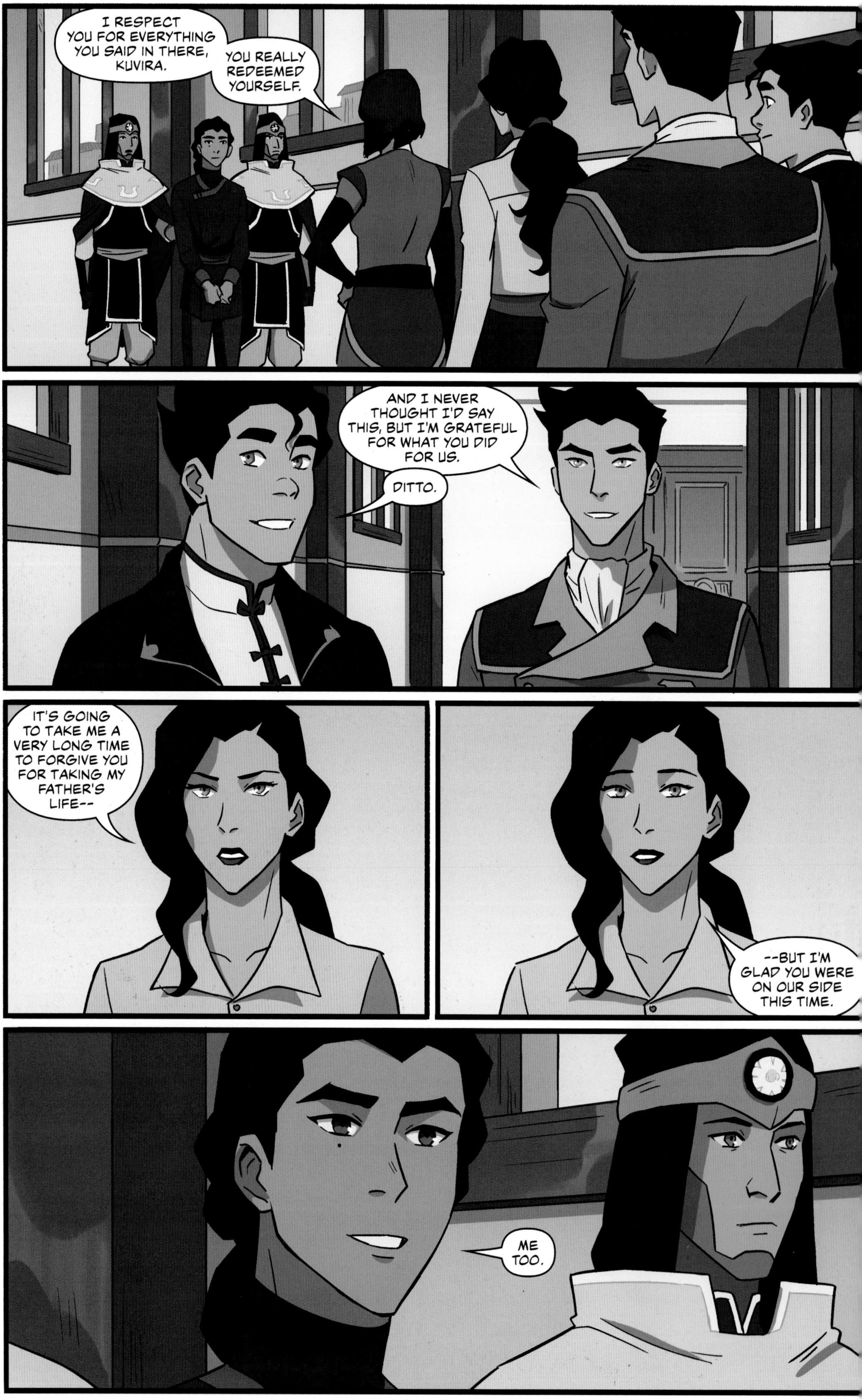
I RESPECT YOU FOR EVERYTHING YOU SAID IN THERE, KUVIRA.
YOU REALLY REDEEMED YOURSELF.
AND I NEVER THOUGHT I'D SAY THIS, BUT I'M GRATEFUL FOR WHAT YOU DID FOR US.
DITTO.
IT'S GOING TO TAKE ME A VERY LONG TIME TO FORGIVE YOU FOR TAKING MY FATHER'S LIFE--
--BUT I'M GLAD YOU WERE ON OUR SIDE THIS TIME.
ME TOO.

I OWE YOU AN APOLOGY, KUVIRA.

WHAT ARE YOU TALKING ABOUT?

I CAN'T HELP BUT THINK THAT IF I HAD BEEN A BETTER MENTOR --A BETTER *MOTHER*-- I COULD HAVE GUIDED YOU ON A MORE APPROPRIATE PATH.

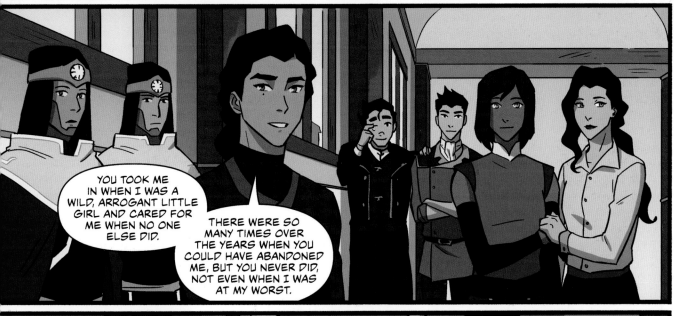

YOU TOOK ME IN WHEN I WAS A WILD, ARROGANT LITTLE GIRL AND CARED FOR ME WHEN NO ONE ELSE DID.

THERE WERE SO MANY TIMES OVER THE YEARS WHEN YOU COULD HAVE ABANDONED ME, BUT YOU NEVER DID, NOT EVEN WHEN I WAS AT MY WORST.

SO, YOU HAVE NOTHING TO APOLOGIZE FOR. I'M THE ONE WHO IS SORRY I NEVER FULLY APPRECIATED WHAT AN AMAZING, SELFLESS MOTHER YOU ARE.

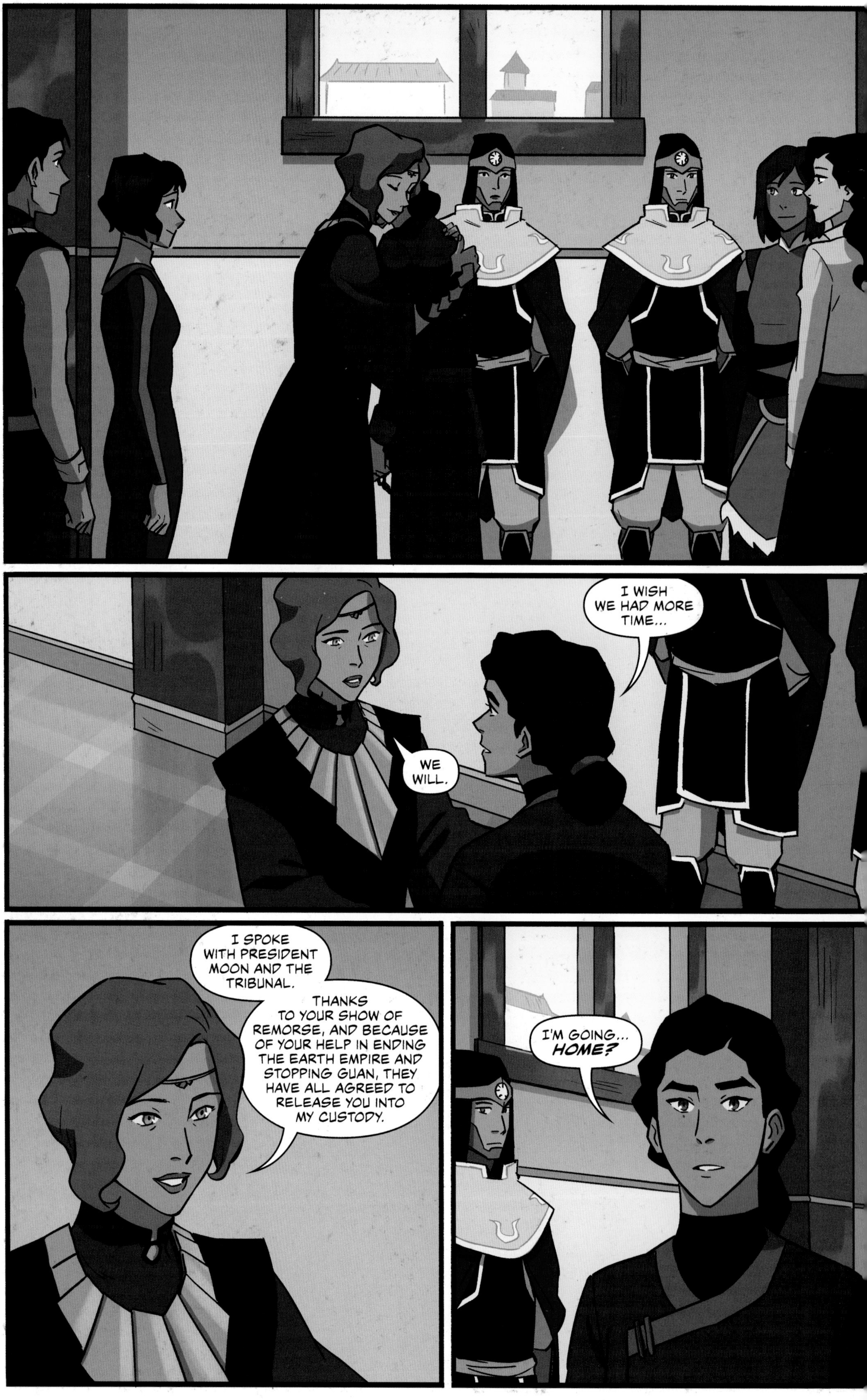
I WISH WE HAD MORE TIME...
WE WILL.
I SPOKE WITH PRESIDENT MOON AND THE TRIBUNAL.
THANKS TO YOUR SHOW OF REMORSE, AND BECAUSE OF YOUR HELP IN ENDING THE EARTH EMPIRE AND STOPPING GUAN, THEY HAVE ALL AGREED TO RELEASE YOU INTO MY CUSTODY.
I'M GOING... HOME?

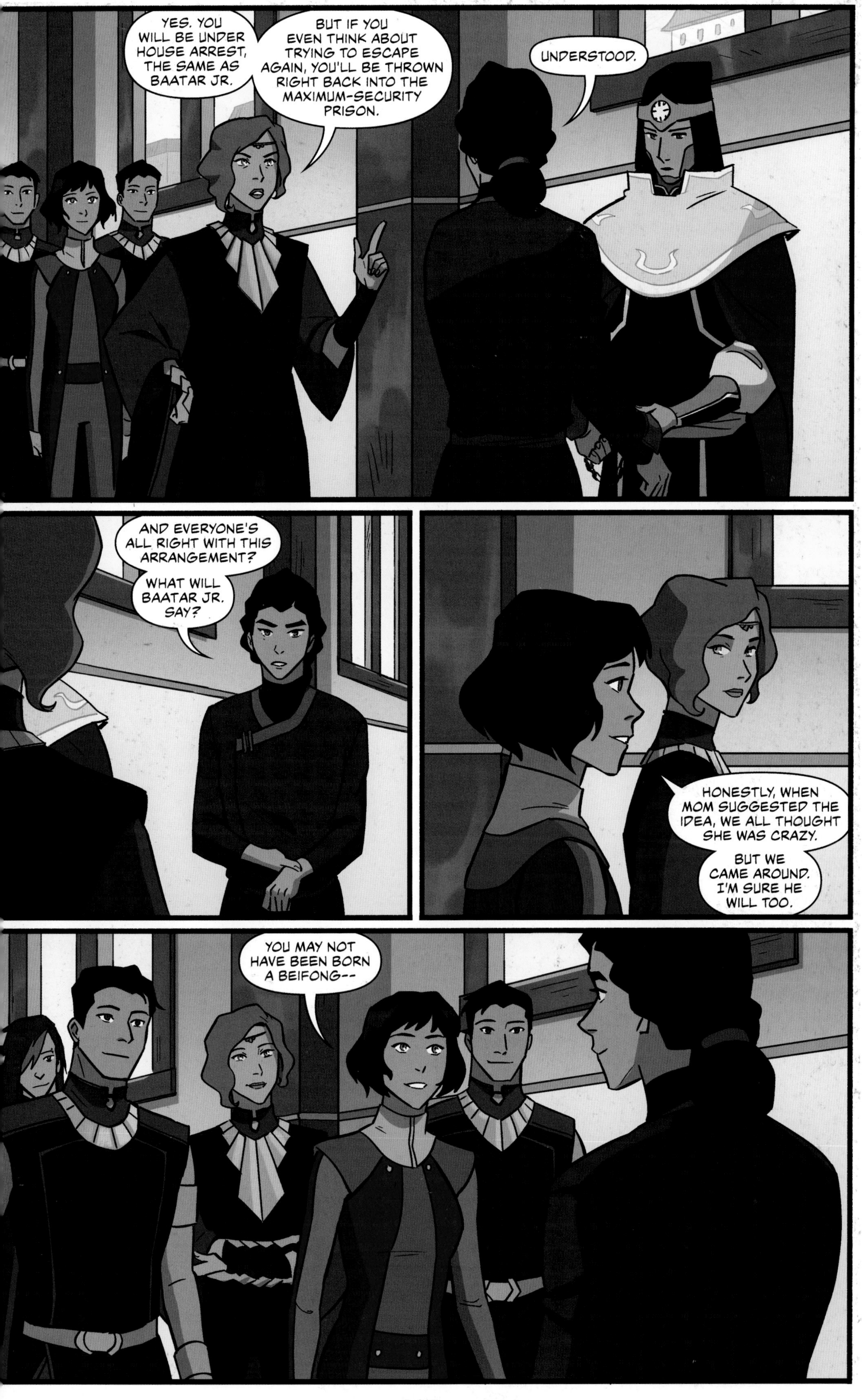
YES. YOU WILL BE UNDER HOUSE ARREST, THE SAME AS BAATAR JR.
BUT IF YOU EVEN THINK ABOUT TRYING TO ESCAPE AGAIN, YOU'LL BE THROWN RIGHT BACK INTO THE MAXIMUM-SECURITY PRISON.
UNDERSTOOD.
AND EVERYONE'S ALL RIGHT WITH THIS ARRANGEMENT?
WHAT WILL BAATAR JR. SAY?
HONESTLY, WHEN MOM SUGGESTED THE IDEA, WE ALL THOUGHT SHE WAS CRAZY.
BUT WE CAME AROUND. I'M SURE HE WILL TOO.
YOU MAY NOT HAVE BEEN BORN A BEIFONG--

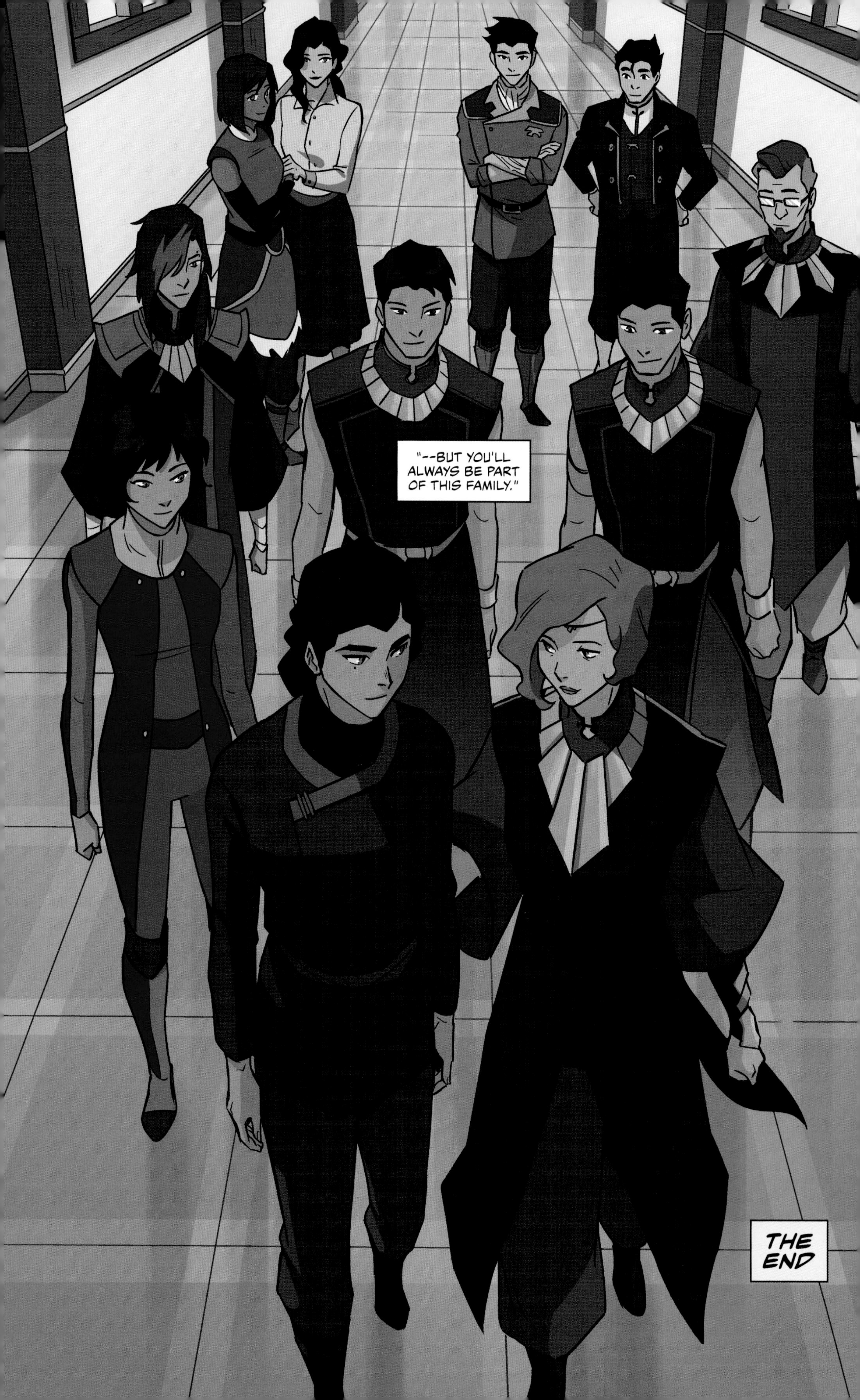
"--BUT YOU'LL ALWAYS BE PART OF THIS FAMILY."
THE END

THE LEGEND OF KORRA

nickelodeon

Process Sketchbook

Illustrations by MICHELLE WONG
with Commentary by RACHEL ROBERTS

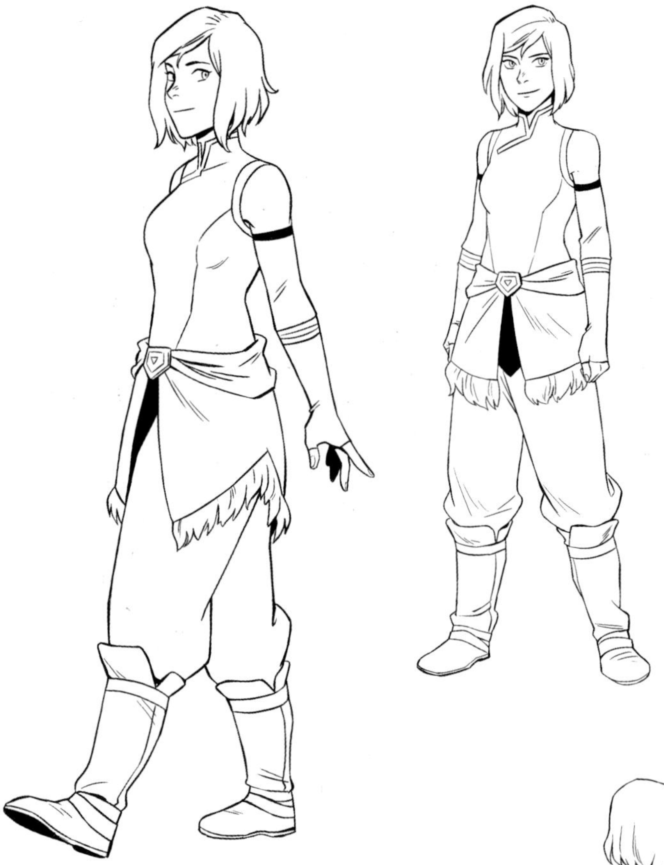

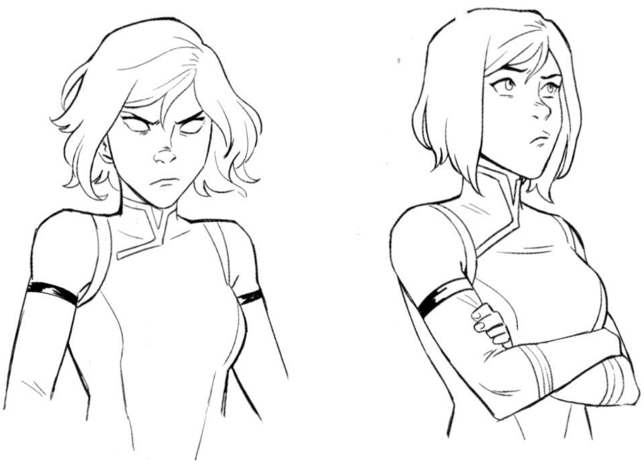

In her foreword, Michelle Wong mentioned her initial style tests—the images shown on this spread. Truth be told, all of us on the team were completely sold on Michelle's style, her confident and bold inking, and her strength with expressions before these drawings were even done. Anecdotally speaking, it was a piece of Voltron: Legendary Defender *fan art on Twitter that made us fall in love with her work.*

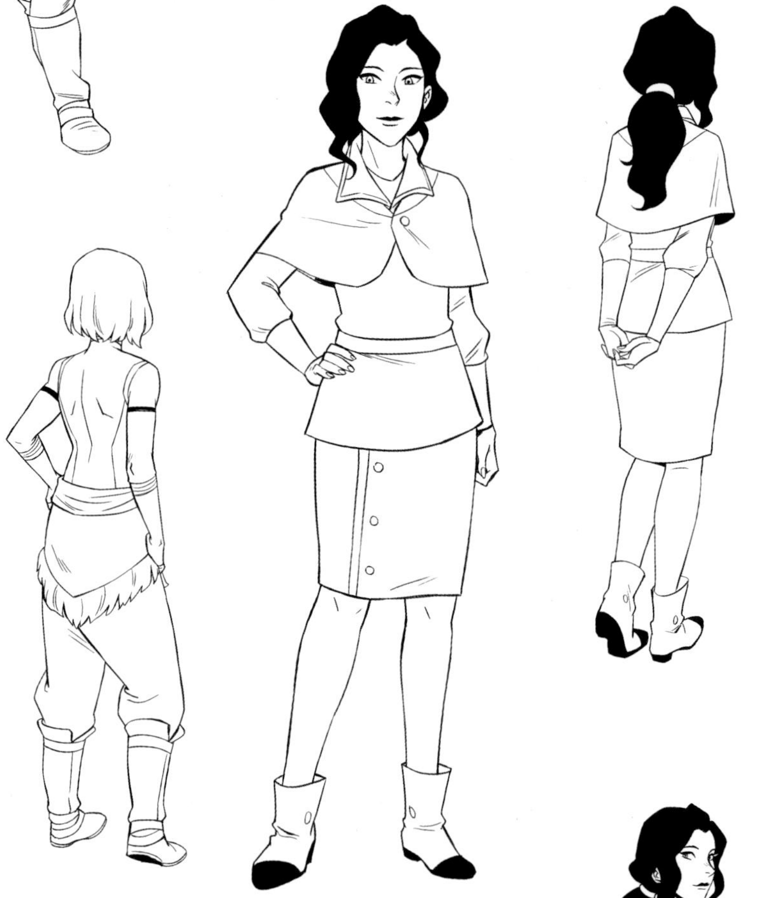

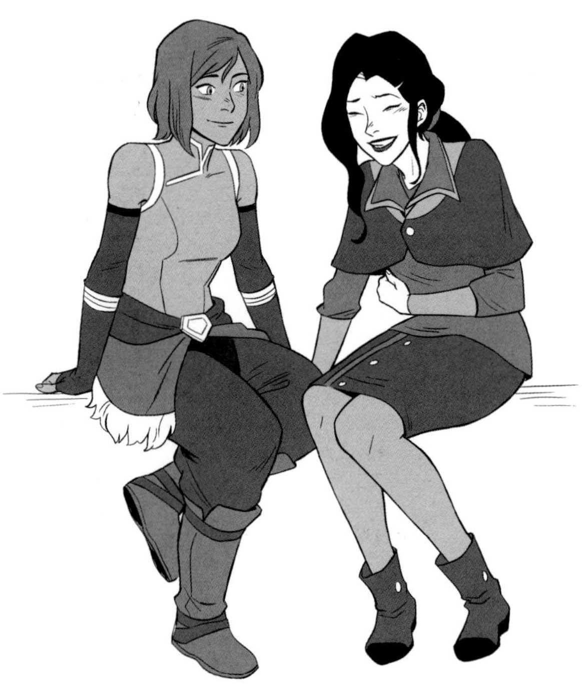

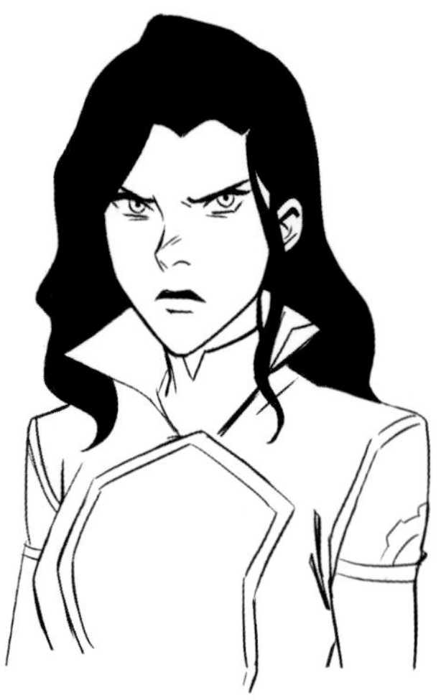

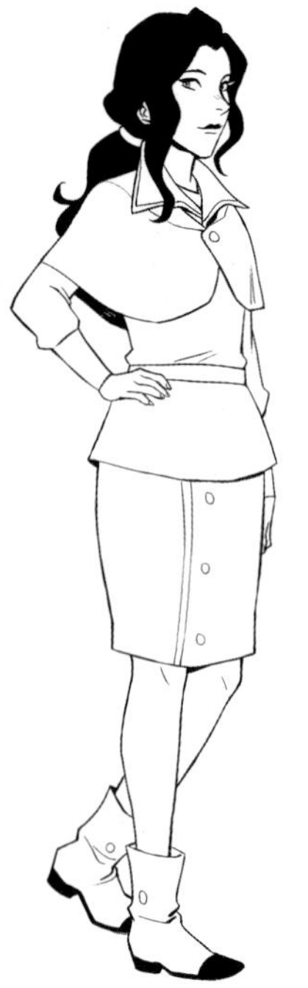

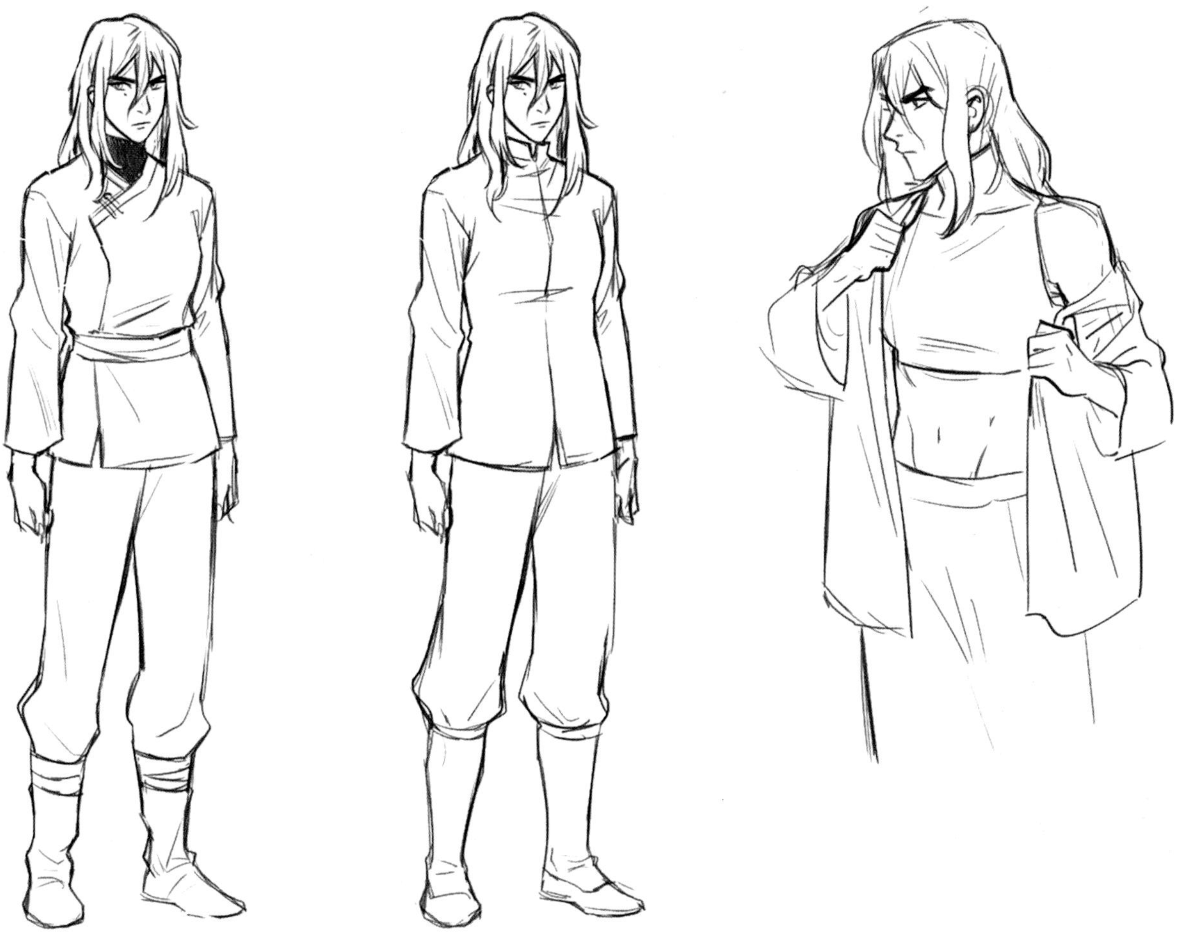

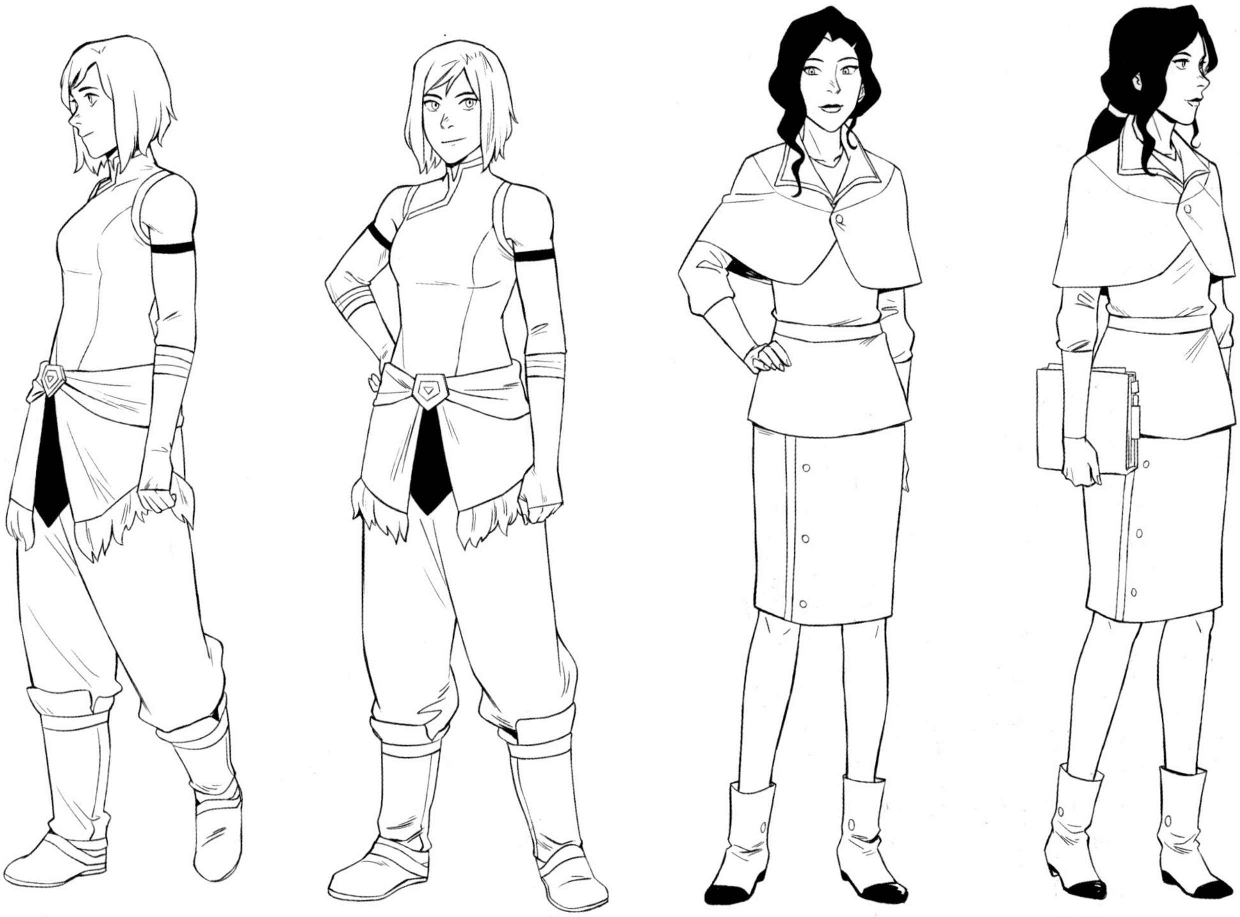

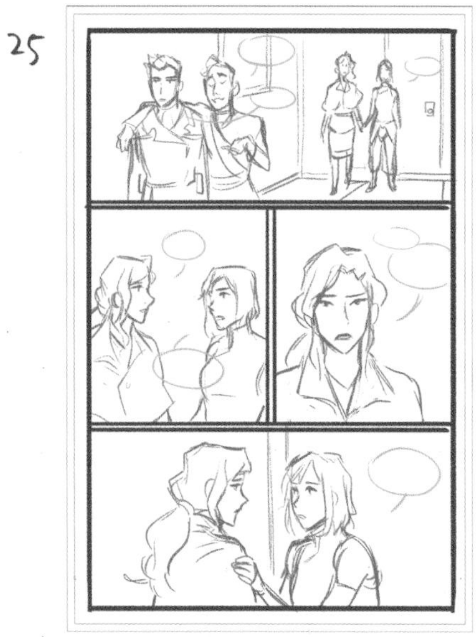
25

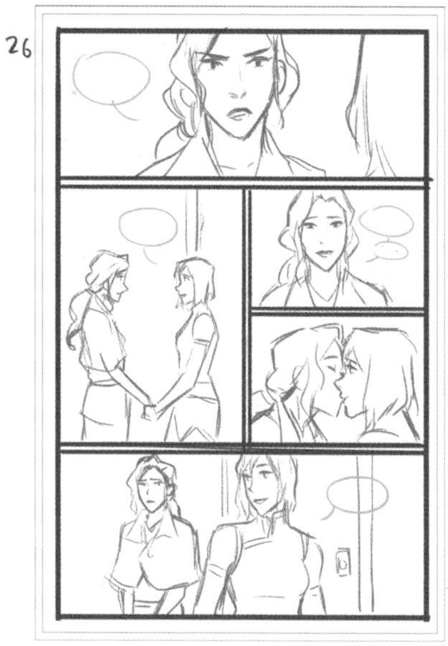
26

Michelle's layouts for various scenes throughout the trilogy, and the process pages for a scene from Part One (below)*. Michelle would often put notes, ideas and sketches, or questions in the layout's margins, which made it easy for us to review with a better understanding of what she had in mind.*

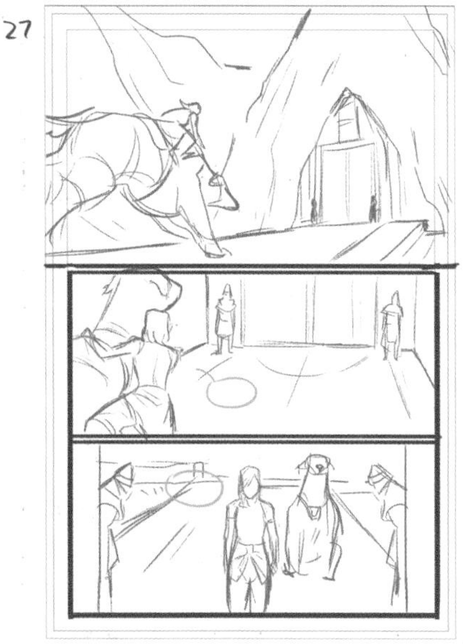
27

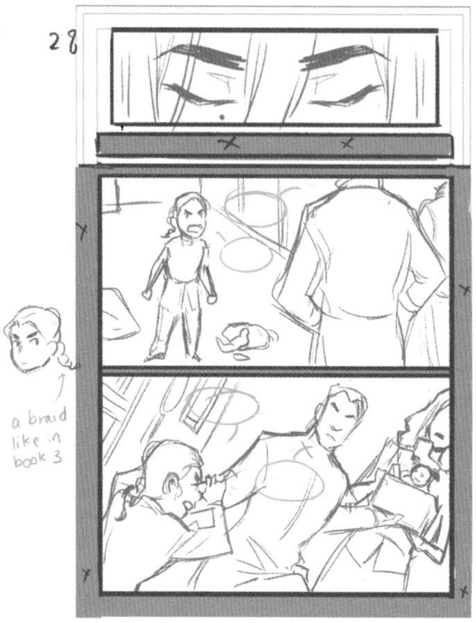
28
a braid like in book 3

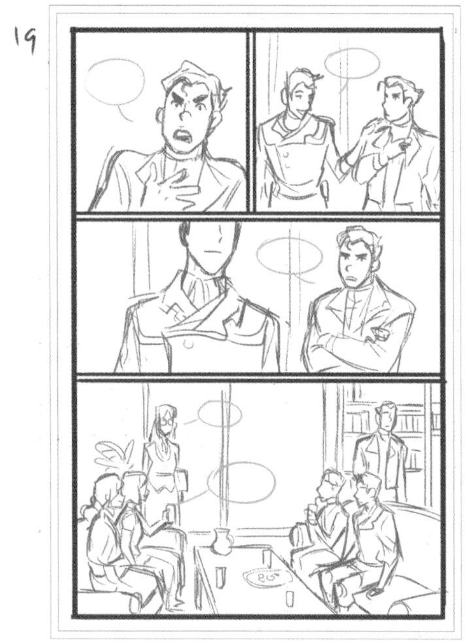
19

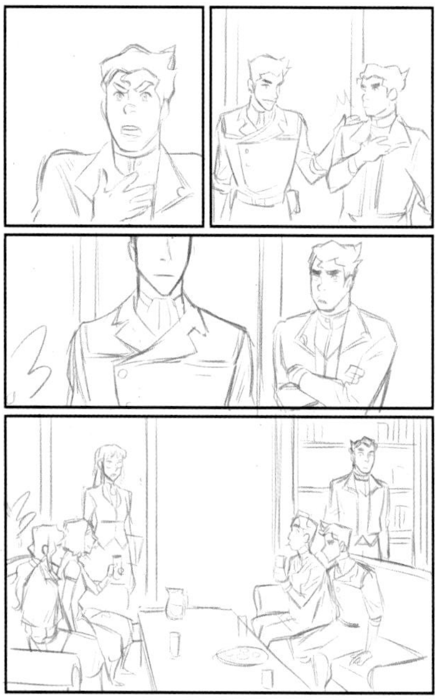

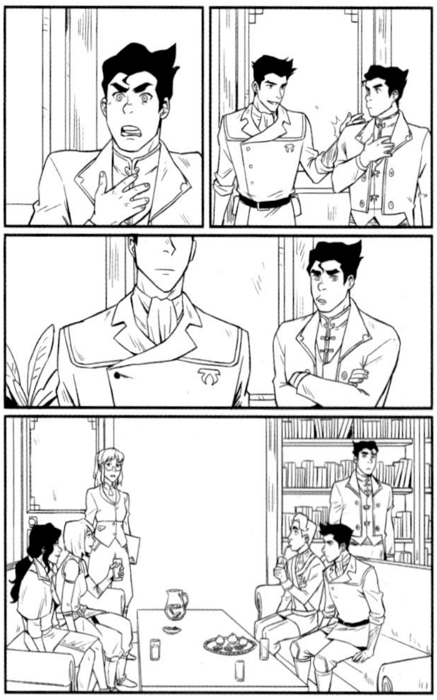

49
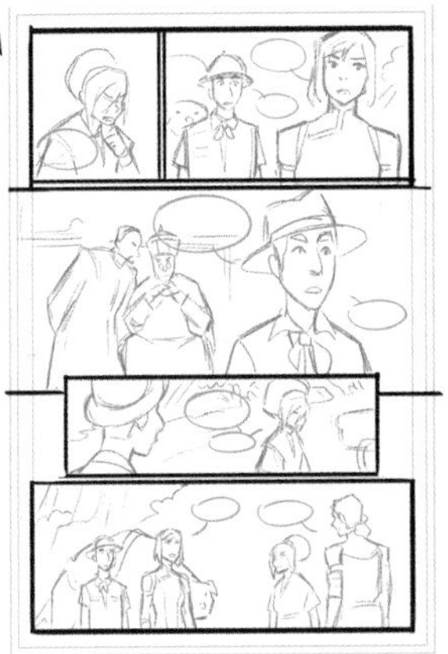

50
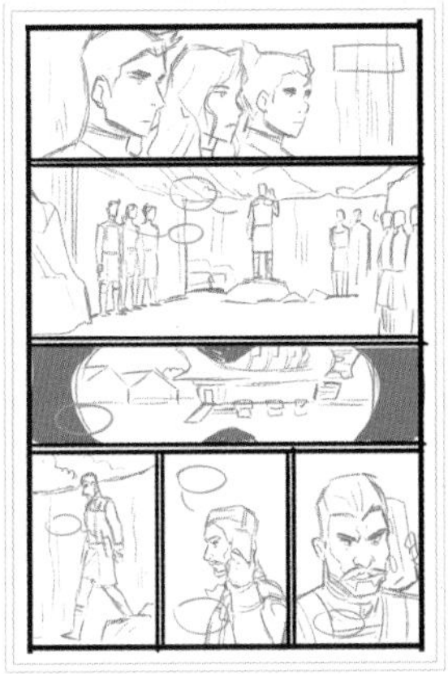

51
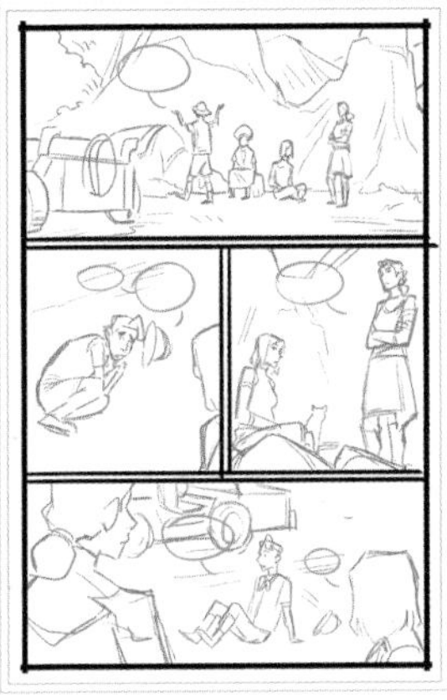

52
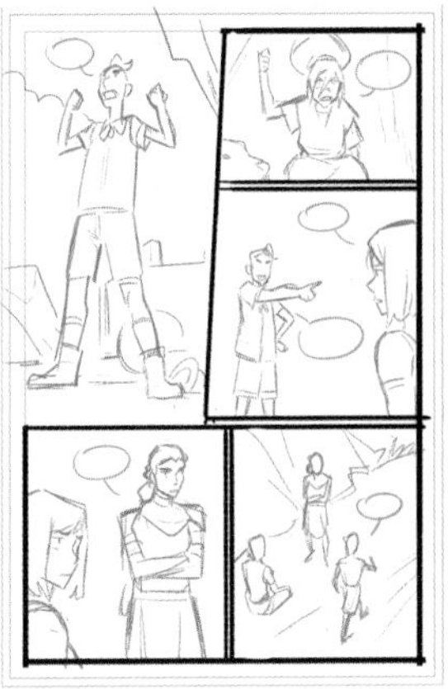

53
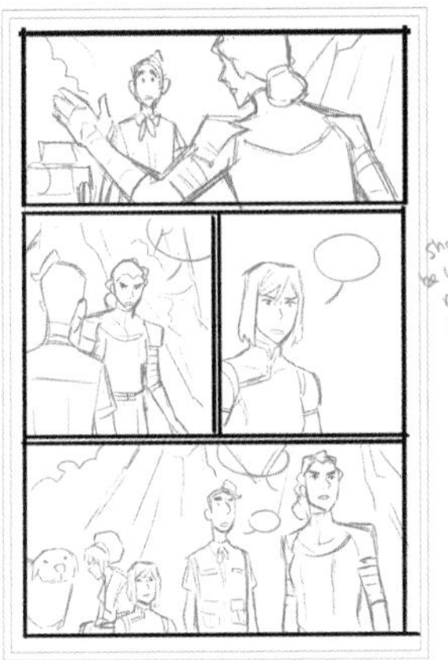

54
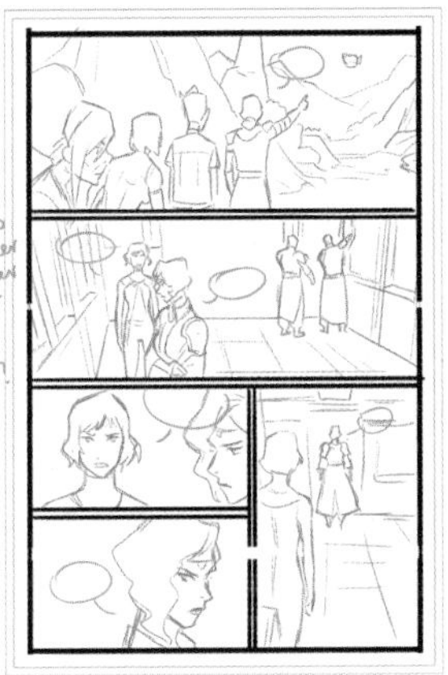

should Su also be wearing her metalbender armor or just her normal outfit?

55
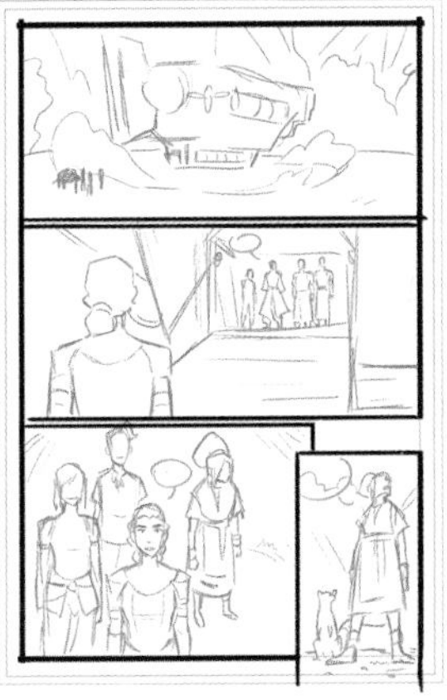

56
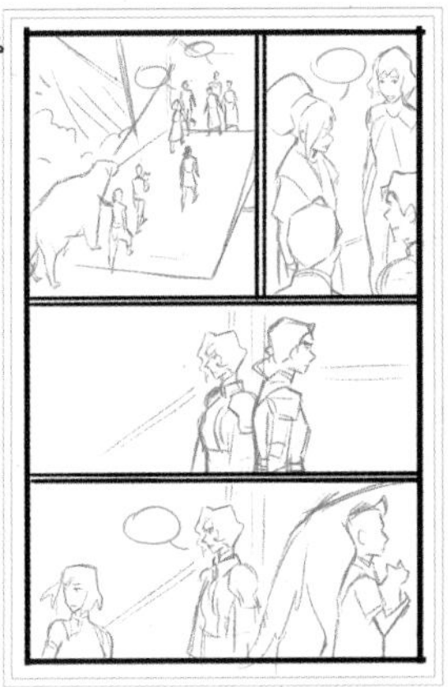

57
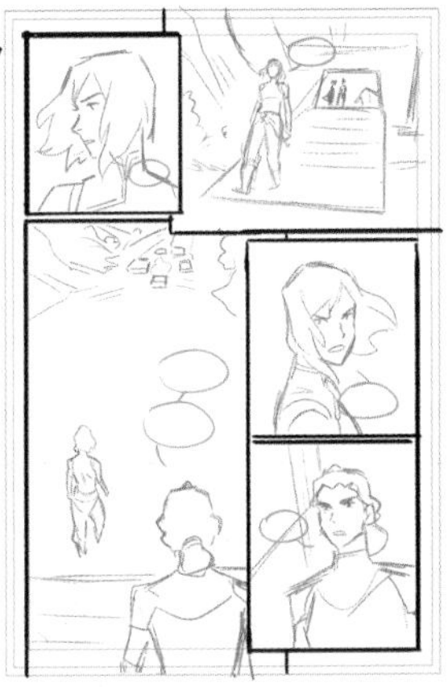

58
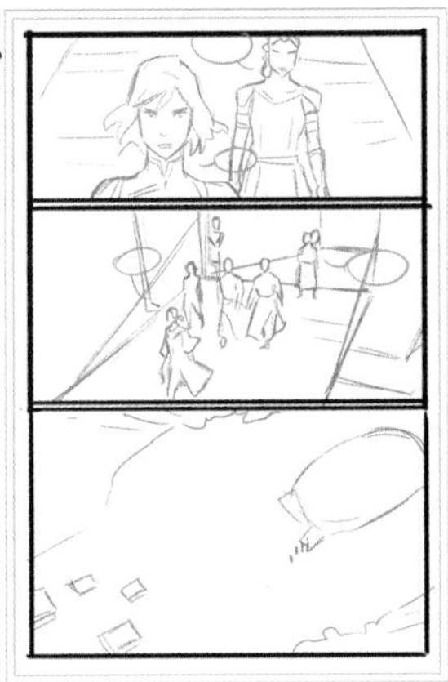

59
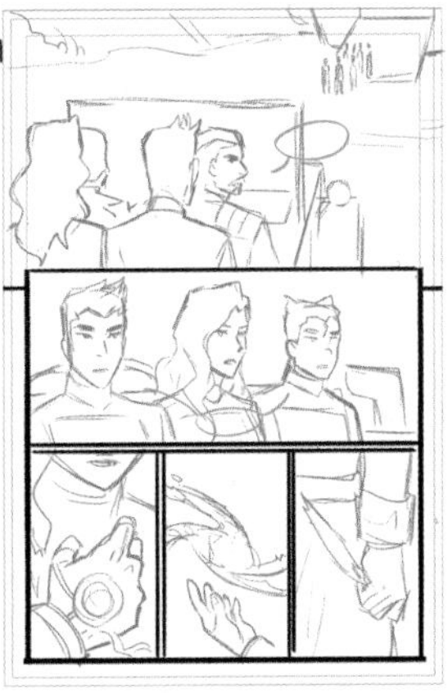

60
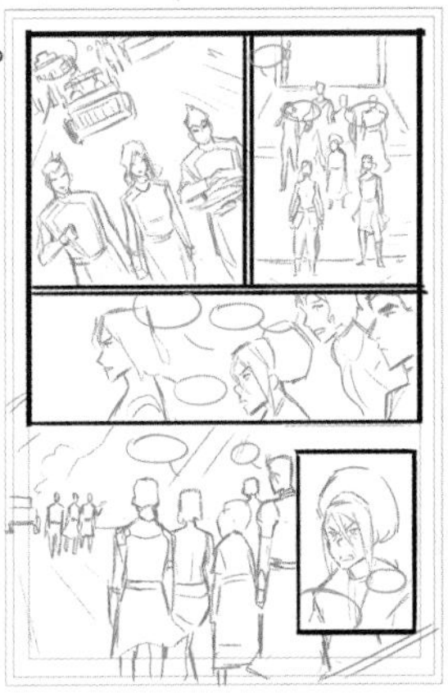

65
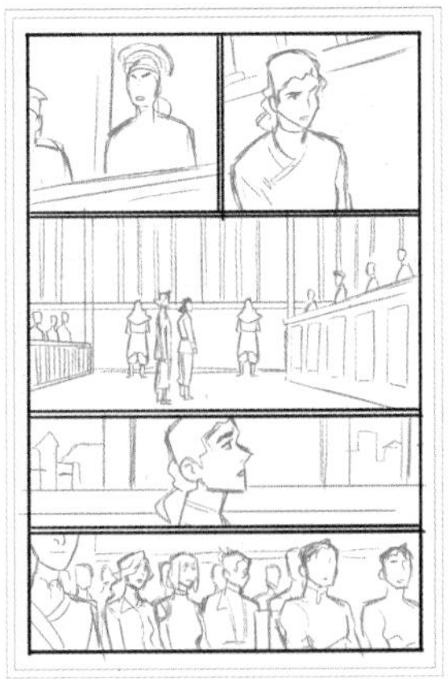

asami wearing one of the outfits from her concepts in Book 4 artbook

66
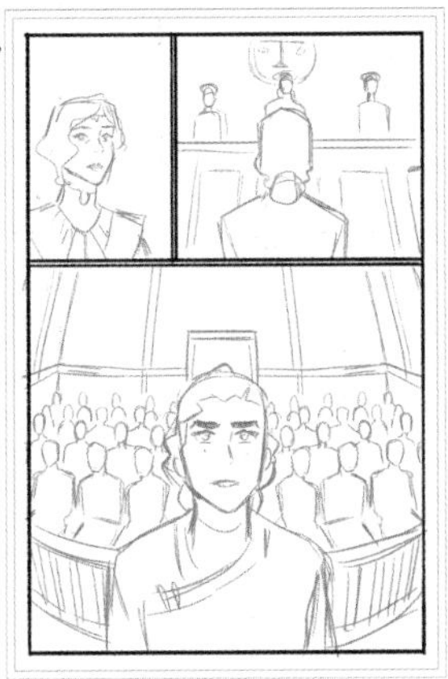

67
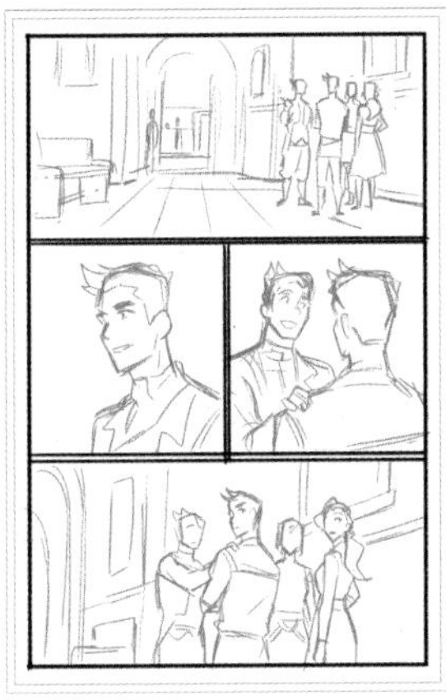

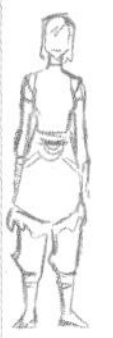

new casual outfit for korra?

68
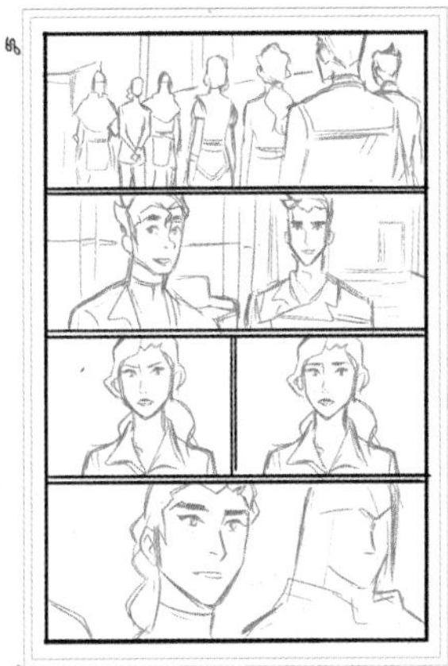

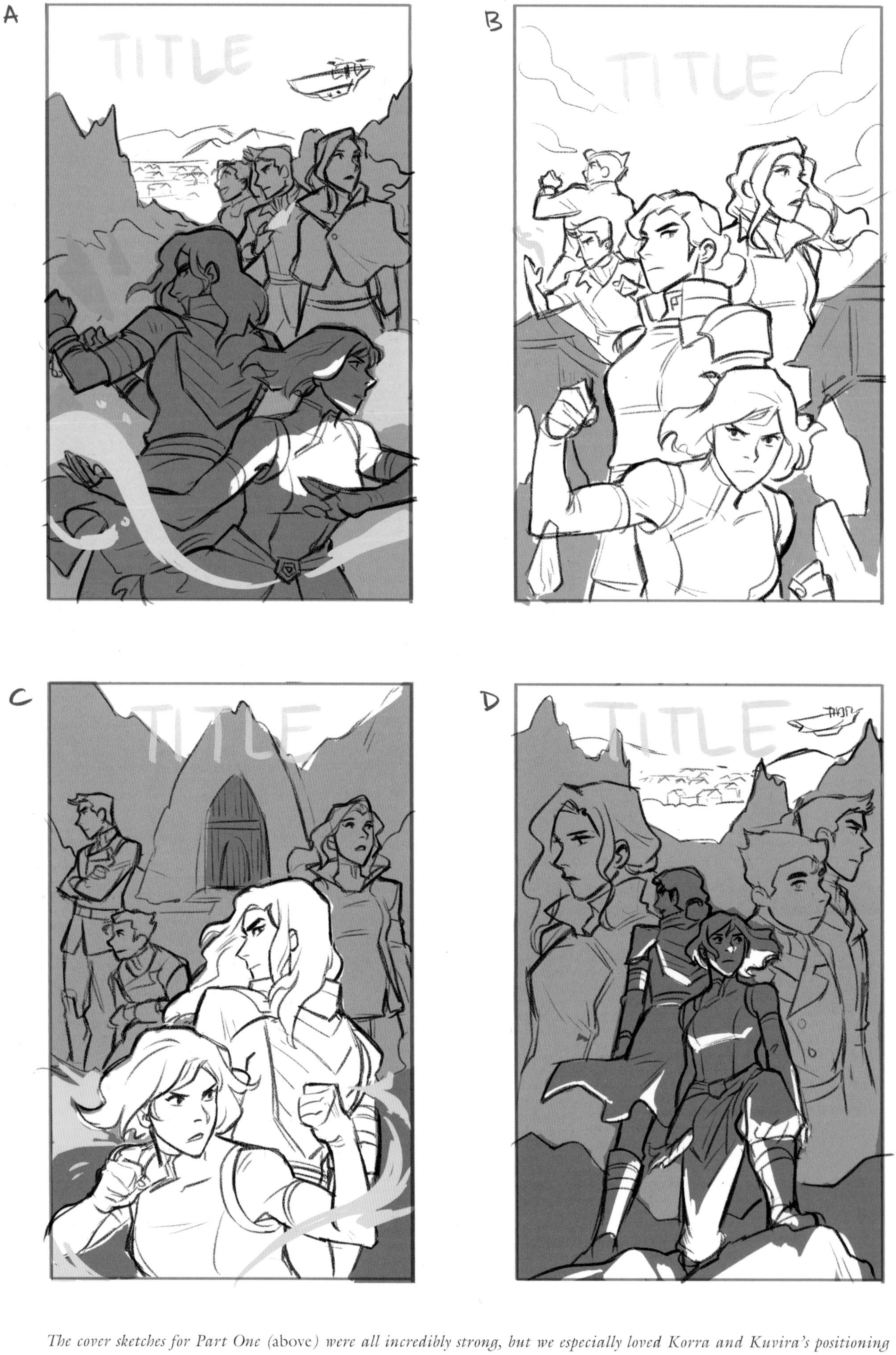
A
TITLE
B
TITLE
C
TITLE
D
TITLE

The cover sketches for Part One (above) *were all incredibly strong, but we especially loved Korra and Kuvira's positioning in option C, not to mention the visual of the White Lotus's prison in the background. Speaking of incredibly strong—one of Bryan's consistent notes for artists is to make Korra beefier* (opposite)*. Getting his notes is always a joy, as they are equal parts educational and charming.*

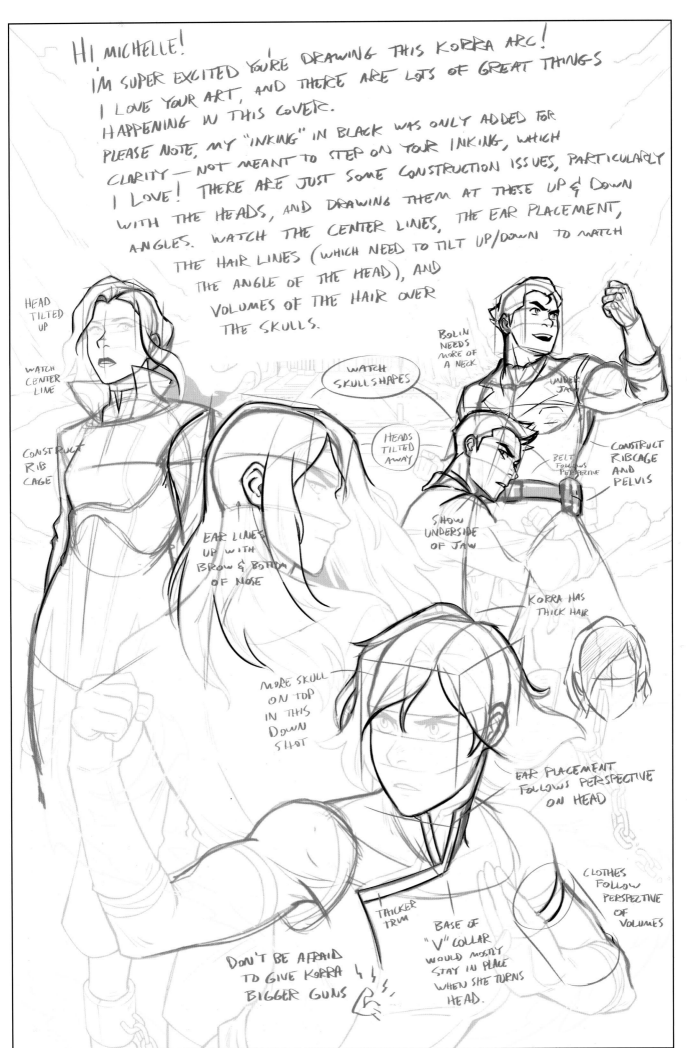

HI MICHELLE!
IM SUPER EXCITED YOU'RE DRAWING THIS KORRA ARC!
I LOVE YOUR ART, AND THERE ARE LOTS OF GREAT THINGS HAPPENING IN THIS COVER.
PLEASE NOTE, MY "INKING" IN BLACK WAS ONLY ADDED FOR CLARITY—NOT MEANT TO STEP ON YOUR INKING, WHICH I LOVE! THERE ARE JUST SOME CONSTRUCTION ISSUES, PARTICULARLY WITH THE HEADS, AND DRAWING THEM AT THESE UP & DOWN ANGLES. WATCH THE CENTER LINES, THE EAR PLACEMENT, THE HAIR LINES (WHICH NEED TO TILT UP/DOWN TO MATCH THE ANGLE OF THE HEAD), AND VOLUMES OF THE HAIR OVER THE SKULLS.

HEAD TILTED UP

WATCH CENTER LINE

CONSTRUCT RIB CAGE

WATCH SKULL SHAPES

HEADS TILTED AWAY

BOLIN NEEDS MORE OF A NECK

UNDER JAW

BELT FOLLOWS PERSPECTIVE

CONSTRUCT RIBCAGE AND PELVIS

SHOW UNDERSIDE OF JAW

EAR LINES UP WITH BROW & BOTTOM OF NOSE

KORRA HAS THICK HAIR

MORE SKULL ON TOP IN THIS DOWN SHOT

EAR PLACEMENT FOLLOWS PERSPECTIVE ON HEAD

CLOTHES FOLLOW PERSPECTIVE OF VOLUMES

DON'T BE AFRAID TO GIVE KORRA BIGGER GUNS

THICKER TRIM

BASE OF "V" COLLAR WOULD MOSTLY STAY IN PLACE WHEN SHE TURNS HEAD.

A

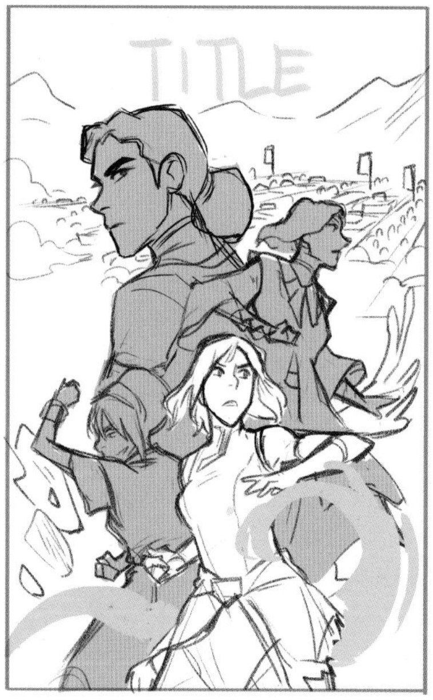
TITLE

B

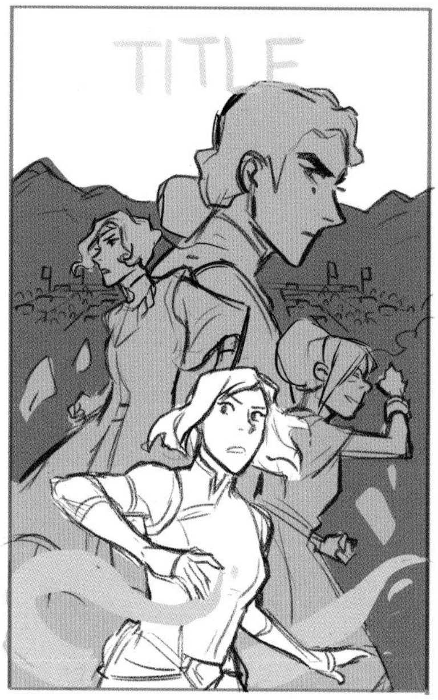
TITLE

C

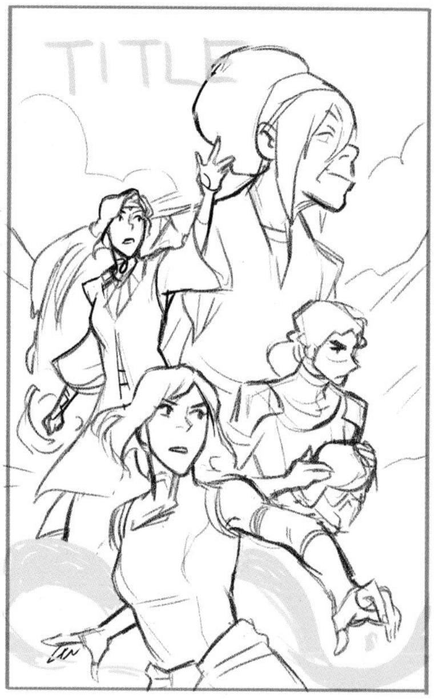
TITLE

D

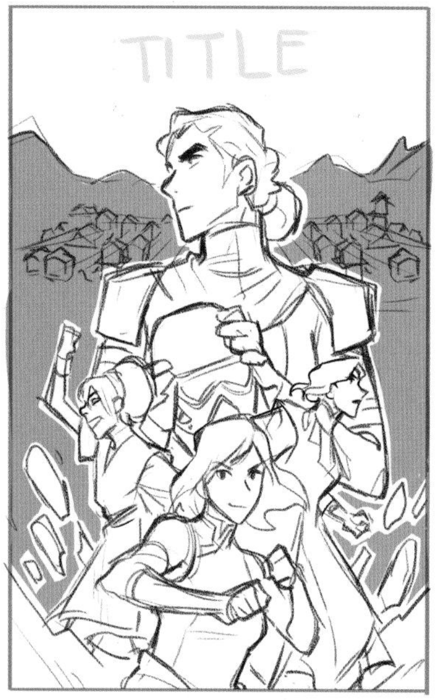
TITLE

Cover sketches for Part Two (above, left) *and Part Three* (below, right). *Again, they all had strong compositions, and it was hard for us to pick favorites! Personally, I was super excited to have Toph on the cover, and hope it was a nice surprise for fans.*

A

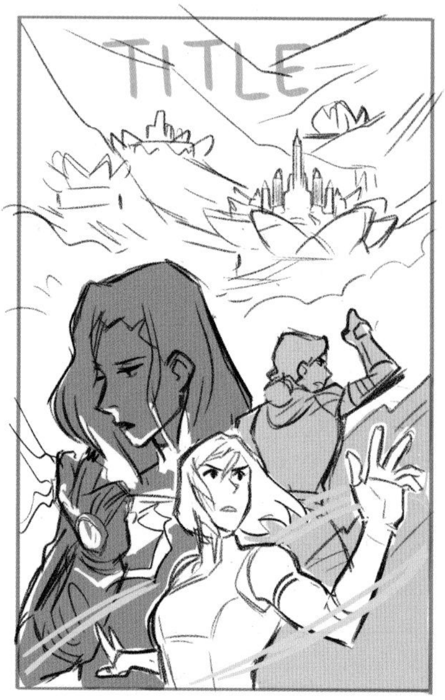
TITLE

B

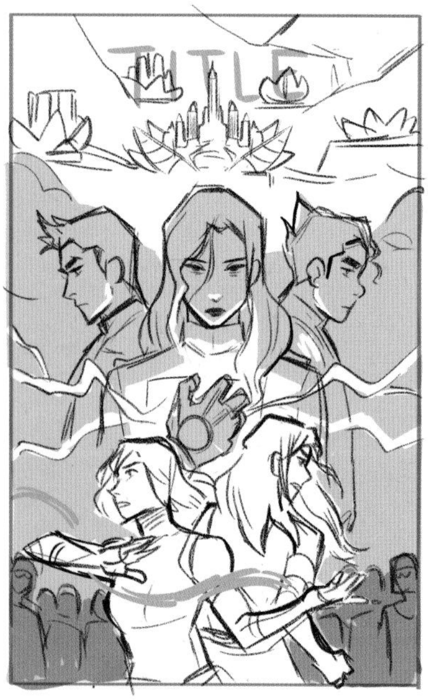
TITLE

C

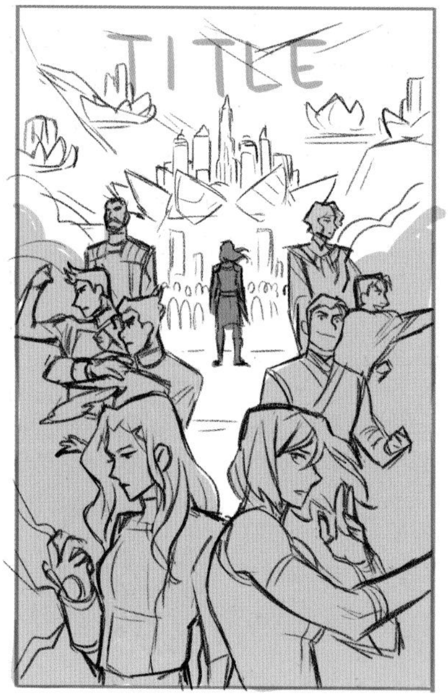
TITLE

D

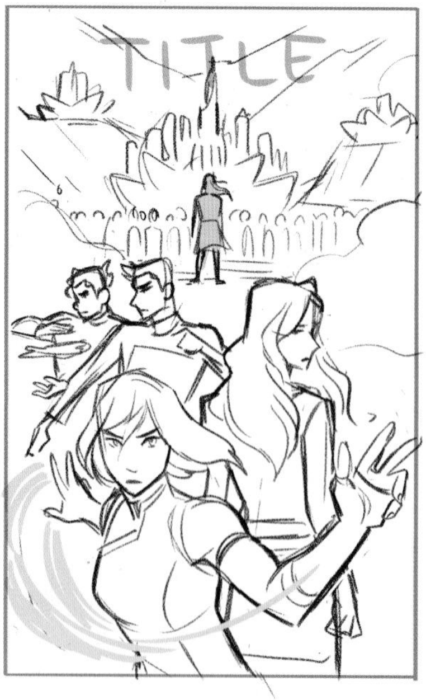
TITLE

ROUGHS

PENCILS

INKS

Michelle's process for the Part Two cover. After approving a sketch, we would rarely see the pencils stage, and instead just receive the final line art. At that point, it would be sent to Killian Ng to color. Killian's color selection and rendering on the final cover are breathtaking, aren't they?

FRONT
BACK

A

B

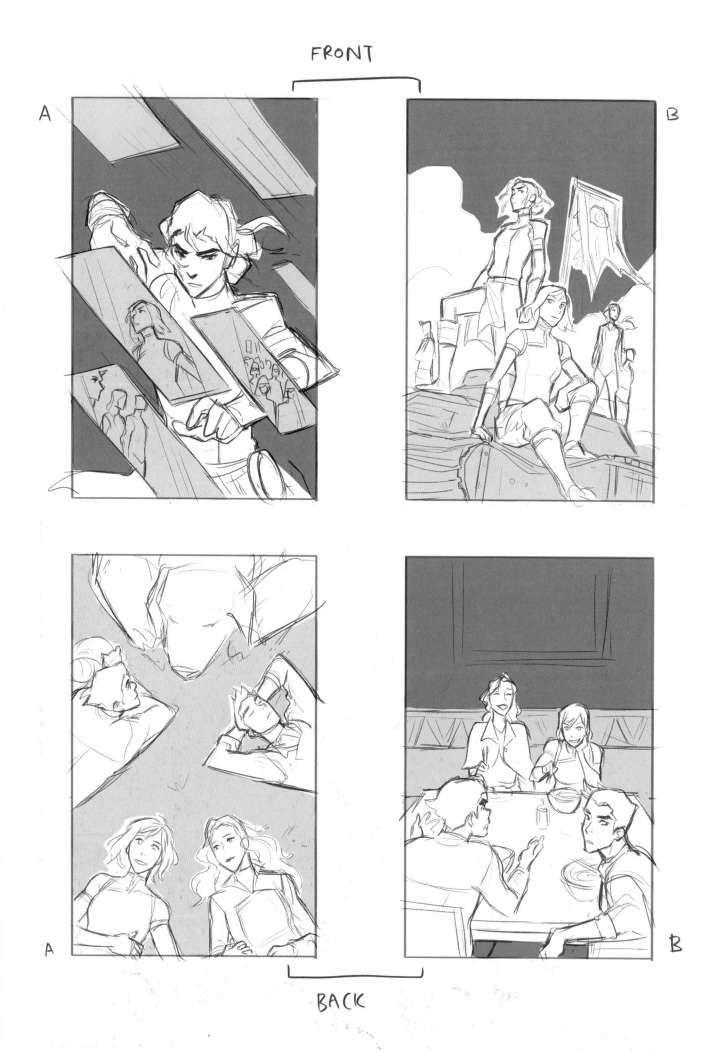

A

B

FRONT
BACK

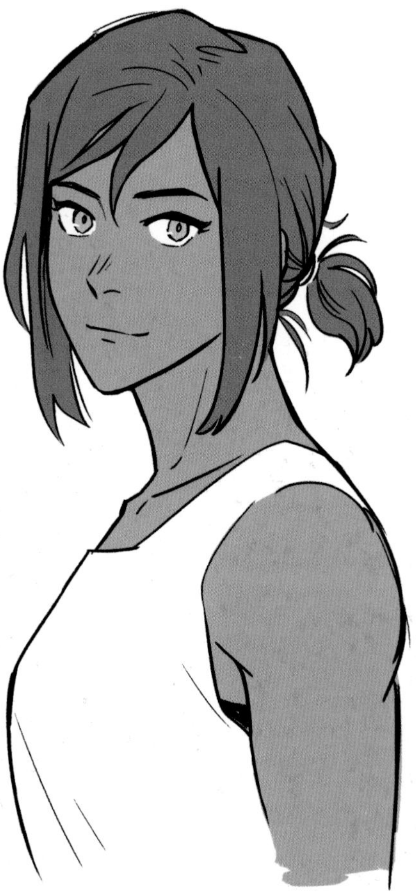

Sketches for this library edition's front and back covers (opposite)*. Approvals for these took a bit longer than usual simply because we couldn't decide which two to go with! I always love illustrations of Team Avatar just having fun and relaxing, but the cool, dynamic shot of Kuvira eventually won for the back cover.*

Finally, some illustrations Michelle did for fun! The lower image of Korra and Asami was done for KorrAsami Day—December 19th, the day the final episode of the animated series aired, and the day Korra and Asami departed for their spirit-y sojourn.

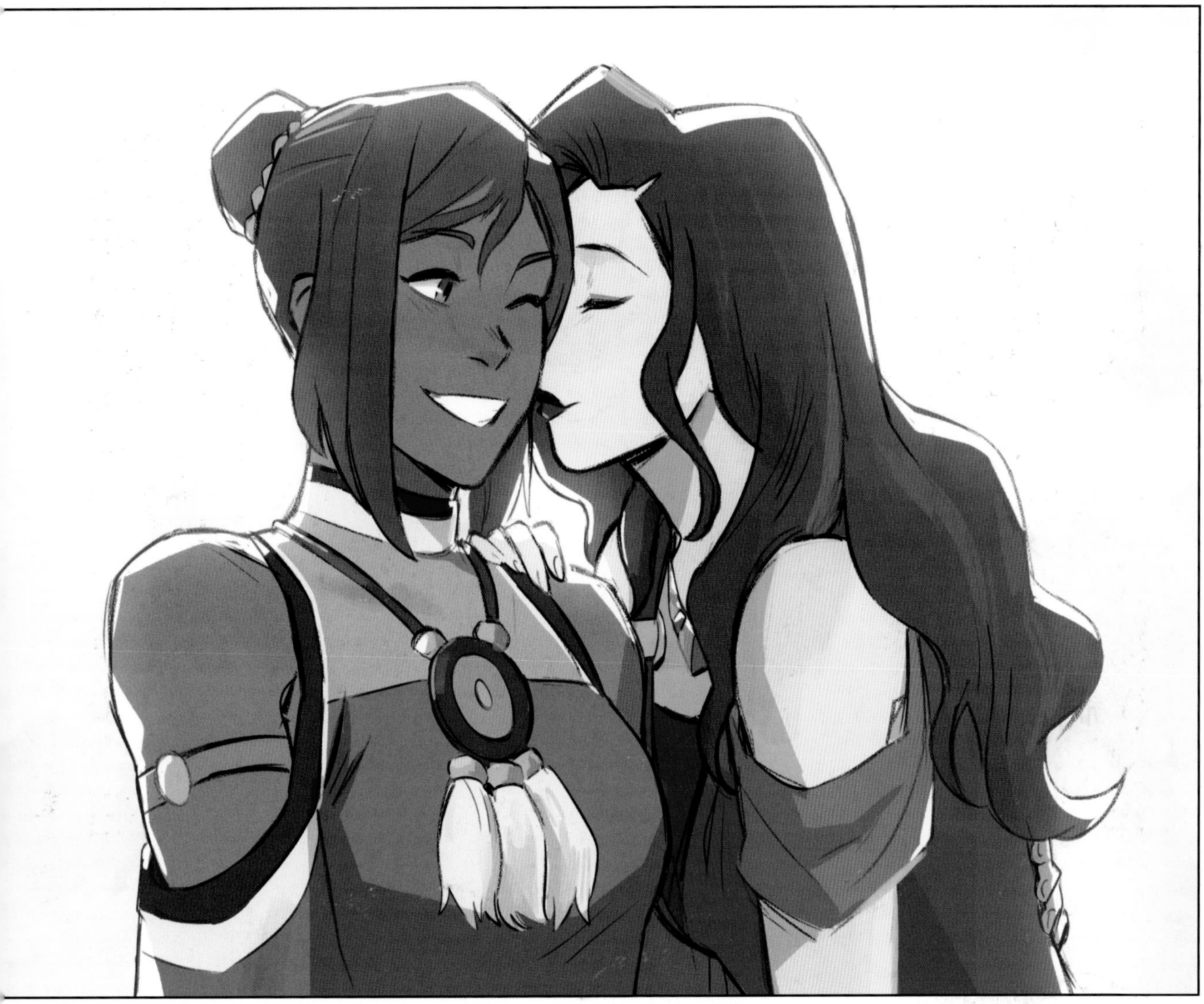

The Legend of Korra
TURF WARS

TURF WARS • PART ONE
TURF WARS • PART TWO
TURF WARS • PART THREE

The Legend of Korra: Turf Wars Library Edition
978-1-50670-202-5 $39.99

The Legend of Korra: Turf Wars Part One
978-1-50670-015-1 $10.99

The Legend of Korra: Turf Wars Part Two
978-1-50670-040-3 $10.99

The Legend of Korra: Turf Wars Part Three
978-1-50670-185-1 $10.99

nickelodeon

THE LEGEND OF KORRA™

JOIN AVATAR KORRA AND TEAM AVATAR IN A NEW AGE OF ADVENTURE!

The Legend of Korra: The Animated Series Book One: Air
978-1-61655-168-1 $34.99

Book Two: Spirits
978-1-61655-462-0 $34.99

Book Three: Change
978-1-61655-565-8 $34.99

Book Four: Balance
978-1-61655-687-7 $34.99

THE ART OF THE ANIMATED SERIES

RUINS OF THE EMPIRE • PART ONE
RUINS OF THE EMPIRE • PART THREE

The Legend of Korra
RUINS OF THE EMPIRE

The Legend of Korra: Ruins of the Empire Part One
978-1-50670-894-2 $10.99

The Legend of Korra: Ruins of the Empire Part Two
978-1-50670-895-9 $10.99

The Legend of Korra: Ruins of the Empire part three
978-1-50670-896-6 $10.99

The Legend of Korra: Ruins of the Empire Library Edition
978-1-50670-893-5 $39.99

AVAILABLE AT YOUR LOCAL COMICS SHOP OR BOOKSTORE! To find a comics shop in your area, visit comicshoplocator.com. For more information or to order direct visit DarkHorse.com or email: mailorder@darkhorse.com

DARK HORSE BOOKS

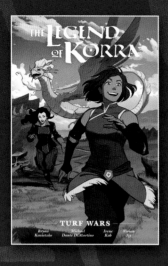

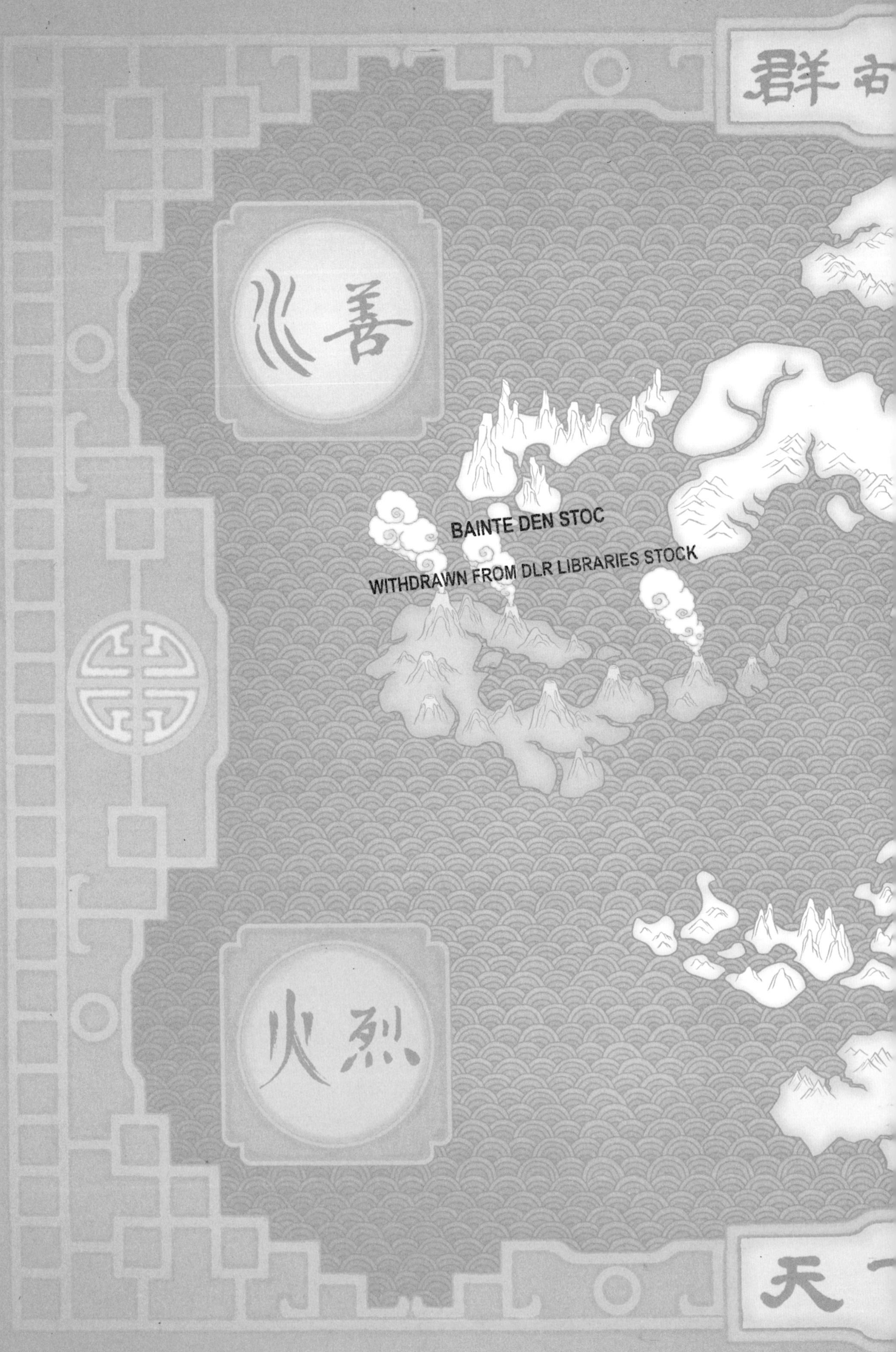
善
烈